How to Do
Everything

Genealogy
Second Edition

George G. Morgan

Mc
Graw
Hill

New York Chicago San Francisco Lisbon
London Madrid Mexico City Milan New Delhi
San Juan Seoul Singapore Sydney Toronto

The McGraw·Hill Companies

Cataloging-in-Publication Data is on file with the Library of Congress

McGraw-Hill books are available at special quantity discounts to use as premiums and sales promotions, or for use in corporate training programs. To contact a special sales representative, please visit the Contact Us page at www.mhprofessional.com.

How to Do Everything: Genealogy, Second Edition

234567890   DOC DOC   019

ISBN   978-0-07-162534-0
MHID   0-07-162534-8

Sponsoring Editor
Megg Morin

Technical Editor
Drew Smith

Composition
International Typesetting
and Composition

Editorial Supervisor
Janet Walden

Copy Editor
Bill McManus

Illustration
International Typesetting
and Composition

Project Manager
Aparna Mathur,
International Typesetting
and Composition

Proofreader
Claire Splan

Art Director, Cover
Jeff Weeks

Indexer
Claire Splan

Acquisitions Coordinators
Carly Stapleton and
Meghan Riley

Production Supervisor
Jean Bodeaux

Contents at a Glance

To the memories of three of my dearest friends, Melvin Orval Brown, Shirley Ruth Neprasch Brown, and Thomas Norman Ryder. While they have passed on and are missed, they have left this world and the genealogical community a richer place.

About the Author

George G. Morgan is an internationally recognized genealogical expert, lecturer, and consultant. He is president of Aha! Seminars, Inc., a Florida-based company providing continuing education to librarians in the United States and genealogy presentations to societies in the United States, Canada, and elsewhere. He also has led genealogy tours to the United Kingdom and has spoken on several genealogy cruises.

He is a prolific author of eight books, including the first and second editions of *The Official Guide to Ancestry.com* (Ancestry Publishing), and the first and second editions of this book. He has written literally hundreds of magazine, journal, and online articles on the subject of genealogy. He currently writes online for *Eastman's Online Genealogy Newsletter* each week, for *Digital Genealogist*, and has written scores of articles articles for the Ancestry.com website. He is a frequent writer for *Ancestry* Magazine, *Everton's Genealogical Helper, Family Chronicle, Internet Genealogy, Discovering Your Family History, Family Tree Magazine*, the FGS *FORUM*, the Association for Professional Genealogists *Quarterly*, and others.

George is the co-host, with his partner Drew Smith, of The Genealogy Guys℠ Podcast, the longest-running genealogy podcast in the world, published each week at **http://genealogyguys.com**. The two also have appeared in the RootsTelevision series "Down Under: Florida" at **www.rootstelevision.com**.

He is the past president of the International Society of Family History Writers and Editors (ISFHWE) and was a director on the board of the Genealogical Speakers Guild. He currently serves as a director for the Florida Genealogical Society in Tampa and as the Public Relations/Publicity Director of the Florida State Genealogical Society. He belongs to more than a dozen other societies in the United States and the United Kingdom.

George has won a number of esteemed awards, including the Genealogy Outstanding Achievement Award and the President's Citation from the Florida State Genealogical Society, the Award of Merit from the Federation of Genealogical Societies, and an Excellence in Writing Award from ISFHWE, among others.

He lives in Citrus Park, Florida, a suburb of Tampa.

About the Technical Editor

Drew Smith, MLS, is a librarian with the University of South Florida in Tampa, and a nationally known genealogy writer and speaker. He is the author of a regular column for *Digital Genealogist magazine*, and is the editor of the Federation of Genealogical Societies' *Voice* newsletter. He also is the author of a new book, *Social Networking for Genealogists* (Genealogical Publishing Company). Since it began in September 2005, he has co-hosted the weekly "The Genealogy Guys℠ Podcast" with George G. Morgan. He is a Director of the Federation of Genealogical Societies, and President of the Florida Genealogical Society of Tampa.

Contents

Acknowledgments

Creating a book is no easy task. It takes dedicated people with talent and specific skills to bring a written work to fruition. I'd like to mention a few of the people who have made this book all that it is.

First, let me extend my sincere thanks to Megg Morin, acquisitions editor at McGraw-Hill. We have had the pleasure of working on both editions of this book to date, and Megg's enthusiasm, humor, and professionalism made the hard work worth every minute.

The team at McGraw-Hill epitomize the meaning of "professional." Special thanks go out to Janet Walden, Carly Stapleton, Perry Norton, Bettina Faltermeier, Bill McManus, and Claire Splan.

Thanks to Drew Smith, the technical editor for this book and my partner in so many genealogical ventures, including "The Genealogy Guys℠ Podcast" at **http://genealogyguys.com**.

Finally, my eternal thanks go to all of my ancestors and their families. Their stories are a rich tapestry that inspires me to be more than I ever thought I could be.

Introduction

Family is forever! That is a lesson I learned at the age of ten when my aunt and grandmother exposed me with pride in our family history. Their stories and enthusiasm sparked an interest in me to explore and learn more on my own. From that day forward, history and geography were no longer just names, dates, and places. They became the world stage on which my ancestors and family members actively participated or observed, and by which they were affected. That perspective has served me well over time because it encouraged me to always try to place my family into context with the places, periods, and events of their lives and to view them as real people.

The first edition of this book was one of the proudest accomplishments in my life, and also one of the most difficult. It was a complex undertaking to summarize more than 40 years of genealogical research experience into a single book. McGraw-Hill's "How to Do Everything" series is one of the most respected catalog of how-to books available. However, my first reaction to being asked to write a genealogy book for the series was, "No one book can teach *everything*. In fact," I said, "volume one of such a work could easily be 15,000 pages long." No one laughed. Those of us who have been working on our genealogy for a while, however, know that the amount of information and resources available to us is nearly incomprehensible and that a work covering literally "everything" would probably occupy an entire bookcase. Still, I believe that you will find in these pages a well-balanced foundation for your family history investigations.

As researchers, we must become methodical detectives who investigate every clue and carefully weigh the evidence we uncover. There are logical processes we can follow and strategies we can employ to help achieve success, even getting past many of the inevitable "brick walls" we encounter. It is not unlike being a crime scene investigator such as those we see on television. I have included scores of illustrations to help you visualize the documents and websites discussed in the text. Many of these are actual documents from my own research collection, while others have been loaned or supplied to me for use in the book. There also are screen shots of web pages that will help you visualize what the providers have to offer.

The new, second edition of this book will provide you with a comprehensive foundation for beginning and continuing your family history research. It covers the major record types available in the United States, Canada, the United Kingdom and Ireland, and Australia and research strategies for successfully locating and evaluating them. The fact that all these geographies are addressed makes this book unique.

This edition also addresses the new technologies and resources that have become a part of the modern genealogist's toolkit. The use of DNA testing and genetic genealogy in our research has become an important topic. Many social networks have burst onto the scene to foster sharing of information and research collaboration. Thousands of brilliant new database collections, many of which contain digitized images of original historical documents and newspapers, present research opportunities we never imagined a decade ago. New websites and updated addresses for others are included to illustrate the best of the Internet resources. And finally, new software programs for the modern range of hardware—from PCs and Macs to handhelds and cellular telephones—are described and links are provided to help you access those resources.

You will find that the book is organized in such a way as to build a strong foundation for you. Regardless of your level of experience and expertise, I think you will find something helpful at every turn. You will learn the basic rules of genealogical evidence and how to use your "critical thinking skills" in evaluating the source materials you find. Along the way, you will learn successful research methods and strategies, including tips and techniques for effectively using the fastest-growing segment of genealogical research tools: the Internet. In addition, an often overlooked or poorly utilized facility, the online catalog of libraries and archives, is discussed in detail and should substantially help your research. The document images, photographs, screen shots, and tables will provide you with visual references to help you understand the material discussed in the text.

Gathering information wherever you go is a given, but many people simply show up unprepared and wander aimlessly in their research. Advance preparation and organization for a genealogical research trip is the key to success, regardless of whether you're planning a visit to your local public library or a once-in-a-lifetime trip to a foreign country in search of records of your family's origins there. I've included an entire chapter covering planning and making a successful genealogical research trip that I'm sure will help you conduct research like a professional. This really is a balanced "how to do everything" book that genealogists have been waiting for.

You are embarking on a fascinating genealogical research odyssey that may last your lifetime. Along the way, you will meet many wonderful people and will come to know your ancestors and their families as real people—and as close personal friends. It is my fervent hope that your research will be successful and that your family tree will prove to be a fruitful source of information to help you better understand your family origins.

Happy hunting!

George G. Morgan

PART I

Begin Your Family History Odyssey

1

Why Explore Your Genealogy?

HOW TO...

- Start at the beginning with yourself and work backward
- Discover sources of information in your own home
- Understand what types of records and materials can help you learn more
- Interview *all* your relatives
- Begin to organize what you find

We are living in fast-paced times, and sometimes it feels as if we are transients without a sense of place. Jobs, marriage, and a wide variety of circumstances draw us away from the places where we were born and raised and separate us from our family members. It isn't unusual at some point to feel the need to reconnect in some way, and often with that need comes the desire to learn more about our family origins. It therefore should be no surprise that researching genealogy, or family history, is the second most popular hobby in the English-speaking world, following online auctions. It also is estimated to be the third most popular use of the Internet after the use of email and reading news sites.

The terms *genealogy* and *family history* are often used interchangeably. While they may seem similar, there actually is a distinction between them:

- Genealogy is the scholarly study of a family's line of descent from its ancestors, during which one develops an understanding of the family's historical context and documents its history and traditions.
- Family history is the study of a family's history and traditions over an extended period of time and may involve documenting some or all of the facts.

A family historian may seek to trace and document specific family members or a branch of the family, and to perhaps write a family history. A genealogist, on the other hand, typically has a much broader view of the family. He or she traces an entire or extended family structure, including brothers, sisters, aunts, uncles, and cousins. This includes both their antecedents (the persons from whom they are descended) and their

descendents. The genealogist actively seeks documentary evidence of many types
to prove and verify facts about the family. In addition, the genealogist seeks to place
family members and ancestors into geographical, historical, and social context in order
to better understand their lives. The genealogist also documents the sources of all the
evidence he or she finds, using standard source citations.

We *are* the product of our ancestry in many different ways. Certainly genetics
play a critical part in our physical makeup, determining our physical characteristics
and potential susceptibility to medical conditions, both physical and mental. However,
the circumstances of place, time, education, economics, experiences, family group
dynamics, and interactions with the personalities of our family members and friends
also distinctly influence our development. They all contribute to the overall person
that we become. The family stories and traditions that we have observed and that
have been passed from generation to generation contribute to our sense of kinship
and belonging. It is no wonder that we want to explore, maintain, document, and
preserve these factors. Documentary evidence is still the most significant resource
used in genealogical research, but genetic genealogy has rapidly become another
component in the genealogist's toolkit.

There are many motivations for genealogical research. Some people trace their
family to help understand their place in it. Others study and document a family's
direct line of descent in order to link to some famous personage. Often this is done in
order to join one or more of the lineage or heritage societies, such as the Daughters of
the American Revolution, the Mayflower Descendants, or the First Fleet Fellowship.
Still others may research their family's history for reasons such as to discover the
family's medical history, try to locate their natural parents, document a family's or
community's history, or help locate heirs. Whatever *your* reasons for tracing and
investigating your own family's history, your search will lead you on an interesting
and exciting journey of discovery. Don't be surprised if your quest lasts a lifetime.

Start at the Beginning: Yourself and Your Family

My genealogical research began on a cold, snowy January day in my North Carolina
hometown when I was ten years old. While snowfall was not unusual, a six-inch
accumulation was rare indeed. There was no school scheduled for several days, and
I spent the days at the home of my aunt, Mary Allen Morgan, and my Grandmother
Morgan while my parents worked. Both women had a strong sense of family and
history, especially my grandmother. She was the daughter and granddaughter of
prominent physicians, as well as the great-great-granddaughter of two North Carolina
Revolutionary War patriots. One of these was John McKnitt Alexander, the secretary
of the group of citizens in Mecklenburg County who formed the provincial committee
that crafted and signed the Mecklenburg Declaration of Independence on 20 May
1775. The other was Major John Davidson, a Revolutionary War military leader after
whose family Davidson College was named.

On that snowy day, the three of us gathered at a drop-leaf table dating back to the 1740s and these ladies proceeded to educate me about our family history. Using a roll of brown parcel paper, a ruler, and pencils, we began drawing a family tree. Fortunately for me, my grandmother was a packrat and had saved generations' worth of materials. We used family Bibles, one of which dated to 1692 in Edinburgh, Scotland; family letters, postcards, and Christmas cards dating back to the late 1930s; a group of old deeds and wills; and *The History of Mecklenburg County from 1740 to 1900* by J. B. Alexander, published in 1902, to construct our family tree. During the process, my 90-year-old grandmother related family stories and anecdotal information dating back to her own childhood in the 1870s. Needless to say, I was hooked, and subsequent visits entailed my appeal to my aunt and my grandmother to "Tell me about when you were a little girl." I have since spent more than four decades in my own quest for more and more information about all branches of my family's origins and history.

You will want to start your own genealogical odyssey with yourself and what you know, and then work your way backward. Along the way you will want to collect documentation to verify every fact *and* keep track of where and when you obtained every piece of evidence. (We will discuss types of evidentiary documents and the process of documentation in more detail in Chapter 3.)

Did You Know? Start with yourself and work backward to connect yourself to previous generations. You are less likely to make a wrong turn and end up researching the wrong ancestors.

A typical research path for you to follow would begin with the following information:

- **Yourself**   Obtain a copy of your own birth certificate. This document provides you with the date, time, and location of your birth, and often information about your physical characteristics at birth, such as weight, length, and hair and eye color. It also indicates the names of your parents, their race or nationality, their ages at the time of the event, the name of the physician attending the birth, and possibly additional details. The content of a birth certificate will vary depending on when and where the document was created. Later certificates may contain more information.
  - Birth certificates can be obtained in the United States from county health departments, state bureaus of statistics, or other governmental agencies.
  - In England and Wales, general registration of births, marriages, and deaths began in 1837, and the General Register Office (GRO), a part of the Home Office Identity and Passport Services, holds a copy of all registrations centrally. Their website is located at **www.gro.gov.uk**. A central index is held at The National Archives (TNA) in Kew, just west of London. Local offices hold copies of their records registered since 1837.

- The General Register Office for Scotland (GROS) is located in Edinburgh and is the contact point for birth, marriage, and death certificates. You may check their website at **www.gro-scotland.gov.uk** for more information.
- The General Register Office of Ireland in Dublin is the depository for many vital records and documents. You will want to visit their website at **www .groireland.ie** and click the link labeled Research.
- In Canada, the responsibility for the civil registration of births, marriages, and deaths lies with the province or territory. The Library and Archives Canada website at **www.collectionscanada.gc.ca** provides links to a vast collection of Canadian genealogical resources grouped into categories, including links to provincial and territorial archives, libraries, and other repositories.
- Like Canada, responsibility for civil registration in Australia lies with the territory or state. The Society of Australian Genealogists has produced an excellent web page concerning Australian civil registration at **www.sag.org.au**.
- If you are researching vital records or civil registration in other countries, you may want to use your favorite Internet search engine and enter the type of document and the name of the country. As an example, I entered the phrase **"death certificate" + singapore** and was rewarded with a link to the Immigration & Checkpoints Authority (ICA) and its web page at **www.ica.gov .sg**, at which I located under eServices & Forms the link to the eXtracts Online system to obtain birth and death extract applications.

- **Your parents**   Learn as much about your parents as possible. Obtain copies of their birth certificates, their marriage license, and any other documents possible. Your mother's maiden name will appear on birth and marriage documents, and sometimes others, and will be an essential part of your research. Ask questions to learn where they grew up, where they went to school, where they lived at every point in their lives, what religious affiliation they have had, and the names and addresses of the religious institutions they attended, what jobs they may have had, what their hobbies and interests are, and anything else you can learn. Take copious notes along the way because this may be the only opportunity you have to gather these important family details. Obtain a copy of the death certificate if a parent is deceased, and seek to obtain copies of any obituaries.
- **Siblings**   Obtain a copy of the birth certificate for each of your brothers and sisters. In addition, obtain any other documents that may have been created for them. Your lives are inextricably linked, and the information you learn about them may reveal other research paths for you.
- **Aunts and uncles**   Your research will extend to your parents' siblings as well. You will want to learn as much about their family groups as you can. After all, the family structure and dynamics can be important in learning more about the factors that influenced your life.
- **Cousins**   Regardless of the family relationship with your cousins, close or distant, try to learn as much about them as possible. They are tangible extensions of your family's line too.
- **Grandparents**   Obtain copies of documents for your parents' parents too. You are tracing a line of descent from these people and want to know as much as possible about them.

Continue expanding outward as far as you can to learn about other family members, their spouses, parents, and children. Don't worry if you can't locate information or obtain all the documents on everyone. This is an ongoing process and, as you progress through this book, you will learn more about how to extend your research reach and locate more and more information. Part of what we, as genealogists, do is fill in gaps in the informational puzzle in order to create a larger picture.

Discover Sources of Information in Your Own Home

Your quest for family information should begin in familiar territory. Start with what you know and work backward. It is probable that you have in your own home or in the homes of your parents, grandparents, and other family members any number of resources that can help you document the family. Take time to consider the following home source materials that you might find around your home and what information they may provide.

Vital and Civil Records

Vital records are those documents that record milestone life events. They include birth certificates, marriage licenses and certificates, divorce decrees, and death certificates issued by governmental agencies. Examples of a birth certificate and a death certificate are shown in Figures 1-1 and 1-2.

The vital records documents issued by governmental entities may or may not contain completely accurate information. A death certificate, for example, will provide the details of an individual's death, such as name, gender, date, cause of death, and the location where the death occurred. This data may or may not be 100 percent correct; however, it is considered to be the official record of the death. Likewise, a coroner's report or the report of an inquest will provide what is deemed the official report on the death.

Other information found on a death certificate, such as the individual's date of birth, parents' names, occupation, and other personal data unrelated to the death, may or may not be correct. This information is typically provided to the official completing the form by a family member or another person, and that informant may or may not have the accurate details. In addition, the person completing the form may make errors in recording or transcribing the information provided. As a result, the details unrelated to the individual's death should be viewed with some skepticism until you have verified them with other independently created sources. We will discuss this in greater detail in Chapter 3.

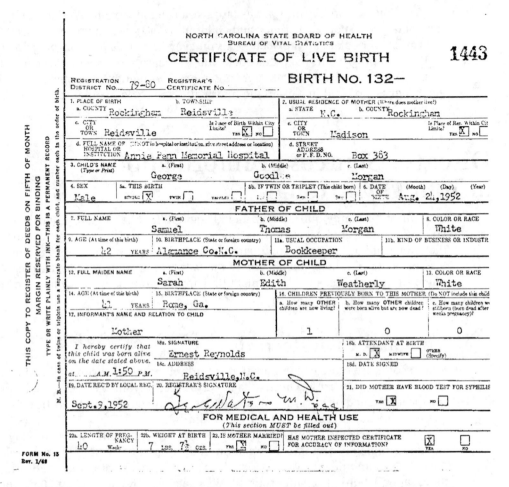

NORTH CAROLINA STATE BOARD OF HEALTH
BUREAU OF VITAL STATISTICS

CERTIFICATE OF LIVE BIRTH   **1443**

BIRTH No. 132–

REGISTRATION DISTRICT No. 79-80   REGISTRAR'S CERTIFICATE No.

1. PLACE OF BIRTH
a. COUNTY Rockingham   b. TOWNSHIP Reidsville
c. CITY OR TOWN Reidsville   Is Place of Birth Within City Limits? YES X NO
d. FULL NAME OF HOSPITAL OR INSTITUTION (If NOT in hospital or institution, give street address or location) Annie Penn Memorial Hospital

2. USUAL RESIDENCE OF MOTHER (Where does mother live?)
a. STATE N.C.   b. COUNTY Rockingham
c. CITY OR TOWN Madison   Is Place of Res. Within City Limits? YES X NO
d. STREET ADDRESS or R.F.D. NO. Box 363

3. CHILD'S NAME (Type or Print)
a. (First) George   b. (Middle) Goodlie   c. (Last) Morgan

4. SEX Male   5a. THIS BIRTH SINGLE X TWIN TRIPLET
5b. IF TWIN OR TRIPLET (This child born) 1st 2nd 3rd
6. DATE OF BIRTH (Month) (Day) (Year) Aug. 24, 1952

FATHER OF CHILD

7. FULL NAME
a. (First) Samuel   b. (Middle) Thomas   c. (Last) Morgan
8. COLOR OR RACE White

9. AGE (At time of this birth) 42 YEARS
10. BIRTHPLACE (State or foreign country) Alamance Co. N.C.
11a. USUAL OCCUPATION Bookkeeper
11b. KIND OF BUSINESS OR INDUSTRY

MOTHER OF CHILD

12. FULL MAIDEN NAME
a. (First) Sarah   b. (Middle) Edith   c. (Last) Weatherly
13. COLOR OR RACE White

14. AGE (At time of this birth) 41 YEARS
15. BIRTHPLACE (State or foreign country) Rome, Ga.
16. CHILDREN PREVIOUSLY BORN TO THIS MOTHER (Do NOT include this child)
a. How many OTHER children are now living? 1
b. How many OTHER children were born alive but are now dead? 0
c. How many children were stillborn (born dead after weeks pregnancy)? 0

17. INFORMANT'S NAME AND RELATION TO CHILD
Mother

I hereby certify that this child was born alive on the date stated above. at 1:50 A.M. P.M.
18a. SIGNATURE Ernest Reynolds
18c. ADDRESS Reidsville, N.C.
18b. ATTENDANT AT BIRTH M.D. X MIDWIFE OTHER (Specify)
18d. DATE SIGNED

19. DATE REC'D BY LOCAL REG. Sept. 9, 1952
20. REGISTRAR'S SIGNATURE
21. DID MOTHER HAVE BLOOD TEST FOR SYPHILIS YES X NO

FOR MEDICAL AND HEALTH USE
(This section MUST be filled out)

22a. LENGTH OF PREGNANCY 40 Weeks
22b. WEIGHT AT BIRTH 7 LBS. 7½ OZS.
23. IS MOTHER MARRIED? YES X NO
HAS MOTHER INSPECTED CERTIFICATE FOR ACCURACY OF INFORMATION? YES X NO

FORM No. 15
Rev. 1/48

I hereby certify that this is a true and correct copy which appears on record in the Office of the Register of Deeds of Rockingham County, North Carolina, in Book 39 , Page 1443.

Witness my hand and official seal, this the 17th day of April 1979.

Irene Pruitt, Register of Deeds

By: _____
    Ass't./Deputy Register of Deeds

FIGURE 1-1   Birth certificates provide essential clues for date and location of birth, names of parents, and other facts. (From the author's collection.)

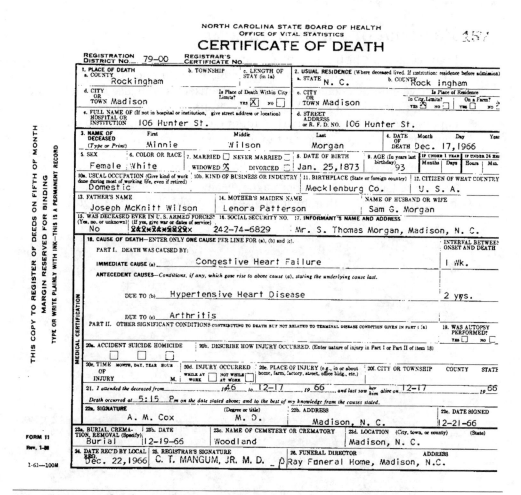

FIGURE 1-2 A death certificate provides information about a person's death. (From the author's collection.)

Religious Records

Ecclesiastical records are often found in the home. Certificates of baptism, christening, confirmation, or records of bar mitzvah or bat mitzvah may be found among family papers. Documents of marriage issued by the church, as opposed to a government-issued marriage license or certificate, may be among the family's treasured documents. Look also for church programs or bulletins issued at the time of and/or commemorating the occasion, because these may contain names of relatives and other information. These also may be recorded in the religious organization's files or archives, along with more detailed accounts of the events and participants. Other congregation publications might include a commemorative congregational history, photographs, newsletters, and other periodicals.

Personal or Family Bible

Pages containing birth, marriage, death, christening, confirmation, baptism, and other events are commonly included in Bibles. Your ancestors or family members may have entered detailed information themselves. You also may find other materials tucked inside a Bible, such as letters, postcards, greeting cards, newspaper clippings, photographs, obituaries, funeral cards, bookmarks, and other items considered special or important to the owner. These may provide invaluable clues to other locations where family information may be found. In one family Bible, I found a page listing the wedding guests at my grandmother's first wedding on 2 February 1898. (See Figure 1-3.) Another page revealed a listing of the bridegroom's death just five months later of "that dreaded disease typhoid fever." (See Figure 1-4.)

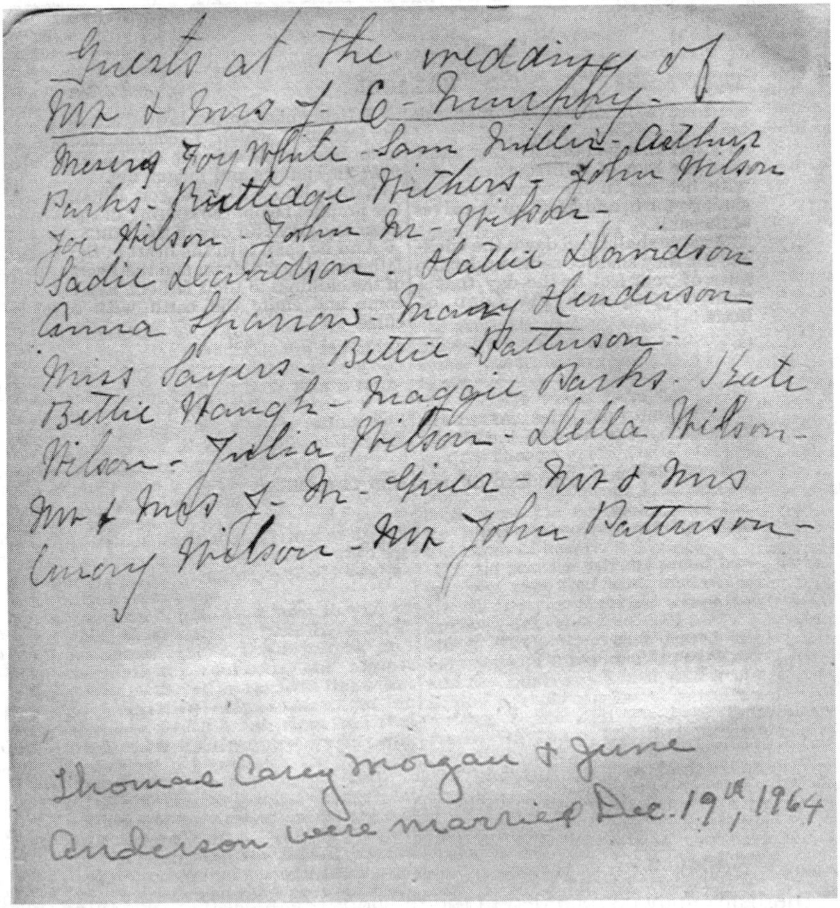
Guests at the wedding of
Mr & Mrs J. E. Murphy.
Messrs Foy White - Sam Miller - Arthur
Parks - Rutledge Withers - John Wilson
Joe Wilson - John M. Wilson -
Sadie Davidson. Hattie Davidson
Anna Sparrow - Mary Henderson
Miss Sayers - Bettie Patterson -
Bettie Waugh - Maggie Parks. Kate
Wilson - Julia Wilson - Della Wilson -
Mr & Mrs J. M. Greer - Mr & Mrs
Emory Wilson - Mr John Patterson -

Thomas Carey Morgan & June
Anderson were married Dec. 19th, 1964

FIGURE 1-3 A personal Bible may include interesting details, such as this example in which the guests at the wedding of Mr. and Mrs. J. E. Murphy are listed. (From the author's collection.)

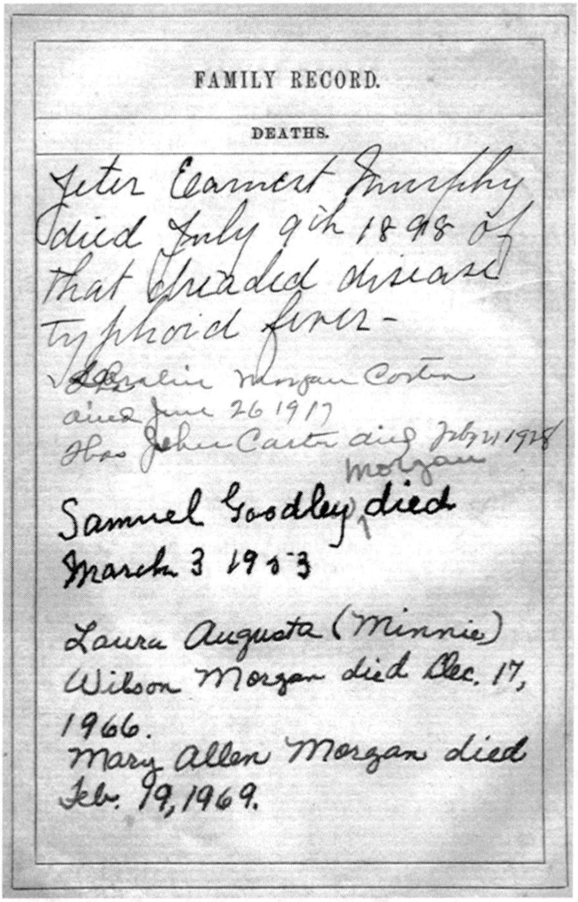

FAMILY RECORD.

DEATHS.

Jeter Earnest Murphy died July 9th 1898 of that Dreaded disease Typhoid fever —

Caroline Morgan Corton died June 26 1917
Thos John Carter died July 11 1918

Samuel Goodley Morgan died March 3 1903

Laura Augusta (Minnie) Wilson Morgan died Dec. 17, 1966.
Mary Allen Morgan died Feb. 19, 1969.

FIGURE 1-4   Jeter Earnest Murphy, the bridegroom at the marriage documented in Figure 1-3, died of typhoid fever just five months and one week after the wedding. The Bible entry is probably the only record of the cause of his death. (From the author's collection.)

Photograph Albums

Family albums may contain photographs and other family memorabilia. If you are very fortunate, photos will be labeled with the name(s) of the subject(s), the location, and the date. If not, be prepared to spend time with other family members and try to identify and label the pictures. This can be an enjoyable experience for everyone and especially rewarding for you as a genealogist. Photographs are keys to understanding your family's history and can be used to help place them in geographical, social, and historical context.

Scrapbooks

A scrapbook often presents a chronicle of life events for an individual or for an entire family group. Newspaper clippings can point you to additional sources for more information and documents. Programs of recitals, plays, sports events, and other occasions may reveal a family member's talents or interests. Obituaries, such as the one shown in Figure 1-5, are full of family history pointers and are often included in scrapbooks or memory books. While an obituary may be undated and the newspaper in which it was published might not be known, the value of the clues found in the obituary can be enormous.

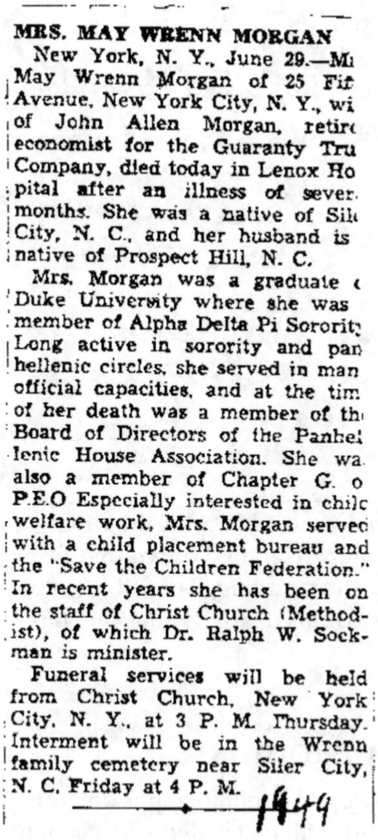

MRS. MAY WRENN MORGAN

New York, N. Y., June 29.—Mi May Wrenn Morgan of 25 Fif Avenue, New York City, N. Y., wi of John Allen Morgan, retire economist for the Guaranty Tru Company, died today in Lenox Ho pital after an illness of sever. months. She was a native of Sile City, N. C., and her husband is native of Prospect Hill, N. C.

Mrs. Morgan was a graduate e Duke University where she was member of Alpha Delta Pi Sororit; Long active in sorority and pan hellenic circles, she served in man official capacities, and at the tim of her death was a member of th Board of Directors of the Panhel lenic House Association. She wa also a member of Chapter G. o P.E.O Especially interested in chile welfare work, Mrs. Morgan servec with a child placement bureau and the "Save the Children Federation." In recent years she has been on the staff of Christ Church (Method- ist), of which Dr. Ralph W. Sock- man is minister.

Funeral services will be held from Christ Church, New York City, N. Y., at 3 P. M. Thursday. Interment will be in the Wrenn family cemetery near Siler City, N. C. Friday at 4 P. M. *1949*

FIGURE 1-5 Obituaries, such as this one, are often found in scrapbooks. (From the author's collection.)

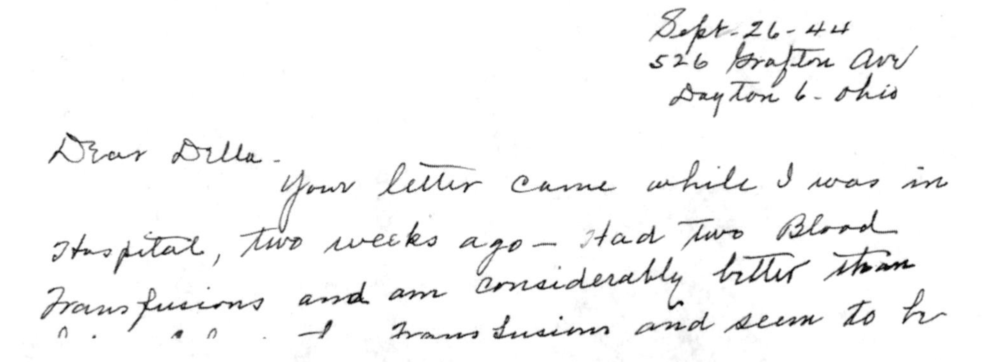
Sept-26-44
526 Grafton Ave
Dayton 6 - Ohio

Dear Della -
Your letter came while I was in Hospital, two weeks ago - Had two Blood Transfusions and am considerably better than
transfusions and seem to be

FIGURE 1-6 A return address on a letter or postcard from a family member may point to the geographical area where they lived and to where other documents may be found. (From the author's collection.)

Letters

Family correspondence is an important chronicle of life events. Letters may provide first-hand accounts of births, graduations, weddings, funerals, and other family occasions. You may uncover details about a person's everyday life, trips they made, their problems and concerns, and news about other family members. Here you may learn more about personal characteristics and family relationships than anywhere else. A return address in the body of a letter, such as in the example shown in Figure 1-6, on the original envelope, or on a postcard may provide an invaluable clue to locating other records about these family members at the time the communiqué was mailed.

Diaries and Journals

Everyday life events and often an individual's innermost thoughts are to be found in diaries and journals. Our ancestors often spent more time recording the details of their lives than we do today, and these cherished volumes can be real treasure troves for the family historian.

Accounting journals for a family farm or business may paint a detailed picture of the lifestyle of the family at the time, the crops and livestock they raised, the costs of supplies and clothing, and weather patterns, to name a few. During the time of slavery in the United States and elsewhere, the names of slaves may have been listed, along with information about their births, deaths, and other events.

Family Histories

An ancestor or another member of the family may already have prepared a historical account of a portion of the family's history. That doesn't mean that the work is already done for you. It merely means that you have a ready-made path to follow and to re-prove the facts and hypotheses already set forth by the other researcher.

MECKLENBURG COUNTY.   149

DR. ISAAC WILSON.

(A practitioner of Medicine from 1825 to 1875.)

The subject of this chapter was a son of Sheriff Wilson, and a nephew of that eminent minister, Rev. John McKamie Wilson, D. D., who was regarded as one of the greatest preachers of his day. Rocky River was his church and home for a number of years. He was so intimately connected with the people of Mecklenburg that no apology is needed for mentioning his name or his greatness. Dr. Isaac Wilson studied medicine under Dr. D. T. Caldwell. He did not have the advantages of attending a medical college, or one of the recent kinds of hospitals, but he gained his knowledge from medical works and bedside experience. His practice covered a large expanse of territory. One day he would start out on the west side, on the next he would go on the east side—so that he was able to see all of his patients once in two days. He carried a very capacious pair of saddlebags, which were replenished every morning with such things as were expected to be needed. One thing in particular was never left out, viz.: his cupping horn. Seventy-five years ago it was very fashionable to bleed in all diseases. Dr. Wilson was not noted for bleeding, but if he did not bleed, he always cupped, hence his horn was never forgotten. It was taken from the head of a two-year-old heifer, scraped so thin you could easily see how much blood was drawn. A nice piece of ivory or horn closed the large end, with a few tacks or wire, and the small end with beeswax, punctured with a pin—through this hole the air is sucked out, and with the teeth the wax is made to fill the hole, and the blood is now poured out in sufficient quantity to relieve the patient.

Dr. Wilson was well known in the northwestern half of the county. In those days when physicians were few and far between, their practice was necessarily extensive; and it was common for a doctor not to see his patients oftener than once in two or three days. In 1830, before quinine was

DR. ISAAC WILSON.

FIGURE 1-7   Local histories may provide ancestors' biographical details found nowhere else. (From the author's collection.)

Local Histories

Don't overlook books, pamphlets, and other publications that focus on the area where your ancestors and family members have lived. These may be in the family collection because of the area and also because information about the family may be included. In the book *The History of Mecklenburg County from 1740 to 1900* by J. B. Alexander, published in Charlotte, North Carolina, in 1902, I was rewarded not only with a biographical sketch of my great-great-grandfather, Isaac Wilson, M.D., but also with the only surviving photographic image of the man. Figure 1-7 shows two facing pages from that book.

Baby Books

The joy of the arrival of a child is recorded in baby books in great detail by parents, guardians, grandparents, and others. You may find that photographs such as the one shown in Figure 1-8, copies of birth documents, and clues to other materials and their location are included in these little books.

FIGURE 1-8   Baby books contain photographs such as this one, along with other important details. (From the author's collection.)

Marriage Books

A wedding provides an occasion for the gathering of families and for the creation of often vivid records. Matrimonial registers signed by attendees, photograph albums, wedding gift lists, and other records may provide excellent resources for your further research. You also may find copies of a marriage license or certificate, and copies of documents from the couple's religious institution(s) to help document the event. These can often lead you to religious membership rolls, and these can sometimes be used to trace family movements from place to place.

Funeral Books and Memorial Cards

Mortuaries and funeral homes have long provided families of the deceased with a funeral or memory book. These can be rich in untapped detail. The name of the deceased and the dates of birth and death are included, as well as the date and place of any services, and the place of interment. Copies of obituaries may be included. The register of persons who attended the visitation or wake will include family members' names and signatures, confirming their presence at the time. An examination of the register may help you reveal the married names of female relatives. In addition, the list of active and honorary pallbearers, as shown in Figure 1-9, should be studied to determine if family members were tapped to participate.

Cards such as the one shown in Figure 1-10 are often distributed at funerals and memorial services. They may commemorate the vital dates of the deceased and/or provide the text for a prayer to be read in unison by participants in the service.

Bearers

Rahn Boyer	Lee Lauten
Frank Lauten	Bobby Steele
Wayne Tilley	Otis Bullins
Gordon Tucker	Dick Anderson

Honorary Bearers

FIGURE 1-9   A page from a funeral book showing names of pallbearers. (From the author's collection.)

IN LOVING MEMORY OF

Mabel Christine Pollock

August 31, 1899
August 23, 1989

The Lord is my shepherd; I shall not want.
He maketh me to lie down in green pastures:
He leadeth me beside the still waters.
He restoreth my soul: He leadeth me in the
paths of righteousness for His name's sake.
Yea, though I walk through the valley of the
shadow of death, I will fear no evil:
for thou art with me; thy rod and
thy staff they comfort me.
Thou preparest a table before me in the
presence of mine enemies:
thou anointest my head with oil;
my cup runneth over.
Surely goodness and mercy shall follow
me all the days of my life:
and I will dwell in the house
of the Lord for ever.

Heeney-Sundquist Funeral Home
Farmington, Michigan

FIGURE 1-10   A memorial or prayer card. (From the author's collection.)

Identification Documents

You might find a number of identification documents that you can use as evidence in your research. A driver's license or passport confirms date of birth, age, physical characteristics, and residence. A Social Security card in the United States can provide an account number that can then be used to obtain a copy of the person's SS-5 application for a Social Security number. A health service card, an insurance card, and other identity papers from a variety of sources can provide leads to their issuers for potentially informative data.

Immigration Papers

On admission to a new country, an immigrant is typically issued some piece of documentation to prove his or her identity. Depending on the country and the historical time period, this may have been as simple as a letter or as formal as a visa, passport, alien registration card, or another document. In addition, vaccination records may also be located among immigration papers that point to the place of vaccination in the previous country of residence.

Naturalization Papers

Many immigrants took the necessary steps to renounce their original citizenship to become citizens of their new country. Some countries have required multiple documents to facilitate the process. In the United States, for example, an immigrant would swear an oath renouncing any allegiance to any foreign "power, sovereign, or potentate" and then sign a Declaration of Intent document. This was done at a courthouse and was the first step in the process to indicate his or her plan to seek citizenship. After a five-year waiting period, the person would file a Petition for Naturalization to initiate the paperwork to verify his or her good record and to request to become a naturalized citizen. While the process and the names of the documents vary in different countries, the process is similar.

The applicant or petitioner usually maintains copies of each document associated with their naturalization process and, finally, of the citizenship document. Figure 1-11 shows a United States Certificate of Naturalization. Not only are these treasured documents, they also provide evidence of citizenship that entitles the person to citizenship privileges such as the right to vote in elections.

FIGURE 1-11   Certificate of Naturalization for Karl Holger Kjolhede, dated 8 July 1946. (Courtesy of Jody Johnson.)

Land Records

Land and property records provide evidence of land ownership and residence. These are among the most numerous and yet the least used documents available for genealogical research. They include land grants, deeds, mortgages, agreements of sale, leases, mortgages, abstracts of title, land contracts, bonds, tax notices, tax bills, homestead documents, liens, legal judgments, dower releases, easements and releases, surveys, and other documents.

Military Records

These documents come in a wide range of record types and formats. Military service statements, disability certificates, discharge papers, separation papers, and pension records are common. Commendations, medals, ribbons, decorations, uniforms, swords, firearms, and other weapons are more tangible evidence of military service. Military regimental histories may also be in the family possession, as may be correspondence between the service person and his or her military branch and with other friends from service.

Directories

City directories, telephone directories, professional directories, alumni lists, personal telephone and address books, and similar items may be found in the home. These may include names, addresses, ages, and other details about family members.

Religious Publications

Newsletters, church bulletins, and other religious publications present a detailed chronology of the congregation's activities. You may find your ancestor or family member's life events announced there, as well as news of their involvement in congregational activities. However, the presence of family members' names in these publications suggests that there are probably membership records available in the congregation's offices.

School Records

Enrollment forms, homework papers/reports/projects, report cards, transcripts, diplomas, honor rolls, fraternity and sorority documents and jewelry, yearbooks and annuals, school photographic portraits, awards, and other materials may be found at home. (See Figure 1-12.) They represent information about family members from a specific period of time. Don't overlook these great resources and the insights they may provide. In addition, alumni directories and other correspondence may provide names and addresses of administrative offices that you may potentially contact for additional information.

LOTUS

LILLIAN BLUE
Gibson, N. C.

Π Θ Μ

Student Council, '24, '25; Secretary Student Body, '24, '25; Y. W. C. A. Cabinet, '23, '24; Fire Marshal, '23, '24, '25; Dramatic Club, '23, '24, '25; Walking Lieutenant '21, '22, '23, '24, '25.

"She strives best who serves most."

When a responsibility comes Lillian's way she assumes it and does her duty, earnestly and well. She has been a capable secretary of the Student Council, and an inspiring example to the rest of us. She is the kindest hearted girl in school and mothers us all.

MARTHA LEE BORDEN
Goldsboro, N. C.

Σ Φ Κ

President of Senior Class, '25; Vice-President of Sigma Phi Kappa Society, '24, '25; President of Cotillion Club, '25; Vice-President of Junior Class, '24; Associate Editor of *Voices of Peace*, '25; President of Preparatory Class, '22; Choral Club, '21, '22, '23, '24, '25; Secretary of Sigma Phi Kappa Society, '24; Secretary of Sophomore Class, '23; Commencement Marshal, '24; Statistics, '23, '25.

"All the gladsome sounds of nature borrow sweetness of her singing."

You have only to look at her picture to know that she possesses irresistible personal charm. She possesses not merely charm, however, but ability as well, for Martha Lee has been for years a strong member of the Class of '25. Peace will miss her, but we know she will make a success in the musical world for has she not a lovely voice—and a Victrola?

Thirty-one

FIGURE 1-12 A college yearbook, such as Peace Institute's 1925 *Lotus*, may yield important biographical information about your ancestor's participation in school activities. (From the author's collection.)

Employment Records

Employers may be reluctant to release records concerning their employees. However, around the home you may locate materials such as résumés, apprentice agreements, indentures of servitude, pay vouchers, paycheck stubs, union documents, life and health insurance policies, severance papers, retirement or pension documents, a Social Security (or Railroad Retirement Board) card, a medical care or prescription benefit card, a National Health Service identification card, or other employment-related materials.

Search for the Less-Than-Obvious Items

In addition to all of the items listed in the preceding sections, don't overlook household items that may contain important clues. Engraved jewelry and silverware may speak volumes to you. For example, an 18-karat gold locket holding tiny photographs of an elderly couple and engraved with the dates "1856–1906" provided the clue I needed to identify them as one set of my great-grandparents. These are the only known surviving pictures of these ancestors. Embroidered samplers, needlework, and quilts often include names and dates. Plaques, coats of arms, and personalized souvenirs offer other information. And don't overlook heirloom furniture and pictures, because you never know what may be incorporated into the design or concealed inside or underneath them.

It is important to investigate *all* the materials at home that may provide information or clues to your family's history. Search through books, letters, papers, trunks, suitcases, boxes, drawers, chests, attics, basements, garages, and everywhere else you can imagine. As you discover each new piece of evidence, keep track of where and when you located it. While that may seem unimportant now, it is definitely a worthwhile part of your documentation. Consider temporarily placing each document in an archival-quality envelope or polypropylene sheet protector sleeve along with a note concerning the name(s) of the person(s) about whom the item concerns, the date you located it, and where you located it. (We will discuss the importance of documenting your source materials in more detail in Chapter 2.)

Interview *All* Your Relatives

You never know where you will find that next piece of information. It could be as close as the family member sitting right beside you or it could be a distant cousin with whom you've never spoken. Your job is to learn as much as you can—*now*! Many a genealogist or family historian has lamented having waited too late to talk with parents and grandparents. However, it is never too late to make contacts with uncles and aunts, cousins, and family friends to learn as much as you can. You also may find that the "missing" family Bible isn't really lost; it may be in the possession of another relative after all.

Genealogy is a lot like journalism. You are seeking information from a variety of sources, asking questions, gathering facts and speculation alike, researching your sources, evaluating what you find, and producing hypotheses. If you do your job in a scholarly manner, you may be rewarded with factual proof as well as a better understanding of your family's story.

A good researcher learns how to ask questions, both of himself or herself and of others. Good interviewing skills are an essential part of your research, and it takes time to become an expert. There is an art to successfully conducting an interview with another family member but, with a little advance preparation and organization, you can become a pro in no time.

An interview need not be an "interrogation" so much as a friendly discussion. You will ask open-ended questions that require more elaboration than just a "yes" or "no" response. You want to get your relative to share knowledge and experiences in a friendly, non-threatening environment. A two-way conversation can be a mutually satisfying experience, blazing a trail for a stronger relationship—and more information—in the future.

Examples of some open-ended questions might include

- Where and when were you born?
- What was it like growing up during the Great Depression?
- What did you do on your first date?
- What kind of trips did you take when you were younger, and which was your favorite?
- What can you tell me about your aunts and uncles?

It is important to realize that there may be sensitive issues in the family that people are uncomfortable about and prefer not to discuss. Scandals, shame, secrets, lies, embarrassment, humiliation, and disgrace are all reasons for reluctance or refusal to discuss a person, place, time, or event. The two most powerful emotions are perhaps pride and the desire to protect the family reputation. Let me give you four examples involving refusals of family members to talk about the past:

- Both of my grandmothers were concerned that no one be aware of their ages. One refused to tell anyone the year of her birth and left instructions in her will that only her date of death be inscribed on her gravestone. The other shaved years from her age at each census until, in 1930, she had "lost" 16 years.
- A woman of Native American descent refused to discuss her parents. She was ashamed that she was an Indian and had inherited from her mother the desire to mask her origin.
- One woman was shocked to learn that the woman she thought was her older sister was, in fact, her mother and that she had been born out of wedlock. When asked about this by the family genealogist, she not only refused to discuss the matter but also made the genealogist swear never to repeat the scandalous information to anyone else in the family. She wanted to protect her own children and other family members from the scandal of illegitimacy.

- Imagine the surprise of the genealogist who discovered that her grandmother had made the family fortune in a most unusual way. Granny always said she didn't want to talk about her husband, and that he was a worthless man who left her before her daughter was born. The genealogist located Granny in the 1910 United States census in Chicago listed as a boarder in the home of two sisters, Minna and Ada Everleigh. Further research revealed that the Everleigh sisters were the proprietors of one of the most famous bordellos in Chicago and that Granny had been an "employee" there.

As you can see, there may be many reasons why family members are reluctant to discuss the past and other family members. However, don't leap to any conclusions. Some people are just not the talkative type.

Did You Know? Interviewing all of your relatives can provide you with invaluable information and clues to other resources. You may also obtain copies of original documentary evidence to verify or refute information.

Consider Several Types of Interview

Most people think of an interview as a face-to-face encounter between two or more individuals. An interview, however, can take one of several forms. In fact, some of the best interviews I've ever conducted with relatives have been done by telephone, and in multiple sessions. Consider the following types of interviews as possibilities for obtaining information from your family members:

- **Face-to-face interview**   This technique involves setting a time and place that is convenient to everyone involved.
- **Family gatherings**   A family reunion, a holiday dinner, a graduation, a wedding or funeral, or just a simple visit with other relatives can stimulate informal conversations from which stories and important family details can be learned.
- **Telephone conversations**   The telephone can be used to schedule and conduct either a casual or a more formal, in-depth interview. Use a "phone visit" as an occasion to ask one or two questions at a time. By establishing ongoing telephone communications with a relative, you not only build and strengthen the relationship between you and the relative, but also can continue asking questions about details over time as you proceed with your research.
- **Written questionnaires**   Use postal mail or email to gather family information. Some researchers prepare open-ended questions in document form and send these to relatives. Beware of sending a lengthy questionnaire, though. Few people are willing to spend a lot of time responding to dozens of questions. A few shorter sets of questions posed over an extended period of time often yield a better response rate. If you choose to use postal mail for your survey, be sure to enclose a self-addressed, stamped envelope (SASE) to encourage replies.

- **Requests for corrections**   Two effective tools used by genealogists to gather information are the family tree chart, commonly referred to as a pedigree chart, and the family group sheet. We will discuss these in more detail in Chapter 3. However, these are the documents that genealogists prepare to organize their family data and present it in report format. You may choose to send a copy of the documents to relatives, along with a SASE. Request that they add to and/or make corrections to the information you have compiled. Be sure to ask for photocopies of any documents they may have that corroborate the facts they provide, and always offer to reimburse them for the cost of their copying, postage, and mileage. Be sure to follow up by sending them a thank you note and an updated copy of the forms.

When preparing your list of questions, leave plenty of space in between them for responses. You will appreciate this when you are conducting an oral interview, and it encourages mail and email respondents to fill in the blank space with their commentary.

You may be surprised at the information gleaned during the oral interview process. I've located family Bibles, marriage certificates, deeds, letters, journals, and a host of other documents this way. Most important, however, has been the wealth of stories I've heard. These tales help bring the family members and their experiences to life. A first cousin related to me a story that her mother told her about two of our retired great-aunts and a train trip they made to Savannah, Georgia, to buy fresh crabs. They made the trip by day, purchased a bucket of live crabs, and then returned to the train station to take a sleeper train back home, booking an upper and a lower berth. During the night, one aunt awoke to use the bathroom. When she returned to her berth, she decided to reach up and pinch her sister's behind. Her sister burst from her berth yelling, "Good heavens! The crabs are loose!" Other passengers were awakened by the racket and peered out of their berths, only to see a woman race to the end of the train car and pull the emergency brake to stop the train. Not only is this a hilarious story, but it also provides some insight for me into the relationship of the two sisters and one's love of practical jokes.

Schedule Interviews for Best Results

It is important to respect your relative's time. It is inconsiderate and rude to show up unannounced to ask a lot of questions for which your relative is unprepared, especially if he or she has another commitment. Your best course of action, regardless of whether you would like to conduct a face-to-face or telephone interview, is to make contact in advance and schedule a mutually convenient time for your encounter. Be prepared for the question, "Well, what is it you want to know?" Before you even make the appointment, you should have decided what information you hope to learn and the questions you want to use to elicit the information.

By knowing the areas about which you want to know and letting the family member know in advance, he or she can mentally prepare for your visit or telephone call. The person also might like to gather together photographs, Bibles, papers, and other items to share with you. By contacting an elderly first cousin in advance and telling her I was interested in her parents and grandparents, I was rewarded with an opportunity to see my great-grandparents' Bible, letters they had written during their courtship, and pieces of heirloom furniture I had not known existed.

If you would like to record the interview, be sure to ask permission in advance. Remember that recording devices can be intimidating and distracting, and can make your subject self-conscious and nervous. If you detect any reluctance on the part of your subject, either in advance or at the time of the interview, don't record. Be prepared instead to take notes of the conversation.

Ask the Right Questions

Know something about the person you plan to interview *before* you make the appointment and *before* you arrive or call to conduct the interview. The last thing you want to do is waste anyone's time, and you want to make the most of the time you have together. That means understanding the person's place in the family structure, where they were geographically located, what other family members he or she would likely have known, and what materials might have come into their possession. Your primary goal should be to learn about the people and their lives. If there are materials that might document their life events, it is a bonus to be able to see them. It is most important, however, to learn *about* the people and their lives so that you can place them into geographical, historical, and sociological context. This will help you anticipate what records might exist to document their lives, where they were created, and where they may be found today.

Your family's origins and background certainly will determine the questions that you will ask. There are many, many places on the Internet where suggested lists of interview questions have been published. The following are a few links I think you will enjoy:

- "Interview Questions" by Juliana Smith
  www.ancestry.com/library/view/news/articles/3425.asp
- "Asking the Right Question" by George G. Morgan
  www.ancestry.com/library/view/columns/george/7041.asp
- "Sparking Family Memories" by Juliana Smith
  www.ancestry.com/library/view/columns/compass/2935.asp
- "Interviewing Grandma" by Michael John Neill
  www.ancestry.com/library/view/news/articles/7206.asp
- "Interview Absolutely Everyone!" by George G. Morgan
  www.ancestry.com/columns/george/04-03-98.htm

Use the Right Equipment for Your Interviews

You should be properly prepared to capture the information you are about to receive. Here are some basic pieces of equipment you will want to take with you to the interview:

- Paper and pencils or pens
- Audio/voice recorder or video recorder
- Conventional or digital camera
- Extra film
- Extra batteries

If you obtained permission in advance to record the interview, you will want to have checked the operation of the recorder in advance. The smaller the recording device, the less intrusive it will be. Be sure you know how to use it and that it is in good working condition before you leave home. When you arrive for the interview, ask again if it is okay to record. If not, move the equipment out of the interview area so that it is not a distraction. If your relative agrees to recording, though, you will be prepared to quickly and efficiently set up the equipment. Perform a sound check on the recording volume before you start, and place the microphone closer to your subject than to yourself. You want a clear recording of the responses and, even though you may not be able to hear all your questions and comments, you should be able to easily relate your subject's responses to your original questions.

Take one or two family items with you to help encourage conversation. I often use an old family photograph as a prop. I ask questions such as "Can you tell me where and when this picture was taken, and can you help me identify all the people in it?" This single question may be the icebreaker you need and the catalyst to open the floodgates of recollection. It literally *can* be worth the proverbial thousand words.

If you own or can borrow a laptop computer and a portable scanner, consider taking them with you as well. Family members may have Bibles, documents, photographs, and other items that can be copied on site. You will find that most of your relatives, regardless of how close they feel to you, are reluctant to let the family treasures out of their possession for any period of time. Some items can be photographed clearly enough using a digital camera to provide a clear and legible image. However, a scanner always provides the best quality image for your records.

Note The books *How to Do Everything: Digital Camera* by Dave Johnson (McGraw-Hill/Professional, 2008) and *How to Do Everything with Your Scanner* by David Huss (McGraw-Hill/Professional, 2003) offer excellent training for maximizing your use of these tools.

Set the Tone of the Interview

It is important in a face-to-face interview especially, but also in a telephone interview, to establish a comfort level for your relative and for yourself. Make sure that there is plenty of time available and that it is a pleasant environment. Interruptions should be kept to a minimum if possible. A third person sitting in on an interview can be a distraction and may prevent the person you are interviewing from opening up to you. Your interviewee may feel uncomfortable or reluctant to discuss people, events, and personal topics with another person present.

Start the interview with a few minutes of lighthearted conversation to set the tone of your time together. Share something with your relative about your life, news of the family, or some other item that might be of mutual interest. It helps break the ice and make your subject feel more at ease. When you begin the actual interview, however, make a tangible transition to that part of the session. In a face-to-face interview, you can do this by straightening yourself in your chair, opening your notebook, setting up a voice recorder (if your subject has already agreed to being recorded), or some other visible transition. If conducting a telephone interview, make the shift with a comment such as, "Well, I don't want to take up a lot of your time, so why don't we get started?" Use your common sense and tact about what is the right method of transitioning with each relative.

Think of yourself as a friendly, non-threatening journalist. Ask open-ended questions that require a response. "Where were you born and when?" is a good starter. You want to learn names, places, and dates, but you also want to know about the people in your relative's life: parents, brothers, sisters, grandparents, aunts, uncles, cousins, nephews, nieces, friends, teachers, ministers, librarians, and anyone else who may have influenced his or her family and life.

There may be topics that are sensitive and uncomfortable to discuss. Don't press the issue. Move on to the next question. The answer to the question may come up in another way, at another time, and perhaps from another relative but, for the present, let the subject drop. Being pushy and insistent can raise barriers between you and your relative that may interfere with the remainder of the interview and with the relationship between you as well.

Keep the interview short, no longer than one or two hours. Be alert to signs of fatigue. If you notice that your subject is beginning to tire, especially older relatives, be considerate and suggest that you continue later. A break may be sufficient but scheduling another session may be a better option. In the interim, both you and your relative will have time to digest what you have already discussed. You may revise your list of questions as a result, and your relative will have time to regroup and perhaps locate photographs and other materials he or she feels will be of interest to you.

Don't Forget the "Thank You"

After the interview, be sure to thank your relative for the time together and for sharing so much wonderful family history with you. Make another appointment, if appropriate, to meet again and talk. After you return home, consider sending a thank you note expressing your appreciation. Building these personal relationships in small ways like this is important. The connections you make are personally gratifying for both of you, and you never know what genealogical dividends they will pay in the future.

Begin to Organize What You Find

As you collect documents, photographs, family artifacts, and the exciting information gleaned from interviewing your relatives, you soon may feel overwhelmed at the volume of materials you are compiling. You're probably wondering what you're going to actually do with all this "stuff."

It is important to keep track of where and when you actually obtained the information and materials, and that will become part of the documentation process we'll explore in Chapter 3. It also is a good idea to develop a filing system early in your research process. Consider creating a large file folder or three-ring binder for each family surname (last name) you identify. Start with your own surname, moving on to your father's surname if it differs from yours, and then your mother's maiden surname. Continue on to the surnames of each of your four grandparents, your twelve great-grandparents, and so on. You may also be interested in setting up files for the spouses of your brothers and sisters, aunts and uncles, cousins, and on and on. I use binders for my filing system, and I file all the records for a surname (such as Morgan) in one binder. Within that binder, I file documents by given name (first name or forename) of each person, and then I file the documents for each of these individuals in chronological sequence. I also file each document in an archival-safe, polypropylene sheet protector. These protective sleeves are available at every office supply store and will help preserve the condition of the documents you obtain.

This is a starting point in your organization process, and your own filing system will be customized to your own research and reference needs. We will discuss organization and preservation in extensive detail elsewhere in the book. In the meantime, you can get started so that the job won't seem so overwhelming later.

Get Started

The starting point for your genealogical research begins with yourself and moves backward to your parents and beyond, as well as to your siblings and their families. Start with what you know and then move on to the unknown territory, actively seeking information and documentation along the way. The more data you obtain and the better you get to know about your family members' lives, the better prepared you are to venture further and learn more. Step by step, you will work your way further back in time and learn more about your ancestry. Placing your ancestors into context with the places and time periods in which they lived, and understanding the social and historical factors that influenced them, will bring these people to life for you. You are, after all, a direct product of these people, their genetic makeup, their circumstances, and the life decisions they made. As you learn more, you will become more self-aware of why you are the person you are, and you'll find yourself wanting to learn even more. Few things are more thrilling than touching a marriage certificate signed by your ancestors 150 years ago or holding an old Bible that was lovingly used by an ancestor. It won't be long before you have joined the tens of millions of other family historians around the world who are involved in the thrill of the research chase and the excitement of discovery.

2

Balance Traditional and Electronic Research

HOW TO...

- Be a modern genealogical researcher
- Understand traditional research
- Discover documentary evidence and where it is found
- Understand electronic research materials
- Learn about different types of electronic resources
- Integrate traditional and electronic research findings

It hasn't been that many years ago that genealogy and family history research was essentially a manual process. Researchers visited libraries and archives to check books, periodicals, and other holdings to determine what evidence might be located in other places, and then they would write letters to request look-ups and copies. They might also visit a nearby Church of Jesus Christ of Latter-day Saints (LDS Church) Family History Center (FHC) to consult the catalog of the Family History Library (FHL) in Salt Lake City, Utah, and identify potentially helpful records that had been microfilmed. They would have the volunteers at the FHC order the microfilm or microfiche from Salt Lake City and would pay a rental fee and use the microform materials at the FHC. The other alternative was to physically travel to facilities where records were held or where evidence might be found. In addition, a researcher might send a written query to a genealogical publication, such as *Everton's Genealogical Helper*, to broadcast his or her interest in locating information about a specific individual. This kind of research was time consuming and potentially very expensive. The wait for responses to letters and inquiries and the arrival of microform materials seemed interminable. As a result, genealogical research progress was a very slow process.

Did You Know?

The term "microform" refers to microfilm, microfiche, and sometimes other formats. It is an archive and storage medium that uses photographic images of documents and other media in a reduced format. The images are reduced about 25 times and stored on a high-resolution photographic film stock. Microfilm consists of images stored on reels of film; microfiche consists of many images stored on film sheets; and ultra fiche is an exceptionally compact form of microfiche or microfilm. Special machines are used to read, and sometimes print, the images from the film. Digital reader/printer machines are available to capture digital images of microform images. Microcards are an obsolete form of microfilming in which images were stored on cardboard cards and read using a magnifying reader.

Be a Modern Genealogical Researcher

The availability of personal computers slowly improved the process of conducting genealogical research. The early Bulletin Board Services (BBSs) in the late 1970s and 1980s facilitated some electronic communication between genealogists. Time passed and online services such as CompuServe, Delphi, GEnie, and America Online were introduced, and each of these services hosted a genealogy area to provide an online meeting place and reference resources to subscribers. Online lectures and chats were conducted using real-time typed exchanges of dialog and comments.

The LDS Church released the first formal genealogy database software, Personal Ancestral File (PAF), as a tool for documenting and organizing data. Users, particularly LDS Church members, were encouraged to use PAF and to submit data files to the LDS Church for inclusion in a large database. Over the years, many other genealogical database programs and utilities have been published. We will discuss those in more detail in Chapter 15.

The introduction of email and the World Wide Web ("the Web") to the public further accelerated the communications technology and promoted the online information explosion. Soon, most commercial companies had a presence on the Web. Further, the introduction of browser software and the inclusion of graphics in web pages made the Internet the most important source of information available.

Genealogists quickly adopted the Internet and began using email mailing lists and online message boards to publish queries about all things genealogical. Websites were created that were devoted to genealogical research. Among the earliest of these were RootsWeb.com (**www.rootsweb.ancestry.com**) and the all-volunteer USGenWeb Project (**www.usgenweb.org**; see Figure 2-1) and WorldGenWeb Project (**www.worldgenweb .org**). These sites provide free "how-to" information and access to data transcribed from original sources by volunteers. The LDS Church established a website, FamilySearch.org (**www.familysearch.org**), to make indexed information available, as well as access to an electronic catalog of its holdings and downloadable PAF software.

Online genealogical subscription services have proliferated on the Internet. These include Ancestry.com (**www.ancestry.com**; see Figure 2-2), Genealogy.com (**http://genealogy.com**), HeritageQuest Online (**www.heritagequestonline.com**),

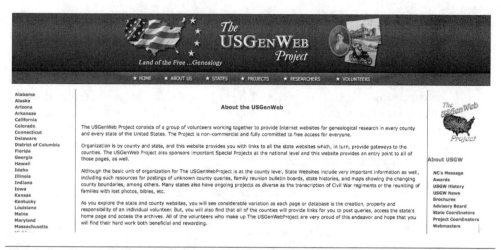

FIGURE 2-1   USGenWeb Project page. (Used with permission of USGenWeb.)

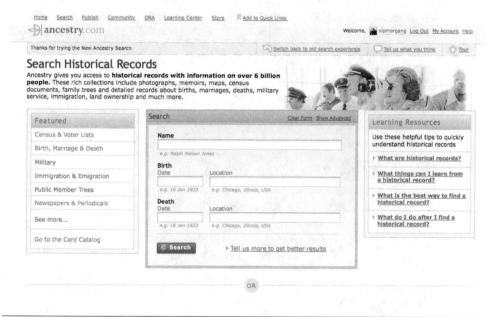

FIGURE 2-2   The Search screen at Ancestry.com. (Used with permission of The Generations Network, Inc.)

Footnote.com (**www.footnote.com**), WorldVitalRecords.com (**www.worldvitalrecords .com**), and many others around the world.

Libraries and archives have kept pace with Internet technology. Almost every library or archive has a website that provides access to their electronic catalog, descriptions of holdings, policies, and other information. LibrarySpot.com (**http://libraryspot.com**) provides a place to begin locating libraries' and archives' websites around the world. OCLC, the Online Computer Library Center, hosts WorldCat (**www.worldcat.org**), another excellent tool for locating specific books and other items in libraries.

Some libraries have digitized materials in their collections that are accessible through their website. The Library and Archives Canada website (**www.collectionscanada .gc.ca**) has digitized Canadian census records, and has produced an impressively informative set of "how-to" and reference resources in its Canadian Genealogy Centre area (see Figure 2-3). The diversity of digitized records that are accessible through libraries' websites is phenomenal.

In addition to the websites maintained by libraries and archives, these facilities frequently subscribe to important database services. Some of these may

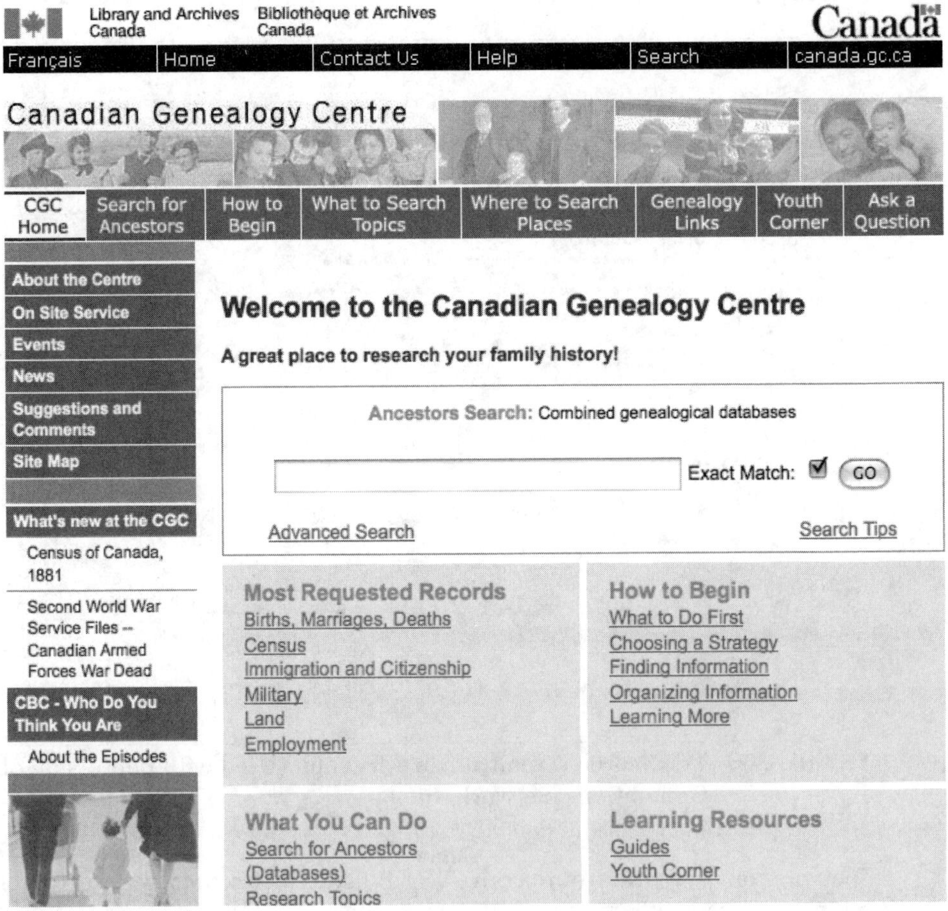

FIGURE 2-3 The Canadian Genealogy Centre page at the Library and Archives Canada

be genealogy-specific while others, such as historical newspapers and obituary databases, may be fully searchable and provide access to invaluable information to help further your research. Most of these are typically accessible from your remote computer with the use of your library card number.

Your favorite web browser software provides you with access to resources worldwide: digitized documents and photographs, newspapers, digitized historical map collections, cemetery information and transcriptions, online newsletters and magazines, and much, much more. We'll explore these further a little later in this chapter and elsewhere in the book.

Understand Traditional Research

Traditional research was and still is the central form of genealogical investigation, and it is essential for acquiring documentary evidence. In Chapter 3, we'll discuss the concepts of original vs. derivative sources and primary vs. secondary evidence. For now, let's just say that the most reliable evidence of a fact is an original document created at or very near the time an event occurred. It is not something transcribed or taken from a word-of-mouth account, because the details may have inconsistencies or may be incorrect.

Traditional research entails looking for clues that direct you to concrete evidence. If you have watched any of the several *Crime Scene Investigation* series on television, you know that building a reliable case means searching for original evidence, studying it, evaluating it in relation to other facts or evidence, developing a hypothesis (or more than one), and substantiating the hypothesis with a strong body of original evidentiary proof. Does that sound complicated? Well, it is and it isn't. Yes, your research should be done in a scholarly manner and must incorporate strong original evidence. However, this will quickly become second nature to you and soon you will be enjoying every aspect of "the thrill of the chase."

Discover Documentary Evidence and Where It Is Found

Traditional research will always entail working with a variety of materials. These include

- Books and periodicals
- Manuscripts
- Maps
- Indexes
- Histories
- Biographies
- Newspapers
- Documents from many traditional locations and sources

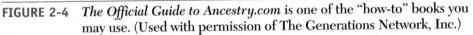

FIGURE 2-4 *The Official Guide to Ancestry.com* is one of the "how-to" books you may use. (Used with permission of The Generations Network, Inc.)

Books and Periodicals

Printed books will always be a source of genealogical information in your research. You will find books that contain everything from "how-to" information, such as this book, to transcribed records, to published images of original records. (See Figure 2-4.) Magazines and journals published by genealogical and historical societies, as well as commercial magazines, may provide details and/or case studies containing information about your ancestor or some facet of his or her life.

Some older historical books are being electronically scanned and indexed, and these are appearing at a number of online sites such as Ancestry.com, HeritageQuest Online, WorldVitalRecords.com, and others. They are every-word searchable and can provide you with access to resources otherwise available only at a remote library or archive.

You will always want to invest time in researching the collections found in libraries, archives, and genealogical societies. They can provide clues to guide you to the original evidentiary records that you want to examine in your research.

Manuscripts

Original, one-of-a-kind manuscripts are seldom found anywhere but inside a library or archive. An unpublished family history may contain a wealth of information and clues that can lead you to genealogical treasure. However, don't expect a manuscript to have been microfilmed or digitized. More than likely, you will need to travel to the repository where it is stored in order to access it.

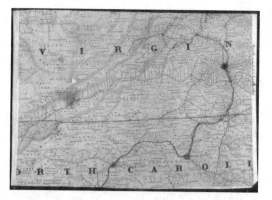

FIGURE 2-5 Map showing Col. John Singleton Mosby's route through Virginia and North Carolina during the U.S. Civil War. (From the Library of Congress collection.)

Maps

Geography is an integral part of genealogical research. It is essential to understand the location where your ancestor lived, where the geopolitical boundaries were, how the boundaries may have changed during your ancestor's residency there, and what governmental body had jurisdiction of the area at a specific time. While many historical maps have been digitized and are on the Internet, most exist only in library collections, archives, university special collections, or the holdings of individuals or organizations (such as the Library of Congress, whose collection includes the map shown in Figure 2-5).

Indexes

There are thousands of published indexes to original records of genealogical importance. P. William Filby's epic and ongoing publication, *Passenger and Immigration Lists Index*, remains the most important reference for identifying information about immigrants to the American colonies and the United States. *Germans to America* is another important reference. However, there are indexes to original documents worldwide. The Civil Registration registers of births, marriages, and deaths for England and Wales, for instance, cover the period from July 1837 to 1983, and more recent registrations are accessible up to 18 months prior to the current date. Indexes to names in censuses, bride and groom marriage indexes, land and property indexes, military service records and awards, and hundreds of other record types have been published. These indexes provide guidance to direct you to the original records, and you can then order copies and examine the exact content for yourself.

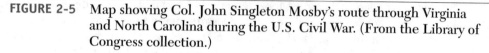

Did You Know? Local histories may contain mentions about your own family. At a minimum, they can convey to you what life was like in the area when your ancestors lived there.

Histories

History books and other historical accounts, such as diaries and journals, may only exist in printed form or as a manuscript. Histories provide you with the context of a place and time in which your ancestor lived. In some cases, a local history may provide the only evidence of your ancestor's presence and activities in an area.

Biographies

Biographies and autobiographies of individuals are important sources of information and clues to original materials. Typically found in library collections, you can use these publications as you would a history book. A biography or autobiography provides an historical context for a time period and describes people, places, locations, and events. For example, while your ancestor's name may never be mentioned, a biography of a military leader under which your ancestor served will likely provide a chronological account of military engagements and details about the circumstances. This information is helpful in understanding that portion of your ancestor's life and the events that influenced him or her and other people.

Newspapers

A newspaper is the chronicle of a community, incorporating news and events about people from all walks of life. Original newspapers are not frequently retained in storage, for a number of reasons. They are certainly a fire hazard, but their physical content produces fumes and other by-products that can be harmful to your health. Finally, newsprint from the late 19th century forward is highly acidic in content, and the acid and lignin can contaminate other materials, causing them to discolor and deteriorate.

Many newspapers have been microfilmed before the originals were destroyed. This is excellent news for researchers. However, unless the newspaper has been indexed in some way, your research will depend on knowing dates or date ranges of issues; otherwise, you may have to comb through image after image on many rolls of microfilm or many sheets of microfiche. These microform records are often found in the library or in an historical archive in or near the place of publication. Copies may also be held in a regional, state, provincial, or national library or archive. You will need to visit that repository to access these records.

A number of the larger newspapers in various countries have been digitized and every-word indexed for complete searchability. Others from across the United States have been scanned and made available at subscription sites such as Ancestry.com (see Figure 2-6). However, because of the varying quality of the microforms from which the digitized images were taken, and the limitations of the optical character recognition (OCR) scanning capability, there may be unavoidable indexing errors.

FIGURE 2-6   Section of the front page of the *Ironwood Daily Globe* in Ironwood, Michigan, on 23 November 1963, from the digitized newspaper database collection at Ancestry.com. (Used with permission of The Generations Network, Inc.)

Documents from Many Traditional Locations and Sources

Your research for original documents or exact copies will take you to many places. This book will help lead you to specific repositories in various locations in order to access those documents. Among them are government offices, health departments, police records repositories, coroners' offices, land and property offices, civil, criminal, and probate courts, churches and religious offices, military records storage repositories, cemeteries and cemetery offices, manuscript collections, libraries, archives at all levels, schools and universities, genealogical and historical societies, and many more. The documents will be unique unto themselves. You will learn more about documents and working with them in Chapter 3 and throughout the book.

Understand Electronic Research Materials

You will find that there are many different types of electronic research resources, and it is sometimes difficult to keep them straight. If you understand the difference between them and what they can provide, it will become easier to decide which resource(s) will be your best tool(s) to use for specific types of research. Let's explore the major kinds of electronic resources you will use. We'll cover all of these in more detail later in the book.

Email and Mailing Lists

Perhaps the most ubiquitous electronic tool in use today is electronic mail, or email. It provides a rapid and inexpensive way to communicate with one or lots of people at once. Email allows you to send and receive textual communiqués and to attach files, such as word processing documents, spreadsheets, digital photos, audio files, videos, and data files, from many software applications.

Electronic mailing lists are a commonly used resource, allowing many people to subscribe and to send and receive messages sent by other subscribers. There are thousands of genealogy-related mailing lists, each with a specific topical purpose. There are surname lists, lists for specific geographical areas, lists concerning locating and working with specific record types, ethnic and religious lists, and a wide variety of other topics.

Message Boards

Electronic message boards are similar to mailing lists, providing a means for exchanging information with others (see Figure 2-7). A message board, however, resides on the Internet, and you must proactively read it and/or post messages to it. (Some message boards also may be set up to notify you via email when there is a new message. However, email doesn't play a role in posting to and working with message boards.)

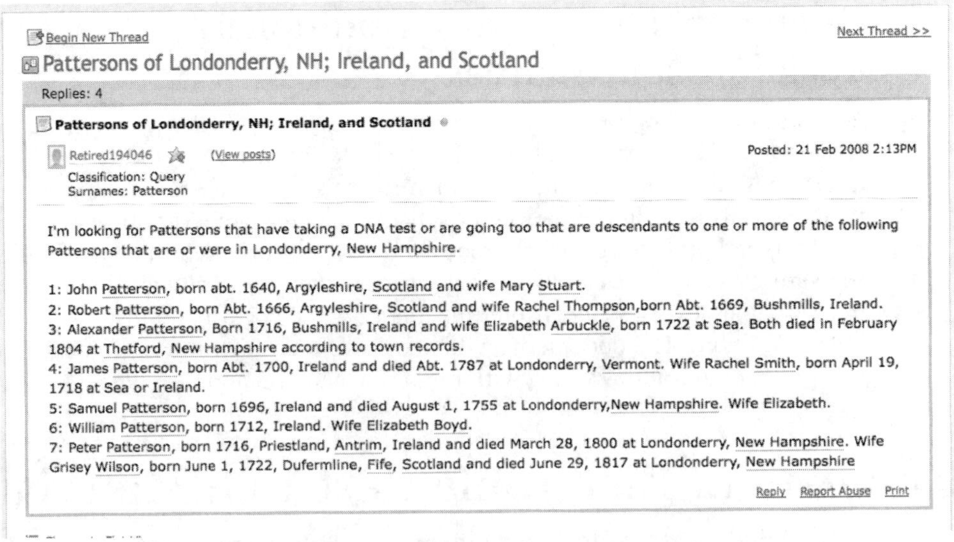

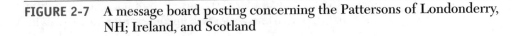

FIGURE 2-7   A message board posting concerning the Pattersons of Londonderry, NH; Ireland, and Scotland

Web Pages

Web pages on the Internet contain a wealth of information, and there are literally billions of web pages accessible by visiting web addresses known to you or that you read about. These may include individual people's web pages, free and subscription websites, subscription databases, as well as blogs (web logs) and other resources. However, your favorite web browser allows you to connect with Internet search engines and to seek out web pages using site names, keywords and phrases, and other criteria.

Compilations and Indexes

There are many websites that have compiled various types of materials for your reference. RootsWeb.com (**www.rootsweb.ancestry.com**) provides "how-to" materials, access to mailing list resources, family trees submitted by you and other researchers, and a variety of online tools. Cyndi's List of Genealogy Sites on the Internet (**www .cyndislist.com**), shown in Figure 2-8, is a compilation of more than 265,000 categorized links to genealogical sites on the Internet. It is *the* starting point for locating all types of research resources. The USGenWeb Project (**www.usgenweb.org**) and the WorldGenWeb

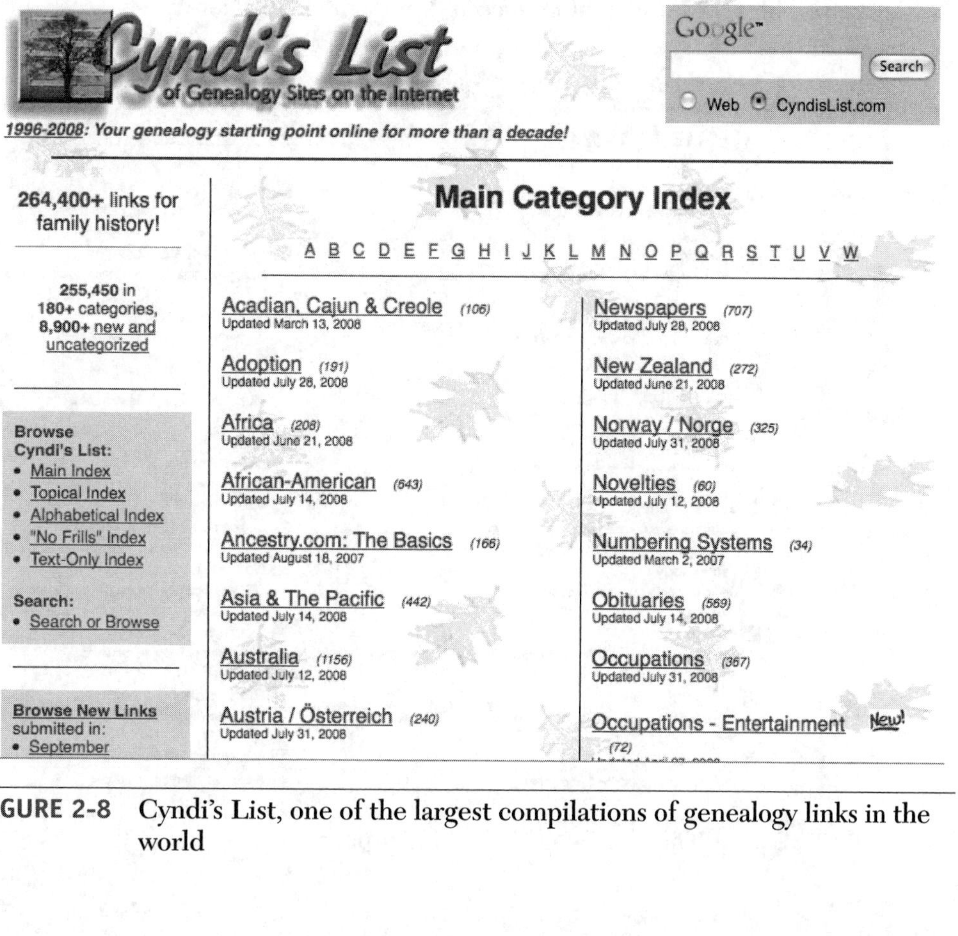

FIGURE 2-8 Cyndi's List, one of the largest compilations of genealogy links in the world

Project (**www.worldgenweb.org**) are two 100 percent volunteer collections for United States and international genealogical information and resources, respectively. Find A Grave (**www.findagrave.com**) is a massive collection of more than 29 million records of cemetery and interment information from around the world that have been transcribed by individuals and entered into a free online database.

Subscription Internet Sites for Genealogy

There are many subscription genealogy sites on the Internet, all of which combined provide access to literally tens of thousands of databases. These databases include indexes to records, digitized and indexed original document images, scanned and searchable books and newspapers, and a host of other great resources. Leaders in this area are Ancestry.com, Footnote.com, Findmypast.com (**www.findmypast.com**), and WorldVitalRecords.com, among others.

Blogs

Blogs are online journals published online about many topics. A great place to locate blogs of interest to you is Chris Dunham's Genealogy Blog Finder at **http://blogfinder.genealogue.com** (see Figure 2-9). There are blogs about national

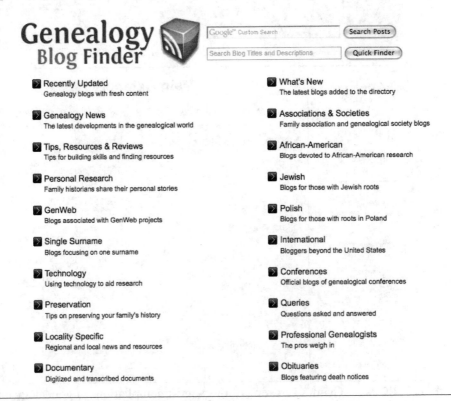

FIGURE 2-9 The Genealogy Blog Finder page

and ethnic origins, religious information, genetic genealogy, software programs, news and events, and much more.

Podcasts and Vidcasts

Podcasts are audio programs that are recorded and published on the Internet. You can listen to them at their website, download and listen to them on your computer or MP3 player/iPod, or burn them to a CD. I am co-host, with my partner Drew Smith, of "The Genealogy Guys Podcast" each week at **http://genealogyguys.com** (see Figure 2-10). The video equivalent of a podcast is referred to as "vidcast" or "vodcast." Genealogy videos are plentiful at Roots Television (**www.rootstelevision.com**), including lectures, interviews, "how-to" programs, and series, such as The Genealogy Guys in "Down Under: Florida."

FIGURE 2-10   The Genealogy Guys Podcast site. (Used with permission of The Genealogy Guys and Aha! Seminars, Inc.)

Social Networking Sites

You have undoubtedly heard of My Space and Facebook, the world's largest social networking sites on the Internet. There are, however, social network sites specifically related to genealogists that allow you to share information with other researchers, add and store your family tree data online at their sites, and collaborate with designated family members on your genealogical research. The following sites are among the social networking sites, as of this writing:

Amiglia	www.amiglia.com
Ancestry.com	www.ancestry.com
Genes Reunited	www.genesreunited.com
GeneTree	www.genetree.com
Genoom	www.genoom.com
Familybuilder	www.familybuilder.com
FamilyHistoryLink	www.familyhistorylink.com
findmypast.com	www.findmypast.com
Famiva	http://famiva.com
Geni	www.geni.com
Kincafe.com	http://kincafe.com
Living Genealogy	www.livinggenealogy.com
MyFamily.com	www.myfamily.com
MyHeritage	www.myheritage.com
NokTree	www.noktree.com
OurStory	www.ourstory.com
SharedTree	www.sharedtree.com
Story of My Life	www.storyofmylife.com
WeRelate	www.werelate.org
Zooof	www.zooof.com

Did You Know? Social networking sites allow you to share information with family, friends, and other researchers. However, be aware that uploading your family information to more than one site means that, when you make changes and additions, you will need to update *all* of the social networking sites you use.

Integrate Traditional and Electronic Research Findings

The overview I have shared with you in this chapter should have piqued your interest in what kinds of resources are available. Hopefully, you now have a better understanding of the differences between so-called "traditional" and "electronic" resources. While you may have thought, "Wow! I can do it all on the Internet!", you would be completely wrong. While there *is* a great deal of material on the Internet, there is much, much more that is not there. Your research must incorporate *and* combine traditional research and resources *with* electronic resources.

This chapter should have prepared you to learn about each of the resources discussed throughout the book. Chapter 3 will lay the complete foundation for collecting and evaluating evidence, organizing and recording it, and creating source citations to effectively document the evidence for future reference. You're already well on your way to building the solid foundation for effective genealogy and family history research. Read on!

3

Organize and Create Your Family Tree

HOW TO...

- Evaluate primary vs. secondary sources
- Recognize and evaluate original vs. derivative materials
- Avoid errors in derivative sources
- Apply critical thinking skills to your genealogical research
- Place your ancestors into context
- Format names, dates, and locations correctly
- Work with pedigree charts
- Work with family group sheets
- Create source citations for your data
- Select a family tree format

Gathering your family information is fun and exciting. I like to think of family history as a large tapestry made up of many colorful threads that, when woven together, present a vivid story. You should recognize, too, that it is important to organize the materials you find in your genealogical quest in order to document and better understand the big picture.

In later chapters, we'll discuss how to go about selecting the genealogy database software program that best suits your needs and how to organize and file your data. Before you make those decisions, though, there are some essential concepts that form the foundation for everything else you do. In this chapter, you will learn about the indispensable methodologies for identifying and properly analyzing the evidence you discover, whether that be documents, books, photographs, microfilm, cemetery markers, or oral stories. The goal is to help you understand these points and to prepare you to dive right into the investigative research process.

Evaluate Primary vs. Secondary Sources

One of the most important considerations in your research is adhering to the basic rules of genealogical evidence. You will quickly learn that not every source of information is equal and that some materials are more reliable than others. That means that you will evaluate every piece of evidence, regardless of the source, and analyze its strength and value.

In many cases, a piece of documentary evidence is generated as the result of some event: birth, marriage, death, sale of property, voting, taxation, court action, probate process, or some other occasion. Sometimes, though, a record is made before the fact and the event never takes place, as in the case of marriage bonds or marriage licenses issued where the marriage never took place, tombstones created for an individual who was never buried in the plot, and agreements of sale that were never executed. Are these valid pieces of evidence too? Of course they are, because they were created to represent intent. And even if the intended action never occurred, the piece of evidence places the person(s) involved in a certain place at a specific point in time and tells you something about his or her life. It may lead you to another clue or source of information.

When evaluating the records of your ancestors' lives, you must always consider the source of the information. Why was it created? When was it created? Who created it? Is it truthful? Source materials can be grouped into two categories: *primary* and *secondary sources*. There are very distinct differences.

Primary sources were created at or very near the actual event being recorded and are therefore more likely to be accurate. Secondary sources were typically created after the fact and, because of the lapse of time and memory, tend to be less reliable than primary sources. Some materials are both primary *and* secondary sources of information. Let's explore some of the most common types of documentary evidence, and evaluate the quality of the information.

Birth Certificates

An example of a primary source is an original or photocopy of a birth certificate. The information on this document was provided at or just after the time of birth and was completed for the purpose of recording the event. An amended birth certificate, such as one issued later that changes the information recorded at the time of the birth, may have been intended to provide more accurate or complete information than that which was entered on the original document. However, there may indeed be other, less correct information placed on that document just because it was done later. A delayed birth certificate, though, which is one issued some time after the event— probably for someone born before birth certificates were issued, born at home with the benefit of a midwife, or whose records were destroyed in a courthouse or other repository—is a secondary source.

Marriage Certificates

Another example of a primary source is a marriage certificate. Prior to a marriage, a couple usually must have obtained a license to marry, and a government office typically issued the license. When the marriage was performed, the person officiating at the ceremony signed and dated the license to indicate that the marriage had been completed according to law. The signed license was then returned to the government office for issuance of the official marriage certificate. The signed license is commonly referred to as a "marriage return," and the information contained in the document was transcribed into a marriage book by a clerk. When the marriage book was filled, it was usually alphabetically indexed in two sequences: by the groom's name and by the bride's name. One of the marriage returns transcribed into a marriage book, such as the one shown in Figure 3-1, would be considered a secondary source even though the information was copied into the book shortly after the event. That is because it has been transcribed, or copied by hand, and there is the possibility that the clerk made a transcription error. The entry of an incorrect maiden name on my great-grandparents' marriage record caused me to spend years searching for the possibility that my great-grandmother had been married before.

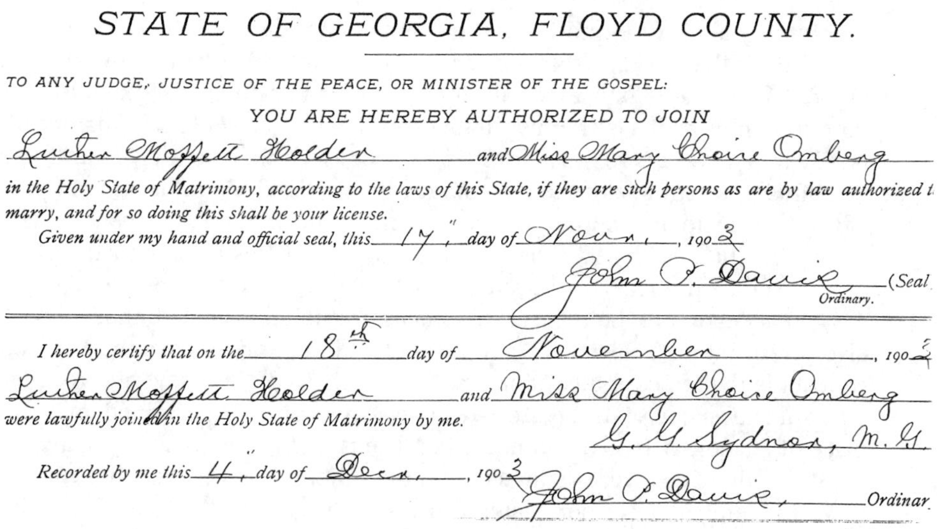

STATE OF GEORGIA, FLOYD COUNTY.

TO ANY JUDGE, JUSTICE OF THE PEACE, OR MINISTER OF THE GOSPEL:

YOU ARE HEREBY AUTHORIZED TO JOIN

Luther Moffett Holder and Miss Mary Choice Omberg

in the Holy State of Matrimony, according to the laws of this State, if they are such persons as are by law authorized t[o] marry, and for so doing this shall be your license.

Given under my hand and official seal, this 17" *day of* Nov., *190*3

John P. Davis (Seal) *Ordinary.*

I hereby certify that on the 18th *day of* November, *190*3

Luther Moffett Holder *and* Miss Mary Choice Omberg

were lawfully joined in the Holy State of Matrimony by me.

G. G. Sydnor, M.G.

Recorded by me this 4" *day of* Dec., *190*3 John P. Davis, *Ordinar[y]*

FIGURE 3-1 A marriage license can be a strong source of information. The upper portion of this document is the license; the bottom portion is the "return," which was completed by the official performing the marriage. It was returned to the clerk for registration. (From the author's collection.)

Death Certificates

Can something be *both* a primary *and* a secondary source? You bet! A death certificate is considered a primary source for information related to the person's death but is a secondary source for all other information, such as date of birth of the decedent, his or her birthplace, names of the parents and spouse, occupation, and other information. A government official or coroner will have completed the information in order to certify the death. Someone else, such as a relative or friend, would supply information to the individual who completed the death certificate, and he or she may not have had adequate knowledge of these details or accurate facts. Sometimes you may even see a death certificate on which some data fields are left blank or are marked "unknown."

Every piece of information that does not directly relate to the event for which the source document was prepared should be considered a secondary source. You certainly can use secondary material as a clue or pointer to other primary materials that verify or refute what is on that death certificate.

Let's examine three examples of secondary sources that also might contain erroneous information.

Obituaries

An obituary is a written notice of the death of an individual. It typically includes the name of the person, where they lived, the date of death, and information about any planned funeral or memorial service. An obituary may also include biographical information provided by family members or friends, as well as the names of surviving family members. There are a number of places where errors may be introduced in an obituary, starting with the informant who provided the information to the writer of the notice. He or she may provide incorrect information. The person taking down the information, such as a funeral home clerk or a newspaper copy desk clerk, may omit a word, alter a fact, or introduce spelling or punctuation errors. The publisher may create errors in the typesetting process, or an editor may either miss catching an error or introduce a mistake. Each person handling the information may potentially contribute to the possibility of errors. The result might be a severe error that leads you on a wild goose chase. In Figure 3-2, my father's obituary contained an error in my place of residence. Instead of indicating "Chicago, Ill.," the obituary stated that I lived in "Fargo, Ill." The error originated with the funeral home clerk who, when taking down the information, abbreviated Chicago as "Ch'go" and the newspaper interpreted the clerk's handwriting to be "Fargo."

As you can imagine, this error might send a genealogical researcher seeking information about me in a location where I never lived. Worse yet, the researcher might waste time looking for a nonexistent location.

SAMUEL THOMAS MORGAN

Funeral services for Samuel Thomas Morgan, 70, of Rt. 2, Madison, were held at 11 a.m. Monday at Ray Funeral Home with Dr. Larry Bennett officiating. Burial was in Woodland cemetery. Mr. Morgan died Friday at Annie Penn Memorial Hospital in Reidsville.

He was a native of Alamance County and a retired industrial engineer with Gem-Dandy Inc. He was was a member of the Madison Presbyterian Church. He joined the Madison Lions Club in 1952 and was a member for 28 years, with perfect attendance 26 years, was secretary from 1956-57; treasurer of the Agricultural Fair Association from 1967-1978, received a Quarter Century award in 1977; 25 years Monarch Award in 1977; Outstanding Award for Lion of the Year in 1966.

Surviving are wife, Mrs. Edith Weatherly Morgan; sons, Carey Morgan of Greensboro, and George Morgan of Fargo, Ill.

FIGURE 3-2 An obituary with an error introduced by the newspaper. (From the author's collection.)

Cemetery Markers

Tombstones, grave markers, and memorial plaques placed in cemeteries, mausoleums, and elsewhere may provide clues to primary and/or secondary sources of information. Some are simple and others are more elaborate and may contain great quantities of information. The name and dates on a marker can lead you to search for documents such as birth and death certificates, church or religious records, military records, obituaries, and other materials.

FIGURE 3-3   This marker indicates the person's membership in an organization. (From the author's collection.)

Some markers may even be adorned with medallions commemorating military rank or membership in some organization, such as the example in Figure 3-3, which indicates that Olin Talley McIntosh was a member of the Society of the Cincinnati. This medallion would encourage you to look for a local chapter of the Society and to obtain copies of the member's records, if possible.

More elaborate markers, like the one shown in Figure 3-4, may provide more information. This stone indicates that Harry was the youngest son of "Benj. & Isabella Green." His date of death is shown as "Oct. 10, A.D. 1871" and his age as "8 years and 6 months." This detailed information provides a link to the parents' information and would encourage you to seek details concerning the child's date of birth and the cause of his death.

Like obituaries, though, gravestones and plaques are created based on information provided to the creator of the marker and may contain erroneous information. It is not unknown for a stone carver to make a mistake. For example, the surname on one gravestone in an old cemetery in downtown Tampa, Florida, is misspelled. Instead of replacing the stone, however, someone returned to carve a slash mark through the incorrect letter and inscribe the corrected letter above. A marker in the historic cemetery in St. Marys, Georgia, was miscarved, and the stonecutter used a stone cement to fill the incorrect letter and then recarved it. The error is still visible on the stone. Remember that the stone carver is only inscribing what was provided and that he or she, too, can introduce errors.

Another problem with tombstones is that, unless you were involved with the purchase or placement of a marker on a grave, you may have no idea when the stone was created or installed. During the Great Depression of the 1930s, families could not always afford a marker for a grave. As a result, it may have been years or decades before a stone was ordered and installed. (The cemetery office may have a record of

FIGURE 3-4   Elaborate marker for Harry Green at Bonaventure Cemetery, Savannah, Georgia. (From the author's collection.)

when the marker was set in place.) While the information you see is "set in stone," always seek corroboration elsewhere of the facts engraved there. I wrote an article for Ancestry.com some time ago that will provide you with additional information on this subject. It is titled "Tombstones Are Secondary Sources" and can be found at **www .ancestry.com/library/view/columns/george/2840.asp**.

Bible Entries

It is a natural assumption for all of us to make that what is entered in the family Bible is correct, but these entries can be misleading as well. Remember that birth, marriage, death, and other information could have been made at any time. There are several things to look for when examining entries made in a Bible that may indicate that they are not primary sources:

- *Always check the publication date of the Bible.* If the date of any entry predates the publication date, you know that it was added later and is therefore secondary material.
- *Examine the handwriting carefully.* The fact that the handwriting is identical doesn't mean much, especially if this was a personal or family Bible. One person may have been the family scribe. However, if you can identify the owner of the handwriting for the entries and can determine that entries were made prior to that person's birth *or* for a logical period when he or she could not have made the entry, you may conclude that the information is secondary in nature.
- *Examine the ink used in the entries.* If all the entries appear to have been made with the same pen and ink, it is possible that someone added a group of entries at one time and not as they occurred. Another tip-off is if any entries for events with dates that precede 1945 are made using a ballpoint pen—they are definitely secondary sources. Why? Because the ballpoint pen was not invented until 1938, was introduced during World War II for military use, and was not sold commercially until 1945.

Recognize and Evaluate Original vs. Derivative Sources

Another consideration in your research is whether the evidence you find is an *original* or *derivative* source. By that, I mean that the material is either an original document *or* that the information has been taken (derived) from some other source. Derivative material might include such things as word-of-mouth accounts, information that was transcribed from other materials, information extracted or abstracted from the original materials, or anything else that is not the genuine, original source.

The original sources you use are indeed the actual documents or other materials created for the purpose of recording something. A marriage certificate would certainly be an original source document. So, too, would be an exact photocopy, a microfilm image, a photograph, or a scanned document image. Anything that is an accurate and exact image of the original document can be considered an original source.

Derivative materials are a different story. As we've already discussed, anytime someone copies or transcribes something, there is a possibility that an error may be introduced. In the course of your genealogical research, you will work with many different materials. Sometimes it is impossible to obtain a photocopy or an exact image of the material. As a result, you will spend time copying information by hand. What you are doing is "deriving" information from the original material, regardless of whether it is a document, a tombstone, an engraved piece of jewelry, or another original source item.

Understand Types of Derivative Sources

Genealogists know that there are three types of derivative sources: a transcription, an extract, and an abstract. Let's discuss the attributes of each of these materials.

Transcription

A transcription is an exact written copy of an original source material. The operative word here is "exact." That means that you are working from the original and are copying its content exactly, word for word, and preserving the spelling and punctuation precisely as it appears in the source document. Since it is possible for you to make transcription errors, it is important that you carefully check your work to ensure that you don't omit or introduce any additional words or characters, and that you don't make any alteration to the content or intent. If you must make a personal notation in the transcription for clarity, enclose it in square brackets and precede your text with the Latin word *sic*. For example, if you encountered a name spelled as Lizzy and you know that it was spelled differently, you might notate it as follows: [*sic*, Elizabeth].

Consider the situation in which a will for a certain man included a list of his six children. The list included "John, Paul, Edward, Polly, Ann, and Elizabeth." If you transcribed these names and omitted the comma between John and Paul, you or a subsequent researcher might read your transcription and conclude that there were only five children instead of six. A conclusion might be drawn that the first name was "John Paul" rather than the two names, John *and* Paul. This could be confusing for you and for other researchers reading your supposedly accurate transcription.

Extract

In the case of a lengthy document, you might decide to copy only portions of the original that pertain specifically to an individual you are researching. An extract is similar to a transcription except that, instead of copying the entire document, you excerpt portions of the original. You still copy the content of the section(s) in which you are interested, word for word, and preserve the spelling and punctuation as it appears in the source document. However, you omit portions that you feel are unimportant to your research.

Extracting from original source materials is a common practice. It also is a source of many errors. An index of names and other information created from original documents can really be an extract or an abstract. People sometimes, in their haste to gather information, make transcription errors or omit important details, which may adversely impact their work and that of other researchers who access and use it. You can protect the integrity of your own research by using extracts, such as indexes, to direct you to the original source material. It is always good to obtain a copy of the entire source document, if at all possible. You can evaluate its contents yourself, and you may find at a later date that you would like to refer to the original to reconfirm your work, provide a copy to another researcher, or look for additional details that may have seemed irrelevant to your earlier research.

Published extracts can be especially problematic in some cases. Remember that, when an extract is prepared, much material is left behind. The loss of details, language, and spelling can adversely impact your or someone else's research. In the case of African-American research, for example, an extract of a slaveholder's will may ignore the names of slaves bequeathed, sold, or freed under the terms of the will. Those details may be unimportant to one of the slaveholder's descendants. However, descendants of the slaves would be very interested in the existence of their antecedents' names in the will. As a result, the extract would be useless to the African-American researcher unless he or she traced the genealogy of the slaveholder and personally examined the original of the will.

Abstract

Another type of derivative work is the abstract. Unlike the transcription or extraction, an abstract does not seek to preserve the content of the original source. Instead, an abstract merely describes the content of the original source. It contains far less detail than even an extract and may only list what the researcher feels is pertinent to his or her research. An abstract represents the researcher's interpretation of the original material. An abstract of the slaveholder's will discussed in the previous section might consist of only the family and heirs of the slaveholder, and might omit altogether any mention of the slaves.

Depending on the knowledge, insight, and skill of the researcher, the information derived from the original and documented in the abstract may contain errors. His or her interpretation, hypothesis, and/or conclusion may be correct but, then again, it may be flawed as a result of taking information out of its original documentary context.

Avoid Errors in Derivative Sources

As you can see, there potentially are problems with each of these forms of derivative materials. If errors are introduced at any point by the researcher, these often are disseminated to other researchers. As a result, an error may be perpetuated and, because it appears again and again in many researchers' work, may come to be considered "fact." You therefore want to use extreme caution when you encounter other people's transcription, extraction, and abstraction work. Try to obtain a copy of the original source material so that you can examine it yourself. Your hypotheses and conclusions may differ from those of another researcher. By personally reviewing and analyzing the original document, you can apply your own knowledge and insight into your own ancestry in arriving at your own conclusions.

You will certainly do your own share of derivative work, and fortunately there are some excellent forms available on the Internet. Among the absolute best are those at Ancestry.com at **www.ancestry.com/trees/charts/researchext.aspx**. Here you will find a Research Extract form, as well as census forms for all of the U.S. federal censuses, 1790–1930; U.K. censuses, 1841–1901; and various Canadian censuses. Genealogy.com also offers an excellent selection of U.S. federal census forms at **www.genealogy.com/00000061.html**. You can also find any number of forms for extracting and abstracting wills, deeds, property descriptions, and other documents by searching on the Internet.

Apply Critical Thinking Skills to Your Genealogical Research

As you have seen, the examination of source materials can tell you a great deal. Personal analysis is a key activity in determining the strength of the evidence you discover. You are acting like an investigative journalist or a crime scene investigator, investigating the scene, the events, the people, and the story. You should always ask about the *who, when, where, what, how,* and *why* of your ancestor's life events. In addition to merely reporting the story, you will analyze information and evidence, and develop realistic hypotheses. Like the journalist, you have equipment, knowledge, skills, and a structured methodology to apply to your investigation. Your job is to bring all of these factors together for the purpose of identifying, classifying, and analyzing the evidence you find.

One thing you will do in your genealogical research is employ your critical thinking skills to the evaluation of the evidence you find. This is an imperative in your work because you have to determine what material you have and its quality. There are five basic evaluation criteria you will use, and these should be applied to everything you evaluate, from printed resources to electronic and Internet materials to physical objects and heirlooms.

A component of your critical thinking skills is what you have learned throughout your life, coupled with a healthy dose of common sense. Another piece is the knowledge you will acquire as you continue encountering and working with new and different types of genealogical source materials. You cannot take anything for granted, but should instead measure the evidence by the five criteria listed here:

- **Origin** You must always question where the material originated, when it was created, who created it, and why. Determine if you are working with an original piece of evidence or an exact facsimile, such as a photocopy, microfilm, or scanned image. If you have a piece of derivative source material, you must determine whether it is a transcription, an extract, or an abstract of the original.

- **Quality and accuracy** The origin of the source material goes a long way toward determining the accuracy of the material. However, recognize that mistakes can be made even in original materials. For example, a census taker could misspell a name on the form he or she is completing. Ask yourself whether the information can be verified (or refuted) by other evidence and, if so, by what other types of evidence and how good (or bad) is that material.
- **Authority** Is the creator or author of the material an authority or expert? How do you know? Have you checked his or her credentials or reputation? Is the information hearsay or is it fact? Is the information you are examining a hypothesis or a proven truth? Again, it is important to consider whether the material being analyzed is original or derivative and primary or secondary material.
- **Bias** Is there any possibility that what you are evaluating is influenced by any bias? Does the creator or author have another agenda? It is possible that you are dealing with partial truth in some instances, especially where individuals' accounts of events are concerned. There may be a reason to lie or to mask the truth. Examples might include a child born out of wedlock; a person misrepresenting his or her age due to vanity or a desire to legally marry, or to qualify for or avoid military service; or the perception of being descended from a particular ethnic or religious group. How do you know that you have not discovered purposely bogus information?
- **Sources** Evaluate the sources from which you have obtained the information. This relates back to origin, quality and accuracy, authority, and bias. However, if you obtain information from another researcher, carefully examine the sources he or she cites, and be prepared to verify everything that person has cited.

With all of this in mind, you should maintain a healthy skepticism in your investigation. Be wary of information that seems too good to be true. You can expect to encounter some brick walls in your research. This book will teach you ways of approaching apparent dead ends and circumventing brick walls in your research, and how to use alternative research strategies and substitute record types in the process.

Place Your Ancestors into Context

English poet John Donne is famous for his *Meditation XVII*, in which he states, "No man is an island, entire of itself…" He asserts that all of mankind is interconnected, and all a part of one another's history and activities. This is as true in our genealogical research of the past generations as it is of today. Our ancestors lived in places and times, and they witnessed and participated in events and activities as surely as we ourselves do.

It is essential during your research process to learn as much about your ancestors' lives and times as possible so that you can better understand them. That means learning about the geography of the places where they lived, including where the jurisdictional boundaries of their state, province, country, or territories were drawn. You also must become a student of the history of the places and times in which your ancestors lived. This will help you understand what their lives were like and perhaps the motivations for some of their actions. Major cataclysms as well as ordinary events shaped the lives of our ancestors. Consider, for example, the Potato Famine in Ireland in the 1840s, which, according to some sources, caused more than 1.5 million starving Irish citizens to migrate to North America. Or perhaps the rule of *primogeniture*, under which the oldest son inherited the land of his father and may have forced one or more younger sons to leave home to make his own way in the world. Your investigation of the place, history, culture, and climate where your ancestors lived—and where they may have migrated—will serve you well in understanding their lives, what records may have been created by and about them, and where these materials may now be located.

Format Names, Dates, and Locations Correctly

Gathering information about your family is one thing; recording it in a format that can be understood and used by others is quite another. Genealogists use a number of standardized forms for this purpose, and genealogy database software programs (which we will discuss in Chapter 15) can produce printed versions of these forms as a result of data entered into and stored in their programs. Let it suffice to say that genealogists have standards for the entry of data. Let's discuss each type of data and the standards that are universally used. Figure 3-5 demonstrates how information should be properly formatted.

Record Names

People's names are entered using their first name (also referred to as a given name or forename), full middle name(s), and surname (last name). A woman's name is always recorded with her first name, her middle name, and her maiden surname. While it is not mandatory to do so, a great many genealogists capitalize the entire surname, as in the following examples:

Green Berry HOLDER
Laura Augusta WILSON

Capitalization of surnames is especially effective in written correspondence, such as letters, emails, online message boards, mail list postings, and other communiqués, because it causes the surnames to be easily seen. If someone is scanning a written document, the capitalized surname jumps out at him or her.

Record Dates

The United States uses a format for dates that is different from the format used in most parts of the world. Whereas most Americans write a date in the format June 14, 1905, in their documents and correspondence, most of the rest of the world writes it as 14 June 1905. From a consistency standpoint, you always want to use the DD

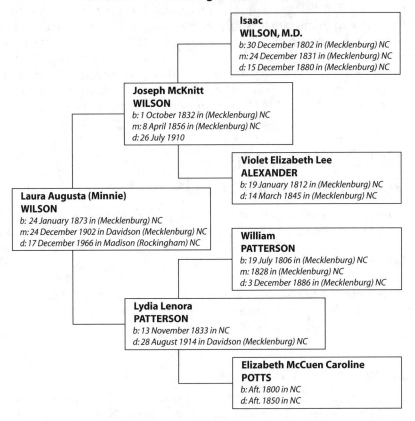

Ancestors of Laura Augusta (Minnie) Wilson

Isaac
WILSON, M.D.
b: 30 December 1802 in (Mecklenburg) NC
m: 24 December 1831 in (Mecklenburg) NC
d: 15 December 1880 in (Mecklenburg) NC

Joseph McKnitt
WILSON
b: 1 October 1832 in (Mecklenburg) NC
m: 8 April 1856 in (Mecklenburg) NC
d: 26 July 1910

Violet Elizabeth Lee
ALEXANDER
b: 19 January 1812 in (Mecklenburg) NC
d: 14 March 1845 in (Mecklenburg) NC

Laura Augusta (Minnie)
WILSON
b: 24 January 1873 in (Mecklenburg) NC
m: 24 December 1902 in Davidson (Mecklenburg) NC
d: 17 December 1966 in Madison (Rockingham) NC

William
PATTERSON
b: 19 July 1806 in (Mecklenburg) NC
m: 1828 in (Mecklenburg) NC
d: 3 December 1886 in (Mecklenburg) NC

Lydia Lenora
PATTERSON
b: 13 November 1833 in NC
d: 28 August 1914 in Davidson (Mecklenburg) NC

Elizabeth McCuen Caroline
POTTS
b: Aft. 1800 in NC
d: Aft. 1850 in NC

FIGURE 3-5 A pedigree or ancestor chart showing properly formatted names, dates, and locations. (From the author's collection.)

MONTH YYYY format for all of your genealogical work. You will find that using this standard makes communicating with other genealogists worldwide easier.

Record Locations

When conducting your research, you will find that boundaries, place names, and political/governmental jurisdictions have changed throughout time, sometimes more than once. It is important for you to seek records in the correct place. That means learning what governmental or other official entity had jurisdiction over a place at the time your ancestor lived there and at the time a specific record was created. It also means working with both contemporary and historical maps. For example, some of my early Morgan ancestors settled in the mid-1750s in what was then Orange County, North Carolina. Today, the exact area in which they settled is divided into Caswell and Person Counties.

The way in which you record locations in your research should reflect the name of the place, the county, parish, or other geopolitical area in which it was located, and the state, province, or country. You can record them with the county, for instance, enclosed in parentheses or separated by commas. Here are some examples:

Location	Record It As	Or Record It As
Madison, North Carolina	Madison (Rockingham) NC	Madison, Rockingham, North Carolina
Rome, Georgia	Rome (Floyd) GA	Rome, Floyd, Georgia
Montreal, Canada	Montreal (Québec) Canada	Montreal, Québec, Canada
Barkham in Berkshire, England	Barkham (Berkshire) England	Barkham, Berkshire, England

Certainly be careful to record the correct geopolitical entity for the location *at the time the event occurred*. This is essential because that is the place where the records will have been recorded and where they are probably still stored. For example, if I wanted to record the marriage of one ancestor in that area in Yanceyville, North Carolina, in 1761, I would record the birth location in the following manner:

Reuben MORGAN   24 August 1761   Yanceyville (Orange) NC

The marriage date of his son, which occurred in the same community after the formation of Caswell County in 1777, would be recorded as follows:

William MORGAN   22 December 1783   Yanceyville (Caswell) NC

The difference in the county name distinguishes the fact that the event occurred under a different governmental jurisdiction. Therefore, if I want to obtain a copy of Reuben's marriage record, I would contact or visit the Orange County courthouse in Hillsborough, North Carolina, whereas I would visit the Caswell County courthouse in Yanceyville, North Carolina, for William's marriage record. Suffice it to say that it is vitally important to properly identify the right location *and* to record it as part of your records.

Work with Pedigree Charts

Now that you know how to collect, evaluate, and analyze evidence, and know how data is to be formatted, it's time to learn about the forms that genealogists use to enter their data.

One of these forms is known as a *pedigree chart*, and is sometimes known by other names, such as "ancestral chart" or "family tree chart." These forms come in a variety of styles and typically represent three or more generations. Let's begin our discussion by looking at some examples. Ancestry.com provides their Ancestral Chart at **http://c.ancestry.com/pdf/trees/charts/anchart.pdf** (see Figure 3-6).

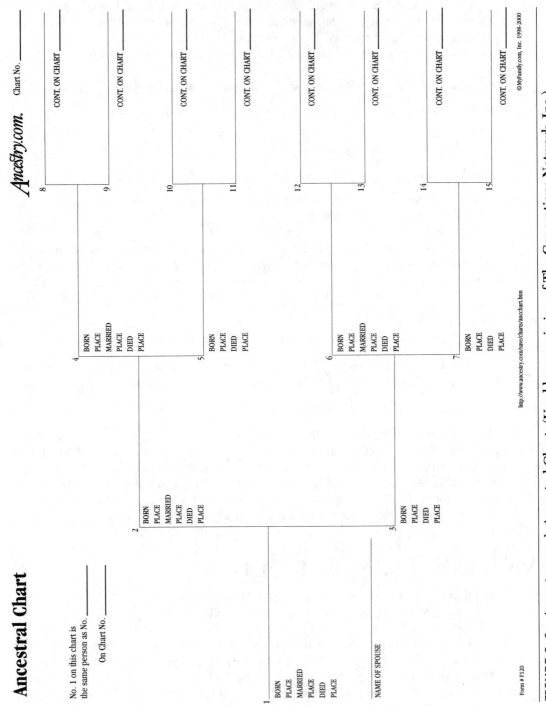

FIGURE 3-6   Ancestry.com's Ancestral Chart. (Used by permission of The Generations Network, Inc.)

Pedigree charts are used to represent multiple generations of direct descent. The downloadable chart shown in Figure 3-6 can be used to represent four generations. Others you might locate through retail stores or on the Internet may represent three or more generations. Some versions may be used to represent as many as 10, 12, 16, or more generations. These latter specimens are usually intended for showy displays, but some genealogists will use the larger format as a working document in order to have their direct family lineage shown on a single sheet.

Let's use your own family as an example and use the Ancestry.com Ancestral Chart form as a worksheet. Remember I said you should start with yourself? That's what you do here. You will note that lines are numbered 1 through 15. Fill in *your name* on line 1 and enter your surname in all capital letters (uppercase). If you have a spouse, you may fill in his or her name on the line below. Remember that you should enter a woman's maiden name as her surname. Under your name on line 1, enter your date of birth (in the format of DD MONTH YYYY such as 10 July 1911), the place of your birth (in the format of City (County) State or similar format), the date of your marriage to the person listed below you, and the place of the marriage. We will assume that you are not yet deceased, of course, so you can leave the areas for date of death and location blank.

The next pair of lines is numbered 2 and 3. Line number 2 represents your father and line number 3 represents your mother. (Even numbers are always male and odd numbers are always female on pedigree charts, with the exception of the individual 1, which may be either male or female.) Enter your father's name with his surname in all capital letters. Enter his birth, marriage, and (if applicable) death dates and locations. Please note that marriage information is always listed on pedigree charts under the male. Enter your mother's name on line 3—this time with her first, middle, and maiden names, and enter her maiden name in capital letters. Enter her birth and, if applicable, death dates and locations. You may not yet have all the names or other information. That's the purpose of genealogical research. Enter as much as you have and enter it in pencil so you can change it later as needed.

The next column consists of lines numbered 4, 5, 6, and 7. Line number 4 represents your father's father and line 5 represents your father's mother. Line 6 represents your mother's father and line 7 represents your mother's mother. Fill in these people's names and any vital information you know.

The next column contains lines numbered 8 through 15. These represent the names and information about your great-grandparents. Fill in as many names, dates, and locations as you can.

You have probably discovered already that you have gaps in your family knowledge. You may also be unsure about some of the information you entered. That's okay, though. That's why we enter the data in pencil, so that we can change or correct it as we locate evidence of the true facts.

Next, you will notice that there are places for chart numbers to be entered. This provides a way for you to organize and cross-reference charts. For example, you may have obtained information on your great-grandparents' (line numbers 8 and 9 on this chart) parents and grandparents. Since you don't have enough room on this chart to represent them, you will need a new pedigree chart for persons numbered 8 and 9. Let's say you start a new chart for your great-grandfather (8). On the new chart, his name will be listed on line number 1. His parents' (your great-great-grandparents) names will then be entered on lines 2 and 3, and so on. You may label this as **Chart 2**. Label the first chart you completed **Chart 1**. Now, cross-reference them as follows:

- Under line number 8 on Chart 1, on the line labeled "CONT. ON CHART ____," enter the number **2** (for Chart 2).
- In the upper-left corner of Chart 2, where it is labeled "No. 1 on this chart is the same person as No. _____ on Chart No. _____," enter the person number as **8** and the chart number as **1**.

You have now cross-referenced the charts for easy navigation back and forth. You will want to create a binder to hold your pedigree charts. We'll discuss organization in detail later in the book but, for now, start by filing the charts in a generational sequence. File your generation on top, followed by other generations in sequence.

Work with Family Group Sheets

While the pedigree or ancestral chart represents a single thread of descent, a *family group sheet* is a representation of a complete family unit: father, mother, and all children. You potentially will prepare a family group sheet for every family unit you document. An example of Ancestry.com's Family Group Record document is shown in Figure 3-7, and a free downloadable version is available at Ancestry.com at **www .ancestry.com/trees/charts/familysheet.aspx**. Some family group sheets include spaces for recording the sources of the information that you have found. The Source Summary for Family Information from Ancestry.com at **www.ancestry.com/trees/ charts/sourcesum.aspx** can be used in conjunction with their Family Group Record document to keep track of the origin of the evidence you use to document the facts. Please take a few minutes to download and print copies of these sheets now.

The family group sheet begins by asking for the name of the preparer and his or her address. In the event you share a copy of this form with another person, he or she will be able to contact you with questions or to share their research with you. You also have a place at the top of the form to cross-reference this sheet to a pedigree chart.

This form contains space for substantially more information than the pedigree chart, but the sources and types of information are pretty self-explanatory. You will note, though, two interesting columns for the children. The first is one with an asterisk (*) at the top, representing whether or not the father and mother are direct ancestors. Remember, some children in a family unit may be from another marriage and may have been adopted by the new spouse. The other column is for Computer ID. You may decide to cross-reference this chart with entries in a computer program, and this column can facilitate that effort.

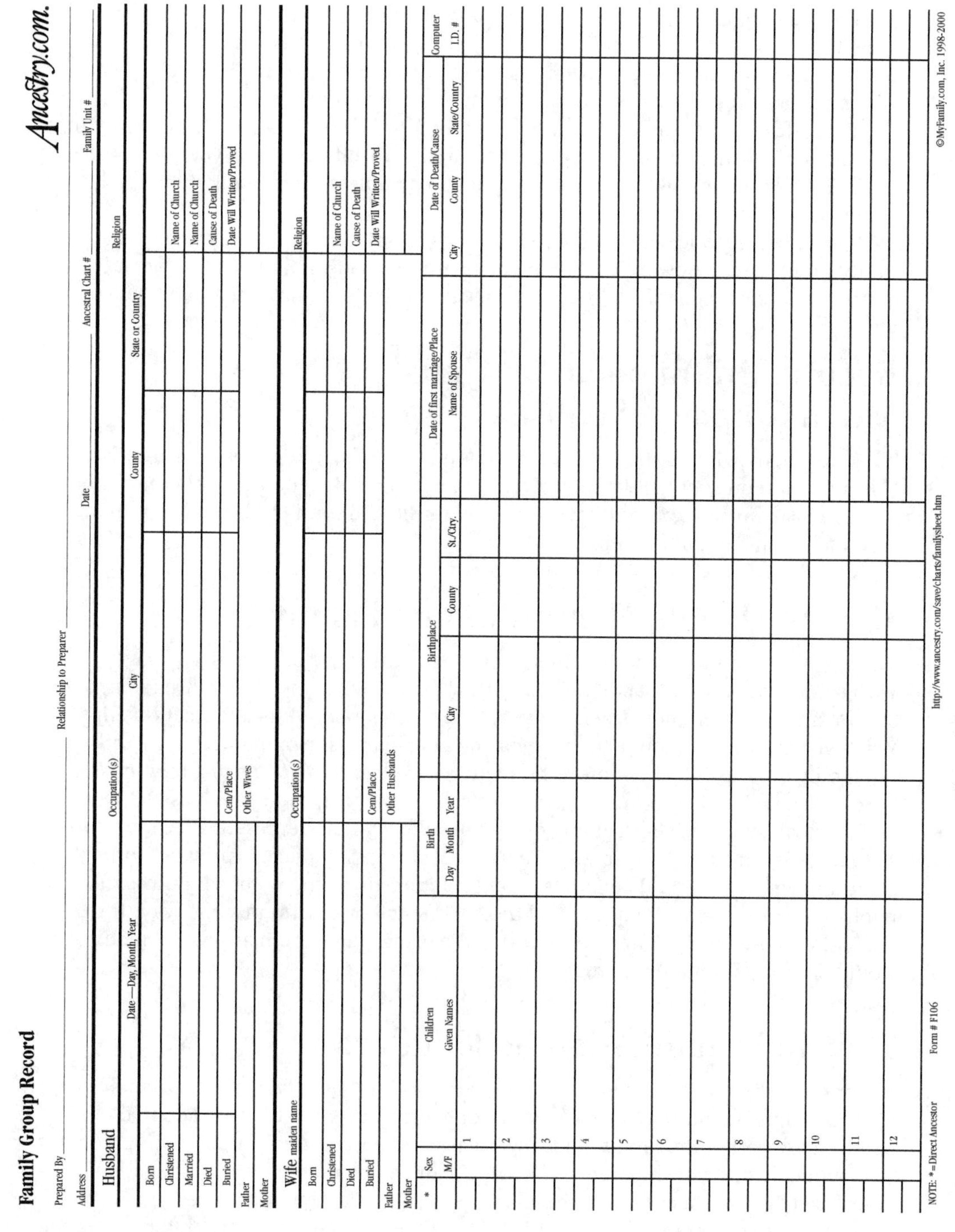

Family Group Record

Ancestry.com.

Prepared By _____

Address _____ Relationship to Preparer _____ Date _____ Ancestral Chart # _____ Family Unit # _____

Husband

Occupation(s) _____ Religion _____

Date — Day, Month, Year | City | County | State or Country

Born			
Christened			Name of Church
Married			Name of Church
Died			Cause of Death
Buried	Cem/Place		Date Will Written/Proved
Father	Other Wives		
Mother			

Wife maiden name

Occupation(s) _____ Religion _____

Born			
Christened			Name of Church
Died			Cause of Death
Buried	Cem/Place		Date Will Written/Proved
Father	Other Husbands		
Mother			

Sex * M/F	Children Given Names	Birth Day	Month	Year	Birthplace City	County	St./Cty.	Date of first marriage/Place Name of Spouse	Date of Death/Cause City	County	State/Country	Computer I.D. #
1												
2												
3												
4												
5												
6												
7												
8												
9												
10												
11												
12												

NOTE: * =Direct Ancestor   Form # F106

http://www.ancestry.com/save/charts/familysheet.htm

©MyFamily.com, Inc. 1998-2000

FIGURE 3-7 Ancestry.com's Family Group Record. (Used by permission of The Generations Network, Inc.)

What if you have the name of one person and not the name of his or her spouse? What if you only know a wife's first name and not her maiden name? What if you know there was a child but you don't know his or her name? Leave the information blank, or add a question mark, backslashes (//), or some other notation to indicate missing data. You can always return to enter it when you locate it.

Take a few minutes to complete a family group sheet for your parents' family unit, and include information about your siblings and yourself. Any facts you don't know can be left blank for now. You can come back to complete them later when you have located documentation of the facts.

You have a good idea now about recording information on a pedigree chart and a family group sheet. However, there are always exceptions in families that need to be recorded. Let's examine three such circumstances that you may encounter.

Record Multiple Family Units with a Common Spouse

What do you do when a spouse died or a couple divorced and a spouse remarried? How do you represent that? The answer is that you create a new family group sheet for the new family couple and for their family unit. Children produced from this union are included on this separate sheet.

How to Handle Nontraditional Family Units

There have always been family units operating without the benefit of marriage. With same-sex marriages taking place in the United States, the United Kingdom, and other countries, there now is a need to record those family units and relationships. Whatever the arrangement and whoever the people are, it is important to record the family unit "as is." Therefore, when you record two individuals in a relationship, portray it on a family group sheet. If there was no marriage, indicate it as **NONE**. Most genealogy database programs today now allow you to represent a relationship status with such codes as "friends," "married," "partners," "single," "private," "other," or "unknown." You should be honest about relationships where known unless the publication of such knowledge would be detrimental or hurtful in some way. If there are children produced from a nontraditional pairing, show them as you normally would, as issue from the union.

How to Handle Adopted Children

A common question is how to handle adopted children on a family group sheet. Should you include them? The answer is, of course, an emphatic yes. Adopted children are part of the family unit, regardless of the identities of their birth parents. The adopted child's birth parents, if known, can be recorded in the notes section of your family group sheet or elsewhere. However, the adoption formalizes the legal relationship between the child and his or her adoptive parents and should become the primary family relationship represented in your records.

Most genealogy database software programs allow for the identification of a child's relationship to the parents. The Family Tree Maker program (by The Generations Network, Inc.), for example, provides values of Natural, Adopted, Step, Foster, Related, Guardian, Sealed, Private, and Unknown.

Remember that adoption may be a sensitive topic for the adoptee, his or her parents, or some other family members. Therefore, you will want to be considerate about publishing the information outside the family circle. That does not mean you shouldn't record it in your records. However, many of the genealogy database programs allow for the omission of the parent-child relationship information when reports are produced or data files are created.

Create Source Citations for Your Data

When you were in school and preparing term papers, you were probably required to prepare a bibliography of your source materials. You may also have used footnotes and endnotes for individual fact or quotation references. This is the scholarly way to document research because it provides details for the reader or subsequent researcher to retrace your work.

As you collect information, evidence, documents, and other materials for your family history research, it is essential to record where you found them. You want to provide a record for yourself and any other genealogical researcher so that he or she can retrace your steps, locate the material you used, and personally examine it. Your interpretation of data may be different from someone else's. The fact that you may actually be looking for different information may influence what you search for, what you believe is important, and the way you interpret it in your family's application. One seemingly insignificant name to you in an ancestor's will may be just the "missing link" that another researcher has been seeking for years.

Your source citations will generally follow standard bibliographic citation standards for books, magazines, journals, and other printed sources. Students and researchers know that there are several citation formats, but typically the style used by genealogists resembles the standards of the Modern Language Association (MLA) or the *Chicago Manual of Style*. The structure of your source citations should contain all essential information that will help another researcher identify and locate the source material you used. However, the citation format may not necessarily adhere precisely to either of these styles. The following are examples of some of the more common source materials.

Book

Mills, Elizabeth Shown. *Evidence Explained: Citing History Sources from Artifacts to Cyberspace*. Baltimore, MD: Genealogical Publishing Co., 2007.

Magazine Article

Morgan, George G. "A Path of No Returns." *Genealogical Computing*, Volume 23.2, (October/November/December 2003).

Newspaper Article

Pilarczyk, Jamie. "Learning History's Lessons." *Tampa Tribune*, 10 September 2008. B3.

Newspaper Article on the Internet

Pilarczyk, Jamie. "Learning History's Lessons." *Tampa Tribune*, 10 September 2008. < http://centraltampa2.tbo.com/content/2008/sep/10/st-learning-history-lessons/ >. Accessed 17 September 2008.

Family Bible (One-of-a-Kind)

Family data, Morgan Family Bible, *The Holy Bible,* new edition (New York, NY: Christian Book Publishers, Inc., 1921); original owned in 2009 by George G. Morgan (229 N. Dalton Street, Anytown, FL 33333).

Print materials make up a sizeable portion of reference material for genealogists. However, we work with an amazing array of materials, including letters, postcards, journals, diaries, deeds, census records, birth certificates, marriage licenses, christening and baptismal records, bar and bat mitzvah records, wills, probate packets, obituaries, ships' passenger lists, naturalization records, medical records, tombstones, jewelry, furniture, embroidered samplers, and much, much more. We work with all types of media as well: paper, microfilm, microfiche, CD-ROMs, computer files, databases, photographs and slides, scanned images, and records found on the Internet or exchanged electronically in such media as email and data files.

As you can imagine, few citation style guides can anticipate every possible source used by genealogical researchers. The MLA standard provides the most appropriate general framework for genealogical source citations. The essential components of every citation are the name of the author or creator, a title or description of the source, where the source was published and who published it, and the date of creation or publication. In addition, if the source is a rare or one-of-a-kind item, it is important to include the place where it resides and/or where you accessed it. Here are examples of some sources unique to genealogical research and appropriate citation formats for them.

Cemetery Marker (Large Cemetery)

Green Berry Holder tombstone; section New Front Addition, Terrace 1, Lot #1, Myrtle Hill. Cemetery, Rome (Floyd County) Georgia; transcribed by the writer on 14 July 1998.

Cemetery Marker (Small Rural Cemetery)

Caroline Alice Whitefield Morgan Carter tombstone, Cooper Cemetery, Caswell County, North Carolina (Ridgeville township, Latitude 36° 17' 15" North, Longitude 079° 12' 02" West) photographed by George G. Morgan on 24 August 2008.

Microfilm of U.S. Federal Census

Green B. Holder household, 1870 U.S. census, Subdivision 141, Floyd County, Georgia, page 102, line 22; National Archives micropublication M593, roll 149.

Email Message

Mary A. Morgan, "Your Great-grandmother Patterson," email message from < mam@auntmary190505.com > (106 E. Hunter Street, Madison, NC 27025) to author, 14 June 2008.

Web Site

Matthews, Elizabeth. "Matthews Family Genealogy Page," online < http://www .matthews.org >. Elmer Watson data downloaded 19 December 2002.

The amount of information included varies with the type of source material you use, what it provides, and in some cases where it is physically located. You will want to learn all about citing your sources so that you do a scholarly job. The best genealogical source citation reference book on the market today is Elizabeth Shown Mills' definitive book *Evidence Explained: Citing History Sources from Artifacts to Cyberspace*, published by Genealogical Publishing Company. (You'll note that I used this work above as a representative source citation example for a book.) It is an excellent resource for the serious genealogist, and I heartily recommend it as a part of your core personal reference library.

The more information you locate, the more important it is to have clearly documented the sources. You will soon learn from personal experience that it is often impossible to recall the origin of a particular piece of information. Source citations are invaluable when retracing your own research and are essential as documentation for other researchers' use in trying to retrace and verify your work.

You will always want to perform effective and scholarly research on your family history. That means identifying and using the best possible source materials you can locate, analyzing them carefully, weighing the evidence, formulating reasonable hypotheses, and drawing realistic conclusions. It combines all the skills discussed so far in this chapter, and these comprise the basic rules of genealogical evidence.

Select a Family Tree Format

Throughout this chapter, I've discussed the mechanics of collecting, analyzing, recording, and citing sources for your family history data. Now is the time to start considering just how to record and display your data.

As you read the header of this section, you probably are thinking, "How can there be more than *one* format of a family tree?" Actually, there are a number of different ways to view family data, and each one can help you analyze what you have

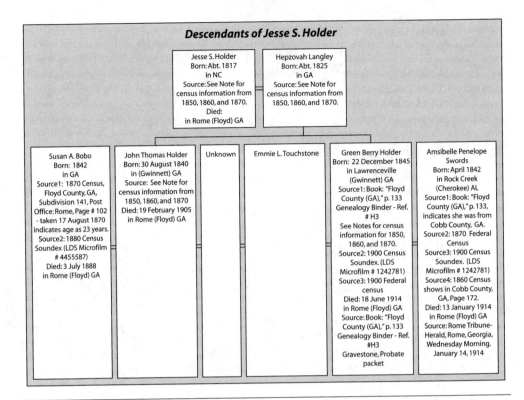

FIGURE 3-8   Ancestry.com's Ancestral Chart. (Used by permission of The Generations Network, Inc.)

discovered in perhaps a different way. Genealogists also have their own preferences about which display format they use. For example, you should know that there are two major family tree display formats: the *standard chart* format and the *fan chart* format. The standard format shown in Figure 3-8 presents a vertical, linear view of two generations. The double, parallel lines linking individuals indicates their marriage or union.

The same data can be displayed in a fan format, as shown in Figure 3-9, starting with the focus individual and his or her spouse, and additional generations' information extending in semicircular bands by generation.

As you are working with your family genealogy, you will find it useful to be able to create both ancestor and descendant tree views. An *ancestor chart* starts with one individual as its focal point and presents a picture of that person's ancestors. A *descendant chart* starts with an individual and shows his or her descendants. The number of generations represented on any chart is your option. In the examples shown in Figures 3-8 and 3-9, only two generations are represented. You also can choose to include as much or as little information as you like. At the very minimum,

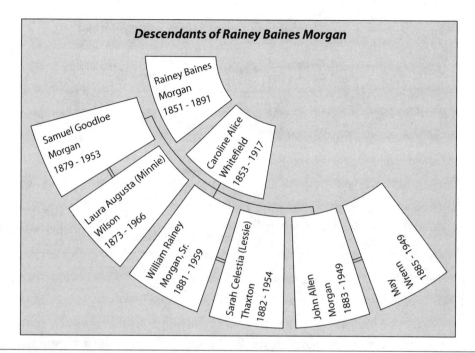

Descendants of Rainey Baines Morgan

Rainey Baines Morgan 1851 - 1891

Caroline Alice Whitefield 1853 - 1917

Samuel Goodloe Morgan 1879 - 1953

Laura Augusta (Minnie) Wilson 1873 - 1966

William Rainey Morgan, Sr. 1881 - 1959

Sarah Celestia (Lessie) Thaxton 1882 - 1954

John Allen Morgan 1883 - 1949

May Wrenn 1885 - 1949

FIGURE 3-9   Sample of descendants chart in fan format

however, you should include each individual's name, date of birth, date of marriage, and date of death. The location of each of these events is important, and you may want to include that data as well.

In addition to the standard and fan formats of the ancestor and descendant chart formats, there are some other formats as well. An *hourglass tree* combines the features of both the ancestor and descendant tree views. In Figure 3-10, my great-grandfather, Rainey B. Morgan, is the focal individual, with his wife, Caroline A. Whitfield, shown at his side and their union being indicated with the double lines linking them. Rainey's parents, Goodloe W. Morgan and Mary L. Woods, and his two sets of grandparents, Reuben Morgan and Mary Merritt, and William Woods and Mary Farley, are shown above him as his ancestors. Rainey's three sons, Samuel G. Morgan, William R. Morgan, Sr., and John A. Morgan, are shown as descendants, and their respective wives are shown beside them, again with the unions represented by double lines.

All of the tree formats discussed above really are just that: tree formats. They are called trees because they begin somewhere with a root individual and branch out from there. The format that you will encounter most for representing lineal family relationships is the pedigree chart that we discussed earlier in the chapter. It is an ancestral tree representation, but is by far the most commonly used representation in day-to-day genealogy work.

Hourglass Tree of Rainey Baines Morgan

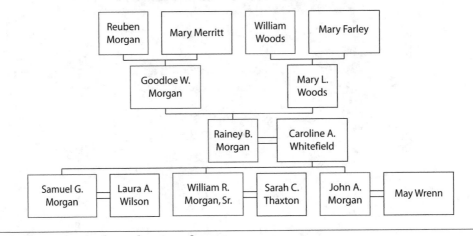

FIGURE 3-10 An hourglass tree format

Blank pedigree charts, as you have seen, can be downloaded from the Internet. They also can be purchased in many formats and range from as few as 3 generations to as many as 12 or even more. Genealogy database software programs can also produce pedigree charts whose contents and formats you can customize.

You will want to experiment with the various formats to determine which one you like best and/or which one best represents your family data. Although it is time-consuming to complete a family tree chart by hand, many people do just that. Sometimes they create a display-quality tree using graphics, photographs, and calligraphic text. These can be framed and displayed as family heirlooms.

On the other hand, you will find that there are a number of genealogy database software programs available. You enter your data and source citations, even photographs, and can produce a variety of customized, computer-generated reports. Those reports include pedigree charts, family group sheets, and family trees in the standard, fan, hourglass, and other formats. Some of these databases also facilitate writing and publishing a quality family history, while others can produce HTML files containing your family data for web pages. We'll discuss a variety of software packages in a later chapter. However, for now, it is important for you to know what is available.

With all this foundation work under your belt now, let's proceed into the wealth of record types and what they can tell us. Let's move on now to Chapter 4.

4

Place Your Ancestors into Context and Locate Vital Records

HOW TO...

- Place your ancestors into context
- Become a student of history
- Establish your ancestor's location at different times
- Use maps to locate the *right* place to research
- Locate birth, marriage, and death records

The most basic record types for establishing an ancestor's locations and life events are birth, marriage, and death records. Government census records can verify his or her location at regular intervals. The use of these records forms a framework for other research of an individual's life. Once you establish an ancestor's location in a specific place at a given point in his or her life, you can pursue your search for other documents and evidence to expand your knowledge and understanding of that person.

This chapter focuses on how to place your ancestors into historical and geographical context so you can be most effective in understanding and using records about their lives. A simple yet extremely effective methodology for the proper use of maps and gazetteers to help locate records is presented. We also will discuss the most basic of genealogical records, the vital records: birth certificates, marriage licenses and certificates, and death certificates. Examples of documents from the United States, the United Kingdom (like the one shown in Figure 4-1), and Canada are included to provide a better understanding of what these documents can offer.

Chapter 5 will continue the discussion of how to place your ancestor into context with a detailed discussion of census records. For now, though, let's concentrate on methodologies for placing your ancestors' lives into context and get started locating these records.

FIGURE 4-1 Certified copy of an 1894 birth entry from Ireland, issued in 1997. (Used by permission of The National Archives, U.K.)

Place Your Ancestors into Context

Our ancestors were real people. They lived in particular locations and were influenced by other people and events, just as we are today. Their curiosity and interest in the world around them was keen. Like the people shown in Figure 4-2, they actively sought out the news of the day, sometimes even traveling considerable distances to obtain

FIGURE 4-2 Our ancestors were interested in the news of the day. (From the Library of Congress collection.)

a newspaper. They lived in a community and interacted with their family members, friends, neighbors, and other people in the area. Climate influenced their lifestyle, and the social, political, and economic environment most certainly played a part in their lives. The type of government and its organization, leadership, and regulations imposed a structure under which they lived as well. All of these factors contributed to the types of records that may have been created for and about your ancestors.

An ancestor who was a farmer was dependent on weather and a market for his or her crop in order to survive and prosper. Another who was conscripted for military service received special training and was assigned duties in a specific area; he may have traveled a great deal and been involved in armed conflict.

Consider, for example, an Irish family in the mid-1840s who was impacted by the Potato Famine. Starving and economically devastated, the father may have sought relief for himself and his family by emigrating from Ireland to America. By studying the history of Ireland in that period, you can understand the factors that motivated someone to want to emigrate elsewhere. By also studying the history of America at that time, and the specific area to which the family immigrated, you can gain an appreciation for what drew the family there: jobs, opportunity, cost of living, and climate, to name but a few.

As you can see, it is impossible to research your ancestors in a vacuum. It is important to place them into geographical and historical context, and that means studying history, geography, economics, sociology, and all sorts of materials that may provide you with insights into their lives and into their motivations for making some of the decisions they made.

Become a Student of History

The study of your family's story also becomes a study of history at all levels. I've found that making the connection between my ancestors and the history of the places and times in which they lived has brought history to life. My ancestors came alive for me beginning on the snowy day spent with my aunt and grandmother in January 1962, and my interest in and appreciation for history, geography, and my family heritage were sparked forever. No longer are historical facts merely a memorization of places, dates, and famous people's names. The exploration of *my* family's history makes me place *them* in a particular place, and I give consideration to what the impact of events in the area at a specific point in time might have had on them. I reflect on what their participation in those events, and that of their contemporaries, might have been. No matter their station in life, they come alive for me, and learning more about them is a vivid and exciting experience!

Consider the circumstances of one of your ancestors who might have lived in Pennsylvania on 1 July 1863 near a little town called Gettysburg. Rumors and reports of approaching armies must have inspired great anxiety. Even if no one in your family was actively involved in military service, imagine the terror your ancestor must have felt at being near the site of the epic Battle of Gettysburg. He or she, and probably the entire family, may have fled the area to escape the advancing armies and the impending destruction that comes with battle. That place and every person there were forever changed by the three days of intense conflict and horror.

Your research will take you into many interesting places where you will discover a wealth of information. There is no doubt that you will become fascinated with contemplating what your ancestors' lives must have been like as you read and learn more about history.

Family Histories

It is possible that someone else may have written a history of your family or an historical account that includes details about your family. Unless one of your ancestors was an eminently famous person whose biography would be of interest to a wide audience, you will find that most family histories are either self-published by the author or privately published. Sometimes an author only produces a few copies of the family chronicle in manuscript form and perhaps donates a copy to the local public library. These gems can be invaluable resources and point you to all sorts of information. However, it is important to use your critical thinking skills to evaluate the content and the source materials. Don't accept any "fact" at face value, even if the family history was compiled and written by Uncle Al or Cousin Becky. Research and verify everything for yourself. You may find that all of their information is correct and well researched, and that the source evidence was meticulously cited. However, there is no substitute for examining the source materials yourself and forming your own conclusions.

County and Local Histories

Histories written about a limited area, such as a town, county, or parish, can provide important details in your research. *The History of Mecklenburg County from 1740 to 1900* by J. B. Alexander, originally published in 1902 by the Observer Printing House in Charlotte, North Carolina, proved a goldmine in my family research. I learned a great deal about the history of Charlotte and the surrounding area, which a number of my ancestors helped settle in the early 1700s. Included were articles concerning agriculture, commerce, and economics through the years, which helped me visualize my ancestors' environment. Other articles discussed individual churches, their histories, and their congregations. Modes of travel, clothing, and medical treatments were described. However, of special interest to me were biographical sketches of several of my ancestors, including my great-great-grandfather, Isaac Wilson, M.D., for whom a photograph was included. (See Figure 4-3.) To my knowledge, this is the only surviving photograph of my ancestor, who was born on 30 December 1802 and died

DR. ISAAC WILSON.

FIGURE 4-3 This photograph of the author's great-great-grandfather, perhaps the only surviving photograph of the man, was discovered in a county history published in 1902. (From the author's collection.)

on 15 December 1880. Imagine my excitement at learning specific details about him, such as the fact that he was a "progressive physician" who practiced between 1825 and 1875. I learned that he eschewed the practice of cupping, in which a cupping glass was used to increase the blood supply to an area of the skin.

My great-great-grandfather organized and participated in both shooting matches and fox hunts. I also learned that he was a Justice of the Peace and officiated at many weddings. This was the first place I learned that he was married three times. Based on what I gleaned from this book, I set off on research to verify the information using other records and found the written account to be extremely accurate.

County heritage books have become popular in the United States and elsewhere over the years. These are primarily compilations of information about places, events, and families whose roots have been based in that area. Organizers solicit articles from area citizens and descendants. Recognize that a great deal of this information may be hearsay or family myth, and may have been written by persons who are neither researchers nor historians. Every fact should therefore be carefully scrutinized and personally verified for accuracy.

There are a variety of places where you can locate local histories. Towns and cities celebrating centennials, sesquicentennials, bicentennials, and other milestone anniversaries often publish booklets commemorating the extended history of the area. Articles and photographs may include your ancestors and other family members. In addition, local newspaper and magazine coverage may include similar genealogical treasures. Don't overlook these resources in your search for family information.

Churches and synagogues preserve many types of records and also can be a source of local historical information. Commemorative books and albums are common and may include names, photographs, and other details that may be useful.

The local or county genealogical and historical societies are essential research resources. They may have unique photographic and documentary materials relating to your family that can be found nowhere else. In addition, these groups undertake transcription and preservation projects. These may involve compiling materials, creating indexes, and generating reports or articles for their newsletter or journal. Such projects might include compiling histories of local businesses, canvassing and indexing cemeteries, and transcribing tax rolls and jury lists. They also may possess diaries, journals, photographs, and correspondence files of local residents. You never know what they have until you ask.

The local public library and nearby academic libraries may have originals or copies of documentary information of local historical value. Besides the privately published family histories mentioned earlier, these repositories may also have file cabinets with miscellaneous documents such as correspondence and obituaries. Some libraries' special collections have acquired unusual sets of records. The University of South Florida in Tampa has acquired the records of several local mortuaries/funeral homes that have gone out of business. The Special Collections department of the Clayton Library in Houston, Texas, owns an impressive collection of materials, including microfilm and manuscripts concerning New England, the Mid-Atlantic States, the Midwest, the Old South, and the New South, described at **www.hpl.lib .tx.us/clayton/special_collections.html**.

State and Provincial Histories

Learning about local history is important, but be sure to learn about state and provincial histories as well. These provide a broader perspective of the historical role played by a town or county. This can lead to a better understanding of the events and influences in your ancestor's life.

Again, historical and genealogical societies can potentially provide excellent resources for your research. Libraries of all types hold books about state or provincial history, particularly state libraries and archives. One of my favorite websites is LibrarySpot.com at **www.libraryspot.com**. Here you will find links to all types of libraries in the United States, links to national libraries in more than 100 countries, and many reference resource links. The UK Public Libraries site at **http://dspace .dial.pipex.com/town/square/ac940/weblibs.html** provides a compilation of links to libraries in the United Kingdom, while the Library and Archives Canada has created a web page of Canadian library websites and catalogs at **www.collectionscanada .gc.ca/gateway/s22-200-e.html**. State, provincial, and national libraries and archives provide extensive materials about history. Many of these facilities also house and preserve original materials, as well as printed, microfilmed, and scanned images. Such collections include

- U.S. National Archives and Records Administration (NARA) at **www.archives.gov**
- Library of Congress at **www.loc.gov**
- Library and Archives Canada at **www.collectionscanada.gc.ca**
- The National Archives of the United Kingdom at **www.nationalarchives.gov.uk**
- National Archives of Australia at **www.naa.gov.au**

Many more such national sites can be located using your favorite search engine and entering terms such as "national library" or "national archive" and the name of the country.

National and World History

The influences of national and international events were important factors in the lives of our ancestors, their families, and their communities. The perspective of history gives us the opportunity to better understand our forebears' place in it. You may think events in France in the late 1700s had little impact on the American continents, but you would be incorrect. On the contrary, following its devastating defeat in the Seven Years' War against Britain (1756–63), France was eager for revenge against the British. When the American Revolution erupted, statesman Benjamin Franklin traveled to Paris, met with French government officials, and the two countries entered into a treaty on 6 February 1778. Franklin met with King Louis XVI and Queen Marie Antoinette on 20 March 1778 to confirm that treaty, and with that the French entered into an agreement to provide aid and support to the American colonies. Following the American Revolution, the French helped broker the signing of the Treaty of Paris at Versailles on 3 September 1783, in which Great Britain recognized the independence of the United States of America. (See Figure 4-4.)

In another treaty, signed on 30 April 1803, the United States successfully completed the negotiations for the Louisiana Purchase from France at a price of about $27 million. The area comprised more than 800,000 square miles extending from the Mississippi River in the east to the Rocky Mountains in the west.

In addition to this impact on North America, the French also occupied Spain in the early 19th century. The occupation severed commerce between Spain and its colonies in Central and South America. Between 1808 and 1826, the Spanish lost all of Latin America, with the exception of Cuba and Puerto Rico. Emulating the example of their neighbors to the north in the new United States, the Spanish colonies rebelled and ultimately claimed their independence.

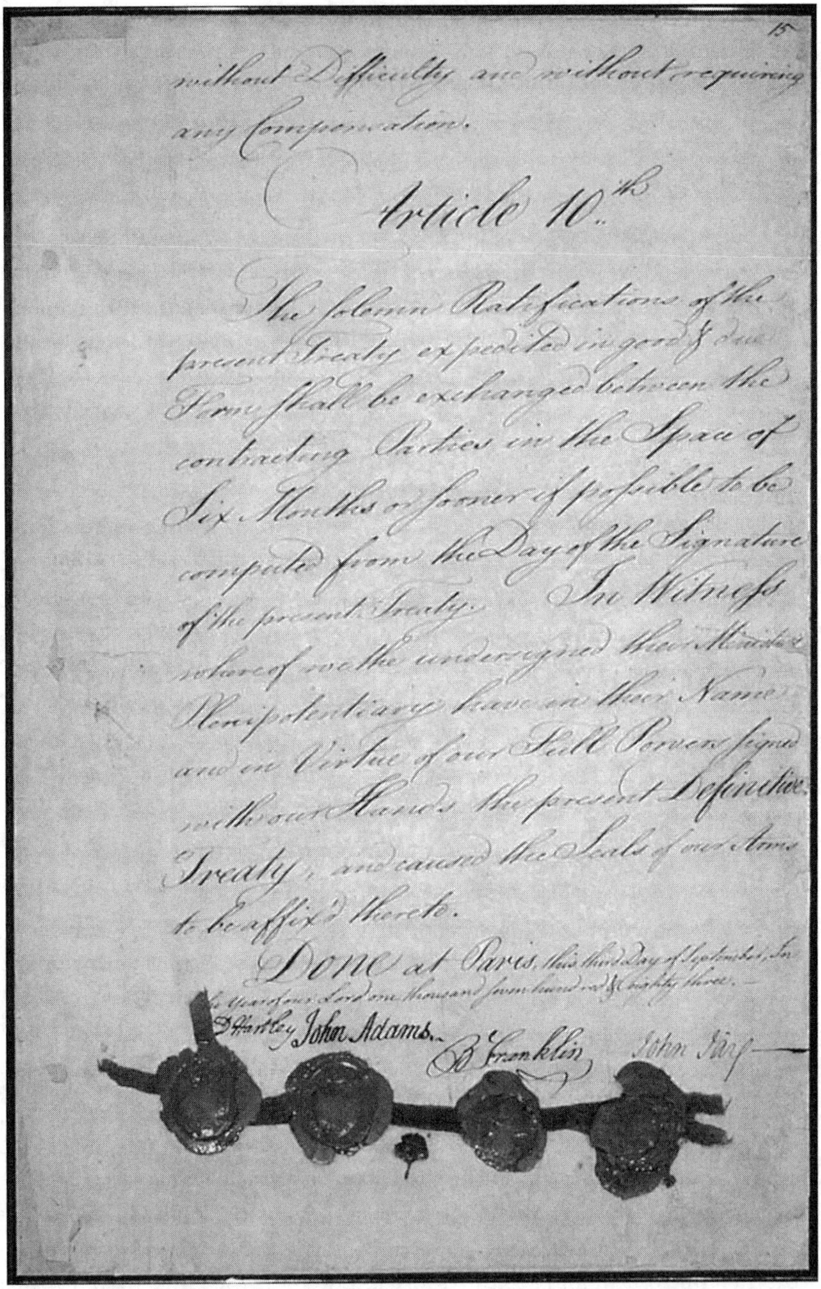

15

without Difficulty and without requiring any Compensation.

Article 10th.

The solemn Ratifications of the present Treaty expedited in good & due Form shall be exchanged between the contracting Parties in the Space of Six Months or sooner if possible to be computed from the Day of the Signature of the present Treaty. In Witness whereof we the undersigned their Ministers Plenipotentiary have in their Name and in Virtue of our Full Powers signed with our Hands the present Definitive Treaty, and caused the Seals of our Arms to be affix'd thereto.

Done at Paris, this third Day of September, In the Year of our Lord one thousand seven hundred and Eighty three.

D Hartley John Adams. B Franklin John Jay

FIGURE 4-4 Signatures on one of two original copies of the Treaty of Paris, signed on 3 September 1783. (From the National Archives and Records Administration collection.)

Another important event in France in the late 1780s was the formation of a group, the Société des Amis des Noirs (Society of Friends of the Blacks), who met in Paris in early 1788 to campaign against the French slave trade. On 4 February 1794, slavery was abolished in the French colonies. The news spread across the Atlantic and slaves were freed in the French colonies. The action did not go unnoticed in the United States. By 1807, the slave trade to all British colonies was abolished and that same year the United States Congress passed legislation prohibiting the importation of slaves into the country and its territories. Slave smuggling persisted through 1862, and President Abraham Lincoln's *Emancipation Proclamation* abolished all forms of slavery in the Southern states, effective on 1 January 1863. The 13th Amendment to the United States Constitution was passed by Congress on 31 January 1865 and ratified on 6 December of that year, ending slavery and involuntary servitude in the United States and greatly expanding the civil rights of Americans.

As you can see, events on a national level had far-reaching and enduring impacts elsewhere. That is why it is important to study history and to consider how the events may have impacted your ancestors and their contemporaries. The French actions described above can be applied to persons of French, Spanish, English, North American, South American, and African descent. You will find that it is imperative to learn something about the history of both the place where your ancestors originally lived *and* about the places to which they migrated. There definitely is a push-pull influence involved that, if you take the time to explore it, may provide a much clearer understanding and appreciation of your heritage.

Use Maps to Locate the *Right* Place to Research

Maps, like the one shown in Figure 4-5, are an essential part of our everyday life. We consult them to plot travel routes as we move from place to place, check them to determine correct postal codes, and use them in a wide variety of other ways. We find maps today printed on paper, on the Internet, and in computer software programs, and the use of Global Positioning System (GPS) technology is becoming more widespread.

Throughout history, maps have changed again and again. Boundaries have moved, towns have come under different jurisdictions, place names have changed, and some places have ceased to exist for innumerable reasons. For this reason, we cannot simply use contemporary maps as references for locating records. We must use a number of types of historical maps in our genealogical research. In order to determine the *right* place to look for records and other evidence, it is essential to understand the geographical history of an area. Many genealogists hit "dead ends" and waste inordinate amounts of time because either they fail to understand the importance of properly using maps in their research or they don't possess the skills to use them.

FIGURE 4-5   Map of Sydney, Australia, dated 1922. (From the Library of Congress Geography and Map Division.)

Avoid Wasted Time and Energy

Imagine the frustration of having planned a vacation that included research at a courthouse in a particular area, only to discover when you arrived that the information you were seeking was actually located in another county's courthouse. It happens all too frequently, especially when a person fails to determine beforehand where his or her ancestors lived *and* which county had jurisdiction over the area at that time.

Perhaps expending the time and expense of a research trip is an extreme example, but it does happen. However, there are many other ways we can waste time and money, researching the wrong materials. You want to avoid the following types of errors:

- Researching in the wrong books
- Checking the wrong census areas
- Using the wrong finding aids and indexes
- Ordering and researching the wrong microfilm reels
- Writing to the wrong courthouse
- Traveling to the wrong location

Worse yet, you could actually be researching the wrong ancestors! When your family has a common name and there are people of the same name in the area, it is entirely possible to latch onto the records of an individual whose details seem "almost right." You might then spend a great deal of time tracing that person's records until you encounter names, places, dates, and other evidence that definitively tell you that you've been on a wild goose chase. Don't think it can't happen to you; it happens to the best of us.

Use Maps for Multiple Purposes

Maps are a necessity in our genealogical research. They help us locate landmarks, waterways, roads and streets, towns, cities, counties, parishes, states, provinces, territories, countries, oceans, continents, islands, and more. Contemporary and historical maps, such as the one shown in Figure 4-6, help us determine the geopolitical jurisdictions in place at a specific time. They provide a visual representation of the geographic spatial relationships between physical locations, and can help us place our ancestors' physical location into perspective. This can help us better understand where they might have been in relationship to events occurring around them.

I happen to use historical maps of and from the 16th to 19th centuries to plot the possible migration paths followed by my own ancestors in the American colonies. This means having studied the history of migration routes north and south as well as across the Appalachian Mountains. The investment in that research has allowed me to plot the potential migration routes for ancestors between two points and to anticipate what their journey entailed. Then, using colored markers, I draw the probable routes(s) on a

FIGURE 4-6 Railroad and Township Map of Massachusetts, dated 1879. (From the Library of Congress Geography and Map Division.)

map and begin researching the interim stops they may have made and the records that may have been created and left behind. The process has been remarkably successful, and I'd like to share it with you.

> **Did You Know?** Because boundaries change frequently over time, using historical maps enables you to find the boundaries that existed at the times your ancestors lived in specific places. It is important for you to know which government had jurisdiction in the area and created official documents. The documents of the period will have remained with the old governmental entity even if the boundaries changed. Check in the offices of the government that had responsibility for the area at the time your ancestor lived there.

Use a Methodology That Works

I have worked with maps for many years and have found a practical methodology for working with maps and other related resources that can improve your success at locating the *right* place to search for records.

Step 1: Start with a Contemporary Map

Obtain a good current map of the area where you believe your ancestors lived in the past. There are many excellent map resources available, including bound atlases, printed individual maps for areas, and maps available from motoring associations such as the American Automobile Association (AAA). In addition, highway department maps at a local, county, or other administrative area level provide excellent detail including secondary and tertiary roads, natural landmarks, churches and cemeteries, and other features. Whatever maps you use should include contemporary boundary lines.

You probably won't want to use cheap maps and atlases because they seldom contain as much detail as you would like, and they sometimes contain errors or omit important features. Maps on the Internet services also are sometimes less than accurate, and seldom contain the detail you need, especially boundaries. Beware of driving directions from these sites, and always compare two sets of driving instructions for conflicting information. Consider the creator of the map, their authority and expertise, the purpose of the map, and the accuracy.

On your good contemporary map, follow this progression and make notes as you proceed:

1. Locate the place you seek.
2. Note the name of the specific county or province in which it is located today.
3. Make specific note of the location within the contemporary boundaries.
4. Note surrounding towns or cities and their direction from your site.
5. Note other surrounding geographic features such as waterways, mountains, and shorelines, and their physical position in relation to the place you located.

It is possible that the place you are searching for isn't listed on the map. Perhaps it is too small or is an unincorporated area, or perhaps the place has been renamed or no longer exists. What do you do? Never fear, there are other resources available to you. Local histories are invaluable in helping locate these places. However, one of the best tools you can use is a *gazetteer*, also referred to as a *place name dictionary*. There are many of these available for different parts of the world, both printed and Web-based. For United States research, I have become addicted to using the book *American Place Names of Long Ago* by Gilbert S. Bahn. The work is based on a portion of Cram's World Atlas, published in 1898, and whose U.S. information was based on the 1890 U.S. federal census returns.

Among the best Internet-based gazetteers are the following:

- United States Geological Survey Geographic Names Information System (also referred to as the USGS GNIS), a massive searchable database of United States national mapping information. Located at **http://geonames.usgs.gov/pls/gnispublic**, the GNIS allows you to search by name and location, and to narrow your search to specific feature type. I often find this facility indispensable in locating somewhat obscure cemeteries. The results include latitude and longitude, as well as links to a number of mapping services that can be used to display maps. Figure 4-7 shows an image from the GNIS in Google Maps.

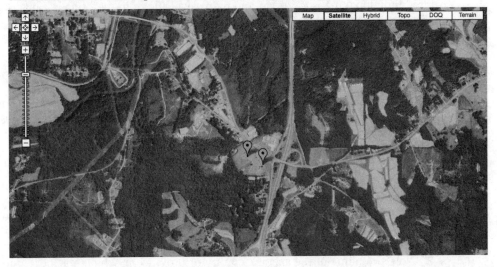

FIGURE 4-7   GNIS in Google Maps (Satellite view) showing Woodland Cemetery in Madison, Rockingham County, North Carolina.

- The University of California's Alexandria Digital Library Gazetteer Server, located at **www.alexandria.ucsb.edu/**, also provides similar detail at a global level. It incorporates data from multiple online cartographic information servers.
- The Atlas of Canada, located at **http://atlas.nrcan.gc.ca/site/english/ dataservices/gazetteer.html**, provides access to the Gazetteer Map Service and allows you to search for place and feature names. You can narrow your search to a specific province and territory and/or feature type. In addition, however, the site contains links to collections of different maps, including a large number of historical maps covering the history of Canada, outline maps, and an archive of images from various editions of the *Atlas of Canada*, going back to the first edition published in 1906.
- The Geoscience Australia Place Name Search facility, hosted by the Australian government and located at **www.ga.gov.au/map/names**, is a compilation of more than 322,000 geographic names provided by members of the Committee for Geographic Names in Australasia.
- The Gazetteer for Scotland at **www.geo.ed.ac.uk/scotgaz/gaztitle.html** is an excellent resource for locating towns and features in Scotland. It also provides an historical timeline feature. In addition, facilities were recently added to allow you to work with areas using either the old Scottish counties or the modern council areas. The former facility is based on the full text of Francis Groome's *Ordnance*

Gazetteer for Scotland, published in 1885. It also includes an historical map layer that includes maps of all the county and parish boundaries, overlaid with 19th-century six-inch Ordnance Survey maps.

- The GENUKI at **www.genuki.org.uk** has compiled a wealth of helpful resources, and its collection of links beginning with the page at **www.genuki.org.uk/big** includes maps of administrative regions, both contemporary and historical, and other online gazetteer materials.

If you are seeking an online gazetteer facility for another country or locale, you can always use your favorite web browser and enter search terms like the ones shown here:

gazetteer *insert country/province name here*

You may be rewarded with search results that you can explore.

You also should consider using the reference resources available to you in libraries of all types. Reference librarians at public and academic libraries are trained to respond to research inquiries from patrons and can direct you to map collections, atlases, and gazetteers. State and national libraries and archives are another resource, and many of them handle reference question requests via telephone and email.

Step 2: Locate and Examine Historical Maps

Your next step is to determine the time period during which your ancestors lived in the area. Locate an historical map of that area from that time period. (See Figure 4-8.) If you are researching your ancestors in the United States, you might want to consult the *Map Guide to the U.S. Federal Censuses, 1790–1920* by William Thorndale and William Dollarhide. This book provides maps of every state for each of the decennial censuses taken between 1790 and 1920. Each map shows the current counties and their boundaries and the counties in existence at the time of the census and their boundaries. This is an excellent tool for a high-level comparison between the contemporary and historical geopolitical boundaries in the United States. You can follow up with a search for and consultation of a detailed historical map of the period. This is the procedure you should follow for other countries and locales as well.

Locate the place you found on your contemporary map in Step 1. Compare it to historical maps from before and after the dates in which your ancestors lived in the area. Make note of the surrounding towns and landmarks you found on your contemporary map and locate these on the historical map. This can be crucial when you are looking for places that changed names or disappeared. More important, though, is to carefully note the administrative boundaries, such as state, parish, or province. If the place you are researching was located in another county at the time your ancestors were there, for instance, you will be seeking to locate records in *that* governmental division's records and not in that of the current governmental unit's repositories. There are some rare cases in which records are transferred to new jurisdictions, such as when new counties are created. It is therefore important to keep this in mind when asking about the availability of records in and from the original government offices.

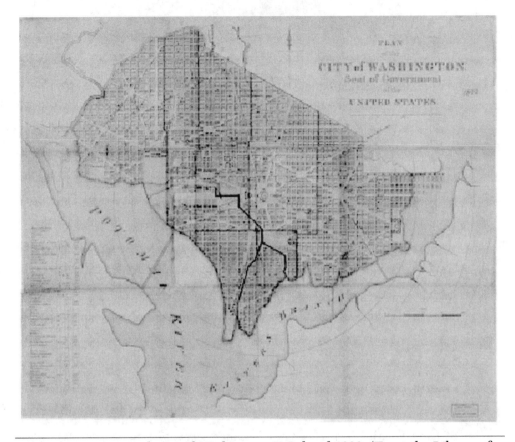

FIGURE 4-8   Historical map of Washington, DC dated 1822. (From the Library of Congress Geography and Map Division.)

Step 3: Fine-tune Your Search Location

The examination of maps is an important factor in locating the *right* place to research records, but there is another step you should perform. While the *Map Guide to the U.S. Federal Censuses, 1790–1920* is an excellent reference work, it only provides detail at the ten-year intervals at which the federal censuses were taken. You may need to determine a more concise date for when the administrative area was formed. Let's look at two examples.

The Pennsylvania county of Wyoming (see Figure 4-9), for instance, was formed in 1842 from Luzerne County. If you were looking for marriage records of your ancestors from 1840, you would seek them in Luzerne County, while if they were married in 1843, you would look in Wyoming County. I was able to determine the county formation dates through use of *Ancestry's Red Book*, published by Ancestry. com, Inc., and *The Handybook for Genealogists*, published by Everton Publishers. I might also search the Internet for information concerning the formation of Wyoming County and its parent county.

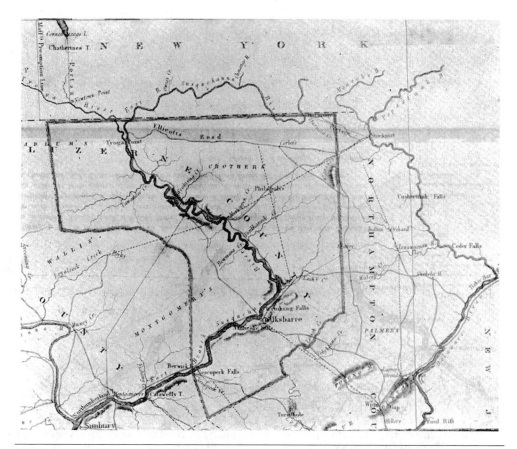

FIGURE 4-9   Historical map of Wyoming County, Pennsylvania, dated 1791. (From the Library of Congress Geography and Map Division.)

Geopolitical boundaries across Europe have changed time and time again. Poland provides perhaps the most vivid example of boundary changes. The country was partitioned between Austria, Prussia, and Russia in 1772 and each country annexed a portion of Poland. In 1793, Russia and Prussia signed a Second Partition Treaty and more of Poland was seized. In 1795, Russia affected yet a third partition and obtained part of the remainder of Poland. While some of the records from these periods may still exist in Polish archives, others would have been created by the three other national governments. And, since the Kingdom of Prussia no longer exists, what would have happened to all of those records? Jumping forward to 20th-century Poland, the invasion by the German army on 1 September 1939 began yet another period of division. The Germans and the Russians partitioned and divided Poland yet again. As you can see, your research of Polish ancestral records would be dependent on the historical time period, the partitioning of the country, and the governmental jurisdiction at the time, as well as a number of other factors.

Step 4: Identify the Records Created and Their Current Location

It is important to read about the types of records created at the time and their purpose. You also will need to determine if they still exist and where they are located. The type of record often dictates its ultimate fate. Some records are of such a temporary nature that, once they have served their purpose, they are discarded or destroyed. Others are of such perpetual importance that they are maintained permanently or for an extended period of time.

Ancestry's Red Book gives detailed descriptions of record types created in each of the United States, the dates when record-keeping for various record types began, and where these records are most likely to be housed today. I say "most likely" because there is the possibility that records may have been relocated for any of a number of reasons.

When researching in England, you will want to learn about The National Archives in Kew, Richmond, Surrey, and at **www.nationalarchives.gov.uk**. The General Register Office for Scotland (GROS) in Edinburgh, and at **www.gro-scotland.gov.uk**, is your starting point to learn what is available there, while the General Register Office in Roscommon, Ireland, at **www.groireland.ie**. The combined Library and Archives Canada site, at **www.collectionscanada.gc.ca**, is accessible in both English and French. It offers excellent, well-organized information about available records. The National Archives of Australia site at **www.naa.gov.au** likewise presents information about its record-keeping and details about available resources.

In addition to all of the places mentioned above, The Church of Jesus Christ of Latter-day Saints (LDS Church), whose members are often referred to as "Mormons," has the largest genealogical library in the world. Their website at **www.familysearch.org** is filled with interesting resources, but one of your best references for locating records is their collection of Research Guides located at **www.familysearch.org/Eng/Search/RG/frameset_rg.asp**.

Step 5: Contact the Repository to Obtain Copies of Records

Once you have determined the *right* place to search for records, make contact with the facility. *Ancestry's Red Book* and the *Handybook for Genealogists* both provide excellent contact information for U.S. state and county/parish records. So, too, do the LDS Research Guides mentioned in Step 4. However, don't assume that they are always correct. Materials sometimes are relocated, are stored off-site in another location, have limited or prohibited access due to legislation or governmental restrictions, or have been lost or destroyed. It is therefore a good idea to make contact with the repository of record to determine what they really have, how accessible the materials are, and how to access or obtain copies. This is especially important if you are planning a research visit. You will want to learn the days and hours of operation, what personal access is permitted, and costs. If records are in off-site storage, you will want to determine how you can gain access to them. This may require filing a special request for retrieval of older archived records so that you can work with them when you arrive at the facility.

Whenever you make contact with a facility, you can avoid some dead-ends by being prepared and by asking open-ended questions. Over the years, I've found that preparing a written set of the questions I want to ask is a way to make certain that I cover everything necessary and all the contingencies. Try this method yourself and I'm certain you will find it helpful.

Begin by performing some advance research and know the names of the persons for whom you are seeking records, what type of records you want, and the correct time period. You should include nicknames and any other names by which a person may have been known. Be certain to use the maiden name of a woman if you are seeking marriage records or other documents created before her wedding date. One distant cousin I always knew to be called "Sudie" actually was born Susan Elizabeth Wilson. It was under her nickname, however, that I found her in some records, and under her birth name that I found her in others.

Open-ended questions are those that require more than a "yes" or "no" answer. For example, if you ask a clerk if their facility has the marriage records from 1902 and he or she responds in the negative, what do you do? Your next question should be, "Can you tell me if the records exist and, if so, where I would be able to locate them?" Otherwise, the clerk may or may not volunteer that information.

Maps Can Equal Success

Libraries, archives, courthouses, records offices, government offices, museums, churches, other physical repositories, and the Internet can all be used to obtain maps. As you can see, this methodology for effectively locating and using maps will substantially improve your chances for success in locating the *right* place for finding your ancestors' records and other evidence. With this in mind, let's proceed to learn about locating some official documents.

Locate Birth, Marriage, and Death Records

The most basic and yet most important records you can locate for your ancestors are ones that record their birth, marriage, and death information. (See Figure 4-10.) These are generally referred to as "vital records" because they record the vital life events. One of my English friends refers to these as the "hatch, match, and dispatch" records. What makes these records so important is that they not only confirm your ancestor or family member in a specific place at a given point in time, but also potentially connect the person to other family members.

The originals or copies of these records may be in your family's possession, and you just need to ask family members for access to them. However, in many instances and especially in cases of older births, marriages, and deaths, you will have to determine if the records were commonly created at the time and, if so, where they are located. You then will have to expend effort to obtain copies of them, either by mail, email, telephone, or personal visit to the repository where they are held.

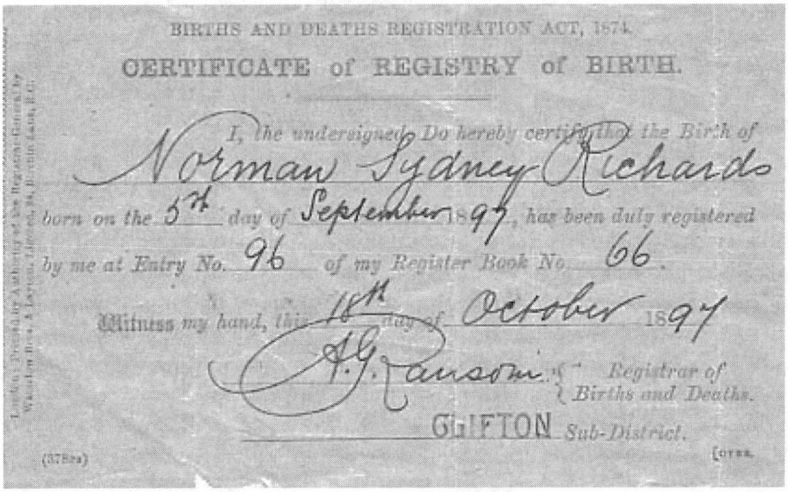

BIRTHS AND DEATHS REGISTRATION ACT, 1874.

CERTIFICATE of REGISTRY of BIRTH.

I, the undersigned, Do hereby certify that the Birth of Norman Sydney Richards born on the 5th day of September 1897, has been duly registered by me at Entry No. 96 of my Register Book No. 66.

Witness my hand, this 18th day of October 1897

A.G. Ransom Registrar of Births and Deaths.

CLIFTON Sub-District.

FIGURE 4-10 Certificate of Registry of Birth from the U.K., dated 18 October 1897. (Used by permission of The National Archives, U.K.)

It is important to recognize right away that you may not be able to obtain copies of some of these records. Creation of a birth certificate, for example, may not have been required at the time your ancestor was born. In the United States, for instance, you may find that some of the counties in a particular state began creating official birth records earlier than others. Kentucky counties, for instance, began creating birth records as early as 1852. In contrast, the North Carolina legislature did not pass legislation requiring counties to create birth and death records until 10 March 1913, and it was not until 1920 that all counties were in full compliance with the law. Civil registration was implemented in England and Wales in 1837 and required the registration of births, marriages, and deaths. However, some people resisted registration for some years. Civil registration legislation was not passed in Scotland until 1854. In Ireland, compulsory civil registration of non–Roman Catholic marriages began on 1 April 1845. The registration of births, deaths, and all marriages began on 1 January 1864. Civil registration began in Canada in the mid-1800s but its implementation varied by province and territory. In Australia, the government of each colony or state implemented civil registration independently. Tasmania was the first area to start, beginning to keep records in 1838, and the Australian Capital Territory was the last to implement it, beginning in 1911.

In some cases, laws may limit access to originals or copies of birth records to the individual for whose birth the document was created and/or his or her parents. Certain information on death certificates may also be masked when copies are created, in order to preserve the privacy of the surviving family members and to prevent the release of information that might be used to steal an identity.

Keep in mind that these three types of records—birth, marriage, and death records—can be used to establish the location of your ancestor or family member at a specific place at a point in time. By extension, that helps you begin locating other records created in the same vicinity, which can expand your knowledge of that person and his or her extended family. When official birth, marriage, and death records are not available for whatever reason, you will need to consider locating alternative record sources to establish the same or similar information. We will discuss this later in the chapter.

Did You Know?

Birth, marriage, and death records are referred to in the United States as *vital records* or *vital statistics*. In the United Kingdom, Canada, and Australia, they are referred to as *civil records* or *civil registration records*.

Locate Birth Certificates

The first document created for many people was a birth certificate such as the one shown in Figure 4-11. We all have had parents and the vast majority of us were probably born with the benefit of some medical attention. And typically there was a record made of the birth in the form of a birth certificate and/or a hospital or other

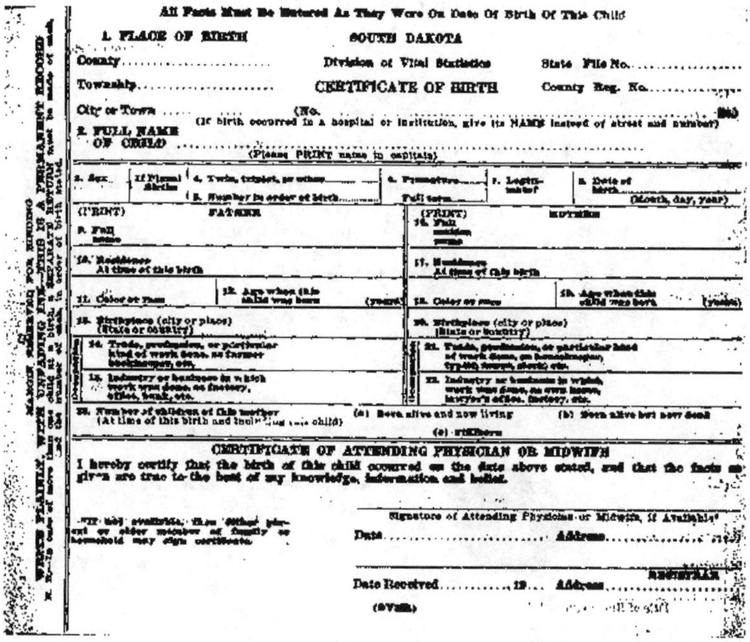

All Facts Must Be Entered As They Were On Date Of Birth Of This Child

1. PLACE OF BIRTH SOUTH DAKOTA

County.................... Division of Vital Statistics State File No....................

Township.................... CERTIFICATE OF BIRTH County Reg. No....................

City or Town .... (No. .... St.)

(If birth occurred in a hospital or institution, give its NAME instead of street and number)

2. FULL NAME OF CHILD ....

(Please PRINT name in capitals)

3. Sex | If Plural Births | 4. Twin, triplet, or other | 5. Number in order of birth | 6. Premature / Full term | 7. Legitimate? | 8. Date of birth (Month, day, year)

(PRINT) FATHER

9. Full name

10. Residence At time of this birth

11. Color or race | 12. Age when this child was born (years)

13. Birthplace (city or place) (State or country)

14. Trade, profession, or particular kind of work done, as farmer bookkeeper, etc.

15. Industry or business in which work was done, as factory, office, bank, etc.

(PRINT) MOTHER

16. Full maiden name

17. Residence At time of this birth

18. Color or race | 19. Age when this child was born (years)

20. Birthplace (city or place) (State or country)

21. Trade, profession, or particular kind of work done, as housekeeper, typist, nurse, clerk, etc.

22. Industry or business in which work was done, as own home, lawyer's office, factory, etc.

23. Number of children of this mother (At time of this birth and including this child) (a) Born alive and now living (b) Born alive but now dead (c) Stillborn

CERTIFICATE OF ATTENDING PHYSICIAN OR MIDWIFE

I hereby certify that the birth of this child occurred on the date above stated, and that the facts as given are true to the best of my knowledge, information and belief.

*If not available, then either parent or other member of family or household may sign certificate.

Signature of Attending Physician or Midwife, if Available*

Date.................... Address....................

REGISTRAR

Date Received.........., 19... Address....................

(OVER)

WRITE PLAINLY, WITH UNFADING INK—THIS IS A PERMANENT RECORD

MARGIN RESERVED FOR BINDING

N. B.—In case of more than one child at a birth, a SEPARATE RETURN must be made of each, and the number of each, in order of birth stated.

FIGURE 4-11 Blank birth certificate form from South Dakota. (From the author's collection.)

medical record. A birth certificate is an important document because it is used to verify identity. From a genealogist's perspective, it can be the basis for beginning research in a specific geographic area for other family members and a wide variety of other records.

You will need to determine *where* the person was born in order to determine if there is a birth certificate from that time. The methodology for using maps to locate the *right* place to search for records is especially helpful.

Ancestry's Red Book, for example, can be used to determine for the United States, state by state, and county by county, when official birth records began to be kept by the government offices in those areas, as well as where to seek them.

Birth certificates come in many formats, with different titles, and contain different amounts of information. At a minimum, you can expect to find the name of the child, the parents' names, the child's date of birth, the child's gender, the location where the birth occurred (or was registered), the name of the attending physician or midwife, and the signature of the registrar. Other information likely to be found on birth records includes the child's birth weight and length, the precise time of birth, and the parents' racial or ethnic background and their occupations. More recent birth certificates may include the child's footprints and perhaps even a photograph. You will find a number of examples of birth certificates in the graphics throughout this chapter. Figure 4-12, for example, shows a certificate issued by a government office in 1942 that confirms a birth entry in the official files dating to 1875. Birth records in different parts of the world may look different and contain different levels of detail, but their intent was to formally record a birth. The Dutch birth certificate shown in Figure 4-13 is a good example of this.

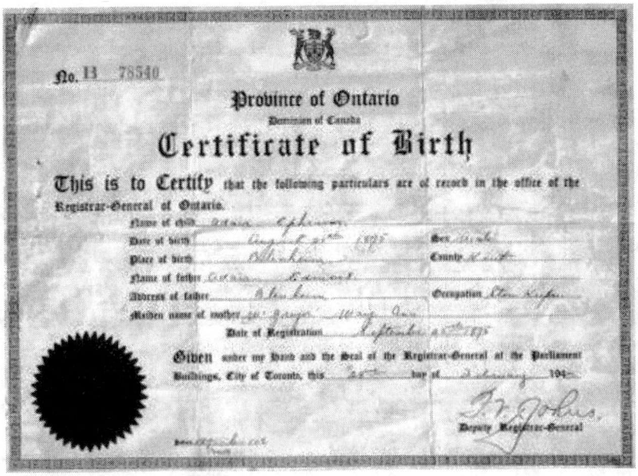
No. B 78540

Province of Ontario

Dominion of Canada

Certificate of Birth

This is to Certify that the following particulars are of record in the office of the Registrar-General of Ontario.

Name of child

Date of birth 1875 Sex

Place of birth County

Name of father

Address of father Occupation

Maiden name of mother

Date of Registration

Given under my Hand and the Seal of the Registrar-General at the Parliament Buildings, City of Toronto, this day of 194

Deputy Registrar-General

FIGURE 4-12 Certificate issued in 1942 attesting to a Canadian birth entry in Ontario in 1875. (From the author's collection.)

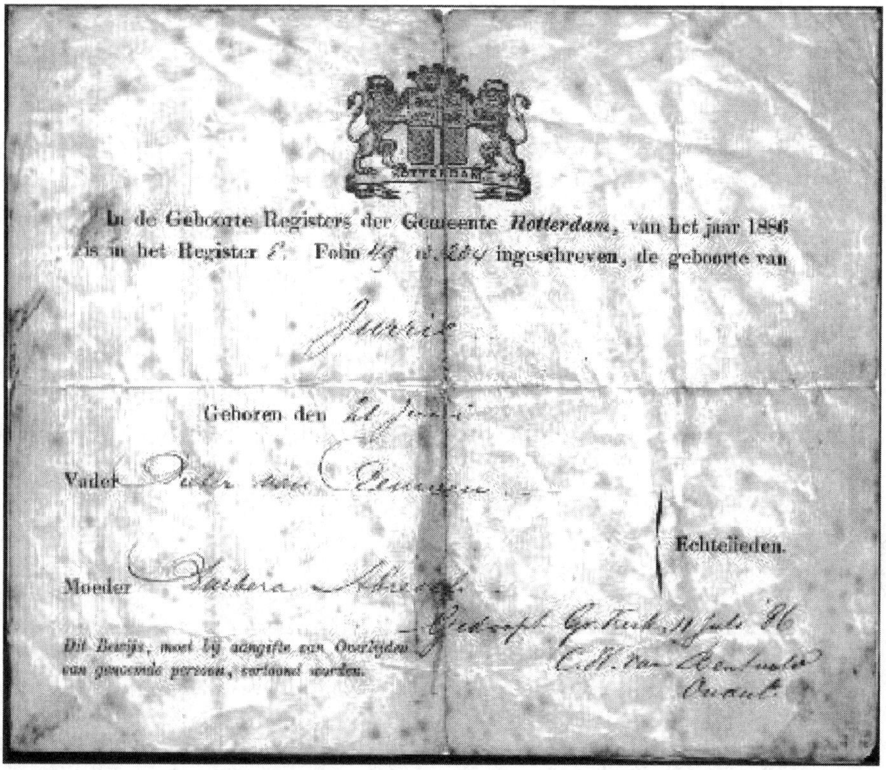
In de Geboorte Registers der Gemeente Rotterdam, van het jaar 1886 is in het Register E Folio n° ingeschreven, de geboorte van

Jurrie

Geboren den

Vader

Echtelieden.

Moeder

Dit Bewijs, moet bij aangifte van Overlijden van genoemde persoon, vertoond worden.

FIGURE 4-13 An original Dutch birth certificate dated 1886. (From the Library of Congress collection.)

You may come across an amended birth certificate from time to time. These are used to change or correct information entered on the original birth certificate. A typical reason for the issuance of an amended certificate is to change or correct the name of the child or its parents. Amended birth certificates are also used in cases of adoption. At the time of the legal adoption, particularly that of an infant or small child, a magistrate orders the creation of an amended birth certificate. This document includes the names of the adopting parents and replaces the original birth certificate in all file locations. The original, which lists the natural or birth parents, is typically removed in United States locations and placed in a court file with the adoption records. In most cases, these records are sealed by the court and require a judicial order to access them. The amended birth certificate is clearly marked to indicate that it is amended and, in the case of adoption, that there was an adoption that caused its creation.

Delayed birth certificates are not uncommon. Governments, in lieu of an original birth certificate, issue these. In cases in which birth records were not created at the time of a person's birth, or where the original records have been lost or destroyed, the governmental office will issue a substitute document. Typically, the applicant needs proof of birth for identification purposes in order to obtain a passport, a visa, or some other document to prove identity or to apply for pension benefits. The person completes an application and presents him- or herself in a governmental facility, and supplies several alternative forms of proof. These might include a family Bible, school enrollment records, church records, military service records, employment records, and affidavits from other people who were alive at the time of the applicant's birth and who can confirm that the applicant is indeed the correct person. These alternative proofs, all of which are usually secondary sources, are reviewed. If they are deemed sufficient, a delayed birth certificate is issued and is considered the legal equivalent of an original birth record. An example of a delayed birth certificate is shown in Figure 4-14.

Alternative records can, of course, be used as evidence of the birth. Remember that you must use your critical thinking skills to evaluate these materials and determine whether they are primary vs. secondary, or original vs. derivative sources. You need to determine whether these materials are sufficient to prove the fact in question, in this case, a birth. Some of the many types of alternative records you might be able to use include the following:

- Baby books created by the parents of other family members might document information about the birth.
- Christening or baptismal records, such as the one shown in Figure 4-15, may be found in family documents or obtained from a church. These typically contain the child's name, date of birth, parents' names, and sometimes names of other family members and godparents.
- A birth announcement published in a newspaper or a church publication may provide clues to the date and location of primary birth records.
- The family Bible may contain entries recording names and dates of birth.
- Letters, journals, and diaries of members of the immediate or extended family may contain information about a birth.
- Affidavits from witnesses at or near the time of the event are useful in obtaining delayed birth certificates but may be helpful to you as well.
- Medical records, although not generally released to persons other than the patient and his or her immediate family members, may provide a date of birth. Medical practitioners often maintained their own records of deliveries they performed.
- School enrollment records are a good secondary source of birth information. Data may be obtained by making a request of the school administration officials, who may provide photocopies or written responses to specific questions.

Another part of your investigative process also involves using your knowledge of history, geography, and your family and coupling that with your creative thinking to consider what other types of record and materials might provide evidence of the event.

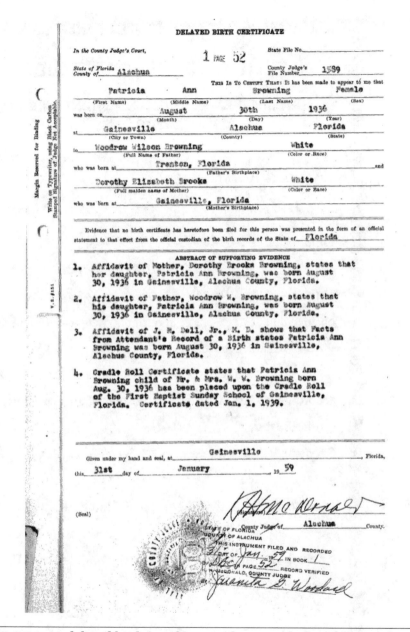

FIGURE 4-14 A delayed birth certificate is often issued when no original was created. Alternate proofs are presented to the government for review. (Courtesy of Jim Powell.)

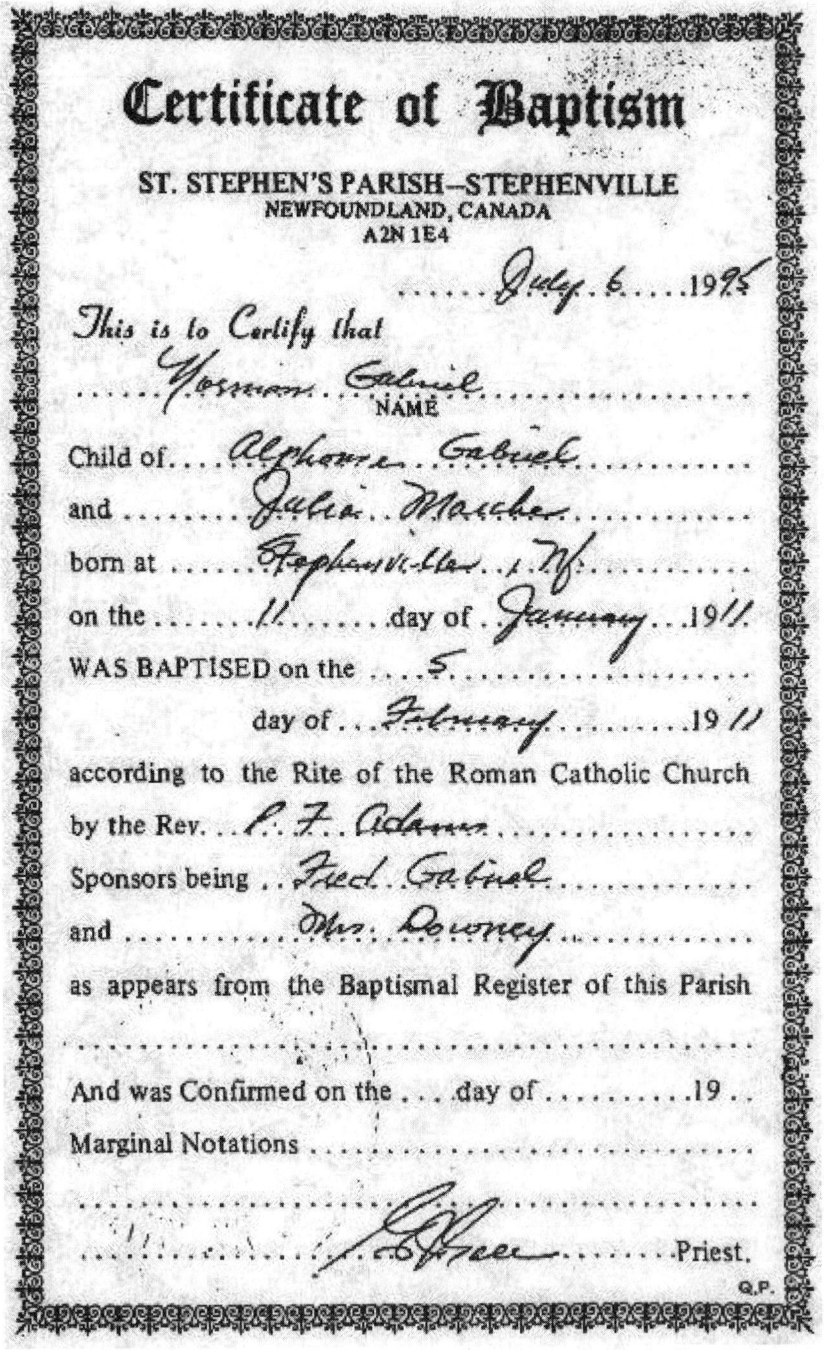

Certificate of Baptism

ST. STEPHEN'S PARISH—STEPHENVILLE
NEWFOUNDLAND, CANADA
A2N 1E4

...... *July 6* 19*75*

This is to Certify that

.... *Norman Gabriel* ....
                    NAME

Child of ..... *Alphonse Gabriel* ....

and .... *Julia Marche* ....

born at ...... *Stephenville, Nf.* ....

on the .... *11* ..... day of .. *January* ... 19*11*

WAS BAPTISED on the ..... *5* ....

.... day of ... *February* 19 *11*

according to the Rite of the Roman Catholic Church

by the Rev. .. *P. F. Adams* ....

Sponsors being .. *Fred Gabriel* ....

and .... *Mrs. Downey* ....

as appears from the Baptismal Register of this Parish

....

And was Confirmed on the .... day of .... 19 ..

Marginal Notations ....

....

.... *Priest.*

Q.P.

FIGURE 4-15 Certificate of baptism from Newfoundland, Canada. (From the author's collection.)

Find Marriage Licenses and Certificates

Marriage records are among some of the oldest records kept. The earliest ones are found in religious institutions, but others can be found among the many places where civil registration records are located. They are often indexed for easy reference, both in groom and bride sequence by surname and then given name.

In some places, such as U.S. courthouses, you will find large ledgers containing copies of marriage license or marriage certificate documents, maintained in chronological sequence. The older ones are handwritten entries made by a clerk (who may also have been known by the title of "ordinary") that indicate the authorization of a couple to be married. The actual license or certificate was then taken to a member of the clergy, a judge, or a justice of the peace, and the ceremony was performed. The original document was then returned to the courthouse, where the clerk transcribed information about the date of the wedding and the name of the officiating individual. As a result, these entries are often referred to as "marriage returns." Figure 4-16 shows an example of a marriage return from the State of Indiana.

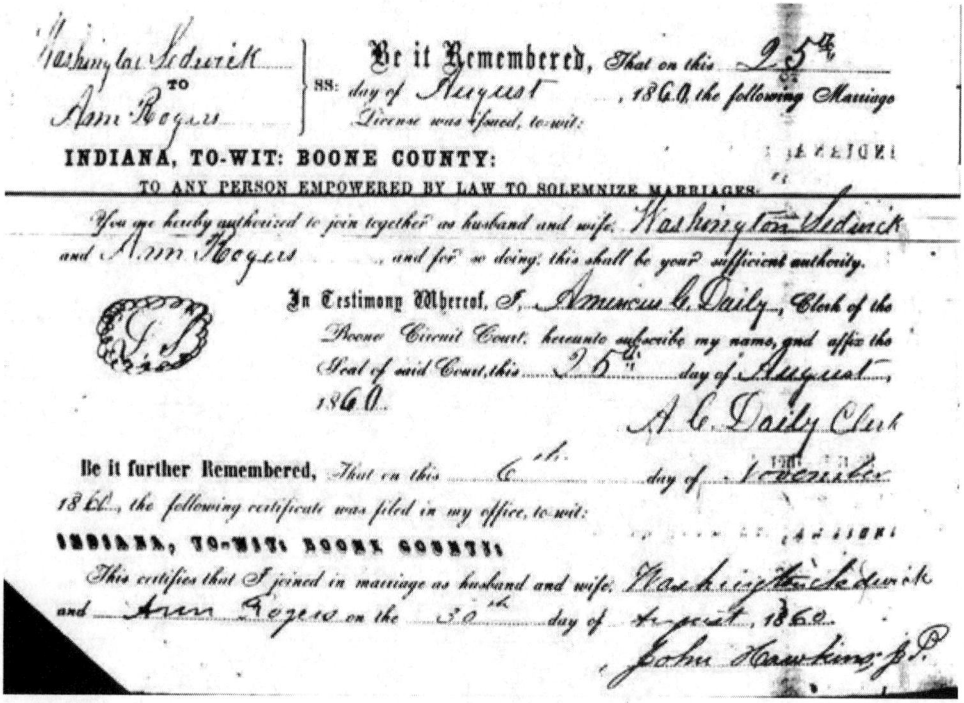
Washington Sedwick TO Ann Rogers SS: Be it Remembered, That on this 25th day of August, 1860 the following Marriage License was issued, to-wit:

INDIANA, TO-WIT: BOONE COUNTY:

TO ANY PERSON EMPOWERED BY LAW TO SOLEMNIZE MARRIAGES.

You are hereby authorized to join together as husband and wife, Washington Sedinck and Ann Rogers, and for so doing, this shall be your sufficient authority.

In Testimony Whereof, I, Americus C. Daily, Clerk of the Boone Circuit Court, hereunto subscribe my name, and affix the Seal of said Court, this 25th day of August, 1860.

A. C. Daily Clerk

Be it further Remembered, That on this 6th day of November 1860, the following certificate was filed in my office, to-wit:

INDIANA, TO-WIT: BOONE COUNTY:

This certifies that I joined in marriage as husband and wife, Washington Sedwick and Ann Rogers on the 30th day of August, 1860.

John Hawkins J.P.

FIGURE 4-16 This 1860 marriage license from Indiana was returned to the county clerk after the ceremony for registration and filing. (From the National Archives and Records Administration collection.)

In other places, there are civil offices or civil registration offices at which the license to wed was issued. In the United Kingdom, the completed marriage document ultimately was sent to the General Register Office (GRO), where it was recorded and filed. Quarterly indexes were compiled by groom's name and bride's name, along with the civil register book and page on which the marriage was recorded. By locating this information, you can order from the GRO a certificate containing the information inscribed on the original marriage document on file.

In some cases, you may find the original documents in a government office, or you may obtain a copy of the document or a certified document, such as the one shown in Figure 4-17, attesting to the content of the marriage entry.

Marriage laws have varied over time in different places. The legal age at which an individual could enter into a marriage contract may have been 16, 18, or some other age. Exceptions to these laws may have been made with the express permission of one or both of the parents of a minor. In addition, laws dictating the permissibility of marriage between couples who shared a certain consanguinity, or blood relationship, were generally closely adhered to. For example, a person might not be permitted by law to marry his or her sibling, first cousin, uncle or aunt, or another close relative.

Marriage licenses are common across the world. What differs, however, are the formats and the amount of information contained on them. The typical marriage record will include the name of the groom, the name of the bride, the date and location, the name or signature of the person who officiated, and the names or signatures of at least two witnesses. Other records may include far more details, such as the ages or even the dates of birth of the bride and groom, the names of their parents, the filing date and location, and the name or signature of the clerk or ordinary. I have even seen a few with addresses of the bride and groom. Others may include the occupation of the fathers of the couple.

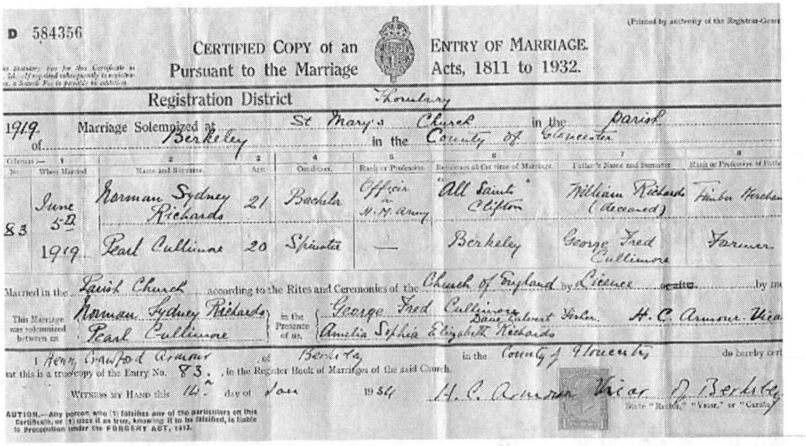
D 584356

CERTIFIED COPY of an ENTRY OF MARRIAGE.
Pursuant to the Marriage Acts, 1811 to 1932.

Registration District Thornbury

1919. Marriage Solemnized at St Mary's Church in the Parish of Berkeley in the County of Gloucester

No.	When Married	Name and Surname	Age	Condition	Rank or Profession	Residence at the time of Marriage	Father's Name and Surname	Rank or Profession of Father
83	June 5th 1919	Norman Sydney Richards	21	Bachelor	Officer in H.M. Army	"All Saints" Clifton	William Richards (deceased)	Timber Merchant
		Pearl Cullimore	20	Spinster	—	Berkeley	George Fred Cullimore	Farmer

Married in the Parish Church according to the Rites and Ceremonies of the Church of England by Licence by me

This Marriage was solemnized between us: Norman Sydney Richards, Pearl Cullimore

in the Presence of us: George Fred Cullimore, Amelia Sophia Elizabeth Richards

H. C. Armour. Vicar

I Henry Crawford Armour of Berkeley in the County of Gloucester do hereby certify that this is a true copy of the Entry No. 83, in the Register Book of Marriages of the said Church.

WITNESS MY HAND this 14th day of Jan 1954 H. C. Armour Vicar of Berkeley

CAUTION.—Any person who (1) falsifies any of the particulars on this Certificate, or (2) uses it as true, knowing it to be falsified, is liable to Prosecution under the FORGERY ACT, 1913.

FIGURE 4-17 The Certified Copy of an Entry of Marriage was issued in Gloucester, England, in 1919 as legal documentation of the marriage. (Used by permission of The National Archives, U.K.)

The elaborate marriage certificate shown in Figure 4-18 appears to have been issued by the church rather than by a governmental office as there is no registration information on it. The couple's names are Germanic, and the bride's name, Adolphine M. Reeb, is followed by the notation, "geb. Kleinknecht." The "geb." is an abbreviation for the German word *geborene*, which is the feminine of the German word for *born* or, in this context, *nee*. This notation indicates that Kleinknecht was the bride's maiden name, and that she has been married before. Also note that another member of her family, Theodor (or Theador), signed the document as one of the witnesses.

The earliest marriage documents recorded royal or noble marriages. Over time, marriage documents became more common and were issued and recorded by churches. These were all handwritten, often in florid script. Later ones used standardized forms. Still others can be found that are extremely ornate, with elaborate artwork, gold or silver leaf, wax or metallic seals, and affixed with ribbons.

FIGURE 4-18   This elaborate marriage certificate, dated 20 April 1881, was probably issued by a church. (From the author's collection.)

There are other records that can be used to help prove a marriage or the intent to marry. The following list includes a number, but certainly not all, of the kinds of alternative record types you might use to help document a marriage:

- Marriage banns are a public announcement, read out on at least three successive occasions in a parish church, of a declaration of intent to marry. These may be documented in church minutes, bulletins, and other publications. Figure 4-19 shows a page from an English parish church's marriage banns in 1796. Before the use of formal marriage certificates, marriage banns found in church records may be the only proof of the joining of a couple.

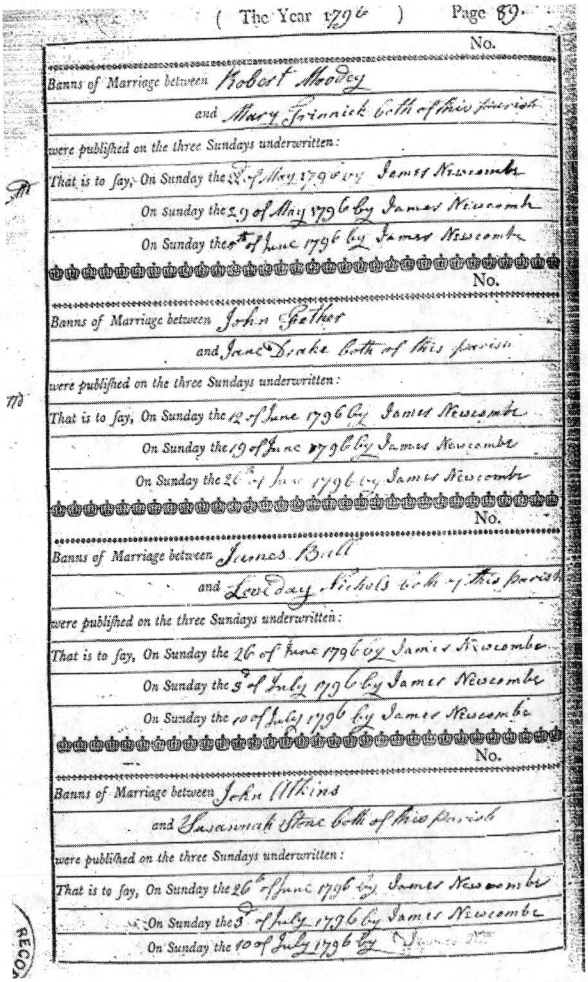

(The Year 1796) Page 89.

No.
Banns of Marriage between Robert Moodey
and Mary Grinnick both of this parish
were published on the three Sundays underwritten:
That is to say, On Sunday the 22 of May 1796 by James Newcombe
On Sunday the 29 of May 1796 by James Newcombe
On Sunday the 5th of June 1796 by James Newcombe

No.
Banns of Marriage between John Gether
and Jane Drake both of this parish
were published on the three Sundays underwritten:
That is to say, On Sunday the 12 of June 1796 by James Newcombe
On Sunday the 19 of June 1796 by James Newcombe
On Sunday the 26 of June 1796 by James Newcombe

No.
Banns of Marriage between James Bell
and Loveday Nichols both of this parish
were published on the three Sundays underwritten:
That is to say, On Sunday the 26 of June 1796 by James Newcombe
On Sunday the 3 of July 1796 by James Newcombe
On Sunday the 10 of July 1796 by James Newcombe

No.
Banns of Marriage between John Wilkins
and Susannah Stone both of this parish
were published on the three Sundays underwritten:
That is to say, On Sunday the 26th of June 1796 by James Newcombe
On Sunday the 3 of July 1796 by James Newcombe
On Sunday the 10 of July 1796 by [illegible]

FIGURE 4-19 Marriage banns were announced or published on several successive Sundays to make public a couple's intention to wed. (Used by permission of The National Archives, U.K.)

- Newspaper announcements of engagements and marriages can provide clues to the date and place of a wedding that you can then follow up to locate primary documents.
- A wedding invitation is an excellent indicator of intent that you may use to help locate a primary marriage record. Remember that dates on a preprinted invitation may have been changed due to unforeseen circumstances.
- Marriage ceremonies performed in a religious institution are typically recorded in their records.
- Civil marriages performed in a city hall or other government office will be found recorded in these governmental offices' files.
- Bible entries may contain marriage information but should be verified with other records.
- Letters, journals, and diaries may discuss details of a wedding, the persons who attended, and other details of the occasion.
- Printed announcements, notices in church publications, or newspaper accounts of milestone anniversary celebrations, such as a 25th, 50th, or 75th wedding anniversary, are pointers back to the date and location of the original event and original documentary evidence.

Marriage records can be helpful in a number of ways. First, they are primary sources of evidence for the marriage. They place a couple in a specific place on a particular date. Using the name of the person officiating at the ceremony, you may be able to refer to a city directory of the time and connect him (or her) with a specific religious institution. That may lead you to individual and family records for the bride and perhaps even to the groom. Membership records may then point you to previous and subsequent places of residence in the form of entries in church minutes where transfers of membership were noted. Names of parents and witnesses may connect you with other family members, friends, and collateral relatives, too. These are examples of how to use your critical thinking skills and creativity to identify other potentially helpful records.

Research Divorce Records

Records of a divorce are far less numerous than marriage records, and so you would think they would be easier to locate. Unfortunately, though, that is not always true. Some courthouses, record offices, and government facilities have done an excellent job indexing the divorces by the names of the husband and wife. In other places, the divorce documentation may only be filed under the name of the plaintiff—the person who sued for divorce. Others, however, may simply have filed divorce petitions and decrees in chronological sequence. This can make your job problematic and may require you to spend hours paging through sheaves of papers. Even if the courthouse or clerks have not been as organized or diligent in their filing, there are other possibilities.

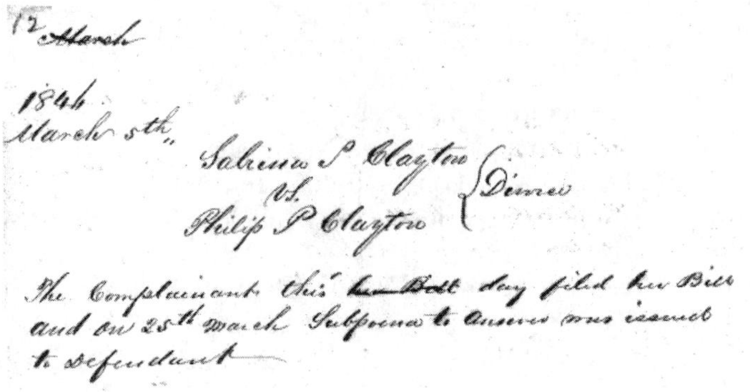

FIGURE 4-20 Simple bill of divorce dated 5 March 1846 found in chancery court records. (Courtesy of Jim Powell.)

Make certain before you undertake a search for divorce records that you determine which court would have handled the process for the period in time when the divorce likely occurred. For example, in one place and time a divorce might have been handled by a civil court, while in another place the hearings may have been held and the dissolution of the marriage may have been finalized in a family court, a high court of justice in the family division, a superior court, a chancery court, or some other judicial division. Figure 4-20 shows an example of a bill of divorce handed down by a chancery court in 1846. Knowing in advance what the laws were at the time *and* the court of law that handled marriage dissolutions at the time can be crucial to your success.

Contact the court that would have handled the divorce petition or suit before you make a trip there. If an index of documents does not exist, request a search of the minutes of the appropriate court. The minute books are well indexed to facilitate location of pertinent documentation, reference to previous court hearings and actions, and the expeditious handling of cases by the magistrate. You may have greater success by obtaining the dates of the filing and hearing in the court minutes, and then going directly to the records filed in chronological sequence.

Early records were handwritten, and reading the clerk's penmanship may be a challenge. Later records, such as the Final Judgment of Divorce shown in Figure 4-21, are typewritten and easier to read.

Death certificates aren't necessarily 100 percent accurate. Death certificates in the United States contain both primary *and* secondary information. Death information is probably quite accurate because the document was created at or near the time of the event. Another person (an informant), however, provided other information, and he or she may not have known correct details about the decedent's date of birth, parents' names, and other data. Always use that data as clues but locate other original primary sources and personally verify the correct information.

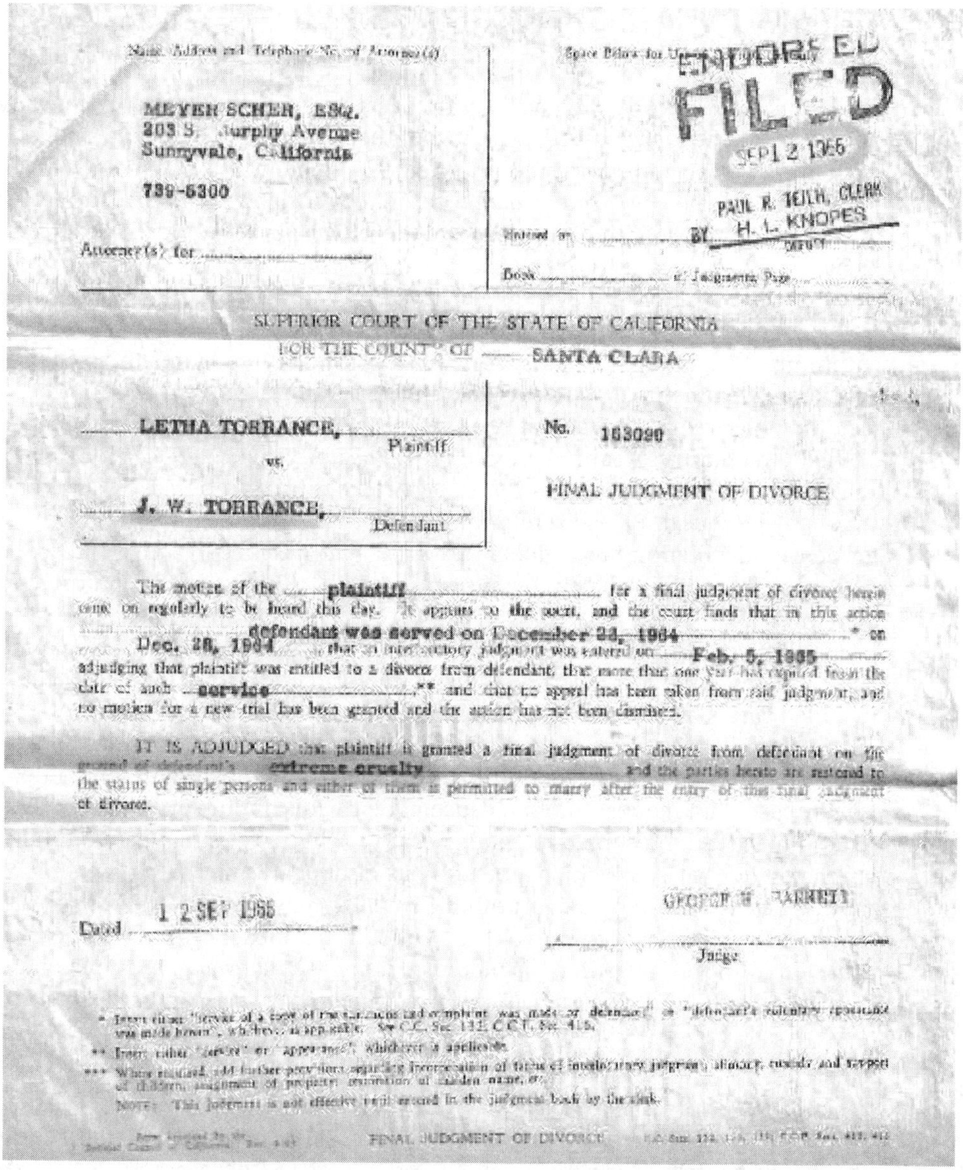

Name, Address and Telephone No. of Attorney(s)

MEYER SCHER, ESQ.
203 S. Murphy Avenue
Sunnyvale, California

739-6300

Attorney(s) for

ENDORSED FILED
SEP 12 1955
PAUL R. TEILH, CLERK
BY H. L. KNOPES DEPUTY

Entered in ... Book ... of Judgments Page ...

SUPERIOR COURT OF THE STATE OF CALIFORNIA
FOR THE COUNTY OF SANTA CLARA

LETHA TORRANCE, Plaintiff
vs.
J. W. TORRANCE, Defendant

No. 153090

FINAL JUDGMENT OF DIVORCE

The motion of the plaintiff for a final judgment of divorce herein came on regularly to be heard this day. It appears to the court, and the court finds that in this action defendant was served on December 28, 1954 * on Dec. 28, 1954, that an interlocutory judgment was entered on Feb. 5, 1955 adjudging that plaintiff was entitled to a divorce from defendant; that more than one year has expired from the date of such service ** and that no appeal has been taken from said judgment, and no motion for a new trial has been granted and the action has not been dismissed.

IT IS ADJUDGED that plaintiff is granted a final judgment of divorce from defendant on the ground of defendant's extreme cruelty and the parties hereto are restored to the status of single persons and either of them is permitted to marry after the entry of this final judgment of divorce.

Dated 12 SEP 1955

GEORGE W. BARNETT
Judge

* Insert either "service of a copy of the summons and complaint was made on defendant" or "defendant's voluntary appearance was made herein", whichever is applicable. See C.C. Sec. 132, C.C.P. Sec. 415.

** Insert either "service" or "appearance", whichever is applicable.

*** Where required, add further provisions regarding incorporation of terms of interlocutory judgment, alimony, custody and support of children, assignment of property, restoration of maiden name, etc.

NOTE: This judgment is not effective until entered in the judgment book by the clerk.

FINAL JUDGMENT OF DIVORCE

FIGURE 4-21 Final Judgment of Divorce, Santa Clara County, California, 1955. (Used by permission of The Generations Network, Inc.)

Locate Death Certificates

The sheer volume of records created as a result of a contemporary individual's death can be enormous. However, you may find that records from earlier times may be nonexistent. The creation and existence of these records will depend on a number of factors. Did the government require them to be kept? Who was responsible for creating them: the government or the church, or both? What information was to be included? Where were these records stored and for what duration? Were there natural or manmade catastrophes that caused records to be lost or destroyed? How will you find out what is and is not available?

A common death record is the death certificate. While a death registration was common in England and Wales from 1837, in the United States the issuance of an official, government-issued death certificate was not required until much later. In fact, a death certificate was not required in many states until the first two decades of the 20th century. Again, *Ancestry's Red Book* or *The Handybook for Genealogists* can help you determine when records were kept in a specific U.S. state and where they may be found. Please remember that a death certificate is a *primary source* for death information but is decidedly a *secondary source* for birth information and other data. This other information should be corroborated with other primary evidence.

Death records come in many forms. The form familiar to most people in the United States is the death certificate, and the format and amount of information included varies by location and time period. Other documents, however, serve a similar or identical purpose for genealogists because they are, after all, official documentation of a death. These might include a coroner's report, an autopsy, the final report of an inquest into the cause of death, or a ruling on evidence of an actual or assumed death presented to a judge or jury. This latter situation would include, among others, a case in which a person has disappeared and, after some period of time, is declared dead by a court of law. You also may encounter or obtain a document that acts as a certified copy of an original death certificate or that certifies the official death entry in the government's records. Figure 4-22 shows an example of a certified copy of a death entry document from the United Kingdom.

Did You Know? Death certificates aren't necessarily 100 percent accurate. Death certificates in the United States contain both primary *and* secondary information. Death information is probably quite accurate because the document was created at or near the time of the event. Another person (an informant), however, provided other information, and he or she may not have known correct details about the decedent's date of birth, parents' names, and other data. Always use that data as clues but locate other original primary sources and personally verify the correct information.

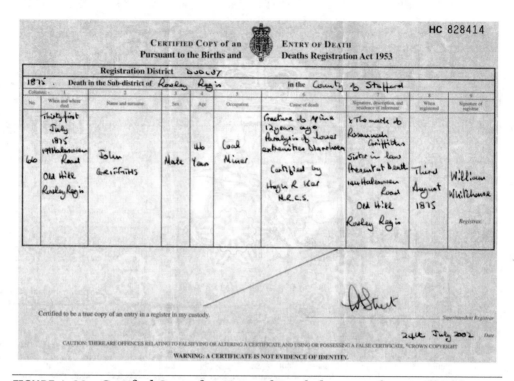

FIGURE 4-22   Certified Copy of an Entry of Death document from Staffordshire, England, for 1875. (Used by permission of the General Records Office, U.K.)

You will remember from our discussion of sources that a death certificate can be both a primary *and* a secondary source of information. Since a death certificate is an official record of a person's death, it is usually created at or very near the time of death in order to record the event. There are exceptions, of course, such as the case noted above of a disappeared person being declared dead. There also are instances of amended death certificates being issued in order to correct or add to information entered on the original document.

The veracity of the information on a death certificate will depend on where the information originated. Information about the identity of the decedent and the death itself are usually obtained from medical, law enforcement, forensic, and other professional persons. It is their job to gather and report the correct information. You would therefore place a significant amount of credence in their data and, if placed on a certificate created at or very near the time of death, consider it to be good primary source information.

Other information found on a death certificate may not be as reliable as that gathered by the professionals. Someone who supposedly knew something about the deceased may have provided the other details included on a death certificate. Another family member or friend is usually solicited to provide the information, and he or she

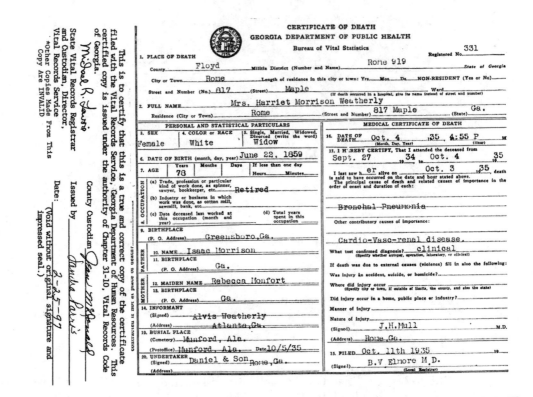

FIGURE 4-23 Certified copy of a death certificate for the author's great-grandmother from Floyd County, Georgia, issued in 1935. (From the author's collection.)

is referred to as the "informant." The informant may or may not know the answers to all the questions that are asked and, on the spur of the moment, may provide what he or she "thinks" is correct. As a result, there are many errors entered on death certificates. Unless the informant has direct, first-hand, and accurate knowledge of facts, the data provided can only be assumed to be secondary in nature. Everything should therefore be verified or corroborated with other sources before you accept those items of information as fact.

As an example, let's examine the death certificate presented in Figure 4-23. The name of the person may or may not be correct, depending on the source of the information. The informant provided information concerning the decedent's date and place of birth, the parents' names, marital status, name of spouse, occupation, place of residence, and other data.

When you request a copy of a death certificate, you may receive an exact copy of the original document, such as a photocopy. However, it is altogether likely that the official office from which you order a copy will issue a certified document attesting to be information correctly copied from the original death registration document. Figures 4-22 and 4-24 show examples of certified copies, the first from the GRO in

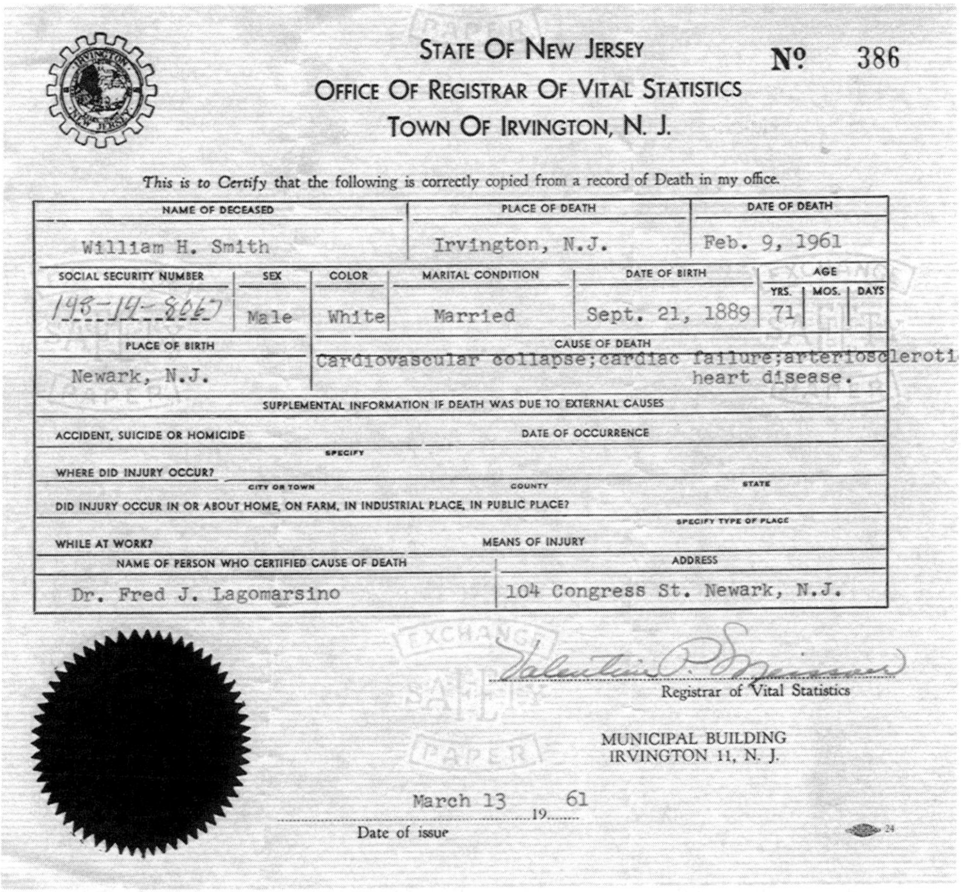

STATE OF NEW JERSEY   N⁰   386
OFFICE OF REGISTRAR OF VITAL STATISTICS
TOWN OF IRVINGTON, N. J.

This is to Certify that the following is correctly copied from a record of Death in my office.

NAME OF DECEASED	PLACE OF DEATH	DATE OF DEATH
William H. Smith	Irvington, N.J.	Feb. 9, 1961

SOCIAL SECURITY NUMBER	SEX	COLOR	MARITAL CONDITION	DATE OF BIRTH	AGE YRS.	MOS.	DAYS
193-19-8067	Male	White	Married	Sept. 21, 1889	71		

PLACE OF BIRTH	CAUSE OF DEATH
Newark, N.J.	Cardiovascular collapse;cardiac failure;arteriosclerotic heart disease.

SUPPLEMENTAL INFORMATION IF DEATH WAS DUE TO EXTERNAL CAUSES

ACCIDENT, SUICIDE OR HOMICIDE   DATE OF OCCURRENCE
SPECIFY
WHERE DID INJURY OCCUR?
CITY OR TOWN   COUNTY   STATE
DID INJURY OCCUR IN OR ABOUT HOME, ON FARM, IN INDUSTRIAL PLACE, IN PUBLIC PLACE?
SPECIFY TYPE OF PLACE
WHILE AT WORK?   MEANS OF INJURY

NAME OF PERSON WHO CERTIFIED CAUSE OF DEATH	ADDRESS
Dr. Fred J. Lagomarsino	104 Congress St. Newark, N.J.

Registrar of Vital Statistics

MUNICIPAL BUILDING
IRVINGTON 11, N. J.

March 13   61
19
Date of issue

FIGURE 4-24   Certified copy of a death record from New Jersey, issued in 1961. (Courtesy of Drew Smith.)

the United Kingdom and the second from the United States. These copies commonly contain far less information than the original document. Remember that an exact copy of the original is your better resource, and that transcription errors might be made despite all caution. If you order a copy of a marriage or death record, request an exact copy of the original rather than a transcribed certified copy, if possible.

Other source materials for determining date of death and other family details include newspaper obituaries (a veritable wealth of clues!), burial permits, transit permits, medical records, family Bibles, tombstones and other cemetery markers, cemetery/sexton records, religious records, mortuary and funeral home records, and wills and probate records, just to name a few.

We've covered a great deal of territory in this chapter. By now, you have a well-grounded feel for how to conduct scholarly research and some excellent methodologies to help ensure your success. Chapter 5 will take you into a thorough examination of census records, which in turn can lead you to a wealth of other records.

5

Use Census Schedules and Records to Locate Your Ancestors

HOW TO...

- Understand and work effectively with United States census records
- Understand and use the Soundex indexing system to locate family members in the census
- Discover the history of the English and Irish censuses
- Learn more about the census in Canada
- Locate information about censuses in other places
- Gain access to census records

Among the most important records that exist for confirming the presence of an ancestor at a particular place at a specific point in time are census records. A *census* is defined as an official count of a population carried out at regular intervals. Censuses have been taken for many centuries in many countries and territories. Over the centuries, censuses were taken for purposes of taxation, to determine legislative representation, to analyze trends in population growth and movement, and for planning purposes.

Census records are the most-used records by genealogists and their use continues to accelerate and grow. This is especially true with the availability and expansion of Internet-based databases containing scanned census document images and searchable indices.

We are going to focus on the available census records in the United States, the British Isles, and Canada in this chapter. Unfortunately, early Australian census records have been destroyed by the government and no known copies exist.

Certainly other countries have taken censuses at various times and, if you are interested in learning more about them and accessing extant records, you can use your web browser to locate archives and other repositories in which the records may be located. Other census indexes, transcriptions, and images are accessible at various websites. For example, Ancestry.de, the German genealogy subscription database, contains some German census records (Volkszälung) such as the image shown in Figure 5-1.

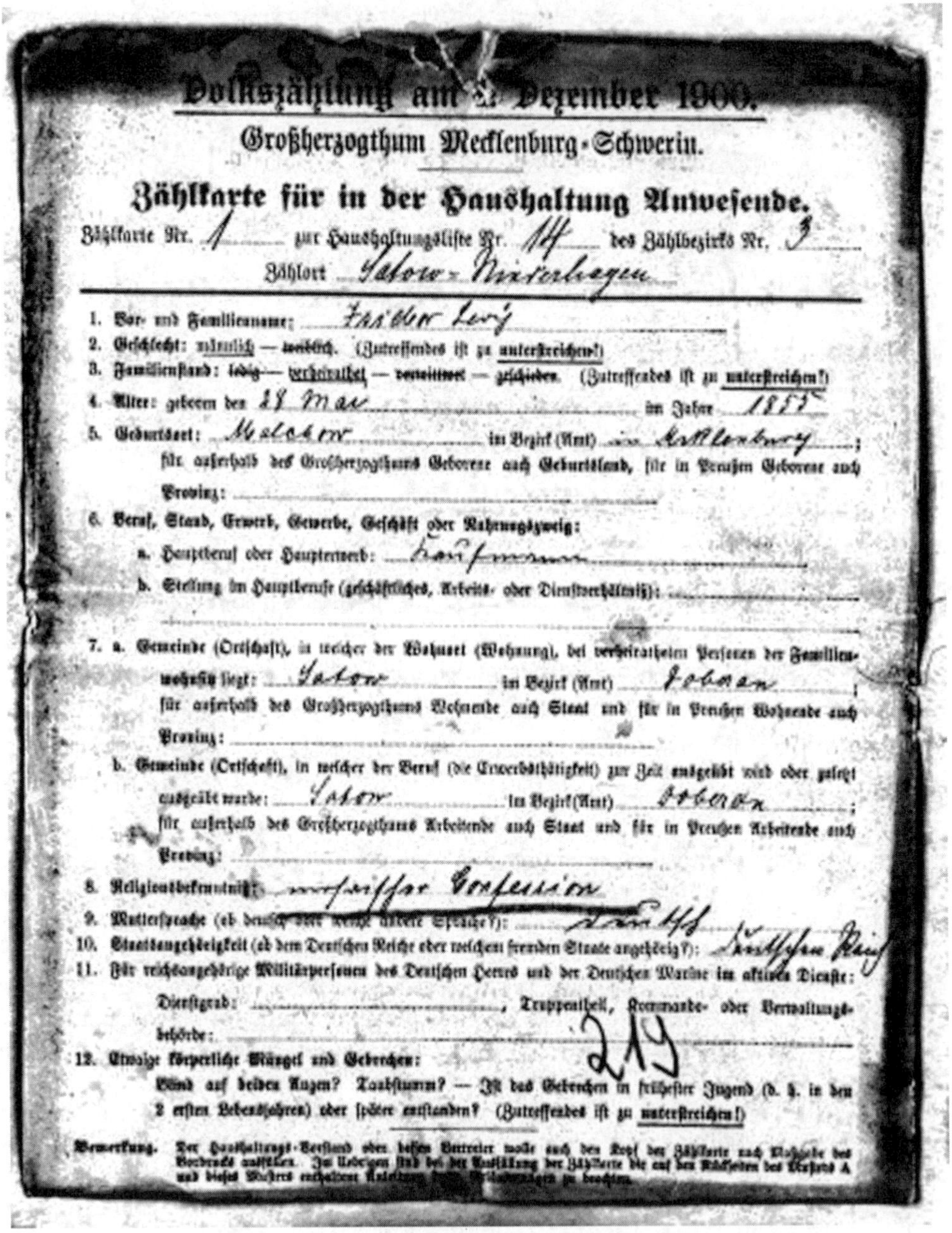
Volkszählung am 1. Dezember 1900.
Großherzogthum Mecklenburg-Schwerin.
Zählkarte für in der Haushaltung Anwesende.
Zählkarte Nr. 1 zur Haushaltungsliste Nr. 14 des Zählbezirks Nr. 3
Zählort Satow - Miekenhagen
1. Vor- und Familienname: Friedrich Lewy
2. Geschlecht: männlich — weiblich. (Zutreffendes ist zu unterstreichen!)
3. Familienstand: ledig — verheirathet — verwittwet — geschieden. (Zutreffendes ist zu unterstreichen!)
4. Alter: geboren den 28 Mai im Jahre 1855
5. Geburtsort: Malchow im Bezirk (Amt) in Mecklenburg;
für außerhalb des Großherzogthums Geborene auch Geburtsland, für in Preußen Geborene auch Provinz:
6. Beruf, Stand, Erwerb, Gewerbe, Geschäft oder Nahrungszweig:
a. Hauptberuf oder Haupterwerb: Kaufmann
b. Stellung im Hauptberufe (geschäftliches, Arbeits- oder Dienstverhältniß):
7. a. Gemeinde (Ortschaft), in welcher der Wohnort (Wohnung), bei verheiratheten Personen der Familienwohnsitz liegt: Satow im Bezirk (Amt) Doberan;
für außerhalb des Großherzogthums Wohnende auch Staat und für in Preußen Wohnende auch Provinz:
b. Gemeinde (Ortschaft), in welcher der Beruf (die Erwerbsthätigkeit) zur Zeit ausgeübt wird oder zuletzt ausgeübt wurde: Satow im Bezirk (Amt) Doberan;
für außerhalb des Großherzogthums Arbeitende auch Staat und für in Preußen Arbeitende auch Provinz:
8. Religionsbekenntniß: mosaischer Confession
9. Muttersprache (ob deutsch oder welche andere Sprache?): deutsch
10. Staatsangehörigkeit (ob dem Deutschen Reiche oder welchem fremden Staate angehörig?): Deutsches Reich
11. Für reichsangehörige Militärpersonen des Deutschen Heeres und der Deutschen Marine im aktiven Dienste:
Dienstgrad: , Truppentheil, Kommando- oder Verwaltungsbehörde:
219
12. Etwaige körperliche Mängel und Gebrechen:
Blind auf beiden Augen? Taubstumm? — Ist das Gebrechen in frühester Jugend (d. h. in den 2 ersten Lebensjahren) oder später entstanden? (Zutreffendes ist zu unterstreichen!)
Bemerkung. Der Haushaltungs-Vorstand oder dessen Vertreter wolle auch den Kopf der Zählkarte nach Maßgabe des Vordrucks ausfüllen. Im Uebrigen sind bei der Ausfüllung der Zählkarte die auf den Rückseiten des Vordrucks A und dieses Musters enthaltenen Anleitungen ... zu beachten.

FIGURE 5-1 German 1900 census record. (Used by permission of The Generations Network, Inc.)

You will not always find entire countries' historical census record images on the Internet. You will need to search websites, particularly those of national archives and libraries, and visit subscription websites to locate what holdings they may have and learn how and where to access them. Some census records also may have privacy limitations that prevent the contents from being revealed for a substantial number of years.

As we discuss census records, be aware that they can be a primary source of information to help establish a person's location in a specific place at a certain point in time. Even that is suspect at times, as you will see. All other information on a census document should definitely be considered secondary source material, and should be verified and corroborated with other sources whenever possible.

Did You Know?

Census records are the documents most frequently used by genealogists. They help you locate your ancestor and his or her family at regular intervals, and the records contain important details about their lives, citizenship, employment, and family members and other people living with them. Let's explore the census records of several important locales.

Understand and Work with United States Census Records

In the United States, there have been censuses taken by the federal government every ten years, beginning in 1790 and continuing to the present. A number of state censuses also have been taken periodically and these can supplement your use of federal census records in American research. Prior to 1790, a few of the original 13 colonies performed partial or complete enumerations of citizens for their own purposes. Some of these records still exist and, in order to locate them, it is a good idea to contact the respective state archive or state library to determine what might have been created, what might still survive, and where to locate the materials. After 1790, too, some states have taken their own censuses. Some of these have been digitized and indexed at Ancestry.com, while others may only be available in original paper records or in a microfilmed format.

The United States Constitution, which took effect on 4 March 1789, established the taking of a national census on a regular basis. Article I, Section 2 specifically called for a census to be taken every ten years. Direct taxation of the population to support the federal government's operation was to be based on census information. The Constitution stated that each free person counted as a whole number, including those bound for service for a term of years, and that free males would be taxed and could vote. Indians living on treaty land were excluded from direct taxation and voting. Other, non-free persons were to be counted as three-fifths of a free person for legislative representation. An Indian who joined the white population was to be considered a "free person" and could vote. The entire text of the Constitution is available at the Library of Congress website at **http://memory.loc.gov/ammem/collections/continental** and an extensive article is available at **http://en.wikipedia.org/wiki/United_states_ constitution**.

Federal decennial censuses have been taken every decade from 1790 through 2000. An official Census Day was established for enumerators to ask questions "as of" that date. The official United States Census Day for each decade is shown here:

1790	2 August
1800	4 August
1810	6 August
1820	7 August
1830 through 1900	1 June
1910	15 April
1920	1 January
1930 through 2000	1 April

The enumerators were given a deadline by which time they were to accomplish their work, instructions to follow, and a set of questions to be used. Census forms for the 1850 to 2000 censuses are available at **http://usa.ipums.org/usa/voliii/tEnumForm.shtml**. The enumerators' instructions for those years can be found at **http://usa.ipums.org/usa/voliii/tEnumInstr.shtml**. Refer also to the website at **http://usa.ipums.org/usa/voliii/tQuestions.shtml** for only the questions.

Assistant marshals of the U.S. judicial districts performed the earliest census enumerations, 1790 through 1870 (see Figure 5-2). At the time of the 1790 census, there were 16 federal court districts. These represented each of the original 13 states and Vermont, which was included in the first census even though it didn't become a state until 1791. The 2 additional districts comprising the 16 were due to the area of Virginia that became Kentucky and the area of Massachusetts that became Maine. These marshals performed the census enumerations in addition to their ordinary duties. They were poorly paid for their work and often had to purchase their own paper, pens, ink, horse feed, and other supplies with their own funds. They had little incentive to do a good job. They sometimes erred in the areas in which they were assigned. When they failed to reach the state and county boundaries they were assigned to enumerate, or when they enumerated past these boundaries, the result was either omitted residents or duplication of other marshals' enumerations. During these decades, Congress provided funding for the enumeration period and a subsequent tabulation only. This funding was usually appropriated in the Congressional session prior to the enumeration year.

The first central Census Office established in Washington, D.C., to coordinate the taking of a decennial enumeration was opened in 1850. When the tabulation was complete, however, the office was disbanded and all census activity was discontinued until the next census. The same process was used in both 1860 and 1870.

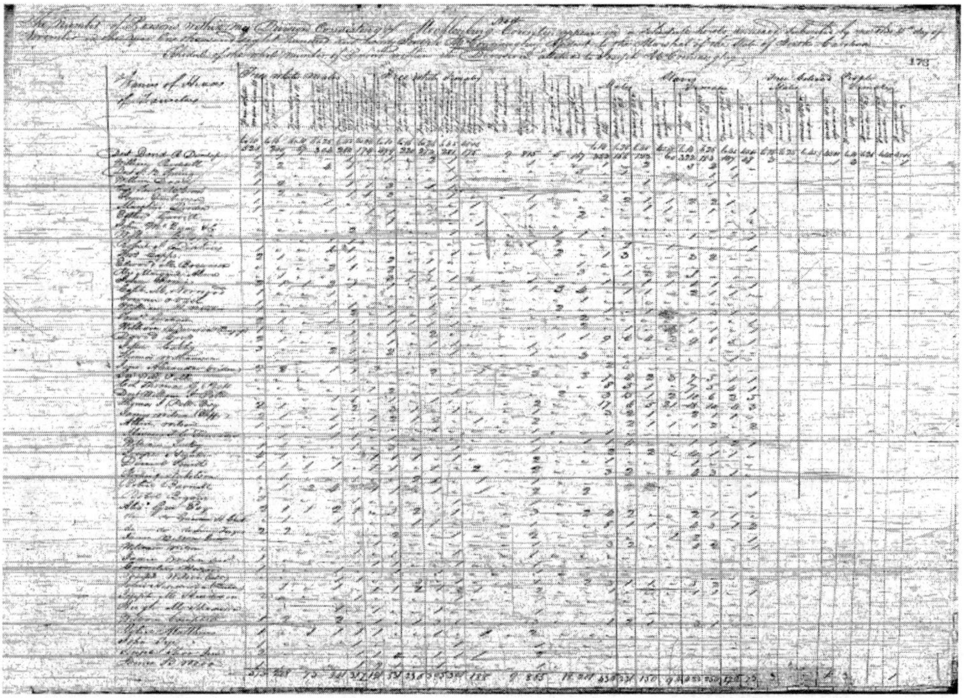

FIGURE 5-2   The 1820 U.S. federal census showing only the names of the heads of household and numerical counts of persons by age group, gender, and free or slave status. (Used by permission of The Generations Network, Inc.)

A Congressional act established and provided funding for a permanent Census Office beginning in 1880. This year was a benchmark in the U.S. federal census in a number of ways. For the first time, the assistant federal marshals were removed from the process. The Census Office hired employees to conduct the enumerations, devised formal Enumeration District maps and descriptions, revised the enumeration instructions, and revised the census forms (or census schedules as they are called). The most common of the federal census documents is the Population Schedule, a sample of which from 1900 is shown in Figure 5-3. These and other schedule documents are discussed next.

It is important to note that the early federal census forms from 1790 through 1840 only contained the names of the heads of household, with the other members of the household represented numerically in categories organized by sex, age, and race. It was not until the 1850 census that the names of all persons within a household were listed. In the 1880 census, the revision of the Population Schedule

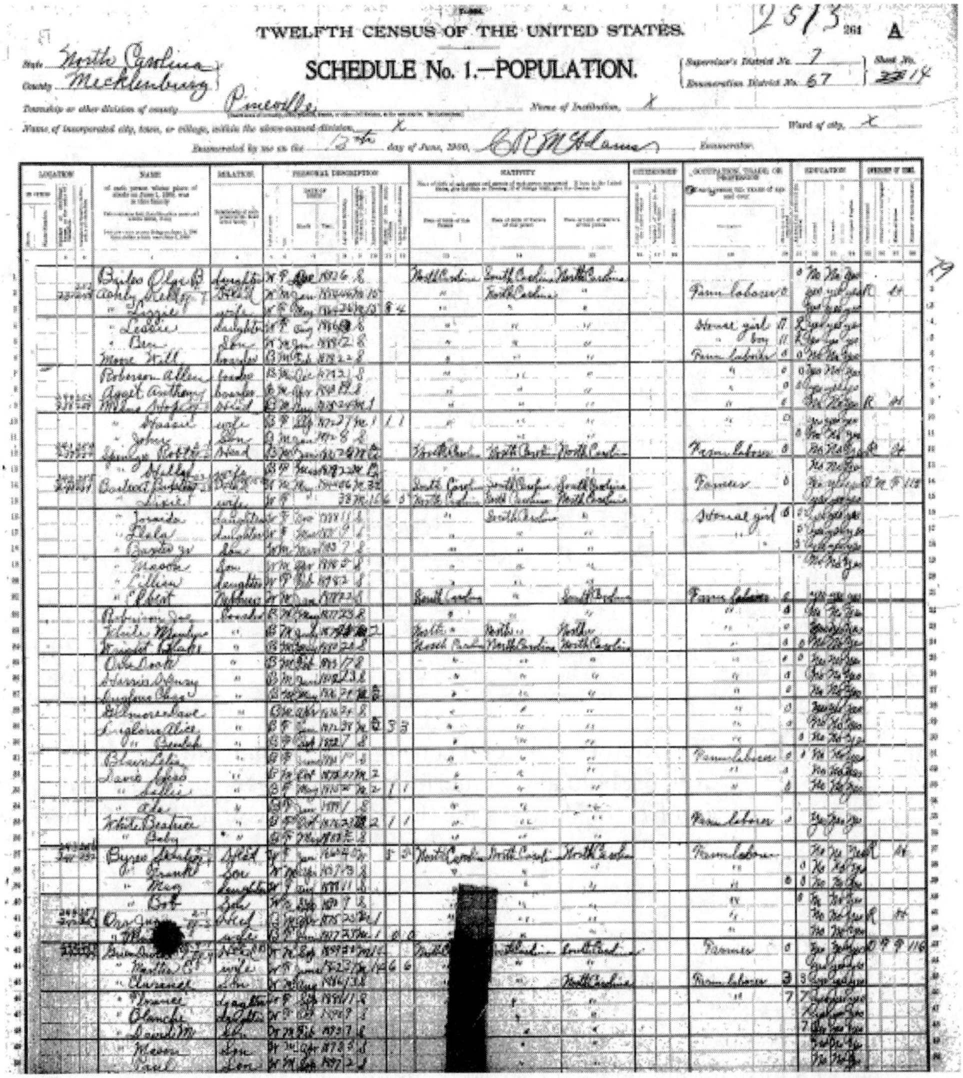

FIGURE 5-3   A 1900 U.S. federal census Population Schedule for Mecklenburg County, North Carolina. (Used by permission of The Generations Network, Inc.)

format called for the names of all inhabitants *and* their relationship to the head of household to be included, and this is an important addition for genealogists. Table 5-4 at the end of this chapter defines for each federal census each of the census forms, or schedules, used for each enumeration year, and what information can be found on each schedule.

Original vs. Copies of Census Documents

There have been various numbers of copies of the original documents created as part of the census enumeration process. From 1790 through 1820, the states sent only summary data to Washington, D.C., and kept their original census documents. The summaries for 1790 through 1810 were destroyed during the War of 1812 when the British burned Washington, D.C.

In 1830, Congress required the states to send all pre-1830 original documents to Washington. Some states complied while others, unfortunately, sent nothing or only partial documentation. As a result, you may find that no census materials exist for certain states for certain years, or that only partial records exist.

If you examine Table 5-1, you will notice that for census years 1830 through 1885, copies of the original census schedules for each state (not summaries) were sent to Washington, D.C., and not the original documents, which were kept by the states. It is important to note that the census schedules that ultimately ended up in the possession of the National Archives and Records Administration (NARA) are the originals returned by the states for 1790–1820. Documents submitted for the 1830 through 1885 censuses were transcribed copies of the original documents completed by the enumerators. The documents for all subsequent enumerations were originals. The copies are transcriptions and, by their very nature, are prone to the possible introduction of transcription errors. In the case of the 1870 census schedules, a transcription of a transcription was actually sent.

TABLE 5-1   U.S. Federal Censuses, Number of Copies, and Disposition. (Used by permission of Aha! Seminars, Inc.)

Year	Enumerator	# Copies Prepared	Sent to Washington
1790	Assistant Marshal	1 original	Summary sent
1800	Assistant Marshal	1 original	Summary sent
1810	Assistant Marshal	1 original	Summary sent
1820	Assistant Marshal	1 original	Summary sent
1830	Assistant Marshal	• 1 original • 1 copy prepared by clerk	Copy sent
1840	Assistant Marshal	• 1 original • 1 copy prepared by clerk	Copy sent
1850	Assistant Marshal	• 1 original • "Clean copy" prepared by Assistant Marshals and sent to state secretary of state ("state copy") • Secretary of state prepared complete copy for federal government ("federal copy")	"Federal copy" sent

(Continued)

TABLE 5-1   U.S. Federal Censuses, Number of Copies, and Disposition. (Used by permission of Aha! Seminars, Inc.) (*Continued*)

Year	Enumerator	# Copies Prepared	Sent to Washington
1860	Assistant Marshal	• 1 original • "Clean copy" prepared by Assistant Marshals and sent to state secretary of state ("state copy") • Secretary of state prepared complete copy for federal government ("federal copy")	"Federal copy" sent
1870	Assistant Marshal	• 1 original • "Clean copy" prepared by Assistant Marshals and sent to state secretary of state ("state copy") • Secretary of state prepared complete copy for federal government ("federal copy")	"Federal copy" sent
1880	Census Office	• 1 original • 1 copy prepared by district supervisor	Copy sent
1885	Census Office and State Enumerators	• 1 original for CO, FL, NE, and Dakota and New Mexico Territories • 1 copy	Copy sent
1890	Census Office	• 1 original • No copy	Original sent (most were destroyed by fire and water)
1900	Census Office	• 1 original • No copy	Original sent
1910	Census Bureau	• 1 original • No copy	Original sent
1920	Census Bureau	• 1 original • No copy	Original sent
1930	Census Bureau	• 1 original • No copy	Original sent

All of the digitized U.S. census documents you find online at sites such as Ancestry.com and HeritageQuest Online (**www.heritagequestonline.com**) were made from microfilmed images of the NARA documents. Therefore, when you work with census images on microfilm and in online databases, remember that the "copy censuses" may be prone to a higher error rate than the originals.

Use Strategies to Work with Population Schedules

The census Population Schedule is the most comprehensive of the U.S. federal census documents, and contains entries for each household. The completeness and accuracy of the enumeration was, of course, dependent on the quality of the work performed by the enumerator, as well as any transcription work done to generate a copy or copies.

Certainly there are omissions in any census. This can be the result of an enumerator missing a residence for whatever reason. An important strategy for every genealogist when working with census records is to locate the family you are researching in one census, and to make note of three to six other families on either side of your family. The reason you will do so is to create a reference group for researching other census years. If you find your family in one census and cannot locate them in the next, check any indexes for that census and look for the neighbors next to them in the previous or subsequent censuses. If you can find the neighbors but your family is not there, there are four possibilities:

- The enumerator omitted or skipped your family's residence.
- Your family was not home, or refused to participate, when the enumerator called.
- Your family moved.
- Your family was deceased, which is more probable when there was only one family member at that location or if the family members were elderly at the time of the previous census.

Another important strategic consideration is that families that lived next door or close to one another, especially in the earlier times, may have intermarried. A check of marriage records in the area may reveal a marriage between families, in which case your "missing" family member may have relocated to live with the newly married couple. I have found numerous examples in my own family ancestry in which a husband died and the wife relocated to live with a son or daughter and their family. Don't be surprised to find a mother-in-law living with her daughter and son-in-law, and even buried in their cemetery plot.

Perhaps the best advice I can give you when doing your genealogical research is to learn how to *misspell* your family members' names. Heaven knows, they misspelled them and so did the other people who created records about them. Consider the many spellings of the surname of SMITH. There are SMITH, SMYTH, SMYTHE, SMIT, SCHMIT, SCHMIDT, and even extended spelling versions of the names such as SMITT, SMITTY, SMITHERS, and many more. One of my ancestors, John Swords, has military service and pension records from the Revolutionary War filed under the spellings of SWORDS, SOARDS, and SORDS, and that doesn't include several other errors in indexes other people have prepared. You can prepare yourself for your research in any type of records by considering the spelling of the surnames, and even the given names, and by preparing a list of alternate spellings and possible misspellings. Using the list, make sure you look for these spellings in census indexes and schedules, or any other records of genealogical importance. By doing so, you can avoid missing records for your own family.

Use Substitutes for the 1890 Census

The eleventh census of the United States, taken in 1890, was different from all others before or since. The Population Schedule included information on only one household per form. It also included a special Veterans and Widows Schedule on which Union soldiers, sailors, and marines, or their surviving widows, were to be enumerated. Again, Congress only financed one copy of the census documents, as it did for all later censuses. States or counties wishing to obtain a copy for their own records would have had to pay for a transcription for their own files. There is no known request having been received for a state or county copy. All original copies of the census documents were sent to the Census Office.

The federal government, recognizing that the tabulation of the 1890 census schedules would be an enormous job, called for a competition to be held for a mechanized method of processing the data to be collected. Herman Hollerith, who had been working on data entry and tabulation machines for a number of years, entered and won this competition. His system utilized punch cards created by use of a manual keyboard resembling a telegraph key. Clerks were able to process an average of 700 cards per day, after which tabulators tabulated an average of 2,000 to 3,000 families per day. As a result, there were over six million persons counted by Hollerith's machines in a single day!

Once the census was complete, the original documents were placed in cartons and stored. In 1896 or 1897, the Census Office destroyed all but the Population Schedules and the Union Veterans and Widows Schedules. The Population Schedules ended up in the basement of the Commerce Building in Washington, D.C., and the Veterans and Widows Schedules were stored on an upper floor. Around 5:00 P.M. on 10 January 1921, a fire broke out in the basement of the building. Records that had not been destroyed by flames had been inundated with water from the firefighters' efforts. The documents were relocated to another storage location but, unfortunately, no salvage was ever performed on the documents. The entire remainder of the 1890 census was destroyed in 1934 or 1935.

The 20-year gap in census records between 1880 and 1900 can seem, at first glance, devastating to your research. However, there are other types of records that can be used as a substitute for this lost census. You will need to use some creativity and refer to reference resources that still exist. These include

- City directories
- Jury rolls
- Voter registration cards and lists
- Land and property records, including plat maps and tax lists
- Newspapers and journals

Use More than Just Population Schedules

The primary type of census document used by the federal government is the Population Schedule. As we have discussed, the amount of information requested and entered on the Population Schedules varied over time. Additional schedule forms were used at various times, and these include the following types of schedules. All of these have been microfilmed and are available from NARA in Washington, D.C., and are accessible at many of their regional branches. In addition, copies of the NARA microfilm are available through the Church of Jesus Christ of Latter-day Saints (LDS Church) Family History Library (FHL) in Salt Lake City, Utah, and the LDS Family History Centers (FHCs). Many have also been made available at Ancestry.com and are noted.

- **Slave Schedules** Used in 1850 and 1860 to determine the numbers, vital statistics, and living conditions of slaves. You can cross-reference the slaveholders' names to Population Schedules on which they were listed. (See Figure 5-4.) Available at Ancestry.com.

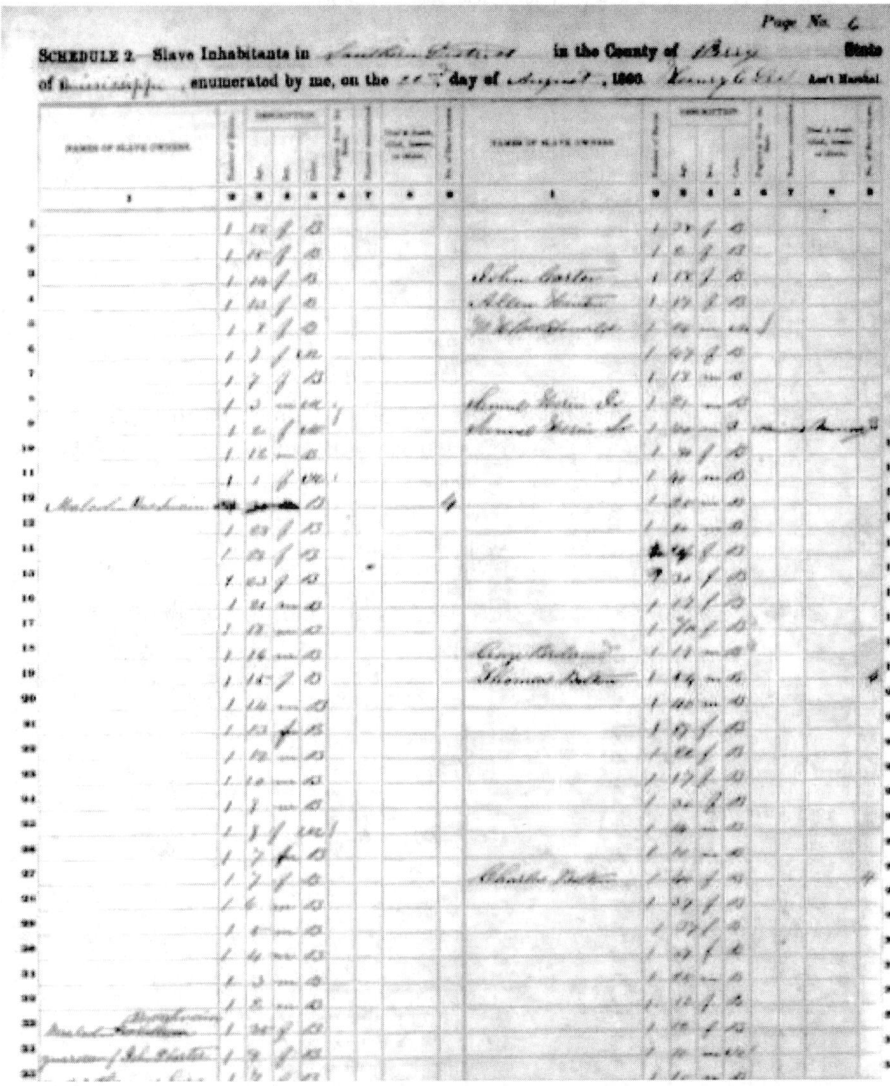

Page No. 6

SCHEDULE 2.—Slave Inhabitants in ... in the County of ... State of ..., enumerated by me, on the ... day of ..., 1860. ... Ass't Marshal.

FIGURE 5-4 A Slave Schedule from the 1860 U.S. federal census of North Carolina. (Used by permission of The Generations Network, Inc.)

- **Mortality Schedules**   Used in the 1850 through 1885 censuses to determine how many persons died in the 12 months prior to Census Day, their vital statistics, duration of illness, and cause of death. (See Figure 5-5.) Available at Ancestry.com.
- **Union Veterans and Widows Schedule**   Used in the 1890 census and was used to enumerate the Union veterans of the U.S. Civil War and widows of Union soldiers. (This is the only complete surviving fragment of the 1890 census—see Figure 5-6.) Available at Ancestry.com.

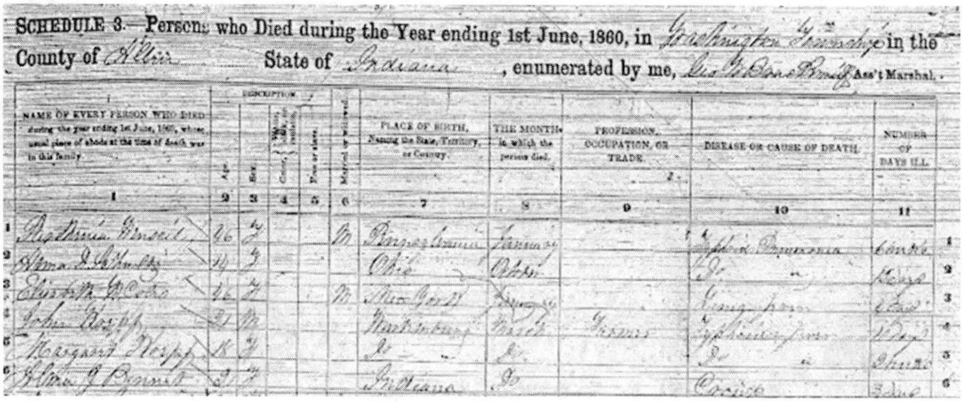

FIGURE 5-5   Portion of a Mortality Schedule from the 1860 U.S. federal census of Indiana. (Used by permission of The Generations Network, Inc.)

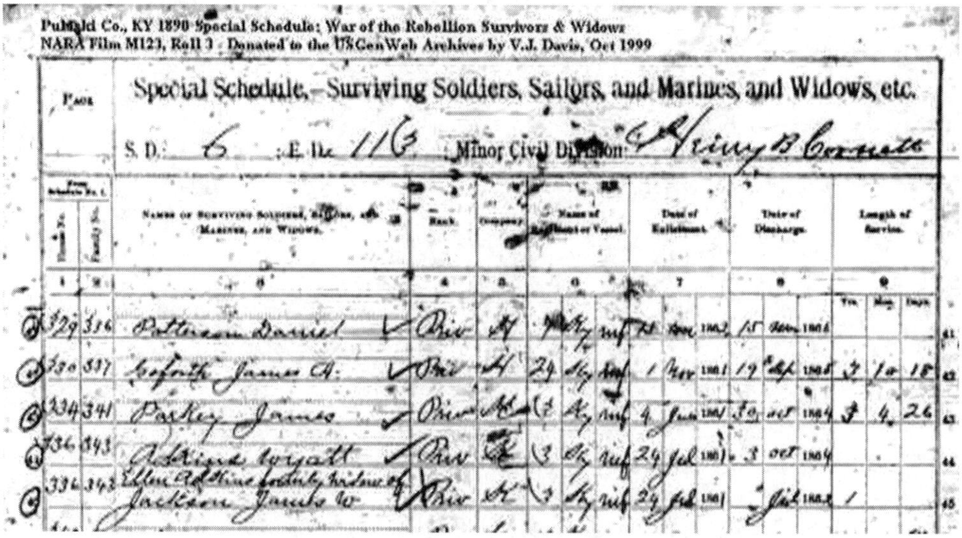

FIGURE 5-6   Portion of a Union Veterans and Widows Schedule. (Used by permission of The Generations Network, Inc.)

- **Agricultural Schedules**   Used in the 1840 through 1910 censuses to determine what agricultural activity was being conducted (farming, ranching, forestry, mining), the value of the land and agricultural output, and production in some key products. These can be used to determine the location and size of an ancestor's land holdings, the commodities in which he was engaged in producing, and the livestock owned.
- **Industry and/or Manufacturing Schedules**   Used in the 1810 through 1910 censuses to determine the industrial and manufacturing activity and output, value of products, and other data. Many of these schedules have been lost or were intentionally destroyed by the federal government. Images of the surviving schedules are mostly poor quality.
- **Defective, Dependent, and Delinquent Classes Schedules**   Used only in the 1880 census. This was a seven-page document that was completed when the enumerator received a response about one of these types of persons on the Population Schedule. The enumerator could also, through personal observation, make an entry in one of the seven categories as defined as follows:
  - **Schedule 1**   Insane inhabitants
  - **Schedule 2**   Idiots
  - **Schedule 3**   Deaf-mutes
  - **Schedule 4**   Blind inhabitants
  - **Schedule 5**   Homeless children (in institutions)
  - **Schedule 6**   Inhabitants in prison
  - **Schedule 7**   Pauper and indigent inhabitants
- **Social Statistics Schedules**   Used in the 1850 through 1880 censuses. Important genealogical information can be gleaned from these schedules. They include information that can be used as a resource to locate specific types of institutions in these years, and trace any surviving records. They include
  - Cemeteries within town borders (names, addresses, descriptions, maps, and other data)
  - Churches, a brief history, affiliation, and membership statistics
  - Trade societies, clubs, lodges, and other social institutions, and statistics about their membership

In addition to all the census schedules, beginning with the establishment of the Census Office for the 1880 census, the area to be canvassed by each enumerator was more clearly defined. The Census Office designated what were known as Enumeration Districts, or EDs. These were defined and represented with textual descriptions and/or ED maps to define the boundaries for each group of enumerators reporting to a district supervisor. Figure 5-7 shows the ED map for a portion of Detroit in the 1930 census. The enumeration districts defined on ED maps sometimes coincided with political or voting areas, but not always. These ED maps exist for federal census areas from 1880 through 1930, and are accessible on microfilm published by NARA.

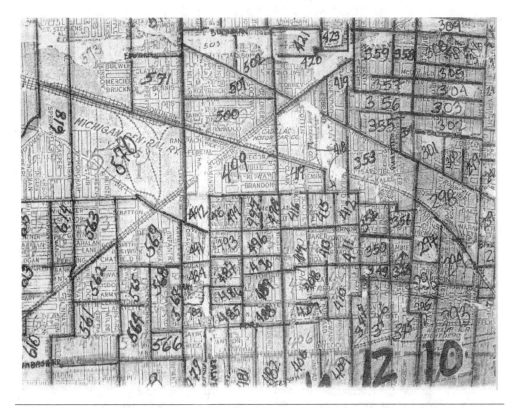

FIGURE 5-7   1930 Enumeration District map showing an area of Detroit, Michigan. (From the National Archives and Records Administration collection.)

In Chapter 4, I told you about the importance of maps in your research, and provided you with a strategy for using maps to find the *right* place to locate your ancestors and their records. The censuses can provide you with another opportunity to use different types of maps. An ED map is helpful if you know your ancestors' address and where in the area that address is situated. And once you know the ED in which your ancestors and family members lived, you greatly improve your chances of quickly locating the right census page(s) to find them, even if the surname was misspelled. There are other resources you can use to help you with this:

- **City directories** are name and address listings published on a fairly regular basis in towns and cities, and were used to help people locate one another. Some of these directories include both individual persons and businesses.
- **Telephone directories**, like city directories, can be helpful in locating addresses.
- **Land and property records**, which we will discuss in some detail later, typically include deeds, indentures, tax rolls, lien papers, and other records indexed by name for easy location by the property clerk, tax assessor, and other government officials. These can provide the names and addresses of the owners, and the governments' maps of property for taxation purposes can be compared with ED maps to help quickly establish a family member's location.

- **Sanborn Fire Insurance Maps** were used in the United States to clearly document urban areas for property and casualty insurance purposes from 1867 until about 1970. These maps provide street-by-street details concerning the buildings, the materials used in their construction, the use of the building, and other information. Additional maps of sub areas provide extensive detail down to the actual shape of an individual building and its construction materials. You can use a Sanborn map in conjunction with directories and land and property records, and compare it against an ED map in order to quickly home in on an ancestor's census records.

Use Census Finding Aids to Locate Your Ancestors

Indexes to the 1790 through 1870 federal censuses are available for most states in book form and can be found in many public libraries with genealogical collections and in academic libraries with genealogical and government documents collections.

Online subscription databases offering access to U.S. federal census indexes include those at the Ancestry.com website and through the HeritageQuest Online census database operated by ProQuest, available through many libraries. Both of these online database services provide links to actual online census population schedule document images. Ancestry.com provides additional indexes for the 1885 federal census enumeration conducted in and for the five states and territories mentioned in Table 5-4 at the end of this chapter. Ancestry.com also provides indexed images to Slave Schedules and Mortality Schedules as noted above.

Use Soundex and Miracode Index Resources

Another important finding aid for locating your ancestors in the census is the sound-alike indexing system. There were two forms of this system that were used in the indexing of census schedules for 1880 through 1930, the Soundex and Miracode systems. They were used for some states in the 1880, 1900, 1910, 1920, and 1930 censuses as follows:

1880	Includes all states but only those households with children aged 10 years and younger
1900	Complete for all households in all states, with separate cards for each adult whose surname differed from the head of household
1910	Includes only 21 states: AL, AR, CA, FL, GA, IL, KS, KY, LA, MI, MS, MO, NC, OH, OK, PA, SC, TN, TX, VA, and WV
1920	Includes all states as well as U.S. territories at the time: Alaska, Hawaii, the Canal Zone, Puerto Rico, Guam, American Samoa, the Virgin Islands, and military and naval institutions
1930	Includes only 12 states: AL, AR, FL, GA, KY, LA, MS, NC, SC, TN, VA, and WV

Soundex and Miracode are similar coding systems that use the first letter of the surname, followed by three numbers to represent the next three remaining consonants (no vowels are used in the numeric portion of the code) in the surname. This number is used to group similar sounding names—such as Smith, Smyth, Smythe, for example—together for ease of location.

The coding for Soundex and Miracode is actually pretty simple. The four-position code begins with the first letter of the surname, whatever it is. The next step is to take the remainder of the surname, discard all the vowels, and retain any consonants. If you have more than three consonants remaining, you discard those additional ones. If you have less than three consonants, don't worry. Whatever you have left at this point will be used to calculate the numeric digits. Zeroes are used to represent a "no consonant" situation. If your family surname is LEE, for example, you would have the letter "L" and no consonants remaining. Your Soundex code would be L000.

You select a numeric code for each of the consonants you have left, using Table 5-2.

TABLE 5-2 Basic Coding Scheme for Soundex and Miracode; Additional Rules Apply

Code #	Represents These Letters...
1	B, F, P, V
2	C, G, J, K, Q, S, X, Z
3	D, T
4	L
5	M, N
6	R
	Disregard A, E, I, O, U, H, W, and Y

Let's take an example. My surname, MORGAN, would be coded as follows:

1. Surname beginning letter is "M."
2. Discard vowels "O" and "A."
3. Remaining consonants are "R," "G," and "N."
4. Equivalent numeric digits to represent "R," "G," and "N" are 6, 2, and 5.
5. Soundex code for MORGAN is therefore M625.

There are some unusual exceptions for which some special rules apply. These are pretty straightforward, however, so don't let them throw you. They actually help you obtain a crisper separation.

- *In surnames with double letters, treat those as a single letter.* For example, the surname SOMMERS would be coded as S562. (The vowels "O" and "E" are discarded, leaving "MM," which is treated as a single "M," an "R," and an "S.")

- *In names with letters side by side that have the same Soundex code value, treat the two letters as one letter.* Here are three examples:
  - MACKEY would be coded M200. (The vowels "A" and "E" are discarded, the "CK" are treated as a single letter and coded as a 2, the "Y" is disregarded and there are no other consonants, and therefore the last two of the four codes are 0 and 0.)
  - TOMCZYAK would be coded T522. (The M is coded as a 5. The vowels "O," "Y," and "A" are discarded, the "CZ" is treated as a single letter and coded as a 2, and the "K" is coded as a 2.)
  - PFISTER would be coded as P236. (The "P" in the double-letter of "PF" is the surname letter, and the "F" is dropped, the "S" is coded as a 2, the "T" is coded as a 3, and the "R" is coded as a 6.)
- *Names with prefixes, such as CON, DE, DI, LA, LE, LO, VAN, and VON, could have been coded either way by the personnel who created the Soundex or Miracode index.* Therefore, you should code the name both ways and check both listings. In all cases, the surnames beginning with MC or MAC are not considered to have used prefixes. These letters are considered part of the entire surname and will be a part of the code.
- *If the two successive consonants have the same Soundex code and are separated by a single vowel ("A," "E," "I," "O," or "U"), the consonant to the right of the vowel is coded, and the other one is ignored.* This could be represented by the example of TOMCZYAK above. However, if an "H" or a "W separates two successive consonants having the same Soundex code" the consonant on the right of the "H" or "W" is not coded. For example, the surname ASHCROFT would be coded A261. (The "S" is coded as 2, the "C" is ignored, the "R" is coded as 6, the "F" is coded as 1, and the "T" is dropped.)

Try the coding system yourself. Dick Eastman, author of *Eastman's Online Genealogy Newsletter*, has a Soundex Calculator at **www.eogn.com/soundex**. I have created a Soundex and Miracode list for myself for all the surnames for which I regularly perform research. I keep a reference card handy with the coding rules, as well as an electronic copy of the card on my iPhone. You may want to create a Soundex reference for yourself.

Special index cards, using either Soundex or Miracode, were created at the request of the Social Security Administration for the 1880, 1900, 1910, 1920, and 1930 censuses in order to help their employees verify the ages of persons applying for retirement benefits. The Works Progress Administration (WPA) created these during the Great Depression in the United States, and they were then grouped and microfilmed by WPA personnel and by some other personnel later. The microfilm is available at NARA, at many libraries with sizeable genealogical special collections, and through the local LDS FHC in your area on loan from the main FHL in Salt Lake City, Utah. Soundex and Miracode card records can point you to the exact census district and census page for the actual census entry for your ancestor or family's member.

Soundex or Miracode microfilm is organized by state, and then in code sequence. Within code, the cards are organized in alphabetical order by the spelling of the surname, and within surname by initials and/or given name of the primary person on the card.

Figure 5-8 shows a Soundex card from the 1920 federal census. For a smaller family, only the one side of the card would have been completed. In this case, however, Lucius Boddie is the head of the household and his family's Soundex card is filed under B300, and then under Boddie, and then under Lucius' name. The Lucius Boddie family consisted of himself, his wife, and seven children. Since the family was so large, the listing was continued to the back of the Soundex card, which is shown in Figure 5-9.

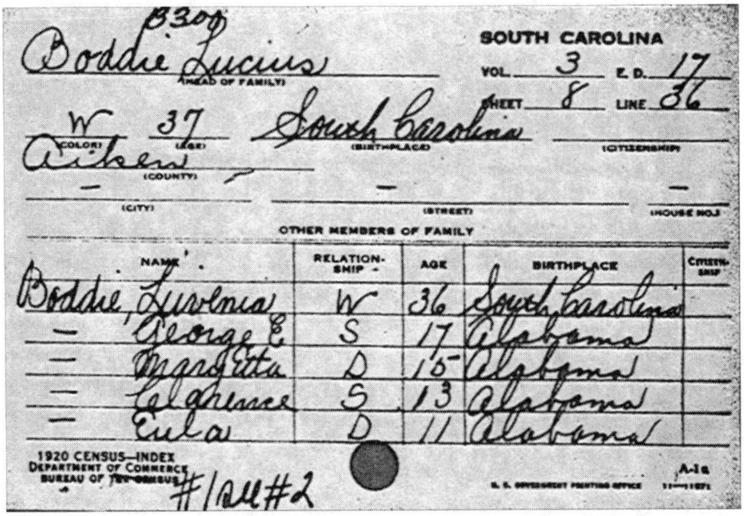

B300
Boddie Lucius (HEAD OF FAMILY)
SOUTH CAROLINA
VOL. 3 E.D. 17
SHEET 8 LINE 36
W (COLOR) 37 (AGE) South Carolina (BIRTHPLACE) (CITIZENSHIP)
Aiken (COUNTY)
(CITY) (STREET) (HOUSE NO.)

OTHER MEMBERS OF FAMILY

NAME	RELATIONSHIP	AGE	BIRTHPLACE	CITIZENSHIP
Boddie, Luvlnia	W	36	South Carolina	
— George E.	S	17	Alabama	
— Margretta	D	15	Alabama	
— Clarence	S	13	Alabama	
— Eula	D	11	Alabama	

1920 CENSUS—INDEX
DEPARTMENT OF COMMERCE
BUREAU OF THE CENSUS
#1 all #2
A-1a

FIGURE 5-8 Soundex card for the 1920 census (front) for the Lucius Boddie family. (Courtesy of Drew Smith.)

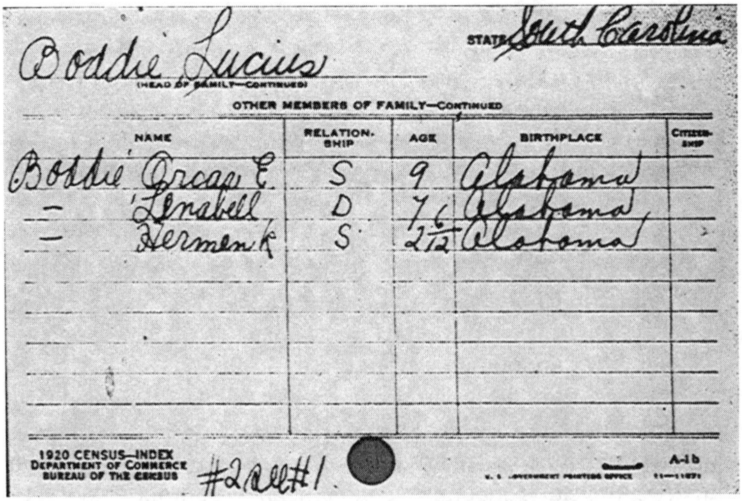

Boddie Lucius (HEAD OF FAMILY—CONTINUED)
STATE South Carolina

OTHER MEMBERS OF FAMILY—CONTINUED

NAME	RELATIONSHIP	AGE	BIRTHPLACE	CITIZENSHIP
Boddie Oscar E.	S	9	Alabama	
— Lenabell	D	7	Alabama	
— Herman K.	S	2 1/12	Alabama	

1920 CENSUS—INDEX
DEPARTMENT OF COMMERCE
BUREAU OF THE CENSUS
#2 all #1
A-1b

FIGURE 5-9 Same Soundex card (back) listing remainder of the Boddie family members. (Courtesy of Drew Smith.)

In other cases, a person who was not a head of household and did not have the same surname as the head had a separate Soundex card created for him or her. That card indicated the name of the head of household with whom this person had been enumerated. Figure 5-10 shows an example of this for Lottie Bodie, who was enumerated with Benjamin F. Tindall. According to the card, she was his daughter.

The Soundex and Miracode indexes were not created for all of the states for the census years mentioned above. Check with your library for more information about what is available for which states. The difference between the censuses coded using Soundex and Miracode is really only in the format of the card and the reference information it provides to the precise location in the census schedules.

The Soundex card provides reference information in the upper-right corner to the actual census volume, the enumeration district, the sheet number (or page), and the line number on the sheet on which the person appears. The Miracode card provides the volume number, the enumeration district, and then the visitation #. This last number refers to the dwelling's sequential number among the total dwellings the census taker visited in the course of enumeration. Please don't confuse this with a street address/house number.

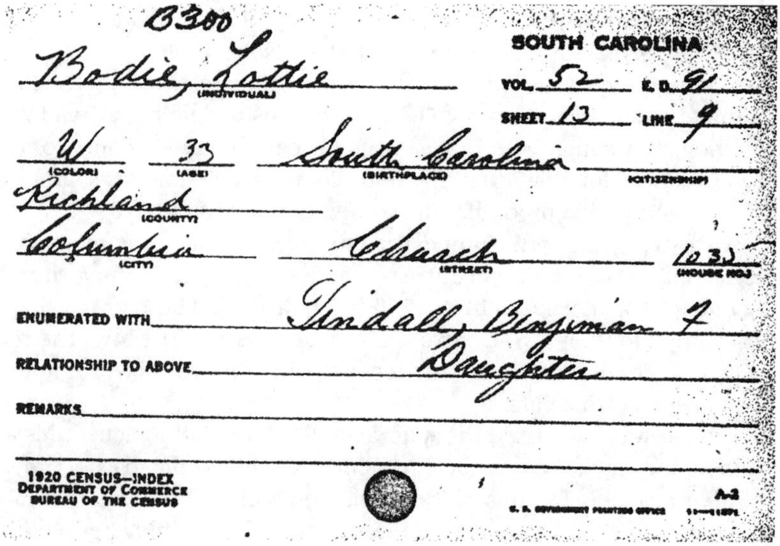
B300
SOUTH CAROLINA
Bodie, Lottie (INDIVIDUAL)
VOL. 52 E.D. 91
SHEET 13 LINE 9
W (COLOR) 33 (AGE) South Carolina (BIRTHPLACE) (CITIZENSHIP)
Richland (COUNTY)
Columbia (CITY) Church (STREET) 1033 (HOUSE NO.)
ENUMERATED WITH Tindall, Benjiman F
RELATIONSHIP TO ABOVE Daughter
REMARKS
1920 CENSUS—INDEX
DEPARTMENT OF COMMERCE
BUREAU OF THE CENSUS
A-2

FIGURE 5-10 Soundex card from the 1920 census showing a person who was enumerated in a household of another surname. (Courtesy of Drew Smith.)

Use Excellent U.S. Federal Census Reference Books

William Thorndale and William Dollarhide's book *Map Guide to the U.S. Federal Censuses, 1790–1920* (Genealogical Publishing Co., Inc., 1987) is an excellent resource for locating places in the correct state and county for each of the U.S. federal censuses. There were also some censuses taken in colonial times, which may have been documented and/or microfilmed by state archives. Ann S. Lainhart's book *State Census Records* (Genealogical Publishing Company, Inc., 2000) is an excellent reference on this subject. Three other excellent books regarding the U.S. federal censuses are William Dollarhide's *The Census Book: A Genealogist's Guide to Federal Census Facts, Schedules and Indexes* (Heritage Quest, 2000), Kathleen W. Hinckley's *Your Guide to the Federal Census for Genealogists, Researchers, and Family Historians* (Betterway Books, 2002), and Loretto D. Szucs and Matthew Wright's *Finding Answers in U.S. Census Records* (Ancestry Publishing, Inc., 2001).

Access the Census Images on Microfilm and in Online Databases

Federal census records were microfilmed decades ago and are available for the years 1790 through 1930 through NARA. You can also rent film through your nearest LDS FHC. Subsequent years' census records are protected through the Privacy Act and are not made public for 72 years. (The 1940 census will be made available in 2012.) You may, however, contact the U.S. Census Bureau to request copies of the census records for your family for 1940 through 1990. There is a fee for this search service, and you will need to provide proof of your connection to the family.

Ancestry.com at **www.ancestry.com** has compiled the most complete online indexes for the U.S. federal censuses and has digitized the majority of the census schedules for all censuses from 1790 through 1930. These are available through a paid subscription to their U.S. Deluxe Collection. Figure 5-11 shows the result of a search at Ancestry.com in the 1920 census records, and you will note a link to view the actual census page for this person.

ProQuest has digitized the federal census Population Schedules and made them available through access to its HeritageQuest Online databases. HeritageQuest Online is available by subscription, and you will find that many public libraries have subscriptions. As a library cardholder for one of those libraries, you may be able to remotely access the HeritageQuest Online databases from your home computer.

The LDS Church has indexed the 1880 U.S. federal census, and this may be accessed at **www.familysearch.org**. At the time of this writing, the LDS Church is indexing and digitizing its microfilm records, including the U.S. census records.

Native American (Indian) censuses conducted over time can be found at Access Genealogy.com at www.accessgenealogy.com/native/census/index.htm.

You will find that some individual census indexing and transcription projects have been undertaken. Some of these have been published in print format, while others

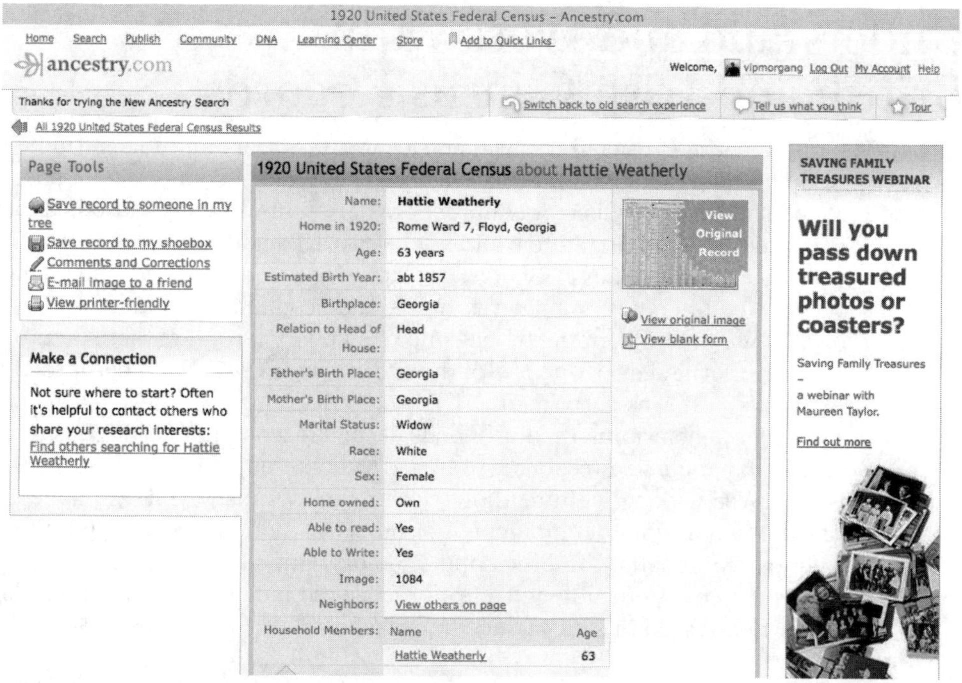

FIGURE 5-11   Census search result record from Ancestry.com with link to the census image. (Used by permission of The Generations Network, Inc.)

have been placed on the Internet at various sites. You can use your favorite Internet search engine to help locate these. Others are included at web pages at the USGenWeb Project site at **www.usgenweb.org**.

Don't Forget to Search State Censuses

In addition to the federal censuses, at certain times a number of the individual states have conducted their own census enumerations. These typically occurred halfway between the decennial federal enumerations—in other words, at the half-decade mark. These records, many of which have been microfilmed and are stored at the respective state's archive or library, can provide evidence of the presence of your ancestor or family member in a particular location. Some of these microfilmed censuses have been digitized, indexed, and placed online as databases in the Ancestry .com U.S. Deluxe Collection.

Ann S. Lainhart has compiled an authoritative reference titled *State Census Records*, which details which states conducted their own censuses, and in what years, whether the records have been microfilmed and/or indexed, and where the records reside.

Understand and Work with British and Irish Census Records

The first modern census in the British Isles was taken in order to determine the makeup of the population and its activities. There had been a period of poor harvests and food shortages. A substantial number of agricultural workers also had joined the military services and therefore could not be involved with working the land.

The Census Act 1800 (41 George III, cap. 15) was enacted and called for a full population enumeration of England, Wales, and Scotland beginning in 1801. The act also called for an enumeration to be conducted every ten years thereafter. A census has been performed ever since, with the exception of 1941 when, because of war, very little census work was performed.

In order to determine the livelihoods of the citizens in the 1801 census, questions were asked that elicited responses to help divide the population into three categories: those involved with agriculture, those working in manufacturing and trade, and those engaged in other types of employment. The population of England and Wales in 1801 was almost nine million, and the population of Scotland was a little over 1,600,000. No names were requested, although a few officials did include names in their documents. The questions asked in 1801 included:

- How many inhabited and uninhabited houses are located within the parish, and how many families live in the inhabited houses?
- How many persons are living in the parish, how many are males, and how many are females? (Military personnel and seamen in military service or on registered vessels were not to be included.)
- How many persons are involved with agriculture, with manufacturing or trade, with handicraft, or in other types of employment?
- How many persons' baptisms and burials have there been within the parish in 1700, 1710, 1720, 1730, 1740, 1750, 1760, 1770, 1780, and in each subsequent year up through 31 December 1800, and how many are there of each sex?

The process of conducting this first census was extensive. Standardized forms were distributed to all households and were to be completed based on persons in a residence as of the census night, 10 March 1801. (See Table 5-3 for census dates.) The information was gathered by enumerators and attached to a copy of the Census Act

British Isles vs. Ireland

The term "British Isles" is controversial, especially to many people in Ireland. The Irish government actually discourages the use of the term. The preferred description is "Britain and Ireland," which is more politically correct. From a census perspective, it is more appropriate to refer to the enumerations by their respective geopolitical areas: England, Wales, Scotland, and Ireland.

1800, and the enumerators presented them to a high constable or other officer and swore an oath as to the accuracy of the information. The returns were gathered by the official, endorsed, and submitted with a list of the names of the enumerators to a town clerk or clerk of the peace. The returns were then summarized into statistical reports, which were then submitted to the Home Office by 15 May 1801.

TABLE 5-3   Census Enumeration Dates for British Censuses 1801–1911

Year	Census Date
1801	Monday, 10 March
1811	Monday, 27 May
1821	Monday, 28 May
1831	Monday, 30 May
1841	Sunday, 6 June
1851	Sunday, 30 March
1861	Sunday, 7 April
1871	Sunday, 2 April
1881	Sunday, 3 April
1891	Sunday, 5 April
1901	Sunday, 31 March
1911	Sunday, 31 March

A similar format with comparable questions was used in the 1811, 1821, and 1831 enumerations. In 1811, a question was added to determine why a house was unoccupied. In 1821, a question was added to elicit ages of men in order to help determine how many men were able to bear arms. It was also in 1821 that Ireland was first included in the census, and its population at that time was calculated to be over 6,800,000. The 1831 census included more-detailed questions concerning economic conditions.

The 1841 census was the first to record the names of the inhabitants, their gender, and their age (the person's age was rounded down to the lower five-year increment for persons over the age of 15), and therefore is the earliest British census used by most genealogists and family historians. In addition, these census documents were sent to a central government location for tabulation and reference. For that reason, they have been preserved and images have been made.

The 1851 census included those persons living on vessels in inland waters or at sea (including the Royal Navy and merchant navy). In addition, persons serving abroad with the armed forces and those working with the East India Company were enumerated, and British subjects residing overseas were also counted.

Between 1861 and 1891, there were few changes in the format and questions asked on the census. The most important additions from a genealogical perspective, however, were the addition of questions concerning the languages spoken. This question was added for enumerations in Scotland beginning with the 1881 census and for Wales beginning with the 1891 census. It is shown in the last column on the example census form in Figure 5-12.

The 1901 census included questions to elicit more precise responses. A good introduction to the British census information can be found at The National Archives website at **www.nationalarchives.gov.uk/catalogue/RdLeaflet.asp?sLeafletID = 326**. Census records' contents are protected in the United Kingdom for a period of 100 years. The 1901 census information was released in 2001. The National Archives, previously known as the Public Record Office (PRO), is custodian of the census records for England and Wales, which also includes the Channel Islands and the Isle of Man. Separate enumerations for Scotland and Ireland were taken, and these records are in the possession of the General Register Office for Scotland (GROS) at **www.gro-scotland.gov.uk** and at The National Archives of Ireland at **www.nationalarchives.ie**, respectively.

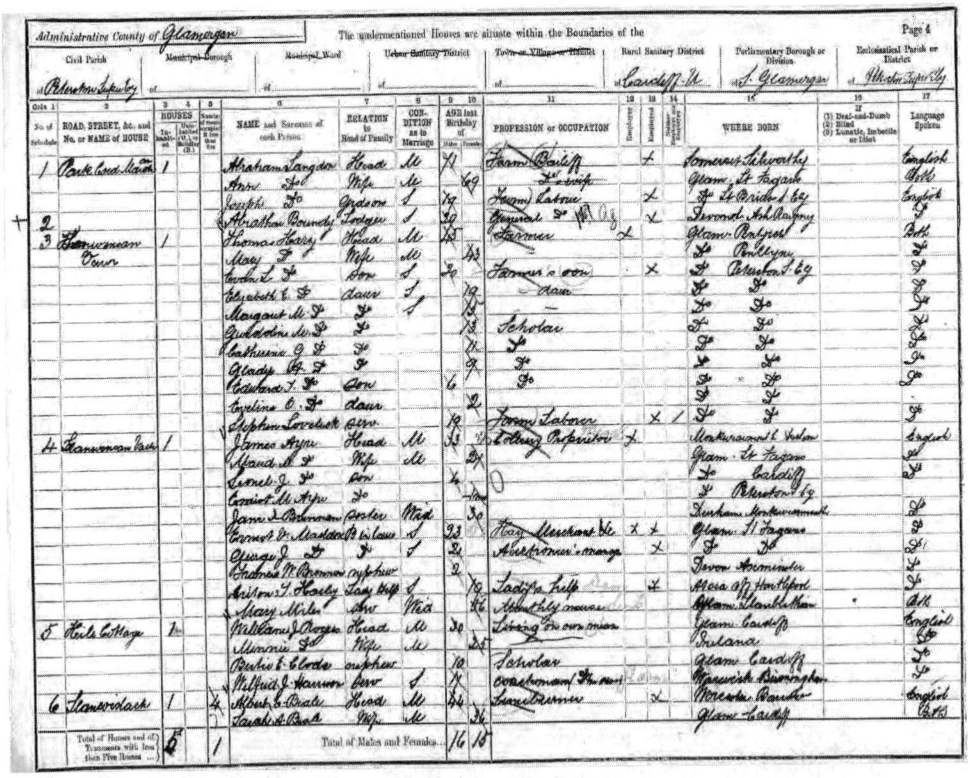
Administrative County of Glamorgan — The undermentioned Houses are situate within the Boundaries of the — Page 4

Civil Parish | Municipal Borough | Municipal Ward | Urban Sanitary District | Town or Village or Hamlet | Rural Sanitary District | Parliamentary Borough or Division | Ecclesiastical Parish or District

No. of Schedule | ROAD, STREET, &c., and No. or NAME of HOUSE | HOUSES | NAME and Surname of each Person | RELATION to Head of Family | CONDITION as to Marriage | AGE last Birthday of Males / Females | PROFESSION or OCCUPATION | Employer | Employed | Neither Employer nor Employed | WHERE BORN | (1) Deaf-and-Dumb (2) Blind (3) Lunatic, Imbecile or Idiot | Language Spoken

Total of Houses and of Tenements with less than Five Rooms — Total of Males and Females

FIGURE 5-12 1891 census form created in the parish of Peterson-super-Ely in Cardiff, South Glamorgan, Wales. (Used by permission of The Generations Network, Inc.)

The U.K. census indexes and images for 1841 through 1901 are accessible through subscription online at **www.ancestry.co.uk**. The 1911 census was released, after some controversy in Parliament concerning early release of the census and possible violation of promised privacy. An index and transcriptions of parts of this census are accessible at the time of this writing at a pay-per-view site, **www.1911census.co.uk**, with more transcriptions available soon.

Work with England's Census Records

Like the United States, the British government defined an "as of" date for use by the respondents, and this date is referred to as the "census night." The individual household schedule was to be completed based on the persons who were in the household during the period of Sunday night to Monday morning on the dates listed in Table 5-3.

It is important that you take into consideration the "as of" date when considering the information found in a census schedule with other genealogical evidence. For example, you might wonder why a person's age is listed as 41 in the 1841 census and only as age 50 in the 1851 census. If you examine the dates in Table 5-3, you will notice that the 1851 census was taken more than a month earlier than the one the previous decade. You could hypothesize that the respondent's birthday fell after 30 March and up to and including 6 June of 1800. Based on that theory, you could then begin searching for proof of the date of birth in other records.

If the head of the household did not properly complete the census form, the enumerator was supposed to have requested the additional information when he called at the house. If the person was illiterate, blind, or for some other reason could not complete the schedule, the enumerator was to have conducted an interview, asked the questions, and completed the document himself.

Descriptions of the enumeration districts can be extremely helpful in locating your ancestors' records. The example shown in Figure 5-13 is from the 1891 census of England and Wales and shows the registration district of Spilsby and the subdistrict of Alford in Lincolnshire.

Learn the Status of Irish Census Records

The Irish government took an independent census in 1813, and then censuses were taken every ten years from 1821 through 1911. Due to the Irish Civil War, no census was taken in 1921, but the next census was done in 1926. The next censuses were taken in 1936 and 1946. From 1946 to 1971, the census was taken every five years. Since 1971, the census has been taken every ten years.

Unfortunately, the Irish census records have not fared well over time. The 1813 census no longer exists. Most of the census information from the 1821 through 1851 censuses was destroyed in a fire in Dublin in 1922, and the censuses from 1861 and 1871 were destroyed by government order shortly after the data was compiled and summarized. The 1881 and 1891 censuses were pulped during World War I because

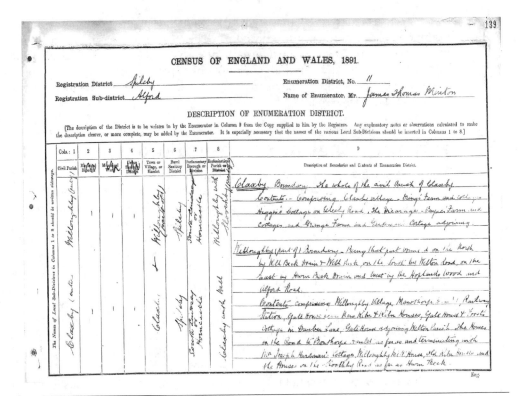

FIGURE 5-13   1891 description of the enumeration district form. (Used by permission of The Generations Network, Inc.)

of a paper shortage. The surviving materials have been microfilmed by the LDS and these films can be obtained through the LDS Family History Library in Salt Lake City, Utah, and through the LDS Family History Centers worldwide.

As a result of the loss of so much of the Irish census material, census substitutes can sometimes be used as alternate evidence sources of residence, age, and other information. These include Old Age Pension Records; Tithe Applotment Books (1823–1838); Griffith's Primary Valuation (1848-1864); and other, later land and property records.

Use Quality Reference Materials when Working with British Census Records

There are excellent resources available for your reference when working with British census records. The best written reference concerning the 1801–1901 censuses is Edward Higgs' *Making Sense of the Census: The Manuscript Returns for England and Wales, 1801–1901*, published in London by Her Majesty's Stationery Office in 1989. Unfortunately, however, it is out of print. If you can locate a copy in a library, it provides an excellent history and perspective of the enumerations of that period. More recently, however, an excellent how-to book by Susan Lumas has been released in its fourth edition, *Making Use of the Census*, one of the Public Record Office Reader's Guide series. The publication of the new edition coincided with the release of the 1901 census records and contains excellent instructions for how to access and use them.

Indexes of censuses have been prepared by a variety of organizations. One excellent starting point is the GENUKI website at **www.genuki.org.uk**, which is concerned with U.K. and Ireland genealogy. Another is the BritishIslesGenWeb Project, which is a subsidiary part of the WorldGenWeb Project (**www.worldgenweb.org**). The BritishIslesGenWeb Project can be accessed at **www.britishislesgenweb.org**, from which you can visit the various county or island sites where information about and links to census resources can be found.

Access the Census Records for the British Isles

We've already mentioned a number of resources for gaining access to census records for England, Wales, Scotland, and Ireland, but let's recap:

- The England and Wales manuscript returns of the 1841 to 1901 censuses are in the possession of The National Archives (formerly known as the PRO). These have been microfilmed and are available for review at The National Archives, at larger libraries with genealogical materials, and through the LDS Family History Library and LDS Family History Centers. (You can locate the Family History Center closest to you by conducting a search through the LDS FamilySearch website, specifically using the search template at **www.familysearch.org/Eng/Library/ FHC/frameset_fhc.asp**.) These census images for 1841 to 1901 are digitized and indexed at Ancestry.com.uk. The 1911 census index and transcriptions are accessible at **www.1911census.co.uk**.
- Surviving Irish census records have been microfilmed. These are available through the Public Record Office of Northern Ireland (PRONI) or through the LDS FHL and FHCs as described above. You can learn more about the 19th century records at **www.proni.gov.uk**.
- Scotland's census records are in the possession of the General Register Office for Scotland (GROS). Census records have been microfilmed. Microfilm can be accessed at New Register House in Edinburgh, Scotland, at larger libraries with genealogical collections that have purchased the film, or through the LDS FHL and FHCs as described above. In addition, the GROS and brightsolid (formerly Scotland Online) have partnered to create and maintain a pay-per-view website called ScotlandsPeople at **www.scotlandspeople.gov.uk**. The site provides a "fully searchable index of Scottish births from 1553–1902, marriages from 1553 to 1927, and deaths from 1855 to 1952. In addition, indexed census data is available from 1881 to 1901. To respect privacy of living people, Internet access has been limited to birth records over 100 years old, marriage records over 75 years, and death records over 50 years." In addition, Ancestry.co.uk has digitized and indexed the census records of Scotland from 1841 to 1901.

Understand and Work with Canadian Census Records

Canada's history is a fascinating study of many people: French, English, Aboriginal, and a mélange of religions, ethnicities, and cultures. The first census in what became Canada was conducted in 1666 by Jean Talon. This enumeration recorded the name, age, marital status, and occupation of each of the 3,215 inhabitants of New France. Between 1666 and the first official Canadian census in 1871, there were no less than 98 different colonial and regional censuses conducted, most of which were performed for purposes of taxation and military conscription. Over time, new questions were added to gather more information about building structures, livestock, crops, firearms, and churches. Religious affiliation—Catholic or Protestant—became another area of interest, and it became important to enumerate other groups, such as the Acadians, Indians (or "First People"), and Blacks. Census returns prior to 1851 are incomplete for most areas.

The Canadian census returns after 1851 used a Population Schedule form for the enumeration by name of every individual in a household, and the Population Schedule was usually accompanied by a separate agricultural schedule that included information about the acreage, land use, buildings, crops, livestock, and valuation.

Library and Archives Canada (**www.collectionscanada.gc.ca**) is the repository for most of the census materials, including those from before Confederation in 1867. However, some of the original documents for New Brunswick, Nova Scotia, and Prince Edward Island prior to 1871 are still in the possession of the provincial archives or libraries. Ancestry.com's Canadian subscription website, at **www.ancestry.ca**, has digitized and indexed many of the provincial, territorial, and national censuses.

Explore the Depth of the 1871 Census

The first official national census was conducted in 1871 and was part of the British North America Act in 1867, which created the Canadian Confederation. The Act stated, "In the general Census of the Population of Canada which is hereby required to be taken in the Year One thousand eight-hundred and seventy-one, and in every Tenth Year thereafter, the respective Populations of the Four Provinces shall be distinguished."

This first census requested a vast amount of information from the respondents and for that reason is extremely important for genealogical researchers whose ancestors and family members lived in Canada at that time. There were nine schedules used to collect information:

- **Schedule 1** Population Schedule by name of every living person
- **Schedule 2** Schedule with the name of every person who died within the previous 12 months
- **Schedule 3** A return listing all public institutions, real estate, vehicles, and implements

- **Schedule 4**   Agricultural return for cultivated produce, such as crops, fruits, and plants
- **Schedule 5**   Agricultural return for livestock, animal products, furs, and homemade fabrics
- **Schedule 6**   Return of industrial manufacturing
- **Schedule 7**   Return of products of forest resources
- **Schedule 8**   Return for shipping concerns and fisheries
- **Schedule 9**   Return for mining and mineral products

You can relate the information found on surviving Schedules 3, 4, 5, 7, 8, and 9 to the name of a person whose name is listed on Schedule 1, the Population Schedule. By doing so, you can expand your knowledge of what that person's economic livelihood entailed, of the extent of their holdings, and of the success or failure of the operation, and you also gain a perspective of the lifestyle of the person or family unit.

The 1881 census eliminated the schedule of industrial manufacturing. Unfortunately, though, only the Population Schedule exists. It has, however, been microfilmed.

The 1891 census returned to nine schedules again, but only the Population Schedule survives and has been microfilmed.

By the time the 1901 census was to be conducted, Canada consisted of: British Columbia, Manitoba, Ontario, Quebec, New Brunswick, Nova Scotia, and Prince Edward Island; two territories, Yukon Territory and Northwest Territories; and the District of Keewatin. Census enumeration areas generally, but not always, corresponded to electoral districts. It is important for you to refer to enumeration area descriptions to help you home in on your family members' locations.

Enumeration was conducted by door-to-door interview, with enumerators individually visiting each house and asking the questions of the "head" of the household. Enumeration was to be completed within 30 days of 31 March 1901. The census commissioners were forced to revise the schedules, however, before being able to compile and send the completed forms to the census office. By the end of August, the central census office in Ottawa had received 98 percent of the forms. The original schedules for British Columbia schedules were lost when the steamer *Islander* sank on 15 August 1901. The census in British Columbia therefore had to be taken all over again, and this delayed the final tabulation of the census data.

The Dominion Bureau of Statistics, at the direction of the Public Records Committee, in 1955 destroyed the original documents from the 1901 census. Fortunately, however, all of the population records (Schedule 1) and most of the buildings, land, church, and school records (Schedule 2) have all been preserved on microfilm, although the quality of the filming is uneven and some images are unreadable. Some instances of the additional schedule forms used can be found among the microfilmed records.

The good news is that Library and Archives Canada has digitized the microfilm images and made them available for browsing at its website (**www.collectionscanada .gc.ca/genealogy/022-911-e.html**) in a searchable database by geographic location. Census districts and maps also are accessible online, which, as you've already learned, can be invaluable in helping you quickly locate your family. A search of the database for the census records for a province and then a geographical area will return a search

1

Province/Territory:	Ontario
District Name:	ESSEX (North/Nord)
District Number:	59
Sub-district Name:	Windsor (City/Cité)
Sub-district Number:	I-1
Schedule:	2
Notes:	Ward/Quartier No. 1
Reference:	RG31 , Statistics Canada
Microfilm Reel Number:	T-6466
Finding Aid Number:	31-40

The following images are associated with this entry:
Associated images: ▼

FIGURE 5-14   Search results from the online index to the 1901 census at the Library and Archives Canada website

results list with records like the one shown in Figure 5-14. It provides you with details about the specific location of the records associated with that place. It also indicates the Record Group (RG) under which Library and Archives Canada has classified and catalogued the records, as well as the reel number for use in accessing the microfilm from which the digital image was produced.

In 1905, the Census and Statistics Act received Royal Assent and defined that a general census would be taken in Canada in 1911 and every ten years thereafter. It also declared that a population and agriculture census was to be taken in Manitoba, Saskatchewan, and Alberta in 1906 and every ten years thereafter. As a result, the following two schedules were prepared and the enumeration was conducted:

- Population and livestock
- Agriculture

Like the 1901 census, microfilm was created of the original records, but the original documents were destroyed in 1955. Library and Archives Canada also has digitized the microfilm images and made these available on its website.

Did You Know? The census documents contain vast amounts of information other than names. Look for addresses, ages, property ownership, occupation, citizenship information, literacy, and more.

Locate Additional Information on the Censuses

Census records can provide you with a huge amount of information and many clues to research. As I've mentioned before, it is important to become a student of history and to learn about the places where your ancestors and family members lived, the time period in which they lived, the documents that may have been created at the time for whatever purposes, which documents have survived, where the surviving materials are located, in what format(s) they exist, and how to gain access to them.

You have seen examples in this chapter of census materials that were created for various purposes. Some have survived while others have been lost to fire or through other causes. Transcripts may have been made or original documents may have been microfilmed, and then the originals may have been destroyed. In some cases, census documents have been digitized and made available on the Internet. You may be able to conduct "armchair genealogy" over the Internet from the comfort of your own home to access images. In other cases, you may have to visit a library or LDS Family History Center in order to access microfilm copies of document images. Other times, you may have to schedule a trip to visit the repository where original documents reside.

Your challenge is to actually trace the documents down in whatever form they may exist, and determine how you can access them. And that does, indeed, mean studying the history of the documents. Fortunately for all of us, the Internet provides a wealth of knowledge we can use in our quest. I often use my web browser and a search engine to learn more about available documentary materials. As an example, when searching for information about Canadian census materials for 1906, I entered the following in the search engine:

canada census 1906

I was rewarded with a huge number of search results, not the least of which was one at the top of the list that happens to be the authoritative site on the subject: Library and Archives Canada's website for the Census of the Northwest Provinces, 1906, **www.collectionscanada.gc.ca/02/020153_e.html**.

Take the time to study each column of a census document. You may find additional information that act as clues to other evidence and resources to aid your understanding of your ancestor and his or her family.

Learn to use the Internet effectively to search and locate information that may be of historical value to your research. In addition, learn how to use online catalogs of libraries, archives, and other facilities so that you can determine what publications may be available to help in your search.

By this time, you have become very knowledgeable indeed about the process of genealogical research and about placing your ancestors into geographical and historical context. The next chapter will take you into some more advanced record types to help further trace and understand your ancestors and family members. You're on your way now with perhaps the most exciting journey you will ever make. Let's move right ahead!

TABLE 5-4   U.S. Federal Census Records, 1790 through 1930. (Used by permission of Aha! Seminars, Inc.)

Census Year	Type of Document	Columns for Information	Comments
1790	Population Schedule	• Head of household • Number of free white males (by age range) • Number of free white females (by age range) • Other free persons and slaves	Name of the head of household was the only name listed.
1800	Population Schedule	Same as 1790 Population Schedule	
1810	Population Schedule	Same as 1790 Population Schedule	
1810	Manufacturing Schedule	• Name of owner, agent, or manager • Type of business • Commodity produced • Value of output • Number of employees	• These schedules may be of limited interest if family operated a manufacturing concern. • All 1810 schedules are lost.
1820	Population Schedule	Same as 1790 Population Schedule, plus the following: • Head of household • Number of free white males (by age range) • Number of free white females (by age range) • Number of slave males (by age range) • Number of slave females (by age range) • Number of free colored males (by age range) • Number of free colored females (by age range) • Aliens • Disabilities (deaf, dumb, blind, insane)	
1820	Manufacturing Schedule	Same as 1810 Manufacturing Schedule	Some schedules are missing or lost.
1830	Population Schedule	Same as 1820 Population Schedule, plus questions on Alien status	
1830	Manufacturing Schedule	Same as 1810 Manufacturing Schedule	Some schedules are missing or lost.

1840	Population Schedule	Same as 1830 Population Schedule, plus the following:	
		• Number involved in variety of trades	
		• Number in school	
		• Number over 21 can read and write	
		• Number insane	
		• Age and name of Rev. War veterans	
1840	Agricultural Schedule	• Name of owner, agent, or manager	• Submitted to Secretary of the Interior to catalog and evaluate the utilization of farmland.
		• Number of acres of improved and unimproved land	
		• Detailed information about crops, timber, mining, livestock, honey, and other commodities	• Excellent insight into family life.
1840	Manufacturing Schedule	Same as 1810 Manufacturing Schedule (mostly statistical information and of very limited use)	Some schedules are missing or lost.
1850	Population Schedule	• Head of household	First census to include the names of every person in the household.
		• All names, ages, gender, and race	
		• Occupation	
		• Real estate value	
		• Place of birth	
		• Married in last year	
		• Literacy	
		• Deaf, dumb, blind, insane	
1850	Slave Schedule	• Name of slave holder	Slave names are seldom listed, but some are included.
		• Number of slaves	
		• Age, sex, and color	
		• Fugitive from a state? Which state?	
		• Number manumitted	
		• Deaf, dumb, blind, insane or idiotic	
		• Number of buildings in which housed	
1850	Mortality Schedule	• Deceased's name	Information on those who died during 12 months prior to Census Day.
		• Whether widowed	
		• Sex, age, and color (white, black, mulatto)	
		• Birthplace	
		• Month of death	
		• Occupation	
		• Cause of death	
		• Number of days ill	

(Continued)

TABLE 5-4   U.S. Federal Census Records, 1790 through 1930. (Used by permission of Aha! Seminars, Inc.) (*Continued*)

Census Year	Type of Document	Columns for Information	Comments
1850	Agricultural Schedule	Same as 1840 Agricultural Schedule	
1850	Industry Schedule	Same as 1810 Manufacturing Schedule, but was retitled Industry Schedule in 1850–1870	Some schedules are missing or lost.
1850	Social Statistics	Included: • Cemeteries within town borders (names, addresses, descriptions, maps, and other data) • Churches, a brief history, affiliation, and membership statistics • Trade societies, clubs, lodges, and other social institutions	Can be used as a resource to locate specific types of institutions in these years, and trace any surviving records.
1860	Population Schedule	Same as 1850 Population Schedule	
1860	Slave Schedule	Same as 1850 Slave Schedule	
1860	Mortality Schedule	Same as 1850 Mortality Schedule	
1860	Agricultural Schedule	Same as 1840 Agricultural Schedule	
1860	Manufacturing Schedule	Same as 1810 Manufacturing Schedule	Some schedules are missing or lost.
1860	Social Statistics	Same as 1850 Social Statistics	
1870	Population Schedule	Same as 1850 Population Schedule, plus the following: • Whether or not parents were of foreign birth • Month of birth if within this year • Month of marriage if within year	
1870	Mortality Schedule	Same as 1850 Mortality Schedule, plus parents' places of birth	
1870	Agricultural Schedule	Same as 1840 Agricultural Schedule	
1870	Manufacturing Schedule	Same as 1810 Manufacturing Schedule	Some schedules are missing or lost.
1870	Social Statistics	Same as 1850 Social Statistics	

1880	Population Schedule	1880 Census Contents:	• First census to include relationship of every resident to the head of household.
		• Head of household	
		• All names, ages, gender, and race	
		• Relationship	• Parents' birthplace information provides information for tracing ancestral records.
		• Marital status	
		• Occupation	
		• Deaf, dumb, blind, insane	
		• Illness or disability	
		• Literacy	
		• Birthplaces (person & parents)	
		• Month of birth if within the year	
1880	Indian (or Native American) Schedule	• Name of each individual in household (Indian and English)	
		• Relationship to head of household	
		• Age, gender	
		• Marital/tribal status	
		• Occupation	
		• Land ownership	
1880	Mortality Schedule	Same as 1870 Mortality Schedule, plus the following:	
		• Where disease was contracted	
		• How long a resident of the area	
1880	Agricultural Schedule	Same as 1840 Agricultural Schedule	
1880	Manufacturing Schedule	Same as 1810 Manufacturing Schedule	Destroyed by act of Congress.
1880	Social Statistics	Same as 1850 Social Statistics	
1880	Defective, Dependent, and Delinquent Classes Schedules	Seven separate schedules to be compiled by the enumerator:	Includes inmates of asylums, orphanages, poor houses, almshouses, prisons, and other institutions, as well as those who the enumerator observed.
		• Schedule 1—Insane Inhabitants	
		• Schedule 2—Idiots	
		• Schedule 3—Deaf-Mutes	
		• Schedule 4—Blind Inhabitants	
		• Schedule 5—Homeless children (institutions)	
		• Schedule 6—Inhabitants in Prison	
		• Schedule 7—Pauper and Indigent Inhabitants	

(Continued)

TABLE 5-4 U.S. Federal Census Records, 1790 through 1930. (Used by permission of Aha! Seminars, Inc.) (*Continued*)

Census Year	Type of Document	Columns for Information	Comments
1885	Population Schedule	Same as 1880 Population Schedule	Special census for which the federal government agreed to share 50 percent of the cost with any state or territory desiring another census. Only five states/territories took advantage of this offer: • Colorado • Dakota Territory (only a part survives) • Florida (four counties missing) • Nebraska (two counties missing) • New Mexico Territory (four counties missing)
1890	Population Schedule	Same as for 1880 Population Schedule, plus the following: • Ability to speak English • Rent or own home • Years in country, and if naturalized • Number of children born and number still living • Whether Civil War veteran or surviving spouse (in which case a separate schedule also was completed—see below)	Each family was listed on a single sheet. • Population Schedules destroyed by fire and water in fire at Commerce Building in January 1921. • Originals destroyed in mid-1930s.
1890	Indian (or Native American) Schedule	Same as 1880 Indian Schedule	
1890	Mortality Schedule	Same as 1880 Mortality Schedule	Destroyed in 1896 or 1897.

1890	Surviving Soldiers, Sailors, and Marines, and Widows, etc. Schedule	• Name of veteran or surviving spouse • Age • Branch of service (Army, Navy, Marines) • Duration of service • Date of enlistment and discharge • Rank, company, regiment, and vessel • Disability	• Survived the 1921 fire. • Union veterans only, but a few Confederates are included. • Partial returns; some counties missing. • Originals destroyed in mid-1930s.
1890	Agricultural Schedule	Same as 1840 Agricultural Schedule	Destroyed in 1896 or 1897.
1890	Manufacturing Schedule	Same as 1810 Manufacturing Schedule	Destroyed in 1896 or 1897.
1900	Population Schedule	Same as 1890 Population Schedule, plus the following additional information: • Exact month and year of birth (only 1900) • Number of years married	This was the first census to enumerate U.S. citizens abroad.
1900	Indian (or Native American) Schedule	Same as 1880 Indian Schedule, plus the following: • Tribe of person and his/her parents • Degree of Indian or White blood • Education	Indian schedules often found at end of state or county returns.
1900	Agricultural Schedule	Same as 1840 Agricultural Schedule	
1900	Manufacturing Schedule	Same as 1810 Manufacturing Schedule	Destroyed by act of Congress.
1910	Population Schedule	Same as 1900 Population Schedule, plus the following additional information: • Year of arrival in United States • Whether veteran and which war (only on the 1910 census)	
1910	Indian Schedule	Same as 1900 Indian Schedule	
1910	Agricultural Schedule	Same as 1840 Agricultural Schedule	

(Continued)

TABLE 5-4 U.S. Federal Census Records, 1790 through 1930. (Used by permission of Aha! Seminars, Inc.) (*Continued*)

Census Year	Type of Document	Columns for Information	Comments
1910	Manufacturing Schedule	Same as 1810 Manufacturing Schedule	Destroyed by act of Congress.
1920	Population Schedule	Same as 1910 Population Schedule, plus the following additional information: • Native tongue	Question regarding whether a veteran (on 1910 census) was not included.
1920	Indian Schedule	Same as 1900 Indian Schedule	
1930	Population Schedule	Same as 1920 Population Schedule plus the following additional information: • Whether owns a radio • Year of naturalization	Indians schedules often found at end of state or county returns.
1930	Indian Schedule	Same as 1900 Indian Schedule	

6

Extend Your Research with Advanced Record Types

HOW TO...

- Use religious records to trace your family
- Obtain and analyze mortuary and funeral home records
- Read between the lines in obituaries
- Discover the wealth of information in cemetery records
- Get inside your ancestor's mind using wills and probate records
- Consider other institutional records

You've learned a great deal about your family so far by locating and using home sources, birth, marriage, and death records, and census resources. Along the way, you also have built a foundation for all of your future genealogical research. You now know how important it is to place your family into context, to conduct scholarly research, to analyze every piece of data you uncover, and to properly document your source materials.

You've made a lot of progress so far, but you probably have only just begun to scratch the surface of your family's rich history. There literally are hundreds of different records that may contain information of value in documenting your forebears' lives.

This chapter discusses some of the more important documentary evidence associated with your ancestor or family member's religion and those associated with the end of his or her life. They can provide a treasure trove of information and clues for you. You just need to know where to look, how to access the records, and how to properly analyze them. You will learn to apply your critical thinking skills to the evidence and formulate reasonable hypotheses, sometimes circumventing the "brick walls" that we all invariably encounter.

Use Religious Records

Religious records are those that relate to a church or some similar established religious institution. Organized religion has provided a source for scholarly philosophical and theological study and writing for many centuries. Documentation reaches far back into human history. Religious groups also have variously maintained documents concerning their operations, administration, and membership. As a result, religious records of many types can provide rich genealogical details and clues to other types of records.

There are a number of challenges you will face in your search for and investigation into these ecclesiastical records. Let's discuss these challenges first, and then we'll explore some of the types of records you might expect to find.

Locate the Right Institution

It is an easy task to contact the place of worship for yourself, your parents, and your siblings. The knowledge of the religious affiliation and where the family members attend worship services is pretty easy to come by. However, as we move backward in time, this information may become obscured. You may make the assumption that your ancestors belonged to the same religious denomination as your family does today, and you may be making a terrible error.

Not every member of a family necessarily belongs to the same religious group. My maternal grandmother's family is a primary example. Her father belonged to the Presbyterian Church and her mother to a Primitive Baptist congregation. Among their six sons and six daughters, I have found them to be members of two Presbyterian, three Baptist, one Methodist, and one Christian Science churches. In addition, some of the people changed churches. Most notable was the entry I found in the membership roll of the First Presbyterian Church of Rome, Georgia, dated 31 October 1926, for one of my great-aunts. It read, "Seen entering Christian Science Church" and her name was lined out. That clue pointed me to the Church of Christ, Scientist, at which I learned that she had formally become a member of its congregation.

In some cases, prior to or upon marriage, one spouse may change his or her religious affiliation to that of the other spouse's affiliation. Many religions want to see children of a marital union raised in their faith, and formal religious instruction and conversion is common.

Determining the religion of an ancestor or other family member is an important part of your research because there may be any number of records to provide more information for your research and pointers to other records. You cannot assume that everyone who lived in England or Wales was a member of the Church of England. Likewise, you cannot assume that all Irish are either Catholic or Protestant. In both areas, other religious congregations are common, including Baptist, Methodist, Presbyterian, Lutheran, Quaker, Jewish, and Muslim. You also cannot assume that the only religions in Germany are Catholicism and Lutheranism.

Look for clues to the religion of a person in the name of the *clergy* who performed marriage ceremonies for the person *and* the spouse, for the person's parents, and for any siblings. Clergy names are typically found on marriage certificates created by churches, such as the one shown in Figure 6-1, and on many marriage licenses filed at government offices after the marriage ceremony has taken place. Look, too, at obituaries for officiating clergy at funerals and memorial services. It is often easy to determine the religious affiliation of the clergyperson and the organization to which he or she was attached in local historical records and city directories, and this can provide an important link to membership rolls and to records of life events associated with the congregation.

The religious affiliation provides one level of information. However, your job is to determine the *right* institution to which your ancestor belonged. If the community in which he or she lived has multiple groups of the same denomination, you may have to contact or visit each one in order to determine if your ancestor

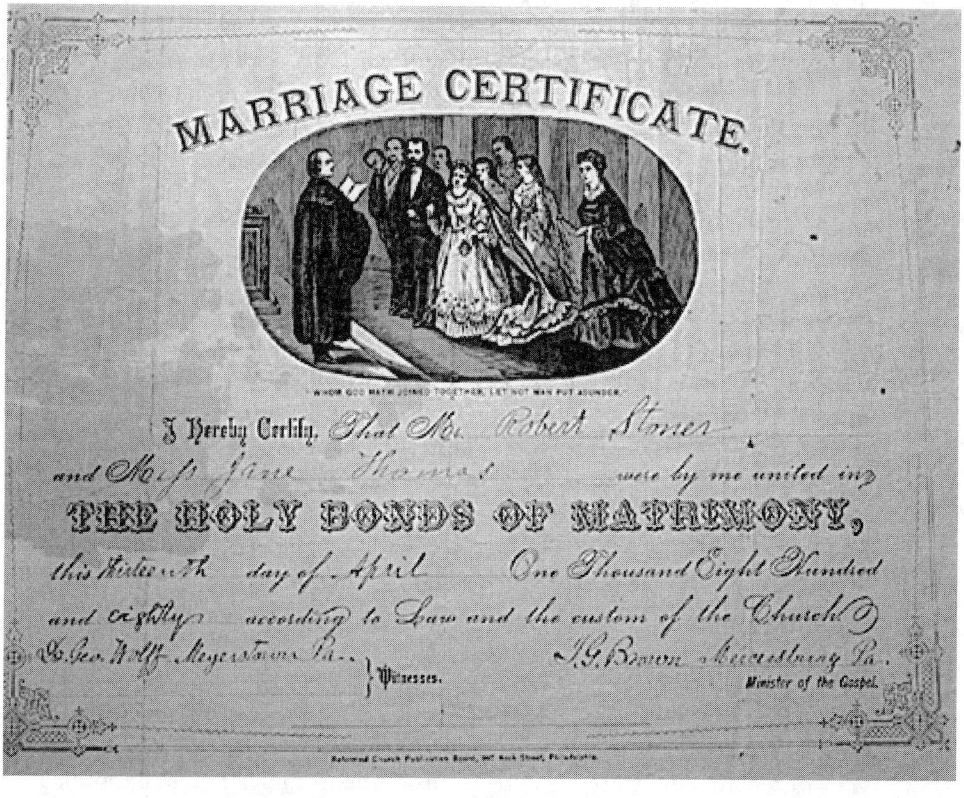

FIGURE 6-1   Marriage certificate issued by a church showing the name of the officiating clergy. (From the author's collection.)

was a member. Depending on the time period in which your ancestor lived in the area, you may research local histories to determine which specific religious groups existed at the time. Your best strategy, however, may be to start with the congregation located closest geographically to where your ancestor or family lived, and work outward. You may also have to escalate your search to an administrative or similar jurisdictional level to locate records for defunct congregations. For example, records for the congregation of a Catholic church that merged with another may have been transferred to the latter church. Alternatively, the records may have been moved to another diocese location or to some other place. Be prepared to escalate your inquiry for a defunct church's records to a higher administrative office. This means doing a little more research into the structure of the religion and its jurisdictional structure.

Determine What Records the Institution Might Have Created

Once you have determined the religious affiliation of your ancestor, it is important to learn something about the organization. Some groups are meticulous about documenting their organizational affairs and their membership information, while others are less inclined. The Catholic Church, for example, maintains thorough documentation of the church business and has created detailed documents about each member, including records for birth, baptism, christening, marriage, death, other sacramental and personal events, and even tithing. Quaker records are also well maintained and full of details. I have found that some Baptist and Primitive Baptist records are often far less detailed or revealing.

Invest some time learning about the history of the denomination and what types of records may have been created by a particular denomination to which your ancestor may have belonged, and what types of records it may have created at the time your ancestor was a member. This will give you a foundation for your research. You will know what types of records to request when you make contact with the particular church or organization, where they were created and by whom, what information is likely to be contained in them, and where they were kept.

Locate the Records Today

Your most immediate consideration is where to locate the records *now*. Congregations sometimes merge with one another, or a congregation may find it can no longer sustain itself financially, and therefore dissolves. What happens to the records?

Your understanding of the history and organization of the denomination can go a long way in helping you locate records. Your study will also help you identify the types of records that were created. For example, some Christian denominations may mark a person's first communion with a ceremony and issue a certificate such as the one shown in Figure 6-2, while others may only record the event in membership

FIGURE 6-2   Certificate of a first communion. (From the author's collection.)

records. While an existing church location may have all of its records dating back to its founding, those records may not necessarily be located on-site at that church. They may be stored in a rectory, parsonage, or vicarage. Records may have been moved to a central parish or diocesan office, or to a regional or national level administrative or storage site.

A good strategy for determining the location of historical records is to contact the clergy or secretary at the specific house of worship. Having learned what records might have been created you can ask about their availability and obtain access to or copies of them. If the records have been moved or sent elsewhere, ask for the name and address of a contact and then follow that lead.

If a congregation no longer exists or you can't find it, contact the local public library and any academic libraries in the area and ask the reference department to assist you in tracing the group and its records. The local, county, state, or provincial genealogical and historical societies are additional resources you should enlist in your research. Their in-depth knowledge of the area and religious groups can be invaluable. Indeed, they may have copied or transcribed indexes, and some ecclesiastical records may even have come into their possession. Again, don't overlook making contact with a higher administrative area of the religious organization. The personnel should be able to provide you with details of the group's history and of the fate of a "missing" congregation's records.

Gain Access to the Records

Another challenge can be gaining access to or obtaining copies of the congregational records you want. Religious groups are, in effect, private organizations and have a right and an obligation to protect their privacy and that of their members. Most are willing to help you locate information about your ancestors and family members, particularly if you do most of the work. Remember that not all church office personnel are paid employees; some are simply members volunteering their time. Not all members of the office staff, and even members of the clergy, know what records they have and what is in them. The old books and papers in their offices may just be gathering dust in a closet or file cabinet. Few of these materials are indexed, such as the document shown in Figure 6-3, which was found among a sheaf of loose papers tucked into a cardboard box in a church office cabinet. It often takes a considerable effort to go through such documents and locate information that may relate to your family.

Be prepared to offer to help the person you contact in the church office. You may have to describe the types of record you are seeking and where they might be located. Reluctance you encounter may be a result of the person's lack of knowledge and experience, lack of time, the cost of making and mailing copies for you, or some other reason. Be kind, patient, and friendly, and offer all the help you can. Be prepared to reimburse all the expenses and to make a donation to the congregation.

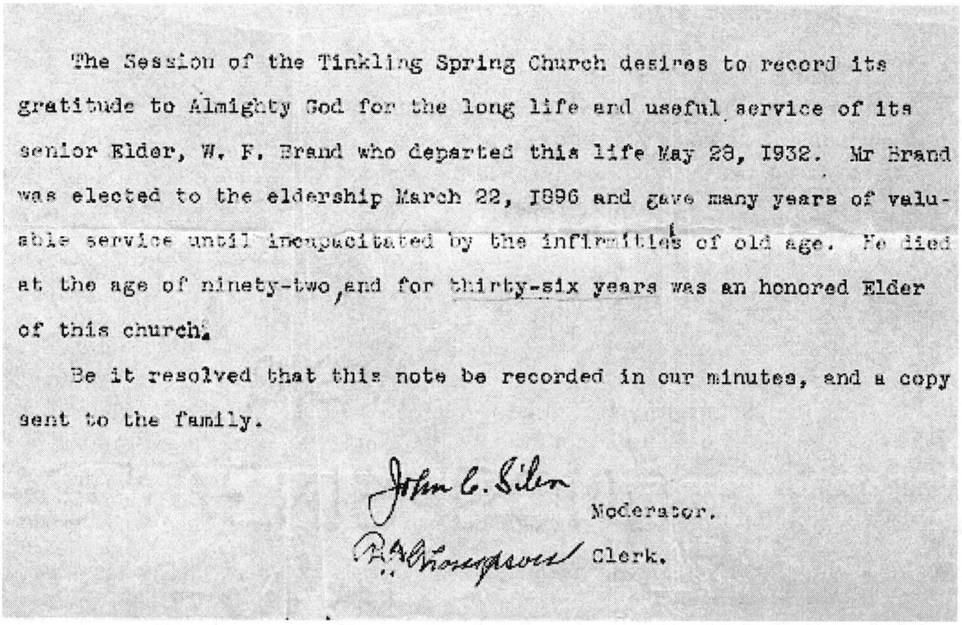

The Session of the Tinkling Spring Church desires to record its gratitude to Almighty God for the long life and useful service of its senior Elder, W. F. Brand who departed this life May 28, 1932. Mr Brand was elected to the eldership March 22, 1896 and gave many years of valuable service until incapacitated by the infirmities of old age. He died at the age of ninety-two, and for thirty-six years was an honored Elder of this church.

Be it resolved that this note be recorded in our minutes, and a copy sent to the family.

John C. Silen   Moderator.

R. A. Thompson   Clerk.

FIGURE 6-3   This loose document from the minutes of a church session commemorating the life and service of a member was found in a box, and it was never indexed. (From the author's collection.)

Interpret, Evaluate, and Place the Records into Perspective

Once you obtain the documents you want, your next step is to carefully read and review them. Interpretation can be a real challenge, particularly if the handwriting is poor, the copies are dim or illegible, or the document is written in a language you do not understand. Many church records are written in Latin, particularly those of the Catholic Church and those of the early Church of England. You may encounter Jewish documents written in Hebrew or other languages, Russian Orthodox Church documents written using the Cyrillic alphabet, and any number of foreign languages and dialects. Old English script and German Fraktur both resemble calligraphy and their character embellishments can be particularly difficult to read. Other older or archaic handwritten materials may be difficult or nearly impossible to decipher. You will want to consider obtaining books on the subject of paleography (the study of ancient writings and inscriptions) and using the skills or services of interpreters. Two particularly good books are *Paleography for Family and Local Historians* by

Hilary Marshall (Phillimore & Co., Ltd., West Sussex England, 2004) and *Reading Early American Handwriting* by Kip Sperry (Genealogical Publishing Co., Baltimore, Maryland, 2008).

As with the other documentary evidence you have obtained, be prepared to evaluate the contents of the documents. Consider the information provided and use it to add to the overall chronological picture you are constructing of your ancestor or family member. Let's now look at specific ecclesiastical records.

Consider a Variety of Religious Records

Your research will present you with a vast array of potential information sources from religious organizations. The following is a list of some of the records you may encounter. Some are more common than others, and the list certainly will vary depending on denomination, time period, and the specific congregation.

Membership rolls	Certificates of membership	Records of excommunication
Meeting minutes	Committee minutes and reports	Hearings and inquiries
Birth records	Baptismal certificates	Christening records
Confirmation records	Records of *bar mitzvah* or *bat mitzvah*	First communion records
Marriage certificates	Records of divorce and annulment	Lists of elders and deacons
Clergy appointments	Office administrative records	Building plans and related documents
Missionary records	Fellowship group records	Photographs
Church bulletins	Newspapers and journals	Donation and tithing records
Death and burial records	Cemetery records	Sexton and administrator records

Any of these documents can provide clues about your ancestor or family member's life. Don't overlook the fact that membership records and meeting minutes also may record the previous place of membership for an individual. I was successful in tracing my maternal grandfather from the church in which he was a member at the time of his death, back through three other churches in which he was a member, to the church in which he was baptized more than six decades before, all through their membership records. A church bulletin, such as the one shown in Figure 6-4, provided details of the election of another family member to the position of head deacon. And another church had a photograph of a grandfather at the ground-breaking ceremony for a new church building. You never know what you will find in the records of religious organizations.

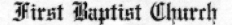

FIGURE 6-4   Church bulletins share news and may point to other types of church records. (From the author's collection.)

Obtain and Analyze Mortuary and Funeral Home Records

Among some of the most detailed records compiled about a person are those that are created at the time of his or her death. The records of an ancestor or family member whose remains were handled by a mortuary or funeral home may hold many important clues. As with religious records, it is important to do some research in advance to determine whether a mortuary's services were used and, if so, which mortuary it was.

A mortuary or funeral home performs a variety of functions, and someone usually selects the specific duties desired for the person who is deceased. The activities of the mortuary or funeral home may include providing a simple coffin or fancy casket, embalming and cosmetic preparation, clothing the corpse, arranging for or conducting services, providing transportation for the family, arranging for interment or cremation, and other, more-specialized services.

Records from a mortuary, funeral home, or crematory relating to the handling of an individual's arrangements may include many documents. You will usually find a copy of a document, such as a death certificate or coroner's report, in the file, along with an itemized accounting or invoice for all the services provided. Figure 6-5 shows a page of detail from a funeral home invoice. Information about the selection of a coffin or casket, a burial vault, and other commodities is often included. A mortuary is often called upon to prepare and handle placement of obituaries in newspapers and other media, and that information or a copy of the obituary information may be included in the file. Look for copies of a cemetery deed and a burial permit, depending on the time period, place, and type of burial. These are the more common documents you might find in these files but occasionally you may find others, such as correspondence and photographs.

Mortuaries and funeral homes are private companies and, as such, are not required to provide copies of their business documents to genealogists. An owner or administrator may decline to provide access to you for reasons of business privacy or to protect the confidentiality of family information. They also are not required to retain and preserve records in perpetuity.

Many of these facilities have disappeared over the years, been sold, or gone out of business. Their records may have been transferred, lost, or destroyed. You may need to work with libraries, archives, and genealogical and/or historical societies to determine the disposition of their records. Some may have been preserved in the special collections of libraries, such as those of several funeral homes in Tampa, Florida, which are now residing in the Special Collections of the University of South Florida Tampa Library.

Read Between the Lines in Obituaries

We're all familiar with obituaries and death notices, those announcements of people's deaths that appear in the newspaper and other media, and now also on the Internet. These published gems often contain a wealth of biographical information in condensed form. You can gather a lot from reading what is printed *and* from reading between the lines.

An obituary is definitely a secondary source of information, derived from one or more persons or documents. You will definitely want to confirm and verify every piece of data listed there. The accuracy of the information included should always be considered questionable because errors can be introduced at any point

Ray Funeral Home

119 NORTH MARKET STREET · MADISON, NC 27025 · (919) 548-9606

PAID

12-20-93

FORBIS & DICK
FUNERAL SERVICE

December 22, 1993

MR. CAREY MORGAN
3606 CALYX CT.
GREENSBORO, NC 27410

The Funeral for EDITH WEATHERLY MORGAN on November 21, 1993

We sincerely appreciate the confidence you have placed in us and
will continue to assist you in every way we can. Please feel free
to contact us if you have any questions in regard to this statement.

THE FOLLOWING IS AN ITEMIZED STATEMENT OF THE SERVICES, FACILITIES,
AUTOMOTIVE EQUIPMENT, AND MERCHANDISE THAT YOU SELECTED WHEN MAKING
THE FUNERAL ARRANGEMENTS.

```
SELECTED SERVICES OF FUNERAL DIRECTOR AND STAFF:
Local Removal . . . . . . . . . . . . . . . . . . . $      90.00
Embalming . . . . . . . . . . . . . . . . . . . . . $     300.00
Other Preparation . . . . . . . . . . . . . . . . . $      75.00
Director and Staff  . . . . . . . . . . . . . . . . $     760.00
SELECTED USE OF FACILITIES AND EQUIPMENT:
Other Use of Facilities . . . . . . . . . . . . . . $     120.00
Use of Visitation Room  . . . . . . . . . . . . . . $     120.00
Equip. for Church Service . . . . . . . . . . . . . $     120.00
SELECTED USE OF AUTOMOTIVE EQUIPMENT:
Hearse  . . . . . . . . . . . . . . . . . . . . . . $     100.00
Family Vehicle  . . . . . . . . . . . . . . . . . . $      80.00
Utility Van . . . . . . . . . . . . . . . . . . . . $      80.00
Service Vehicle . . . . . . . . . . . . . . . . . . $      80.00
                                                      ----------
        FUNERAL HOME SERVICE CHARGES  . . . . . . . $    1925.00

SELECTED MERCHANDISE:
Lexington Maple . . . . . . . . . . . . . . . . . . $    2765.00
Continental . . . . . . . . . . . . . . . . . . . . $     994.00
Register Books  . . . . . . . . . . . . . . . . . . $      25.00
Acknowledgement Cards . . . . . . . . . . . . . . . $      10.00
Rita Barber #6749 . . . . . . . . . . . . . . . . . $     100.00

THE COST OF OUR SERVICES, EQUIPMENT, AND MERCHANDISE
THAT YOU HAVE SELECTED. . . . . . . . . . . . . . . $    5819.00
```

AT THE TIME FUNERAL ARRANGEMENTS WERE MADE, WE ADVANCED CERTAIN
PAYMENTS TO OTHERS AS AN ACCOMMODATION. THE FOLLOWING IS AN
ACCOUNTING FOR THOSE CHARGES.

EDITH WEATHERLY MORGAN
Page 1

FIGURE 6-5   Detail page from a funeral home invoice. (From the author's collection.)

in the publication process. The informant for the information may or may not be a knowledgeable family member, or the person may be under the stress of the occasion and provide inaccurate details. The person who takes down the information may introduce an error, a newspaper employee may transcribe something incorrectly, and an editor may miss a typographical error.

Some of the information and clues you can look for in obituaries include the following:

- Name and age of the deceased
- Date, location, and sometimes cause of death
- Place of residence
- Names of parents and siblings
- Names and/or numbers of children and grandchildren
- Places of residence of living relatives
- Names of and notes about deceased relatives
- Where and when deceased was born
- When deceased left his/her native land, perhaps even the port of entry and date
- Naturalization date and location
- Place(s) where deceased was educated
- Dates and locations of marriage(s), and name of spouse(es) (sometimes maiden names)
- Religious affiliation and name of congregation
- Military service information (branch, rank, dates served, medals, and awards)
- Place(s) of employment
- Public office(s) held
- Organizations to which he/she belonged
- Awards received
- Events in which he/she participated
- Name and address of funeral home, church, or other venue where funeral was to occur
- Date and time of funeral
- Name(s) of officiating clergy
- List of pallbearers
- Date, place, and disposition of remains
- Statement regarding any memorial services
- Directions regarding donations or memorial gifts

I use obituaries as pointers to locate primary record sources. I certainly use them to help corroborate other sources of evidence, and to help verify names, dates, and locations of events. They may include the names and locations of other family members, and may identify alternative research paths to get past some of the "dead ends" I may have encountered.

One of my most successful uses of obituaries occurred when researching a great-grandmother. I had tried unsuccessfully for years to trace back and identify her parents. I finally visited the town where she lived in 1997 and was able to access the actual 1914 newspaper in which her obituary had been printed. The obituary included the names of three surviving sisters whose married names I had not known. Two of the three were dead ends, but records for the third sister and her husband were easily located. I transferred my research attention to that sister and pretty quickly was able to identify and locate the parents' records. I then used a will to "connect downward" and prove that my great-grandmother was one of their children. Suddenly the doors opened and, within a matter of months, I had traced my lineage back to a great-great-great-grandfather who had fought in the American Revolution and I had obtained copies of his military service and pension records.

Locate and Delve into Cemetery Records

Most people's perception is that a cemetery is a lonely place, devoid of any activity other than the interment of remains and the visits by families and friends of those who have passed before. However, if you have ever participated in the process of making arrangements for a family member, spouse or partner, or a friend, you know that there can be a lot of paperwork involved. And where there is paperwork, there are pieces of potentially valuable genealogical evidence. Some of these materials are accessible to you, the researcher, and others are not. However, let's examine the processes involved with handling the death of an individual and the documentation that may have been created.

Cemeteries are much more than graveyards. They are representations in a community of the society, culture, architecture, and the sense of the community. Many genealogists and family historians arrive at a cemetery, wander around looking for gravestones, copy down the names and dates, perhaps take a few photographs, and then leave, thinking they have found all there is to be found. In many cases, they have merely drifted past what might have been a treasure trove.

Did You Know? A marker may have been installed in a place in which the decedent was not interred. These markers are known as *cenotaphs*. In other cases, a marker may have been installed at an intended gravesite, and a person may not have been buried there. Look for the absence of a death date, and always check with the cemetery office or administrator to confirm that an interment did or did not take place.

It is important to know that a tombstone or other type of marker isn't necessarily the only record to be found in or associated with a cemetery. You also should recognize that these memorial markers are not necessarily accurate *primary sources* of evidence. That is because the markers are not always created at or near the time of death, and incorrect information may have been provided and/or inscribed. While a marker may have been placed within a short time of the interment, you cannot always determine if that is the case. In other cases, a marker may have been installed in a place in which the decedent was not interred. These markers are known as *cenotaphs*. Also, understand that the information carved on a tombstone or cast in a metal marker is actually a transcription of data provided, and that one or more errors may have been made. For example, there is a granite marker in an old cemetery in St. Marys, Georgia, on which an incorrect name was carved. Rather than replace the entire stone, the stonecutter used a composite stone paste to fill in the incorrect letter. After the paste set, the correct letter was carved. Unfortunately, the flaw is still visible on the stone (see Figure 6-6).

Someone or some organization owns and/or is responsible for a cemetery. A visit to the local city government office that issues burial permits, to the office that handles land and tax records, or to the closest mortuary can usually provide you with the name of the owner or a contact individual. The next step is to make contact with the person or agency responsible for the maintenance of the cemetery. That may be an administrator or sexton, and this contact may yield important information.

Cemeteries typically consist of lots that are subdivided into plots into which persons' remains are interred. Someone owns the lot and has authorized the burials there. If a government is involved, there may have been a burial permit or similar document created to allow a grave to be opened and an individual's remains to be interred. A crematory's information concerning the commitment of the cremains to a columbarium niche may also be included. Other documents may well have been created, and they may have been given to the cemetery administrator or sexton for inclusion in the cemetery's files. As a result, making contact with the cemetery may help you obtain copies of documents that are available nowhere else. Let me give you a few examples.

FIGURE 6-6 Grave marker showing a stonecutter's error and correction. (From the author's collection.)

When I was searching for the burial location of my great-grandparents, Green Berry Holder and his wife, Penelope Swords, I knew they were buried in Rome, Georgia, in the Myrtle Hill Cemetery. I contacted the Rome city administrative offices to determine who was responsible for the cemetery's administration and maintenance. I was directed to the Rome Cemetery Department, which is responsible for five municipal cemeteries. I made a call and spoke with the sexton of Myrtle Hill Cemetery. He was able to quickly pull the records for Green Berry Holder while we were on the telephone and told me the following:

- The date of the original purchase of the cemetery lot
- The identification information of the lot (lot number and location)
- The names of each person buried in the lot, their date of death, their ages, and the dates of their interments
- The date on which two plots in the lot were resold to the owner of an adjacent lot

I also asked about a great-uncle, Edward Holder, whom I believed was also buried in that cemetery. There was, in fact, a joint grave marker for him and his wife, shown in Figure 6-7, although his year of death was incomplete. I had assumed that he was buried there; however, the sexton told me that only his wife was interred in this cemetery. It turned out that my Great-uncle Ed actually was buried in another municipal cemetery on the other side of town beside another woman bearing his surname. I learned that he had a *second* marriage about which neither I nor anyone else in the family was aware.

Based on the information the sexton was able to provide, I had much better details with which to research my family members interred in both of the cemeteries. I also had information about approximate dates of death that I followed to the Floyd County Health Department to obtain copies of all the death certificates. I also headed to the county courthouse for a marriage record for my Great-uncle Ed's second marriage

FIGURE 6-7   Grave marker for the author's great-uncle, who is buried in another cemetery with his second wife. (From the author's collection.)

and to the library to work with microfilmed newspapers, looking for marriage announcements and obituaries. Had I located the obituary of the great-uncle earlier, I would have known he was buried in the other cemetery *and* that his second wife survived him.

These clues led me to others, including the name of the current owner of the local funeral home that handled most of the family members' funerals over the decades, to church records in multiple congregations, to land and property records, to wills and estate probate files, and more.

An on-site visit to the cemetery sexton's office also provided me the opportunity to see the physical files maintained there. My great-grandmother, Penelope Swords Holder, died prior to Georgia's requirement that counties issue death certificates. However, there were copies of her obituary, a burial permit, and a note to the sexton from my great-grandfather asking that my great-grandmother be buried in a specific plot adjacent to one of their grandchildren. In addition, the sexton checked an ancient interment ledger and found recorded there the cause of death—pneumonia. This was important because, in the absence of a death certificate, the entry confirmed the family story of her cause of death.

There are other documents that you may find in a cemetery's office. These include requests for burial, such as the ones shown in Figures 6-8 and 6-9. A burial permit, such as the one shown in Figure 6-10, is often required in order to control and keep track of the interment, and as another source of local tax revenue.

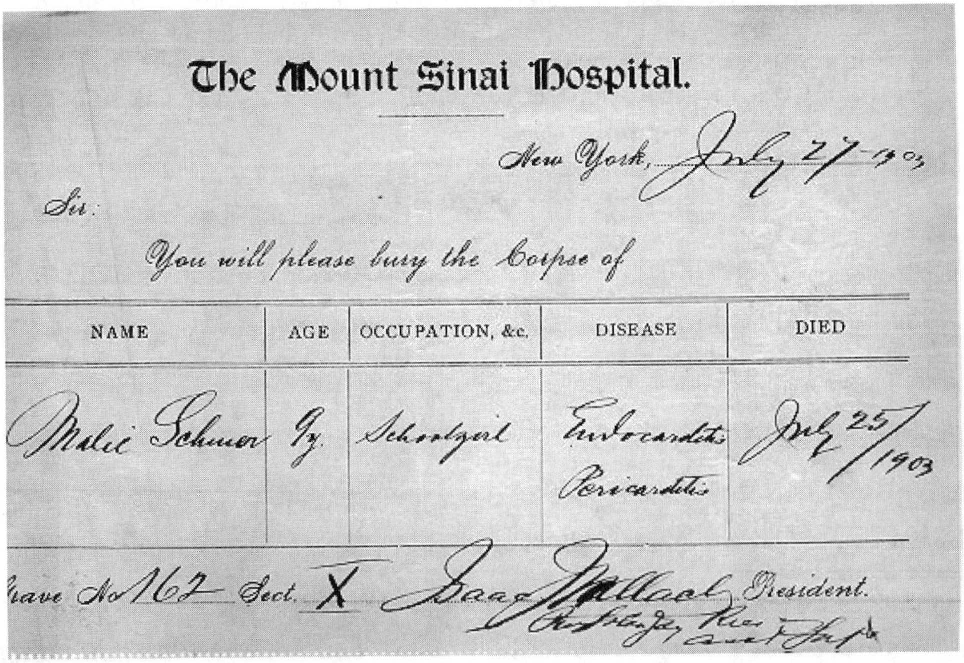

The Mount Sinai Hospital.

New York, July 27 1903

Sir:

You will please bury the Corpse of

NAME	AGE	OCCUPATION, &c.	DISEASE	DIED
Malie Schuner	9y	Schoolgirl	Endocarditis Pericarditis	July 25/1903

Grave No 162 Sect. X Resident.

FIGURE 6-8 A request for burial found in a cemetery file. (From the author's collection.)

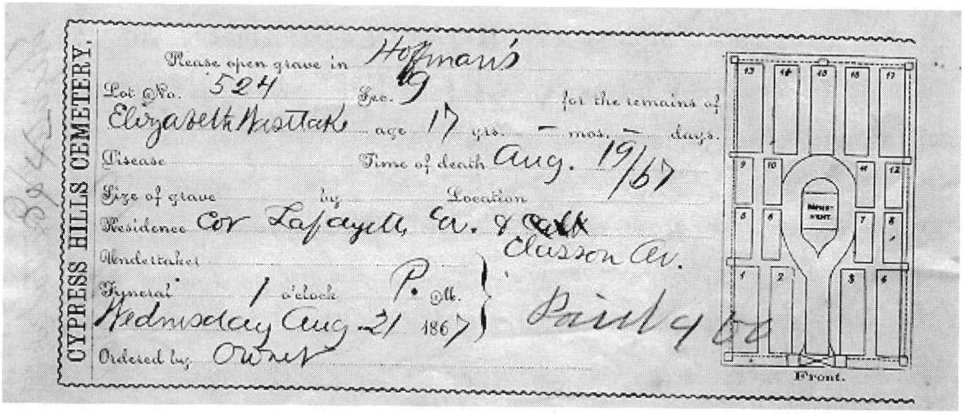

CYPRESS HILLS CEMETERY,

Please open grave in Hoffman's
Lot No. 524 Sec. 9 for the remains of
Elizabeth Westlake age 17 yrs. — mos. — days.
Disease Time of death Aug. 19/67
Size of grave by Location
Residence Cor Lafayette Av. & Classon Av.
Undertaker
Funeral 1 o'clock P. M. Wednesday Aug. 21 1867
Ordered by Owner
Front.

FIGURE 6-9 A cemetery's form requesting the opening of a grave. (From the author's collection.)

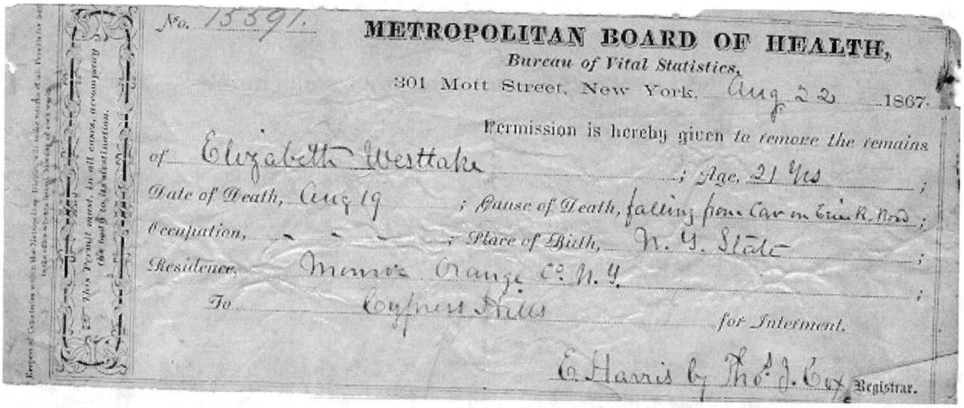

No. 13591.

METROPOLITAN BOARD OF HEALTH,
Bureau of Vital Statistics,
301 Mott Street, New York, Aug 22 1867.

Permission is hereby given *to remove the remains*
of Elizabeth Westlake ; Age, 21 Yrs ;
Date of Death, Aug 19 ; Cause of Death, falling from Car on Erie R. Road ;
Occupation, ; Place of Birth, N. Y. State ;
Residence, Monroe Orange Co. N. Y. ;
To Cypress Hills *for Interment.*

E. Harris by Thos. J. Cox Registrar.

FIGURE 6-10 A burial permit from New York, 1867. (From the author's collection.)

Transit permits are used to facilitate the movement of human remains from one political jurisdiction to another. Two examples are shown in Figures 6-11 and 6-12. These documents are usually completed in multiple copies. The original document accompanies the body to the place of final interment; the issuing governmental office retains another copy (or coupon); and other copies may be provided to the transportation carrier(s) en route. A transit permit, such as the one shown in Figure 6-11, may contain a significant amount of information about the deceased, including the age, address, cause of death, the names of the physician and coroner, the name of the undertaker, and the mode of transportation.

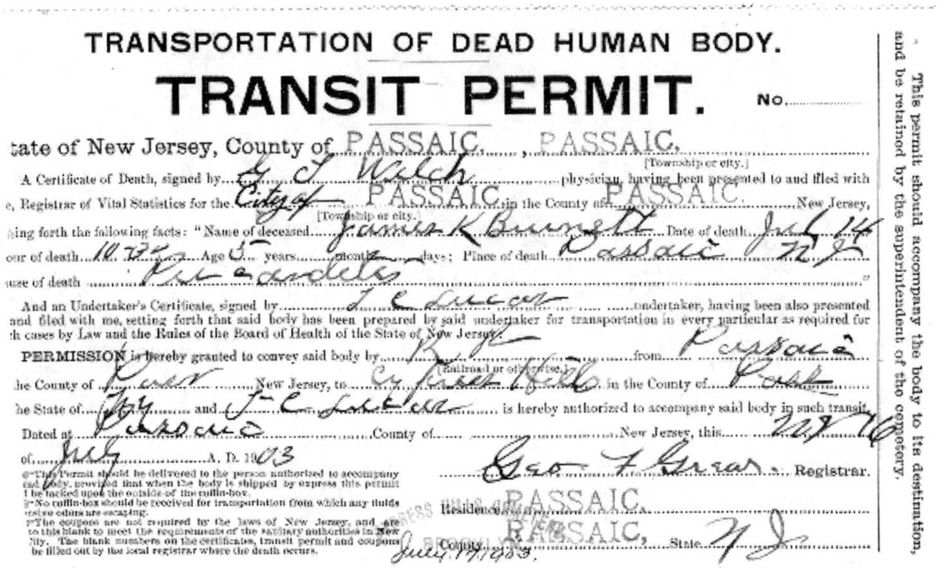
TRANSPORTATION OF DEAD HUMAN BODY.

TRANSIT PERMIT. NO.

State of New Jersey, County of PASSAIC, PASSAIC.
(Township or city.)

A Certificate of Death, signed by G. T. Welch physician, having been presented to and filed with the Registrar of Vital Statistics for the City of PASSAIC in the County of PASSAIC New Jersey, setting forth the following facts: "Name of deceased James K Burnett Date of death July 14 Hour of death 10 Age 5 years months days; Place of death Passaic N J Cause of death

And an Undertaker's Certificate, signed by undertaker, having been also presented and filed with me, setting forth that said body has been prepared by said undertaker for transportation in every particular as required for such cases by Law and the Rules of the Board of Health of the State of New Jersey,

PERMISSION is hereby granted to convey said body by from Passaic the County of New Jersey, to in the County of the State of and is hereby authorized to accompany said body in such transit.

Dated at Passaic County of New Jersey, this of July A. D. 1903

Geo F. Greer Registrar.

Residence PASSAIC.

County PASSAIC, State N J

This permit should accompany the body to its destination, and be retained by the superintendent of the cemetery.

FIGURE 6-11 This 1903 transit permit contains many details that can be researched. (From the author's collection.)

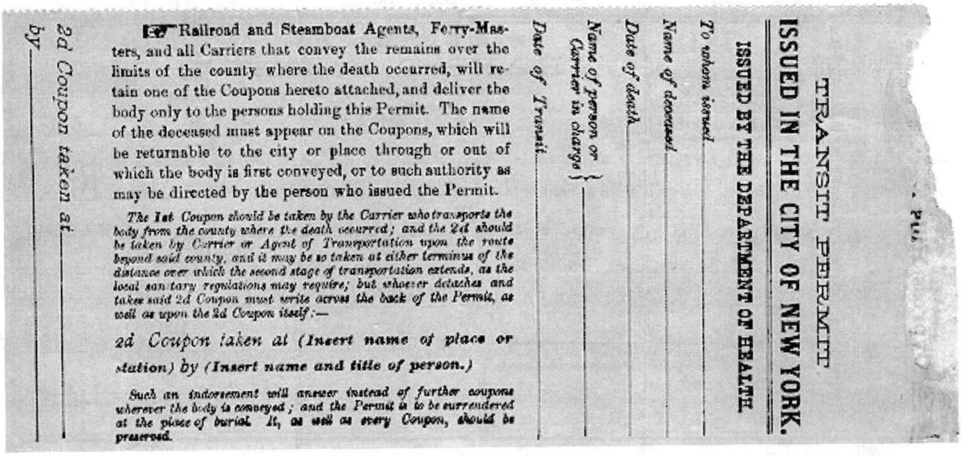
TRANSIT PERMIT

ISSUED IN THE CITY OF NEW YORK.

ISSUED BY THE DEPARTMENT OF HEALTH.

To whom issued

Name of deceased

Date of death

Name of person or Carrier in charge

Date of Transit

Railroad and Steamboat Agents, Ferry-Masters, and all Carriers that convey the remains over the limits of the county where the death occurred, will retain one of the Coupons hereto attached, and deliver the body only to the persons holding this Permit. The name of the deceased must appear on the Coupons, which will be returnable to the city or place through or out of which the body is first conveyed, or to such authority as may be directed by the person who issued the Permit.

The 1st Coupon should be taken by the Carrier who transports the body from the county where the death occurred; and the 2d should be taken by Carrier or Agent of Transportation upon the route beyond said county, and it may be so taken at either terminus of the distance over which the second stage of transportation extends, as the local sanitary regulations may require; but whoever detaches and takes said 2d Coupon must write across the back of the Permit, as well as upon the 2d Coupon itself:—

2d Coupon taken at (Insert name of place or station) by (Insert name and title of person.)

Such an indorsement will answer instead of further coupons wherever the body is conveyed; and the Permit is to be surrendered at the place of burial. It, as well as every Coupon, should be preserved.

2d Coupon taken at

by

FIGURE 6-12 This City of New York transit permit includes less information, but it can still provide clues to locating a death certificate and other records. (From the author's collection.)

Some transit permit formats provided very little information, such as the example shown in Figure 6-12. Transit permits were used when shipping bodies of soldiers back home from other locations, and a copy may be found in the mortuary records, in cemetery files, and in surviving military personnel files.

Search for burial and transit permit records in the county or municipal district in which the death occurred. Depending on the location, they may or may not have survived in the issuing governmental office.

Search for Other Death-Related Documents

Death certificates, obituaries, and burial permits are not the only documents relating to death that you may locate that contain genealogical information. Nor are mortuaries, funeral homes, crematoria, and cemeteries the only places to look for these documents.

Table 6-1 includes a number of important documents, data that they may contain, and where you may search for them.

TABLE 6-1   Other Death-Related Documents and Where to Locate Them. (Used by permission of Aha! Seminars, Inc.)

Type of Document and Description of Its Use	Information You Likely Will Find on the Document	Where You Are Likely to Locate the Document
Death Certificate—Used to document a death. It is an excellent *primary source* for death information, but a *secondary source* for all other information. Death certificates may not exist in many places prior to 1900. Consult *Ancestry's Red Book* for specifics in U.S.	• Date and place of death • Name of mortuary or funeral home handling body • Name and location of the place of interment	• County department of health • County courthouse • Government offices of health or vital statistics • Mortuary or funeral home records • Files of the cemetery administrator or sexton
Coroner's Report—Used to document cases of unusual, suspicious, or accidental death.	• Date and place of death • Cause of death • Name of mortuary or funeral home handling the body • Name(s) of investigating officials • Final determination	• Office of the coroner or medical examiner • Courthouse with jurisdiction over location of death at the time • Probate court records • Other court records

(Continued)

TABLE 6-1 Other Death-Related Documents and Where to Locate Them. (Used by permission of Aha! Seminars, Inc.) (*Continued*)

Type of Document and Description of Its Use	Information You Likely Will Find on the Document	Where You Are Likely to Locate the Document
Transit Permit—Used to document the movement of the deceased's remains from one political jurisdiction to another, i.e., state to state or country to country.	• Date and place of death • Cause of death • Sometimes includes the address and age of the decedent • Name and location of the originating mortuary or funeral home • Name and location of the destination mortuary or funeral home • Sometimes includes the name and location of the place of interment	• Government office of the place of origin of the body's departure • County department of health • County courthouse • State department of health or vital statistics • Mortuary or funeral home records • Files of the cemetery administrator or sexton
Burial Permit—Used to record the opening of a grave and allow the interment of remains. This may be issued by the government entity that had ownership and administrative control of the cemetery.	• Name of the deceased • Date and place of death • Name of cemetery • Interment location (lot and plot identity, tomb or mausoleum identity, or columbarium identity) • Scheduled date of interment • Name and location of mortuary or funeral home • Sometimes name of the person or company authorized to open and close the grave • Authorizing agency, signature, and date of issue	• Issuing agency, usually the owner or administrator of a municipal-, county-, state-, or federal-owned/operated cemetery • Files of the mortuary or funeral home • Files of the cemetery administrator or sexton for the cemetery • For military service personnel, may find a permit for a burial in a military cemetery in the individual's military personnel file
Interment Ledger—Used in some cemeteries in older times to record interments.	• Name of the deceased • Date of death • Sometimes includes the cause of death and location • Location of interment in the cemetery • Date of interment	• Office of the cemetery administrator or sexton for the cemetery

Cemetery Lot Deed or Land Title—Used to record the sale of a cemetery lot and sometimes the sale of individual plots.

- Name of purchaser
- Name of seller
- Date of the sale
- Location and description of the lot (or plot)
- Amount paid for the parcel

- Office of the cemetery administrator or sexton for the cemetery
- May also be recorded in county clerk's office along with other property records
- May find a copy in the files of the mortuary or funeral home that handled the arrangements, particularly if this was the first interment in the lot

Obituary—Used to publicly announce a death, location, and date(s) of arrangements.

- Name of deceased
- Date and location of death
- Extensive or abbreviated information about the person's life, survivors, and other personal information
- Date and location of funeral or other services
- Location of interment

- Newspapers, church bulletins and newsletters (local and regional), union and fraternal organization publications, professional publications
- Libraries and archives with microfilmed holdings of the above publications
- Internet-based obituary transcriptions

Public Notices—Used to advertise a death, and both to announce the collection of debts for the estate and to request presentation of claims.

- Name of deceased
- Date of death and residence
- Name of administrator
- Sometimes place of death and place of interment are listed if different from place of residence

- Newspapers
- Libraries and archives with microfilmed holdings of the newspapers
- Estate and probate packets
- Probate court minutes

Cemetery Canvasses and Gravestone Transcription Projects—Compilations and publications to record the interments in a cemetery or other place of interment for posterity.

- Any information inscribed or cast onto a tombstone or other grave marker
- May or may not be all-inclusive, including epitaph
- May or may not include photographs
- May or may not be published

- Genealogical societies in the area and at the state level
- Historical societies as above
- Libraries and archives
- Genealogy society periodicals, which can be located using the Periodical Source Index (PERSI) online at Ancestry .com and then ordered from genealogical libraries

(Continued)

TABLE 6-1 Other Death-Related Documents and Where to Locate Them. (Used by permission of Aha! Seminars, Inc.) *(Continued)*

Type of Document and Description of Its Use	Information You Likely Will Find on the Document	Where You Are Likely to Locate the Document
County and Local Histories—Used to record information of historical significance in a specific geographical area.	May contain a variety of information about individuals, families, ethnic groups, and other facts to help you locate religious, public, private, and family places of interment.	• Genealogical societies in the area and at the state level • Historical societies in the area and at the state level • Libraries and archives
Military Histories and Regimental Histories—Used to record information of historical significance relating to a specific military event or military unit.	May contain a variety of information about individuals serving in the military, their families, ethnic groups, and other facts to help you locate religious, public, private, family, and military places of interment.	• Genealogical societies in the area and at the state level • Historical societies in the area and at the state level • Libraries and archives
Military Service Papers—Used to document the military service and pension information for an individual.	May contain a variety of information about an individual and his or her military service. May also include information about death benefits paid and interment in a military cemetery in the U.S. or abroad.	• Military service and pension files (different locations) • American Battle Monuments Commission website (for WWI, WWII, Korean War, and Vietnam War) at **www.abmc.gov** • Other web-based sites
Funeral or Condolence Books—Provided by the mortuary or funeral home to allow persons visiting the family of the deceased to sign their name and write a message.	May contain a variety of information, but also may specify date and location of interment.	• Family effects
Websites—Many websites contain information related to places of interment.	The Internet contains a wealth of information concerning deaths and interments, and using a search engine can be of some assistance.	• Ancestry.com databases, **www.ancestry.com** • RootsWeb databases, **www.rootsweb.com** • USGenWeb Project, **www.usgenweb.org** • WorldGenWeb Project, **www.worldgenweb.org**

Get Inside Your Ancestor's Mind Using Wills and Probate Records

Wills and probate packets are extremely interesting and revealing collections of records. A person's last will may be one of the most honest statements about his or her relationships with other family members and friends. And the probate packet's contents may provide information and insights into the person that you may never find anywhere else.

Did You Know?

A person's last will may be one of the most honest statements about his or her relationships with other family members and friends. Documents included in the probate packet are an estate inventory, lists of debts owed and due, financial reports, and a list of all potential heirs' names, addresses, and other details.

Understand the Meaning of a Will and Testament

Let's first discuss some of the terminology. A *will* is a legal document in which a person specifies the disposition of his or her property after death. The person who makes the will is called the *testator*, and the will may also be referred to as the *last will and testament*.

At the time a testator dies, he or she is referred to as the *decedent* or the *deceased*. The process of proving a will's authenticity or validity is called *probate*, taken from the Latin word *probatim* or *probare*, which means "to examine." The legal body responsible for reviewing and examining materials related to the handling of an estate in the United States is the *probate court*. From the 13th century until 1857 (with the exception of the period of the interregnum, 1653–1660) in England and Wales, ecclesiastical courts handled the probate process, and this usually dealt only with nobility and wealthy landowners. The Court of Probate Act 1857 established a civil court, the Principal Probate Registry, which started functioning on 10 July 1858. Probate law in the United States, Canada, Australia, and certain other countries is based on the English model.

The person appointed by a court to oversee or administer the affairs of the estate during the probate process is known as the *executor*. Alternatively or in conjunction with an executor, one or more *administrators* may be appointed.

Did You Know?

Historically, the terms "testator" and "testatrix" and "executor" and "executrix" were used to designate the gender of individuals. The former terms indicate a male and the latter terms indicate a female. In modern times, however, most probate courts no longer use the terms "testatrix" and "executrix." The masculine terms are used to recognize either gender.

Depending on the size of the estate and/or the amount of detail to which the testator went, a will may be a short document or a lengthy one. A will does not need to be drawn up by a lawyer or solicitor; an individual may write his or her own. It is a legal document so long as the testator signs it. Usually, however, it is advisable to have two or more witnesses to the signing of the document. This makes the probate process, or proving of the will, simpler because it assures that the signature or mark of the testator is genuine.

If the testator decides to change the will after it is made and signed, a new will can be drawn up, signed, and witnessed. Sometimes, if there are minor changes or if there is an expedient required (such as an interim change to a will while an entirely new one is being drawn up), a codicil can be drafted and signed. A *codicil* is simply a supplement to a will, usually containing an addition or a modification to the original will.

The Probate Process Defined

Medieval English law and legal customs influence the United States, Canada, and Australia. The terms "will" and "testament" originally referred to separate portions of an individual's estate, and the documents were usually separate documents handled by separate courts. A "will" was used to dispose of one's real property, or real estate, and the "testament" was used to bequeath personal property. A study of history in the British Isles will reveal that the courts that were used to probate an estate changed over time from ecclesiastical ones to civil courts. In Wales and England, the last will and testament became a single probated entity and this practice spread to other places. If you are researching wills and probate in the United Kingdom, an understanding of the history of the process, the courts, their jurisdictions, and the documents' contents in England, Wales, Scotland, and throughout Ireland, respectively, is essential.

In the United States, though, the use of the singular last will and testament document is generally found to be the norm. This is the case of the probate process we will explore below. Of course, there are exceptions and special circumstances as with any legal documentary process. However, in the interest of clarifying the probate process, let's focus on a rather straightforward definition.

Did You Know? The person making a will is called the *testator*. A person appointed by a court to oversee and perform the activities associated with settling an estate is called the *executor* or *administrator*. A minor change or a temporary amendment to a will is called a *codicil*.

A person's last will and testament is intended to express his or her wishes for what is to be done with their possessions after death, as illustrated in the case of Isaac Mitchell, whose will is shown in Figures 6-13 and 6-14. In some cases, there are heavy religious overtones to the document. This is perhaps understandable under the circumstances because, at the time this document is written, the testator is giving

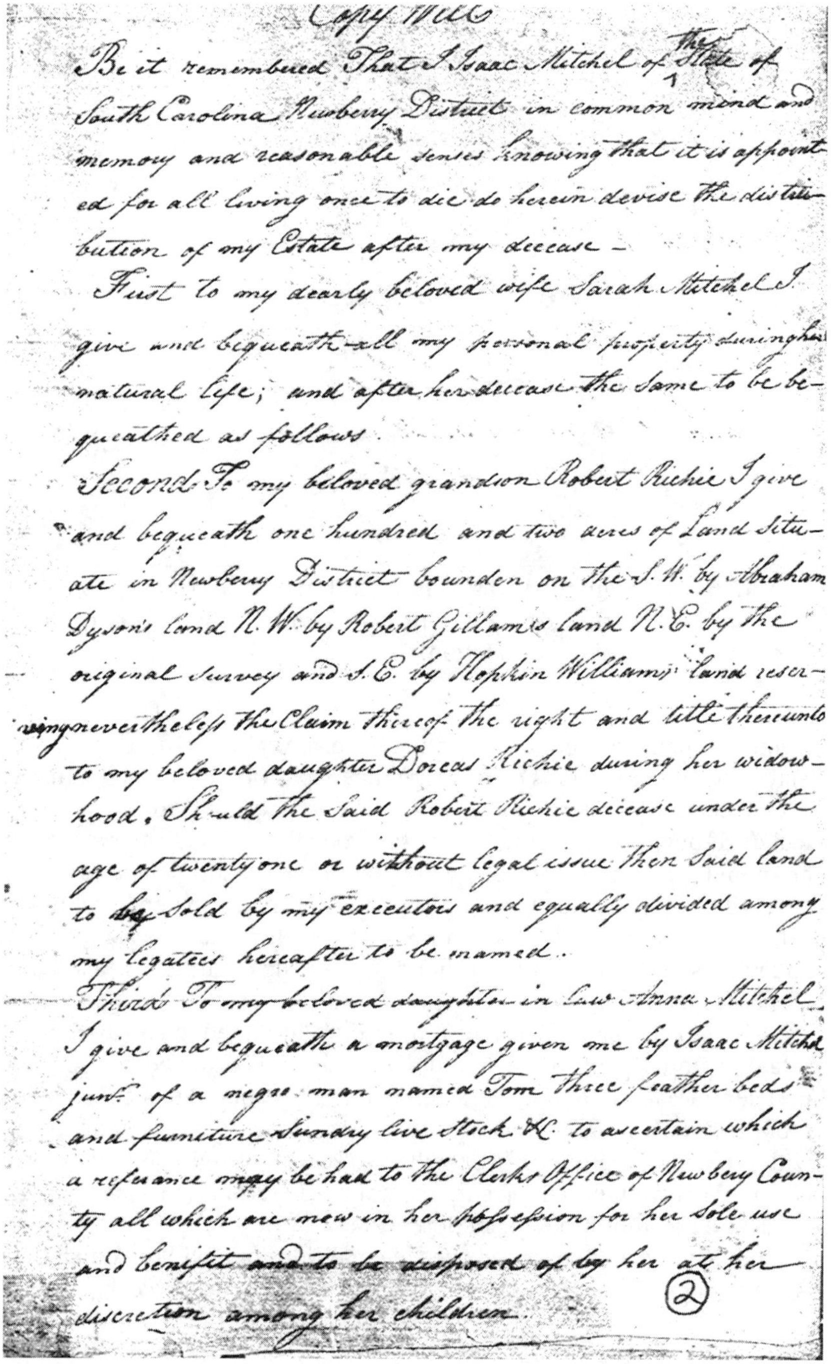

Copy Will

Be it remembered That I Isaac Mitchel of the State of South Carolina Newberry District in common mind and memory and reasonable senses knowing that it is appointed for all living once to die do herein devise the distribution of my Estate after my decease –

First to my dearly beloved wife Sarah Mitchel I give and bequeath all my personal property during her natural life; and after her decease the same to be bequeathed as follows.

Second: To my beloved grandson Robert Richie I give and bequeath one hundred and two acres of Land Situate in Newberry District bounden on the S.W. by Abraham Dyson's land N.W. by Robert Gillam's land N.E. by the original Survey and S.E. by Hopkin Williams land reserving nevertheless the Claim thereof the right and title thereunto to my beloved daughter Dorcas Richie during her widowhood. Should the Said Robert Richie decease under the age of twenty one or without legal issue then Said land to be Sold by my executors and equally divided among my legatees hereafter to be named.

Third: To my beloved daughter in law Anna Mitchel I give and bequeath a mortgage given me by Isaac Mitchel junr. of a negro man named Tom three feather beds and furniture Sundry live Stock &c. to ascertain which a reference may be had to the Clerks Office of Newbery County all which are now in her possession for her Sole use and benifit ~~and to be disposed of by~~ her at her discretion among her children.

(2)

FIGURE 6-13 Part one of the will for Isaac Mitchell of Newberry District, South Carolina, taken from the copy transcribed into the county will book. (From the author's collection.)

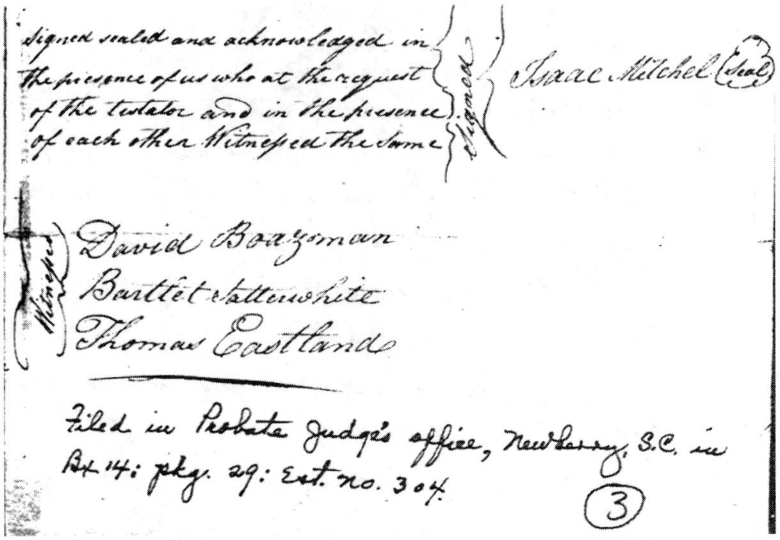
Signed sealed and acknowledged in the presence of us who at the request of the testator and in the presence of each other Witnessed the same

Signed

Isaac Mitchel (Seal)

Witnesses

David Boazman

Bartlet Satterwhite

Thomas Eastland

Filed in Probate Judge's office, Newberry, S.C. in Bx 14: pkg. 29: Est. no. 304

3

FIGURE 6-14 Signature area of Isaac Mitchell's will showing names of the witnesses and the probate clerk's filing reference details. (From the author's collection.)

careful thought, no doubt, to meeting his or her Maker. In many cases, a person's will may include instructions concerning the disposition of the body, funeral directions, and/or memorial instructions. A will may be revoked through the creation of a new will or through a document known as a codicil. A codicil can be used to revoke and/or amend specific sections of a will without the person having to write an entirely new will. It may also be used to append additional, supplemental instructions to an existing will. In all cases, however, a will or codicil must be signed by the individual and witnessed by at least two other persons. The document is also sometimes witnessed by a notary public.

The probate process is a legal procedure intended to certify that a person's estate is properly disposed of, and the process has changed very little over the past centuries. Where there is a will and it is presented to a court to be proved, there is usually a probate process that takes place. In cases where a person dies without having written or left a will, also known as dying *intestate*, a court may become involved in making sure the person's estate is correctly valued, divided, and distributed to appropriate beneficiaries.

While there may be some special conditions of a will or codicil that add additional steps to the process, here's how a simple probate process works:

1. The testator makes his/her will and any subsequent codicil(s).
2. The testator dies.

3. Someone involved in the testator's legal affairs or estate presents the will/codicil(s) to a special court of law called the probate court. The probate court and its judge are concerned with the body of law devoted to processing estates. (Minutes and notes concerning the estate and any probate court proceedings related to the estate are recorded throughout the process and should not be overlooked in your research of the estate.)

4. The will/codicil(s) is/are recorded by the probate court. The persons who witnessed the testator's signature are called upon to testify or attest to, in person or by sworn affidavit, that they witnessed the actual signature to the document(s). This is part of the "proving" of the will—that it is the authentic document on which the testator signed his/her name.

5. The probate court assigns an identifying code, usually a number, to the estate and enters it into the court's records. A probate packet is created for the court into which all documents pertaining to the settlement of the estate are placed. If the will or codicil(s) named one or more persons to act as the executor and/or administrator of the estate, the probate court issues what is called "letters testamentary." (If a named executor cannot or will not serve, the court may name another person to act in that capacity.) This document authorizes that person or persons to act on behalf of the estate in conducting business related to settling all claims.

6. Potential beneficiaries named in the will/codicil(s) are identified and contacted. If any are deceased, evidence to that effect is obtained, and if the intent of the will indicates that others besides the deceased beneficiaries are to benefit from the estate, they are identified and contacted.

7. The executor and/or administrator publish a series of notices, usually in newspapers circulated in the area where the testator lived, concerning the estate. Persons having claims on or owing obligations to the estate are thereby given notice that they have a specified amount of time to respond.

8. The executor and/or administrator conducts an inventory of the estate and prepares a written list of all assets, including personal property, real estate, financial items (cash, investments, loans, and other instruments), and any other materials that might be a part of the estate.

9. The executor and/or administrator settles any debts, outstanding claims, or obligations of the estate, and then prepares an adjusted inventory of the deceased's assets. This document, along with any supporting materials, is submitted to the probate court and becomes a permanent part of the probate packet.

10. The probate clerk reviews all the documentation for completeness and submits it to the probate judge for review. The probate court rules that the estate is now ready for distribution to beneficiaries.

11. Inheritance taxes and other death duties are paid.

12. The estate is divided and distributed and, in many cases, beneficiaries are required to sign a document confirming their receipt of their legacies.

13. Following the distribution, the executor and/or administrator prepares a final statement of account and presents it to the probate court.

14. The probate court rules that the estate has been properly processed, that all assets have been divided and distributed, and that the estate is closed.
15. The probate packet is filed in the records of the probate court.
16. The estate is closed.

Special arrangements specified in wills and codicils, such as trusts and long-term bequests, may require additional steps in the process. In some cases, the final settlement of an estate may be deferred for many years until certain conditions are satisfied. A trust, for instance, may require the establishment of a separate legal entity, and the estate may not be settled until a later date. Some people leave wills that skip a generation, perhaps leaving property and/or monies to grandchildren, in which case the estate may not be settled for a generation or more and may require extended administration. In the case of any estate whose settlement extends to multiple years, the executor and/or administrator must prepare annual reports for the probate court. Receipt of these reports is entered into the probate court record and the reports usually are placed into the probate packet.

During the process, the executor and/or administrator typically pays to publish one or more notices in the press as a public notice that all claims against the deceased's estate should be presented and all debts owed to the estate are to be presented by a specific date. As a result, not only will you be looking in the courthouse and the probate court minutes and files, but you also should be looking in the local newspapers and other publications.

Learn What a Will Can Tell You—Literally and by Implication

Some of the most interesting insights into an individual's personality and his or her relationships with other family members can be found by looking at probate records. A wife may have been provided for through a trust. It is not unusual in older wills to see a bequest such as, "To my beloved wife, Elizabeth, I leave her the house for her use for her lifetime, after which it is to be sold and proceeds divided between my children." One of the most amusing bequests I've seen was, "I leave my wife, Addie, the bed, her clothes, the ax and the mule." What a generous husband! However, the husband actually may, at that specific period in time, have legally owned all of his wife's clothing.

Farther back, you will find that laws sometimes dictated that the eldest son inherited all of the estate, a custom known as the *law of primogeniture*. Sometimes the eldest son is not listed in the will at all because this law dictated that all real property automatically came to him. In other cases, the eldest son may be named and may be given a double share of the otherwise equally divided estate. In some cases, the testator may apply the rule of primogeniture in order to accomplish some goal, such as keeping an estate from being divided. *Ultimogeniture*, also known as postremogeniture or junior right, is the tradition of bestowing inheritance to the last-born. Ultimogeniture is much less common than primogeniture.

You will often see a father leave his daughter's share of his estate to her husband. Why? Often it was because a woman was not allowed to own real property or because it was felt that she could not manage the affairs of the bequest. Sometimes, because a father may have settled a dowry on his daughter when she married, the father's bequest may be a smaller one than to other, unmarried sisters. It is also possible that a will may leave an unmarried daughter a larger amount than her sisters, in order to make them equal in their overall share of the father's estate.

A father who did not possess a large estate may have made arrangements for the placement of a son as an apprentice or indentured servant. This was a common means of guaranteeing the care and education of a son when there would not have been enough from the estate to support him. If you find such a statement in a will, investigate court records for the formalization of the arrangement. The guardian became responsible by law for the apprentice or servant.

The absence of a specific child's name may or may not indicate that he or she is deceased. The omission may indicate that the child has moved elsewhere and has not been heard from for some considerable time. It might also indicate some estrangement, especially if you can determine that the child was, in fact, still alive at the time of the death. Otherwise, it is more likely that the testator would leave an equal part to that child and the court would probably have charged the executor with locating the child. You should investigate each of these possibilities.

It also is possible that, before a will was prepared and signed, an individual may have personally prepared an inventory of his or her possessions or may have engaged the services of an appraiser. Such an inventory would help determine the value of items of real and personal property and therefore facilitate the decisions concerning how to divide them in an equitable fashion.

Examine the Contents of a Probate Packet

You may be amazed at what is or isn't in a probate packet. Some courts are very meticulous in their maintenance of the packets, in which case you may find vast amounts of documents. Other courts are less thorough, and documents may have been misplaced, incorrectly filed, lost, or even destroyed. It is important when examining probate packets to also review probate court minutes for details. (I once found a missing document from one ancestor's probate packet filed in the packet of another person's packet whose estate was heard the same day in court. It had been misfiled.) The most common items found in a probate packet are the following:

- **Will**   These documents are the core of a probate packet and include names of heirs and beneficiaries, and often the relationship to the deceased. Married names of daughters are great clues to tracing lines of descent, and names of other siblings might be located only in these documents.
- **Codicil**   Look for these amendments to a will as part of the probate packet. They also are noted in the minutes of the probate court, along with the judge's ruling on the validity of the will and the changes included in the codicil. Figure 6-15 shows the first codicil to the will of John Smith of Chelsea, London, making an

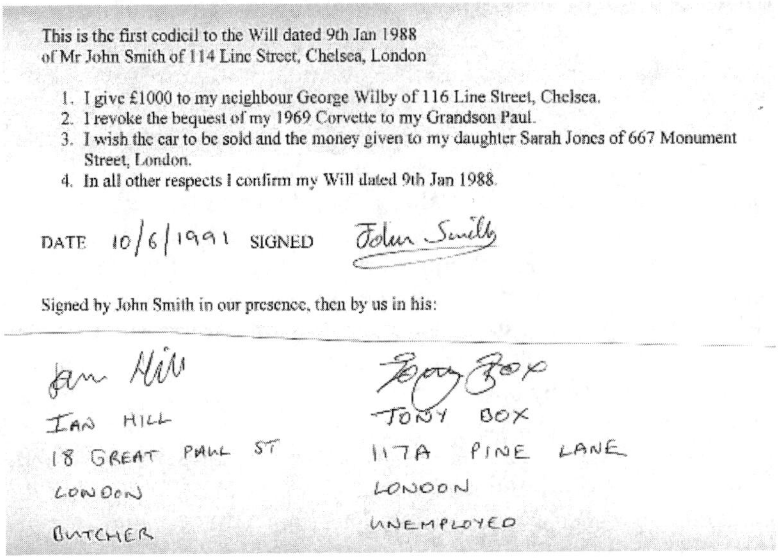

This is the first codicil to the Will dated 9th Jan 1988
of Mr John Smith of 114 Line Street, Chelsea, London

1. I give £1000 to my neighbour George Wilby of 116 Line Street, Chelsea.
2. I revoke the bequest of my 1969 Corvette to my Grandson Paul.
3. I wish the car to be sold and the money given to my daughter Sarah Jones of 667 Monument Street, London.
4. In all other respects I confirm my Will dated 9th Jan 1988.

DATE 10/6/1991 SIGNED *John Smith*

Signed by John Smith in our presence, then by us in his:

IAN HILL
18 GREAT PAUL ST
LONDON
BUTCHER

TONY BOX
117A   PINE LANE
LONDON
UNEMPLOYED

FIGURE 6-15   Codicil of John Smith. (From the author's collection.)

additional bequest of £1,000 to a neighbor, revoking the bequest of an automobile to his grandson, and calling for the sale of the car and the distribution of the proceeds to a daughter.

- **Letters testamentary**   Look for a copy of this document in the probate packet. If it isn't there, look in court records. The name(s) of the actual executor and/ or administrator may well be different from the person named in the will. You will want to determine the actual person(s) and their relationship (if any) to the deceased. It is important to know if and why the named executor did not serve. Was the person deceased or did he or she decline to serve?

- **Inventory or appraisal of the estate**   The inventory reveals the financial state of the deceased, and this is a good indicator of his/her social status. The inventory of personal property, such as the example shown in Figure 6-16, provides indicators to the person's lifestyle. The presence of farm equipment and livestock may indicate the person was a farmer; an anvil and metal stock might point to blacksmithing as a profession; hammers, chisels, nails, a level, and other tools may reveal carpentry. In an 18th-century estate inventory, the presence of books indicates education and literacy, and the possession of a great deal of clothing and shoes indicates an elevated social position. The inclusion of slaves, as shown in the inventory in Figure 6-17, is indicative of a position of some wealth. There are many indicators that may direct you to other types of records. You may even find items listed in the inventory that confirm family stories, such as military medals.

- **List of beneficiaries**   A list of persons named may differ from the list of names in the will. Beneficiaries may be deceased, they may have married and changed names, they may not be locatable, their descendants or spouses may become inheritors, and so on. This list will tell you much about the family.

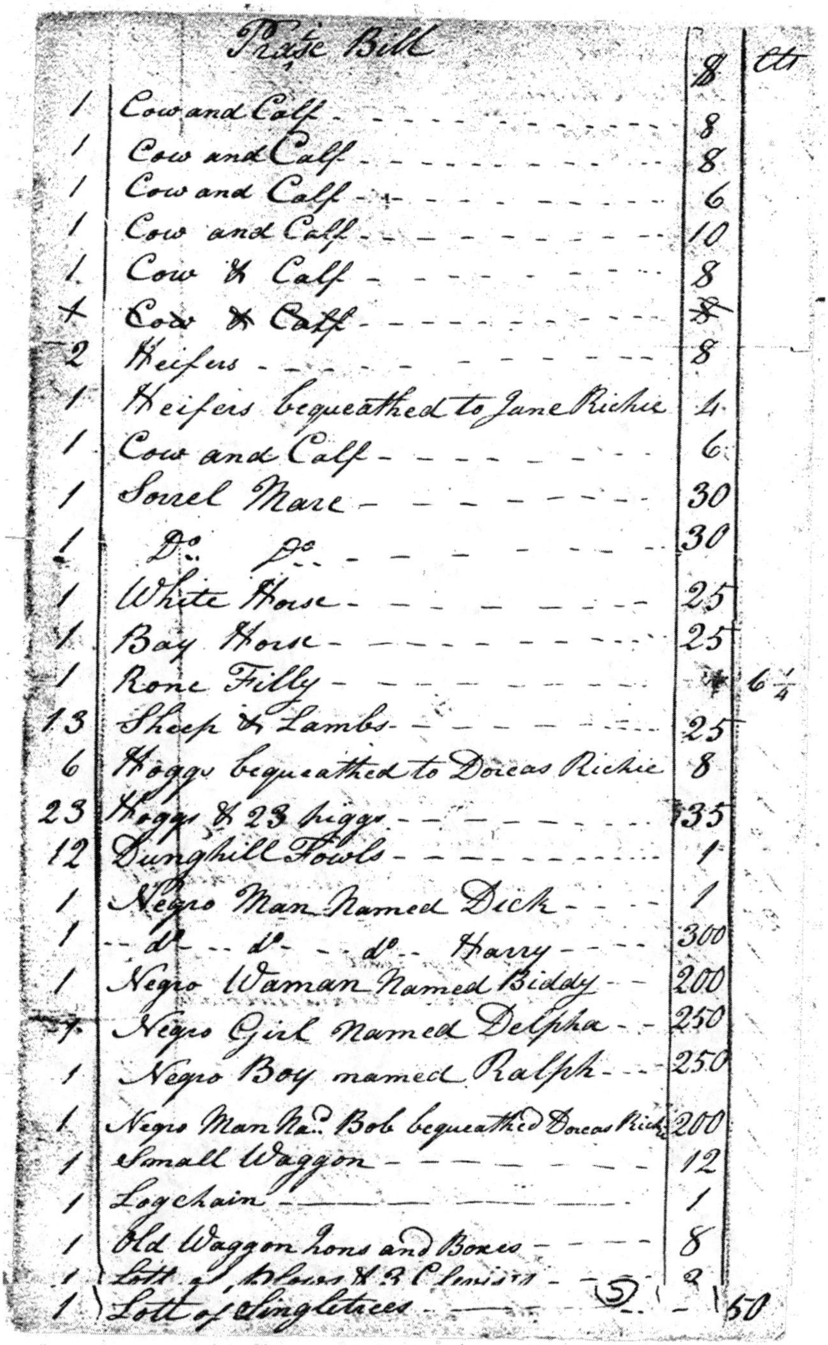

FIGURE 6-16 Estate inventory of a wealthy Southern man's estate file. (From the author's collection.)

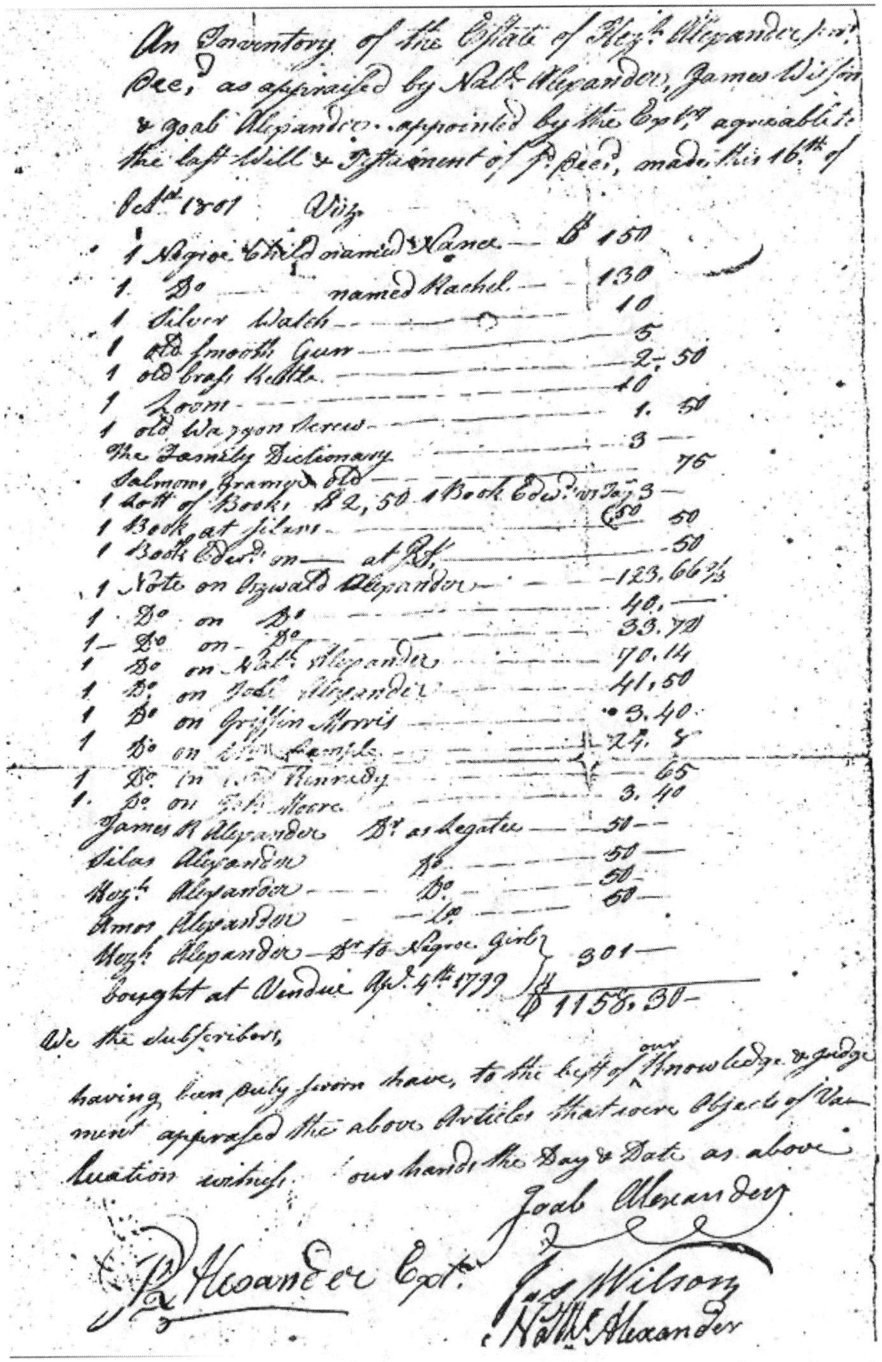

FIGURE 6-17 Estate inventory dated 1801 that includes the names of slaves. (From the author's collection.)

- **Records of an auction** Sometimes all or part of an estate was auctioned. Sometimes assets were liquidated to pay bills or to raise money for the surviving family. Auction records reveal much about estate contents and their value. It was common for relatives to participate as bidders/purchasers at an estate auction, and you may find people with the same surname (or maiden name) as the deceased. These may be parents, siblings, or cousins you will want to research.
- **Deeds, notes, bills, invoices, and receipts** There may be a variety of loose papers in the probate packet that point to other persons. Deed copies point you to land and property records and tax rolls. Names appearing on other papers may connect you to relatives, neighbors, friends, and business associates whose records may open doors for you.
- **Guardianship documents** Letters and other documents relating to the guardianship and/or custody of widows and minor children are common in probate packets. These can point you to family court documents and minutes that formally document the legal appointment of guardian(s). Figure 6-18 shows a petition for the appointment of a guardian for minor children, and Figure 6-19 shows a combination petition for and granting of guardianship from probate court records in 1911.
- **Accounting reports** Reports filed with the probate records can provide names of claimants and entities holding estate debts, including names of relatives.
- **Final disposition or distribution of the estate** A final estate distribution report is of vital importance. You may find the names and addresses of all the beneficiaries, and what they received from the estate. This will ultimately point you to the locations where you will find other records for these persons.

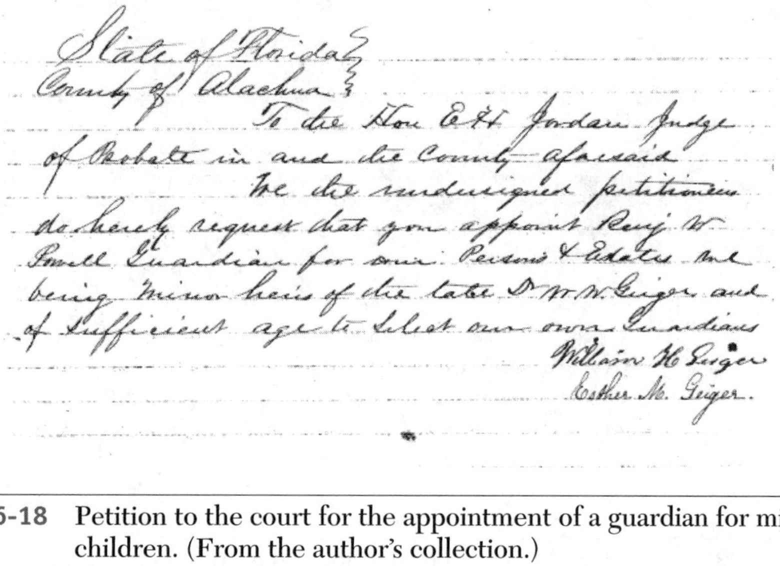
State of Florida }
County of Alachua }
To the Hon E.H. Jordan Judge of Probate in and the County aforesaid
We the undersigned petitioners do hereby request that you appoint Benj. W. Powell Guardian for our: Persons & Estates we being minor heirs of the late Dr. W. W. Geiger and of sufficient age to select our own Guardians
William H Geiger
Esther M. Geiger

FIGURE 6-18 Petition to the court for the appointment of a guardian for minor children. (From the author's collection.)

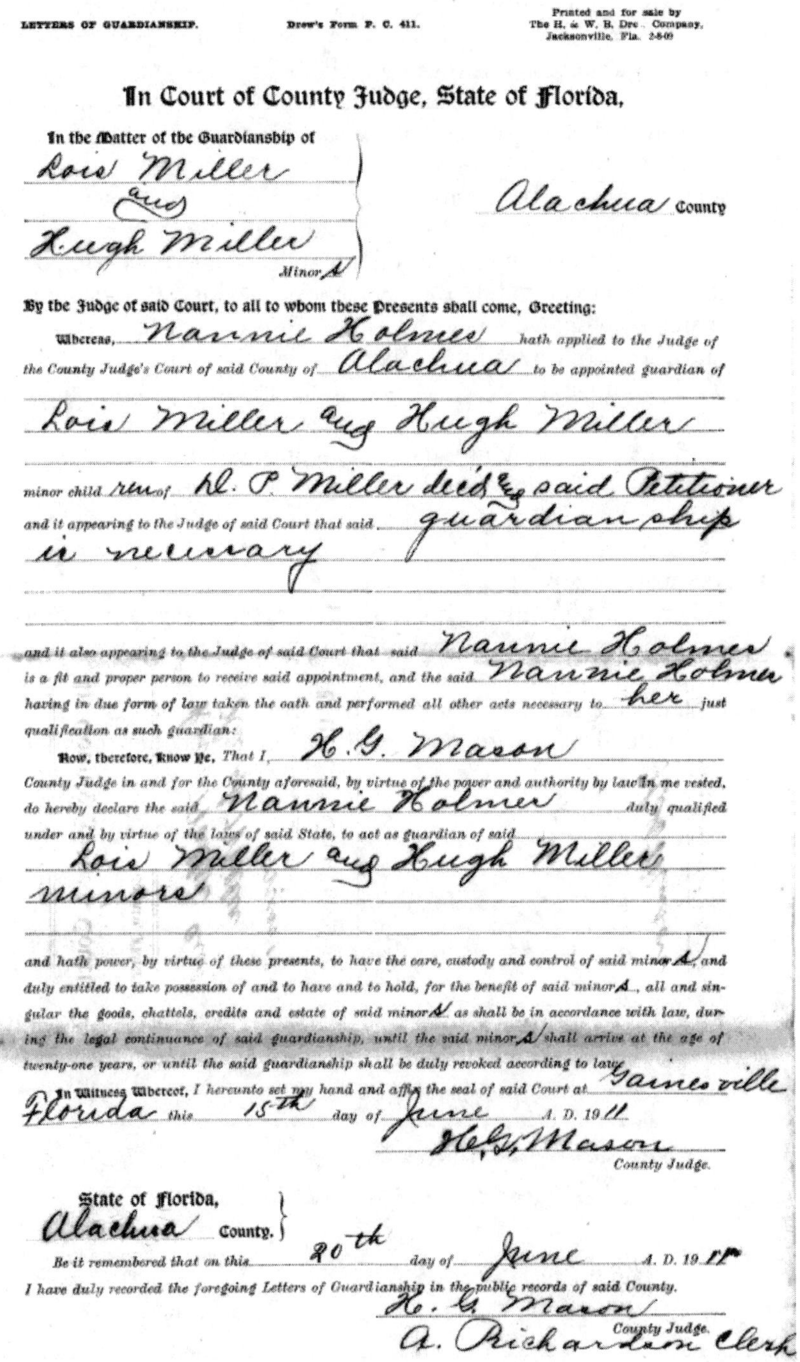
LETTERS OF GUARDIANSHIP. Drew's Form P. C. 411. Printed and for sale by The H. & W. B. Drew Company, Jacksonville, Fla. 2-8-09

In Court of County Judge, State of Florida,

In the Matter of the Guardianship of Lois Miller and Hugh Miller Minors — Alachua County

By the Judge of said Court, to all to whom these Presents shall come, Greeting:

Whereas, Nannie Holmes hath applied to the Judge of the County Judge's Court of said County of Alachua to be appointed guardian of Lois Miller and Hugh Miller minor children of H. P. Miller dec'd & said Petitioner and it appearing to the Judge of said Court that said guardianship is necessary

and it also appearing to the Judge of said Court that said Nannie Holmes is a fit and proper person to receive said appointment, and the said Nannie Holmes having in due form of law taken the oath and performed all other acts necessary to her just qualification as such guardian:

Now, therefore, Know Ye, That I, H. G. Mason County Judge in and for the County aforesaid, by virtue of the power and authority by law in me vested, do hereby declare the said Nannie Holmes duly qualified under and by virtue of the laws of said State, to act as guardian of said Lois Miller and Hugh Miller minors

and hath power, by virtue of these presents, to have the care, custody and control of said minors, and duly entitled to take possession of and to have and to hold, for the benefit of said minors, all and singular the goods, chattels, credits and estate of said minors as shall be in accordance with law, during the legal continuance of said guardianship, until the said minors shall arrive at the age of twenty-one years, or until the said guardianship shall be duly revoked according to law.

In Witness Whereof, I hereunto set my hand and affix the seal of said Court at Gainesville Florida this 15th day of June A. D. 1911.

H. G. Mason
County Judge.

State of Florida,
Alachua County.

Be it remembered that on this 20th day of June A. D. 1911
I have duly recorded the foregoing Letters of Guardianship in the public records of said County.

H. G. Mason
County Judge.
A. Richardson Clerk

FIGURE 6-19 Combination petition for and granting of guardianship for minor children. (From the author's collection.)

Watch for Clues and Pointers in the Probate Packet

You will almost always find clues and pointers in wills and probate packet documents that point to other types of records. As such, you will soon come to recognize that you must work with these documents in tandem with other documents. Let's discuss some of these clues and pointers.

A will or probate file may contain information about land and property—including personal property. These references point you to other areas of the courthouse. You may go into land records, tax rolls, court records, and other areas. If any of the assets of the estate were auctioned, check the auction records. These are generally a part of the probate packet too, and may have been entered into the court minutes. Here you may find connections to other relatives of the same surname who came to purchase items.

Guardians are appointed to protect the interests of children (as shown in Figures 6-18 and 6-19) and, in some cases, young widows. Remember that in many locations, if the father dies and leaves a widow and minor children, the children are considered to be "orphans." Most often, the guardians appointed by the court are relatives of the deceased or of the spouse. A different surname of a guardian may be a clue to the maiden name of the widow. Start looking for guardianship papers and possibly adoption papers. If you "lose" a child at the death of one or both parents, start searching census records (beginning with the U.S. federal census of 1850 and the U.K. census in 1851) for the child being in another residence, particularly in a relative's home. In the absence of relatives, the county, parish, state, or province may have committed the child to an orphanage, orphan asylum, or a poorhouse. Leave no stone unturned. Check the respective court minutes and files for the year following a parent's death for any evidence of legal actions regarding a child. You might be surprised at what you locate.

Witnesses are important. By law, they cannot inherit in a will; however, they may be relatives of the deceased. It is not uncommon to find an in-law as a witness. Bondsmen involved in the settlement of an estate are often relatives. If the wife of the testator is the executor of the estate, the bondsmen are usually *her* relatives. (If you do not know the maiden name of the wife, check the surnames of the bondsmen carefully because one of them may be her brother.)

You will almost always find an inventory of the estate in the probate packet. The executor or administrator(s) of the estate is first charged by the court to determine the assets, the debts, and the receivables of an estate in order to properly determine what needs to be done to divide or dispose of it. The inventory often paints a colorful picture of the way of life of the deceased. The type of furniture and the presence or absence of books, farm equipment, livestock, real and personal property listed all tell us what type of life and what social status the person enjoyed—or did *not* enjoy.

Obviously, there are many things to consider when reviewing wills and probate packet contents. The location, the laws in effect at the time, the religious affiliation of the testator, the size of the estate, the presence or absence of a spouse, children, brothers, sisters, and parents—these are just a few.

You Really Want to Examine Documents Yourself

There are many ways to obtain information about a will or probate packet. Since most of us cannot afford to travel to all the places where our ancestors lived, we may need to do some "mail order" business, writing or emailing for copies of courthouse records.

One of the problems with will and probate documentation published in books, magazines, periodicals, and on the Internet is that someone *else* has looked at the documents. Since these are not their ancestors, they may not have the family perspective and insight that you have. If they have transcribed the document *verbatim*, it might be correctly done but you can't be sure unless you review it yourself. Even worse, materials that have been extracted or abstracted often contain omissions of details that might be of significant importance to your research. As an example, one will listed nine children's names, some of which were double-barrel names, such as Billy Ray and Nita Beth. The insertion of extra commas in the transcription, extract, or abstract of these two children's names could easily turn these two children's names into *four* children—and wouldn't you play havoc trying to straighten that out?

Watch wills carefully for names of children. Don't make any assumptions. One of my friends researched her great-great-grandfather's family and was convinced that there were seven children in the family. That was until she studied the actual will of the great-great-grandfather. In the will, the names Elizabeth and Mary had no comma between them. This led her to suspect that there was one daughter named Elizabeth Mary, rather than two daughters. Further investigation of marriage records in the county contradicted the one-daughter theory because she found that there were individual marriage records for two daughters, one married a year after her father's death and the other two years later. Further, Elizabeth and Mary and their respective spouses settled on land that was part of their father's holdings and appeared on census records thereafter.

Locate and Obtain Copies of Wills and Probate Documents

Wills, testaments, codicils, and other probate documents can be found in a variety of places. It is important to start in the area in which the person lived and make contact with the courts that had jurisdiction at that time, if they still exist.

In England, this may be difficult for older wills that at one time were handled by different levels of ecclesiastical courts that no longer exist. From the 13th century until 1858, church courts handled all the probate process. Their jurisdictions sometimes overlapped and their administrative powers were not always clear. In addition, English wills that required the probate of an estate containing multiple pieces of land could be complicated if the parcels were in multiple church administrative districts. In those cases, a level of ecclesiastical court whose administrative level included all of the districts in which the lands were located handled the probate process. Those early ecclesiastical records were written in Latin and may present you with difficulty, both with the language used *and* the ancient handwriting style. It is important to understand the structure of the jurisdictions in the specific time period you are researching before undertaking a search for your English ancestor's will. It was not until 1858 that civil courts began handling probate and a more standard approach was imposed.

Probate documents may be encountered in many forms. The original documents may still exist and may be filed with the records of the court that handled the process. Look for court minutes and other evidence of the proceedings. Many courts and administrative offices have microfilmed their court records. Microfilm provides for compact storage of these voluminous records while preserving the originals. Microfilm also allows for the economic duplication of the records for access and use in multiple locations, and makes printing and copying simple and inexpensive.

You may also find that some original probate documents have been digitized and made available on the Internet. The Scottish Archive Network has made more than half a million Scottish wills and testaments dating from 1500 to 1901 accessible in digital format at **www.scotlandspeople.gov.uk**. Individual counties, municipalities, and courts also have digitized records. A particularly impressive effort has been accomplished in Alachua County, Florida, with the ongoing digitization of the county's Ancient Records Archives. This collection of indexed and, in some cases, transcribed documents can be seen at **www.clerk-alachua-fl.org/Archive**.

Obtain Information from the Social Security Administration and Railroad Retirement Board

The Social Security Administration was established by an act of the U.S. Congress in 1935, in the depth of the Great Depression. President Franklin D. Roosevelt's administration was hard at work trying to help the United States recover economically through a number of social and financial programs. One area that required attention was that of old-age pensions. Older Americans were at significant risk of disaster during the Depression, and previously the only old-age pensions were available from some state and local governments. Many of those pension programs were faltering or had collapsed, and Congress was under pressure from the administration and from the public to take action.

The Social Security Act of 1935 established a national program for Americans over the age of 65 to receive benefits, and set up the structure and criteria for participation of those people in the work force and their employers to contribute to their retirement security. The program would not begin for several years and credit would not be given for any service prior to 1937.

In the meantime, railroad employees clamored for a program that would provide credit for prior service *and* an unemployment compensation program. Legislation passed in 1934, 1935, and 1937 established the Railroad Retirement program for employees of the U.S. railroads. More about that later.

At the beginning, in order to determine which persons would immediately be eligible to receive unemployment benefits, the Social Security Administration (SSA) used the 1880 U.S. federal census as a reference to help verify the age of recipients.

The SSA formed a special branch called the Age Search group to handle this function. That branch still exists today to perform the same function. The Age Search group quickly determined that searching the 1880 census population schedules for a single person's enumeration listing was a highly laborious process. The SSA therefore commissioned the creation of an indexing system to assist in the search process. It was at that time that the Soundex coding system was developed for this program, and the first index was created for the 1880 census. Index cards were prepared by a group of employees of the Works Progress Administration (WPA), and these cards were only created for households in which there were children aged 10 and under. After the 1880 census was Soundexed, indexes were prepared for entire households in the 1900, 1910, 1920, and 1930 censuses. This is the same Soundex and Miracode coding scheme described in Chapter 5.

In order to pay retirement pension benefits, the SSA required that an applicant must prove his or her age eligibility. While the Soundex system was used by the Age Search group, the person applying for benefits had to a) have applied for and been assigned a Social Security number (SSN), b) prove his or her identity, and c) provide evidence of his or her age. (Persons with disabilities who could not work also later became eligible for Social Security benefits, and the requirements were the same for them.)

SSNs were assigned by offices in each state and territory, with each geographical division (state and territory) having been assigned a block of numbers. The number consists of three groups of digits: the first group of three digits represents the area in which the assignment was made; the next two digits represent a group; and the last group of four digits is a serial number, chronologically assigned. These numbers were assigned at the time that the SS-5 application form, such as the one shown in Figure 6-20, was completed to obtain the SSN. The *first* group of three represents where the applicant's

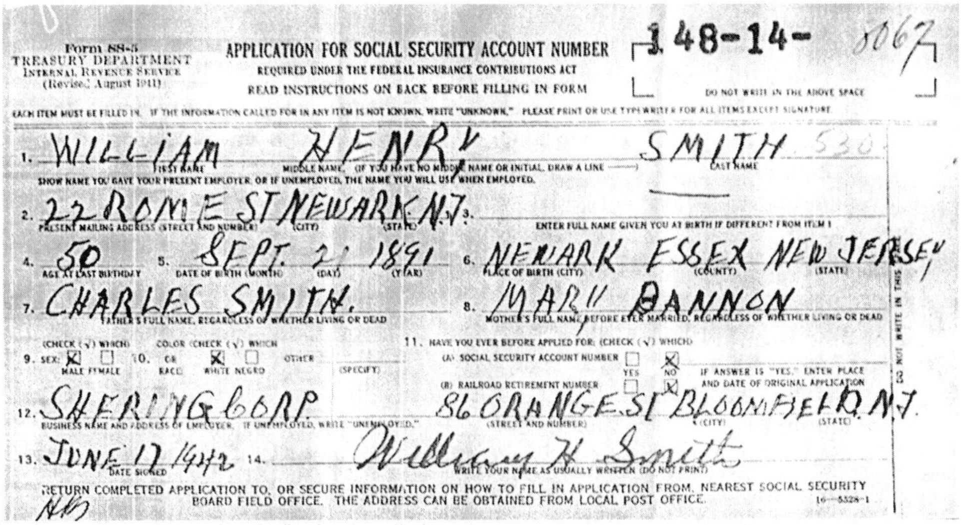

Form SS-5
TREASURY DEPARTMENT
INTERNAL REVENUE SERVICE
(Revised August 1941)

APPLICATION FOR SOCIAL SECURITY ACCOUNT NUMBER
REQUIRED UNDER THE FEDERAL INSURANCE CONTRIBUTIONS ACT
READ INSTRUCTIONS ON BACK BEFORE FILLING IN FORM

148-14-5067

DO NOT WRITE IN THE ABOVE SPACE

EACH ITEM MUST BE FILLED IN. IF THE INFORMATION CALLED FOR IN ANY ITEM IS NOT KNOWN, WRITE "UNKNOWN." PLEASE PRINT OR USE TYPEWRITER FOR ALL ITEMS EXCEPT SIGNATURE.

1. WILLIAM (FIRST NAME) HENRY (MIDDLE NAME, IF YOU HAVE NO MIDDLE NAME OR INITIAL, DRAW A LINE) SMITH (LAST NAME)
SHOW NAME YOU GAVE YOUR PRESENT EMPLOYER, OR IF UNEMPLOYED, THE NAME YOU WILL USE WHEN EMPLOYED.

2. 22 ROME ST NEWARK N.J. (PRESENT MAILING ADDRESS (STREET AND NUMBER) (CITY) (STATE))
3. ENTER FULL NAME GIVEN YOU AT BIRTH IF DIFFERENT FROM ITEM 1

4. 50 (AGE AT LAST BIRTHDAY) 5. SEPT. 21 1891 (DATE OF BIRTH (MONTH) (DAY) (YEAR)) 6. NEWARK ESSEX NEW JERSEY (PLACE OF BIRTH (CITY) (COUNTY) (STATE))

7. CHARLES SMITH. (FATHER'S FULL NAME, REGARDLESS OF WHETHER LIVING OR DEAD) 8. MARY BANNON (MOTHER'S FULL NAME BEFORE EVER MARRIED, REGARDLESS OF WHETHER LIVING OR DEAD)

9. SEX: (CHECK (✓) WHICH) MALE [X] FEMALE [ ] 10. COLOR (CHECK (✓) WHICH) WHITE [X] NEGRO [ ] OTHER RACE (SPECIFY)

11. HAVE YOU EVER BEFORE APPLIED FOR: (CHECK (✓) WHICH)
(A) SOCIAL SECURITY ACCOUNT NUMBER YES [ ] NO [X]
(B) RAILROAD RETIREMENT NUMBER YES [ ] NO [X]
IF ANSWER IS "YES," ENTER PLACE AND DATE OF ORIGINAL APPLICATION

12. SHERING CORP (BUSINESS NAME AND ADDRESS OF EMPLOYER. IF UNEMPLOYED, WRITE "UNEMPLOYED.") 86 ORANGE ST BLOOMFIELD N.J. (STREET AND NUMBER) (CITY) (STATE)

13. JUNE 17 1942 (DATE SIGNED) 14. William H. Smith (WRITE YOUR NAME AS USUALLY WRITTEN (DO NOT PRINT))

RETURN COMPLETED APPLICATION TO, OR SECURE INFORMATION ON HOW TO FILL IN APPLICATION FROM, NEAREST SOCIAL SECURITY BOARD FIELD OFFICE. THE ADDRESS CAN BE OBTAINED FROM LOCAL POST OFFICE.

16—5328-1

DO NOT WRITE IN THIS SPACE

FIGURE 6-20 A photocopy of the SS-5 application form from the Social Security Administration. (Courtesy of Drew Smith.)

SSN was assigned, and *not* necessarily where the person was born. This is an important distinction, and a source of confusion and misunderstanding among many genealogical researchers. In order for an individual to receive a SSN, an application form (known as the SS-5) was completed.

When a beneficiary dies, it is a legal requirement that the SSA be notified so that payments are immediately stopped. A benefit check for the last partial month of the person's life usually must be returned, and the SSA has a procedure for handling the final payment. The SSA does not require a copy of a death certificate or other form of written proof of death. In some cases, a simple telephone call or the return of the check with a notation that the person is deceased is sufficient for the SSA to update its database. In some cases, a surviving spouse may collect the benefits of the deceased.

The SSA's records were maintained on paper until the early 1960s. At that time, data from the SS-5 forms of all known living persons with SSNs (along with the last known address) and information from all new applicants' SS-5 forms were entered into a computer database. In addition, the SSA began maintaining benefit information by computer and entering death information as notifications of the deaths of recipients were received. Beginning in 1962, the Social Security Death Master File began to be produced electronically on a regular basis. Initially, it contained only about 17 percent of the reported deaths, but that increased to more than 92 percent in 1980. The percentage of completeness has varied up and down since then, and will never be 100 percent complete. The file has since come to be known as the Social Security Death Index, or SSDI. Genealogists with family members in the United States have used this valuable tool to locate the place of last residence or benefit payment in order to locate other records.

It is important to understand that the SSDI contains only information about deceased individuals, in compliance with both the Privacy Act, which protects individuals' information for 72 years, and the Freedom of Information Act, which makes information available to the public. There are four criteria for a person's information to be included in the SSDI:

- The person must be deceased.
- The person must have had a Social Security number assigned to him or her.
- The person must have applied for and received a Social Security benefit payment.
- The person's death must have been reported to the Social Security Administration.

If a person was assigned a SSN and is deceased, but never received a benefit of any sort, he or she will not be found in the SSDI. For these persons, and for those persons who died prior to the computerization of the SSA records, you can still obtain a copy of their SS-5 application form from the SSA. All you need to do is write the SSA Freedom of Information Officer, provide the full name, address, and birth date of the individual, and request the SS-5. If you can provide the person's SSN, the cost of obtaining an SS-5 at this writing is $27; without the SSN, the cost is $29. In addition, you can request a copy of a printout from the SSDI database known as a Numident. The Numident is nothing more than the data entered into the SSA database. The price of this document is $16 but is only available when you can provide the person's SSN. Requests for SS-5 forms and Numident printouts should be directed to:

Social Security Administration
Office of Earnings Operations
FOIA Workgroup
300 N. Greene Street
P.O. Box 33022
Baltimore, Maryland 21290-3022

Your request to the SSA for a copy of the application (SS-5) for a person who never received a benefit and for whom the SSA wasn't notified of the death may be denied. However, if you can supply evidence of the person's death, such as a copy of a death certificate, you can appeal the decision and, in fact, then receive the copy of their SS-5 form.

The SSDI is available online at a number of websites, including Ancestry.com (**www.ancestry.com**) and RootsWeb.com (**http://ssdi.rootsweb.ancestry.com**), and these sites also provide the ability to automatically produce a request letter for you. You may also submit your request electronically at **www.ssa.gov/foia/html/foia_guide.htm#Requests**.

The U.S. Railroad Retirement Board (RRB) is the administrative body for the railroad workers' retirement pension benefits system. The Railroad Retirement program is similar to Social Security but is administered by the RRB in Chicago, Illinois. Up until 1963, persons who worked for a railroad in the United States at the time they applied for a SSN were assigned a number between 700 and 728. Therefore, if you locate any document that lists a SSN whose first three digits are in that numbering range, you will know that the person worked for the railroad industry at the time he or she was assigned the number. You also will know to check first with the RRB for records.

A person who worked exclusively in the railroad industry will apply for and receive old-age pension benefits from Railroad Retirement. An individual who worked for both the railroad industry and elsewhere would have contributed to both a Railroad Retirement pension account and to Social Security during his or her working career. At the time of retirement, the person had to apply for a retirement pension benefit from either one or the other, but not both plans.

The RRB records you obtain may be more detailed, including earnings reports, copies of designation of beneficiary forms, and perhaps more. The address to which you would send your request, along with a check for $27 made payable to the Railroad Retirement Board, is

Office of Public Affairs
Railroad Retirement Board
844 North Rush Street
Chicago, Illinois 60611-2092

For more information about the RRB, visit their website at **www.rrb.gov** and specifically their genealogy web page at **http://rrb.gov/mep/genealogy.asp**.

Consider Other Institutional Record Types

You can see now how the investigative work you are doing and the scholarly methodologies you are using can begin to pay big dividends. In many of the examples I've shown in this chapter, I have tried to convey the ways that one record may provide clues and pointers to others.

As you encounter new sources of information, use your critical thinking skills to read between the lines. Consider the other institutional records that might add to your knowledge. These could include records from employers, unions, schools, professional organizations, civic and social club memberships, and veterans groups, just to name a few. Just as with cemetery offices, you never know what information might be in these organizations' files.

7

Use the Many Types of Military Service Records

HOW TO...

- Expand your knowledge of the military services
- Identify possible sources for military records
- Find facts in registration, conscription, and enlistment records
- Learn from military pension records
- Discover other military records

In the previous chapters you have learned the importance of building a firm foundation on your ancestors' and family members' records of many types. We discussed census records in Chapter 5, and you saw that there are cases in which a census document may have included information about someone's military service record. The U.S. federal census of 1840 was the first to call for the name and age of American Revolutionary War veterans, and the 1890 census included a separate census schedule specifically for Civil War veterans and their widows. In Great Britain, the 1851 census included those persons living on vessels in inland waters or at sea, including members of the Royal Navy and the Merchant Navy. In addition, persons serving abroad with the armed forces and those working with the East India Company were enumerated. As you can see, census materials may provide information about an ancestor that can spur you to search for military records. Even if you are unsure whether or not your ancestor or a family member served in the armed forces of a particular country, it is wise to invest some amount of time researching the official rosters and/or indexes to see if a familiar name appears there. You would be surprised how often people make the discovery of a military ancestor when they didn't know or think there was one. Registration and enlistment records can help link a person to other relatives, and they may provide a physical description of the individual. Military service and pension records also can provide more detailed insight into a person's life than you could imagine. There is sometimes a link between military service and other records. For example, the U.S. federal government compensated some military personnel with land rather than or in addition to paying them cash. These "bounty lands" were granted to persons in reward for their military service or for rendering goods and services to the government and/or troops. We'll discuss bounty land in more detail in Chapter 8.

Other sources you may encounter may refer or point to military records. Some examples of these are obituaries, wills and probate records, tombstones, naturalization records, and other resources. I often find references to a person's military service in death-related records, and military documents have often been used as a form of identification and/or to apply for some benefit such as a voter's registration, naturalization without having to file a Declaration of Intent document, educational benefit (such as the G.I. Bill), a housing subsidy, low-interest loans, retirement pension, medical assistance, and death benefit for the surviving spouse and family.

Military records in the British Isles, as you will see, have become more accessible in the past several years. Many of these are available on microfilm at The National Archives at Kew. These can contain exceptionally detailed history for an individual. Military medals cards from World War I have been digitized and are accessible for a small fee through DocumentsOnline at The National Archives (**www.nationalarchives.gov.uk/documentsonline**).

Many genealogists fail to follow through with a search for military service records and pension files. The reason for these omissions or oversights can generally be attributed to a lack of understanding of the history of the area where their ancestors and family members lived, the military history of which might have played a very significant role in their lives. However, another contributing factor is that military records are not always located together. Sometimes the military service records are in one archive, the pension files are in another, and perhaps other pertinent records are in the possession of another governmental office. This can be confusing if you haven't taken the time to determine what records were created at a particular time, what part of the government or military used them, what they were used for, and what was done with those records when they were no longer needed. Context is important!

With all of this in mind, let's set out to become experts in the research of military records. I think you will find that these are fascinating types of records, and that they provide insights into history you never imagined.

Expand Your Knowledge of the Military Services

Military service is a job and, as such, can produce a vast amount of written documentation. Census records provide information at ten-year intervals, which is a huge span of time between milestones. Military records, on the other hand, provide a more regular form of documentation, at shorter intervals, than a census. From the date of registration, conscription, or enlistment, there will have been official military records maintained. These may include the following record types:

Draft registration cards	Draft notices
Enlistment forms and related documentation	Medical records
Quartermaster or provisions records	Educational testing and training reports/diplomas
Duty assignments	Muster rolls
Payroll records and pay stubs	Announcements/postings of promotions
Records of the awarding of medals and awards, such as the medal shown in Figure 7-1	Casualty reports
Service files or dossiers	Discharge papers
Records of courts martial	Pension applications
Pension files containing affidavits, correspondence, payment records, and other documents	Pension payment vouchers
Veterans records	Veteran's life insurance certificate
Benefits records	Death and burial records

That is an impressive list. It is important to note that not every country generated or maintained this broad a range of documents, and that fewer types of records were created the farther back in history you research. Specific personnel units, too, may have required the use of additional or unique records. Still, the sheer volume of military documentation of a soldier's daily, monthly, or annual affairs can present you with a detailed insight into his or her life at that time. Remember, too, that military assignments take a person to many locations and expose him or her to a wide range of experiences. That exposure may influence the decisions made later in life to select a particular profession, to relocate to another area, or to take some other course of action.

In addition to the official file contents listed above, you may find items among materials in the home that can further your research, such as uniforms, dog tags, insignia, patches, badges, medals, ribbons, certificates and awards, correspondence, and photographs. Each of these can provide clues and pointers to other military records.

Investigate Military History for the Appropriate Time Period

Every time I visit a library or a bookstore, I am impressed by the number of books and periodicals available on the subject of military history. There are books available about armies, navies, and every conceivable military branch. Innumerable historical accounts and analyses of military units, engagements, and strategies from the present and extending back to ancient times have been published in books, magazines,

FIGURE 7-1 The Congressional Medal of Honor is the United States' highest military award.

journals, and other media. There are specialty book and magazine titles that discuss the uses of horses, wagons, tanks, jeeps, ships, airplanes, helicopters, land-sea transports, landing vehicles, and other transportation modes in warfare. Every manner of weapon you can imagine is documented in intricate detail, from swords, scimitars, cutlasses, spears, lances, maces, sabers, knives, and bayonets to pistols, rifles, cannon, mortars, bombs, bazookas, flamethrowers, missiles, fighter aircraft, computer-assisted weapons, and other types of armaments.

You already know the importance of placing your ancestors and family members into geographical, historical, and social context. This is also emphatically true when it comes to researching the history of someone who may have performed some military service. You will benefit from the study of the history of the country in which your ancestor lived and particularly about the military establishment there at the time, military service requirements, and the military conflicts in which the country was engaged. This information can help you better understand what records you might expect to find. In a time of war, you could expect to find that a government would impose conscription or impressments to force enrollment of personnel in the military service. In the United States in 1917 and 1918, a series of draft calls were made by the U.S. federal government to quickly build the armed forces for involvement in "The Great War" in Europe. Men in certain age ranges, such as 19-year-old Charles Ray Morrison shown in Figure 7-2, were required to present themselves at the office of their local draft board to complete a draft registration card. Knowing that every male between certain ages was required to complete a card will prompt you to attempt to obtain a copy of the record for your research. Likewise, if you had a male ancestor living in Prussia in 1816, it is important to know that compulsory military service had been imposed, even in peacetime. You might therefore want to investigate the existence of military service records that documented his date and place of birth and other details that might be included about him.

FIGURE 7-2   Charles Ray Morrison, born in 1899, was enrolled in the United States' Third Draft Registration on 12 September 1918. (From the author's collection.)

Sometimes you will find that individual records may no longer exist, in which case you will need to seek out alternate sources of information. State, county, parish, and local histories can be beneficial in that regard because they frequently include sections about military units that originated from the area and rosters of the people who served in them. Even if your ancestor or other family member is not listed by name, identifying the military unit(s) from that area can be an important clue to lead you to other materials.

Biographies of legendary military leaders, such as Vice Admiral Lord Viscount Horatio Nelson, George Washington, General Robert E. Lee, General George S. Patton, and others, provide minute details of their lives and military leadership. Military unit histories, analyses of battles and strategies, diaries, and memoirs are abundant. Following the U.S. Civil War and throughout the remaining decades of the 19th century, former officers and veterans penned exhaustive memoirs and historical accounts of their experiences. These narratives often contain complete rosters of the people serving with them and anecdotal materials about them. In some cases, these accounts may contain the only surviving details about the fates of individual soldiers lost in battle or to disease.

Historians also have chronicled military units' histories and their engagements, compiling official records and personal accounts to re-create a chronological account of events. Military-related heritage societies also organized to honor the veterans, their families, and their descendants, and to perpetuate the history of their service. Organizations such as the Daughters of the American Revolution, the Sons of the American Revolution, the United Daughters of the Confederacy, and the Sons of Confederate Veterans foster education, caretaking activities for historical materials, maintenance of cemeteries, and publication of information relating to their respective group. The Home Service Military Service Society (Northern Ireland) "was formed to preserve the heritage of The Ulster Defence Regiment and the Royal Irish Regiment Home Service Battalions and to maintain and promote an awareness of the contribution and sacrifice of our servicemen and servicewomen in pursuit of peace in Northern Ireland." There are other organizations whose members may or may not be descendants of veterans of specific military personnel but who are interested in preserving information and materials and encouraging the study of a specific area or period. Examples of these groups would include The English Civil War Society (**http://english-civil-war-society.org**), the Military Historical Society of Australia (**www.mhsa.org.au**), the Scottish Military Historical Website (**www.btinternet .com/~james.mckay/dispatch.htm**), and the United Empire Loyalists' Association of Canada (**www.uelac.org**).

In addition, there are many magazines with military and historical themes, among them *World War II, Military History, Civil War Times, America's Civil War, History Magazine, Naval History, The Beaver: Canada's History Magazine, Canadian Journal of History, BBC History Magazine*, and *Living History* (United Kingdom). You may want to purchase a copy of a magazine at the newsstand to determine if it contains information of interest or help to you. You can then subscribe to one or more publications that will contribute to your growing knowledge of the subject. These publications can help contribute to placing your military ancestors into context with their time and branches of the armed forces. You can expect to locate vast amounts of military unit information both in book and magazine form, and also on the Internet. Whenever you begin to research an ancestor who was or may have been in the military service, do some preliminary investigative work into the history of the area and time period, and into the records that may have been created for the military command and the personnel. Once you know what was created, you can then begin tracking down the locations where those materials may be stored and the procedures for accessing them.

Identify Possible Sources for Military Records

Military records are government documents. You will find that for a particular country or government, military records may well be distributed across a number of document depositories. This is a primary reason why it is important to study history. In the United States, military records are held by both the National Archives and Records Administration (**www.archives.gov**) and its National Personnel Records Center (**www.archives.gov/st-louis**) in St. Louis, Missouri. In Canada, most of the military service records are held by Library and Archives Canada (**www.collectionscanada. gc.ca/genealogy/022-909-e.html**). In the United Kingdom, a significant collection of military records, including service and pension records, is held by The National Archives (**www.nationalarchives.gov.uk**). Other military records, however, may still be in the possession of the Ministry of Defence. The National Archives of Australia holds army, navy, and air force records (**www.naa.gov.au/collection/explore/ defence/services.aspx**). Please note that, if your ancestor served in the military forces in other than his or her native country, the records for that service will be in the other country's possession. Let's examine each of these governments' records in detail.

Many indexes, transcripts, and abstracts of military records have been prepared. These include summary personnel records, muster rolls, casualty lists, medical reports, and many other types of records. These can point you in the direction of original, primary source documents, a copy of which you will want to obtain for your own review.

Locate Military Records in the United States

The United States, as a comparatively young nation, has a considerable military history, and a vast collection of military records from colonial times still exists. You will find that the earlier the era, however, the less complete the military records will be. Documents may have been lost or destroyed, or they may simply have deteriorated before they were gathered together for archiving and preservation.

Learn About Early Records

The earliest recorded military conflicts are perhaps those that occurred at Jamestown in the colony of Virginia. The Native American attack on the settlement in March of 1622 killed more than 300 settlers and almost destroyed it. The English retaliated and, over the next 22 years, almost decimated the Native Americans in the area. Documents in the form of correspondence and historical accounts do exist from these years, both among the documents in the United Kingdom and in the United States at the Library of Virginia.

Other conflicts between the English and French colonies (in territory that is now split between the United States and Canada) and against the Native Americans are numerous. However, no appreciable military documents exist *per se*. Rather, correspondence and anecdotal accounts form what historical materials exist, and these are in the hands of various archives in the United Kingdom, Canada, the United States, and some of the states' and provinces' libraries or archives.

Military forces serving in what is now the United States during the colonial era consisted primarily of European military personnel from the countries controlling specific respective areas. The Spanish governed Florida on multiple occasions, California, and some southern areas. The English governed the eastern colonies and Florida for a time. The French governed the Louisiana Territory. In addition, Mexico governed what now are the states of Texas, New Mexico, Arizona, and part of California. And the Russian Empire owned Alaska until it was sold to the United States on 30 March 1867.

Research Your Ancestors in the American Revolutionary War

American colonists supplemented the British troops with local military units and militia. It was not until the mid-1700s that the 13 original colonies began to actively oppose British governance. The American Revolutionary War (1775–1783) was the first really organized armed conflict by the Americans themselves, and there are unique military-related documents that were generated as a result of the clashes that occurred. There are four major sources for discovering who actually served during that war:

- Lists of veterans compiled by each state early in the 19th century.
- Pension applications filed by veterans or their surviving spouses and family members, found at the federal and/or state levels.
- The 1840 U.S. federal population schedule, which asked for the names and ages of pensioners of the American Revolutionary War and other military services.
- Records of applicants to the Daughters of the American Revolution (DAR). These may include detailed documentation, both official papers and personal materials, of the military record of members' ancestors.
- The Library of the National Society of the Sons of the American Revolution (NSSAR) holds more than 58,000 items of genealogical interest.

However, these are not the only resources you might expect to find. Let's look at one excellent example. Let's say that you are looking for an ancestor's records relating to his military service during the period of 1775 to 1783 in what is now the United States. You will be seeking records relating to the American Revolutionary War, and you will be looking in a number of places. It is important to know first of all the state from which he served. For our example, let's choose North Carolina.

You next need to know or investigate whether your ancestor served in the local regulators, the state militia, or the Continental Army (or a combination of the three). You therefore are going to be dealing with records originally created at the local/county, state, and/or national level. This makes a great deal of difference in how you approach locating any surviving records.

If your ancestor served with the local regulators, he was probably assigned to policing and protecting the area in which he lived. If he served in North Carolina's state militia, the records relating to his military service *and* his military pension, if any, would have been created and maintained at the state level. Records of regulators and state militia are most likely to be found in the North Carolina State Archives, the state library, or state with the state historical society. That is assuming, of course, that he enlisted in the state in which he lived.

If your ancestor served in the Continental Army, his military service and pension records, if any, would have been generated at a higher level and would be among the records maintained at the national level today. Records for the Continental Army would be found among the records at the National Archives and Records Administration (NARA).

Your ancestor may have served in one or more military units at all three levels, in which case your research might reveal records in multiple places. Your ancestor may have begun service in the local regulators, for example, and then enlisted in the state militia or the Continental Army. Similarly, he may have served his term in the state militia and then may have enlisted in the Continental Army. His unit, too, may have been sent by the state to be attached to the Continental Army. Your study of military units' history for that state's soldiers would help you understand where to seek existing records. You may find, as I did, that your ancestor collected a federal Revolutionary War pension and, upon its termination, applied for and was granted a state military pension for his service on behalf of the state in the Revolutionary War. What's more, all of these documents will be unique, created at different times by different government, military, or judicial officials, and therefore will contain different documents and potentially more information about your ancestor's service.

Find Later Military Records

Military records of different eras also may be located in different places. Military service records in the United States are located at NARA for the period from 1775 to 1916. The United States' World War I draft registration cards were created during three calls for registration in 1917 and 1918, as shown in Table 7-1. These draft registration cards are in the possession of NARA at its Southeast Region Branch in Morrow, Georgia. They have also been digitized and indexed by Ancestry.com. Understanding the history of the World War I draft registration process helped me determine that Charles Ray Morrison, shown previously in Figure 7-2, who was born in Munford, Talladega County, Alabama, on 27 March 1899, was not required to register until the Third Registration Day on 12 September 1918. I was able to locate his registration card and obtain additional personal details about him from that record. This is one example of how understanding the historical background of the period for a specific area can help you to locate records that can further your research.

TABLE 7-1 United States World War I Draft Registration Calls and Age Ranges of Eligible Registrants. (Used with permission of Aha! Seminars, Inc.)

Registration Call & Date	Ages at that Time	Persons Born Between These Dates
First Registration Day 5 June 1917	All males between the ages of 21 to 31	5 June 1886 and 5 June 1896
Second Registration Day 5 June 1918	Males who reached the age of 21 since 5 June 1917	6 June 1896 and 5 June 1897
Supplemental Second Registration Day 24 August 1918	Males who reached the age of 21 since 5 June 1918	6 June 1897 and 24 August 1897
Third Registration Day 12 September 1918	All males aged 18 to 20 and 31 to 45 who had not previously registered	12 September 1872 and 12 September 1900

You can request copies of the military service records held by NARA by completing NATF Form 86. You may request copies of military pension file records by completing NATF Form 85, or by submitting a request via the Internet. However, you will want to use NARA's eVetRecs site at **www.archives.gov/veterans/evetrecs** to create a customized order form to request copies of military service records. NARA has produced tens of thousands of rolls of microfilmed military records. Their *Military Service Records: A Select Catalog of National Archives Microfilm Publications* is available in printed form but is also available in its entirety online. Visit their Publications web page at **www.archives.gov/publications/microfilm-catalogs.html**. These microfilmed records are accessible at their facilities, a complete listing of which can be found at **www.archives.gov/locations**. (Be sure to check this site and contact the branch in advance to verify their microfilm holdings, because not all branches maintain a complete collection of all microfilm materials.) In addition, contact or visit your nearest LDS Family History Center (FHC) to determine if they can obtain the microfilm from the Family History Library (FHL) in Salt Lake City, Utah, for your research use.

United States military service records for circa 1917 to present are maintained by the National Personnel Records Center (NPRC) at 9700 Page Avenue, St. Louis, Missouri, 63132. Unfortunately, a fire on 12 July 1973 at the facility destroyed an estimated 16–18 million military personnel files. Approximately 80 percent of the U.S. Army personnel records for persons discharged between 1 November 1912 and 1 January 1960 were destroyed. An estimated 75 percent of U.S. Air Force personnel records were lost for persons discharged between 25 September 1947 and 1 January 1964. There were no duplicates or microfilm records of these records. Some of these records in files were damaged but not destroyed, and these have been refiled. The NPRC, on receipt of a veteran's or surviving family member's request, will attempt to reconstruct a destroyed service record for an individual using other sources when possible.

As you can see, there was some overlap between the military records held by NARA and by the NPRC. Again, by doing some research in advance of making requests for documents, you may avoid the expense and disappointment of coming up empty-handed because you requested material from the wrong place.

You can obtain copies of surviving military personnel records from 1917 and later if you are the veteran or the next-of-kin either by completing Standard Form 180 and submitting it to the St. Louis address, or by completing an online request document at the eVetRecs website at **www.archives.gov/research**, printing it, signing it, and mailing or faxing the form within 20 days. If you are not a next-of-kin relative, you can still complete and submit the Standard Form 180. However, your request may be denied or you may be provided with a limited amount of information.

This all might be confusing if you don't take the time to understand the historical background of the period in which your ancestor lived, the military service requirements at the time, the years and military conflicts in which he or she might have been serving, the branch of the military, the types of records created, and where they might be stored. For U.S. military records, the best book currently available is James C. Neagles' *U.S. Military Records: A Guide to Federal and State Sources—Colonial America to Present*. Published by Ancestry, Incorporated, in 1994, this book provides excellent descriptions of the records created and where they are located. There are no Internet addresses in the book and, since its publication, some government departments have been renamed and their addresses and telephone numbers may have changed. However, you can use your Internet search skills to locate current governmental contact information.

Locate Canadian Military Records

Canada is a fascinating combination of French, British, and aboriginal cultures and a study of strength and courage of individuals carving life out of a rich but often harsh wilderness. It is interesting to read and learn about military conflicts between all of these groups, plus the clashes with the Americans to the south. In addition, Canadians have participated in both world wars and in other military conflicts around the world. If you are researching your Canadian ancestors, written histories may provide information to the portrait of those individuals and their families.

Early Records

Library and Archives Canada (LAC) (**www.collectionscanada.gc.ca**) is the primary source for the majority of the military records that exist, and has done an excellent job of indexing materials for ease of location. You can access these materials by visiting the main web page and clicking the link for the Canadian Genealogy Centre. Select the Military topic in the list in the middle of the page, and then choose the subtopic for the military records about which you would like to learn more.

The earliest military materials in colonial materials relate to records of the French Regime, records concerning British regiments that were stationed in Canada, and a variety of United Empire Loyalists resources from the time of the American Revolutionary War (1775–1783). The latter group also includes some petitions to the

Crown as reward for their loyalty and service. Some collections are broken up into two sections, Upper Canada and Lower Canada.

Unfortunately, however, few military records of any genealogical value exist for the period prior to World War I, with the exception of records for the South African (or "Boer") War, which lasted from 1899 until 1902. Earlier records consist of little more than muster rolls and pay lists, and these contain very little information other than the name of the soldier. Most of these records also have not been indexed, which means that you will need to know the regimental unit in which your ancestor may have served.

LAC's collection of British military and naval records includes materials with references to the British army units in Canada, Loyalist regiments during the period of the American Revolutionary War, the War of 1812, Canadian militia records, and some other materials. The index to this collection and the collection itself may be available through inter-institutional loan. The index includes a short description of the document, the date, the volume number in the collection, and the page number.

The military service personnel records for soldiers who served in the South African War are in the possession of LAC. They have been organized in alphabetical order and have been microfilmed.

Records from World War I

LAC holds an extensive collection of records relating to World War I, accessible from the main page at **www.collectionscanada.gc.ca** by clicking the link for the Canadian Genealogy Centre. It is an excellent research tool to locate the information held there concerning such topics as the 600,000 Canadians who enlisted in the Canadian Expeditionary Forces (CEF) during World War I and to access the CEF's units' War Diaries from that period. The database of Soldiers of the First World War (1914–1918) is searchable by name, and results for an individual provide the regimental number and the specific location in LAC for the person's original service records. A link takes you to a web page with information about ordering copies of documents. In some cases, images of documents are accessible through the website.

Each CEF unit was required to maintain a daily account of its field activities from the beginning of World War I. These accounts were known as "War Diaries" and are actually detailed unit histories. They include reports, maps, copies of orders, casualty listings, and other documents. Many of the War Diaries have been digitized and placed online, and are searchable by unit name and date. When you locate one that you wish to view, enter the collection and you will find the contents' images listed in chronological sequence by date and page. Click the link, and the document, or facing pages, will be displayed. Some images will be displayed at full size. Others may be resized using your browser to fit in its display window. If your browser has resized the image and it can be enlarged, there is a simple way to zoom in for easier reading. To zoom in on the image, move your mouse cursor to the lower-right corner of the image and pause. If it can be enlarged, a small orange box with blue arrows pointing outward from the four corners will pop up. Click that box and the image will be expanded to full size. While the contents of these War Diaries have not been indexed to make them searchable by keyword or phrase, you will find that the details of your ancestor's or family member's unit's activities will provide a clear picture of day-to-day life.

You might also want to visit the Veterans Affairs Canada (VAC) website at **www .vac-acc.gc.ca** for some of the best historical material about Canada's recent military past. Visit its Canada Remembers area where you can search the Canadian Virtual War Memorial, a registry of more than 116,000 names of Canadians and Newfoundlanders with information about their graves and memorials. The site provides access to a searchable database of personnel information, which includes the soldier's name, date of death, service number, branch, regiment, and unit. The cemetery name, location, directions to it, and the precise burial location are included. Another website you will want to visit is the Commonwealth War Graves Commission at **www.cwgc.org**. Here, too, you can search by name for an individual. At this site, which represents war memorials for the entire British Commonwealth, there is even more information, including rank and nationality, as well as a link to provide details about the cemetery of interment.

The VAC also maintains the Canadian Merchant Navy War Dead Database at **www.vac-acc.gc.ca/remembers/sub.cfm?source = history/secondwar/atlantic/ merchant_search**. This database can be used to search for the names of sailors killed while serving in Canada's Merchant Marines. It can also be used to search for the names of Canadian Merchant Navy vessels. You can enter the name of one of the Canadian Merchant Navy war dead, the vessel they served on, or both.

Some but by no means all of the Canadian military records are available on microfilm through the LDS Family History Centers. Microfilmed records are available for research at the LAC or through inter-institutional loan arrangements.

Military Records After 1918

LAC holds personnel records for more than 5.5 million former military personnel of the Canadian Armed Forces and civilian employees of the Federal Public Service. You can request copies of records from LAC in writing, using their Application for Military Service Information form, an Access to Information Request Form, or by letter. All requests are subject to the conditions of Canada's Access to Information Act and the Privacy Act.

Other military records not held by LAC are referenced by links to other websites.

Locate Military Records in the United Kingdom

Military records are of great interest in the United Kingdom because they are inextricably linked with documenting the history of the British Isles going back as far as William the Conqueror. You will find during your research that literally hundreds of books have been written about military conflicts that have involved the British Isles and their residents. The authors have used manuscripts and historical accounts of the military units and individuals, and have worked with the wealth of records that have been preserved. The Naval & Military Press, for example, is one of the largest independent booksellers in Britain, and their focus is on specialized titles concerning military conflicts. You can visit their website at **www.naval-military-press.com** to view or search for specific titles and subjects.

Understand the Historical Background

It is important with any research in the British Isles to spend time understanding the historical background of the time period and the geographical area in which your ancestors lived. This is especially true when seeking military records, because understanding the military structure at that time can help you determine what might be available and where any existing records may be located.

The English Civil War (1642–1649) is an important milestone in your military research. Prior to that period, there were no standing armies in England and Wales. Armed forces were raised as needed to fight in specific wars or special circumstances. Parliament raised the New Model Army, an organization of professional soldiers, in February of 1645 in order to more effectively fight the forces of King Charles I. This was the first real army in England. The Union of 1707 brought England and Scotland together, and Scottish regiments became part of the English armed forces after that period.

A significant number of army documents exist from about 1660, and some fragmentary military records from slightly earlier can also be found. However, it is not until you begin researching military units dating from the early 1700s that you will find that large numbers of military documents have survived and have been preserved. Still, the records from these periods are records of organizations and not documents about specific individuals.

King Henry VIII's reign (1509–1547) saw the formation of the first permanent British navy. A few naval records exist from approximately 1617. The majority of the surviving records, however, date from about 1660, the same era as those of the army.

Soldiers were organized into specific units that were known by various designations depending on the function of the organization. It helps to know that infantry troops were organized into regiments, and that subdivisions of these regiments were battalions and companies. Cavalry regiments were subdivided into squadrons, while the artillery units were subdivided into batteries. The subdivision distinctions were typically named in earlier times after their commanding officers, and it was not until the 1700s that numeric designations and a description were used to distinguish one from another. That does not mean that commanders' names were no longer used in references to the units, because you still might encounter a reference to a numeric designation along with a reference to a specific commander's group. Don't be surprised to find multiple commanders' names associated with a specific group, as there were changes in leadership over time. It is therefore wise to focus on *both* a commander's name *and* a specific unit number and description. Other designations you will find for military units on active duty include armies, corps, divisions, brigades, and others. If your ancestor was an officer, there may be specific records concerning his service and command. However, if he was not an officer, it may be more difficult to locate specific records for him unless you know the unit in which he served, especially in the military records prior to the 20th century, which may not have been well organized and indexed.

If all of this seems confusing to you, don't feel that you are alone. The designations and names that were used have changed over time, and this just serves to illustrate the importance of learning more about your ancestor's origins and the military history of the era *and unit* in which he or she may have served. This can be especially important if your ancestor did not serve in the government's army but instead served in a volunteer militia.

Locate the Repositories Where Records Are Held

The National Archives (TNA) in Kew, Richmond, Surrey, is the best starting point for your military research. TNA was formed in April 2003 from the Public Record Office (formerly known as the PRO) and the Historical Manuscripts Commission (HMC). Movement of the holdings of the HMC to Kew was completed in the autumn of 2003, and everything is now housed and accessible at one location. When you are reading reference materials that refer to the PRO or the HMC, remember that these now refer to the holdings of The National Archives, whose website is at **www.nationalarchives .gov.uk**.

Military documents at TNA have been organized, stored, and cataloged in groups for ease of access, and a majority of these records have been microfilmed. Therefore, TNA's holdings form a huge body of reference material that can help you learn more about and more successfully locate military documents for your ancestor. In addition, you will find that specific governmental and civilian organizations can provide information and reference assistance.

Army Records   Army records prior to 1914 are held at TNA. Officers' records from 1914–1920 have been transferred from the Army Records Centre (ARC) to TNA, but those from 1920 and later remain at the ARC. All records of enlisted personnel from 1914 and later remain at the ARC.

You will want to visit the Army Museums Ogilby Trust website's "Ancestor Research" pages at **www.armymuseums.org.uk/ancestor.htm** to determine what is in their holdings and what may have been transferred to TNA, especially as this situation changes over time. You also will want to visit their Useful Addresses page at **www.armymuseums.org.uk/addr.htm** for postal, email, and website addresses that may supplement your research.

Navy Records   Naval records can be a bit more problematic to locate. Royal Navy records prior to 1914 are held at TNA, while the Ministry of Defence in Whitehall, London, retains the post-1914 records. The location of records, however, is subject to change periodically. Some good references for the location and accessibility of naval records are found at the website of the Mariners Mailing List at **www.mariners-l.co .uk/UKRNPersonnel.html** and **www.mariners-l.co.uk/UK20thCSeamen.html**. In addition, be sure to check the United Kingdom Maritime Collections Strategy website at **www.ukmcs.org.uk** for links and access to specific sites holding maritime materials that may be of help in your research.

Ministry of Defence   The Ministry of Defence's Veterans UK website was created in 2007 and is the ideal place to begin your inquiry for personnel service records and pension information for those who served in the armed forces from World War II and later. The website at **www.veterans-uk.info** contains links for Service Records, Medals, and other information. The A–Z index, the site map, and the Frequently Asked Questions areas are particularly helpful. There is a charge for records requests for family history/genealogical research purposes.

Military Museums of Note   Military museums hold fascinating collections of historical military materials that may be useful in your research. Inquiries for information and guidance usually receive prompt responses. The following list highlights some of the best of these resources:

- Imperial War Museum   **www.iwm.org.uk**
- National Army Museum   **www.national-army-museum.ac.uk**
- National Maritime Museum   **www.nmm.ac.uk**
- Royal Air Force Museum   **www.rafmuseum.org.uk**
- Royal Marines Museum   **www.royalmarinesmuseum.co.uk**
- Royal Naval Museum   **www.royalnavalmuseum.org**
- Royal Navy Submarine Museum   **www.rnsubmus.co.uk**

Other Helpful Resources   Don't overlook the resources of local public and academic libraries in the area in which your ancestors lived or from which they may have served. Other helpful resources in locating military records and historical materials include the following organizations:

- Federation of Family History Societies (FFHS)   **www.ffhs.org.uk**
- Gazettes Online (London, Edinburgh, and Belfast)   **www.gazettes-online.co.uk**
- GENUKI—British Military Records page   **www.genuki.org.uk/big/BritMilRecs .html**

Types of Military Records in the United Kingdom

Military records may vary across the different branches of service. There are document types that you may expect to locate, especially among the more modern era.

- **Attestation Form**   Attestation forms were completed by most recruits when they applied to be admitted for service in the military. This is the equivalent of an enlistment form in other military organizations, such as the U.S. armed forces. The attestation form usually asked for the person's name, date and place of birth, place of residence, occupation and/or skills, and physical description. Later forms asked for parents' names and other information.
- **Muster Rolls and Pay Lists**   Military units tracked the physical presence of troops and their attendance using muster rolls. Regular assembly of troops included roll calls and reports of persons missing. These rolls exist by unit and can be used to verify your ancestor's presence or status in a specific location at a precise point in time. Pay records exist in various forms ranging from payroll lists to individuals' payment stubs and/or receipts.
- **Personnel Records**   These, too, vary in their existence and content over time.
- **Casualty Lists and Returns**   As a result of muster calls, observations, reports, and medical information, casualty lists were created for the military unit. Depending on the time period, individual forms may have been created to document a person's injuries or death. These can take the shape of a letter or form, and there may also be copies of correspondence in an individual's personnel or service file and/or in the military unit's files.

- **Medical Records** Medical records may be included in an individual's personnel file, in the records of the military unit or the appropriate echelon, or may still exist in the archives of the medical facility in which the individual was treated. Summary reports were often sent to the military unit for its records, while sometimes the records are quite extensive. Figure 7-3 shows a single page from a lengthy medical summary for an English soldier wounded by shrapnel in World War II and who underwent several years' treatment for his wounds.

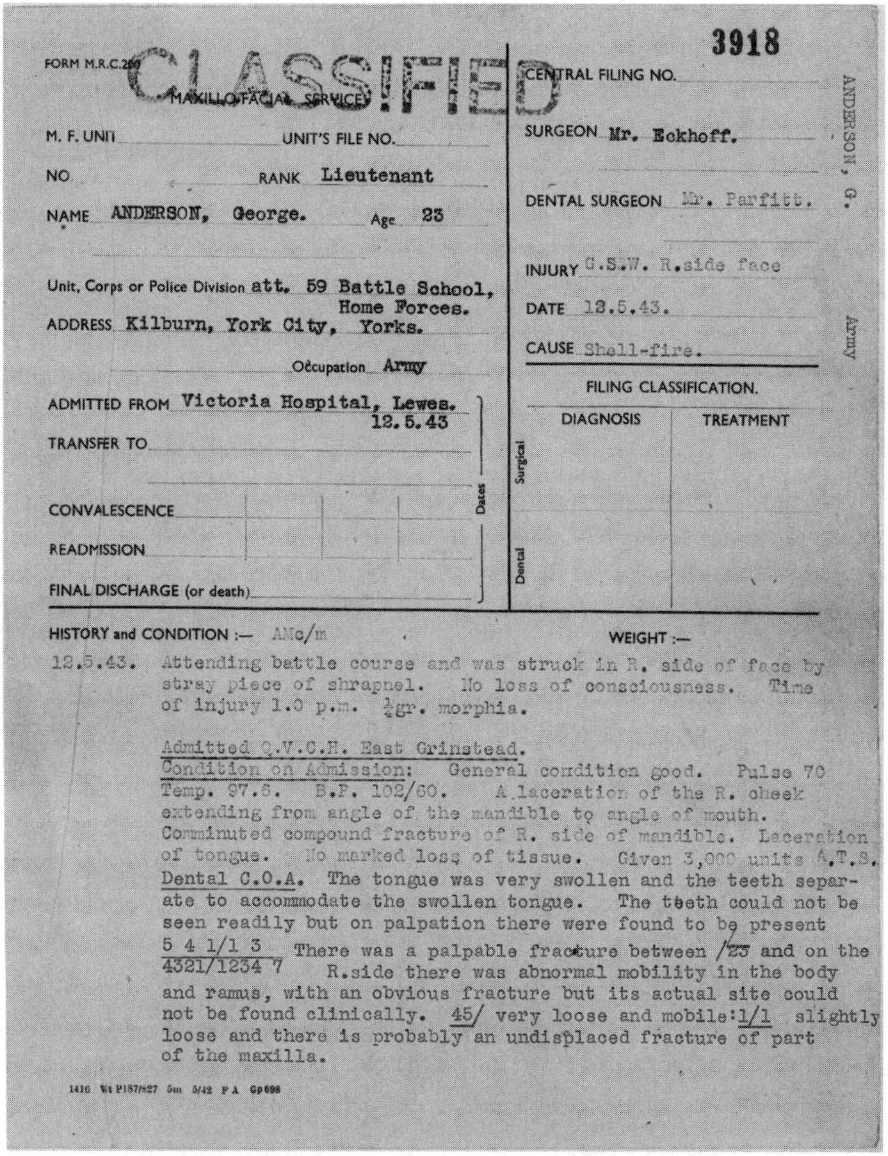

FORM M.R.C.200 CLASSIFIED
MAXILLO-FACIAL SERVICE
3918
CENTRAL FILING NO.
ANDERSON, G.
Army

M. F. UNIT UNIT'S FILE NO.
SURGEON Mr. Eckhoff.
NO. RANK Lieutenant
DENTAL SURGEON Mr. Parfitt.
NAME ANDERSON, George. Age 23
INJURY G.S.W. R.side face
Unit, Corps or Police Division att. 59 Battle School, Home Forces.
DATE 12.5.43.
ADDRESS Kilburn, York City, Yorks.
CAUSE Shell-fire.
Occupation Army
FILING CLASSIFICATION.
ADMITTED FROM Victoria Hospital, Lewes. 12.5.43
TRANSFER TO
CONVALESCENCE
READMISSION
FINAL DISCHARGE (or death)
Dates

	DIAGNOSIS	TREATMENT
Surgical		
Dental		

HISTORY and CONDITION :— AMc/m WEIGHT :—

12.5.43. Attending battle course and was struck in R. side of face by stray piece of shrapnel. No loss of consciousness. Time of injury 1.0 p.m. ¼gr. morphia.

Admitted Q.V.C.H. East Grinstead.
Condition on Admission: General condition good. Pulse 70 Temp. 97.6. B.P. 102/60. A laceration of the R. cheek extending from angle of the mandible to angle of mouth. Comminuted compound fracture of R. side of mandible. Laceration of tongue. No marked loss of tissue. Given 3,000 units A.T.S.
Dental C.O.A. The tongue was very swollen and the teeth separate to accommodate the swollen tongue. The teeth could not be seen readily but on palpation there were found to be present
5 4 1/1 3
4321/1234 7 There was a palpable fracture between /23 and on the R.side there was abnormal mobility in the body and ramus, with an obvious fracture but its actual site could not be found clinically. 45/ very loose and mobile: 1/1 slightly loose and there is probably an undisplaced fracture of part of the maxilla.

1416 Wt P187/827 5m 5/42 F A Gp698

FIGURE 7-3 Page from the medical records of a wounded English soldier in World War II. (Courtesy of Gillian M. Anderson.)

- **Records of Deserters** Military life was difficult at the best of times, and harsh conditions induced some individuals to desert. Military units maintained lists of deserters, and records were included in the individual's file. In addition, the British military published lists of deserters in public newspapers and in the *Police Gazette*. You will find that these records may be helpful if your ancestor "disappeared" from the military at a particular time.
- **Records of Courts Martial** Military discipline was notoriously harsh, and a great deal was made of conducting and publicizing the court martial of personnel. Military court and tribunal records include records of hearings and trials, and detailed records are to be found in unit records and in an individual's service records. In addition, accounts of a high-profile person's court martial may sometimes be found in newspapers of the period.
- **Discharge Papers** Discharge papers vary greatly from different periods. The earliest ones are nothing more than handwritten statements confirming the name, dates, and regiment in which the individual served, signed either by an officer or clerk in the organization. Later there were forms used that provided space for the name, rank, military unit, dates of service, places where the individual served and campaigns in which he had participated, any wounds suffered, physical condition at the time of discharge, and statements concerning the individual's character and performance. Later versions of the forms used included inoculation records and other data.
- **Pension Files** Veterans and/or their surviving spouse and/or family members were entitled to certain pension benefits. In order to obtain a benefit, a person had to make an application. This might take the form of a written petition or an appearance before a court or hearing board. Documentation is therefore likely to exist in one or more places. You may find pension records and related documents in the possession of The National Archives or through a specific veterans' organization. Veterans' groups and organizations that formed to assist veterans in obtaining benefits may be particularly helpful to your research. The Ministry of Defence's Veterans UK site (**www.veterans-uk.info**) maintains a page of web links to ex-service organizations and registered charities.

Military Records for Ireland

Military records for Ireland and its citizens who served in the military during the time that it was under the British government will be found among those records at The National Archives. Ireland has its own army, navy, and air corps forces, and those more modern records will be in the possession of the Irish government. An excellent website to begin your research for more contemporary Irish military history and records is the Defence Forces site located at **www.military.ie**.

As you can see, there are many, many avenues of research available for your search for military records in the British Isles. It is therefore important to conduct your preliminary historical research in advance so that you are better informed concerning what records may or may not be available and where to search for them.

Locate Australian Military Records

The National Archives of Australia holds records of its defense forces from the time of Federation in 1901. This includes Australian Army records from the Boer War, World War I, service between the wars, World War II, and service subsequent to World War II. The Royal Australian Navy records include two categories: service up to 1970 and service after 1970. The Royal Australian Air Force Records are also grouped into two categories: service before World War II and service after World War II. The archives also hold a number of other types of records relating to wartime service. You can learn about all of the holdings by visiting the website at **www.naa.gov.au**.

The Australian Ancestry.com site at **www.ancestry.com.au**, a part of The Generations Network, Inc., genealogy database subscription, includes several military databases for Australian servicemen and women. They can be found by using the Ancestry Card Catalogue under the Search link. These include at this writing:

- **ANZAC Memorial**   This database contains *The Anzac Memorial*, a book compiled to commemorate those who served in the Australian and New Zealand Army Corps (ANZAC) and died in World War I. The digitized book contains the Roll of Honour and is organized in alphabetical sequence by surname and is searchable.
- *Australia's Fighting Sons of The Empire: Portraits and Biographies of Australians in the Great War*   This book contains biographical text and photographs of thousands of Australians who served in World War I. It is digitized, indexed, and searchable. (Enter **Portraits and Biographies** in the Title box in the Ancestry Card Catalogue search template.)

Another excellent site for locating information is the World War Two Nominal Roll website at **www.ww2roll.gov.au**. It "was created to honour and commemorate some one million people who served in Australia's defence forces and the Merchant Navy" during World War II. It contains the service details of individuals who served during the period 3 September 1939 to 2 September 1945. The number of individuals collected for the Nominal Roll includes some 50,600 members of the Royal Australian Navy (RAN), 845,000 members of the Australian Army, 218,300 members of the Royal Australian Air Force (RAAF), and approximately 3,500 merchant mariners. This database is searchable by name, service number, honor awarded, or location (within Australia or elsewhere). For each search result, you can print a certificate (see Figure 7-4), see a full explanation of all the details in the record, or request a copy of the actual records from the National Archives of Australia.

Examine Samples of Military Records

I find that one helpful strategy in investigating military records is to examine specific representative examples of records created during the period I am researching. Army, navy, marine, and air force records created during World War II in the United States all contain similar if not identical information. Military records from the same period

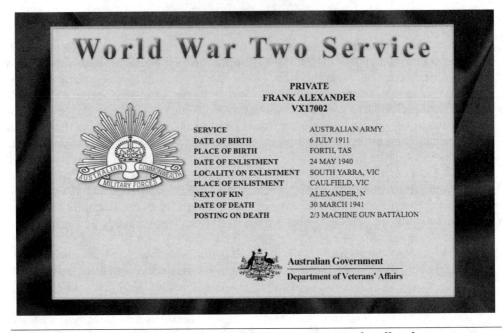

FIGURE 7-4 A certificate from the World War Two Nominal Roll website

in the United Kingdom will all contain information of a similar type as defined and required by the central governmental organization. Examining these materials can provide insight into just what types of data *were* recorded, and this helps me focus my search on those records as well as other locations where identical or similar data were collected. Therefore, if I am unable to locate the information in one place, I can investigate alternate research paths to possibly locate it elsewhere.

There are many reference books available that can help you learn more about military records and their contents. James C. Neagles' books, *U. S. Military Records: A Guide to Federal and State Sources, Colonial America to the Present* and *Confederate Research Sources: A Guide to Archive Collections*, are both excellent American references. Mark D. Herber's book, *Ancestral Trails: The Complete Guide to British Genealogy and Family History*, contains an exhaustive study of available military records for that area. Other works, such as John J. Newman's book about United States World War I draft registrations, titled *Uncle, We are Ready! Registering America's Men, 1917–1918*, provide comprehensive, definitive information to help you research specialized topic areas and record types. You will find that these and other reference works can help you significantly with your research. You just need to start investigating what is available.

Your research into military records can provide you with many details about the individual. Let's look at a number of specific examples of military records from the United States. These are not arranged in chronological sequence by when these records were created, but rather in something of a logical order in which they might occur in the career of a serviceperson.

Enlistment and Draft Registration Records

Some of the most detailed and descriptive records you will find are those relating to the enlistment or conscription of personnel. They contain name and address, date and location of birth, parents' names, a personal physical description, and other information, depending on the era. Bear in mind, however, that the information supplied on these documents should be corroborated with other sources. For example, it is not unusual for a minor to lie about his or her age in order to enlist in the military. It was not until well into the 20th century, when formal birth certificates were created, that a person was required to present such official proof of his age.

Figures 7-5 and 7-6 show both sides of a sample World War I draft registration card from the files at NARA. On the front are spaces for a serial number for the registration, the registrant's name, address, date of birth, whether U.S. citizen, nearest relative, employer's name and address, and the signature of the registrant. The back includes spaces to provide a physical description of the registrant, the signature of the registrar, and the date. The stamp of the local draft board that had jurisdiction over the area in which the applicant registered was also applied.

The information on this draft card may point you to city directory listings, a voter registration, driver's license, land and property records, religious congregations in the area, employment records, and other records. The name of the nearest relative provides yet another research clue for you. In this case, E. E. Holder is indicated as the registrant's brother, and you might look for census records, city and telephone directories, land and property records, death certificate, a will and probate record, obituaries, and other evidence to locate that person in Rome, Georgia, and trace other family members. You might also search earlier census schedules to locate the two brothers together with their parents.

Military Muster Rolls and Pay Records

Military units regularly muster their troops to verify attendance, issue orders, make announcements, drill, and perform other functions. Muster roll records for a military unit and muster cards for individual soldiers can be found in many U.S. military service files from the colonial period forward. In addition, unit payroll records and payment stubs or receipts can provide important information to help place your ancestor at a specific place and time. The pay stub shown in Figure 7-7 for my ancestor, John Sords [sic, Swords], indicates that he was paid "Three Pounds, five Shill^s, & eight Pence half Penny Sterling" for 43 days of military duty in 1782. Coupled with other military records, such as his sworn affidavit of service found in his Revolutionary War pension file, it is possible to link John Swords with a particular military command at that date. Further, by researching military history for that unit, I can determine where he traveled and what military action he saw.

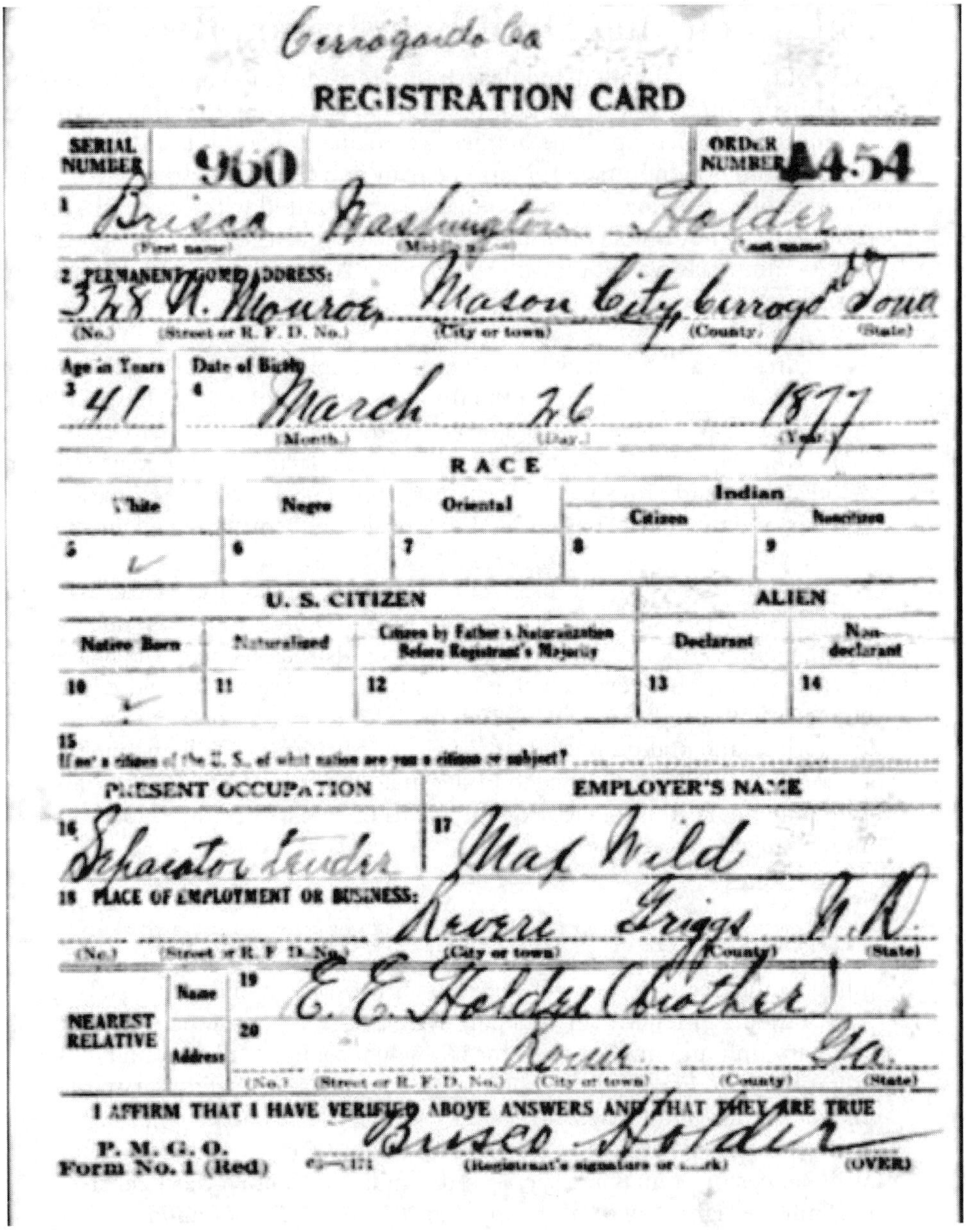

Cerrogordo Co

REGISTRATION CARD

SERIAL NUMBER 960 ORDER NUMBER A454

1 Brisco Washington Holder
(First name) (Middle name) (Last name)

2 PERMANENT HOME ADDRESS:
328 N. Monroe Mason City Cerrogordo Iowa
(No.) (Street or R. F. D. No.) (City or town) (County) (State)

Age in Years	Date of Birth		
3 41	4 March	26	1877
	(Month.)	(Day.)	(Year.)

RACE

White	Negro	Oriental	Indian	
			Citizen	Noncitizen
5 ✓	6	7	8	9

U. S. CITIZEN			ALIEN	
Native Born	Naturalized	Citizen by Father's Naturalization Before Registrant's Majority	Declarant	Non-declarant
10 ✓	11	12	13	14

15 If not a citizen of the U. S., of what nation are you a citizen or subject?

PRESENT OCCUPATION	EMPLOYER'S NAME
16 Separator tender	17 Max Wild

18 PLACE OF EMPLOYMENT OR BUSINESS:
Revere Triggs N.D.
(No.) (Street or R. F. D. No.) (City or town) (County) (State)

NEAREST RELATIVE
Name 19 E. E. Holder (brother)
Address 20 Rome Ga.
(No.) (Street or R. F. D. No.) (City or town) (County) (State)

I AFFIRM THAT I HAVE VERIFIED ABOVE ANSWERS AND THAT THEY ARE TRUE
Brisco Holder
P. M. G. O.
Form No. 1 (Red)
(Registrant's signature or mark) (OVER)

FIGURE 7-5 Front of a U.S. World War I draft registration card. (Used by permission of The Generations Network, Inc.)

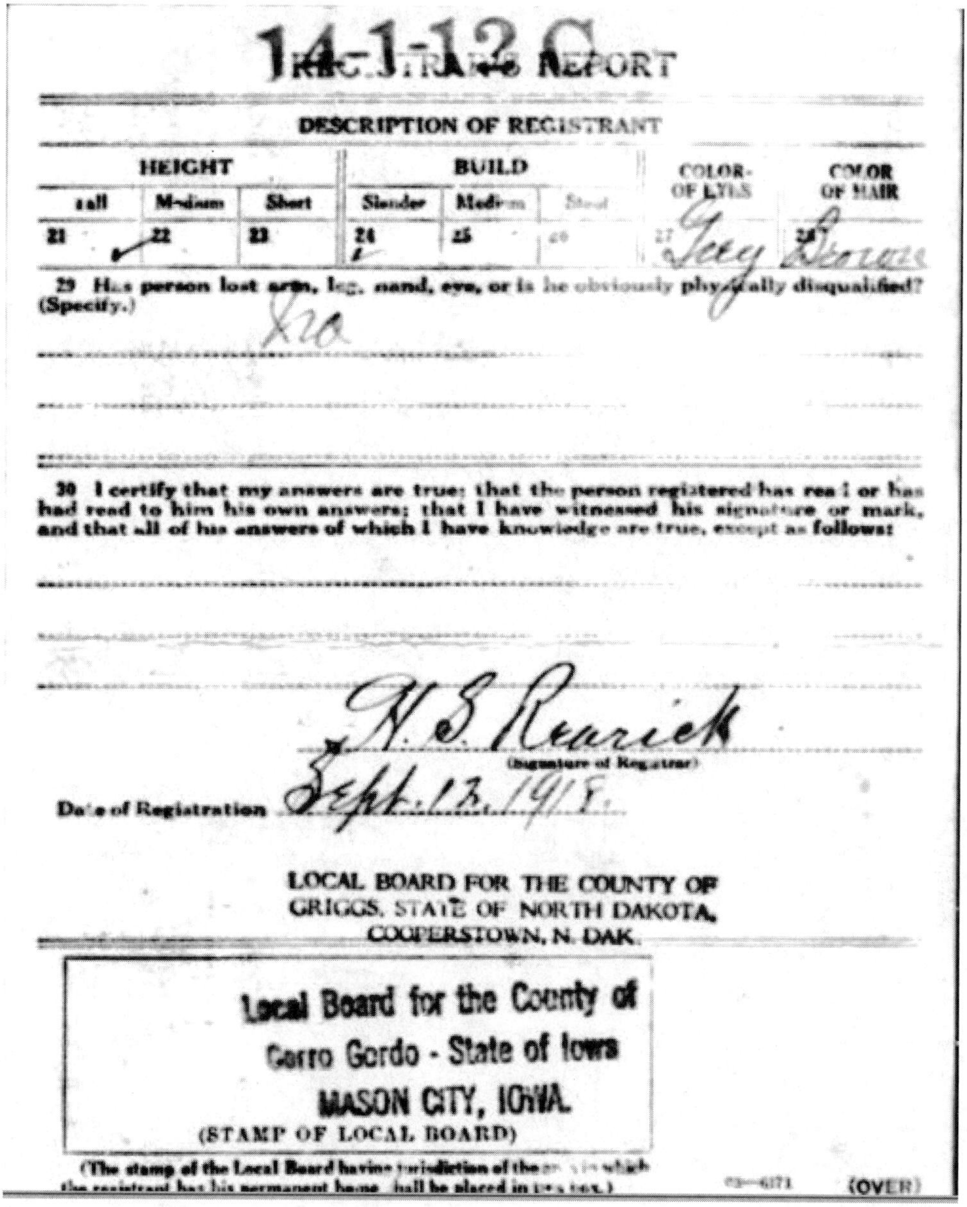

14-1-12 REGISTRAR'S REPORT

DESCRIPTION OF REGISTRANT

HEIGHT			BUILD			COLOR- OF EYES	COLOR OF HAIR
Tall	Medium	Short	Slender	Medium	Stout		
21	22	23	24	25	26	27 *Grey*	28 *Brown*

29 Has person lost arm, leg, hand, eye, or is he obviously physically disqualified? (Specify.)

No

30 I certify that my answers are true; that the person registered has read or has had read to him his own answers; that I have witnessed his signature or mark, and that all of his answers of which I have knowledge are true, except as follows:

N. S. Rearick
(Signature of Registrar)

Date of Registration *Sept. 13, 1918.*

LOCAL BOARD FOR THE COUNTY OF
GRIGGS, STATE OF NORTH DAKOTA,
COOPERSTOWN, N. DAK.

Local Board for the County of
Cerro Gordo - State of Iowa
MASON CITY, IOWA.
(STAMP OF LOCAL BOARD)

(The stamp of the Local Board having jurisdiction of the area in which the registrant has his permanent home shall be placed in this box.)   03—6171   (OVER)

FIGURE 7-6   Back of a U.S. World War I draft registration card. (Used by permission of The Generations Network, Inc.)

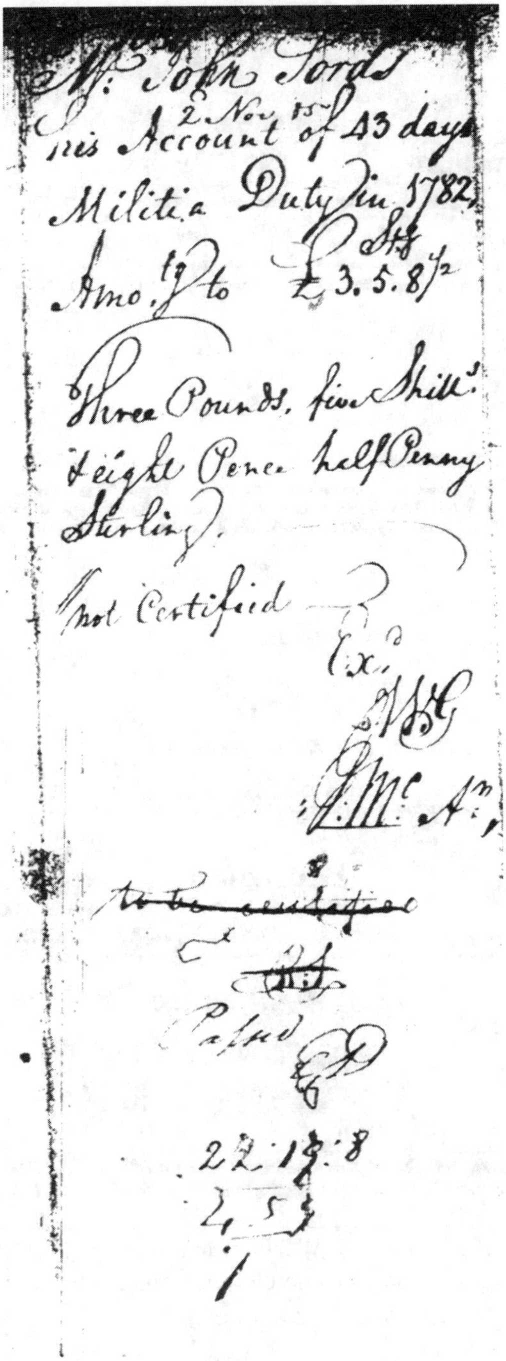
Mr. John Sords
2 Nov 15
his Account of 43 days
Militia Duty in 1782
Stg
Amo.t to £3.5.8½
Three Pounds, five Shill.s
& eight Pence half Penny
Sterling
Not Certified
Ex.d
Passed
22.13.8
4.5

FIGURE 7-7 Copy of a Revolutionary War pay record for John Sords' [sic, Swords'] military service in 1782, obtained from a NARA pension file. (From the author's collection.)

Educational and Training Records

Military personnel are trained to perform their jobs at an optimal level. We are all familiar with the idea of infantry troops going through their drills of marching, combat assault, hand-to-hand combat, rifle practice and marksmanship, use of artillery equipment, bivouac, flight training, seamanship, and a wide range of operations training. Military service records may contain information about the education, testing, and evaluation of an individual's skills and any specialized education or training provided. The records you may encounter in an individual's personnel files and/or the service files may include test scores, correspondence documenting successful completion of training, certificates, and diplomas. Figure 7-8 is an example of a certificate of completion of an Air Force medical training course.

BE IT KNOWN ___A2C CAREY T. MORGAN___ IS A GRADUATE OF

USAF MEDICAL UNIT TRAINING COURSE

IN TESTIMONY WHEREOF AND BY AUTHORITY VESTED IN US, WE DO CONFER UPON HIM THIS DIPLOMA. GIVEN AT

___2130 Communications Squadron, RAF Croughton___

THIS ___29th___ DAY OF ___SEPTEMBER___ 19___62___

TSGT JAMES E. LONG, JR.
Instructor

JAMES R. HOWERTON, MAJOR, USAF
Commander

FIGURE 7-8   Certificate of completion of a medical training course. (Courtesy of Carey T. Morgan.)

Station and Duty Assignment Orders

Personnel are assigned to specific locations and are attached to specific units. Documents are created to order the individual to report to a location and to perform explicit duties or functions. These documents are often referred to as "orders," and the individual is typically charged with delivering his or her orders to the new unit's commanding officer or clerk. A copy of the orders is retained in the individual's service file. Figure 7-9 shows an example of a Permanent Change of Station Order. Again, the information in this document can be used to verify the movement of an individual from one place to another and to help relate his or her service to the activities of the military unit at that time.

Promotions and Commissions

A successful individual may, in the course of his or her military service, be promoted to higher levels of authority and greater responsibility. In the U.S. armed forces, there is a distinction made between recruits, noncommissioned officers (also known as NCOs), and commissioned officers. You can learn more about the various ranks by researching the individual branches of the military service and their history at the time your ancestor or family member served. There are typically several documents associated with a personnel promotion or a commission.

A promotion of a noncommissioned officer is usually documented with a written notice to the serviceperson, a copy to every level of command under which the person serves, a copy to the person's file, and a notice posted in a unit's communication media, such as on a bulletin board, in a newsletter, or in some other venue.

An officer's commission is more formal. A congratulatory letter is delivered to the individual formally announcing the commissioning. The notification processes throughout the echelon are similar. In addition to the letter, an example of which is shown in Figure 7-10, a formal certificate like the one shown in Figure 7-11 commemorating the new appointment is created and presented to the individual.

A promotion or commissioning, the awarding of medals, ribbons, clusters, and special insignia, and the awarding of a commendation and other recognition to the unit or to an individual is a ceremonial occasion. The ceremony may be as simple as an announcement made at a unit formation or as formal as an occasion at which dress uniforms are worn, a military band performs, troops march in formation, rifle salutes are fired, and high-ranking officers and other dignitaries speak. In any case, records are created and become part of the military record for the individual and for the military unit.

Discharge and Separation Records

You will find that the normal conclusion of an individual's military service generates a significant number of important documents. A document detailing the permanent change of duty assignment or station order may be created, along with other internal administrative documentation that may or may not be included in an individual's personnel file. There will be, however, some record of discharge or separation. These documents vary depending on the time period. Let's examine three examples.

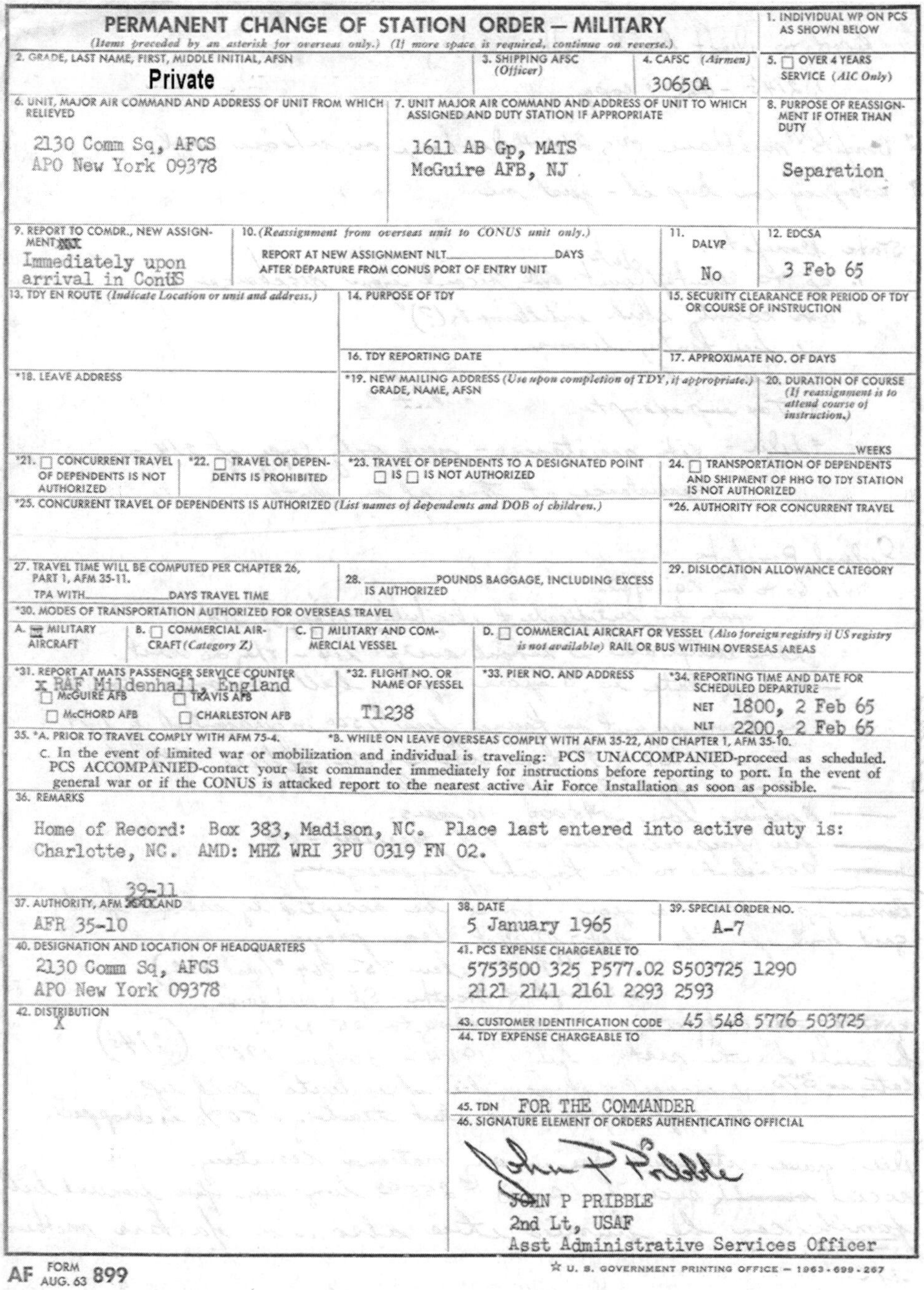

PERMANENT CHANGE OF STATION ORDER — MILITARY
(Items preceded by an asterisk for overseas only.) (If more space is required, continue on reverse.)

1. INDIVIDUAL WP ON PCS AS SHOWN BELOW

2. GRADE, LAST NAME, FIRST, MIDDLE INITIAL, AFSN
Private

3. SHIPPING AFSC (Officer)

4. CAFSC (Airmen)
30650A

5. ☐ OVER 4 YEARS SERVICE (A1C Only)

6. UNIT, MAJOR AIR COMMAND AND ADDRESS OF UNIT FROM WHICH RELIEVED
2130 Comm Sq, AFCS
APO New York 09378

7. UNIT MAJOR AIR COMMAND AND ADDRESS OF UNIT TO WHICH ASSIGNED AND DUTY STATION IF APPROPRIATE
1611 AB Gp, MATS
McGuire AFB, NJ

8. PURPOSE OF REASSIGNMENT IF OTHER THAN DUTY
Separation

9. REPORT TO COMDR., NEW ASSIGNMENT XXX
Immediately upon arrival in ConUS

10. (Reassignment from overseas unit to CONUS unit only.)
REPORT AT NEW ASSIGNMENT NLT_____ _____DAYS AFTER DEPARTURE FROM CONUS PORT OF ENTRY UNIT

11. DALVP
No

12. EDCSA
3 Feb 65

13. TDY EN ROUTE (Indicate Location or unit and address.)

14. PURPOSE OF TDY

15. SECURITY CLEARANCE FOR PERIOD OF TDY OR COURSE OF INSTRUCTION

16. TDY REPORTING DATE

17. APPROXIMATE NO. OF DAYS

*18. LEAVE ADDRESS

*19. NEW MAILING ADDRESS (Use upon completion of TDY, if appropriate.) GRADE, NAME, AFSN

20. DURATION OF COURSE (If reassignment is to attend course of instruction.)
_____WEEKS

*21. ☐ CONCURRENT TRAVEL OF DEPENDENTS IS NOT AUTHORIZED

*22. ☐ TRAVEL OF DEPENDENTS IS PROHIBITED

*23. TRAVEL OF DEPENDENTS TO A DESIGNATED POINT ☐ IS ☐ IS NOT AUTHORIZED

24. ☐ TRANSPORTATION OF DEPENDENTS AND SHIPMENT OF HHG TO TDY STATION IS NOT AUTHORIZED

*25. CONCURRENT TRAVEL OF DEPENDENTS IS AUTHORIZED (List names of dependents and DOB of children.)

*26. AUTHORITY FOR CONCURRENT TRAVEL

27. TRAVEL TIME WILL BE COMPUTED PER CHAPTER 26, PART 1, AFM 35-11.
TPA WITH_____DAYS TRAVEL TIME

28. _____POUNDS BAGGAGE, INCLUDING EXCESS IS AUTHORIZED

29. DISLOCATION ALLOWANCE CATEGORY

*30. MODES OF TRANSPORTATION AUTHORIZED FOR OVERSEAS TRAVEL

A. ☐ MILITARY AIRCRAFT

B. ☐ COMMERCIAL AIRCRAFT (Category Z)

C. ☐ MILITARY AND COMMERCIAL VESSEL

D. ☐ COMMERCIAL AIRCRAFT OR VESSEL (Also foreign registry if US registry is not available) RAIL OR BUS WITHIN OVERSEAS AREAS

*31. REPORT AT MATS PASSENGER SERVICE COUNTER
☒ RAF Mildenhall, England
☐ McGUIRE AFB   ☐ TRAVIS AFB
☐ McCHORD AFB   ☐ CHARLESTON AFB

*32. FLIGHT NO. OR NAME OF VESSEL
T1238

*33. PIER NO. AND ADDRESS

*34. REPORTING TIME AND DATE FOR SCHEDULED DEPARTURE
NET 1800, 2 Feb 65
NLT 2200, 2 Feb 65

35. *A. PRIOR TO TRAVEL COMPLY WITH AFM 75-4.   *B. WHILE ON LEAVE OVERSEAS COMPLY WITH AFM 35-22, AND CHAPTER 1, AFM 35-10.
c. In the event of limited war or mobilization and individual is traveling: PCS UNACCOMPANIED-proceed as scheduled. PCS ACCOMPANIED-contact your last commander immediately for instructions before reporting to port. In the event of general war or if the CONUS is attacked report to the nearest active Air Force Installation as soon as possible.

36. REMARKS

Home of Record: Box 383, Madison, NC. Place last entered into active duty is: Charlotte, NC. AMD: MHZ WRI 3PU 0319 FN 02.

39-11

37. AUTHORITY, AFM XXX AND
AFR 35-10

38. DATE
5 January 1965

39. SPECIAL ORDER NO.
A-7

40. DESIGNATION AND LOCATION OF HEADQUARTERS
2130 Comm Sq, AFCS
APO New York 09378

41. PCS EXPENSE CHARGEABLE TO
5753500 325 P577.02 S503725 1290
2121 2141 2161 2293 2593

42. DISTRIBUTION
X

43. CUSTOMER IDENTIFICATION CODE 45 548 5776 503725

44. TDY EXPENSE CHARGEABLE TO

45. TDN   FOR THE COMMANDER

46. SIGNATURE ELEMENT OF ORDERS AUTHENTICATING OFFICIAL

John P Pribble

JOHN P PRIBBLE
2nd Lt, USAF
Asst Administrative Services Officer

AF FORM AUG. 63 899

☆ U. S. GOVERNMENT PRINTING OFFICE — 1963-699-267

FIGURE 7-9   Permanent Change of Station Order. (From the author's collection.)

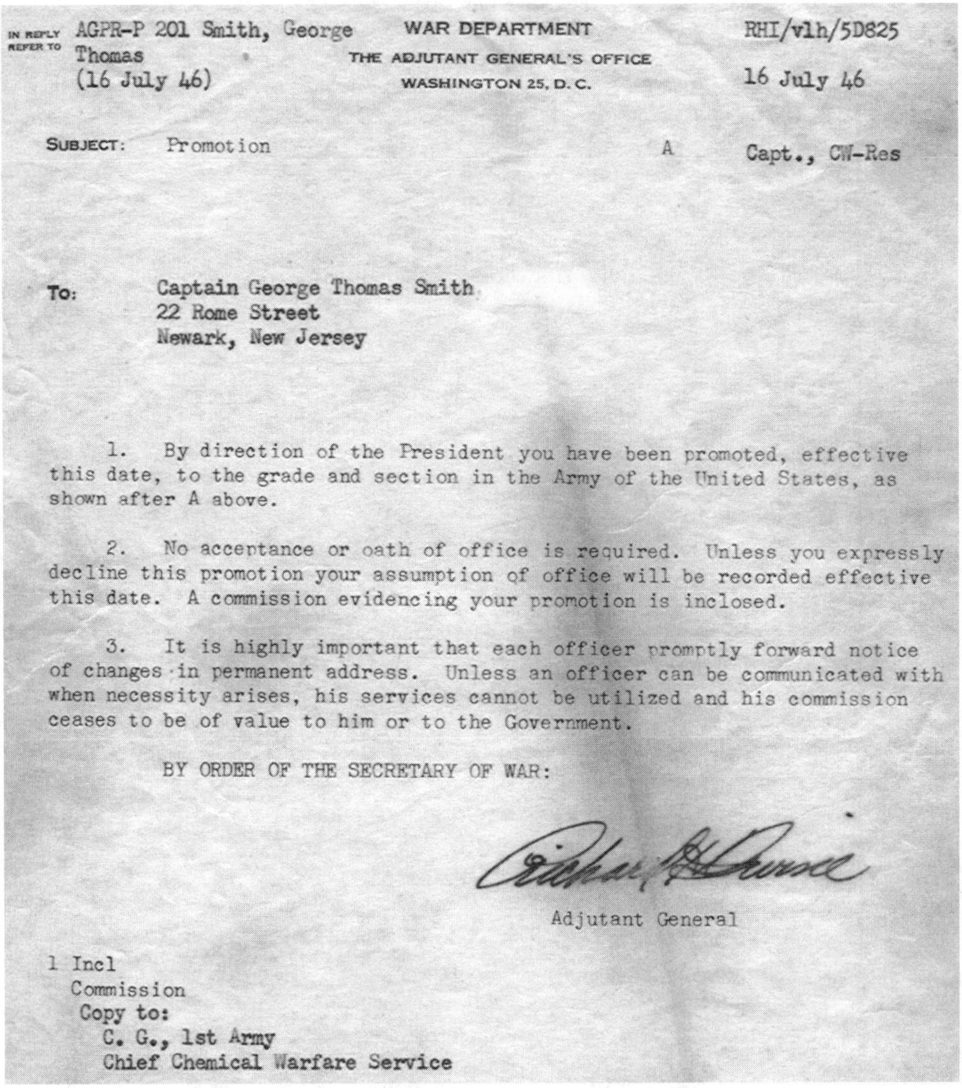

IN REPLY REFER TO AGPR-P 201 Smith, George   WAR DEPARTMENT   RHI/vlh/5D825
Thomas   THE ADJUTANT GENERAL'S OFFICE
(16 July 46)   WASHINGTON 25, D. C.   16 July 46

SUBJECT: Promotion   A   Capt., CW-Res

To: Captain George Thomas Smith
         22 Rome Street
         Newark, New Jersey

    1.   By direction of the President you have been promoted, effective
this date, to the grade and section in the Army of the United States, as
shown after A above.

    2.   No acceptance or oath of office is required. Unless you expressly
decline this promotion your assumption of office will be recorded effective
this date. A commission evidencing your promotion is inclosed.

    3.   It is highly important that each officer promptly forward notice
of changes in permanent address. Unless an officer can be communicated with
when necessity arises, his services cannot be utilized and his commission
ceases to be of value to him or to the Government.

    BY ORDER OF THE SECRETARY OF WAR:

                                        Adjutant General

1 Incl
 Commission
 Copy to:
   C. G., 1st Army
   Chief Chemical Warfare Service

FIGURE 7-10   Letter notifying George Thomas Smith of his promotion to Captain.
(Courtesy of Jeff Smith.)

World War I

Emil I. Hoffman's Honorable Discharge from the United States Army, dated
9 January 1919, is shown in Figure 7-12. This document is important for a
number of reasons. It states that he was born in Smorgan, Russia, and that "he
was 30 years of age and by occupation a Salesman" when he enlisted. Further,
it describes him physically as being 5 feet 4 ¾ inches in height with brown
eyes, brown hair, and a ruddy complexion.

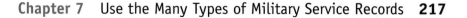

FIGURE 7-11   Certificate commissioning George Thomas Smith to Captain.
(Courtesy of Jeff Smith.)

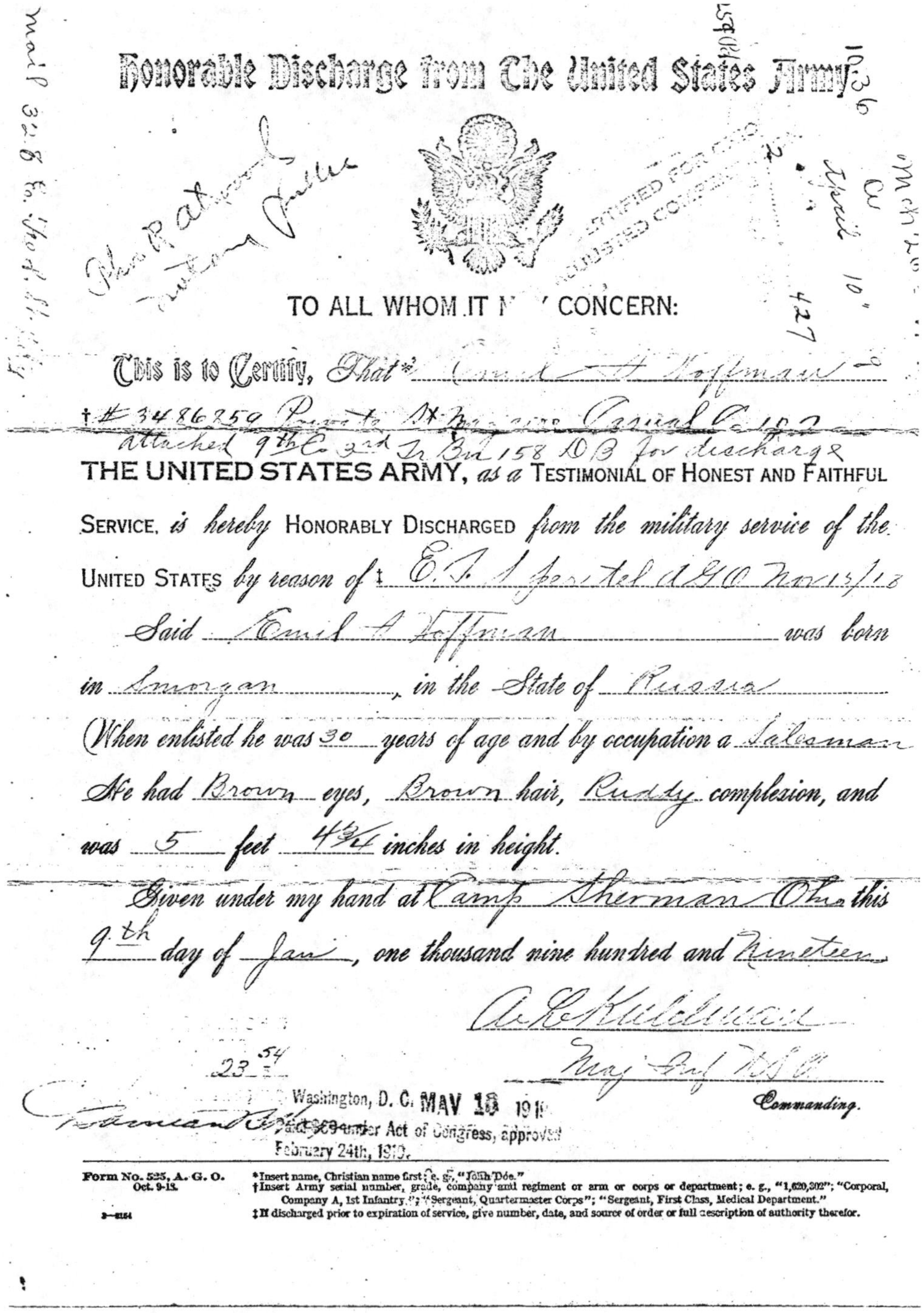

FIGURE 7-12   World War I Honorable Discharge from the U.S. Army for Emil I. Hoffman. (Courtesy of June H. Roth.)

On the reverse side of the Honorable Discharge certificate is his enlistment record, shown in Figure 7-13. This document is filled with great information, starting with the date of his enlistment on 27 May 1918 at Youngstown, Ohio. He was not an NCO, and he served with the AEF (Allied Expeditionary Forces) from 22 July 1918 until 24 December 1918. He was married and deemed to be of excellent character. He was vaccinated against typhoid fever and was in good health when he was discharged. A stamp in the upper-right corner and a notation indicates that he received a bronze Victory Lapel Pin on 16 September 1919. The remarks indicate that there was no A.W.O.L. or absence from duty. He also was entitled to travel pay.

World War II

The documentation changed somewhat by the time of World War II. In fact, there are even more documents that comprise the military service record and the certificates awarded to the individual.

The Honorable Discharge document and Enlistment Record for George Thomas Smith, which occupy the front and back of a single sheet and which are shown in Figures 7-14 and 7-15, are very similar to those from World War I.

In addition to those records, the separate Honorable Discharge certificate on heavy paper stock, shown in Figure 7-16, was presented to the individual.

Another two-sided document was created and given to the individual at the time of separation. The Certificate of Service shown in Figure 7-17 was another form of honorable discharge documentation. On the reverse side is the detailed Military Record and Report of Separation, which is shown in Figure 7-18.

The Military Record and Report of Separation contains name, rank, serial number, military organization and occupation, permanent civilian address, date and place of birth, race, a physical description, and marital status. The detailed military history includes the locations where the individual served, decorations and citations, education and training schools attended while enlisted, areas of service outside the United States, and information about continuation of insurance. His right thumbprint was applied as another form of identity confirmation.

One additional document of interest was awarded to the individual, the Army Air Forces Certificate of Appreciation for War Service, shown in Figure 7-19. I find this document particularly interesting in terms of the patriotic text that appears in the second paragraph: "Together we built the striking force that swept the Luftwaffe from the skies and broke the German power to resist. The total might of that striking force was then unleashed upon the Japanese."

Post–World War II

The mix of military documents changed somewhat following World War II. In 1950, a new document, the Report of Transfer or Discharge from Active Duty, was introduced. It was used to facilitate the transfer of personnel between branches of the armed services and to provide documentation for separation and discharge. The document has become most commonly known as and referred to by its form number, DD 214, and an example is shown in Figure 7-20. In addition, a certificate of Honorable Discharge was issued.

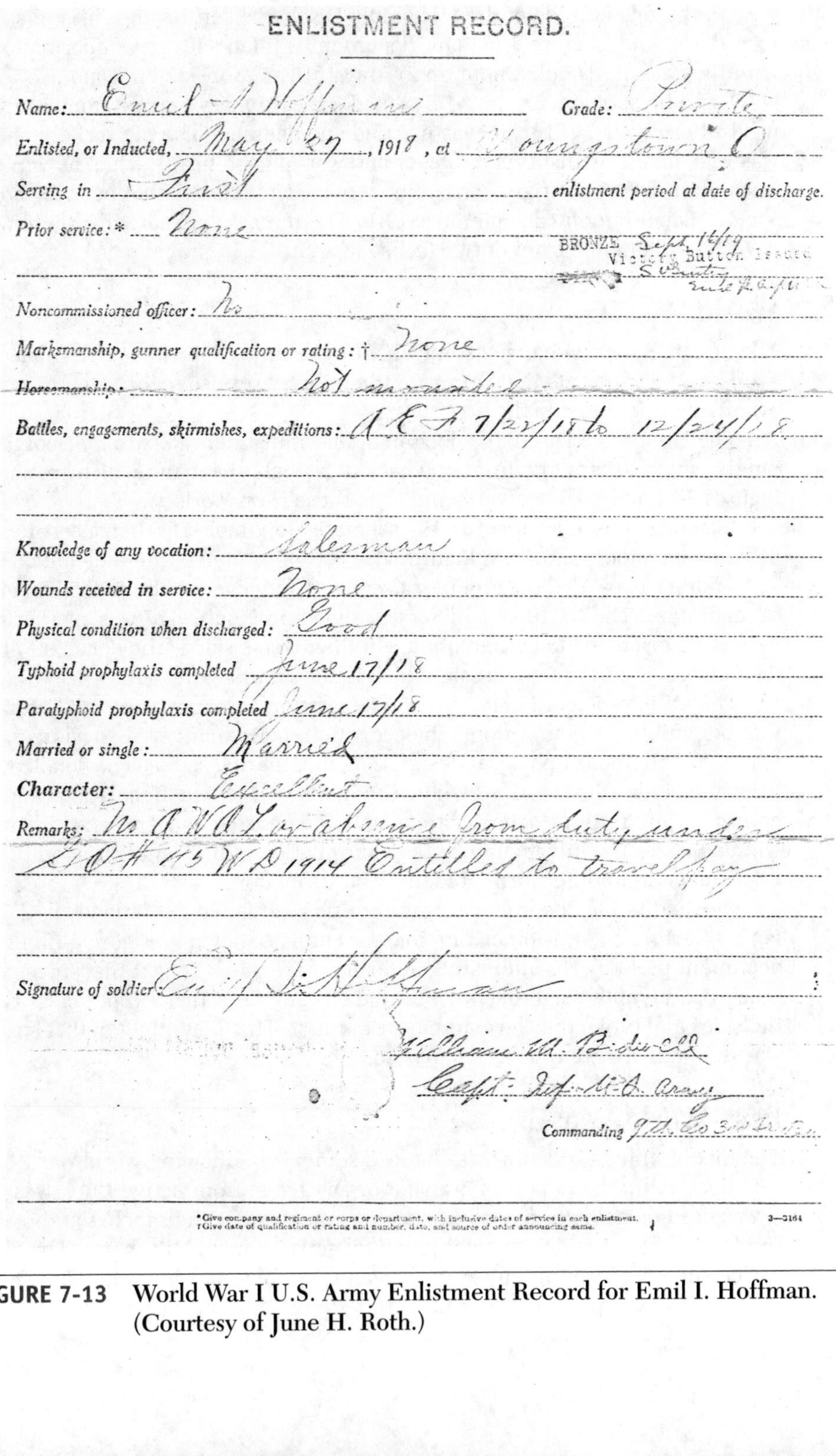

ENLISTMENT RECORD.

Name: *Emil I. Hoffman*   Grade: *Private*

Enlisted, or Inducted, *May 27*, 1918, at *Youngstown, O.*

Serving in *First*   enlistment period at date of discharge.

Prior service: * *None*

BRONZE *Sept. 16/19*
Victory Button Issued

Noncommissioned officer: *No*

Marksmanship, gunner qualification or rating: † *None*

Horsemanship: *Not mounted*

Battles, engagements, skirmishes, expeditions: *A.E.F. 7/27/18 to 12/24/18*

Knowledge of any vocation: *Salesman*

Wounds received in service: *None*

Physical condition when discharged: *Good*

Typhoid prophylaxis completed *June 17/18*

Paratyphoid prophylaxis completed *June 17/18*

Married or single: *Married*

Character: *Excellent*

Remarks: *No AWOL or absence from duty under*
GO # 45 WD 1914 Entitled to travel pay

Signature of soldier *Emil I. Hoffman*

William W. Bidwell
Capt. Inf. U.S. Army
Commanding *7th Co. 3rd Inf...*

*Give company and regiment or corps or department, with inclusive dates of service in each enlistment.
†Give date of qualification or rating and number, date, and source of order announcing same.*   3—3164

FIGURE 7-13   World War I U.S. Army Enlistment Record for Emil I. Hoffman.
(Courtesy of June H. Roth.)

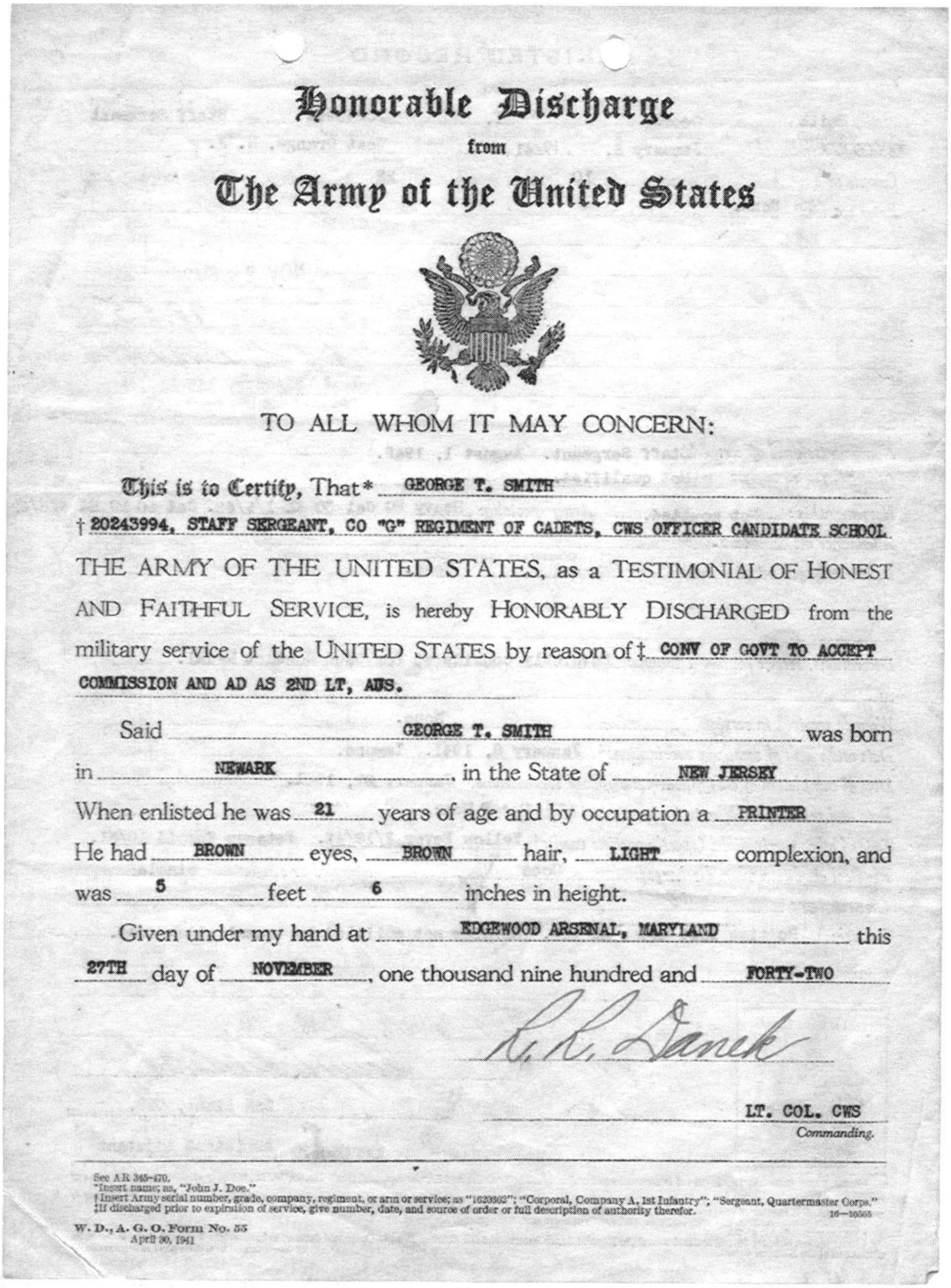

Honorable Discharge

from

The Army of the United States

TO ALL WHOM IT MAY CONCERN:

This is to Certify, That* GEORGE T. SMITH

† 20243994, STAFF SERGEANT, CO "G" REGIMENT OF CADETS, CWS OFFICER CANDIDATE SCHOOL.

THE ARMY OF THE UNITED STATES, as a TESTIMONIAL OF HONEST AND FAITHFUL SERVICE, is hereby HONORABLY DISCHARGED from the military service of the UNITED STATES by reason of ‡ CONV OF GOVT TO ACCEPT COMMISSION AND AD AS 2ND LT, AUS.

Said GEORGE T. SMITH was born in NEWARK, in the State of NEW JERSEY

When enlisted he was 21 years of age and by occupation a PRINTER

He had BROWN eyes, BROWN hair, LIGHT complexion, and was 5 feet 6 inches in height.

Given under my hand at EDGEWOOD ARSENAL, MARYLAND this 27TH day of NOVEMBER, one thousand nine hundred and FORTY-TWO

C. R. Danek

LT. COL. CWS
Commanding.

See AR 345-470.
*Insert name; as, "John J. Doe."
†Insert Army serial number, grade, company, regiment, or arm or service; as "1620802"; "Corporal, Company A, 1st Infantry"; "Sergeant, Quartermaster Corps."
‡If discharged prior to expiration of service, give number, date, and source of order or full description of authority therefor.
16—16565

W. D., A. G. O. Form No. 55
April 30, 1941

FIGURE 7-14 World War II Honorable Discharge from the U.S. Army for George T. Smith. (Courtesy of Jeff Smith.)

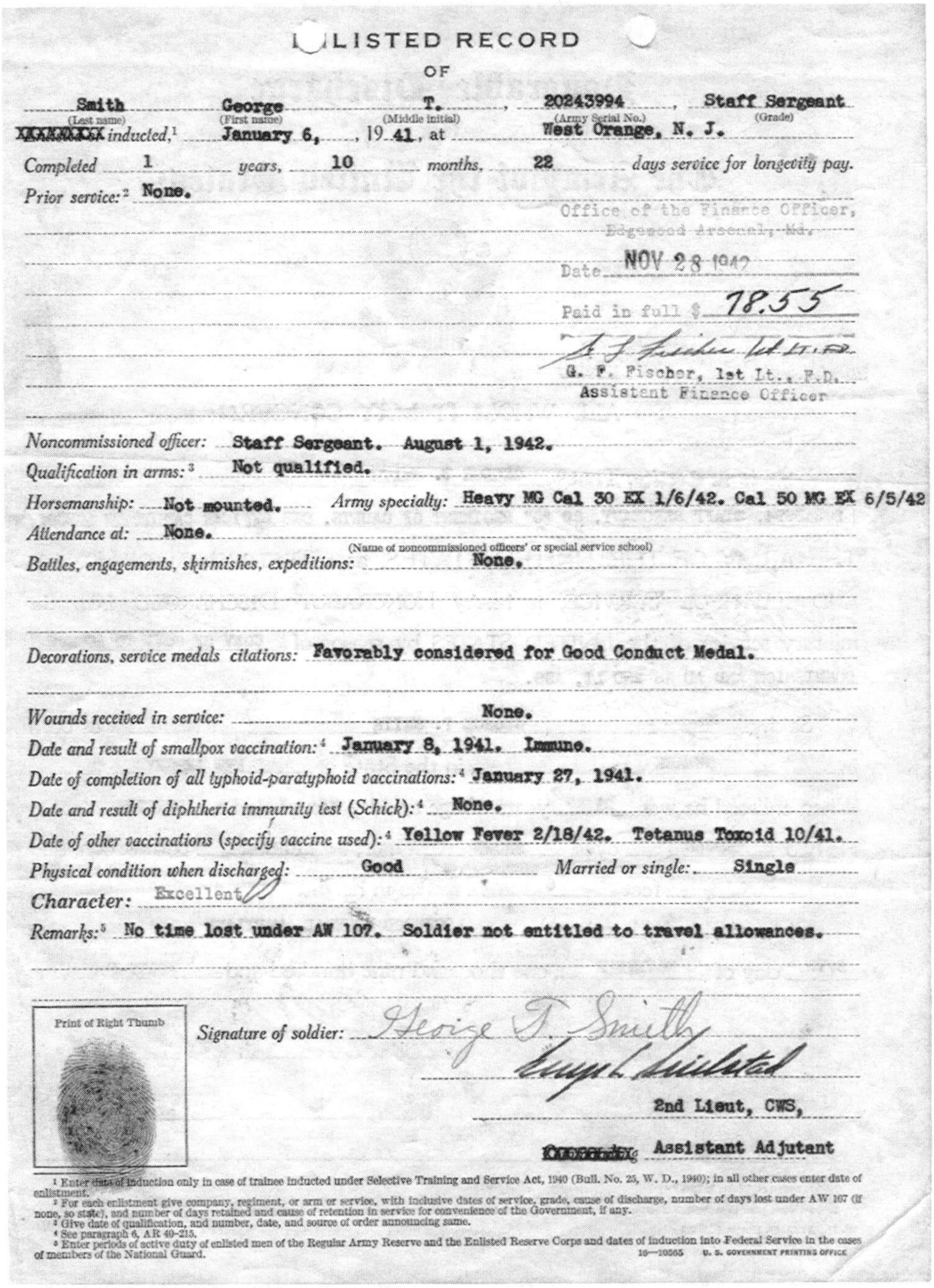

ENLISTED RECORD
OF

Smith (Last name) George (First name) T. (Middle initial), 20243994 (Army Serial No.), Staff Sergeant (Grade)

XXXXXXXX inducted,[1] January 6, 19 41, at West Orange, N. J.

Completed 1 years, 10 months, 22 days service for longevity pay.

Prior service:[2] None.

Office of the Finance Officer,
Edgewood Arsenal, Md.
Date NOV 28 1942
Paid in full $ 78.55
G. F. Fischer, 1st Lt., F.D.
Assistant Finance Officer

Noncommissioned officer: Staff Sergeant. August 1, 1942.

Qualification in arms:[3] Not qualified.

Horsemanship: Not mounted. Army specialty: Heavy MG Cal 30 EX 1/6/42. Cal 50 MG EX 6/5/42

Attendance at: None. (Name of noncommissioned officers' or special service school)

Battles, engagements, skirmishes, expeditions: None.

Decorations, service medals citations: Favorably considered for Good Conduct Medal.

Wounds received in service: None.

Date and result of smallpox vaccination:[4] January 8, 1941. Immune.

Date of completion of all typhoid-paratyphoid vaccinations:[4] January 27, 1941.

Date and result of diphtheria immunity test (Schick):[4] None.

Date of other vaccinations (specify vaccine used):[4] Yellow Fever 2/18/42. Tetanus Toxoid 10/41.

Physical condition when discharged: Good Married or single: Single

Character: Excellent

Remarks:[5] No time lost under AW 107. Soldier not entitled to travel allowances.

Print of Right Thumb

Signature of soldier: George T. Smith

2nd Lieut, CWS,
XXXXXXXX Assistant Adjutant

[1] Enter date of induction only in case of trainee inducted under Selective Training and Service Act, 1940 (Bull. No. 25, W. D., 1940); in all other cases enter date of enlistment.
[2] For each enlistment give company, regiment, or arm or service, with inclusive dates of service, grade, cause of discharge, number of days lost under AW 107 (if none, so state), and number of days retained and cause of retention in service for convenience of the Government, if any.
[3] Give date of qualification, and number, date, and source of order announcing same.
[4] See paragraph 6, AR 40-215.
[5] Enter periods of active duty of enlisted men of the Regular Army Reserve and the Enlisted Reserve Corps and dates of induction into Federal Service in the cases of members of the National Guard.

16—10565 U. S. GOVERNMENT PRINTING OFFICE

FIGURE 7-15 WWII Enlistment Record for George T. Smith. (Courtesy of Jeff Smith.)

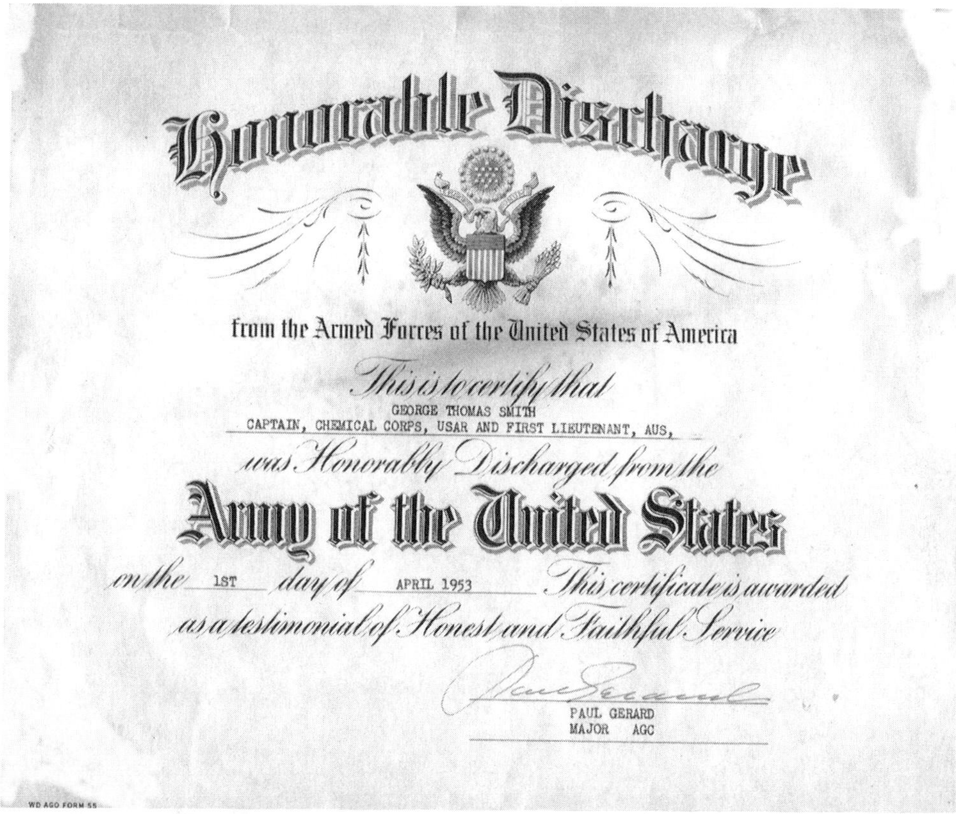
Honorable Discharge

from the Armed Forces of the United States of America

This is to certify that

GEORGE THOMAS SMITH

CAPTAIN, CHEMICAL CORPS, USAR AND FIRST LIEUTENANT, AUS,

was Honorably Discharged from the

Army of the United States

on the 1ST day of APRIL 1953 This certificate is awarded

as a testimonial of Honest and Faithful Service

PAUL GERARD

MAJOR AGC

WD AGO FORM 55

FIGURE 7-16 Honorable Discharge certificate for George T. Smith. (Courtesy of Jeff Smith.)

Death and Burial Records

An inevitable consequence of military service for some is the loss of life. The U.S. military is meticulous in its communications with surviving family members and in offering support. When military personnel were killed overseas in World War II, they were interred in military cemeteries and families were contacted to determine whether to return the remains to the United States for burial. One case I have reviewed is that of 1st Lieutenant William J. Smith, who died in England in 1943. (He was the brother of George Thomas Smith, whose records are included above.) William J. Smith was initially interred in the military cemetery at Brookwood, England. After a series of detailed written communications, the family decided that his remains should stay in England rather than be returned to the United States, and the U.S. War Department arranged for permanent interment in the U.S. Military Cemetery in Cambridge, England. Figure 7-21 shows the letter received from the War Department.

Army of the United States

CERTIFICATE OF SERVICE

This is to certify that

FIRST LIEUTENANT GEORGE T SMITH   CHEMICAL WARFARE SERVICE
803RD CHEMICAL COMPANY AIR OPERATIONS
BUCKLEY FIELD COLORADO

honorably served in active Federal Service

in the Army of the United States from

28 NOVEMBER 1942   *to*   27 DECEMBER 1945

Given at SEPARATION CENTER FORT DIX NEW JERSEY

on the 27TH *day of* DECEMBER   *19* 45

FOR THE COMMANDING OFFICER

C H TALL LT COL INF

FIGURE 7-17   Certificate of Service for George T. Smith. (Courtesy of Jeff Smith.)

CF 14A   17
MILITARY RECORD AND REPORT OF SEPARATION
CERTIFICATE OF SERVICE

1. LAST NAME - FIRST NAME - MIDDLE INITIAL	2. ARMY SERIAL NUMBER	3. AUS. GRADE	4. ARM OR SERVICE	5. COMPONENT
SMITH GEORGE T	Private	1ST LT	CWS	AUS

6. ORGANIZATION	7. DATE OF RELIEF FROM ACTIVE DUTY	8. PLACE OF SEPARATION
803RD CHEMICAL COMPANY AIR OPERATIONS BUCKLEY FIELD COLORADO	27 DEC 45	SEPARATION CENTER FORT DIX NEW JERSEY

9. PERMANENT ADDRESS FOR MAILING PURPOSES	10. DATE OF BIRTH	11. PLACE OF BIRTH
22 ROME STREET NEWARK NEW JERSEY	8 NOV 17	NEWARK NEW JERSEY

12. ADDRESS FROM WHICH EMPLOYMENT WILL BE SOUGHT	13. COLOR EYES	14. COLOR HAIR	15. HEIGHT	16. WEIGHT	17. NO. OF DEPENDENTS
SEE 9	BLUE	BROWN	5'6"	130 LBS.	1

18. RACE	19. MARITAL STATUS	20. U.S.CITIZEN	21. CIVILIAN OCCUPATION AND NO.
WHITE X NEGRO OTHER (specify)	SINGLE MARRIED X OTHER (specify)	YES X NO	ROTOGRAVURE PRESSMAN 4-48.060

MILITARY HISTORY

SELECTIVE SERVICE DATA ▶	22. REGISTERED YES NO X	23. LOCAL S. S. BOARD NUMBER	24. COUNTY AND STATE	25. HOME ADDRESS AT TIME OF ENTRY ON ACTIVE DUTY
				305 BOULEVARD HASBYOUCK HEIGHT NEW JERSEY

26. DATE OF ENTRY ON ACTIVE DUTY	27. MILITARY OCCUPATIONAL SPECIALTY AND NO.
28 NOV 42	CHEMICAL WARFARE UNIT COMMANDER 1413

28. BATTLES AND CAMPAIGNS

NONE

29. DECORATIONS AND CITATIONS

EUROPEAN AFRICAN MIDDLE EASTERN THEATER CAMPAIGN RIBBON   AMERICAN DEFENSE SERVICE MEDAL

30. WOUNDS RECEIVED IN ACTION

NONE

31. SERVICE SCHOOLS ATTENDED	32. SERVICE OUTSIDE CONTINENTAL U. S. AND RETURN		
CHEMICAL WARFARE SCHOOL EDGEWOOD ARSENAL MARYLAND AIRFORCE MUNITIONS SCHOOL LEICESTER ENGLAND	DATE OF DEPARTURE	DESTINATION	DATE OF ARRIVAL
	17 JAN 44	EUROPEAN TH	28 JAN 44

33. REASON AND AUTHORITY FOR SEPARATION		
RELIEF FROM ACTIVE DUTY TWX AAF PDC TF2/REK/2741 25 SEP 45RR1-5 DEMOB	7 AUG 45 U S A	20 AUG 45

34. CURRENT TOUR OF ACTIVE DUTY						35. EDUCATION (years)		
CONTINENTAL SERVICE			FOREIGN SERVICE					
YEARS	MONTHS	DAYS	YEARS	MONTHS	DAYS	GRAMMAR SCHOOL	HIGH SCHOOL	COLLEGE
1	5	26	1	7	3	8	4	0

INSURANCE NOTICE

IMPORTANT   IF PREMIUM IS NOT PAID WHEN DUE OR WITHIN THIRTY-ONE DAYS THEREAFTER, INSURANCE WILL LAPSE. MAKE CHECKS OR MONEY ORDERS PAYABLE TO THE TREASURER OF THE U. S. AND FORWARD TO COLLECTIONS SUBDIVISION, VETERANS ADMINISTRATION, WASHINGTON 25, D. C.

36. KIND OF INSURANCE			37. HOW PAID		38. Effective Date of Allotment Discontinuance	39. Date of Next Premium Due (one month after 38)	40. PREMIUM DUE EACH MONTH	41. INTENTION OF VETERAN TO		
Nat. Serv.	U.S. Govt.	None	Allotment	Direct to V.A.				Continue Continue only Discontinue	
X			X		31 DEC 45	31 JAN 46	* 13.75	X	*

42.	43. REMARKS (This space for completion of above items or entry of other items specified in W. D. Directives)
RIGHT THUMB PRINT	ASR SCORE(2 SEP 45)75 LAPEL BUTTON ISSUED

44. SIGNATURE OF OFFICER BEING SEPARATED	45. PERSONNEL OFFICER (Type name, grade and organization - signature)
George T. Smith 1st Lt CWS AC	F P PORTER 2ND LT SIG C ASST ADJ F P Porter

WD AGO FORM 53-98
1 November 1944

This form supersedes all previous editions of WD AGO Forms 53 and 280 for officers entitled to a Certificate of Service, which will not be used after receipt of this revision.

FIGURE 7-18   The Military Record and Report of Separation for George T. Smith. (Courtesy of Jeff Smith.)

ARMY AIR FORCES

Certificate of Appreciation

FOR WAR SERVICE

TO

GEORGE T. SMITH

I CANNOT meet you personally to thank you for a job well done; nor can I hope to put in written words the great hope I have for your success in future life.

Together we built the striking force that swept the Luftwaffe from the skies and broke the German power to resist. The total might of that striking force was then unleashed upon the Japanese. Although you no longer play an active military part, the contribution you made to the Air Forces was essential in making us the greatest team in the world.

The ties that bound us under stress of combat must not be broken in peacetime. Together we share the responsibility for guarding our country in the air. We who stay will never forget the part you have played while in uniform. We know you will continue to play a comparable role as a civilian. As our ways part, let me wish you God speed and the best of luck on your road in life. Our gratitude and respect go with you.

COMMANDING GENERAL
ARMY AIR FORCES

FIGURE 7-19   Certificate of Appreciation for War Service presented to George T. Smith. (Courtesy of Jeff Smith.)

SAFEGUARD ...

LEGEND: Insert N/A in the items below which are not applicable

PERSONAL DATA

1. LAST NAME - FIRST NAME - MIDDLE NAME: Private
2. SERVICE NUMBER: Private
3. a. GRADE, RATE OR RANK: A1C b. E-4
b. DATE OF RANK (Day, Month, Year): 1 OCT 63
4. DEPARTMENT, COMPONENT AND BRANCH OR CLASS: AIR FORCE REGAF
5. PLACE OF BIRTH (City and State or Country): MEBANE, NORTH CAROLINA
6. DATE OF BIRTH: DAY 31 MONTH AUG YEAR 40
7a. RACE: CAUCASIAN
b. SEX: MALE
c. COLOR HAIR: BLACK
d. COLOR EYES: GREEN
e. HEIGHT: 5'10"
f. WEIGHT: 147
8. U.S. CITIZEN: [X] YES [ ] NO
9. MARITAL STATUS: MARRIED
10a. HIGHEST CIVILIAN EDUCATION LEVEL ATTAINED: COLLEGE 2
b. MAJOR COURSE OR FIELD: RELIGION

TRANSFER OR DISCHARGE DATA

11a. TYPE OF TRANSFER OR DISCHARGE: RELEASE FROM ACTIVE DUTY
b. STATION OR INSTALLATION AT WHICH EFFECTED: MCGUIRE AFB NEW JERSEY
c. REASON AND AUTHORITY: (SDN 411) COG, PAR 3C, AFR 39-14
d. EFFECTIVE DATE: DAY 5 MONTH FEB YEAR 65
12. LAST DUTY ASSIGNMENT AND MAJOR COMMAND: 2130 COMM SQ (AFCS)
13a. CHARACTER OF SERVICE: HONORABLE
b. TYPE OF CERTIFICATE ISSUED: DD FORM 217AF

SELECTIVE SERVICE DATA

14. SELECTIVE SERVICE NUMBER: 31 80 40 351
15. SELECTIVE SERVICE LOCAL BOARD NUMBER, CITY, COUNTY AND STATE: LB# 80 REIDSVILLE (ROCKINGHAM) N. C.
16. DATE INDUCTED: DAY MONTH NA YEAR
17. DISTRICT OR AREA COMMAND TO WHICH RESERVIST TRANSFERRED: AFRES

SERVICE DATA

18. TERMINAL DATE OF RESERVE OBLIGATION: DAY 13 MONTH FEB YEAR 67
19. CURRENT ACTIVE SERVICE OTHER THAN BY INDUCTION
a. SOURCE OF ENTRY: [X] ENLISTED (First Enlistment) [ ] ENLISTED (Prior Service) [ ] REENLISTED [ ] OTHER: AFQT 79-85-II
b. TERM OF SERVICE (Years): 4
c. DATE OF ENTRY: DAY 14 MONTH FEB YEAR 61
20. PRIOR REGULAR ENLISTMENTS: NA
21. GRADE, RATE OR RANK AT TIME OF ENTRY INTO CURRENT ACTIVE SERVICE: AB
22. PLACE OF ENTRY INTO CURRENT ACTIVE SERVICE (City and State): CHARLOTTE, NORTH CAROLINA
23. HOME OF RECORD AT TIME OF ENTRY INTO ACTIVE SERVICE (Street, RFD, City, County and State): BOX 383 MADISON ROCKINGHAM NORTH CAROLINA
24. STATEMENT OF SERVICE

		YEARS	MONTHS	DAYS
a. CREDITABLE FOR BASIC PAY PURPOSES	(1) NET SERVICE THIS PERIOD	03	11	22
	(2) OTHER SERVICE	00	00	00
	(3) TOTAL (Line (1) + line (2))	03	11	22
b. TOTAL ACTIVE SERVICE		03	11	22
c. FOREIGN AND/OR SEA SERVICE		02	09	09

25a. SPECIALTY NUMBER AND TITLE: COMM & CRYPTO EQP SYS RPMN CAFSC 30650A
b. RELATED CIVILIAN OCCUPATION AND D.O.T. NUMBER: NONE
26. DECORATIONS, MEDALS, BADGES, COMMENDATIONS, CITATIONS AND CAMPAIGN RIBBONS AWARDED OR AUTHORIZED:
SAEMR SO# G-62, HQ UK COMM RGN, 1964
AFGCM SO# G-19 HQ UK COMM RGN 1964 (14FEB61 - 13FEB64)
27. WOUNDS RECEIVED AS A RESULT OF ACTION WITH ENEMY FORCES (Place and date, if known): NONE
28. SERVICE SCHOOLS OR COLLEGES, COLLEGE TRAINING COURSES AND/OR POST-GRADUATE COURSES SUCCESSFULLY COMPLETED

a. SCHOOL OR COURSE	b. DATES (From-To)	c. MAJOR COURSES
SHEPPARD AFB TEXAS	MAR 61 - NOV 61	ELECT COMM CRYPTO RPMN
LACKLAND AFB TEXAS	DEC 61 - MAR 62	F& O MAINT TSEC/K/W-26

29. OTHER SERVICE TRAINING COURSES SUCCESSFULLY COMPLETED: GED COLLEGE

VA DATA

30. a. GOVERNMENT LIFE INSURANCE IN FORCE: [ ] YES [X] NO
b. AMOUNT OF ALLOTMENT: NA
c. MONTH ALLOTMENT DISCONTINUED: NA
31. a. VA BENEFITS PREVIOUSLY APPLIED FOR (Specify type): NONE
b. VA CLAIM NUMBER: C- NA

AUTHENTICATION

32. REMARKS:
BLOOD GROUP AB-POS NO TIME LOST GEN 80 ADMN 85 MECH 60 ELECT 85 DTD FEB61
PAID FOR 32 DAYS ACCRUED LEAVE NOT ELIGIBLE MOP NAC COMPLETED 11DEC61 FILED
4TH DIST OSI RE-3/93 CDSD 3FEB65 SSN: 246-56-3258
33. PERMANENT ADDRESS FOR MAILING PURPOSES AFTER TRANSFER OR DISCHARGE (Street, RFD, City, County and State): BOX 383 MADISON, ROCKINGHAM, NORTH CAROLINA
34. SIGNATURE OF PERSON BEING TRANSFERRED OR DISCHARGED: Private
35. a. TYPED NAME, GRADE AND TITLE OF AUTHORIZING OFFICER: PAUL E. O'BRIEN, MAJOR USAF
b. SIGNATURE OF OFFICER AUTHORIZED TO SIGN: Paul E. O'Brien

DD FORM 1 NOV 55 214 (8 Part) REPLACES EDITION OF 1 JUL 52 WHICH IS OBSOLETE

ARMED FORCES OF THE UNITED STATES REPORT OF TRANSFER OR DISCHARGE 1

FIGURE 7-20 Report of Transfer or Discharge from Active Duty, also known as the DD 214. (From the author's collection.)

WAR DEPARTMENT
OFFICE OF THE QUARTERMASTER GENERAL
WASHINGTON 25, D. C.

5 January 1949

1st Lt William J. Smith, ASN O 661 675
Plot B, Row 7, Grave 25
Headstone: Cross
Cambridge U. S. Military Cemetery

Mr. William H. Smith
22 Rome Street
Newark, New York

Dear Mr. Smith:

This is to inform you that the remains of your loved one have
been permanently interred, as recorded above, side by side with com-
rades who also gave their lives for their country. Customary military funeral services were conducted over the grave at the time of
burial.

After the Department of the Army has completed all final interments,
the cemetery will be transferred, as authorized by the Congress, to the
care and supervision of the American Battle Monuments Commission. The
Commission also will have the responsibility for permanent construction
and beautification of the cemetery, including erection of the permanent
headstone. The headstone will be inscribed with the name exactly as
recorded above, the rank or rating where appropriate, organization,
State, and date of death. Any inquiries relative to the type of headstone or the spelling of the name to be inscribed thereon, should be
addressed to the American Battle Monuments Commission, the central
address of which is Room 713, 1712 "G" Street, N. W., Washington 25, D. C.
Your letter should include the full name, rank, serial number, grave
location, and name of the cemetery.

While interment activities are in progress, the cemetery will not be
open to visitors. However, upon completion thereof, due notice will be
carried by the press.

You may rest assured that this final interment was conducted with
fitting dignity and solemnity and that the grave-site will be carefully
and conscientiously maintained in perpetuity by the United States Government.

Sincerely yours,

Thomas B Larkin

THOMAS B. LARKIN
Major General
The Quartermaster General

FIGURE 7-21   Letter from the U.S. War Department concerning final interment
of 1st Lieutenant William J. Smith. (Courtesy of Jeff Smith.)

Congress established the American Battle Monuments Commission (ABMC) at the request of General John J. Pershing to honor the accomplishments of the American Armed Forces where they have served since World War I. The Commission is responsible for the establishment and maintenance of war memorials and cemeteries in foreign countries. Its website at **www.abmc.gov** provides access to databases of World War I, World War II, and Korean War casualties buried overseas. The site provides detailed information about the name, rank, unit, date and place of death, cemetery where the individual is interred, and information about services that the ABMC can provide to help honor and commemorate individuals buried in these places.

The Vietnam Veterans Memorial Wall USA website at **http://thewall-usa.com** has a searchable database of all U.S. casualties in the Vietnam War, and vast amounts of information is accessible there. A separate website exists for the United States Defense Prisoner of War/Missing Personnel Office, at www.dtic.mil/dpmo.

Learn from Military Pension Records

Military pension records can be tremendously informative. In order to qualify for benefits, a veteran or surviving spouse or family member must present evidence of identity and proof of military service. As you have seen, the military records from the 20th century that veterans received at the time of separation are easily sufficient to document an application for pension benefits. However, it has not always been so easy.

Individuals who fought in the American Revolutionary War, for example, had to swear an affidavit in a court of law concerning their military service. In addition, they had to bring forward witnesses who served with them and/or who were personally familiar with the service of the individual. The witnesses also had to swear oaths or affidavits concerning their knowledge.

The sworn statements of the veteran typically include details about the dates and places of service, the units in which they served, the names of commanding officers, and details concerning the engagements in which they had participated. Some of these accounts are vivid with details. If the widow of a man who served applied for survivor pension benefits, she was required to swear an oath and provide some evidence of her marriage to the deceased. It is not surprising that sometimes the pension files contain original marriage certificates or pages taken from the center of the family Bible on which marriages, births, and deaths were recorded. Figure 7-22 shows one of several pages from a family Bible that are included as part of the Revolutionary War pension file for my ancestor, John Swords, at the South Carolina State Archives and History Center. These documents were worth more when submitted as evidence to collect monetary benefits than as family documentation.

In addition, pension files may include receipts or payment stubs that document annuity payments. These and correspondence in the file may document the life events, medical conditions, and death of the veteran and/or the surviving spouse and other family members. The example shown in Figure 7-23 is a payment document

[677]

FAMILY RECORD.

MARRIAGES.

John Swords and Eleanor Swancy was married April 24th 1782 —

MARRIAGES.

Rosa was born Febry 28th — 1828

Elmer was born Febury 14th 1830

Saraan was born March 10th 1832

Sopha was born January 19th 1841

86

4 R

FIGURE 7-22 Page from the Swords family Bible that was included in the pension file of John Swords. (From the author's collection.)

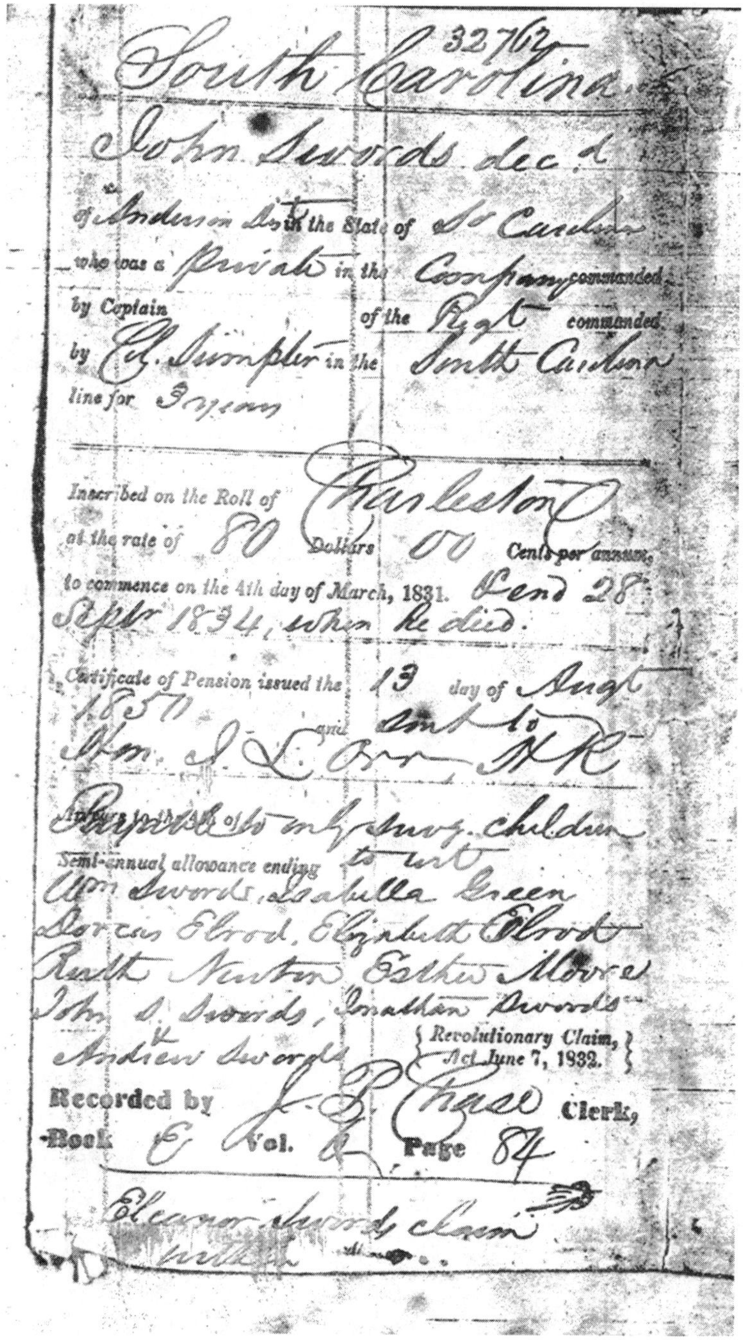

South Carolina 32762

John Swords dec'd

of Anderson Dist in the State of So Carolina
who was a Private in the Company commanded
by Captain of the Regt commanded
by Col. Sumpter in the South Carolina
line for 3 years

Inscribed on the Roll of Charleston
at the rate of 80 Dollars 00 Cents per annum,
to commence on the 4th day of March, 1831. Ending 28 Sept 1834, when he died.

Certificate of Pension issued the 13 day of Augt 1850 and sent to
Hon. J. L. Orr H.R.

Arrears to the 4th of
Payable to only surv. children
Semi-annual allowance ending to wit
Wm Swords, Isabella Green
Dorcas Elrod, Elizabeth Elrod
Ruth Newton, Esther Moore
John S. Swords, Jonathan Swords
and Andrew Swords

Revolutionary Claim, Act June 7, 1832.

Recorded by J. P. Chase Clerk,
Book E Vol. 8 Page 84

Eleanor Swords claim

FIGURE 7-23 Record of payment to the widow of John Swords that lists the names of his surviving children. (From the author's collection.)

for John Swords. This single document indicates that he served in the army for three years from South Carolina, and that he died on 28 September 1834. It also tells me that his wife collected pension benefits, tells me that she is deceased, and lists the names of all the surviving children as of 13 August 1851.

Pension files for those who served in the Revolutionary War, the War of 1812, and for Union veterans of the United States Civil War can be found at NARA. You can order these from NARA electronically. Visit the NARA website at **http://archives .gov/research/order** for more information and to initiate an order online.

You may also find that both the federal and state governments paid military pensions, as I found for John Swords. I obtained a Revolutionary War pension file from NARA with more than 20 pages of copies of microfilmed documents. A number of years later, I was researching at the South Carolina Archives and History Center and discovered another, different pension file with more extensive records. In fact, his sworn statement in that file provided details of his capture and imprisonment by the British at the Battle of Savannah. Those details were not included in the statement in the NARA file, and I therefore gained more information and insight into his life.

You will now find that U.S. military pension records are digitized and available online at the Footnote.com subscription database service (**www.footnote.com**) and in the HeritageQuest Online database, available through many U.S. public libraries.

Military records, as you have seen, can be a gold mine of detail if you know where to look. Your investment in the study of the history and geography of the areas where your ancestors and family members lived and from where they may have served in the military can prepare you for locating records more effectively.

8

Understand and Use
Land and Property Records

HOW TO...

- Locate and use land and property records in the United States
- Understand and use land and property records in Canada
- Learn about land and property records in the United Kingdom
- Locate land and property records online
- Place your ancestors into context with property records

Land and property records are among the most numerous records in existence. However, they also are some of the most poorly understood and least used resources by genealogical researchers. The common perceptions are that a) they are cryptic and unfathomable, and b) they contain little of genealogical value.

Like military records, land and property records require some advance research into the history of the geographical area and the types of records that were created at specific periods. In addition, the methods used to define boundaries and register the ownership and transfer of property also need to be understood. However, this is not an insurmountable problem, and once you have invested the time to learn about land and property records, you will find that they are a tremendous source of information. And yes, they *can and do* contain vast amounts of genealogical information to help further your research.

There are many excellent books and reference materials available to help you understand land and property records in various locations, such as libraries, bookstores, and on the Internet. However, as a beginning, let's explore the basics of land and property records in the United States, Canada, and the United Kingdom. These overviews should provide you with some basic knowledge to get started in locating your ancestors' records in those places, and give you ideas on how to approach similar research in other countries in which your ancestors lived and may have owned property.

Locate and Use Land and Property Records in the United States

The United States' history is a colorful combination of Spanish, English, French, Dutch, Mexican, Russian, and Native American influences. Nearly every American schoolchild is taught that Christopher Columbus discovered America in 1492 and, although the place that Columbus "discovered" was not exactly a part of what we know to be the United States of today, this definitely was the beginning of centuries of colonization, conflict, and amazing expansion.

The history of the United States makes for a fascinating study and its settlement parallels that of Canada in many ways. You will find in the course of your genealogical research in both the United States and Canada that land and property records development is similar because of the efforts of both France and England to colonize vast areas of the North American continent. The influence of the Spanish in Florida and the southeast, in California and the west, and in other areas brought Spain's form of government, its religion, its governmental processes, and its forms of record-keeping with it. Each time there was a change in government, the land and property records process was impacted from the perspectives of documentation and taxation. However, this also could be said for many areas of what is now the United States.

Consider for a moment the Spanish possession of Florida in the 1500s. Spain's Catholic and Jesuit priests spent decades trying to make Christians of the Native Americans in that area. It was a bloody conflict from the outset but the Spanish continued to colonize and settle the area. In fact, the oldest permanent European settlement in the United States is St. Augustine, Florida, established in 1565. Spain divided Florida into two administrative regions, east and west. This action continues to influence the state to this day as its capital, Tallahassee, is in the panhandle of the state. The panhandle was a much more populous area than the lower portion of the peninsula, and the capital was sited there in the 19th century. As a result, Tallahassee became and has remained the capital despite the explosive population growth to its southeast. Britain gained possession of what was primarily east Florida in 1763 and ruled there until 1783 when the Spanish regained control. During the period of British rule of Florida, residents sought proof from Spain of their ownership of land. The documents created are referred to as "memorials" and "concessions," and these really were petitions for proof of land ownership. These are written in Spanish and are among some of the earliest land documents that exist for Florida. The Board of Land Commissioners was established in 1822 by the U.S. government to settle all Spanish land grant claims in the territory that Spain ceded to the United States in 1821. These records are held by the Florida State Archives (**http://dlis.dos.state.fl.us**).

Spain and France also competed for possession of what we know as the Louisiana Territory, with both struggling to colonize and control this vast area. In 1800, Spain signed a secretly negotiated treaty in which it signed over its control of the entire territory to France. When the U.S. government learned in 1802 that France, and not Spain, had authority over the area, it began negotiations to acquire the territory for itself. This culminated in 1803 with the Louisiana Purchase.

Spanish rule continued in Florida until 1821, which is when the U.S. government obtained possession of the area under a reparation treaty negotiated in 1819. At that time, Florida became and remained a territory of the United States until March of 1845, when it became a state. Mexico fought for independence from Spain and gained its sovereignty in 1821. Texas declared its independence from Mexico in 1836 and won its freedom at the Battle of San Jacinto that same year. The Dutch founded New Netherland, a territory that covered parts of the states of Maryland, Delaware, Pennsylvania, New Jersey, New York, Connecticut, and Rhode Island. New Amsterdam on the island of Manhattan, the site of what is now New York City, was founded in 1624. In 1621, the Dutch West India Company received its charter. The English battled the Dutch for the area and finally received the territory in 1674. It was renamed New York. Russia's influence is centered on Alaska, which was purchased for the United States by Secretary of State William H. Seward in 1867.

This short "thumbnail" history is only one example of the kind of historical research that is important to understand as part of your preparation to conduct effective research, especially in the area of land and property records from these early periods. You will want to study the history of the areas and historical periods during which your ancestors lived there to learn more about the boundary changes at all levels, the government(s) having jurisdiction, the records that were created, and the ultimate disposition of those particular records.

Did You Know? Refer to histories of the area in which your ancestors lived, at the time they lived there. Understand what government had jurisdiction at the time, and then determine where the records of that time period are stored. You can then arrange to access them or order copies.

Learn About the Organization of State and Federal Lands

Land and property research in the United States can yield vast amounts of genealogical information if you understand the organization of the materials and where to search. There are two distinct types of what I'll call "land organization" in the United States: State-Land States and Federal-Land States. Understanding the distinction between them is important because the way they are measured and recorded differs. The descriptions provided in this chapter are intended only as an introduction for you. There are many books on the subject of land records in the United States and I would refer you to them for a more detailed study. Perhaps the best of these is E. Wade Hone's book *Land and Property Research in the United States* (Ancestry, Incorporated, 1997).

State-Land States

The term "State-Land States" refers to the fact that the land was originally controlled by the state and sold or distributed by the state itself. Any subsequent land transactions were conducted between private individuals and are therefore often referred to as "private lands." If you examine the following list, it is immediately apparent that many of the State-Land States were part of the original 13 colonies under the control of the British Crown. Others, such as West Virginia, were derived from an original colony. And other foreign governments controlled others, such as Texas and Hawaii. The State-Land States are Connecticut, Delaware, Georgia, Hawaii, Kentucky, Maine, Maryland, Massachusetts, New Hampshire, New Jersey, New York, North Carolina, Pennsylvania, Rhode Island, South Carolina, Tennessee, Texas, Vermont, Virginia, and West Virginia.

Following the Revolutionary War, some of the original colonies claimed extensive westward territories as part of their jurisdictions. However, with the formation of the U.S. federal government and based on individual negotiations with the states, most of the land outside what are the current state boundaries was ceded to the federal government. These lands and other territorial acquisitions by the federal government became what were used to create Federal-Land States.

State-Lands Survey Methods

The common method of land measurement in the State-Land States is referred to as "metes and bounds." This scheme is based on the use of physical natural features such as rocks, trees, and waterways as reference points and the surveyor's chain as a unit of measure. Table 8-1 shows a high-level conversion from surveyor's measurements to feet and inches. You will want to refer to a complete surveyor's conversion table in another reference work.

TABLE 8-1 Surveyor's Measurement Conversion

Surveyor's Measure	Equivalent
1 link	7.92 inches
25 links	1 rod, 1 pole, or 1 perch
100 links	1 chain (also referred to as a Gunter's chain)
1 chain	66 feet
80 chains	1 mile
625 square links	1 square rod
16 square rods	1 square chain
10 square chains	1 square acre

The metes and bounds surveying method dates back to the earliest colonial days, and you will find that, as a result, there are some very strangely shaped land parcels. Some surveys included the placement of stakes for use in later surveys. However, since a stake could be physically moved, a parcel of land always had to be completely resurveyed to verify the accuracy of the land holding. You will therefore find, in many surveys and land description records, references to physical features, stakes, and other people's property, as well as the use of standard surveyor's measurements. The surveyor used compass directions stated as north, south, east, west, or combinations, a compass direction in degrees, and a distance measured in surveyors' units, such as chains.

Figure 8-1 shows a surveyor's report prepared for the estate of one Eli Jones, who owned property in Caswell County, North Carolina. The report includes representations of roads and waterways, and incorporates references to roads, stakes, pointers, sweet gum trees, and other persons' properties. It uses surveyor's chain measurements to illustrate and describe the property. You will also note that, at the upper end of the drawing of the parcel, there are references to "Dower" and "Dower line." This indicates that the owner of the parcel cited was married. By law, the property could not be sold or transferred without the consent of the wife. We will discuss "dower release" shortly.

Figure 8-2 shows a detailed section from another survey report that includes a detailed metes and bounds description of the parcel of property.

A separate system of measurement was used in the Federal-Land States and is commonly referred to as the "Township and Range" system. We'll discuss that in the "Federal-Land States Records" section later in this chapter. However, be aware that a combination of metes and bounds and township systems, along with some other less widely used schemes, has been used in some areas. In Texas, for example, the Spanish land measurement method of "leagues and labors" was used in some areas. In Louisiana, the French used the "River Lot System" of slender lots laid out perpendicular to waterways, and these are referred to as *arpents*. Ohio used several land measurement systems depending on the area and the measurement scheme used at the time.

State-Land States Records

You will find a wealth of varied and interesting land records in use in State-Land States. The original process of acquiring land began with a land grant. The grant simply defined the terms under which the land would be made available by the grantor to the grantee. The terms "grantor" and "grantee" continue to be used to this day in land transactions. In order to obtain an original grant, an individual (or organization) was required to make an application. A successful application resulted in the issue of a land warrant. A land warrant is simply an official order or directive for a survey to be performed. The survey was conducted and returned to the appropriate land office, where it was recorded. At this point, a patent was prepared. The patent is a title document signifying that the entire acquisition process has been conducted, including the exchange of any money or other consideration. The land patent was then recorded and the title process was complete.

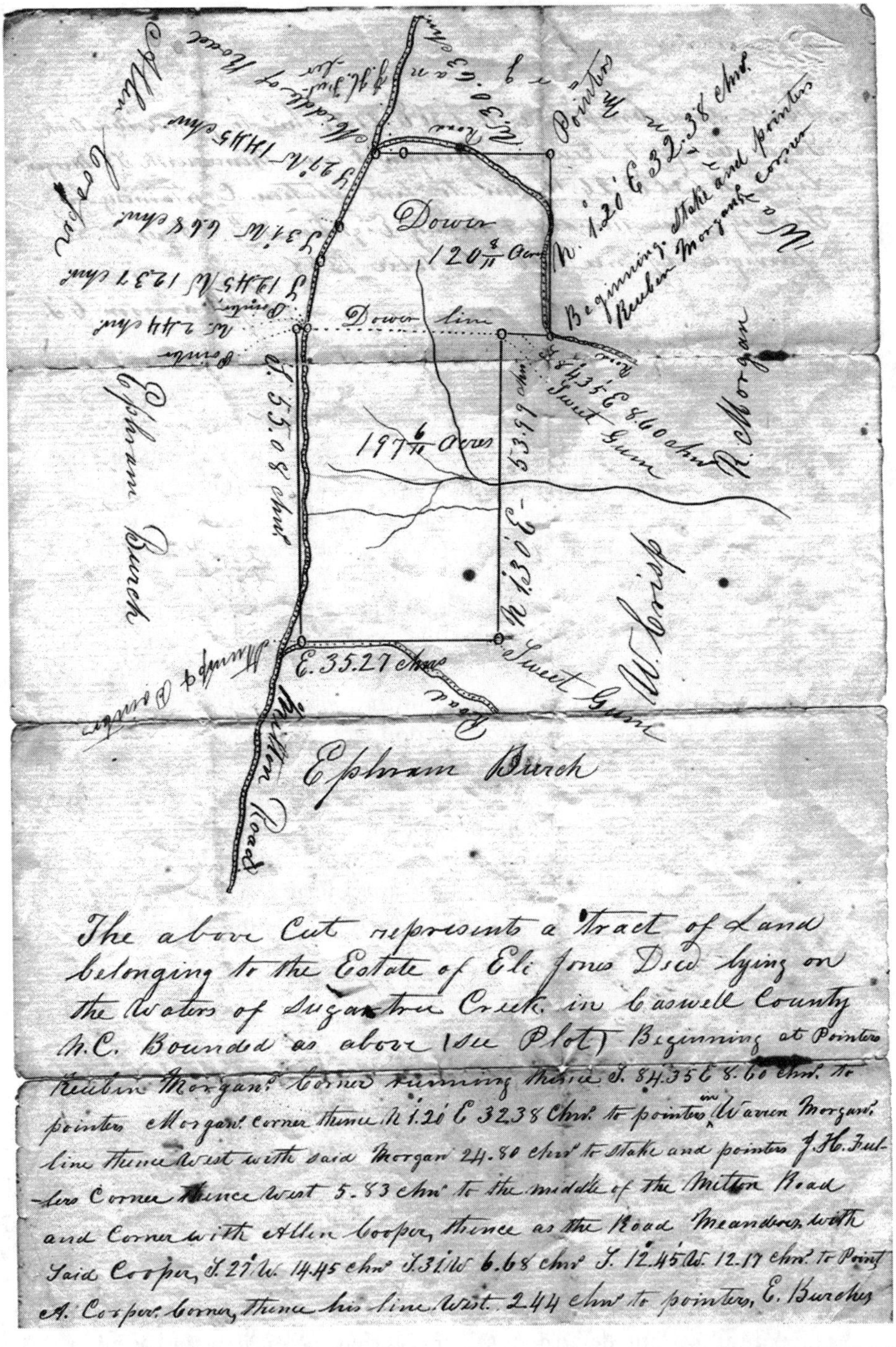

The above Cut represents a Tract of Land belonging to the Estate of Eli Jones Dec'd lying on the Waters of Sugartree Creek in Caswell County N.C. Bounded as above (See Plot) Beginning at Pointers Reuben Morgan's Corner running thence S. 84.35 E 8.60 chns. to pointers Morgan's Corner thence N 1.20 E 32.38 chns to pointers in Warren Morgan's line thence West with said Morgan 24.80 chns to Stake and pointers J. H. Ful-lers Corner thence West 5.83 chns to the middle of the Milton Road and Corner with Allen Cooper, thence as the Road meanders with Said Cooper, S. 27 W. 14.45 chns S. 31 W. 6.68 chns S. 12.45 W. 12.17 chns. to Point A. Cooper Corner, thence his line West 2.44 chns to pointers, E. Burches

FIGURE 8-1 Survey report for a parcel of land in North Carolina that used the metes and bounds survey method. (From the author's collection.)

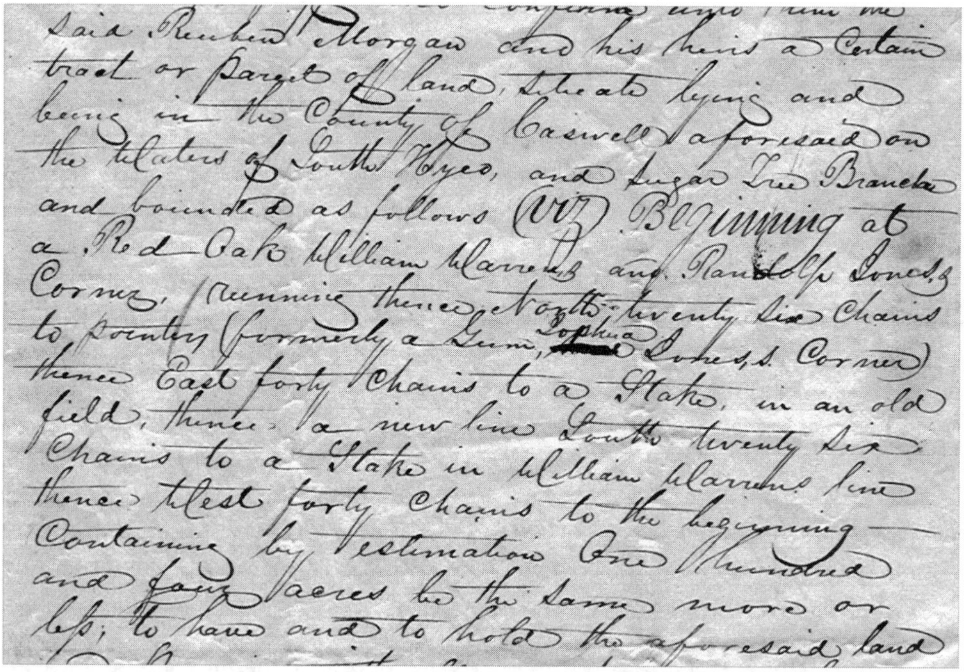
said Reuben Morgan and his heirs a Certain
tract or Parcel of land, Situate lying and
being in the County of Caswell aforesaid on
the Waters of South Hyco, and Sugar Tree Branch
and bounded as follows (viz) Beginning at
a Red Oak William Warren's and Randolph Jones's
Corner, running thence North twenty six Chains
to pointers (formerly a Gum, Sophia Jones's Corner)
thence East forty Chains to a Stake, in an old
field; thence a new line South twenty six
Chains to a Stake in William Warren's line
thence West forty Chains to the beginning
Containing by estimation One Hundred
and four acres be the same more or
less; to have and to hold the aforesaid land

FIGURE 8-2 Detail of a metes and bounds property description from a land survey. (From the author's collection.)

You will find that the subsequent land transfer process typically was continued, as property ownership moved from person to person, with the use of indentures (or agreements), a property survey, and various sale transaction documents, ultimately resulting in the preparation and recording of a deed. Figures 8-3 and 8-4 show both sides of a copy of an indenture for the purchase of a piece of property in Caswell County, North Carolina, dating from 1792. (This document is a transcription prepared by the Register of Deeds on 7 November 1838 from the Deed Book in his office, as indicated by the clerk's statement at the bottom of the second page.)

During the American Revolution, there was no formal federal government and therefore no treasury. Soldiers were paid as possible, but some were rewarded for their service with what became known as "bounty land." There were both federal and state bounty land warrants issued. States that produced their own bounty-land warrants to compensate its citizens for service were Georgia, Maryland, Massachusetts, North Carolina, Pennsylvania, South Carolina, and Virginia. A sample bounty land warrant is shown in Figure 8-5. In order to obtain bounty land, an individual had to make application and go through a documentation process to prove eligibility to receive the land. Military service or providing supplies or other aid were reasons for eligibility, so don't be surprised to find the occasional woman's name on a bounty land application or warrant. The number of acres granted depended on the person's rank and service.

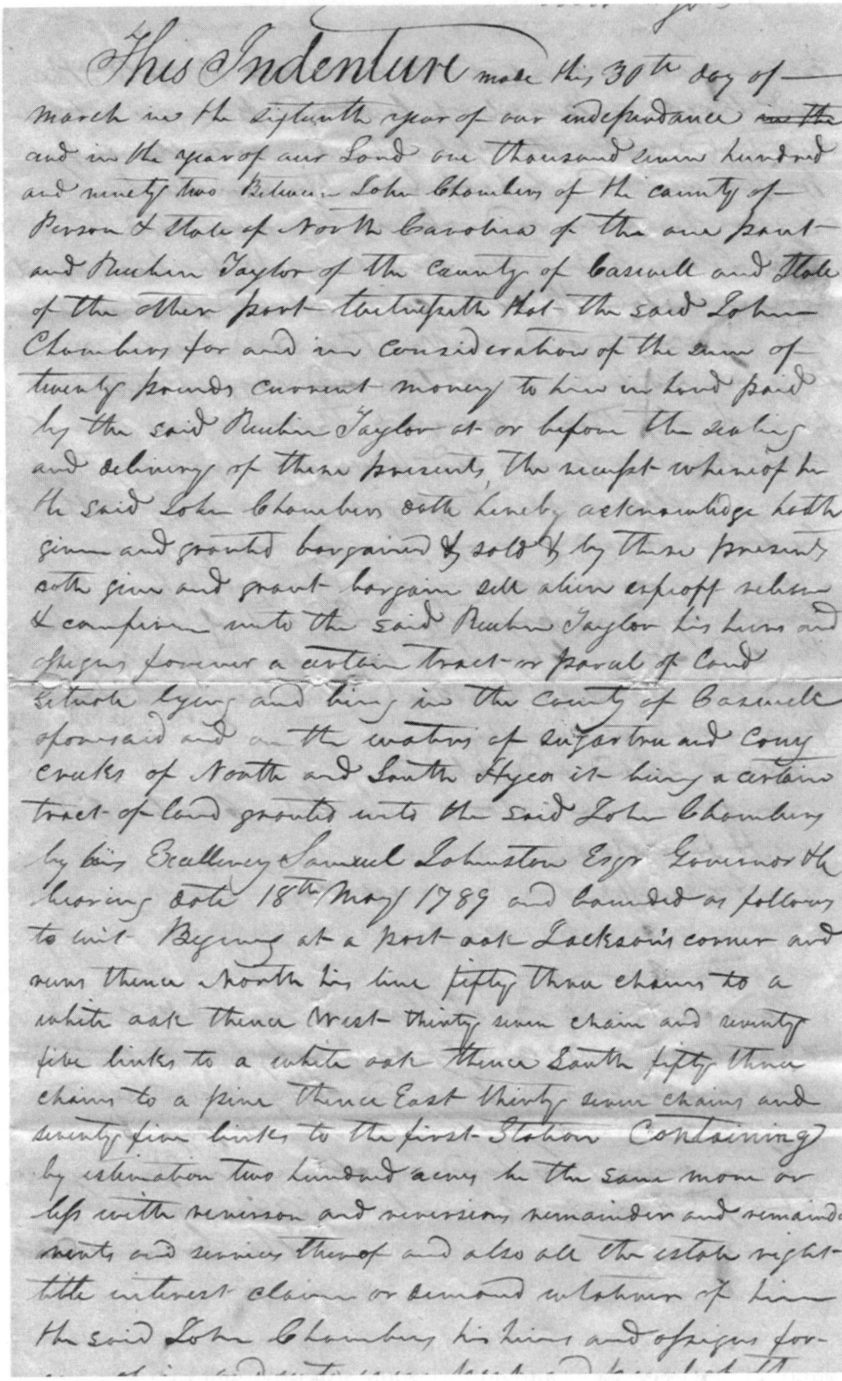

This Indenture made this 30th day of
March in the sixteenth year of our independance ~~in the~~
and in the year of our Lord one thousand seven hundred
and ninety two Between John Chambers of the County of
Person & State of North Carolina of the one part
and Reuben Taylor of the County of Caswell and State
of the other part Witnesseth that the said John
Chambers for and in consideration of the sum of
twenty pounds current money to him in hand paid
by the said Reuben Taylor at or before the sealing
and delivery of these presents, the receipt whereof he
the said John Chambers doth hereby acknowledge hath
given and granted bargained & sold & by these presents
doth give and grant bargain sell alien enfeoff release
& confirm unto the said Reuben Taylor his heirs and
assigns forever a certain tract or parcel of land
situate lying and being in the County of Caswell
aforesaid and on the waters of Sugartree and Cony
creeks of North and South Hyco it being a certain
tract of land granted unto the said John Chambers
by his Excellency Samuel Johnston Esqr Governor &c
bearing date 18th May 1789 and bounded as follows
to wit Beginning at a post oak Jackson's corner and
runs thence North his line fifty three chains to a
white oak thence West thirty seven chain and seventy
five links to a white oak thence South fifty three
chains to a pine thence East thirty seven chains and
seventy five links to the first Station Containing
by estimation two hundred acres be the same more or
less with reversion and reversions remainder and remainders
rents and services thereof and also all the estate right
title interest claim or demand whatsoever of him
the said John Chambers his heirs and assigns for-

FIGURE 8-3 Front page of an indenture for the purchase of land in 1792. (From the author's collection.)

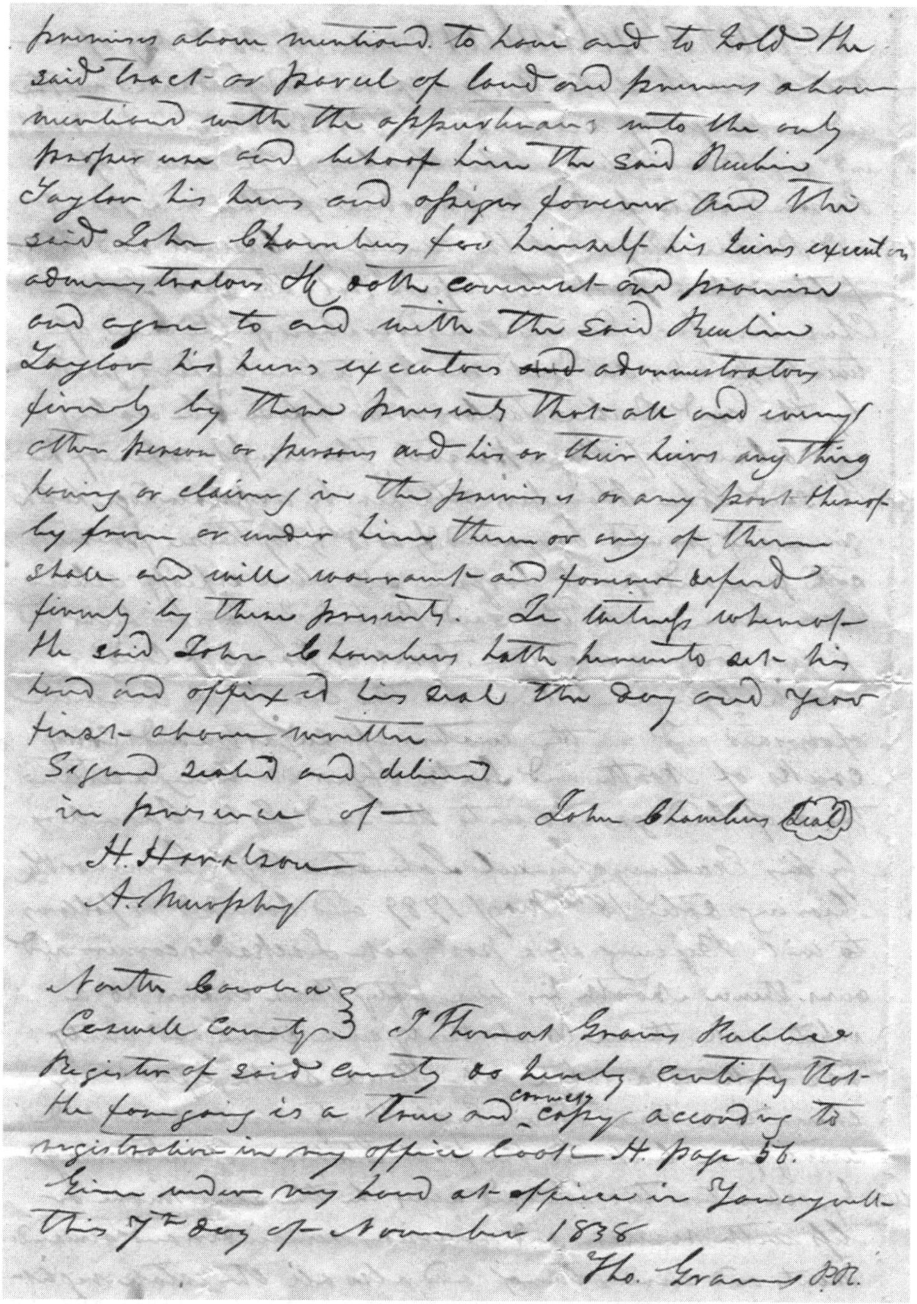

premises above mentioned. To have and to hold the
said tract or parcel of land and premises above
mentioned with the appurtenances unto the only
proper use and behoof him the said Reubin
Taylor his heirs and assigns forever And the
said John Chambers for himself his heirs executors
administrators doth covenant and promise
and agree to and with the said Reubin
Taylor his heirs executors ~~and~~ administrators
firmly by these presents that all and every
other person or persons and his or their heirs any thing
having or claiming in the premises or any part thereof
by from or under him them or any of them
shall and will warrant and forever defend
firmly by these presents. In testimony whereof
the said John Chambers hath hereunto set his
hand and affixed his seal the day and year
first above written
Signed sealed and delivered
in presence of — John Chambers (Seal)
H. Haralson
A. Murphey

North Carolina }
Caswell County } I Thomas Graves Public
Register of said County do hereby certify that
the foregoing is a true and correct copy according to
registration in my office book H. page 56.
Given under my hand at office in Yanceyville
this 7th day of November 1838
Tho. Graves P.R.

FIGURE 8-4 Back page of the same indenture shown in Figure 8-3, showing the clerk's notation of his transcription made in 1838. (From the author's collection.)

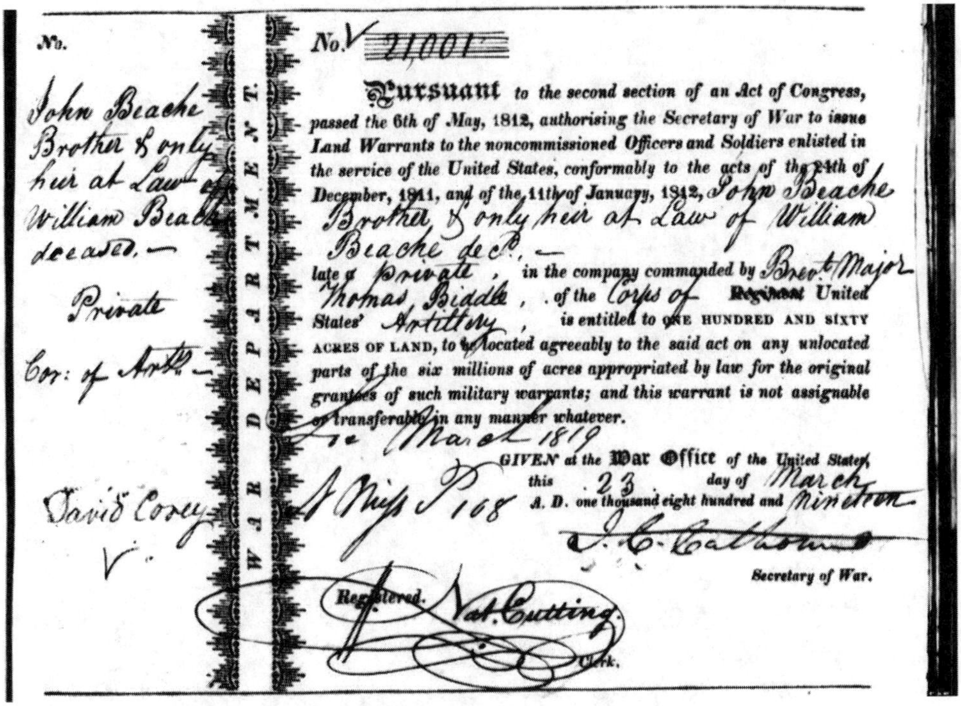
No.
John Beache
Brother & only
heir at Law of
William Beache
deceased. —
Private
Cor: of Artl. —
David Corey
V.

WAR DEPARTMENT.

No. V 21001

Pursuant to the second section of an Act of Congress, passed the 6th of May, 1812, authorising the Secretary of War to issue Land Warrants to the noncommissioned Officers and Soldiers enlisted in the service of the United States, conformably to the acts of the 24th of December, 1811, and of the 11th of January, 1812, John Beache Brother & only heir at Law of William Beache decd, — late a Private, in the company commanded by Brevt Major Thomas Biddle, of the Corps of Regiment United States' Artillery, is entitled to ONE HUNDRED AND SIXTY ACRES OF LAND, to be located agreeably to the said act on any unlocated parts of the six millions of acres appropriated by law for the original grantees of such military warrants; and this warrant is not assignable or transferable in any manner whatever.

2d March 1819

A Miss P 168

GIVEN at the War Office of the United States, this 23 day of March A. D. one thousand eight hundred and nineteen

J. C. Calhoun
Secretary of War.

Registered. Nat. Cutting
Clerk.

FIGURE 8-5 Bounty land warrant to John Beache, brother and only heir at law of William Beache. (Used by permission of The Generations Network, Inc.)

Bounty land documents may be found in county records, state land offices, and/or in state archives. Bounty land warrants continued in use until 1855, with some finalized and dated in 1858. Many federal bounty land records have been digitized and indexed by Ancestry.com, Footnote.com, and HeritageQuest Online.

As you can see, there are some interesting and diverse land survey schemes used in the State-Land States that have their origins in their colonial past. You will want to do some preliminary research into the state and area in which your ancestors lived and owned property in order to learn what system(s) might have been in use at that time.

Measurements for Federal-Land/Public-Land States

Following the American Revolution, the new federal government instituted several processes to control territorial land it acquired. There were several reasons for this. First, the government wanted to raise revenue to build its reserves and pay off debts incurred as a result of the Revolutionary War. Second, it wanted to compensate soldiers and other supporters from the war with land rather than pay money. Finally, with all this new territory, the government wanted to encourage westward migration and settlement. As a result, documentation dating from this period is some of the richest genealogical evidence you will find.

In order to organize these Federal-Land areas, also known as Public-Land or Public Domain States, the federal government had to define a system of measurement so that parcels could be defined. Rather than using the older metes and bounds system, the government decided to use a cartographic reference system using meridians. A *meridian* is an imaginary north–south line running from the North Pole to the South Pole. Thirty-seven principal meridians were established over a period of time to form the basis of the Public Land Survey System (PLSS). Additional imaginary north–south lines are defined as guide meridians, and these are located 24 miles to the east and to the west of the principal meridians or of the previously established guide meridians. A horizontal line, running east to west and intersecting the principal meridians and guide meridians, is referred to as a *base line*. It is used to measure distances from north to south. These imaginary reference lines are used to facilitate a quick reference for locating a physical location.

Meridian regions are divided into tracts, each of which is approximately 24 miles wide. Each tract is subdivided into 16 townships, each of which is approximately six miles square.

You also will encounter the term "range" in your research of townships. Ranges are imaginary north–south lines within a meridian that are set six miles apart. Remember that six miles is the width of a township. A count of the number of ranges to the east or west of a meridian and to the north or south of a base line indicates a specific township. For example, if you encounter a description that indicates "T2S and R2E," this means that the township being defined or described is two townships south of the base line and two townships east of the range line.

Each township is further subdivided to provide a more finite means of locating a specific piece of property. Each township is subdivided into sections. There are 36 square sections in a township, each of which comprises approximately 640 acres. Sections are numbered from 1 to 36, with the position of the numbers being dependent on whether the township is north or south of a baseline or east or west of a range line.

A section is most often subdivided into a variety of different-sized parcels. (There are exceptions to this, particularly in Ohio and other states in which the township, range, and section scheme was not clearly in place at the time of the initial surveys or where specific governments dictated other methods.) These subdivisions of sections are typically square or rectangular in shape. That is not to say that different parcels of land might not be subdivided and shaped differently. However, land descriptions you will encounter in Federal-Land States usually refer to townships, ranges, and sections to help define the location and size of a parcel.

There are 30 Federal-Land States: Alabama, Alaska, Arizona, Arkansas, California, Colorado, Florida, Idaho, Illinois, Indiana, Iowa, Kansas, Louisiana, Michigan, Minnesota, Mississippi, Missouri, Montana, Nebraska, Nevada, New Mexico, North Dakota, Ohio, Oklahoma, Oregon, South Dakota, Utah, Washington, Wisconsin, and Wyoming.

Federal-Land States Records

The Public Lands in the Federal-Land States were distributed in a variety of ways over different time periods. Others were auctioned or sold by lottery. Initial sales of land were conducted by auction with the land going to the highest bidder. Land offices opened and did the proverbial "booming business" in selling land to individuals wishing to settle on undeveloped properties to the west.

There were a number of transactions used for transferring ownership from the federal government to an individual (or organization). In order to purchase a parcel of land, an individual had to be a native-born citizen of the United States or must have filed a Declaration of Intent document to initiate the naturalization process. The exception to this requirement was in the case of bounty-land warrants.

The process of acquiring property usually began with the individual filing an application for a desired parcel of land. The person had to pay cash or present evidence of some form of credit. At that time, a warrant for survey was issued to accurately define the property description and to ensure that someone else did not already own the property. A completed survey report was submitted to the government and was recorded in a township plat book. The plat book consisted of a map of the township and a listing of the parcels. The surveys recorded here also included descriptions of the physical characteristics of the property, such as rocks, streams, forests, and other features.

Next, the information about the transaction was recorded in the tract book. You can use the tract books' contents to point to specific townships to locate individual landowners' records. All of the paperwork created and documentation supplied so far was then gathered together and sent to the General Land Office. The materials were placed in what is commonly known as a land-entry case file and the files were reviewed. There should be a case file for every application processed, regardless of whether it was approved or rejected. The General Land Office reviewed the land-entry case file and, if approved, issued to the applicant a document referred to as a 'final certificate.' This indicated that all of the required steps had been taken and that a land patent for the parcel had been approved. The actual land patents were generated by the General Land Office and were sent to the local land office, where the applicant could then exchange the final certificate for the actual land patent. Figure 8-6 shows the land patent for my great-great-grandfather, John N. Swords, dated 10 August 1849, for a parcel of land in the area of Lebanon, Alabama.

The land patents have been digitized and indexed by the U.S. Bureau of Land Management General Land Office (BLM-GLO). These can be searched in a database at **www.glorecords.blm.gov**, viewed, and printed. You also can order a certified copy of the document from that agency.

Places to Locate Land and Property Records

Subsequent sales and transfers of titles occurred as private transactions without the participation of the U.S. federal government unless a question concerning the original patent or title arose. Agreements of sale, indentures, mortgages, surveys, receipts, and deeds are probably the most common documents found.

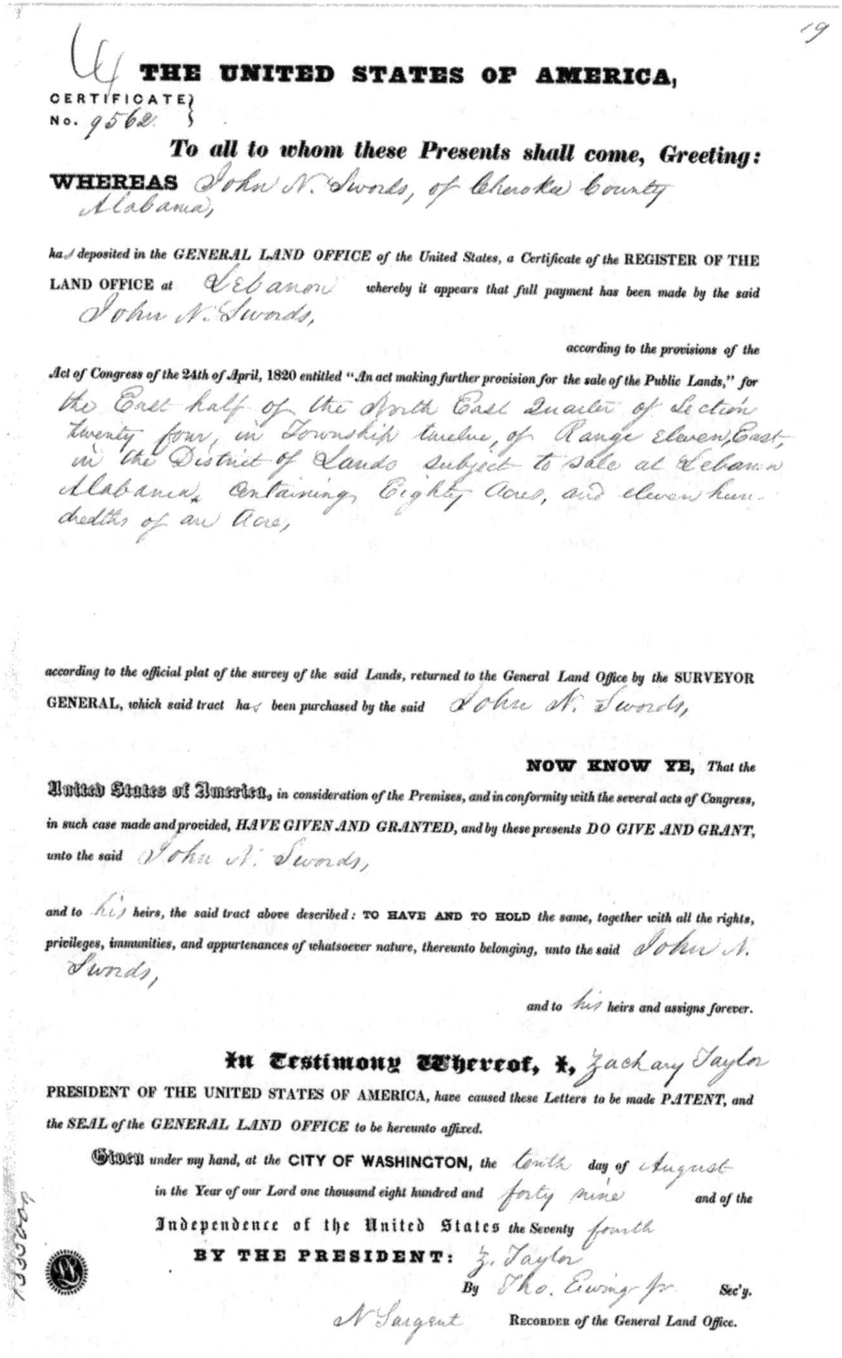

19

4 THE UNITED STATES OF AMERICA,

CERTIFICATE No. 9562

To all to whom these Presents shall come, Greeting:

WHEREAS John N. Swords, of Cherokee County Alabama,

has deposited in the GENERAL LAND OFFICE of the United States, a Certificate of the REGISTER OF THE LAND OFFICE at Lebanon whereby it appears that full payment has been made by the said John N. Swords,

according to the provisions of the Act of Congress of the 24th of April, 1820 entitled "An act making further provision for the sale of the Public Lands," for the East half of the North East Quarter of Section twenty four, in Township twelve, of Range eleven, East, in the District of Lands subject to sale at Lebanon Alabama, containing Eighty Acres, and eleven hundredths of an Acre,

according to the official plat of the survey of the said Lands, returned to the General Land Office by the SURVEYOR GENERAL, which said tract has been purchased by the said John N. Swords,

NOW KNOW YE, That the United States of America, in consideration of the Premises, and in conformity with the several acts of Congress, in such case made and provided, HAVE GIVEN AND GRANTED, and by these presents DO GIVE AND GRANT, unto the said John N. Swords,

and to his heirs, the said tract above described: TO HAVE AND TO HOLD the same, together with all the rights, privileges, immunities, and appurtenances of whatsoever nature, thereunto belonging, unto the said John N. Swords,

and to his heirs and assigns forever.

In Testimony Whereof, I, Zachary Taylor PRESIDENT OF THE UNITED STATES OF AMERICA, have caused these Letters to be made PATENT, and the SEAL of the GENERAL LAND OFFICE to be hereunto affixed.

Given under my hand, at the CITY OF WASHINGTON, the tenth day of August in the Year of our Lord one thousand eight hundred and forty nine and of the Independence of the United States the Seventy fourth

BY THE PRESIDENT: Z. Taylor

By Tho. Ewing Jr Sec'y.

N Sargent RECORDER of the General Land Office.

FIGURE 8-6 Land patent issued to John N. Swords dated 10 August 1849. (From the author's collection.)

Land and property documents may be located almost anywhere. Some documents will be in the possession of the individual or family, while others will be found in courthouses, recorders of deeds offices, registrars' offices, tax assessors' offices, county offices, state archives, NARA, the BLM-GLO, and other places. Remember that city directories, voter registration lists, jury lists, and many other records may provide clues to property ownership and associated records.

Learn About Types of Records

Deeds are used to transfer title of property from the grantor to the grantee. Deeds are perhaps the most common document you will find in your property research, and they can contain extensive genealogical information. In the case of a piece of property owned by someone who has died, the transfer of property as part of an estate in probate may contain a great deal of information. The name of the deceased and his or her date of death are often shown to designate the reason for the transfer of ownership. The names and relationships of the devisees/heirs can be a gold mine in your research. However, this information also serves as a pointer to other records, such as a will and probate packet or marriage documents.

Did You Know? A married man in many U.S. locations could not, by law, sell land unless his wife consented. She was interviewed apart from her husband and swore she was under no compulsion or duress from her husband regarding the sale. She then swore and signed a dower release.

Another important piece of genealogical information that appears in land records is that of "dower release." In referencing Figure 8-1 earlier in this chapter, I called attention to the "dower line" shown on that particular survey report. When a woman had a legal interest in the ownership of property, laws in earlier times required that the woman sign a dower release in order to allow the sale of the property. The woman was interviewed separately from her husband and was asked if she voluntarily exercised her right to relinquish ownership or interest in the property to allow for its sale or transfer. Figure 8-7 shows a copy of a deed recorded in the deed books of Alachua County, Florida, dated 7 June 1873. At the bottom of the document is a record of Priscilla McCall's dower release for that piece of property.

Warranty deeds are those instruments used in property transactions in which the grantor fully warrants good clear title to the property. A warranty deed offers the greatest protection of any deed and you will find references to and copies of these among the land and property records you research. Figure 8-8 shows an example of a cover page of a warranty deed. The remainder of the text of the warranty deed is virtually identical to other deeds but, in this case, proof of title has been presented at the time of transfer to ensure the veracity of the title.

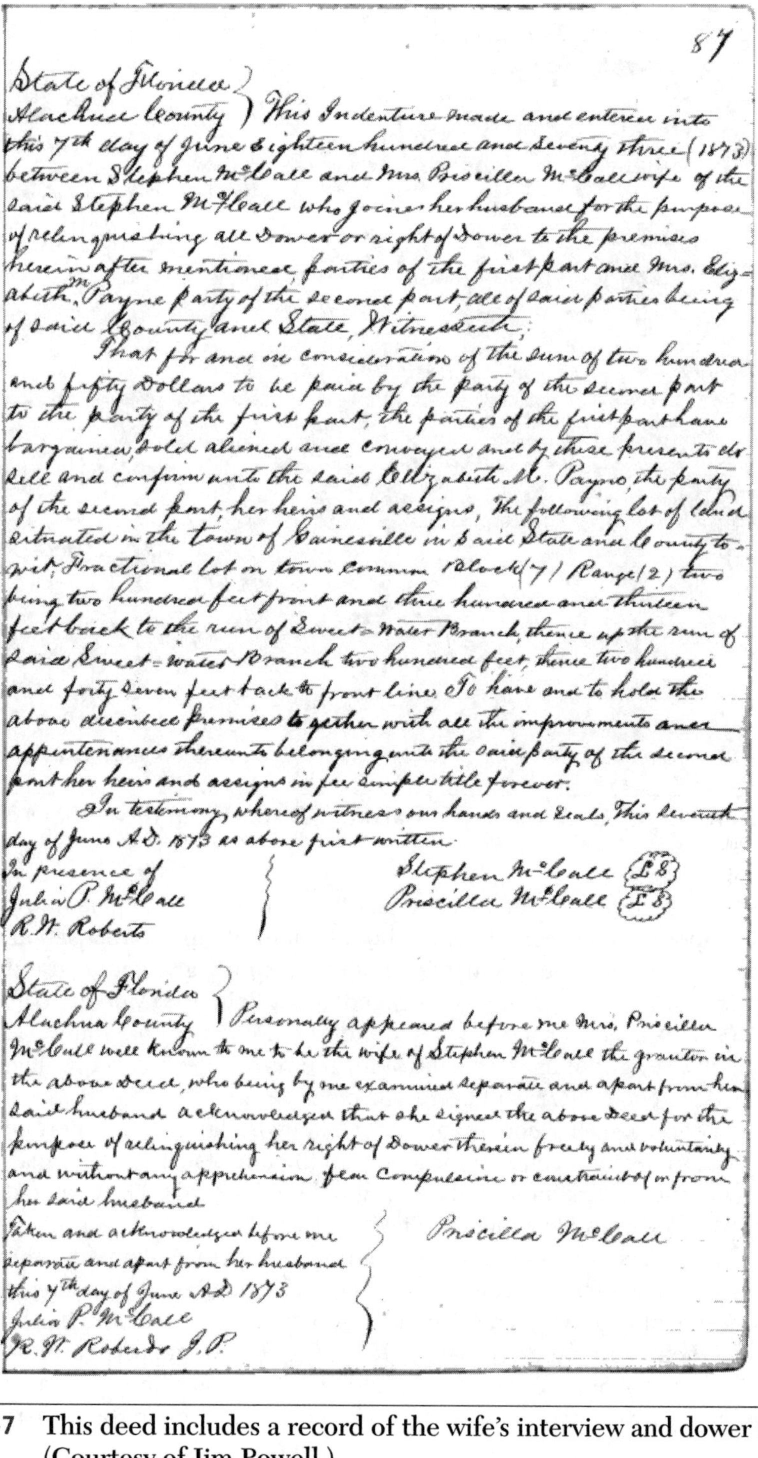

87

State of Florida }
Alachua County } This Indenture made and entered into this 7th day of June Eighteen hundred and Seventy three (1873) between Stephen McCall and Mrs. Priscilla McCall wife of the said Stephen McCall who joins her husband for the purpose of relinquishing all Dower or right of Dower to the premises hereinafter mentioned parties of the first part and Mrs. Elizabeth M. Payne party of the second part, all of said parties being of said County and State, Witnesseth;

That for and in consideration of the sum of two hundred and fifty Dollars to be paid by the party of the second part to the party of the first part, the parties of the first part have bargained, sold aliened and conveyed and by these presents do sell and confirm unto the said Elizabeth M. Payne, the party of the second part, her heirs and assigns, the following lot of land situated in the town of Gainesville in said State and County to-wit; Fractional lot on town Common Block (7) Range (2) two being two hundred feet front and three hundred and thirteen feet back to the run of Sweet-Water Branch, thence up the run of said Sweet-water Branch two hundred feet, thence two hundred and forty seven feet back to front line. To have and to hold the above described premises together with all the improvements and appurtenances thereunto belonging unto the said party of the second part her heirs and assigns in fee simple title forever.

In testimony whereof witness our hands and seals, this seventh day of June A.D. 1873 as above first written.

In presence of
Julia P. McCall
R.W. Roberts

Stephen McCall (L.S.)
Priscilla McCall (L.S.)

State of Florida }
Alachua County } Personally appeared before me Mrs. Priscilla McCall well known to me to be the wife of Stephen McCall the grantor in the above Deed, who being by me examined separate and apart from her said husband acknowledged that she signed the above Deed for the purpose of relinquishing her right of Dower therein freely and voluntarily and without any apprehension fear compulsion or constraint of or from her said husband

Taken and acknowledged before me separate and apart from her husband this 7th day of June A.D. 1873
Julia P. McCall
R.W. Roberts J.P.

Priscilla McCall

FIGURE 8-7 This deed includes a record of the wife's interview and dower release. (Courtesy of Jim Powell.)

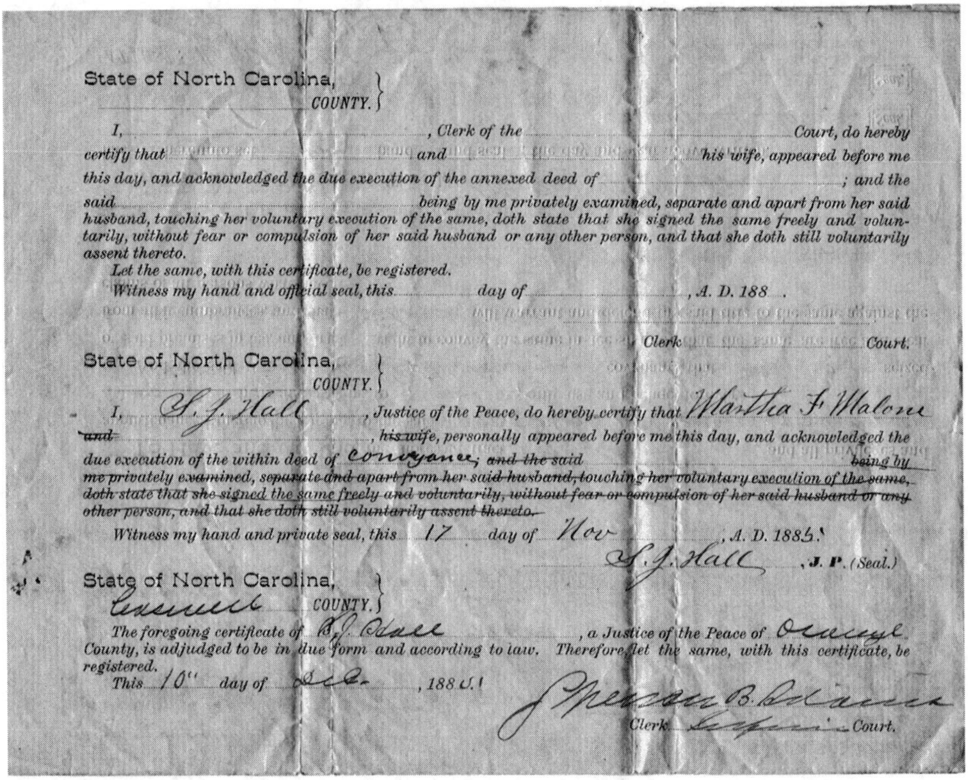

State of North Carolina,
COUNTY.

I, ..., Clerk of the .... Court, do hereby certify that .... and .... his wife, appeared before me this day, and acknowledged the due execution of the annexed deed of ....; and the said .... being by me privately examined, separate and apart from her said husband, touching her voluntary execution of the same, doth state that she signed the same freely and voluntarily, without fear or compulsion of her said husband or any other person, and that she doth still voluntarily assent thereto.

Let the same, with this certificate, be registered.

Witness my hand and official seal, this .... day of ...., A. D. 188 .

Clerk .... Court.

State of North Carolina,
COUNTY.

I, S. J. Hall, Justice of the Peace, do hereby certify that Martha F Malone ~~and~~ ...., ~~his wife~~, personally appeared before me this day, and acknowledged the due execution of the within deed of conveyance; ~~and the said .... being by me privately examined, separate and apart from her said husband, touching her voluntary execution of the same, doth state that she signed the same freely and voluntarily, without fear or compulsion of her said husband or any other person, and that she doth still voluntarily assent thereto.~~

Witness my hand and private seal, this 17 day of Nov, A. D. 1885.

S. J. Hall, J. P. (Seal.)

State of North Carolina,
Caswell COUNTY.

The foregoing certificate of S. J. Hall, a Justice of the Peace of Orange County, is adjudged to be in due form and according to law. Therefore let the same, with this certificate, be registered.

This 10" day of Dec, 1885.

[illegible]

Clerk Superior Court.

FIGURE 8-8 Cover page of a warranty deed. (From the author's collection.)

Another type of deed is a "deed of gift" in which one person transfers ownership of property to another person without benefit of any compensation or remuneration. Figure 8-9 shows the original deed of gift from my great-great-grandfather, Goodlow W. Morgan, to his son, my great-grandfather, Rainey B. Morgan, dated 17 December 1885. This deed transfers ownership of the home tract of land to Rainey but reserves Goodlow's right of use and control for the remainder of his life. The deed is registered in a deed book in Caswell County, North Carolina.

There are other documents associated with land and property ownership in the United States that you may find helpful to your research. Particularly useful are those documents that point you to the original land records. These include property tax bills such as the example shown in Figure 8-10.

Other documents might include tax liens, court judgments, and auction records, to name just a few. As you can see, the wide range of documents and the possible contents may provide you with a great many clues. It should be obvious to you by now, though, that there is a lot to learn about U.S. property records. You will want to learn more about the records available in the areas where your ancestors lived at the times they were there. By doing so, you can begin to tap these marvelous resources.

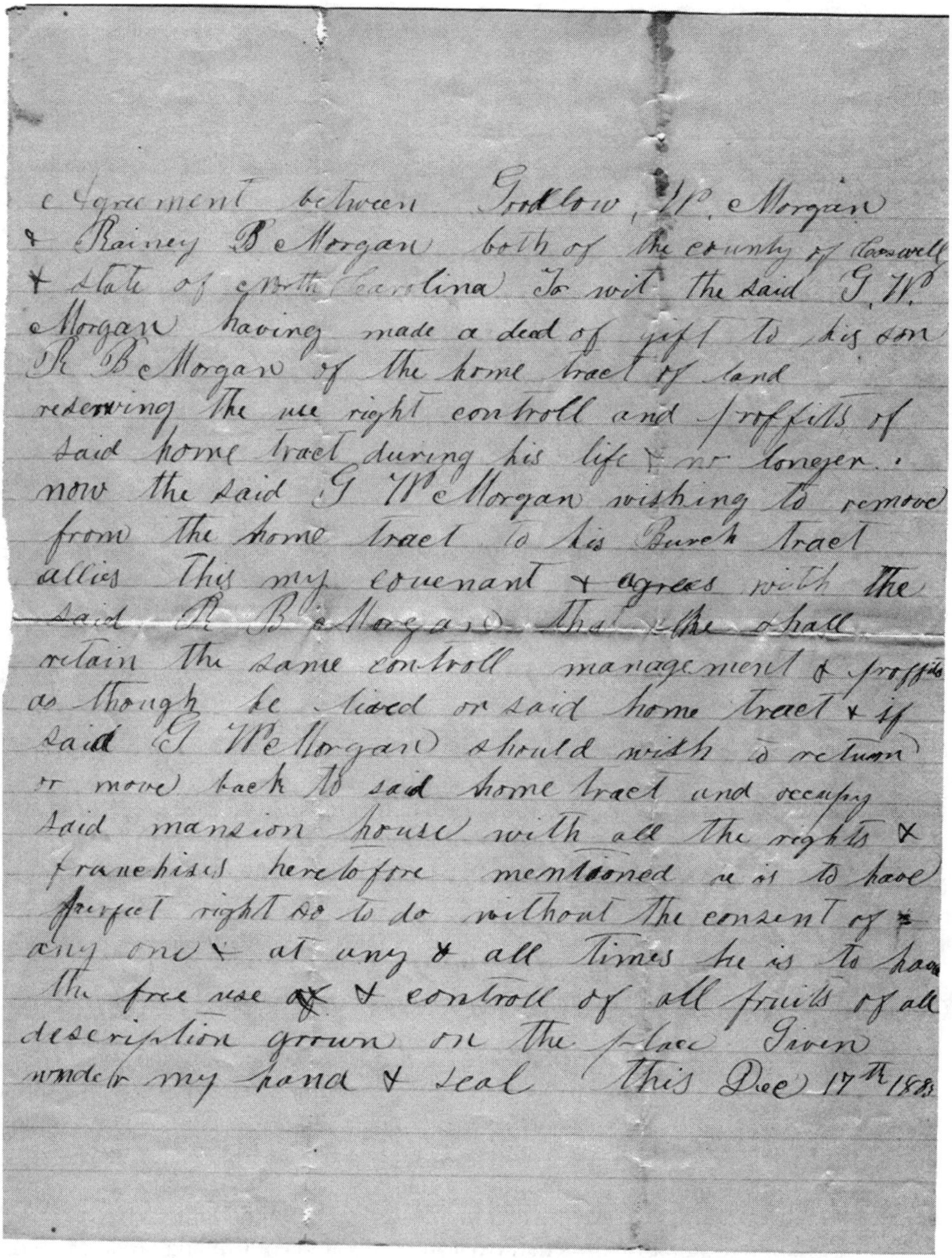

Agreement between Goodlow W. Morgan & Rainey B. Morgan both of the county of Caswell & State of North Carolina To wit the said G. W. Morgan having made a deed of gift to his son R. B. Morgan of the home tract of land reserving the use right controll and proffitts of said home tract during his life & no longer. now the said G. W. Morgan wishing to remove from the home tract to his Burch tract allies This my covenant & agrees with the said R. B. Morgan that the shall retain the same controll management & proffits as though he lived on said home tract & if said G. W. Morgan should wish to return or move back to said home tract and occupy said mansion house with all the rights & franchises heretofore mentioned is to have perfect right so to do without the consent of any one & at any & all times he is to have the free use of & controll of all fruits of all description grown on the place Given under my hand & seal   This Dec) 17th 1885

FIGURE 8-9   Deed of gift from the author's great-great-grandfather giving ownership of the home property to the author's great-grandfather. (From the author's collection.)

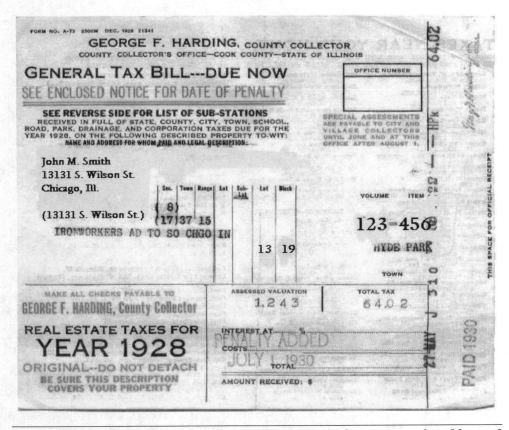

FIGURE 8-10 Sample of a real estate tax bill, which can direct you to the address of a specific piece of property and confirm the name(s) of the owner(s) of record. (From the author's collection.)

Land and Property Records in Canada

Canada was an attractive destination for people from both France and the British Isles. Over the centuries, people were drawn to immigrate by the availability of land. In fact, both governments recruited people to settle there, and examples of advertisements exist in the holdings of the archives of both countries. Many parcels of land were granted in payment for military service. Additionally, people migrated northward from the 13 American colonies and the United States.

Among the first records that exist in many areas of Canada are land records as people settled and migrated westward. In many cases, land records will be the only records available that document people who lived in the area. What is interesting is the high percentage of early settlers who did own land. While this is encouraging, remember that these records may be handwritten in French or English by persons whose literacy and knowledge of legal affairs were not always the best. As a result, you may find that some records are particularly challenging to read and use.

Since settlement began in the eastern area and spread westward, you can expect to find the oldest records among the surviving documentation in those areas. Most formal land records in eastern Canada, however, date from the late 1700s. Land records in New France were based on the feudal system of *seigneuries*, which were landed estates. In Canada, the holder of a *seigneurie* was referred to as a *seigneur*, as in a member of the landed gentry.

These land records include land petitions, conveyances, warrants and fiats (permissions), which authorized the granting of land in payment for a service, land grants and patents, Loyalist land grants, deeds, indentures, quit-claim deeds, titles, transfer documents, leases, mortgages, liens, and a variety of other land instruments. The documents that are available for research will vary based on the time period, the government having jurisdiction at the time, and the laws of the period.

Transcriptions of the documents were recorded in the government land offices in the various areas where the transactions occurred. Records of legal claims and actions may also be found in court records.

Land Measurement in Canada

As you work with property records in Canada, you will undoubtedly encounter the use of surveyors' measurements, just as in the State-Land States in the United States. Surveyors used units of measurement based on the length of a surveyor's chain. Refer again to Table 8-1 for a brief overview of conversions from surveyors' measurements to feet and inches.

Land Systems Used in Canada

Several land systems have been used in Canada throughout the centuries. In the course of your research, you may encounter these systems and will need to understand a little about them in order to successfully work with the land records. There are four organizational systems you are likely to encounter:

- **Dominion Land Survey**   This is by far the most common organizational system used in Canada. It is based on the U.S. Public Land Survey System and began being used in Canada in 1871. The basis of this system is the use of townships and sections. A township consists of 36 square miles and is subdivided into 36 sections, which are one mile square. Each section is subdivided into four 160-acre areas referred to as quarter sections. This is the smallest unit of this land system. A parcel of land is typically described in its deed or other document as lying in a particular township, section, and quarter section.

- **Patchwork System**   This system used natural land features such as rocks, rivers and streams, and trees to indicate the beginning and end of a specific boundary. For example, a boundary might be described as "beginning at the large oak near the edge of Twenty-Mile Creek and traveling west, ending at the eastern edge of the creek." Canada is not unique in its use of such descriptive land measurements; this system also was used in areas of the United States for many years, and you will find later physical features noted, along with surveyors' measurements, to more fully describe a piece of property. This system was widely used in Newfoundland, Nova Scotia, and the Maritime Provinces.
- **River Lot System**   The use of this system is generally attributed to the land holding system developed and used in New France. Lands along rivers and streams were defined as long, relatively slender lots running perpendicular to the waterway.
- **Rectangular Lot System**   This system uses a Township or Parish system, which should not be confused with the designation of the use of township, section, and quarter section used in the Dominion Land Survey described above. Used primarily in Ontario, Québec, and the Maritimes, this system employs the use of a formal Township or Parish as its largest unit, and then individual parcels were subdivided into individual lots of a uniform size and rectangular in shape. The size of the lot might range from 100 acres on up, and common sizes were 100 or 200 acres.

The land office with which you are working can help you to understand and locate specific parcels of property. They typically have produced information sheets or leaflets that describe the system or systems in use in their records and will provide them to you on request. In addition, they will also have detailed land maps of the area going back a long time and, using the property description found on a document, can help you pinpoint its precise physical location.

Taxation and Duty Records

Throughout your research for the land records themselves, don't overlook the taxation and duty records associated with the land. Property taxes and duty records associated with land transactions can provide another source of information for you. In addition, those records may include names and references to military service, land descriptions, previous and subsequent residences, wills and estates, and other clues that can further your research.

Locate the Land Records

The most logical place to start your land and property research is in the area where you think your ancestor lived. That means making contact with Library and Archives Canada (LAC) to determine what they may have in their possession. Start at their website at **www.collectionscanada.gc.ca**.

Getting Past Penelope Swords

My great-grandmother, Penelope Swords Holder, was an enigma, and represented perhaps my most difficult research "brick wall." I have mentioned her several times in this book because the methods I used to get past the gridlock are good examples of alternative research strategies that you will sometimes need to employ.

Defining the Problem

My childhood memories are peppered with recollections of my mother's and her three sisters' discussions of their own mother's parents, Green Berry Holder (1845–1914) and his wife, Penelope Swords (1842–1914), of Rome, Floyd County, Georgia. It was not until my early twenties that I began to look in all seriousness

Ansibelle Penelope Swords Holder (1842–1914). (From the author's collection.)

at the ancestry in my maternal line. When I did, it was comparatively simple to document—first, my mother and her sisters, and second, my grandmother, Elizabeth Holder, and her five sisters and five of her six brothers. My great-grandfather, Green Berry Holder, had been a Confederate soldier, the first postmaster of two federal post offices, a farmer, a merchant, founder of the North Georgia Fertilizer Company, owner and president of the Rome Mercantile Company, board member of two banks, the elected representative to the Georgia State Legislature for two non-consecutive terms, a real

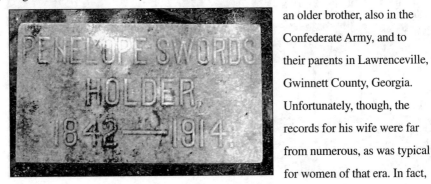

Gravestone of Penelope Swords Holder, Myrtle Hill Cemetery, Rome, Georgia. (From the author's collection.)

estate investor, an insurance salesman, a member of the United Confederate Veterans, and a member of the Rome Presbyterian Church.

As you can imagine, there were lots of records about him and from those I was able to link him to an older brother, also in the Confederate Army, and to their parents in Lawrenceville, Gwinnett County, Georgia. Unfortunately, though, the records for his wife were far from numerous, as was typical for women of that era. In fact, for quite a while, the only real record I had was her gravestone. My research problem was to locate information about Penelope, identify her parents, and be able to continue my research in her ancestral line. ●

Start with What You Know and Work Backward

We've discussed the importance of beginning your research with what you know and with searches for information, sources, and evidence found at your family home or in the possession of other family members. When you hit a "brick wall" in your research, go back and review in detail all the information you have acquired. Reread everything in chronological sequence and look at the total picture of your subject's life. I personally found myself doing this again and again in the course of my

research on my great-grandmother, and ultimately the pieces fell into place. Let's examine my research process in this case study.

Family Tradition

The family story (or tradition) had it that my great-grandmother Penelope died the morning after the birth of one of my mother's sisters. My aunt, Carolyn Penelope Weatherly, was born on 12 January 1914, in Green Berry and Penelope's home on Broad Street in Rome, and the child was named Penelope for her grandmother. Starting with that clue, I began my search from home for records.

Look for Death-Related Records

While some Georgia counties and cities did maintain birth and death records from earlier years, it was not until 1919 that Georgia required the registration of all births and deaths in the state. Unfortunately, Floyd County and Rome did not create these records until 1919 and so there was no death certificate for Penelope Swords Holder.

I next contacted the Genealogy Department of the Sarah Hightower Regional Library in Rome to determine if they might have microfilm of the local newspapers from 1914 from which an obituary could be obtained. I was informed that their microfilm of the *Rome Herald-Tribune* was incomplete, and that 1914 was one of the years that they did not have.

Locate a Marriage Record

My next step was to contact the Floyd County Courthouse in Rome to try to obtain a marriage record for Green Berry and Penelope. I hoped the marriage license might provide the bride's parents' names, her age, and/or her place of residence. The response from the courthouse included a document that showed Greenberry [sic] Holder wedding Miss A. P. Sanders (or Sauders) on 27 December 1866 (see Figure 1). This was a surprise. Could Penelope have been married before? I considered five possibilities:

- Penelope was supposedly born in 1842 and married Green Berry in 1866. She would have been twenty-four years old, a somewhat advanced age for a woman to be married at that time.
- The marriage occurred following the U.S. Civil War and, considering Penelope's age, it was possible that she had been married before to a man whose surname was Sanders or Sauders and that she had been widowed.
- The entry from the Floyd County Marriage Book (vol. A, page 347, # 1359) clearly states Miss A. P. Sanders, supposedly an unmarried woman.
- Was it possible that Green Berry married before, or could the clerk entering the record on 15 April 1868 have made an error in reading or transcribing the name?
- The couple's first child, Edward Ernest Holder, was born on 28 January 1868. The couple was therefore probably married before April of 1867.

I contacted the Floyd County Courthouse again to determine if there was any record of another marriage for Green Berry Holder on file or any record of a divorce from A. P. Sanders. I was informed that there were no such records.

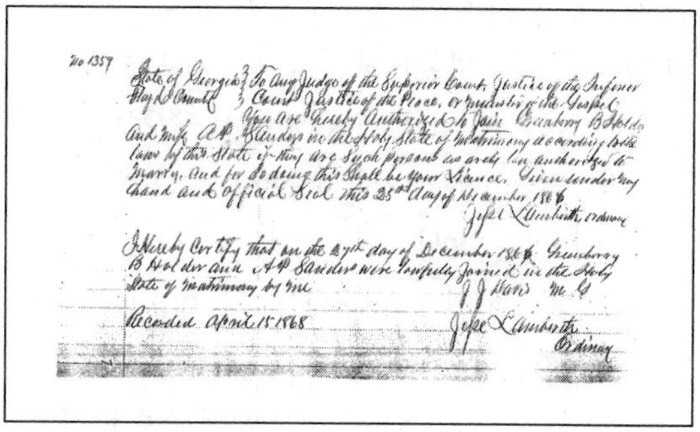
No 1357 State of Georgia } To any Judge of the Superior Court, Justice of the Inferior Floyd County } Court, Justice of the Peace, or Minister of the Gospel.
You are hereby authorized to join Greenberry B Holder and Miss A P Sanders in the Holy State of Matrimony according to the laws of this State if they are such persons as are by law authorized to marry, and for so doing this shall be your License. Given under my hand and official seal this 25th day of December 1866
Jesse L Lambeth, Ordinary

I hereby certify that on the 27th day of December 1866 Greenberry B Holder and A P Sanders were lawfully joined in the Holy State of Matrimony by me
J J Davis M G

Recorded April 15 1868 Jesse L Lambeth Ordinary

Figure 1. Marriage record from the Floyd County, Georgia, marriage book. (From the author's collection.)

Check the Census Records

Based on the information I had found so far, I decided to check in the U.S. federal census for Georgia for various years. Knowing that Green Berry married in 1866, I checked the 1870 census for his entry. I found a listing for him in Subdivision 141 of Floyd County, Georgia, along with his wife, "Ancybelle P.," and sons "Edward W.," age 2, and "Willis I.," age 3/12 years (3 months). This gave me two important clues. "Ancybelle P." certainly agreed with the "A. P." initials on the marriage record, and the age of the first son certainly agreed. The wrong middle initial for Edward did not concern me too much because the name of the second son was really William Ira Holder and not "Willis." These two errors, the spelling of "Ancybelle," and the fact that the original 1870 census records were transcribed and the copy was sent to Washington all point to either enumerator spelling errors or transcription errors.

The 1880 census showed Green B. Holder in Enumeration District 11 of Floyd County, age 34. His wife is recorded as Ansabelle, age 34, and nine children are listed: Edward (son – 13 years old), Willis (son – 11), Scott T. (son – 9), Ida (daughter – 7), Annie (daughter – 5), Luther (son – 4), Ella (daughter – 3), Brisco (son – 1), and Emma (daughter – 4/12).

The next available federal census, in 1900, shows Green B. Holder in Supervisor's District 7, Enumeration District 153, Lindale District in Floyd County, with his wife, "Nancy B.," and the following children: William I. (born November 1869), Ida L. (July 1872), Anna L. (April 1874), Luther M. (July 1875), Ella E. (October 1876), Emma E. (December 1879), Charles W. (May 1881), Nita M. (June 1882), and Lizze B. (July 1885). Note that family tradition always indicated that the last child, my grandmother Elizabeth Holder, was called by the nickname she gave herself as a baby, "Lizzie Bep."

The 1910 census, the last enumeration before both Green Berry and Penelope died in 1914, shows them at 808 South Broad Street, Supervisor's District 7, Enumeration District 69, 5th Ward, the Rome Militia District. Green B. Holder is 65, wife "Annie" is 67, and living with them are three of their daughters: Ida (age 32), Anna (28), and Emma (26). A further clue indicates that "Annie" was born in Alabama, and that both of her parents were born in South Carolina.

It was now time to move backward from the marriage certificate to try to identify and connect Ansibelle Penelope to her parents and family. I next went looking through 1860 federal census indexes in Georgia, looking for the surname of Swords. I located a printed index of Cobb County, Georgia, for that year and it pointed me toward the First District, Roswell Post Office, in Cobb County. There I found the J. N. Swords family, including Penelope at age 18—the correct age if she was born in 1842 as indicated on her gravestone (see Figure 2). I now had the names of her parents, J.N. and Rebecca Chapman Swords, both of whom were born in South Carolina, and Penelope born in Alabama.

Make a Very Successful Genealogy Trip

I felt that I had done just about all I could do from the comfort of home and with the assistance of the genealogical and history collections in local libraries and archives. It was time to make a road trip.

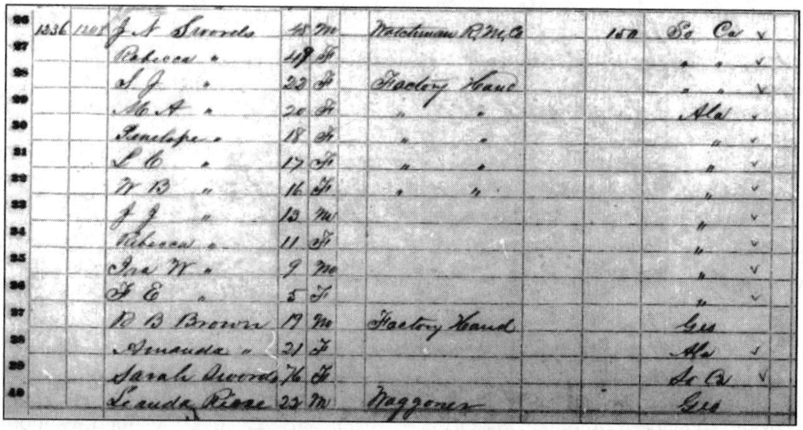

26	1336	1205	J A Swords	48	M	Watchman R M Co	150	So Ca
27			Rebecca "	49	F			"
28			S J "	23	F	Factory Hand		"
29			M A "	20	F	" "		Ala
30			Penelope "	18	F	" "		"
31			S C "	17	F	" "		"
32			W B "	16	F	" "		"
33			J J "	13	M			"
34			Rebecca "	11	F			"
35			Ira W "	9	M			"
36			F E "	5	F			"
37			R B Brown	19	M	Factory Hand		Geo
38			Amanda "	21	F			Ala
39			Sarah Swords	76	F			So Ca
40			Leander Rice	22	M	Waggoner		Geo

Figure 2. Detail from the 1860 U.S. federal census, Cobb County, Georgia. (Used with permission of The Generations Network, Inc.)

Following the procedures described in Chapter 14, I pulled all my information together about Green Berry Holder, Ansibelle Penelope Swords, and their children, organized it, and prepared a research plan. I did my preliminary research on the Internet, contacted the genealogy librarian at the Sarah Hightower Regional Library, and made contacts with the Rome Municipal Cemetery Department and the Northwest Georgia Genealogical Society for appointments to meet with people on-site. Two months later, in July 1997, I drove from my home in Tampa, Florida, to Rome, Georgia, for what would be one of the best research trips of my life.

The library in Rome proved to contain a wealth of information for my research. The genealogy librarian there at the time, Gwen Billingsly, was an outstanding help. City directories in the library's collection helped me place Green Berry and his sons at specific addresses in Rome. The papers of local historian, George Magruder Battey, contained correspondence with some of the Holder daughters and with others that discussed the town's history and my great-grandfather's role in the community. Local histories also helped in my quest. The microfilm collection of the *Rome Herald-Tribune* was incomplete, as I had learned before. However, Ms. Billingsly knew that the missing years' original newspapers were stored in the county school district administration's records retention facility. Apparently the library had run out of funds to microfilm all the years of publication. She contacted the administrator there and arranged for me to visit and examine these original newspapers.

When I arrived at the storage facility, I was warmly greeted and led through a warehouse to the area where the complete, leather-bound volumes of 1908, 1909, 1913, and 1914 were stored. The year 1914 was the one of most interest, since my great-grandmother died on 13 January 1914 and my great-grandfather followed her in death on 18 June 1914. It was easy to locate their obituaries and, working with the fragile newsprint and without the benefit of a photocopier, I carefully transcribed both obituaries. (These newspapers were subsequently microfilmed, by the way.) There were, of course, many clues in my great-grandmother's obituary in the *Rome Herald-Tribune*, Rome, Georgia, on Wednesday morning, January 14, 1914, page 1, which reads as follows:

> *Mrs. G.B. Holder, aged 71 years, an old and honored resident of Rome, died Tuesday night at 11:10 at the family residence, 808 South Broad Street, after a brief illness of pneumonia. The deceased was born at Rock Creek, Alabama, in 1848. She married in 1867, G.B. Holder, of this city, and has since resided in Rome. Her husband is a prominent business man of the county. Mrs. Holder was a member of the Primitive Baptist church and always took an active part in the church work.*
>
> *She is survived by 11 children, five sons and six daughters. The sons are Ed Holder, Will Holder, Scott Holder, Brisco Holder and Charlie Holder. The daughters are Misses Isa [sic, Ida] Holder, Anna Holder and Emma Holder, Mrs. A.D. Starnes, Mrs. Walton Weatherly and Mrs. Wyatt Foster. She is also survived by three sisters, Mrs. Cal Menton and Mrs. Davis of Alabama, and Mrs. George Black, of Cedartown.*
>
> *The funeral services will be conducted from the residence at 3 o'clock this afternoon, the Rev. J. W. Cooper officiating. Interment will follow in Myrtle Hill cemetery.*
>
> *The following pall-bearers will meet at 2:30 o'clock at Daniels Furniture Company: Honorary, J.G. Pollock, B.F. Griffin, Capt. J. H. May, M.W. Formby, H.V. Rambo, Tom Sanford. Active: J.M. Yarbrough, G.G. Burkhalter, Sanford Moore, W.A. Long, Dr. R.M. Harbin, C.B. Geotchius.*

The most significant facts for my research beyond my great-grandmother into her siblings, parents, and other ancestors were the names of two of her surviving sisters. However, it took me a while to get past another self-imposed "brick wall."

First, I discounted "Mrs. Davis of Alabama" as being nearly impossible to locate. However, I did search the Alabama census records for the Menton surname and for a man whose forename might have been Calvin, Calvert, Calbert, Calhoon, and other variations, all without success. I next did the same search with different spellings of the surname, including Minton. It was not until I realized that the custom of the time was that a married woman used her husband's first and last names, and that a widow used her own first name and the surname of her husband. Mrs. Cal Menton, as it turned out, was Mrs. Caroline Minton. "Cal" was a nickname for Caroline. When I later located her, it turned out that she was the daughter listed variously as L. C. Swords or Lydia Swords; her full maiden name was Lydia Caroline Swords.

"Mrs. George Black of Cedartown," a town south of Rome in Polk County, Georgia, was easier to locate. I searched the probate records while at the Floyd County Courthouse in Rome for all of the Holders and happened to look for Black, Davis, and Swords. It turned out that there was a probate packet for George S. Black that specifically mentioned his wife, Martha. Another marriage record in Floyd County showed George Black married Martha Ann Swords on 27 December 1866. I had another connection!

Take Another Look at Census Records

I went back to look at the census records again. In the 1860 census, two other daughters of J. N. and Rebecca Swords are listed: M. A. Swords (age 20) and L. C. Swords (age 17).

Next I went to the 1850 census and, based on the 1860 census and the ages of the children born in Alabama, I worked with census indexes. I found the family in the 1850 census in the 27th District, Cherokee County, Alabama. The parents were listed as John N. Swords and his wife, Rebecca. Among the children listed, I found a seven-year-old daughter named Lydia, an eight-year-old named Nancy, and a ten-year-old named Martha, all of whom had been born in Alabama (see Figure 3). I'd found the right place, the right people, and the right person. The name "Nancy" in the 1850 census corresponded with the same name in the 1900 census and was certainly similar to "Ansabelle" and "Annie" in other censuses, and the names of the sisters were correct. I had the correct family and the correct individuals.

Contact Other Courthouses

I still had that burning question about the surname of Sanders (or Sauders) on the Floyd County marriage document, so I considered that it was possible that Ansibelle Penelope Swords might have been married prior to her 1867 marriage to Green Berry. Therefore, I wrote the courthouses in the counties of Cobb and Floyd, and the counties in between—Bartow, Cherokee, Gordon, Paulding, Pickens, and Polk—to try to have a check made of bride indexes in their marriage books between 1860 and 1867 for a woman with the surname of Swords and a forename of Ansibelle and/or Penelope, or with the initials A. P. All the responses indicated that no such names appeared in their marriage indexes.

Other Information Discovered Along the Way

The appointment with the cemetery administrator in Rome reconfirmed dates of death and interment for Penelope Swords Holder in the Myrtle Hill Cemetery

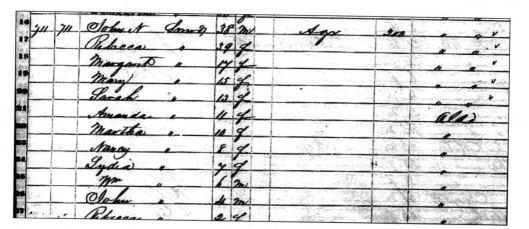

Figure 3. Detail from the 1850 U.S. federal census, Cobb County, Georgia. (Used with permission of The Generations Network, Inc.)

Interments ledger, which also listed the cause of her death as pneumonia, and for Green Berry later that year. I also learned that their daughter, Emma Dale Holder, sold three spaces in the family cemetery lot in 1956 to the owners of the adjacent lot, the family of George and Martha Black. It turns out that Penelope and her sister Martha were buried toe-to-toe in the cemetery.

I obtained the marriage entries from the Floyd County Courthouse for all of Green Berry and Penelope's children who married there, as well as copies of death certificates for eight of their children. I located the graves of all eight of those children, including Edward E. Holder, who was widowed and then remarried, and who was buried in a cemetery other than the one in which his original, pre-inscribed tombstone had been placed.

In the Floyd County Courthouse, a clerk's preliminary search of land and property records showed more than thirty-eight pages of entries in their deed index for G. B. Holder, A. P. Holder, Penelope Holder, and for their sons, Edward,

William, Scott, and Luther Holder. I have reserved an entire future trip to study the actual land and property entries and learn what they can reveal to me.

Finally, after all of the census research, it finally dawned on me where the nickname for my great-aunt, Ella Edna Holder, had come from. She was called "Little Annie" after her mother because she always scurried around taking care of her siblings.

From the clues obtained along the way in my search for Ansibelle Penelope Holder's family, I was able to significantly expand my knowledge and documentation of the entire family unit's genealogy. However, the clue that John N. Holder's and his wife, Rebecca's, parents were both born in South Carolina carried me back to both their families. In addition, I've since been able to locate copious amounts of documentation about John N. Swords siblings and their parents, a Revolutionary War soldier named John Swords and his wife, Eleanor Swancey, both of whom are mentioned in other parts of the book. And my search continues for more and more information.

Next, you will want to make contact with the appropriate provincial or territorial archives to determine what records are in their possession, or for recommendations of additional contacts in their area. LAC maintains a complete list of addresses and web links to the provincial and territorial archives, and to major genealogical societies in those areas, at **www.collectionscanada.gc.ca/genealogy/022-809-e.html**.

Be sure to use your local public and academic libraries as reference resources, and visit the nearest LDS Family History Center for help determining what materials you can access.

Learn About Land and Property Records in the United Kingdom

Some of the more complicated land and property records, from the perspective of organization, are those found in the British Isles. The manorial system in use in England dates back to before the *Domesday Book*, which was commissioned in 1085. The manorial system is an amalgamation of an agricultural estate system and the feudal system of military tenures. In effect, the king owned all the land. A tenant-in-chief received his ability to "hold" the large piece of land from the king. The tenant-in-chief could grant the privilege of "holding" to those persons who might be his retainers or valued representatives. These retainers are also referred to as *mesne lords*. The mesne lord could also grant "holdings" to his persons. Throughout the structure, however, each of these persons could and did create their own manorial area, complete with tenants, servants, and other lower persons.

Did You Know?

The Domesday Book is the record of the great survey of England that was completed in 1086 on behalf of King William I (William the Conqueror). Men were sent to each shire to find and record what or how much each landowner possessed in land and livestock, and its value. The process was much like a census, but was used to assess value for taxation purposes. The Domesday Book is held at The National Archives in England. It has been digitized and can be seen at **www.nationalarchives.gov.uk/domesday**.

A lord and his manor at any level owed his existence to the person from whom he received his holding, and his tenants and other residents of the manor owed their service and existence to the lord of the manor. That included fields for farming and the raising of livestock, forests for hunting, cottages, the church, and common necessary services such as mills and smithies. Tenants, both free and unfree, and other residents not only provided service to the lord, but they also contributed a portion of the produce of the labor to support the lord and the manor. The lord, in turn, paid taxes and tribute to the king and provided men, materials, and service to the monarch as required. These services were originally called "tenures" and there were multiple types of these, including the lowliest of the tenants, the free tenures and non-free tenures. These persons were also known as serfs, bondsmen, or *villeins*.

Tenures were slowly replaced by monetary payments, known as *socage*, and military tenures were abolished in 1660.

> **Did You Know?** The National Archives (TNA) has a portion of the Manorial Documents Register (MDR) digitized and online on its website at **www.nationalarchives.gov.uk**.

How Many Manors Were There?

You might be surprised to learn that there were tens of thousands of manors in England in medieval times. By some calculations, there may have been as many as 25,000 to 65,000 manors. There were approximately 11,000 parishes in the 1500s and 1600s. There were manors of various sizes and with varying numbers of people affiliated with each one. Some parishes had more than one manor associated with them.

One point of confusion with English land records concerns the fact that manorial lords were often more than simply landlords. In many cases they acted as the administrative and judicial authority, hearing and ruling on all types of claims and complaints. Further, some of the lords also claimed jurisdiction to rule on and administer the wills and estates of their tenants. Beginning in the 14th century, however, the responsibilities of the manorial courts were transferred to other bodies. These included church courts, secular courts, ecclesiastical parish authorities, and finally to the local authorities. Manorial courts still operated, however, into the 19th century for the purpose of handling property transactions on the manor itself.

There really were three types of manorial court. The Court Leet was the most common court, established by the lord of the manor. Its purpose was to assist in the administration of activities in the manor, and its functions included acting as a court of minor law and, in some cases, monitoring the quality of the produce of the manor. The Court Customary dealt with feudal matters, and particularly with disputes and other matters between the unfree tenants, or *villeins*. The Court Baron dealt with matters of tenure, feudal services, feudal dues, and disputes between free tenants. Obviously, there was more to these courts than this, and their functions varied from manor to manor, in different places, and at different periods. However, this should give you a brief idea of their purposes.

Manorial Records

The good news is that many manorial records have survived for centuries, going as far back as the 13th and 14th centuries. These manorial rolls consist primarily of the minutes of the courts dealing with a vast array of issues. The bad news, however, is that the earliest of these records are written in Latin. With the exception of some records dating from 1653–1660, it was not until the early 1730s that manorial court records began to be written in English, albeit they include many Latin abbreviations and subsidiary notations.

All that said, however, manorial records can contain a great deal of important and helpful genealogical information. The National Archives maintains the Manorial Documents Register (MDR) and Manorial Lordships records.

The MDR was established in 1922 as a result of the abolishment of the use of "copyhold" in British property law. Copyhold is a form of tenure according to manorial law, and used as title deeds until their abolished. Proof of property ownership, however, was often contained in the original books and rolls of the manorial courts, and it was imperative that references to the original copyhold entries be easily locatable in order to expedite the handling of land and property transactions. The MDR is maintained by TNA on behalf of the Master of the Rolls. It maintains a record of the locations of all manorial records, excluding title deeds, throughout England and Wales. Manorial records survive today in many national and local record offices and, in some cases, in private hands. The MDR, therefore, is an essential tool for locating the records you might be seeking.

Some of the MDR is available online at **www.nationalarchives.gov.uk/mdr**. A detailed description of the MDR and Manorial Lordships records is available at **www.nationalarchives.gov.uk/catalogue/RdLeaflet.asp?sLeafletID = 385**. However, you may (at the time of this writing) search the MDR for Wales and for Hampshire, Isle of Wight, Norfolk, and the three Ridings of Yorkshire. A search of the database will provide you with information about the number and types of available manorial records and where they are located. Manorial Lordships records are of little genealogical help; lordships can be sold. The Land Registry site at **www.landregistry. gov.uk** may be of help to you if you are searching for lordship titles and associated land holdings.

Your research into British land and property records will require you to do some historical research into the locations and periods in which your ancestors lived. There are many excellent reference works available concerning manorial records and other land records. Among the best is Mark D. Herber's *Ancestral Trails: The Complete Guide to British Genealogy and Family History* (Genealogical Publishing Co., 2006).

Locate Land and Property Records Online

More and more materials are being made available on the Internet each month. The MDR is one example of land and property reference materials that may be found online. However, there are numerous free and subscription databases that can help further your research. Don't overlook the government websites of the places your ancestors lived; they may have indexed and/or digitized many of their documents.

The Cyndi's List website at **www.cyndislist.com** includes many links to land and property records. These are located under the Land Records, Deeds, Homesteads, Etc. category and under the resources under England, Wales, Scotland, and Ireland.

Place Your Ancestors into Context with Property Records

Land and property records can most emphatically be used to place your ancestors and family members into geographical and historical context. While a census record may establish an individual's presence in a location at one point every decade, property tax records created on an annual basis can reconfirm the presence (or absence) of an ancestor. When you determine that an ancestor is no longer paying a property tax, you may then direct your research toward deed and property indexes, wills and probate documents, city directories, and other research paths to determine if the property changed hands and, if so, the reason for the change. In addition, when other government documents are lost or destroyed, property records are almost always re-created in some manner. It is essential for a government to quickly reconstruct these records in order to establish property ownership and to continue the taxation that is a primary source of its revenue.

There are numerous types of land and property records that you may encounter. As I mentioned at the beginning of the chapter, some of these may be linked to military service. They might include bounty land warrants, homestead and other tax exemptions, military pension loan programs such as the United States' G.I. Bill, and others. You also can link property records with other documents, such as wills and probate records, jury lists, voter registration, divorce settlements, lawsuits, census enumeration districts, and more.

The wide range of documents attached to the purchase, ownership, sale, and transfer of land records is extensive. And while they may at first glance seem complicated or convoluted, the processes employed and the documentation created actually are quite logical. Now that you have an understanding of the types of land and property records that are used and where they might be found, you are prepared to begin searching for those that have been created for your ancestors and their families. Combine your study of history and geography with your genealogical research skills and you really can expand the chronicle of your family's history in a given area.

9

Locate and Use Immigration and Naturalization Records

HOW TO...

- Understand why people migrate
- Locate and use U.S. immigration and naturalization records
- Locate and access Canadian immigration records
- Locate and access Australian immigration records
- Use strategies for determining your ancestor's ship
- Use other strategies for determining your ancestor's place of origin
- Expand your family's story by tracing their migrations
- Locate and use immigration records
- Locate and access Canadian Immigration Records
- Understand the naturalization process and work with those documents

You've learned a great deal about your family so far by locating and using home sources, vital and personal records, and census resources. Along the way, you also have built a foundation for all of your future genealogical research. There are literally hundreds of different record types that may contain information of value in documenting your forebears' lives. You now know how important it is to place your family into context, to conduct scholarly research, to analyze every piece of evidence you uncover, and to properly document your source materials.

This chapter discusses some of the more important document types and presents successful methodologies for locating records of emigration, immigration, and naturalization and evaluating their content. Working with these documents will help you learn much more about the details of your ancestor and his or her family members' lives, and you will come to know them more intimately. A variety of other, less commonly used materials will also be referenced in this chapter, along with recommendations for where to locate them and how to incorporate their information into your family research and documentation.

Understand Why People Migrate

Since the dawn of time, it is a natural state of affairs for all creatures to migrate from place to place in order to survive and to make a better existence. It is the natural order of things, and humankind is no different. People moved from one place to another for a variety of reasons, sometimes moving multiple times until they found a place that suited them. While there are many reasons for moving from one place to another, the following are some of the principal motivations:

- **Natural Disasters** Droughts, floods, earthquakes, volcanoes, fires, tornadoes, hurricanes, and other natural disasters were life-altering catastrophes that caused people to leave one place and move to another. Floods in Germany in 1816 and 1830, for example, displaced thousands of people. Hurricane Katrina in August 2005 is an example of a more recent natural disaster that dispersed thousands of people, many of whom did not return to their homes.

- **Drought, Crop Failure, and Famine** Drought and plant diseases are common natural causes of famine; wars, land mismanagement, and other human-caused disasters also result in famine. Famine in Ireland in 1816–17 and the potato famines in 1822, 1838, and between the years 1845 and 1850 caused tens of millions of people to emigrate, particularly to the United States and Canada. Famines in France in 1750, 1774, and 1790 and then the general famine across Europe in 1848 caused French, German, Italian, Dutch, and Scandinavian people to immigrate to the United States.

- **Economic Problems** The economic problems of an area can cause people to migrate. Consider the mass migrations resulting from the Great Depression of the 1930s when people relocated to any place they could find work.

- **Political Turmoil or Oppression** Millions of people have emigrated from their native lands in search of asylum in another place in order to avoid political instability, conflict, persecution, violation of personal rights or freedoms, and other problems.

- **War** War is undoubtedly the greatest catalyst of change. Military conflicts have been caused by colonization, land hunger, economic advantage, and social issues, and the destruction they cause have long been a primary reason for migration, relocation, and evacuation.

- **Accompanying or Following Family and Friends** Many people accompanied or followed other family members or friends who had already moved somewhere else. The lure of employment opportunities, better living conditions, and political and religious freedom was often irresistible.

- **Adoption** Adoption forces the movement of the adoptee from one place to another without his or her control. Single-child and multiple-sibling adoptions have been common, especially when one or both parents died. The Orphan Trains carried children from cities across North America and placed as many as 150,000 to 200,000 children in new homes in 47 states, Canada, and South America.

Orphaned and indigent children were transported from the British Isles to Canada and Australia for adoption at various times. And during World War II, children from Britain, Holland, Belgium, and other countries were often evacuated to relatives or through social agencies to other locations in order to protect them.

- **Religious or Ethnic Persecution**   One overwhelming reason for the migration by our ancestors was their desire to live in freedom, to practice their religious beliefs without persecution, or to pursue the lifestyle of their ethnic group. The Pilgrims are an excellent example of the early settlers who emigrated from England to the American colonies. In the 20th century, the emigration of Jews and other persecuted peoples from Europe to Britain, the United States, Australia, South America, and Israel provide vivid examples of persons fleeing persecution.

- **Slavery**   Slave trade was responsible for destroying families and entire communities, and for the forced relocation of hundreds of thousands of persons over the ages. The sale or exchange of human beings removed people from Africa to the New World, and then from place to place as a result of sale, barter, kidnapping, and theft. Invading conquerors enslaved native peoples of the Americas, and substantial numbers also were transported back to Europe as curiosities and as victims of enforced servitude.

- **Forced Relocation of Native Americans**   Native Americans were seen as an imminent danger to settlers and an impediment to progress. Armed conflicts between them and white settlers, and later the U.S. army, ultimately resulted in treaties calling for the ceding of Native American lands and permanent relocation of Native Americans to parcels referred to as "reservations." Many died in the relocation marches, such as those who were removed to the Oklahoma Territory in the notorious "Trail of Tears," and in other relocations.

- **Criminal Incarceration/Deportment**   Criminals, debtors, and political dissidents were transported to colonial settlements to eliminate them from society and serve sentences of hard labor. Others were offered the option of relocating to a colony rather than face execution or prolonged imprisonment in their homeland.

- **Primogenitor or Ultimogenitor**   It was common in the Middle Ages (and later) for the eldest son to inherit most or all property on the death of his father. In laws or societal rules primogenitor, the eldest son could then allow his mother and other siblings to remain or he could force them to leave. In some places, a separate custom called *borough English* or *ultimogeniture* required that the youngest son inherit all the land. In either case, sisters were usually married off, and other brothers were encouraged to leave and fend for themselves.

These reasons cannot possibly encompass the universe of factors that influenced our ancestors to make a move. However, placing your own ancestors into context goes a long way toward understanding their motivations. One of my favorite reference websites for a chronological representation of historical events is the Timelines of History website at **http://timelines.ws**.

Did You Know? It's important to consider both the possible reasons for migration and the possible reasons why your ancestors settled in a particular place. People didn't just move for just any reason; there was a motivation. Likewise, something drew them to a new location, such as family, friends, land, or employment opportunities. Apply the "push and pull" rationale to your search for all your ancestors that moved.

Locate and Use U.S. Immigration and Naturalization Records

The desire to trace one's ancestors back to the place of origin is one of the principal motivations for family history researchers. Many of us will spend our entire genealogical research career investigating family members in the country in which they settled, and that is also commonly the same one in which we live and with which we are familiar. However, the impetus to continue the quest backwards to our ancestors' native land(s) will take many of us on another, more rigorous research trek.

Placing your ancestor in geographical and historical context becomes a research imperative when you begin retracing his or her migration path across an ocean and back to the place of birth. It is essential that you consider the country and place of origin *and* the destination country, their geographies, the social and historical environments at the time, and the motivations for both leaving the old country *and* going to a particular location in the new country. For a great many of us, the knowledge of the place of our family's origin has been lost to time and we will have to use all sorts of clues to reconnect a migration path backward. The pointers we'll use may include letters, photographs, books, family stories or traditions, immigration records, passenger lists, naturalization documents, census records, passports and visas, and a host of other primary and secondary evidence. This may seem a daunting task, but it is certainly one of the most rewarding and insightful experiences you can imagine.

Earlier we discussed some of the motivating factors that compelled our ancestors and their family members to migrate to a new place. Deciding to undertake a move of this magnitude was no small matter; it took a great deal of courage and planning and usually meant leaving family, friends, and everything familiar forever. Our ancestors were literally risking everything, including their lives. Under extreme circumstances, some people fled their homes with little preparation. However, a majority of the emigrants left their ancestral home place for another part of the world with some plan for where they would go and what they would do to survive when they arrived. These people were courageous and endured terrible conditions in order to make a new life for themselves and their families.

Our Ancestors Came in Ships

For most of us, our ancestors traveled in ships. One of the most familiar images to many immigrants or first-generation Americans is that of the immigration processing station Ellis Island. Millions of people, such as those shown in Figure 9-1, arrived there between 1 January 1892 and 12 November 1954. These immigrants may have left their hometowns on foot, in wagons and carts, and even on trains, but ultimately they had to cross an ocean. Millions upon millions of people did so in ships and, depending on the time period, the type of ships on which they traveled determined the duration of the voyage and the living conditions in which they traveled. It was not until well into the 20th century that people emigrated via airplane and, when they began doing so, many of the records we seek were no longer created—in particular, the ships' passenger lists and manifests.

You will find that immigration and naturalization are inextricably linked together, not just because one event occurred before the other but also because, to become naturalized citizens in the new country, proof of when, where, and how your ancestors arrived there was required. We're going to concentrate on immigration to the United States and the naturalization process to become an American citizen. However, we also will explore the wealth of records concerning immigration to Canada and Australia from the British Isles and resources for tracing ships from other countries to these destinations as well.

FIGURE 9-1   Immigrants arriving from Italy, ca. 1911. (From the Library of Congress collection.)

Many migration routes have been used over the centuries, depending on the location you are researching, the time period, the method of transportation from place to place, and the destination. There are many excellent websites for your review, depending on your area of interest. They include the following:

- German emigration to the United States at **www.spartacus.schoolnet.co.uk/USAMgermany.htm**
- Irish emigration to the United States at **www.spartacus.schoolnet.co.uk/USAEireland.htm**
- Italian emigration to the United States at **www.spartacus.schoolnet.co.uk/USAEitaly.htm**
- Swedish emigration to the United States at **www.spartacus.schoolnet.co.uk/USAEsweden.htm**
- Immigrants to Canada at **http://ist.uwaterloo.ca/~marj/genealogy/thevoyage.html**
- Museum Victoria's "Immigration to Victoria [Australia] - A Timeline" at **http://museumvictoria.com.au/DiscoveryCentre/Websites-Mini/Immigration-Timeline**

Did You Know? Geopolitical boundaries have frequently changed throughout history. Use historical maps of the areas in which your ancestors lived to help understand where they were located, and make sure you look at maps from the same time period to make sure you are looking for the records in the right repository.

In the United States, I have two favorite collections of historical maps online. The first is the Perry-Castañeda Library Map Collection at the University of Texas at Austin, located at **www.lib.utexas.edu/maps**. Once at that site, click the link labeled "Maps of the United States including National Parks and Monuments," and then click the link labeled "Historical Maps of the United States." You will find several groups of maps on this page, including "Exploration and Settlement" and "Territorial Growth," excellent references for migration routes. Also on that page, under the section labeled "Later Historical Maps," are a number of maps that were compiled from the 1870 U.S. federal census showing concentrations of population settlements of Chinese, English and Welsh, British American, German, Irish, and Swedish and Norwegian people. All of these are dated 1872.

My other favorite collection is the David Rumsey Map Collection at **www.davidrumsey.com**. You have a choice of four viewer tools of the maps at the time of this writing. The new LUNA browser is simple to use and provides splendid viewing results. It runs in the Internet Explorer, Firefox, and Safari browsers. The in*sight* Java Client, which requires a free download of software that installs on your computer, is another excellent viewing option. This collection is searchable in a variety of ways and the images are wonderful. (You may need to turn off any pop-up blocker software on your computer in order to access the map images.)

Learn About the History of Ships' Passenger Lists

Passenger lists, also referred to as "passenger manifests," will vary in format and content, depending on who created them, why they were created, the time period, and other factors. For example, persons transported in bondage from England—that is, prisoners transported to a colony as punishment and/or to permanently get rid of them—may be documented in court records in the country of origin. The person may also be listed on a prisoner ship's records. In other places, there may be no immigration lists available at the destination location but there may well be emigration lists and/or ships' manifests at the point of departure.

In addition, and perhaps most important of all, it is absolutely imperative to remember that you must always look for the obvious records *and*, in the event that you can't find those, investigate the possibilities that there may be alternative record types that can help document the migration. For example, if there are no ships' passenger lists, look for immigration records to document the arrival. Also, in the United States, you can use the decennial federal census records starting in 1790 to help document and trace your immigrant ancestors. For example, the 1880 census asked for the place of birth of each person as well as of his/her father and mother. The 1900, 1910, 1920, and 1930 federal censuses all asked for the year of immigration and whether the person had been naturalized. Census Population Schedules also may include the language spoken, or "mother tongue," and that can help lead you to the place of origin. These records therefore can be the bonanza you need in the way of pointers to other records and/or can be used as alternative, supplemental, and corroborative evidence and documentation.

Figure 9-2 shows detail from the 1910 U.S. federal census for the Frances Farina family in San Francisco, California. His wife, Mary, their two sons, one daughter, and his widowed mother-in-law live together. You now have Mary's probably maiden name, Nani. The three adults were born in Italy, as were their respective parents. The three children, however, were born in California, and their parents are shown as Italian. To the right of these birth locations is a two-column set of critical information for your search. The year of arrival in the United States is listed in the first column. You can see that Frances arrived in 1886, and Mary arrived in 1889. Mary's mother arrived in 1906. Based on this information, you now have a target year in which to search for these people on passenger lists.

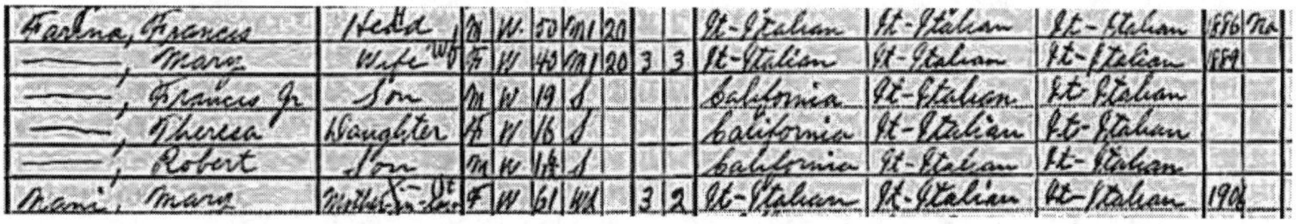

Farina, Frances	Head	M	W	50	M1	20			It-Italian	It-Italian	It-Italian	1886	Na
——, Mary	Wife	F	W	49	M1	20	3	3	It-Italian	It-Italian	It-Italian	1889	
——, Frances Jr	Son	M	W	19	S				California	It-Italian	It-Italian		
——, Theresa	Daughter	F	W	16	S				California	It-Italian	It-Italian		
——, Robert	Son	M	W	14	S				California	It-Italian	It-Italian		
Nani, Mary	Mother-in-law	F	W	61	Wd		3	2	It-Italian	It-Italian	It-Italian	1906	

FIGURE 9-2 1910 U.S. federal census detail showing places of birth, arrival year, and naturalization status. (Used with permission from The Generations Network, Inc.)

The last column in this census indicates the naturalization status. In this case, Frances' entry contains a code "Na," indicating that he is naturalized. That should be a clue to begin tracing his naturalization records. It appears that neither his wife nor his mother-in-law was naturalized by 1910. However, a check of the 1920 census shows both women, now listed as "Marie" Farina and "Marie" Nani, have been naturalized. That tells you to also look for *their* naturalization papers. The name of the ship on which they arrived and the date of arrival will be listed on the naturalization documents, as you will see a little later in this chapter.

Let's look at the United States and ships' passenger arrival lists that you may want to research and examine. In order to understand what is available, we need to briefly examine the history of these records.

A Chronology of Ships' Passenger Lists in the United States

Prior to the Revolutionary War, there was no formal attempt to require passenger arrival lists. Indeed, any requirements were instituted by the colonies themselves as they had control over their own affairs. Because the 13 colonies were, in fact, British, and close to 80 percent of the white immigrants arriving before 1790 came from England or British-governed countries, there was little or no need to record the arrivals. Any documentation about passenger movement was created or maintained by the ships' owners and operators; the colonial government maintained any information concerning shipping commerce. The primary concern was the taxation on incoming and outgoing goods, and government officials had little interest in passenger arrivals other than those of Crown prisoners and indentured servants.

If you are seeking information about early arrival colonies, it is important to look for alternative records, as mentioned before, such as "lists of departure" in the original country. Some of these are in national archives or in the collections of libraries and archives, or in local government record repositories near the port of departure. (In Spain and Portugal, there are extensive archival holdings relating to shipping and passenger movements that trace back in many cases into the 1300s, and hence we have a solid historical record of much of the global exploration from those periods.) Histories of individual colonies and settlements may also provide you with information about arrivals of individuals or families and their participation in the community affairs.

There are, as mentioned above, a few exceptions to the pre-Federal period's lack of passenger arrival lists. In Pennsylvania, for instance, beginning in 1727 that colony required that non-British immigrants be identified. The persons identified in the listings that were created were primarily of German nationality. There were essentially three lists compiled, consisting of: 1) the ship captain's list, made on board ship, of names from the manifest; 2) lists of oaths of allegiance to the British king that were signed by all males over the age of 16 who could march to the local magistrate at the port of arrival; and 3) lists of the signers of the oath of fidelity and abjuration, a renunciation of any claims to the throne of England by "pretenders," also signed by males over the age of 16 who could walk to the courthouse. One estimate is that only about two-fifths of the ships' passengers actually signed these oaths, and not all of the ledgers and documents have survived. Still, these are a source of considerable interest to researchers with German ancestors who went to Pennsylvania in that time period. The surviving documents are in the possession of the Pennsylvania Archives.

Did You Know?

Nearly 100 percent of the passenger arrivals in U.S. ports were recorded on passenger lists prepared by ships' captains. The ports' custom officers were required to prepare a monthly summary of passenger arrivals and send them to Washington, D.C. Those reports have been used as replacements for those passenger lists that were lost or destroyed. The complete chronological set of lists and/or reports was microfilmed by the National Archives and Records Administration (NARA) and has been digitized and indexed at Ancestry.com.

The year 1820 is a bellwether for historians and genealogists from an immigration perspective. In that year, Congress passed legislation calling for passenger lists to be filed by each ship's master with the customs officer in the port of arrival. Manifests of goods being brought into port were already being prepared and delivered to the customs officer. However, passenger manifests were something new. These documents are referred to as the "customs passenger lists" or "customs passenger manifests." Two copies of the passenger list, like the ones shown in Figures 9-3 and 9-4, were created on board the ship and listed every passenger. Births and deaths occurring during the voyage were also to have been added to the list. The names of crew members were not required. On arrival at port, the ship's master was required to deliver both copies of the document to the customs collector. The master then swore under oath that the lists were complete and correct, and then both he and the customs officer signed the documents. One copy remained with the customs collector and the other copy was retained by the ship's master. The collectors prepared an abstract of the lists quarterly

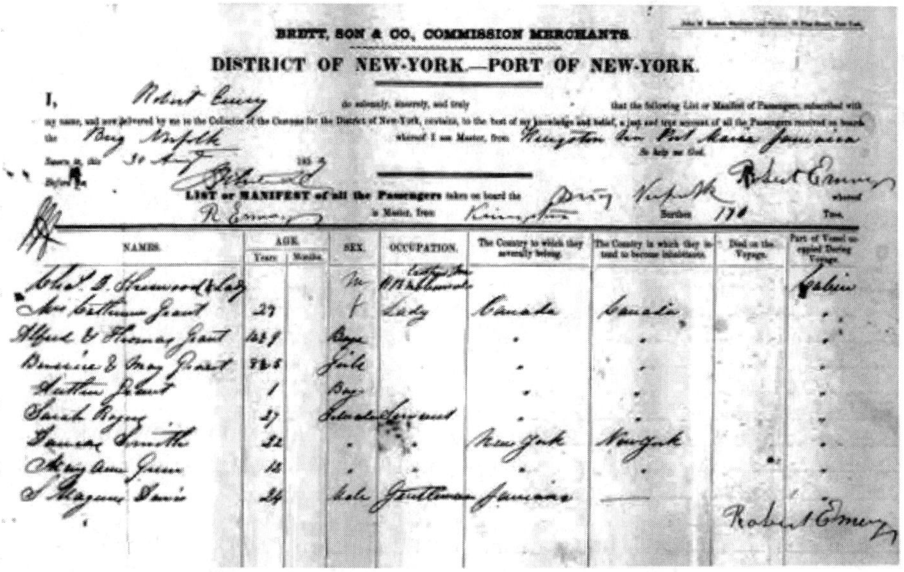
BRETT, SON & CO., COMMISSION MERCHANTS

DISTRICT OF NEW-YORK.—PORT OF NEW-YORK.

LIST or MANIFEST of all the Passengers taken on board the

NAMES.	AGE. Years	AGE. Months	SEX.	OCCUPATION.	The Country to which they severally belong.	The Country in which they intend to become inhabitants.	Died on the Voyage.	Part of Vessel occupied During Voyage.

FIGURE 9-3 Passenger list of the Brig *Norfolk*, which arrived in New York on 30 August 1859. (Used with permission of The Generations Network, Inc.)

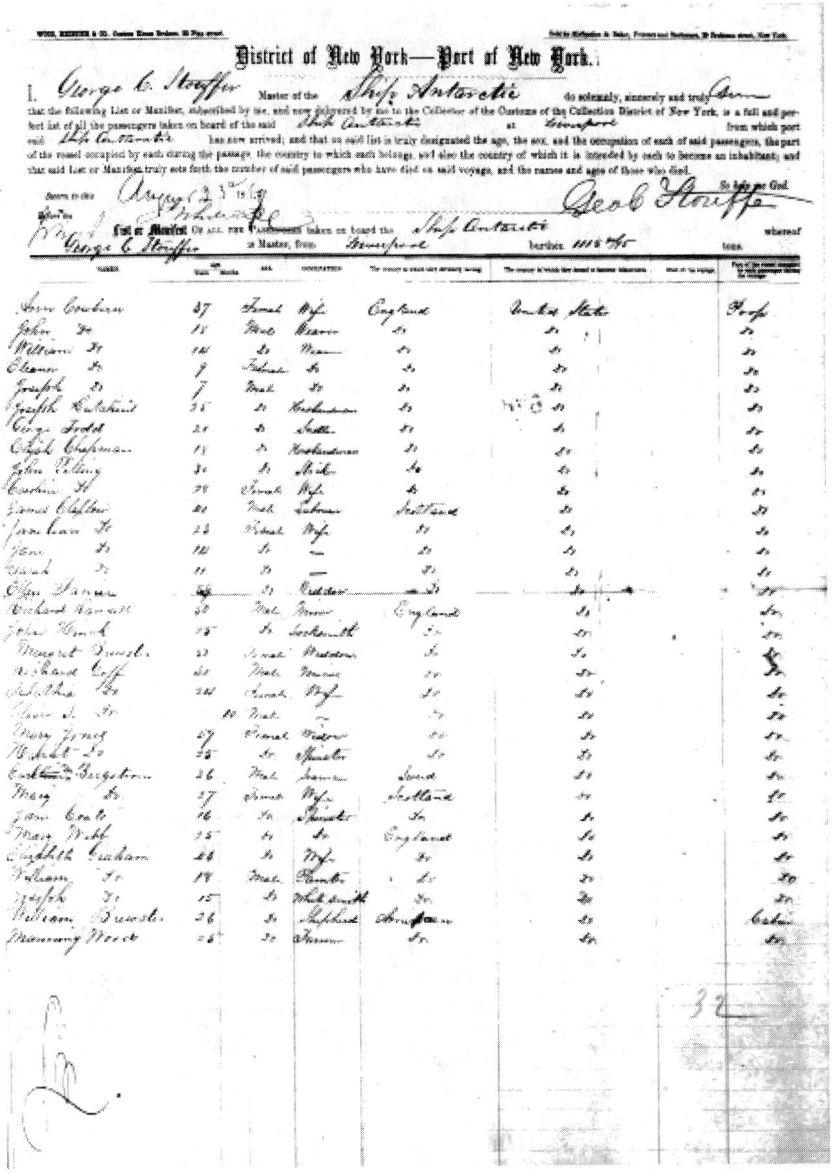
District of New York—Port of New York.

FIGURE 9-4 Manifest of the *Antarctic*, which arrived in New York on 23 August 1859. (Used with permission of The Generations Network, Inc.)

and sent it to the secretary of state in Washington, D.C. The abstract listed the name of every vessel; the port of origin; any intermediate ports of call; the date of arrival; each respective ship's master's name; and the names, gender, and ages of all passengers.

A Congressional act passed in 1882 required that federal immigration officials record all immigrants arriving in the United States. The lists produced date from

1883 for the port of Philadelphia and from 1891 for most other ports, and these have been microfilmed by NARA. These lists include the name of the master, the name of the ship, the ports of departure and arrival (including intermediate stops), the date of arrival, the name of each passenger, their place of birth, last residence, age, occupation, and gender, and any other remarks. The intermediate ports of call may be important for tracing your ancestors' stages of migration.

The year 1891 is a watershed in the United States for a number of reasons. In that year, a separate federal governmental agency was formed whose purpose was specifically to oversee immigration. This was the Office of Immigration, and its head was the Superintendent of Immigration. For the first time, this new bureau strictly oversaw this function and, as a result, the records created became more detailed. Between 1891 and 1906, responsibility for the collection and maintenance of the forms passed through several federal departments, finally becoming the province of what was the Immigration and Naturalization Service, which was formed in 1906.

Standardized forms, such as the one shown in Figure 9-5, began to be used in every embarkation port around the world and were to be prepared *before* the departure of

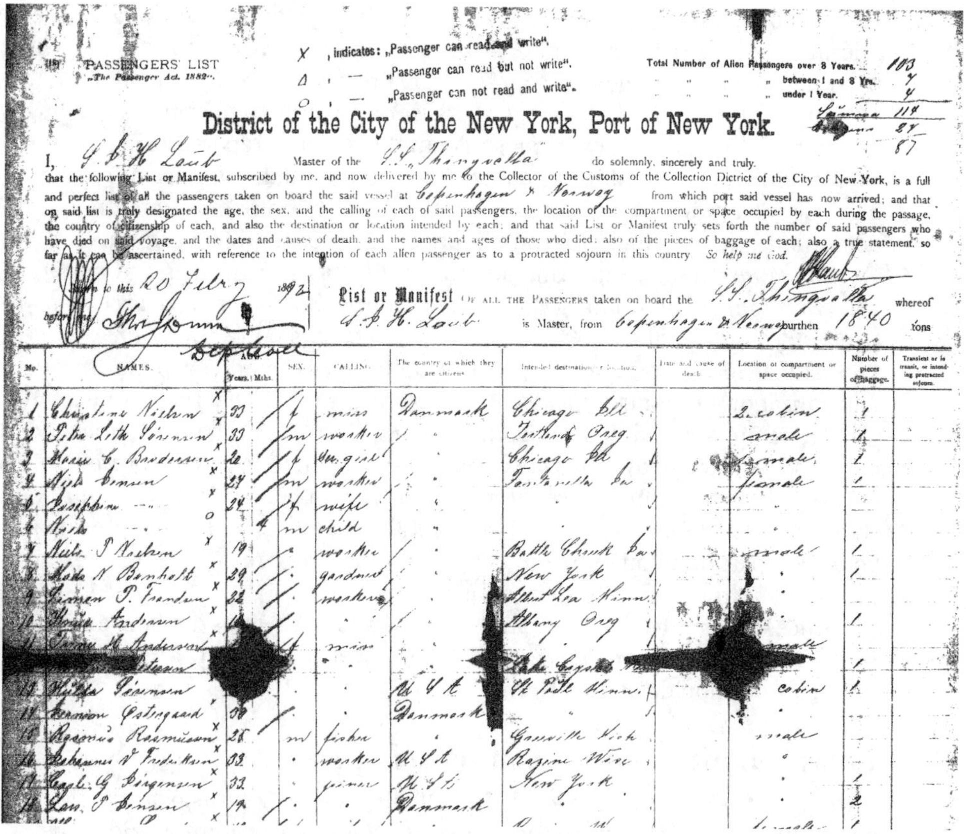

PASSENGERS' LIST
„The Passenger Act. 1882".

X , indicates: „Passenger can read and write".
Δ , — „Passenger can read but not write".
O , — „Passenger can not read and write".

Total Number of Alien Passengers over 8 Years. 103
between 1 and 8 Yrs. 7
under 1 Year. 4

District of the City of the New York, Port of New York.

I, G. F. H. Laub Master of the S.S. „Thingvalla" do solemnly, sincerely and truly, that the following List or Manifest, subscribed by me, and now delivered by me to the Collector of the Customs of the Collection Dictrict of the City of New-York, is a full and perfect list of all the passengers taken on board the said vessel at Copenhagen & Norway from which port said vessel has now arrived; and that on said list is truly designated the age, the sex, and the calling of each of said passengers, the location of the compartment or space occupied by each during the passage, the country of citizenship of each, and also the destination or location intended by each; and that said List or Manifest truly sets forth the number of said passengers who have died on said voyage, and the dates and causes of death, and the names and ages of those who died; also of the pieces of baggage of each; also a true statement, so far as it can be ascertained, with reference to the intention of each alien passenger as to a protracted sojourn in this country. So help me God.

Sworn to this 20 Febr 1892

List or Manifest of all the Passengers taken on board the S.S. Thingvalla whereof G. F. H. Laub is Master, from Copenhagen & Norway burthen 1840 tons

No.	NAMES.	AGE. Years. Mths.	SEX.	CALLING.	The country of which they are citizens.	Intended destination or location.	Date and cause of death.	Location of compartment or space occupied.	Number of pieces of baggage.	Transient, in transit, or intending protracted sojourn.

FIGURE 9-5 Detail from the passenger list of the S.S. *Thingvalla*, arriving in New York on 20 February 1892. (Used with permission of The Generations Network, Inc.)

the ship. Therefore, any changes would have been noted *prior* to entry into any U.S. port. Only births, deaths, and the discovery of a stowaway would have caused the manifest to be changed en route.

Again, the forms were to be presented to the Customs and Immigration Service officers at the port of arrival. The forms became known as Immigration Manifests or Immigration Passenger Lists. When these forms were introduced in the early 1890s, they required more information than ever before to be provided. (Please see Table 9-1.) Further columns were added in later years, all of which provide more information for our genealogical use.

The federal immigration department requested that all early passenger arrival records be sent to that office. Unfortunately, though, that was easier said than done. The original documents had been stored in customs houses, courthouses, customs collectors' homes, and other places. Some had been damaged, destroyed, or simply lost. Fortunately, a vast majority of the original customs passenger lists from 1820 to 1905 survived for seven U.S. ports, as have a majority of the customs collectors' abstract reports. They are in the possession of NARA and have been microfilmed. In fact, where the original passenger list has not survived, NARA has used the customs officers' reports as substitutes to fill in gaps in chronological sequence in the microfilmed records. While these abstracts don't contain as much detail as the original passenger manifests, they do supply critical nominal information and other details.

As the years passed, passenger lists were prepared with more forethought to their clarity and accuracy. Many of these documents were prepared using a typewriter, such as the example in Figure 9-6, which certainly makes for easier reading. However, because the typewritten passenger lists were likely prepared from other handwritten documents, the possibility of transcription and typographical error is increased.

For more extensive information about ships' passenger lists and manifests, you will want to read John Philip Colletta's definitive how-to book, *They Came in Ships* (Ancestry Incorporated, 2002), articles in Ancestry's book, *The Source* (Ancestry Publishing, 2006), and Loretto D. Szuc's definitive reference book for immigration and naturalization reference, *They Became Americans* (Ancestry Incorporated, 1998).

There are any number of indexes and finding aids to these records, and all three of the books cited above provide excellent guidance to help you locate these indexes. Perhaps the most definitive is the mammoth set of books by P. William Filby, the *Passenger and Immigration Lists Index* (Gale Research, Inc., 1985 to present). These books are part of an ongoing project to index as many resources of ships' passenger information from as many sources as possible.

Ancestry.com has digitized and indexed all of the ships' passenger lists for all U.S. ports. These images can be accessed at their website at **www.ancestry.com** as part of their subscription database offering.

Learn About the American Ports of Entry

Although passengers arrived at about 100 different U.S. ports over the years, most ports saw only infrequent traffic. Sometimes only a few ships would arrive in a given year. During the early years, most of the immigration traffic tended to be directed to one of five major ports: Boston, New York, Philadelphia, Baltimore, and New Orleans.

TABLE 9-1   Required Contents for Passenger Manifests Arriving in the United States. (Used with permission from Aha! Seminars, Inc.)

Time Period	Passenger List Columns/Contents
1820–1891	• Passenger Name • Age • Gender • Occupation • Nationality
1892	• Passenger Name • Age • Gender • Occupation • Nationality • Marital status • Last residence • Intended final destination in the U.S. • Whether ever in the U.S. before and, if so, where, when, and for what duration • Name, address, and relationship of any relative in the U.S. which the immigrant planned to join • Whether able to read and write • Whether in possession of a train ticket to the final destination • Who paid the passage to America • Amount of money (in dollars) the immigrant was carrying • Whether the person was a convict, indigent, insane, or a polygamist • State of the immigrant's health
1903	All of the information as in 1892, plus: • Race or people
1906	All of the information as in 1903, plus: • Personal description (height, complexion, hair color, eye color, and any other identifying marks)
1907	All of the information as in 1906, plus: • Name and address of the closest living relative in the native country

FIGURE 9-6 Page from a passenger manifest of a ship arriving in New York on 1 May 1923. (From the author's collection.)

Although Philadelphia had been the most popular of these ports during the colonial era, within the first two decades of federal immigration regulation, New York emerged as the preferred port of arrival.

By 1850, more immigrants arrived in New York than in all other ports combined. This is a likely result of the construction of the Erie Canal and its expansion. The canal became a primary conduit for migration to western New York, Pennsylvania, Ohio, and further west by means of passenger ships plying the Great Lakes. New York had become the nation's largest seaport since the 1820s. By the 1850s, New York also was a major railroad hub offering access to nearly every part of the country. It is no wonder that it became the primary immigration port of entry.

Because of the waves of immigrants entering the city, New York was the first port to open an immigration depot. Castle Garden, shown in Figure 9-7, was located at the Battery in lower Manhattan. It was the immigration processing center for the Port of New York prior to the opening of Ellis Island on 1 January 1892. It was a massive stone structure originally built in 1808 as a fort. It later served as an opera house until 3 August 1855 when New York State authorities transformed it into an immigration landing and processing station.

Castle Garden's primary purpose was not to inspect, but to protect new arrivals from the thieves, swindlers, confidence men, and prostitutes who prowled the piers looking for easy marks. Inside Castle Garden, immigrants could exchange money, purchase food and railway tickets, tend to baggage, and obtain information about boarding houses and employment. More buildings were erected outside the original Castle Garden to handle the additional volume of people as immigrant arrivals increased. Brick walls were constructed to enclose the large complex. On 18 April 1890, the last immigrants were processed through Castle Garden. During its lifetime, more than eight million immigrants had passed through Castle Garden.

FIGURE 9-7   View of Castle Garden in New York. (From a stereoscope card in the author's collection.)

Control over the immigration processing in New York shifted to the U.S. Superintendent of Immigration, and the Barge Office became an interim landing depot, pending the opening of a new immigrant processing center on Ellis Island on 1 January 1892.

Public pressures increased to regulate immigration and protect American jobs. With this pressure, a major new piece of legislation was introduced and passed, the Immigration Act of 1891. This act established the federal office of Superintendent of Immigration, which later became the Immigration Bureau. Over time, the Immigration Bureau exerted more and more control over the immigration lists and other documents, including their creation, content, distribution, processing, and retention. The Immigration Bureau was ultimately merged with the Bureau of Naturalization and became the Immigration and Naturalization Service that we have long known. It now is known as the U.S. Citizenship and Immigration Services (USCIS).

Did You Know? Ellis Island wasn't the first immigration processing center in New York. Ellis Island opened on 1 January 1892 and replaced Castle Garden.

Another important milestone in 1891 was the completion of the new Ellis Island immigration processing site in New York Harbor. Ellis Island replaced Castle Garden, and opened on 1 January 1892. Immigrants such as those shown in Figure 9-8 arrived

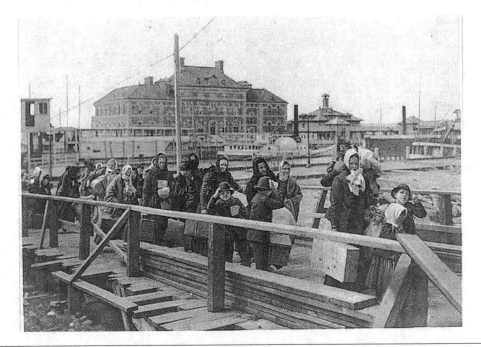

FIGURE 9-8   Immigrants arriving at Ellis Island. (From the Library of Congress collection.)

at a modern, well-organized facility where they were given physical examinations, helped with completing forms by interpreters who spoke their language, and processed efficiently through customs.

On 14 June 1897, however, fire destroyed the Ellis Island facility, and with it went the administrative records of Castle Garden (1888–1890) and Ellis Island (1890–1897). These were administrative records only and it is believed that very few passenger list documents, if any, were lost. The passenger lists that had already been handled over Ellis Island's years of operation to that date were perfectly safe and already in the custody of the Bureau of Customs and the Bureau of Immigration. The Ellis Island facility was reconstructed, this time using fireproof materials, and it reopened on 15 December 1900. It served as the immigration processing site for New York until 1954. You will want to research passenger arrivals at the Ellis Island Foundation site at **www.ellisisland.org**. Stephen P. Morse has developed an excellent website that can help you get past some of the limitations of the official Ellis Island Foundation site, and his site can be accessed at **http://stevemorse.org**. Here you will find numerous search tools for Castle Garden and Ellis Island immigrant arrivals.

New immigration forms were implemented at different times in different ports depending upon a number of factors, most notably who was in charge of the port at the time. Some ports were immediately regulated by federal immigration officials beginning in 1891, while other ports were regulated and administered by local officers contracted by federal officials. Any lists created under the authority of the Immigration Bureau are considered and referred to as "immigration passenger lists." This distinguishes their content and handling from that of the customs collectors and the "customs passenger lists" and the associated processing that was used from 1820 until 1891.

Contrary to popular myth, the employees of the immigration processing centers did not arbitrarily change immigrants' names as they arrived. You may have seen photographs of immigrants queued up for interview or inspection in which a paper tag was attached to their clothing. The tag actually bore the name of the ship on which the person had arrived and the line number on the passenger manifest on which his or her name was listed. The processing stations used these tags to facilitate the expeditious processing of persons who spoke little or no English. The tags assisted in directing the new arrivals into proper lines for processing. There also was a small army of translators available to assist in the arrival and inspection process. Many immigrants actually changed their own names prior to sailing, on arrival in the new country, or later in order to become more quickly assimilated into the new environment. Versions of the same forms used in the United States at various times have included a place to indicate the name under which the person arrived in the country.

Virtually all of the later immigration passenger lists survived and were eventually acquired by NARA after its creation. In the 1940s and 1950s, thousands of bound volumes of these lists (about 14,000 volumes of Ellis Island records alone) were microfilmed. Since the project was completed relatively early in the history of microfilming, the quality is not always good. Some estimates indicate that as much as 6 percent of the lists are difficult or impossible to read, with that number reaching as high as 15 percent for the pre-1902 lists. The passenger lists were destroyed after microfilming, though, making it impossible to create new digital images from the originals. Ancestry.com, however, has digitized and indexed all of the surviving passenger lists for all U.S. ports of arrival.

Locate Ships' Passenger Lists for Immigrants Arriving in the United States

The ships' passenger lists for arrivals into the United States, as I mentioned before, have been microfilmed by NARA and digitized by Ancestry.com. You can use the indexes such as those produced by William Filby, colonial, state, and local histories, and transcriptions in both print and on the Internet to locate ships whose port of origin and time period seem appropriate candidates to search. Federal census schedules, too, can be used as part of your research strategy. For example, the following years' U.S. federal census Population Schedules contain important clues:

- **1880**   Nativity columns ask for place of birth for the named person on the census form, as well as his or her parents.
- **1900**   Nativity information is again requested. In addition, the year of immigration is requested, as well as number of years in the United States and status of naturalization.
- **1910**   Nativity information is again requested. In addition, the year of immigration, whether naturalized, and language spoken if not English were included.
- **1920**   Year of immigration, naturalization status, and year of naturalization are requested. Place of birth and mother tongue are requested for the named person on the census and his or her parents.
- **1930**   Place of birth of named person on census and parents were requested, as well as language spoken in home before coming to the United States. Year of immigration and naturalization status were included.

All of these years' census schedules can provide pointers to dates and locations of immigration, including the language or "mother tongue" spoken. A response of Yiddish certainly points to a Jewish background, and a reply such as Polish, French, or Urdu would indicate another national or ethnic origin.

Naturalization documents, which we will discuss later in the chapter, can name the date, port of arrival, and name of the ship on which the person arrived.

If you are unsure of the ship on which your ancestor arrived, it is possible to use other clues such as language, place of birth, or spelling of the surname to narrow your search. If you have a good idea of the country of origin, you may be able to use microfilm of newspapers and read the shipping news. Ships' arrivals, name of the port of origin, intermediate ports of call, and shipping company can help you avoid having to read every entry for every ship in a given year. In addition, with the names of shipping lines arriving from your ancestor's country of origin, you may also be able to locate ships' manifests created and filed on the other side of the ocean.

The Immigrant Ships Transcribers Guild (ISTG) at **www.immigrantships.net** is an all-volunteer effort and is making great strides in locating, accessing, and producing accurate transcriptions of ships' passenger lists and manifests from the 1600s to the 1900s from all over the globe.

Did You Know? The Immigration and Naturalization Service, begun in 1906, became the U.S. Citizenship and Immigration Services (USCIS). You can access that site at **www.uscis.gov/portal/site/uscis** and learn about its history and the necessary requirements for obtaining information from that agency.

Locate and Access Canadian Immigration Records

There are many, many records available for the Canadian researcher. One important website with which to begin your research is inGeneas, created and maintained by genealogy professionals in Ottawa. Located at **www.ingeneas.com**, the site provides searchable databases, including passenger and immigration records from the 1700s to the early 1900s. Search results provide listings of matches, and following the links may present you with information about a person's age, the year of the record, and a description. You can then order transcripts of records you want more information on, or you can also order a photocopy of the original microfilmed document.

Another excellent website with many links is Immigrants to Canada, located at **www.ist.uwaterloo.ca/ ~ marj/genealogy/thevoyage.html**. Included are scores of links, including compilations of ships for specific years, written/transcribed accounts describing the voyages, emigrant handbooks, extracts from government immigration reports of the 19th century, and many, many nationalities' emigration/immigration website links. Don't miss this one!

The Generations Network, Inc., completed the digitization and indexing of all the surviving Canadian passenger lists in 2008. This digital collection encompasses the years 1865 to 1935 and includes more than 7.2 million names. It is part of the Ancestry.com and Ancestry.ca subscription database collections. Figure 9-9 shows an example from 1934.

Library and Archives Canada

Library and Archives Canada, at **www.collectionscanada.gc.ca**, provides its content in both English and French. Here you will find a wealth of information for your research. On the main page, click the Canadian Genealogy Centre link. Here you can search any of the databases related to genealogy. You can also view the list of all the available databases. Click a link and explore the available information.

FIGURE 9-9   Canadian passenger list from 1934. (Used with permission of The Generations Network, Inc.)

First, you should know that there are no comprehensive lists of immigrant arrivals in Canada prior to 1865. Until that year, shipping companies were not required to create, retain, or supply their passenger lists to the government offices. There are apparently a few of the lists that include passenger names, and the Miscellaneous Immigration Index in the archives' reference room is accessible for locating those few records. The contents relate to immigrants from the British Isles to Québec and Ontario between the years 1800 and 1849. That information also is included in the inGeneas website as a result of volunteers' work to index and enter it.

> **Did You Know?**
>
> Immigration passenger lists were not required in Canada until 1865. The originals are at Library and Archives Canada (LAC), and they have been digitized at Ancestry.com and Ancestry.ca. The LAC site is an excellent site at which you can learn more about history and context of these records.

Please note that records from 1 January 1936 are still in the custody of Citizenship and Immigration Canada. Privacy of individuals is protected, and certain requirements exist. Border Entry records also are available for immigrants arriving across the U.S./Canadian border between April 1908 and December 1935. However, not all immigrants were recorded. Some persons immigrated without being processed through ports when they were closed or where no port or governmental station existed. Others, for whom one or both parents were Canadian or who had previously resided in Canada, were considered "returning Canadians" and were not listed.

There also are registers of Chinese immigrants to Canada who arrived between 1885 and 1949.

It is important to know that the records are arranged by name of the port of arrival and the date of arrival, with the exception of the years 1923–1924 and some records from 1919 to 1922 when a separate governmental reporting Form 30A (individual manifest) was used. In addition, the Pier 21 Society of Halifax, Nova Scotia, has worked with Library and Archives Canada in inputting passenger list data from 1925–1935 and border entry record data into ArchiviaNet, the On-line Research Tool. Information about and access to ArchiviaNet is accessible at **www .collectionscanada.gc.ca/archivianet/020123_e.html**. The search template for ArchiviaNet is shown in Figure 9-10.

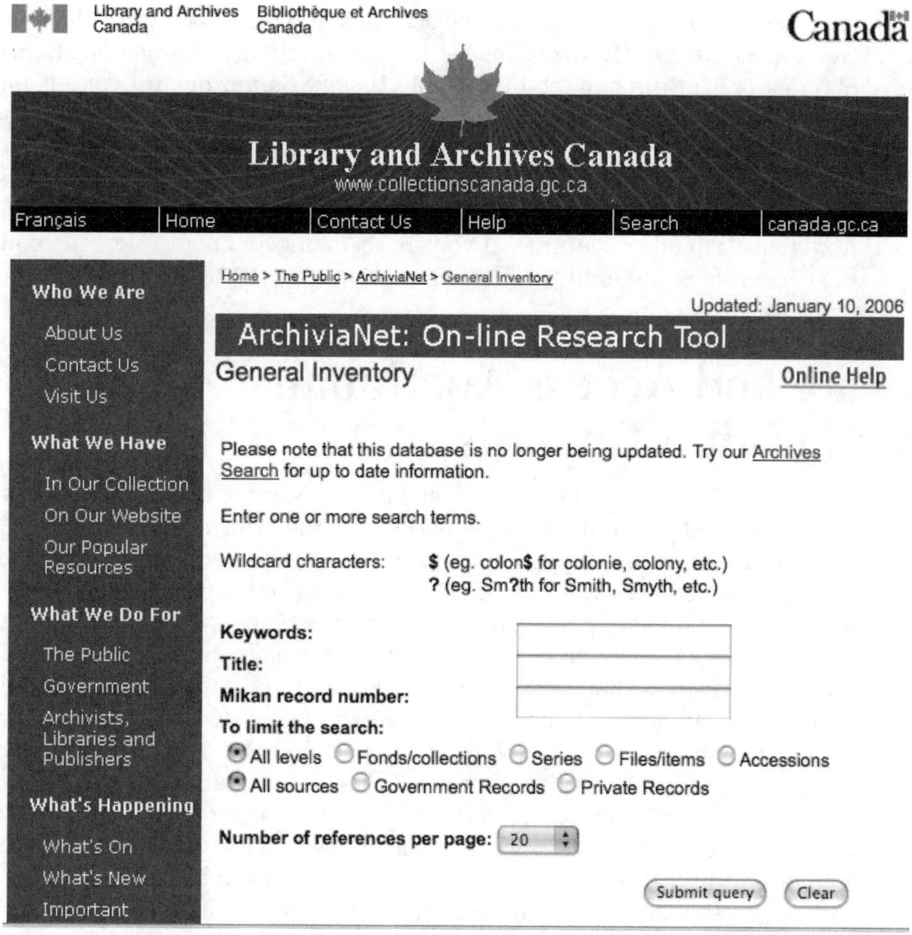

FIGURE 9-10   The search template for ArchiviaNet

Home Children is a term used to designate the more than 100,000 children who were sent from Great Britain to Canada between the years of 1869 and 1930. The intent was to supposedly provide a better, healthier, and more moral life for them. These were primarily poor or orphaned children, and rural Canadians welcomed them as cheap labor for their farms. (You may learn more about this phenomenon at the Young Immigrants to Canada website at **www.dcs.uwaterloo.ca/ ~ marj/genealogy/ homeadd.html**.) The archive contains a great deal of correspondence from sponsoring and administrative agencies for these children. Members of the British Isles Family History Society of Greater Ottawa are locating and indexing the names of these Home Children found in passenger lists in the custody of Library and Archives Canada. Details about the record holdings and a searchable database of these children are accessible at **www.collectionscanada.gc.ca/genealogie/022-908.009-e.html**.

Passenger lists and other records from before 1865 may exist in the provincial or territorial libraries, archives, and/or at maritime museums. The passenger arrival records in the custody of Library and Archives Canada that date from 1865 to 1935 have been microfilmed. They can be accessed in person by visiting them at 395 Wellington Street in Ottawa, Canada, through interlibrary loan among Canadian libraries, and/or through the LDS Family History Center nearest you. As mentioned before, digitized images are indexed and accessible at Ancestry.com and Ancestry.ca.

An excellent strategy for researching immigrants into Canada would be to start with Library and Archives Canada and then seek additional resources in the appropriate province or territory. Please note that Canada *does not* maintain records of emigrations from Canada to other countries. If you are searching for an ancestor who emigrated to the United States, for example, you will need to refer to U.S. immigration records.

Locate and Access Australian Immigration Records

The history of Australia is a rich one, and it is the story of two peoples: the indigenous Aboriginals and the immigrants, primarily from the British Isles. Most people know that Australia was originally a penal colony, and that most of the original, colonial settlers were, in fact, convicts who were transported from the United Kingdom since 1788, along with the military personnel assigned to the colony. Nowadays it is the "in thing" to descend from a convict. In fact, Australian citizens often express the sentiment that the more convicts in the family tree, the merrier—and the more "ocker" (Australian) one becomes. So let's look at convicts first. The earlier your ancestor arrived in Australia, the greater the probability that you are descended from a convict or from a member of the Crown government, an army or naval person, or a member of a ship's crew.

It is important to recognize early on that the National Archives of Australia on Queen Victoria Terrace in Canberra is the archives of the Commonwealth government. The records in that collection therefore date mostly from the Federation in 1901. The archives do not possess the records of convicts, of colonial migration, or of 19th-century Australian history concerning such periods as the early exploration, the gold rushes, or colonial administration. They also do not have information about functions administered by the state and territory governments such as births, deaths, and marriages registers, or land titles. To obtain further information on these topics, it is necessary to contact the relevant state or territory registrar.

What the National Archives of Australia does have, however, are immigration records relating to the 20th century dating primarily from 1924. They do have some older records dating to the 1850s, but most of the records will be found in the respective state and territory archives. The National Archives' Fact Sheets page can be accessed at **www.naa.gov.au/about-us/publications/fact-sheets/index.aspx**. You will also want to review specific fact sheets for records held in other offices of the archives as follows:

Fact Sheet 56	Passenger records held in Perth **www.naa.gov.au/about-us/publications/fact-sheets/fs56.aspx**
Fact Sheet 64	Passenger records held in Sydney **www.naa.gov.au/about-us/publications/fact-sheets/fs64.aspx**
Fact Sheet 172	Passenger records held in Melbourne **www.naa.gov.au/about-us/publications/fact-sheets/fs172.aspx**
Fact Sheet 184	Passenger records held in Hobart **www.naa.gov.au/about-us/publications/fact-sheets/fs184.aspx**

Fact Sheet 2, located at **www.naa.gov.au/about-us/publications/fact-sheets/fs02.aspx**, is perhaps your most valuable online reference in the search for historical documents related to your genealogical research. It contains the addresses, contact information, and web address links for all of the major Australian archival institutions.

Learn About Australian History

Many criminal offenses in England during previous centuries could be punished with extremely harsh and cruel sentences, ranging from public floggings to an appointment with the hangman, or to an executioner with an axe, if you were a "special" prisoner. During the 17th century, a more humane method of punishment was sought, and *transportation* to a distant wilderness environment was seen as an ideal solution. Thus, transportation began from the United Kingdom to the American colonies. Debtors' colonies and criminal settlements existed for those condemned to a penal servitude or for a term of years or for life. The outbreak of the American Revolutionary War halted transportation of criminals and undesirables to that destination in 1775. While sentences of transportation were still passed by the courts, the convicts were remanded to prison. Before long, prison overcrowding created dire conditions. The government began to acquire older, perhaps no longer seaworthy ships, which were referred to as "the hulks." These were fitted to house criminals, and thousands of convicts were sentenced to terms of imprisonment in these floating jails moored in coastal waters. The deplorable living conditions in both the prisons and on board the hulks reached a crisis stage, with rampant disease and escalating death tolls. The government sought a new penal colony as a solution. In 1787, what has been called the "First Fleet" set sail from England for Botany Bay in Australia. A number of penal colony settlements were founded and maintained over the next 70 years. Transportation as a punishment was effectively stopped in 1857, although it was not formally abolished until 1868.

As you begin your research for Australian ancestors, you will want to familiarize yourself with the history of the judicial system in the United Kingdom at the time in question, and about the history of the penal colonies in the various areas of Australia. You also will want to try to locate the records of the criminal proceedings against your ancestor, the details of sentencing, and to what colony he or she was transported. This will help you trace the migration path.

You also can trace the path backward, although it may be more complicated to make that leap without understanding the ancestor's circumstances and his or her offense. In either case, however, it is important to learn as much about your ancestor as possible before you begin. At a minimum, you will want to know the exact name, age, approximate date of arrival, and the port of disembarkation. Any additional information you can glean in advance may be the crucial factor in distinguishing *your* ancestor from another person bearing the same name. Again, most of these records will be in the possession of the respective state or territory to which the person was transported.

Use Strategies for Determining Your Ancestor's Ship

By now, you should have a much better idea of the types of information that are available for the various time periods and what you are likely to find at various points in time. The actual *locating* of the records is, of course, the real challenge. The following are some strategies you may consider employing in order to locate these records for your ancestors.

Start with What You Know

As with all effective family history and genealogical research, start with the most recent period and work your way backward. Any other approach, especially when researching back "across the pond," can be disastrous. As you proceed backward, start with what other family members may know. Look for home sources, including documentary materials that may have recorded immigration and/or naturalization details. These include Bibles, letters, naturalization papers, voter registration documents, obituaries, and other documents. Another, older relative may even recall having heard Grandpa or Grandma discuss his or her trip to the new country, or something they recall having heard from another family member. While the intervening years may have dimmed or distorted the memory, there is likely to be a glimmer of truth or a kernel of fact with which to begin researching.

Refer to Vital Documents

Marriage and death certificates, as well as any ecclesiastical records, may provide crucial information concerning your ancestor's origins.

Don't Overlook Voter Registration Records

One important record overlooked by many researchers is the voter registration record. These records typically are maintained at the county level across the United States and in governmental offices in other countries. Most times they are in a list format but sometimes the original voter registration application cards still exist. In order to vote in an election, an individual had to be a citizen, and the voter registration records may include areas to indicate the place of birth, whether naturalized and when, and how many years a resident in this voting precinct, ward, and so on.

Look for Passport Records

Passports were issued as early as 1797 in the United States to citizens traveling to other countries. It is possible that your ancestor had to obtain a passport to return to and visit his or her homeland (and even to bring other relatives to America). Ancestry.com has digitized and indexed more than 1.5 million passport applications dating from 1795 to 1925. Figure 9-11 shows the passport application for Samuel L. Clemens, also known as author Mark Twain, from 5 May 1891.

Locate and Use the U.S. Federal Census Population Schedules

Don't overlook the information included on U.S. federal census records from 1880 forward concerning place of birth of the individual, his or her parents, and naturalization information details. We saw an example of the 1910 census in Figure 9-2. The information in the census documents often provides direct clues. However, be aware that a stated place of birth may have been in a different geopolitical jurisdiction at the time of birth than it is now, and your understanding of the history and geographical boundary changes is crucial to your successful research into your ancestor's origins.

Study Published Histories

It is important to locate histories of the country and the locale from which your ancestor(s) may have come. Some of these published chronicles include the names of emigrants, their reasons for emigration, the migration paths they took, the time periods in which they relocated, and, in some cases, the names of the shipping lines (and ships) used.

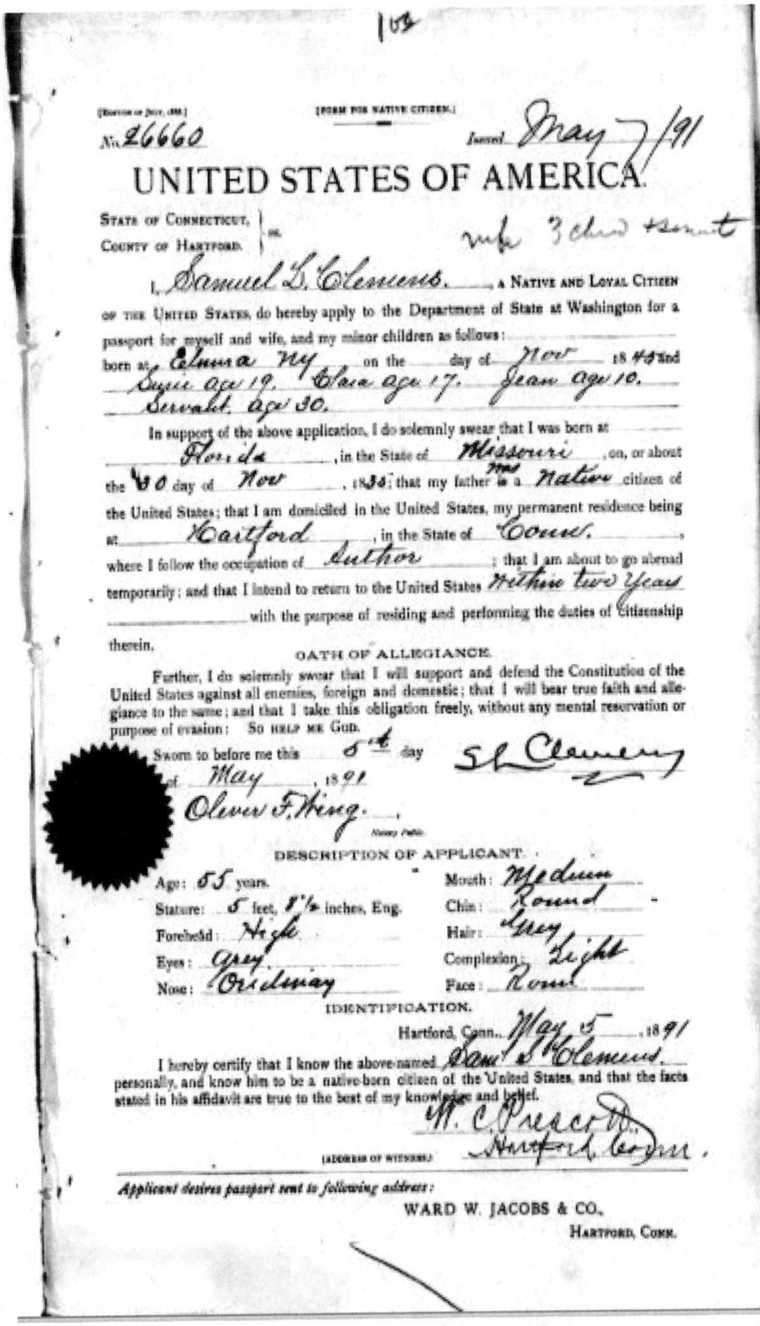

[Edition of July, 188_] [FORM FOR NATIVE CITIZEN.]

No. 26660 Issued May 7/91

UNITED STATES OF AMERICA.

State of Connecticut,
County of Hartford, ss.

I, Samuel L. Clemens, a Native and Loyal Citizen of the United States, do hereby apply to the Department of State at Washington for a passport for myself and wife, and my minor children as follows: born at Elmira NY on the day of Nov 1845 and Susie age 19. Clara age 17. Jean age 10. Servant age 30.

In support of the above application, I do solemnly swear that I was born at Florida, in the State of Missouri, on, or about the 30 day of Nov, 1835; that my father was a native citizen of the United States; that I am domiciled in the United States, my permanent residence being at Hartford, in the State of Conn., where I follow the occupation of Author; that I am about to go abroad temporarily; and that I intend to return to the United States within two years with the purpose of residing and performing the duties of citizenship therein.

OATH OF ALLEGIANCE.

Further, I do solemnly swear that I will support and defend the Constitution of the United States against all enemies, foreign and domestic; that I will bear true faith and allegiance to the same; and that I take this obligation freely, without any mental reservation or purpose of evasion: So help me God.

Sworn to before me this 5th day of May, 1891 S L Clemens

Oliver F. Wing.
Notary Public.

DESCRIPTION OF APPLICANT.

Age: 55 years.	Mouth: Medium
Stature: 5 feet, 8 1/2 inches, Eng.	Chin: Round
Forehead: High	Hair: Grey
Eyes: Grey	Complexion: Light
Nose: Ordinary	Face: Round

IDENTIFICATION.

Hartford, Conn., May 5, 1891

I hereby certify that I know the above-named Saml L Clemens personally, and know him to be a native-born citizen of the United States, and that the facts stated in his affidavit are true to the best of my knowledge and belief.

W. C. Prescott

[Address of witness.] Hartford Conn.

Applicant desires passport sent to following address:

WARD W. JACOBS & CO.,
Hartford, Conn.

FIGURE 9-11 Passport application for Samuel L. Clemens (aka Mark Twain) from 5 May 1891. (Use with permission from The Generations Network, Inc.)

One category of histories that should not be overlooked is the British genealogies that mention relatives who have gone to the New World. In the 16th and 17th centuries, heralds from the College of Arms would visit the various counties and record the pedigrees of families who aspired to *armigerous* status (meaning that they would have a coat of arms). Occasionally, there would be references to younger sons who had migrated or emigrated elsewhere.

In the 18th and 19th centuries, ambitious compilers of county histories would include pedigrees of the principal families of the county. Again, there would be the occasional reference to a relative who had gone to America, and perhaps even to a specified destination.

Finally, in the 19th and 20th centuries, the various volumes of pedigrees of landed gentry, peerage, and baronetcies, published by Burke's Peerage & Gentry (**www.burkes-peerage.net**), contain many references to American settlers.

Look for Books About Early Settlers

By the same token, the companion to the histories discussed above would be the historical publications concerning arriving immigrants at the other end of your ancestors' journey. Often these books include the names, origins, and biographical sketches of literally hundreds of persons who lived first in a particular area after their immigration from Europe.

Google Books (**http://books.google.com**) is an excellent place to search for books referencing your ancestors and their relatives. Google has digitized many thousands of older books and they are completely searchable.

Seek Supplemental Information on the Internet

Don't forget to conduct research for historical text, records, and other information on the Internet! Learn to use Boolean searches with your favorite browser(s) and start exploring using creative combinations of keywords and phrases. We will discuss research on the Internet in depth in Chapter 11.

Consult Indexes

P. William Filby's set of indexes, mentioned earlier in the chapter, at the end of the section "A Chronology of Ships' Passenger Lists in the United States," remains a monumental reference work. However, there are many, many other indexes you can use. The Soundex index of the passenger records that are in NARA's possession provides an exceptional reference. Similar indexes in other locations, including in the archives of states, counties, and other entities, may be equally as helpful. And don't forget the national archives of other countries for emigration lists, criminal transportation records, shipping company records, crew lists, and other documents.

Search for Shipping News

Newspapers of the period in a location can provide important information about ships' departures and arrivals. Shipping was big business! For example, one researcher accessed microfilmed newspaper records for the port of Bremen and identified every ship sailing during a particular three-month (autumn) sailing season to the port of Boston. Armed with that narrowed-down information, she then researched the incoming shipping records in the Boston newspapers. Using the arrival dates, she then sought—and found—that there were several likely ships on which her own ancestors might have arrived. She went on to locate the passenger manifests and more information about the ships themselves in maritime books and on the Internet. From those records, she was able to reconstruct her ancestors' voyage, including the weather and sailing conditions, and finally located the records she sought. The picture she constructed through her research is a rich tapestry of life at the time for her emigrant/immigrant ancestors.

Use Other Strategies for Determining Your Ancestor's Place of Origin

By now, you should understand more clearly that there are more paths to follow than just one in the search for your ancestors' records. When the place of birth, previous residence, or other indication of native origin is conveniently and clearly marked, you can be thankful for more modern records. However, when you don't have such crystal-clear directional markers, what are you to do?

Determining your ancestral origin can be a tricky thing but it is not always impossible to ascertain. Numerous strategies are employed, so let's look at a few. This list can never be complete because each nationality has its own nuances, but you must invest some thought and ingenuity to reach out to your ancestors' stories and traits.

Use Photographic Images

If your ancestors came to America between 1850 and present, photographs of them very well may exist, especially in family photographic collections. An examination of clothing, hair styles, shoes, jewelry, and other objects in the picture may be helpful. On older photographs mounted on cabinet card stock, there may even be the name of a photographer and a location. Researching these can be an interesting study as well, and it is not unusual to find a particular photographer having taken photos in a specific area or neighborhood in which a national or ethnic group lived.

Look for Letters Written in Another Language at Home

If you encounter letters written in another language among the family possessions, or Bibles and books in another language, start asking questions. These may be indicative of the nativity of members of your family or your ancestors. It may also be possible to have these items translated into your language so that you can understand them and potentially gain more clues.

Did You Know? Specific family clues can point to the country or region of origin for your ancestors. Consider language spoken, family traditions, ethnic recipes, and other clues.

Consider Family Customs

Are there specific customs in your family you don't understand? One researcher wondered why the family always ate marinated herring at Christmastime, only to discover later that it was a residual custom from her maternal grandmother, whose family always ate it at their home outside Uppsala, Sweden. And are there songs in another language that are sung, such as lullabies? They might be an important clue.

Culinary Styles Can Provide Clues

Ethnic or national cooking is always an interesting tip-off, though not always. Your grandmother's Hungarian goulash may be indicative that she is one of Zsa-Zsa Gabor and her sisters' cousins! Maybe not, but don't overlook the possibility that some culinary trait might point to a particular ethnic or national heritage.

Pay Attention to Family Physical Traits

One African-American friend heard a lecture at the National Genealogical Society Conference in Valley Forge, Pennsylvania, in 1997, by another African-American researcher. In that lecture, she learned that there are physical characteristics of some African peoples that may be used to trace ancestry of slave ancestors back to the geographical area and perhaps to a specific group. The physical traits in this case were the size and shape of the ear, the shape of a nose, and the physical size of the ulna. It is a very interesting approach, and it might really matter.

Use Alternative Record Types to Identify Clues

It is important to use your creativity to identify and locate alternative records that might help you trace your ancestors to their native origins. Remember that ships' manifests are not the only possible extant records that may record that information. Consider the following record types: religious records, including letters of membership transfer; marriage records; census records; naturalization papers; death records; newspaper articles; obituaries; cemetery records; wills and probate packet documents; family histories; published local and provincial histories; genealogical and historical society documents; maritime museums and archives; and academic libraries and archives and their special collections.

Each of these is a possible source for prospecting for your immigrant ancestors' origins.

Use the Resources at the U.S. Citizenship and Immigration Services Website

The U.S. Citizenship and Immigration Services website, as mentioned before, provides some of the most important historical and reference materials for your immigration and naturalization research. USCIS is located at **www.uscis.gov**. Under the Services & Benefits tab is a link labeled Genealogy. Here you will find information concerning the fee-based search and copy services for genealogists to obtain naturalization information. Under the Education & Resources tab is a link labeled Immigration Legal History. Here you will find a number of PDF files for specific time periods. Taken together, they provide a rich historical perspective that can help you home in on your ancestor's naturalization requirements and processes. From any page at the USCIS site, you can enter search keywords or phrases for specific items, such as "genealogy."

Understand the Naturalization Process

As our forebears began their new lives in new communities, they strove to "fit in" and to normalize in the new environment. Many realized they would never return to their past lives, and they eagerly embraced their new circumstances. This meant renouncing their political ties to their motherland and applying to become citizens of their new country.

The naturalization process has varied in every location we will discuss here, and has evolved over time to produce more consistent practices with more standardized and detailed records. United States naturalization is discussed below, but your study of naturalization practices in England and Wales, Scotland, Ireland, Canada, Australia, and other locations can provide you with the knowledge and legal background to help understand those places' laws and customs.

Naturalization in the United States, like the ships' passenger lists and manifests, has changed over the last two and a quarter centuries of the country's existence. Different methods of handling the process, different laws and requirements, different forms, and different places where the process was handled all add up to what can be a challenging research effort. There are many intricacies and exceptions and, as a result, we have to do some self-education to learn the details of the history of naturalization in the United States. To that end, Loretto D. Szuc's book *They Became Americans: Finding Naturalization Records and Ethnic Origins* wins my applause for the best volume on the process, and is illustrated with scores of document examples. However, in short, there are four principal documents associated with naturalization in the United States:

- **Declaration of Intention** This document (also referred to as *first papers*) is signed by the immigrant, renouncing citizenship in his/her previous country and any allegiance to the country and/or its ruler or sovereign. It expresses the individual's intent to petition the United States to become a citizen after all requirements are met. The format varied over time, as you can see from the examples in Figures 9-12 and 9-13.

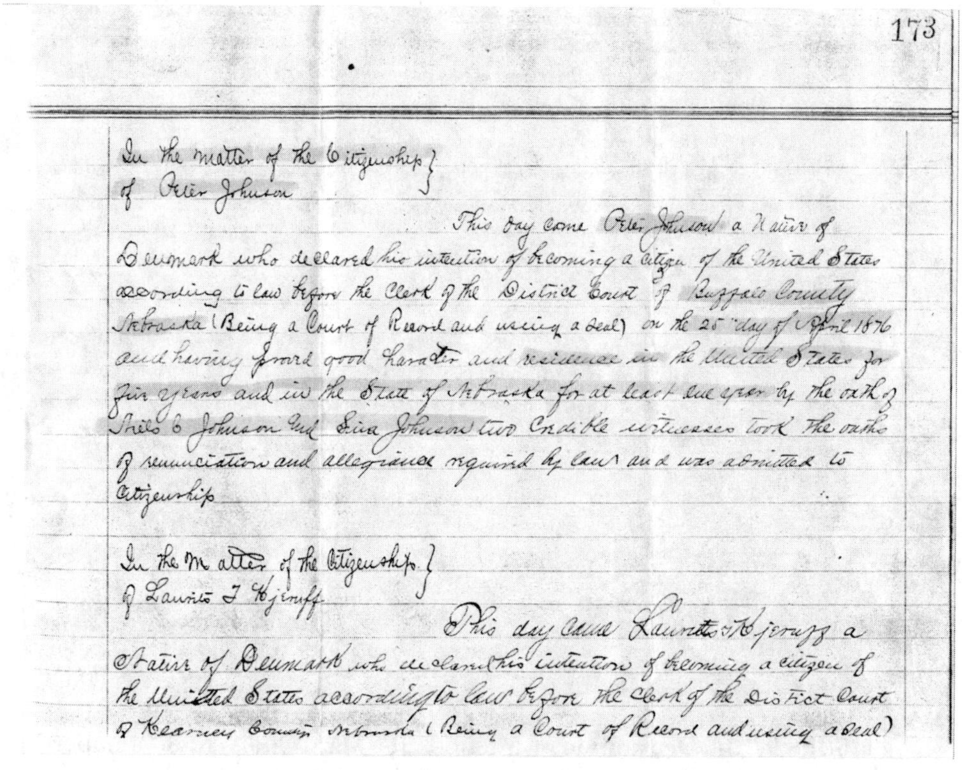
173

In the matter of the Citizenship
of Peter Johnson

This day come Peter Johnson a Native of Denmark who declared his intention of becoming a citizen of the United States according to law before the Clerk of the District Court of Buffalo County Nebraska (Being a Court of Record and using a Seal) on the 25 day of April 1876 and having proved good character and residence in the United States for five years and in the State of Nebraska for at least one year by the oath of Niels C Johnson and Lina Johnson two Credible witnesses took the oaths of renunciation and allegiance required by law and was admitted to Citizenship

In the matter of the Citizenship
of Laurits T Hjeruff

This day came Laurits T Hjeruff a Native of Denmark who declared his intention of becoming a citizen of the United States according to law before the Clerk of the District Court of Kearney County Nebraska (Being a Court of Record and using a Seal)

FIGURE 9-12 Handwritten Declaration of Intention for Peter Johnson, 25 April 1875, Buffalo County, Nebraska. (Courtesy of Jody Johnson.)

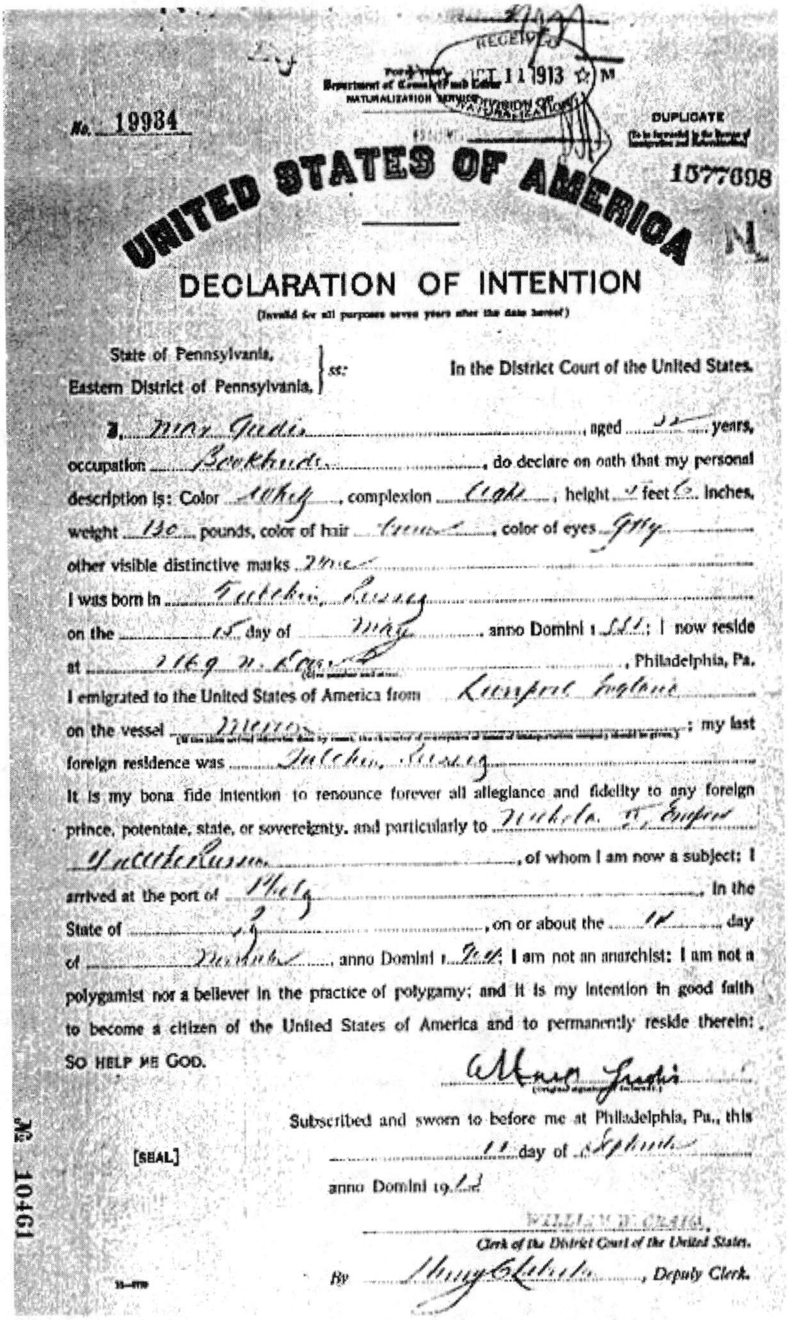

No. 19934

RECEIVED OCT 11 1913

Department of Commerce and Labor
NATURALIZATION SERVICE
DIVISION OF NATURALIZATION

DUPLICATE

1577608

UNITED STATES OF AMERICA

DECLARATION OF INTENTION

(Invalid for all purposes seven years after the date hereof)

State of Pennsylvania,
Eastern District of Pennsylvania, } ss: In the District Court of the United States.

I, Mary Gudis, aged ___ years,
occupation Bookbinder, do declare on oath that my personal
description is: Color white, complexion light, height ___ feet ___ inches,
weight 130 pounds, color of hair brown, color of eyes grey
other visible distinctive marks none
I was born in ___ Russia
on the ___ day of May anno Domini 1___; I now reside
at 2169 N. ___, Philadelphia, Pa.
I emigrated to the United States of America from Liverpool England
on the vessel Merion; my last
foreign residence was ___ Russia
It is my bona fide intention to renounce forever all allegiance and fidelity to any foreign
prince, potentate, state, or sovereignty, and particularly to Nicholas II, Emperor
of all the Russias, of whom I am now a subject; I
arrived at the port of Phila, in the
State of Pa, on or about the ___ day
of ___, anno Domini 1___; I am not an anarchist; I am not a
polygamist nor a believer in the practice of polygamy; and it is my intention in good faith
to become a citizen of the United States of America and to permanently reside therein:
SO HELP ME GOD.

Mary Gudis
(Original signature of declarant.)

Subscribed and sworn to before me at Philadelphia, Pa., this
11 day of September
anno Domini 1913

[SEAL]

WILLIAM W. CRAIG
Clerk of the District Court of the United States.

By ___, Deputy Clerk.

No. 10461

FIGURE 9-13 Declaration of Intention for Mary Gudis, 11 September 1913, filed in Pennsylvania. (From the National Archives and Records Administration collection.)

FIGURE 9-14   Petition for John Wolf, 4 February 1885. (Courtesy of Sherrie Williams.)

- **Petition for Naturalization**   This document (also referred to as *final papers*) is the application that the person completes and submits to request the granting of citizenship, typically after satisfying residency requirements and after filing first papers. Figure 9-14 shows an example of this document, and Figure 9-15 shows the court document granting permission to take the oath of naturalization. Both examples originated in the Dakota Territory in 1885.
- **Oath of Allegiance**   This is the document that is signed by the petitioner for citizenship at the time citizenship is granted (or restored), swearing his/her allegiance and support to the United States. This may or may not be included in the naturalization file for your ancestor.
- **Certificate of Naturalization**   This is the formal document issued to the petitioner to certify that he/she has been naturalized as a citizen of the United States. Figure 9-16 shows a certificate from 1946.

One change required by the revised statute of 1906 was the addition of a step in the process to verify the arrival/admission of the immigrant in the United States. On the Declaration of Intention document, the individual was required to state the place from which he/she emigrated, the arrival point in the United States, the name under which he/she arrived, the date of arrival, and the vessel on which he/she arrived. Copies of the form were forwarded to the port of arrival, where clerks verified the data against the immigration manifests. If the record was found, the INS issued an additional document: the Certificate of Arrival, a sample of which is shown in Figure 9-17. Between its institution in 1906 and 1 July 1924, the Certificate of Arrival was an essential document to process a Petition for Citizenship. Beginning in 1924,

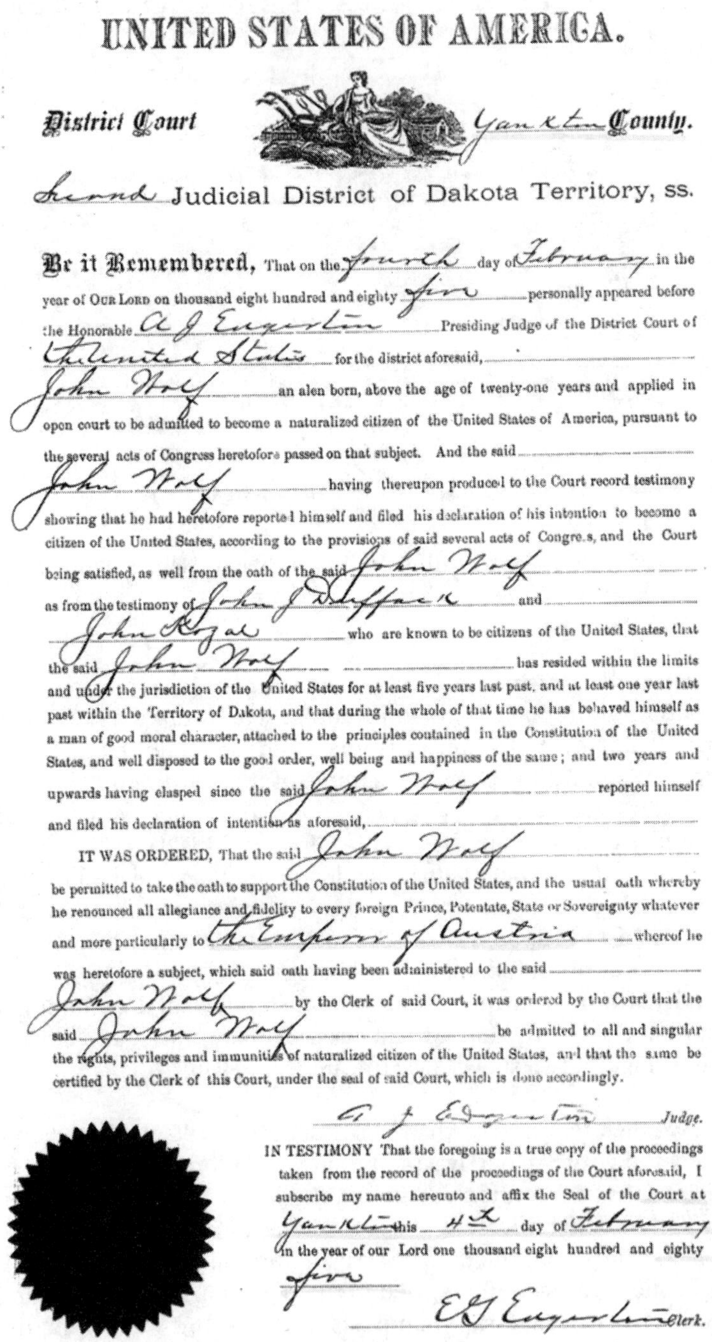

UNITED STATES OF AMERICA.

District Court   **Yankton County.**

Second Judicial District of Dakota Territory, ss.

Be it Remembered, That on the *fourth* day of *February* in the year of Our Lord on thousand eight hundred and eighty *five* personally appeared before the Honorable *A. J. Edgerton* Presiding Judge of the District Court of *the United States* for the district aforesaid, *John Wolf* an alen born, above the age of twenty-one years and applied in open court to be admitted to become a naturalized citizen of the United States of America, pursuant to the several acts of Congress heretofore passed on that subject. And the said *John Wolf* having thereupon produced to the Court record testimony showing that he had heretofore reported himself and filed his declaration of his intention to become a citizen of the United States, according to the provisions of said several acts of Congress, and the Court being satisfied, as well from the oath of the said *John Wolf* as from the testimony of *John J. Duffack* and *John Royal* who are known to be citizens of the United States, that the said *John Wolf* has resided within the limits and under the jurisdiction of the United States for at least five years last past, and at least one year last past within the Territory of Dakota, and that during the whole of that time he has behaved himself as a man of good moral character, attached to the principles contained in the Constitution of the United States, and well disposed to the good order, well being and happiness of the same ; and two years and upwards having elapsed since the said *John Wolf* reported himself and filed his declaration of intention as aforesaid,

    IT WAS ORDERED, That the said *John Wolf* be permitted to take the oath to support the Constitution of the United States, and the usual oath whereby he renounced all allegiance and fidelity to every foreign Prince, Potentate, State or Sovereignty whatever and more particularly to *the Emperor of Austria* whereof he was heretofore a subject, which said oath having been administered to the said *John Wolf* by the Clerk of said Court, it was ordered by the Court that the said *John Wolf* be admitted to all and singular the rights, privileges and immunities of naturalized citizen of the United States, and that the same be certified by the Clerk of this Court, under the seal of said Court, which is done accordingly.

                                                    A. J. Edgerton Judge.

IN TESTIMONY That the foregoing is a true copy of the proceedings taken from the record of the proceedings of the Court aforesaid, I subscribe my name hereunto and affix the Seal of the Court at *Yankton* this *4th* day of *February* in the year of our Lord one thousand eight hundred and eighty *five*

                                                    E. J. Edgerton Clerk.

FIGURE 9-15   Court document granting John Wolf's petition and authorizing him to take the Oath of Allegiance. (Courtesy of Sherrie Williams.)

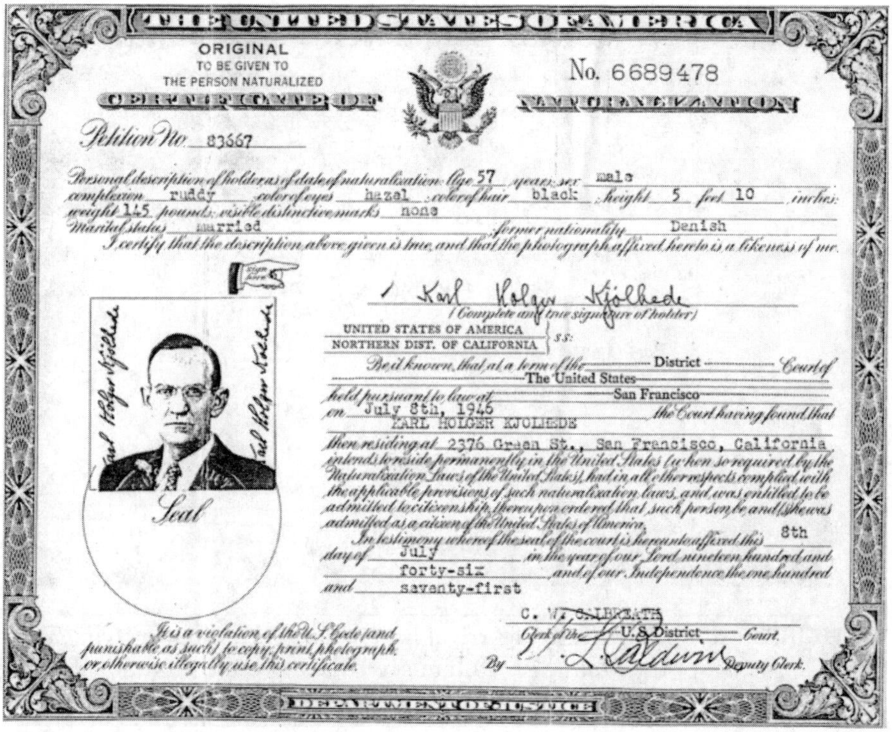

THE UNITED STATES OF AMERICA

ORIGINAL
TO BE GIVEN TO
THE PERSON NATURALIZED

No. 6689478

CERTIFICATE OF NATURALIZATION

Petition No. 83667

Personal description of holder as of date of naturalization: Age 57 years; sex male
complexion ruddy color of eyes hazel color of hair black height 5 feet 10 inches
weight 145 pounds; visible distinctive marks none
Marital status married former nationality Danish
I certify that the description above given is true, and that the photograph affixed hereto is a likeness of me.

Karl Holger Kjolhede
(Complete and true signature of holder)

UNITED STATES OF AMERICA
NORTHERN DIST. OF CALIFORNIA } SS:

Be it known, that at a term of the District Court of The United States
held pursuant to law at San Francisco
on July 8th, 1946 the Court having found that
KARL HOLGER KJOLHEDE
then residing at 2376 Green St., San Francisco, California
intends to reside permanently in the United States (when so required by the Naturalization Laws of the United States), had in all other respects complied with the applicable provisions of such naturalization laws, and was entitled to be admitted to citizenship, thereupon ordered that such person be and (s)he was admitted as a citizen of the United States of America.
In testimony whereof the seal of the court is hereunto affixed this 8th
day of July in the year of our Lord nineteen hundred and
forty-six and of our Independence the one hundred
and seventy-first

Seal

C. W. CALBREATH
Clerk of the U.S. District Court.
By L. Baldwin Deputy Clerk.

It is a violation of the U.S. Code (and punishable as such) to copy, print, photograph, or otherwise illegally use this certificate.

DEPARTMENT OF JUSTICE

FIGURE 9-16 Certificate of Naturalization for Karl Holger Kjolhede, issued 8 July 1946. (Courtesy of Jody Johnson.)

the INS began collecting immigrant visas, and these documents ultimately replaced the need to have verification clerks search the immigration manifests. The visas were presented to an immigration inspector on arrival in the United States, and were filed. Visas for nonimmigrants were filed in the port of arrival, while visas for immigrants were forwarded to the INS in Washington, D.C., for filing and future reference.

Another important document that may possibly be of help to your research is the Alien Registration Card. Concerned by the possibility of war and related espionage, the United States enacted the Alien Registration Act (also known as the Smith Act) in 1940. Between 1940 and 1944, every alien was required to register as they applied for admission to the country, regardless of their origin. They completed a two-page form and were fingerprinted, and they were given an alien registration receipt card to present if asked to confirm their compliance with the law.

There are a number of other types of naturalization documents that were used during the 20th century. The scope of this book makes it impractical to list all of them here. However, Loretto Szucs provides an excellent reference list of documents issued by the INS since 1906, along with their abbreviations, on page 169 of her book *They Became Americans: Finding Naturalization Records and Ethnic Origins* (Ancestry Incorporated, 1998).

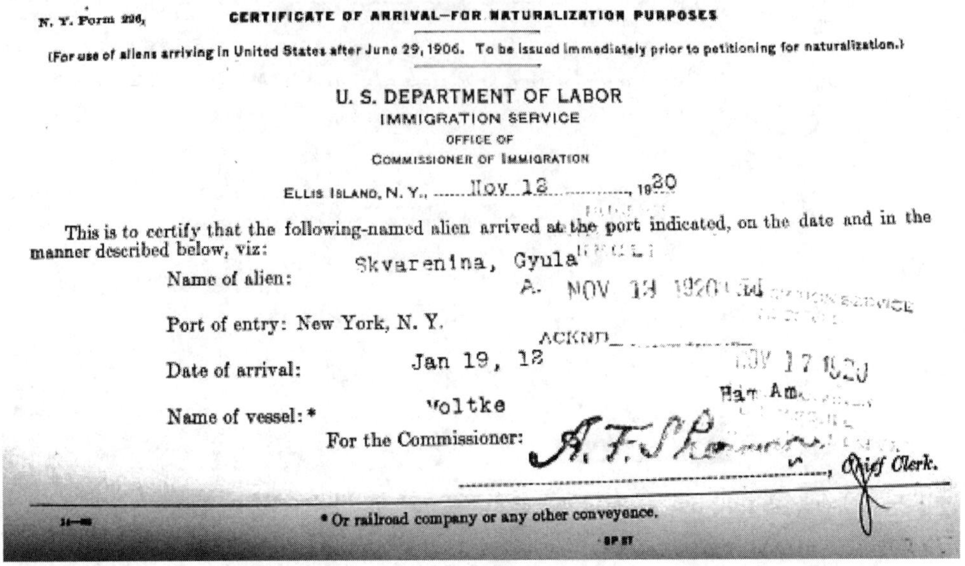

N. Y. Form 226, CERTIFICATE OF ARRIVAL—FOR NATURALIZATION PURPOSES

(For use of aliens arriving in United States after June 29, 1906. To be issued immediately prior to petitioning for naturalization.)

U. S. DEPARTMENT OF LABOR
IMMIGRATION SERVICE
OFFICE OF
COMMISSIONER OF IMMIGRATION

ELLIS ISLAND, N. Y., Nov 12, 1920

This is to certify that the following-named alien arrived at the port indicated, on the date and in the manner described below, viz:

Name of alien: Skvarenina, Gyula

Port of entry: New York, N. Y.

Date of arrival: Jan 19, 12

Name of vessel:* Moltke

For the Commissioner: A. F. Sh..., Chief Clerk.

* Or railroad company or any other conveyance.

FIGURE 9-17 Certificate of Arrival for Gyula Skvarenina verifying arrival on the *Moltke* on 19 January 1912. (From the National Archives and Records Administration collection.)

Locate Repositories Where Naturalization and Related Documents Are Housed

Locating the original documents is your goal, and you certainly will hope to find definite data or clues as to the origins of your ancestor and how he or she traveled to America. As you conduct your research, please remember that an individual may begin the naturalization process, filing a Declaration of Intention, in one place and complete the naturalization process in another place. Therefore, the physical documents may be located in different areas altogether.

The sheer volume of naturalization indexes and documents described above can be mind-boggling. You should be aware that a significant number, but certainly not all, of the extant naturalization documents themselves that have been unearthed have been forwarded to the INS and, in turn, to NARA for microfilming and storage. As a general rule, NARA does *not* have naturalization records created in state or local courts. However, some county court naturalization records have been donated to the National Archives and are available as National Archives microfilm publications. For a reference to the holdings of naturalization materials at NARA, please refer to their website on the topic located at **www.archives.gov/genealogy/naturalization**. This is essential reading for the researcher!

Did You Know?

U.S. naturalization documents are held in the NARA repository that holds the U.S. District Court records for the geographical area in which the naturalization documents were filed. You may find that your ancestor filed a Declaration of Intention and a Petition for Naturalization in different places, and the records may therefore be in different NARA branches.

NARA, for example, has none of the naturalization documents for the State of Utah. These reside with the U.S. District Court for the District of Utah, and some of the older records reside with the Utah State Archives and Records Service. There certainly are many, many other exceptions.

What you will find is that the original naturalization records in NARA's possession have been stored in the National Archives Regional Archives facility that serves the state in which the federal court is located. As an example, NARA's Southeast Region in Morrow, Georgia, is the repository for documents relating to Alabama, Florida, Georgia, Kentucky, Mississippi, North Carolina, South Carolina, and Tennessee. It is important that you determine what NARA Regional Archive serves the state in which your ancestor would have lived at the time he or she filed the Declaration of Intent and/or Petition for Citizenship. Then you need to determine if the NARA Regional Archive does, in fact, have the documents you seek. You can begin your research by visiting the NARA website at **www.archives.gov**, and then visit to **www.archives .gov/locations** for the NARA Regional Archives. Within each one of these, you will find a link to Historical Records and Court Records, and to other resources. Within the resulting pages, you will find a listing of their holdings. Not every NARA Regional Archive has genealogical records.

In the process of your research, it would be prudent whenever you are preparing to conduct a search for naturalization documents to visit the NARA website, check the holdings list of microfilm publications and/or in their online catalog, and consider making a telephone call to their reference desk. The reference staff can help you determine if the records you seek are or are not part of NARA's holdings, whether those documents have been indexed and/or microfilmed, and how to obtain copies. Be sure to check in advance of making a trip to a NARA Regional Archive to confirm that they do, in fact, have the microfilm and/or records you might want to view.

Don't overlook the use of your local LDS Family History Center as a resource to borrow the NARA microfilm from the Family History Library in Salt Lake City. This is an economical means of accessing and working with the materials locally, rather than traveling to a NARA facility.

Finally, Footnote.com is, at this writing, in the process of digitizing the indexes to naturalization indexes and records and placing the images in a searchable database at their subscription website at **www.footnote.com**.

In any event, inasmuch as naturalization records research can involve searching in multiple facilities and potentially working with both archives *and* court repositories, the NARA Regional Archive staff can provide excellent guidance for your research.

Work Immigration, Naturalization, and Census Records in Tandem

You will find it natural to work between using the immigration and naturalization records for your ancestors and family members, and using census records for many clues. Working backward, you can use the naturalization records to isolate the date of arrival, the port, and the name of the vessel. If your ancestors arrived during the implementation of the Certificate of Arrival (1906–1926), this document can provide a strong piece of evidence for you because the arrival date, place, and ship were researched at the time of naturalization. In addition, if the person had changed his or her name since immigration, the name under which he or she arrived would have had to be provided in order to locate and verify the arrival on a passenger list. With naturalization information in hand, tracing the ship can be greatly simplified. You can then trace to the port of departure to determine if other documents exist. These might contain more information to help you trace your immigrant to the hometown.

On the other hand, if you have already discovered the ship on which the person traveled and the port of arrival, you can begin to look for other evidence about them in that vicinity. Use the port of arrival as a central point, and seek other documents, including city directories and newspapers. Focus on other relatives or in-laws, both of the immigrant and a spouse, in the country and check census records, city directories, court records, and other documents in their areas. Your immigrant may have settled temporarily or for an extended period in that vicinity.

Using the knowledge you are already developing about genealogical record types and research methodologies, you can incorporate immigration and naturalization documents into your work. You're increasing your knowledge of each individual you study *and* you are constantly expanding the overall story of your family. As you do so, remember to apply your critical thinking skills to the evidence and formulate reasonable hypotheses.

PART II

Research Methods and Strategies

10

Discover Where to Locate Documents About Your Family

HOW TO...

- Determine where to look for different document types
- Use indexes, compilations, and other finding aids
- Use libraries and archives
- Use an LDS Family History Center
- Consult reference books and other resources
- Deal with closed or limited access to materials
- Order document copies by postal mail and email
- Keep track of your correspondence
- Use a research log

The previous chapters have addressed the foundations of your genealogical research and discussed a broad selection of record types. By this time, you should have a pretty good idea of what you want to do with your genealogical research. You should know about a variety of common document types and how to use your critical thinking skills to evaluate and assess them.

In this chapter, we will discuss processes you can use to locate major repositories where documents or copies are held, and how to access the materials. Advance preparation is essential for your success in accessing documentary evidence, and there are many tools available to you. These include indexes, compilations, and other printed finding aides. Electronic tools include the Internet, online databases, library and archive catalogs, and CD-ROM products.

You will want to gain access to the original primary source documents whenever possible and obtain copies for your reference and documentation. Photocopies and reproductions can usually be obtained if you make an on-site visit to a facility. Many original documents have been digitized, indexed, and made available online. You also can write letters and email to request copies if you cannot make a trip to the repository.

If you are an active researcher, your correspondence may be extensive, and it is not uncommon in such situations to lose track of the status of all of your requests for copies. A correspondence log and a little dedication to maintaining it can provide a process you can use to maintain control and to generate follow-up messages.

You will visit many research facilities and examine literally hundreds of books, journals, periodicals, and documents in the pursuit of your family's genealogy. As a result, it is easy to forget what you have already examined and, consequently, waste both time and money conducting duplicate research. A research log allows you to keep track of what materials you have already researched and what you did or did not find in those resources.

The topics covered in this chapter will provide you with some methodologies for becoming a more efficient and effective researcher. Over time, each strategy will become part of your standard operating process.

Determine Where to Look for Different Document Types

You began your family history research in Chapter 1 when you began looking for home sources such as Bibles, letters, diaries and journals, scrapbooks, and copies of original records. Having only one place to search is a lot easier than having to conduct research to locate places where you *can* conduct research. Yet that is what we have to do.

We can expect to find particular documents in specific places. For example, we know we can usually find probate files at the courthouse where the probate court conducts its business. In other cases, however, the place where document copies reside may not be where we might at first expect to find them. For example, a birth record might be found at a county health department office, a courthouse, a state or provincial vital records or vital statistics office, or elsewhere. The challenge we face as researchers is not just evaluating the records; very often it involves tracking down the records themselves.

We have already discussed the importance of studying geography and history to place our ancestors into context. However, this can be equally as important when trying to locate the documents for our family members. The type of record, the person or organization that generated it, the reason(s) for the document's production, the place it was created, and the time period, all contribute to our determining the location.

The place where a document was once stored might not be where it is stored today. The document may have been moved elsewhere, such as to another storage location. This is common when one facility exhausts its storage space or when older documents are needed infrequently for reference. They may be packed up and sent to a warehouse or other off-site storage facility. Some documents created by one governmental entity may have been generated in one place and then sent to a central governmental archive or storage facility. For example, the U.S. government in 1830 requested all states to forward their 1790 to 1820 census schedules to Washington to replace the summaries that were destroyed when the British burned the city on 24 August 1814. The 1830 census documents and those for all subsequent censuses have been sent to Washington. Additionally, in some cases there have been multiple copies of certain documents produced, possibly as exact duplicates or as supposedly exact transcriptions, and one or more copies forwarded elsewhere for someone else's use. A good example of this would be a death certificate. The original and at least one copy are typically produced. The issuing governmental office retains the original and a copy is forwarded to a central office, such as a state or provincial records bureau. Other copies may have been provided to the undertaker, to the executor or administrator of the estate, to the probate court, to the coroner, and to other persons or organizations. If you know that duplicates were produced and held by different official organizations, and you know when the process began, you can begin planning to obtain a copy of a particular document from one or the other office.

Did You Know?
The U.S. government in 1830 requested all states to forward their 1790 to 1820 census schedules to Washington to replace the summaries that were destroyed when the British burned the city on 24 August 1814.

A document may have been microfilmed or digitized and the original placed in storage or destroyed. This, too, is something you will find to be a common practice.

Use Indexes, Compilations, and Other Finding Aids

There are many published materials to help you with your search. Some are available through traditional publishers and commercial companies, while genealogical or historical societies and individuals publish others. Still other materials are published in the form of databases, CD-ROMs, and/or on the Internet. Let's explore some examples of these resources.

Indexes

An index is defined as an ordered listing of people, places, topics, or other data that includes references allowing the user to quickly locate specific information. The format of the listing is dependent on the data being indexed. We're all familiar with the index found in the back of a book. This book's index is arranged alphabetically by subject, type of document, and so on, with page number references that point you to specific information. There are at least four major categories of indexes that will be of interest to every genealogist. Let's briefly discuss each of these.

Indexes in Courthouses and Government Facilities

We've discussed a number of types of records that you will find in courthouses. This includes marriage and divorce records, wills and probate packets, judicial records of all sorts, jury lists, land and property records, property maps, taxation maps and records, voter registration records, guardianship records, poorhouse records, lunacy records, and many more. Depending on the location you are researching and the time period, the responsibilities of the government in that locality will determine what records were created at the time. As jurisdictions changed, the records usually remained in the possession of the original governmental entity. However, some of the records may have been physically transferred to (or copies made for) the new jurisdictional entity, depending on the record type and the need for the new office to have immediate access to the documents.

Most of the records are organized and filed in some manner and indexes have been prepared. An index is typically prepared at a later date than the original entries are made. You will encounter both hand-written and typed indexes. Marriage records are usually indexed twice, once in an alphabetical list of grooms' names and again in an alphabetical list of brides' names. Both are created in *surname sequence*, and then in forename or given name order. Women's surnames are entered using their maiden name for single women or the surname from a previous marriage for divorced or widowed women. However, don't be surprised to find a previously married woman's maiden name sometimes listed in the bride index. That means that you should always check for *both* possible surname entries. Land and property entries also are typically indexed in two ways, once in grantor sequence and once in grantee sequence. The indexes you find in courthouses and other governmental facilities will point you to specific places where you will find the material you want to use. Figure 10-1 shows

GRANTORS				GRANTEES	KIND OF INSTRUMENT	Date of Filing			Where Recorded	
FAMILY NAMES	ABCDEFGH	IJKLMNO	PQRSTUVWXYZ			Mo.	Day	Year	Book	Page
Burge,		Louisa O.		Williams, M. D.					M	384
Buffington,			T. A.	Darby, Thos, A.					M	514
Butler,	Geo. A.			Thomas, Joseph					M	941
Burt,		James		Calhoun, Wm. L.					M	958
Buffington,			T. A.	Darby, T. A.	W D	June	25	1881	M	514
Burke,		M. A.		Tucker, Mamie W.	W D	Feb	17	1882	N	72
Bunker,		L. V.		Tison, W. O.	W D	July	19	1882	N	568
Bush,	Eliza J			Sikes, W. W.	W D	Sept	8	1882	N	692
Burroughs,		Jno. W.		Carroll, Eliza A/	W D	Oct	7	1882	N	784
Burroughs,		Jno. W.		Bevill, Francis B.	W D	Oct	9	1882	N	787
Burroughs,		Jno. W.		Berrien, Harriet C.	W D	Dec	16	1882	N	946
Burge,		L. O. extx		Mc Ewen, Chas A.	W D	Feb	21	1883	O	124

FIGURE 10-1   Detail of a grantor index to deed entries. (Courtesy of Jim Powell.)

the detail of a grantor index. If you were researching the transfer of property from Jno. W. Burroughs to Harriet C. Berrien, investigation into the grantor index indicates the transaction was filed on 16 December 1882 and that the detail can be found in an entry on page 946 of Deed Book N.

Indexes in Libraries, Archives, and Other Research Facilities

Libraries and archives are veritable gold mines for your research. The most common items you will use in these research facilities are the printed books, journals, periodicals, and electronic databases to which they may provide access. There are thousands of indexes that have been published to many original records. Let me provide a few examples for you, along with bibliographic citations.

Census Indexes

Gibson, Jeremy and Mervyn Medlycott. *Local Census Listings: 1522–1930: Holdings in the British Isles*. 3rd ed. Baltimore, MD: Genealogical Publishing Co., 1997.

Steuart, Bradley W., ed. *Virginia 1870 Census Index*. 4 volumes. Bountiful, UT: Precision Indexing, 1989.

Immigration Lists

Glazier, Ira A., ed. *Germans to America: Lists of Passengers Arriving at U.S. Ports*. 4 vols. to date. Wilmington, DE: Scholarly Resources, 2002–to date.

Glazier, Ira A. and P. William Filby, eds. *Germans to America: Lists of Passengers Arriving at U.S. Ports*. 67 vols. to date. Wilmington, DE: Scholarly Resources, 1988–to date.

Marriage Index

Daniell, Anne C. *Talladega County, Alabama, Marriage Book "A-1834," 1833–1846: An Alphabetical Listing of Grooms' Names with an Index to the Names of the Brides*. Anniston, AL: AlaBenton Book Shop, 1986.

Land and Property Records Indexes

Hughes, B. H. J. *Jottings and Historical Records with Index on the History of South Pembrokeshire: Manorial Accounts, 1324–33*. Pembroke Dock, Wales: Pennar Publications. 1996.

Shuck, Larry G. *Greenbrier County, (West) Virginia, Records*. 8 vols. Athens, GA: Iberian Publishing Co., 1988–1994.

Wills and Probate Records Indexes

Johnston, Ross B. *West Virginia Estate Settlements: An Index to Wills, Inventories, Appraisements, Land Grants, and Surveys to 1850*. Baltimore, MD: Genealogical Publishing Co., 1978.

Webb, Cliff, comp. *An Index of Wills Proved in the Archdeaconry Court of London, 1700–1807*. London, UK: Society of Genealogists, 1996.

As you can see, there are published indexes for many types of records from around the world. The preceding examples represent only a tiny fraction of the record types that have been indexed in printed form.

Online Database Indexes

The explosive growth of the Internet in the last 20 years accelerated the already popular genealogical research to new heights. Individuals created their own websites to display their genealogical data and/or they uploaded the contents of their databases to genealogy service providers' sites. The largest area of Internet growth for genealogists, however, has been in the area of online databases, both free and fee-based subscription services. These databases include indexes to original source records, digitized images of original documents, and other content.

A wealth of other online databases provides access to general or specific types of data. Some of these include the following:

- Ancestry.com (**www.ancestry.com**) is a subscription site that has placed literally thousands of indexed and searchable databases online. Some of the databases are free to access but most are available only on a subscription basis. Ancestry.com's collections are truly international in scope and are simple to search. A search will yield a full list, such as that shown in Figure 10-2, of every database at Ancestry.com

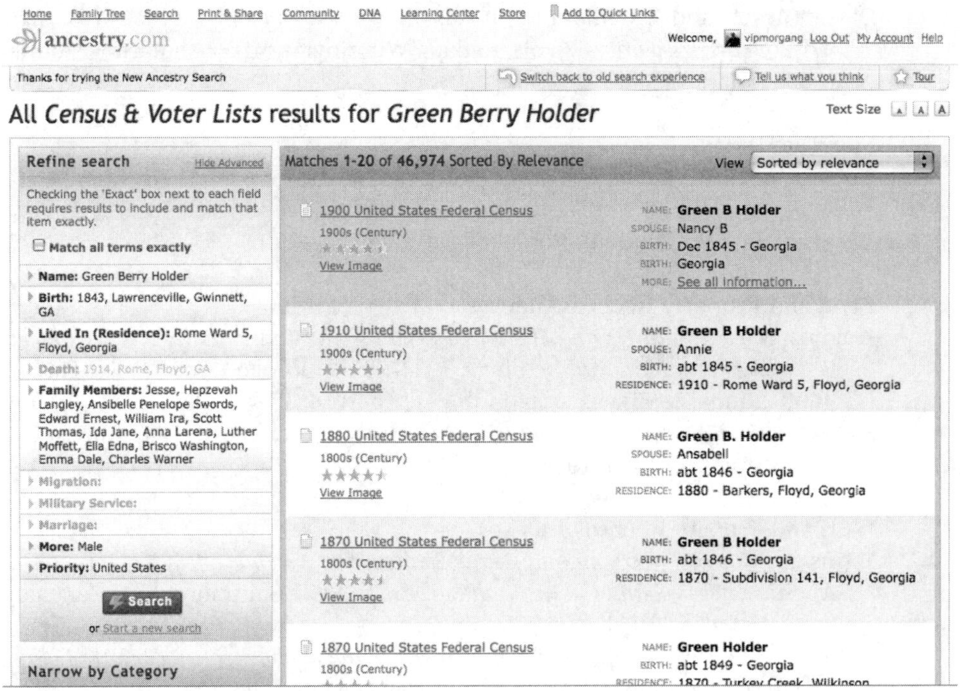

FIGURE 10-2 Search results list at Ancestry.com. (Used with permission of The Generations Network, Inc.)

that contains that name. Among their premier subscription databases are the U.S. Census Records and Images Collection, the U.K. Census Collection, U.S. Immigration Passenger Lists, World War I Draft Registration Cards, and the impressive Historical Newspaper Collection containing hundreds of indexed, searchable newspapers dating from the 1700s to 2000 from the United States, Canada, and the United Kingdom. Ancestry.com's Ancestry Library Edition database offering is marketed to libraries, and can often be found as part of public and academic libraries' subscription database collections. That edition does not provide access to all the databases available at Ancestry.com because of licensing arrangements made by The Generations Network, Inc., with some of their database providers. (Other Ancestry subscription sites include, at this writing, Canada, the United Kingdom, Australia, France, Germany, Italy, Sweden, and China.)

- Footnote.com (**www.footnote.com**) is a subscription site that provides access to millions of digitized U.S. document images, including military service and pension records, widows' pension records, naturalization index cards, city directories, photographs, and much more. Figure 10-3 shows the main page at Footnote.com.

FIGURE 10-3   The main page at Footnote.com. (Used with permission of Footnote.com.)

- HeritageQuest Online, a product offering from ProQuest Company, is a major collection of subscription databases. These include U.S. census images, images of Revolutionary War records, Freedman's Bureau images, access to the Periodical Source Index (PERSI), access to the U.S. Serial Set, and a collection of more than 25,000 digitized, indexed, and fully searchable books. HeritageQuest Online can often be found as part of public and academic libraries' subscription database collections and is often accessible to registered library patrons from their home computers.
- inGeneas (**www.ingeneas.com**) provides a collection of database materials related to Canadian genealogy, as well as links and access to professional genealogical researchers for hire.
- The Origins Network (**www.origins.net**), whose main website screen is shown in Figure 10-4, provides genealogical databases about the British Isles, including British Origins (**www.britishorigins.com**), Irish Origins (**www.irishorigins .com**), and Scots Origins (**www.scotsorigins.com**).

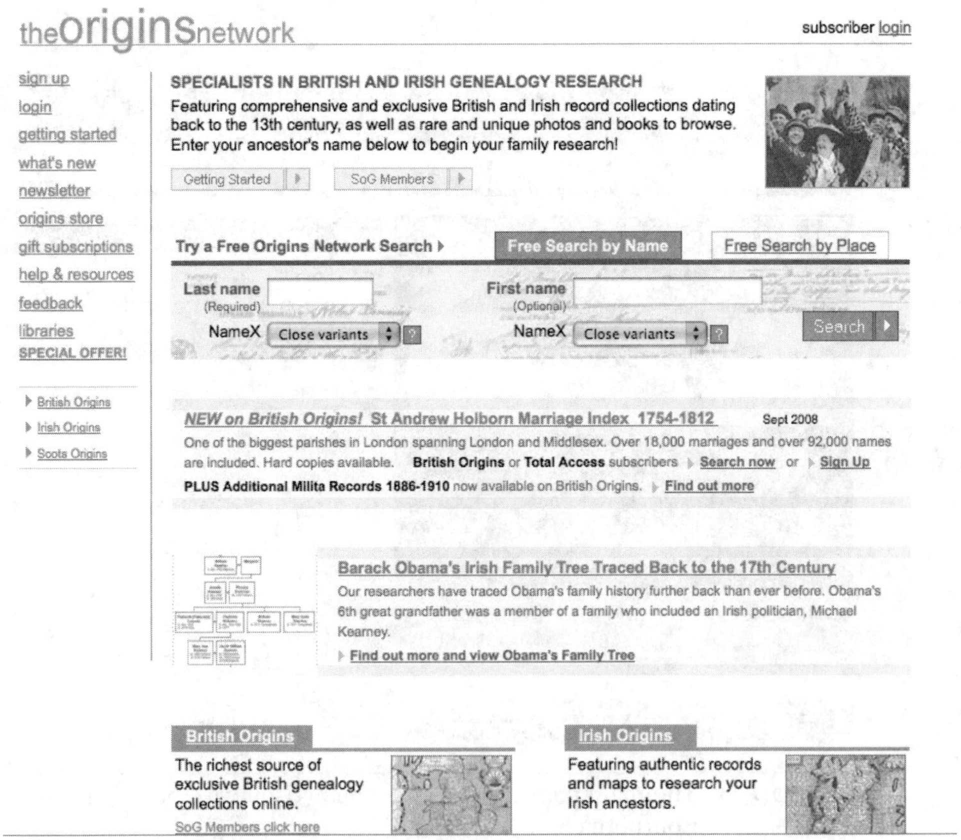

FIGURE 10-4   The main page at the Origins Network

- Digital Sanborn Maps (**http://sanborn.umi.com**) is a subscription database that provides digital access to more than 660,000 large-scale maps of more than 12,000 American towns and cities. Sanborn Fire Insurance Maps were widely used in the United States by property and casualty insurance companies, underwriters, and government agencies from 1867 to 1970. In electronic form, the Sanborn Maps take on much improved value over the microfilm versions of the same maps, allowing for greater flexibility of use and improved viewing possibilities. Users can easily manipulate the maps, magnify and zoom in on specific sections, and layer maps from different years. This digitized map database is part of the ProQuest collection and may be accessible through your library's subscription to the ProQuest products.

Governmental agencies have also provided online databases of materials in their possession, although the concerns for individuals' privacy and identity theft have prevented making many records accessible online, either in index or image form. An excellent example of this is the Alachua County, Florida, Clerk of Court's website for the county archives at **www.alachuaclerk.org/Archive**. Ancient Records Coordinator Jim Powell has scanned tens of thousands of original documents and placed them online at the Alachua County Archives Entry page shown in Figure 10-5. He also has

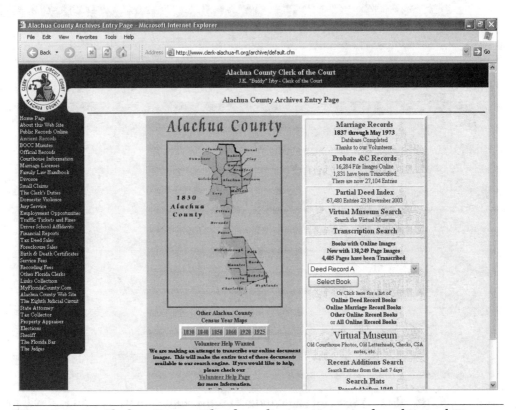

FIGURE 10-5   Alachua County, Florida, online ancient records archive website

recruited a small army of genealogical volunteers from across the United States to index the records by name and keyword and transcribe thousands of these documents. This ongoing volunteer project, sanctioned and supported by Alachua County Clerk of the Court J. K. "Buddy" Irby, is an excellent model for what can be done.

Search Engines' Indexes

Whenever you use a search engine on the Internet, you are using a sophisticated index. A search engine combs the Web electronically and, when it connects to and accesses a web page, reads every word on the page. That includes the text, labels, and filenames of graphics on the web page, as well as the "hidden" meta tags used in the source code of the HTML or XHTML document that produced the page. The search engine indexes every word and then, when you enter a word or phrase in the engine's search box or template, presents matches to your entries in the form of a search results list. Figure 10-6 shows the beginning of the search results list for the words *genealogy database georgia*. Each search engine indexes the Web differently and uses its own relevancy ranking criteria to order and display the search results. We will discuss the use of search engines and other tools to perform research on the Internet in the next chapter.

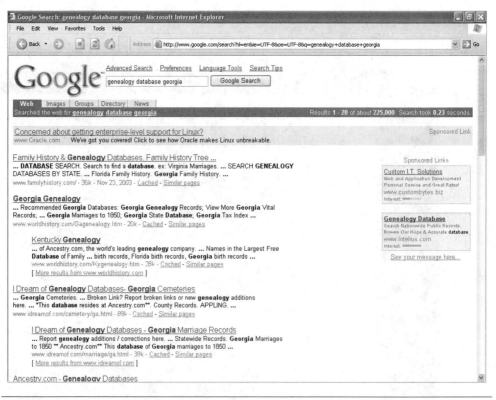

FIGURE 10-6 A search engine indexes words found on web pages and will present a search results list.

Compilations

A compilation is a gathering of information from a variety of places into a useful directory or organized listing. You could consider this book a compilation of a wide variety of useful information. A directory of materials on the Internet can also be considered a compilation. Perhaps the largest and best-known web-based genealogical compilation is Cyndi's List (**www.cyndislist.com**), shown in Figure 10-7, which contains more than 264,000 links to other websites.

There are many excellent compilation websites, including Linkpendium (**www .linkpendium.com**), the USGenWeb Project (**www.usgenweb.org**), the WorldGenWeb Project (**www.worldgenweb.org**), GENUKI (**www.genuki.org.uk**), JewishGen (**www.jewishgen.org**), RootsWeb (**www.rootsweb.ancestry.com**), and the Canadian Genealogy & History Links website (**www.islandnet.com/ ~ jveinot/cghl/cghl.html**). You can always find resources to help your genealogy research by visiting Cyndi's List, locating the geographic or topic area you wish to pursue, and accessing the web page resources linked there.

Other Finding Aids

The term *finding aid* shouldn't confuse you. It simply refers to any resource you can use to further your genealogical search, and includes tools such as the following:

- Maps
- Gazetteers (or place name dictionaries)

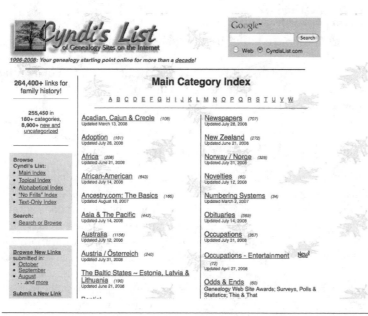

FIGURE 10-7   Main page of Cyndi's List, one of the largest genealogy compilations of web links on the Internet

- Surname dictionaries by national, ethnic, or religious group
- Dictionaries of contemporary and archaic terminology
- Dictionaries of abbreviations and acronyms of different areas and time periods
- Language translation dictionaries
- Histories of geographic areas, towns and communities, different population groups, and cultural histories
- Reference works to aid in reading old handwriting
- Genealogy references, "how-to" books, and guides to working with record types
- Compilations of Internet sites related to genealogy
- Online indexes and databases, as discussed previously

Anything that you can use to gain insight into your ancestral search and access to quality source materials can be considered a valid finding aid. Look around you, and use your imagination and insight.

Use Libraries and Archives

Libraries, archives, and their staff are among the best resources you can have. I consider a good librarian to be a "personal information broker." While you can't expect every librarian to know everything about genealogical research and records, you can always rely on a librarian's willingness to help you and his or her ability to conduct quality research on almost any topic. A well-trained librarian or archivist understands research methods and resources of all types, and knows how to locate and access information. Furthermore, he or she is always willing to share their skills with you if you are willing to invest the time to listen and learn.

The facilities that libraries and archives provide to their users, or patrons, vary significantly depending on the content of their collection, their service population, and their stated mission. Special collections such as genealogy and local history materials usually are not circulated but are, instead, reserved for in-house reference. There are ways, however, to gain access to the materials without physically visiting the facility, and we'll discuss those shortly.

Learn to Use the Library Catalog

It has not been too many years ago that libraries had no computers. The primary finding aid for its holdings was a card catalog. There were card catalog cabinets in a central area filled with small paperboard cards, all hand-typed and filed in alphabetical sequence by author, title, and subject. Each item in the collection for which there was a card also was coded with a reference using the classification system employed by that library. Public libraries in North America and the United Kingdom typically use the Dewey Decimal Classification system, while most North American academic libraries use the Library of Congress Classification system. Academic libraries in the United Kingdom use a combination of systems. Other archives and repositories may use another system based on the type of holdings in their collections, including one of their own devising that fits the unique needs for organizing and accessing their special collection. It is to your advantage to learn a little about the Dewey Decimal and Library of Congress systems. Understanding these systems helps you understand how any library is physically organized, and you can then quickly and effectively locate and access materials in their collections. You can learn about the Dewey Decimal Classification system and its contents at the BUBL LINK site at **http://bubl.ac.uk**, and about the Library of Congress Classification scheme at **www.loc.gov/catdir/cpso/lcco**.

Some things in libraries and archives have changed over time while others have remained static. Computers changed information storage and retrieval expectations, and libraries understood the importance of changing their printed and typed card catalogs to computerized systems. Standardized online catalog computer programs were developed and implemented in libraries.

> **Did You Know?**
>
> Most catalogs in public libraries use the Dewey Decimal Classification system while academic libraries (in the United States) use the Library of Congress Classification system. Archives most often use systems specifically focused on their collections, sometimes unique and developed especially for them.

Online catalog software can be and has been integrated into libraries' websites, and multimedia capabilities have been added. It now is not unusual for a library to have incorporated graphic and sound files of their holdings into their online catalogs, complete with links to directly access those materials. The public access catalog is sometimes called the iPAC, or Internet Public Access Catalog.

Throughout all of this evolution, the principles of organization, cataloging, and standardizing catalog entries for resources have been maintained and expanded. There are standards in place within the library industry to utilize technology to its maximum, integrate as many materials as possible into the online systems, and provide excellence in customer access and customer service.

Start with What Has Already Been Done

Many of us conduct a substantial amount of our genealogical research, or pre-research, from the comfort of our homes. Perhaps you find yourself sitting in front of the computer, searching on the Internet for records concerning your ancestors. Perhaps it is three o'clock in the morning; you're there in your pajamas, sipping a glass of milk, and munching on chocolate chip cookies. What a life!

Fortunately, the Internet and the online catalogs of libraries and archives are accessible 24 hours a day, 7 days a week, and 365 days a year. If you are conversant with the use of the catalog, you can make a tremendous amount of headway with your research into the available resources without assistance.

For a genealogist, one of the first steps in doing research is to locate any published family histories and/or local histories that may contain information about ancestors and other family members. Family histories and many local histories are not usually the type of book that you're likely to find in your neighborhood bookstore, or even in a typical online bookstore. Instead, to locate such books, you'll have to visit a library, or look in their online catalogs. The next step is to locate the indexes and other finding aids that help you find the resources you want or need. Fortunately, the Web has made that process easier.

If you don't know which library or libraries have a copy of a particular book, contact your reference librarian and ask for help. You can search a free online database called WorldCat at **www.worldcat.org**. Figure 10-8 shows the main page at WorldCat. You can search for books, DVDs, CDs, and articles, and the search results will provide you with the locations of facilities that hold a copy. I recommend that you create a free ID and password for WorldCat and sign in. When you conduct a search, you can enter a location and WorldCat will sort the list of libraries for you from nearest to farthest. Using this sort feature, you can find libraries nearby that you can visit, or you can check the availability of an item near to a place you might be visiting.

Once you have the information on a specific book, a sample of whose record from the John F. Germany Public Library in the Hillsborough County Public Library Cooperative based in Tampa, Florida is shown in Figure 10-9, you now have all you need to visit the library and locate the book. (Notice in Figure 10-9 that you could add the title to a booklist, which you can later print or email to yourself, and place a hold on the title to make sure it doesn't get checked out before you get there. This always requires that you have a library card with that library or that your library has a reciprocal borrowing agreement of some sort with that library.)

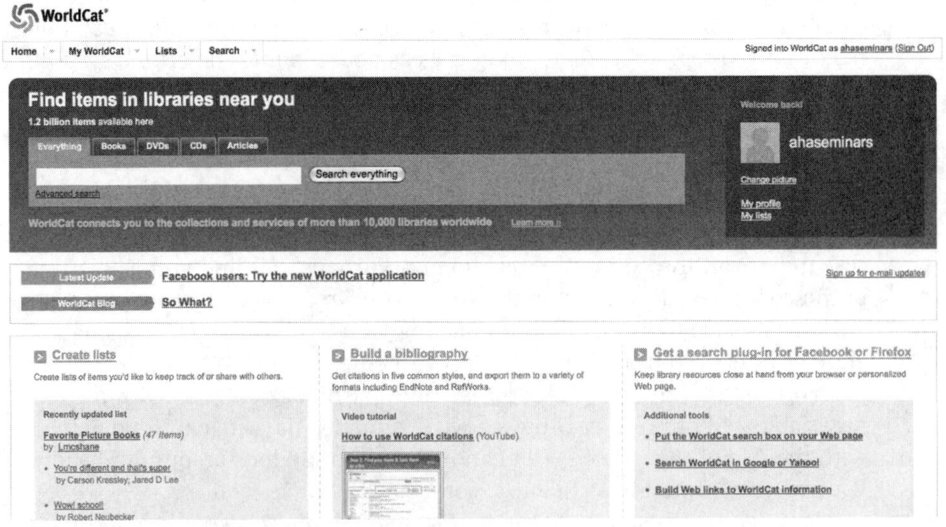

FIGURE 10-8 The main page at WorldCat

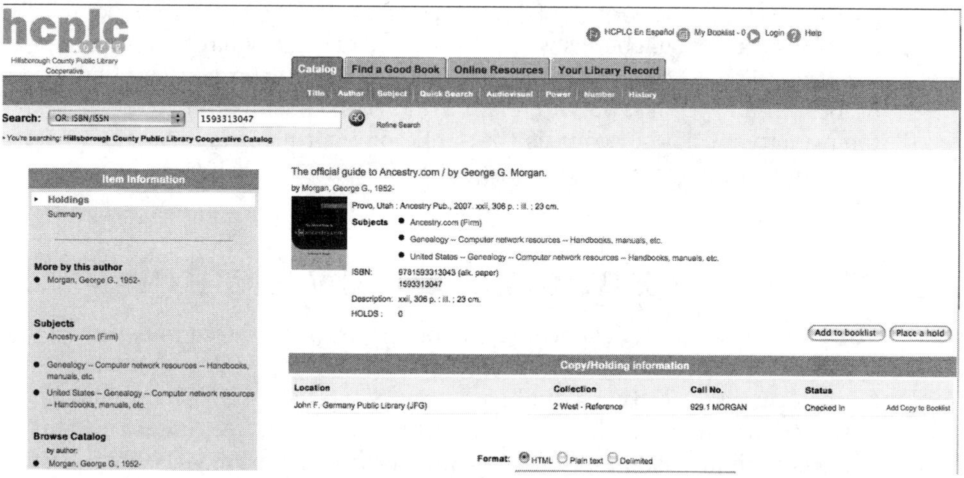

FIGURE 10-9   The catalog record at the Hillsborough County Public Library Cooperative shows the book at the John F. Germany Public Library.

If you are unable to visit the library, there is another option open to you: interlibrary loan, also referred to as ILL in the United States and Canada. (In the United Kingdom, this is often spelled as Inter-Library Loan.) ILL is a service that allows patrons of one library to request the loan of a book from its owning library to their own. However, since most genealogy and local history collection materials are non circulating reference materials, it is unlikely that you can actually have your library borrow the book. But all is not lost! ILL can be used to request that *photocopies* be made of certain pages and sent to you or to your library for pickup. You might want to make two ILL requests. The first will request a copy of the pages of a book's index for the surname(s) you are seeking, and a second request after you've received the index pages will ask for copies of the text pages from the book in question. Keep in mind that, when requesting text pages, you might want to request one or two additional pages *before and after* the pages shown in an index. This helps alleviate the problem that arises when meaningful descriptive text begins on a previous page or continues to a subsequent page.

As you can see, there is tremendous value to having performed advance research in an online library catalog. Let's now look at some specific library catalogs.

The Library of Congress Online Catalog

Sometimes, you'll hear about a book from a friend or a fellow genealogist, or you may see it referred to in some publication. Unfortunately, you may find that you are missing either the author's name or the title of the book, or that one of those is incorrect or incomplete. Your first step should be to pin down the exact title of the book and the full name of the author. This will make later searching much easier and more productive.

The online catalog of the Library of Congress (LC) is often a good place to begin searching for unusual books when you don't necessarily have all of the information you need. The LC does not lend (or circulate) their materials classified as genealogy or local history. Unless you are planning a trip to Washington, D.C., in the near future, the primary purpose of your use of the LC online catalog is to obtain information about the book so that you can then look for it in a closer library.

Use the LDS Family History Center

The largest collection of genealogy manuscripts, printed materials, and microfilm in the world is undoubtedly the Family History Library (FHL) in Salt Lake City, operated by the Church of Jesus Christ of Latter-day Saints. The LDS Church has microfilmed many family and local histories and, for a small rental fee, lends the film from the FHL through its system of local Family History Centers (FHCs) throughout the world. In order to identify what books it has, visit the FamilySearch website at **www .familysearch.org**. Once there, click the Library tab, and choose Library Catalog in its drop-down menu. Like the LC online catalog, the FHL catalog has a button for searching by author, by title, or by subject. Unlike the LC online catalog, the FHL catalog is designed specifically for genealogy, and so the buttons on their catalog search screen have additional labels.

If you do not know the location of the nearest FHC, follow the Family History Centers link in the Library drop-down menu so that you can locate it with the search tool provided. The people who work at the FHC can help you learn how to use their materials and how to request the loan of microfilm and CD-ROMs from the FHL in Salt Lake City.

> **Did You Know?** The LDS is currently involved in digitizing and indexing all of its microfilmed records, and will place these on their website over the next several years.

Consult Reference Books and Other Resources

Some of the best resources at your disposal are reference books that focus on different record types and the locations of those records. Among my personal favorites for general reference are the following titles:

- *The Source: A Guidebook of American Genealogy, Third Edition*, edited by Loretto Dennis Szucs and Sandra Hargreaves Luebking (Ancestry Publishing, 2006), provides the most comprehensive reference for U.S. records of all types and research methodologies. Information about conducting research about specific record types, what can be found in them, and how to locate and then assess the content are discussed in detail. Used in conjunction with the *Red Book: American State, County, and Town Sources*, discussed next, this is an unbeatable reference set for U.S. genealogy.

- *Red Book: American State, County, and Town Sources*, edited by Alice Eichholz (Ancestry Publishing, 2004), provides a state-by-state reference. Historical background about the formation of each state is provided, along with descriptions of all major record types, when they began being created, and where they reside. For each state, there is a county boundary map and a table showing each county, its contact information, details about its formation, and the years when each of the following record types began being created: birth, marriage, death, land, probate, and court.

- *French-Canadian Sources: A Guide for Genealogists*, by Patricia Keeney Geyh et al. (Ancestry Publishing, 2002), is a compilation of scholarly chapters written by experts in French-Canadian research. The book covers the entire history of the French in Canada from establishment in 1605 of Port Royal in what is now Nova Scotia, and details the many types of records created over the centuries by the French, English, and Canadian governments. Among the elegant appendixes are a collection of French vocabulary words and phrases you are likely to encounter; charts and descriptions of Canadian census records and substitutes; and an extensive compilation of French-Canadian research addresses.

- *Ancestral Trails: The Complete Guide to British Genealogy and Family History, Second Edition, Revised and Updated*, by Mark D. Herber (Genealogical Publishing Co, Inc., 2006), is the most extensive and comprehensive guide to tracing your British heritage, presented in an orderly fashion and in easily understandable language. It provides clear descriptions of all major and many obscure records, and will help you understand the church and governmental structures employed over the centuries in creating and maintaining the records.

- *Tracing Your Irish Ancestors: The Complete Guide, Third Edition*, by John Grenham (Genealogical Publishing Co., 2006), provides an excellent primer on how to begin your ancestral quest, and examines the major sources such as civil records, censuses, church records, land and property documentation, wills, emigration papers, deeds, registry sources, newspapers, and directories. A complete table of Roman Catholic parish registers' reference information is included, as are detailed materials about available research services, genealogical and historical societies, and contact information for an array of libraries and record repositories.

- *A Genealogist's Guide to Discovering Your Scottish Ancestors*, by Linda Jonas and Paul Milner (Betterway Books, 2002), is a straightforward guide for Americans tracing Scottish immigrant ancestors. Clear, concise descriptions and illustrations of many document types are complemented by step-by-step guidelines to conducting research in U.S. and Scottish records.

The preceding books form a strong core of reference works for your use. You may decide to purchase some of these as components of your personal genealogical reference collection. Your local public library also may own a copy of each of these books in its own collection. However, if not, you certainly can recommend acquisition to the person responsible for the library's collection development.

Locate the Repository on the Internet

Web pages typically provide the most current information about a facility or document repository you might want to access. Just as libraries and archives maintain a Web presence, usually with an embedded online catalog, government agencies, companies, organizations, societies, and other entities create and maintain websites. If you know the web address of the facility, you can quickly access their site and check on their holdings. If you don't know the address, you can use your favorite Internet search engine to locate the site. For example, I decided I wanted to locate information about local government offices in the area near the town of Chelmsford, located northeast of London in the United Kingdom. I entered the following in the Google search engine:

chelmsford government

I was rewarded with search results that included a number of links, including those for Chelmsford, Massachusetts. However, I accessed a direct link to the Chelmsford Borough Council's site at **www.chelmsford.gov.uk**. Another search result was that of the LocalLife site for Chelmsford at **www.locallife.co.uk/chelmsford/ governmentoff3.asp**, which included links to government offices' sites. Knowing that Chelmsford is located in Essex, I searched for **essex government uk**. The first item in the search results list was the Essex County Council website at **www.essex.gov.uk**.

Researchers seeking information about vital records in the United States and its territories will want to visit the website at **www.vitalrec.com**. Also included is a link to a web page describing how to file a consular report of the birth or death of an American citizen abroad, or a marriage ceremony abroad in which at least one party was an American citizen. Instructions for applying for a certified copy of one of these consular reports also are provided.

Contact the Repository

While we hope that the "official" websites of government agencies and other entities are maintained with up-to-date information, the truth is that a vast number of websites are less than current. The old adage of "phone first!" certainly applies here.

Another complication that occurs is when the facility withdraws the materials temporarily for microfilming, scanning/digitization, repair, or other maintenance. By contacting the repository in advance, you can learn if the materials you want to access will, in fact, be available when you visit or if you request them through ILL, postal mail, or email.

You will frequently find that many materials of genealogical interest may not have been cataloged. You have already seen typical catalog records in this chapter and can understand the effort required to create a single catalog database record. Imagine, then, the loose documents, correspondence, maps, folders, and other materials that may be a part of a library's or archive's holdings. It is expensive and labor-intensive to catalog each and every item. Sometimes there may be a single catalog entry to reference a group of related materials, such as the correspondence files of a local historian. In other cases, there may be no catalog record at all. For these and other reasons, it is important that you *always* ask the question of a reference professional at the library or archive, "Are there any materials of genealogical or local historical significance in your collection that have not been cataloged?" More often than not, the answer will be in the affirmative. It's then time to form a strong bond with this reference person to learn what is available, the content and scope of those holdings, and how to access the materials.

Making individual contact with the repository also allows you to confirm the location, travel directions, hours of operation, costs of printed copies of materials, and policies for security, access, and use of the materials. Obtaining that information in advance helps you plan your research visit and the time there more efficiently.

In addition, if you believe there are specific materials that you want to use, you can confirm that they will be available. If you find that they are unavailable, you can adjust your schedule or your research plan. If you find out that the materials you are seeking have been relocated elsewhere, you can then pursue what happened to the records and how to gain access to them at the new location.

Seek Help from a State, Provincial, or National Library or Archive

The personnel at a local repository may be unable to tell you about specific materials of genealogical importance. The individual may not have the knowledge or training to help you, or may just be overwhelmed with his or her duties and unwilling to give that little extra something to help you make your connection with the materials you want or need. Don't overlook the use of the expert professionals who staff libraries and archives having a broader focus than local ones. Their collections are most often substantially larger, their training has been more intensive, and their perspective of documents, records, books, journals, microfilm, and digitized materials broader than local libraries' or county governments'.

When I have been unable to locate specific geographical locations on maps of a particular state, I have called on the state library or state archive for assistance. Their collections of historical maps, gazetteers, and other reference materials are extensive and the staff members are well trained in effectively using these resources. In addition, I have used the telephone and email reference services of academic libraries, the National Archives and Records Administration (NARA), the Library of Congress, the U.S. Geological Survey, and other types of facilities to obtain answers to questions and to locate materials that either were difficult to find or had been relocated.

Contact Genealogical and Historical Societies at All Levels

Genealogical and historical societies are among your best resources. They are actively involved with the study of history, culture, society, and documentation in their respective areas. Their business is research and, in many cases, preservation of information, documentation, and artifacts. Think of these societies as "networks" of individuals with knowledge and experience in the materials in their area. If you contact one person who does not have an answer to your question, he or she usually knows where to look or who to put you in contact with to help you. It is possible that a society may have acquired records, photographs, or artifacts that have not been accessible to researchers before. The society may be indexing or cataloging records or indexes in preparation perhaps for publishing them or donating them to a library or archive. They also may be involved with collecting and organizing information that is not yet available in any other way.

There are two excellent examples in Florida that immediately come to mind. One is a genealogical society's ongoing project of indexing articles concerning individuals who lived in or passed through their county in the territorial period prior to Florida statehood in 1845. The other is an ongoing project by one county's genealogical society to canvass and document every gravestone in every cemetery in the county, and to publish indexes for all of those cemeteries. The Florida State Genealogical Society is pleased to announce ongoing projects of this type at their website at **www .flsgs.org**; in the drop-down list on the left, under "About FGS," click the item labeled "Projects Registry." Both of the societies' work products, however, may be unique and found nowhere else.

It also is not unusual for these societies' members to respond to your problem by jumping in to help you with the research. They may look up records for you, make copies, take photographs, or provide assistance in other ways.

Engage a Professional Researcher

Finally, if you are seeking records that you believe should exist somewhere but have been otherwise unable to locate them, you may want to engage the services of a professional genealogical researcher. You will want a person who has the experience and credentials to conduct a scholarly research effort for you and provide status reports and a final report with copies and fully documented source citations as the final project deliverable. There are a number of organizations that test and accredit professional researchers. Some of these are listed here:

- Board for Certification of Genealogists (BCG)
  www.bcgcertification.org
- International Commission for the Accreditation of Professional Genealogists (ICAPGen)
  www.icapgen.org
- Accredited genealogists who became accredited through The Church of Jesus Christ of Latter-day Saints Family History Department prior to October 2000
- Association of Professional Genealogists
  www.apgen.org
- Association of Professional Genealogists in Ireland
  www.apgi.ie

Did You Know?   You can contract with certified professional researchers to help get you past your brick-wall research problems.

Deal with Closed or Limited Access to Materials

Some records are not accessible to the public, or access may be restricted. Since the terrorist attacks in the United States on 11 September 2001, many legislators and government agencies around the world have taken steps to prevent access to information and records that might be used to falsify an identity or otherwise engage in illegal activities. As a result, a number of official documents previously available for research may be off-limits or require verification of your identity in order to use them. Vital records or civil records, including birth certificates, are highly protected because of their use in obtaining identity cards, driver's licenses, passports, and other official documents.

Some government documents are completely closed to the public and may never be opened, regardless of anything you might do. One type of these is adoption records, which, in most cases, cannot be accessed by anyone, even the adoptee or the adoptive parents, without a court order or the intervention of a judge or magistrate. Others include court-ordered, sealed files concerning some divorce settlements, civil lawsuit settlements, coroners' reports, and inquests.

Private companies and organizations also are reluctant to release any information about their clients, employees, or members for whatever reason. Some may divulge information and provide copies of records to persons who are immediate relations of an individual; however, many will refuse inquiries and requests unconditionally. As private entities, they have the right to hold information confidential and there is little you can do to circumvent their position.

Religious institutions also may choose to maintain the privacy of their records and those of their members.

These brick walls can certainly seem like insurmountable problems. There are, however, several methods you may take to help gain access to otherwise restricted or closed records. Let's explore a few of these approaches.

Be Prepared to Provide Proof of Your Relationship

You will almost always be asked to explain the reason for requesting someone else's information, even though that person may have been deceased for some time—even decades or centuries. Your best response will be that you are researching your family and that you can provide proof of your relationship to the individual whose records you are requesting. As a good genealogist, you will already have traced your family backward from yourself and will have collected documentation of your lineage.

It is important to be able to present your identification wherever you go but, if your surname is different from that of the person you are researching, you may have to present some additional proof. Be prepared by carrying a copy of a pedigree chart with you, along with copies of birth certificates, marriage licenses, death certificates, obituaries, and any other documentation that might prove your relationship. The fact that you *are* prepared to prove your relationship speaks volumes to the people from whom you make these requests. They are usually so impressed by your preparation, your openness, and the evidence that you present that they often will open access to otherwise closed or restricted materials.

Offer to Pay All the Expenses

Demonstrate your seriousness about the subject by offering to pay for the expenses associated with making copies, mailing them to you, and whatever else might be required. Be sure that the person you are dealing with knows this from the beginning. If you are working with a religious institution or a nonprofit organization, such as a genealogical or historical society, offer to make a small contribution as a gesture of appreciation and to help offset the person's time.

Provide Letters of Authorization or Permission to Access

Your relationship to the individual you are researching may not be a direct one. Perhaps you are searching for records for your grandfather's brother's children. Since you are not a direct relative, you may be challenged and blocked from access to some or all records. This can sometimes be resolved by providing a letter of authorization or affidavit from a descendant or other direct blood relative. The letter or affidavit should be signed, dated, and legalized by a registered notary public. It also helps to be able to prove your relationship to the family in the same way described previously, only this time you should be able to show your ancestral connection to this collateral, branch line of the family.

Invoke the Use of the Freedom of Information Act

In the United States, the Freedom of Information Act, also referred to as the FOIA, requires government agencies to disclose records requested in writing by any person. Certainly there are some restrictions that relate to national security, and certain privacy laws pertaining to living individuals may apply. However, it is important to recognize that you can invoke the FOIA in certain circumstances to overcome artificial obstacles and refusals.

The United States Department of Justice (DOJ) maintains a web page at its site that specifically addresses FOIA requests. You can visit that site at **www.usdoj.gov/ oip**. Consult their DOJ FOIA Reference Guide for specific details concerning what can and cannot be accessed and the procedures for making your request. The U.S. Department of State's online Electronic Reading Room at **www.state.gov/m/a/ips** provides an overview and additional FOIA reference materials.

Different countries' governments will have legislation that regulates access to information. It is wise to research these laws in each location.

Obtain a Court Order

Some documents are closed or restricted to the public by governments and individuals. One effective approach is to apply to a court of law for a court order to open records or to provide copies of specific items. You must be prepared to present a convincing argument of your need to access the materials and to prove your relationship. One of the most persuasive arguments presented in contemporary court hearings of this sort is the necessity of medical information. The need to identify blood type, genetic predisposition to a disease or medical condition, or similar reason is often an effective argument for the issuance of a court order. You may or may not require a legal representative's help in preparing and presenting your request to the court. The use of a legal professional can be expensive, but the cost may be justified if this is your last resort.

Order Document Copies by Postal Mail and Email

Letter writing has become something of a lost art, and people tend to forget the importance of using effective correspondence to get results. Younger genealogists also may not know what informational components are required in order to get the best results, and older genealogists may not be using modern technology to achieve success.

It isn't always convenient or cost-effective to make a visit to a particular place to obtain copies of documents you want or need for your research. Therefore, you will do what genealogists have done for decades: write letters and/or complete forms to obtain copies of documents. The difference between the way we handled this now and 20 years ago is that email is available in addition to traditional postal mail. Since email is so fast, the slower postal mail has acquired the name of "snail-mail."

Your first step, as always, is to determine the correct place to inquire about the records you want to obtain. You certainly can use the Internet and a search engine to locate the website of a particular facility. For example, if you were looking for the contact information for Augusta County, Virginia, governmental offices, you might enter the following into your favorite search engine:

"augusta county" virginia government

The search results list includes the county government's website at **www.co.augusta .va.us**. From that page, you could navigate to other pages containing the addresses and telephone numbers of the Circuit and District Courts. You could then write a letter to the clerk of the appropriate court and mail it, along with a self-addressed, stamped envelope (SASE). This is a professional gesture that encourages a response.

You also can obtain copies of required document request forms from some archives and libraries. The U.S. National Archives and Records Administration (NARA) requires you to use their preprinted, multipart forms to request searches for and copies of specific records or use their online ordering facilities that were discussed earlier in the book. You can obtain these forms by visiting NARA's website at **www.archives.gov** and using the links under Research & Order on the left side of the page. When generating a request to any person, organization, or institution requesting anything, use the standard business letter format. Include your complete return address and the date of your letter. The heading should include the name and complete address for the entity you are writing. If you have the name of a specific contact individual, include that name, preceded with the title (Mr., Ms., Mrs., etc.), in the header. See the examples here:

Alamance County Offices
Attn.: Department of Vital Records
124 W. Elm Street
Graham, NC 27253

Ms. Iris Garden
Clerk of Court
Alamance County Courthouse
124 W. Elm Street
Graham, NC 27253

Next comes the salutation, followed by a colon. Use the person's name and title, if you know it. If you don't know the name, use the generic salutation. Look at the following examples:

Dear Ms. Garden:
Dear Gentlemen and Ladies:
To whom it may concern:

The body of the letter must communicate clearly what you are seeking. Include the full name of the person whose record you want to obtain. Include any nickname and, for women, the maiden name, and define these alternative names as what they are. Here is the text from the body of a letter that I wrote concerning my paternal grandparents:

I am seeking a copy of the marriage record for my grandparents who were married on 24 December 1902 in Davidson, Mecklenburg County, North Carolina. Their names and information are as follows:

Groom: Samuel Goodloe Morgan (born 6 April 1879)
Bride: Laura Augusta (Minnie) Wilson Murphy (born 25 January 1873)

Laura Augusta Wilson was also known as "Minnie" and may be listed as such in the marriage records. Also, she had been previously married to a Mr. Jeter Earnest Murphy in 1898 but was widowed the same year.

I have tried to provide as much information as possible above. I hope it will be enough for you to locate this record for me. Please advise me of the cost of locating and providing me with copies of these records. I will send a check immediately or provide credit card information, whichever you prefer. I am enclosing a SASE for your reply.

If you do not have these records, please advise me if they have been transferred to another location, the state archive, to a library, or other facility so that I may continue my search there.

Thank you in advance for your invaluable help with my family quest.

You will notice that I included a paragraph asking that, if the records are no longer in that facility, the person should let me know where they may have been sent or transferred. Many clerks are overwhelmed with work and, if you don't ask the question, they may not automatically supply you with that invaluable information.

The signature block of your letter should include a complimentary closing such as "Yours" or "Sincerely." Include your full name and, if you wish, your title (Mr., Mrs., Ms.) and any professional or educational credential abbreviations that are appropriate (DDS, PhD., etc.).

Address your mailing envelope clearly so that it matches the header block of your letter, and be certain to include your return address. Enclose a clearly addressed SASE with ample postage to encourage a reply.

Another way to streamline the letter-writing process is to create a template in your word processor and save it. This can reduce the amount of typing you have to do. You might consider creating a separate letter template document for use in requesting marriage records, one for death certificates, another for wills and probate records, and yet another for land and property records. Each template will have the specific verbiage you need to specify and obtain copies. You also might consider a mail merge document in your word processor, which is one in which you can define specific fields of the letter and code them in such a way that you simply enter data into one document and then cause it to be merged into the template, creating multiple documents. Check the Help facility of your word processor program for detailed instructions for how to create document templates for these letters and/or mail merge documents. You actually could create multiple mail merge documents. Use the data entry document as the single place you type in information and then allow it to produce the letters and produce a sheet of mailing labels for envelopes. You also can create a number of self-addressed envelopes at one time and then you only need to add the stamp and enclose it with your letters. It really is simple to automate the process. It requires a little time investment in the beginning to set everything up. However, after that, the letter-writing process itself can be a breeze.

Keep Track of Your Correspondence

My genealogy correspondence used to be a terrible mess. I would write letters to courthouses for copies of documents, send off forms to obtain copies from NARA, and shoot off email messages to many other researchers. I was so busy sending things out that I wasn't really sure what I had done and what I had not. I ended up duplicating my efforts again and again, and yet never followed up on anything because I didn't keep control of it. It is particularly embarrassing when you send the same request two or three times to the same person, and it gets expensive sending money multiple times to the same courthouse or archives and receiving the same documents more than once. Yes, it *can* happen to you!

The simple solution is to maintain a correspondence log and get into the habit of entering information about all of your correspondence, including both postal mail and email. The correspondence log is merely a formatted record of what you have written to someone else about, when you wrote it, when you received a response, and what results you obtained.

Some people choose to maintain a record of their correspondence at the surname level and, by doing so, have only one place to check for every letter or email sent and received for an entire family. I know other people who maintain a control log based on geography, or even surname and geography, to get a little more granular. There are a number of options for setting up and maintaining a correspondence log. You will have to choose the format and organizational scheme that works best for you based on the people you are researching.

You have a number of options in terms of format. Ancestry.com provides a free downloadable Correspondence Record form at **http://c.ancestry.com/pdf/trees/charts/correc.pdf**; RootsWeb offers another format at **www.rootsweb.com/~cokids/forms/pics/corresp.jpg**; and *Family Tree Magazine* provides yet another document at **www.familytreemagazine.com/upload/images/pdf/correspondence.pdf**. There are other examples on the Internet that you can find by typing **genealogy forms** into your favorite search engine.

Another option is to create your own form using a word processor or spreadsheet program. You can define whatever columns you would like and format them to suit your own research needs. At a minimum, you will want to keep track of the following data fields:

- Date on which you made the request
- Name and address of the person or institution
- Type of information requested
- Type of information received
- Any money that you sent along with the request

I use a spreadsheet program for my genealogy correspondence log. Microsoft's Excel or Apple's Numbers programs are good choices for a PC or Mac, respectively. By setting up multiple columns for surname, forename/given name, and middle initial, I can sort the data in the spreadsheet into whatever sequence I like. Excel allows me to sort in ascending or descending order for every field. For example, perhaps I want to see all correspondence I've generated for all persons in alphabetical order. I could sort the surnames alphabetically as the primary sort, then by forename as the secondary sort, and middle initial as a tertiary sort. That would present a spreadsheet in all alphabetical sequence by name. I also could add another sort to place the correspondence in date sequence within person—or in surname. Perhaps I want to see what correspondence I've sent to a specific person or organization. I could sort the spreadsheet in addressee name sequence and then, if I like, add additional sorting within that by date and by surname. As you can see, using a spreadsheet program can provide a great deal of flexibility in viewing the data. That way you can generate follow-ups for correspondence for which you have received no reply.

Using a correspondence log requires a little investment in setup time and a commitment to the process of using and maintaining it. The payback, however, comes in the elimination of redundant written correspondence and in being able to maintain control over what can be an overwhelming activity.

Use a Research Log

Keeping track of all the places you have conducted research and all the resources that you have consulted can be difficult. The danger is that you may duplicate your research, which can be a terrible waste of time and money. It is important to keep track of what resources you have investigated in the past, even those that yielded nothing of value, so that you don't duplicate your efforts. A research log or research calendar can help you record your progress. You can maintain your log by surname, by individual, by geographic area, in a combination of any of these, or in whatever organizational structure makes you most effective.

All of the information discussed in this chapter will help you home in on different record types in all types of locations. In the process, using correspondence and research logs can help you identify the materials you have already used and thereby avoid an enormous duplication of work effort and waste of money making photocopies, ordering document copies, and purchasing books.

Now that we have covered so many different record types, and discussed various printed references and finding aids, let's proceed to Chapter 11 and discuss how to locate information on the Internet about your ancestors.

11

Learn How to Successfully Research Your Ancestors on the Internet

HOW TO...

- Categorize the major types of genealogical web page resources
- Structure effective searches to locate information
- Use online message boards to share information and collaborate with others
- Subscribe to and use genealogy mailing lists
- Write effective messages and postings that get results
- Locate and use additional Internet resources to help your research

Genealogical research is one of the top uses of the Internet, and it is no surprise that so many of us are confused by all the options and overwhelmed by the information we find. Making sense of what you find on the Internet means understanding what you are looking at. Understanding the various types of Internet resources is not unlike visiting your local public library and recognizing that dictionaries are vastly different resources than fiction and nonfiction books, magazines are different than journals, and microfilm is different than the Internet. You use your critical thinking skills every time you visit the library to differentiate between materials you want to use; to recognize what is current vs. noncurrent information; and to discern between quality, authoritative, and unbiased information as opposed to that which is not.

This chapter focuses on the different types of Internet resources, how to evaluate them, and how to incorporate them with the "traditional" documents, print materials, and other resources you use. Ultimately, you will work all of these sources in tandem to obtain more comprehensive results and make yourself a more effective researcher.

Categorize the Three Major Types of Internet Resources

Many people equate "the Internet" only with web pages. It is, however, much more than that. Certainly there are billions of web pages, but the Internet really is a collection of numerous tools. These can be grouped into three main categories:

- Web pages
- Electronic mail (email)
- Message boards and mailing lists

Within web pages are other subsidiary contents, including text, graphics files, sound files, video files, forms for inputting data, search templates, archives of files that can be transferred or downloaded, chat rooms, and a number of other resources.

Email is the most widely used form of communication on earth today. Many billions of electronic messages are sent and received each day. Some are individual person-to-person messages while others are one-to-many messages, such as those sent to an email mailing list or distribution list. Email has, like web pages, become more than just textual. Messages can contain multimedia graphics, sound, and video files within the body of the message and as attachments.

Message boards and mailing lists are Internet tools that allow you to reach many persons at once who share an interest in a particular topic. Genealogy message boards are used by tens of thousands of persons each day to post queries concerning persons with a specific surname, questions about a geographical area, or questions concerning some other subject area. A mailing list uses email messages to communicate to persons who have subscribed to that particular list whose messages are focused on a specific surname, geographical area, or topic. Message boards and mailing lists are discussed in greater detail later in this chapter.

Web pages, email, message boards, and mailing lists are different media and are used for different purposes. If you understand their uses up front, you are better prepared for what you may *and* may not expect to find when you use them.

One of the best pieces of advice I can give you is to look for "help" resources on the websites you use in your research. Most websites and Internet resources include a "Help" facility. This may also be titled "Tips and Tricks" or some other name. You may also discover Frequently Asked Question (FAQ) facilities that provide information to assist your use of the site. You can always become more conversant and more effective in the use of any online facility by accessing and reading the Help text area. This area will explain what is and is not available in the way of functionality. Often you will find examples of how to access content effectively and, if there is a search facility available, how to optimize your use of it. These "mini-tutorials" are intended as primers for you and usually are not long, drawn-out, dry narratives.

Categorize the Major Types of Genealogical Web Page Resources

No matter whether you're just starting your genealogical odyssey on the Internet or you're a seasoned web researcher, there is always something new to be discovered there. What you must remember is that websites change over time. New content is added, content is updated, dead links and outdated materials are removed (hopefully!), and websites evolve to become easier to use. Let's explore the major types of websites you will encounter and assess what you can expect to find there.

Compilation Sites

Compilation sites are websites that gather significant resources together in an organized fashion. The materials are presented in a format that allows you to locate materials by reviewing the logical groupings of materials or hierarchical structures to find what you want. Some of these sites may include a search function that allows you to locate specific resources by keyword or phrase. Following are some examples of compilation websites and suggested areas to explore at each:

- Ancestry.com **www.ancestry.com**
  Visit the main page and locate and click the Learning Center link. Click the tab labeled Keep Learning. On the left side of the next page is a list of links. Click the one labeled Ancestry Archive; the next page, shown in Figure 11-1, allows you to browse all the Ancestry.com and *Ancestry* Magazine articles by year and month. You'll also see a Search Topics box that allows you to perform a simple search of the Archive. Click the Advanced Search link and you can search by topic, publication dates, category, and author.
- Canadian Genealogy & History Links **www.islandnet.com/~cghl**
  Visit the main page (shown in Figure 11-2) and click the Nunavut link, and then click the Teaching & Learning About Nunavut link to see a map and to learn more about this area.
- Cyndi's List **www.cyndislist.com**
  Look for Cyndi Howells' group of information on Wills & Probate. Scroll through the entire page to see what is there. Then, go back to the top and try the Search function to locate a listing for Delaware. Then, return to the top of the page and type **delaware** in the Search box and see what all is at her site. You can narrow the search to locate wills in Delaware by typing the two words, **delaware wills**.
- GENUKI **www.genuki.org.uk**
  Visit the main page and click the link labeled Researching UK and Irish Genealogy from Abroad and, on that page, read the section "Commissioning Research."

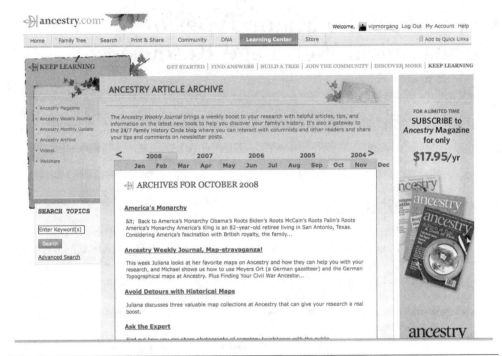

FIGURE 11-1 The Ancestry.com Archive. (Used with permission of The Generations Network, Inc.)

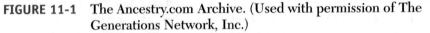

FIGURE 11-2 Main page from the Canadian Genealogy & History Links website

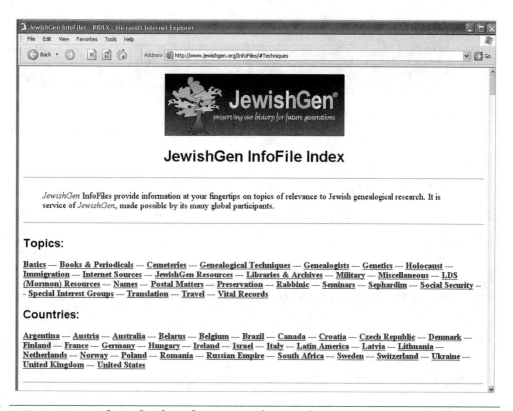

FIGURE 11-3   The InfoFile Index page at the JewishGen.org site provides the most comprehensive set of links to Jewish resources on the Internet.

- JewishGen   **www.jewishgen.org**
  Visit the main page and locate and click the link labeled JewishGen InfoFiles (under Learn), which takes you to the page shown in Figure 11-3. Click the Genealogical Techniques link at the top of the page to move to that area on the web page. Click the EEFAQ—Jewish Genealogical Research in Eastern Europe link and learn how to conduct research for ancestors and relatives from that part of the world.
- USGenWeb Project   **www.usgenweb.org**
  This all-volunteer effort provides access to information about all 50 states and their countries. Visit the site, whose main page is shown in Figure 11-4, and click the States menu. (There are other selections you'll want to explore as well.) Use one of the links to the map, table, or text to access the listing of states. Select "Virginia" and then explore what is there.
- WorldGenWeb Project   **www.worldgenweb.org**
  This is the international companion site to the USGenWeb Project. Visit this site and click on the link for CenEuroGenWeb, located on the left side of the page. On the next page, click the link for Germany or the subsidiary list of states and visit the page for the resources listed there.

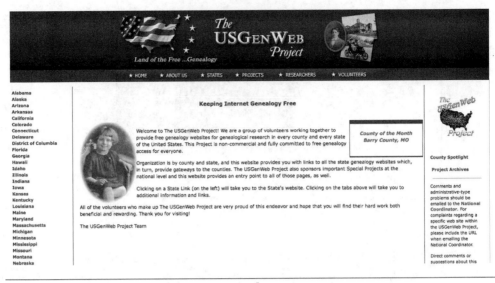

FIGURE 11-4 Main page of the USGenWeb Project site

As you can see, each of these websites is a compilation of many different types of information. Within some of these are "how-to" materials, databases, maps, dictionaries, and links to other sites. While Cyndi's List offers an exceptionally comprehensive collection of reference links across many subject areas across the Internet, a compilation by topic area provides an excellent focal point for your research concerning a specific topic area. The esteemed JewishGen site, for example, provides categories of general and geography-specific information and links, making it the preeminent website for Jewish ancestral research guidance.

Did You Know? Cyndi's List at **www.cyndislist.com** is the work of genealogy maven Cyndi Howells, and is one of the largest compilations of genealogy websites on the Internet. Started in 1996, the site now has more than 264,000 links and continues to grow.

"How-to," Educational, and Reference Sites

This category includes "how-to" articles that provide instruction, as well as articles, columns, tips, and other online reference materials. The following are representative examples of this category:

- AfriGeneas (African Ancestored Genealogy from Africa to America)   **www .afrigeneas.com**
  Visit the main screen and click Records at the top of the page for a drop-down menu. Click Library Records. Select one of the items on the page to investigate.

- FamilySearch.org (LDS Church)   **www.familysearch.org**
  This is the genealogical database website of The Church of Jesus Christ of Latter-day Saints and it provides access to information about the church's genealogical materials. There is a tremendous amount here. However, let's focus on excellent instructional materials. On the main web page, select (but don't click) the Library menu at the top of the page and click the Education link in the drop-down menu. On the next page, click the Research Guidance link for a list of all the locations for which research guides are available. Click Sweden. You will now be presented with selections of birth, marriage, and death categories with date ranges presented. Under Birth, click 1860–Present. You are presented with three tabs: Historical Background, For Beginners, and Search Strategy. Click each one in turn. Under each is a link that you may click to be displayed as a web page. You also may click the link for a printable version of the document. As a resource for strategies in various areas, these are unbeatable instructional sheets for your research.
- Genealogy.com   **www.genealogy.com**
  Visit the main page and click the Learning Center link at the top of the page. Choose one of the areas of interest to you on the page and visit that page.
- RootsWeb Guide to Tracing Family Trees   **http://rwguide.rootsweb.ancestry.com**
  Visit this web page and select one or more subjects that are of interest to you in your research. You might want to try the Land Records (U.S.A.) link for interesting information.

Genealogy Charts and Forms

In the course of your research, you will probably find a number of types of forms useful in recording information you uncover. In particular, census transcription forms and forms for abstracting wills, deeds, and other documents can be great tools. You certainly can create forms for your own work style, but there also are free forms available at a number of sites:

- Ancestry.com   **www.ancestry.com/trees/charts/ancchart.aspx**
  Some of the best charts and forms are available at the Ancestry.com site. These include census forms for the United States, United Kingdom, and Canada, and other forms. These are in Adobe PDF file format and are downloadable here.
- *Family Tree Magazine* online   **www.familytreemagazine.com/forms/download.html**
  Family Tree Magazine has perhaps the most complete collection of genealogy forms on the Internet, available in both PDF and plain text formats.
- Genealogy.com   **www.genealogy.com/00000061.html**
  There are census forms here that provide another format option to those at Ancestry.com.

These are just a few of the many places on the Internet where you can obtain free forms to download and/or print. Additional free forms can be found by entering **genealogy forms** in your favorite search engine.

Online Databases

The fastest growing area of the Internet for genealogical resources is in online databases. There are both free databases and fee-based databases. Some sites offer a combination of databases. Various payment arrangements are available to access data at the fee-based sites. They include: access on an annual or monthly subscription basis; pay-per-day; pay-as-you-go; or pay-per-record downloaded or printed. A number of the database sites will give you a free demonstration or sample subscription. It is wise to try the site on a short-term basis before committing yourself to a lengthy subscription.

In this category of web resources, you should consider exploring as far as you possibly can in these areas, *and* returning often to these sites for new and updated materials. Some of the best of the databases are listed here:

- Ancestry.com (free and pay databases) **www.ancestry.com**
  Ancestry.com contains the U.S. collection of databases. However, there currently are international collections for the United Kingdom (**www.ancestry.co.uk**), Canada (**www.ancestry.ca**), Australia (**www.ancestry.au**), Germany (**www.ancestry.de**), France (**www.ancestry.fr**), Italy (**www.ancestry.it**). Sweden (**www.ancestry.se**), and China (**www.jiapu.cn**). You can use the search template at Ancestry.com to enter name, location, time period, and/or other data and conduct a search of all the databases. Alternatively, however, you can examine the full list of available databases at Ancestry.com by visiting their Card Catalog at **http://search.ancestry.com/search/CardCatalog.aspx**. You may either browse the entire list (which I strongly recommend in order to see what is there) or filter the titles by collection. You will be amazed at the scope and diversity of Ancestry.com's international databases. Among their Images Online premium databases are the U.S. federal census population schedules (1790–1930), the Immigration Ships Passenger Lists, the Historical Newspaper Collection, the United Kingdom Censuses, the Civil War Pension Index, Pallot's Marriage and Baptism Indexes for England (1780–1837), and the United States WWI Draft Cards, to name just a few. More databases are in the process of being digitized, indexed, and placed online, which means that you should check back often to locate additional records. (My book, *The Official Guide to Ancestry.com*, available in its second edition at the time of this writing, describes how to use this subscription database site.)
- FamilyHistoryOnline (pay-per-view databases) **www.familyhistoryonline.net**
  The Federation of Family History Societies in the United Kingdom provides access to more than approximately 17 million records for England and Wales at the FamilyHistoryOnline website. These records have been compiled by local genealogy societies and include indexes for baptisms, marriages, burials, monument inscriptions, and census records, and some of the records include more extensive details. The site continues to expand as additional counties and records are compiled and placed online.

- FamilySearch.org (LDS Church)   **www.familysearch.org**
  The LDS Church website is a fast-growing resource for your genealogical reference. The LDS Church is working to digitize, index, and make available on this site all of the microfilmed records they have captured over the decades. Visit the main page, shown in Figure 11-5, and click the Advanced Search link. There are a number of databases here, and it is important that you know what these include. Searches of some of these will present you with a file number and/or microfilm number. You can present these at the nearest LDS Family History Center (FHC), whose staff can work with you to arrange to order the rental microform materials from the Family History Library (FHL) in Salt Lake City, Utah.

Did You Know?   The LDS Church is working to digitize, index, and make available on FamilySearch .org all of the microfilmed records they have captured over the decades.

The search databases include the following:

- **Ancestral File**   This data has been researched and uploaded to the LDS site by individuals. It may contain research errors.
- **Census**   This area contains the 1880 United States, 1881 British Isles, and 1881 Canadian census material. This has been independently compiled and indexed by the LDS Church and can be ordered on microfilm.
- **International Genealogical Index**   This is an indexed database of materials collected and microfilmed by the LDS Church. There are indexing errors but this remains an excellent resource to film of the original records.

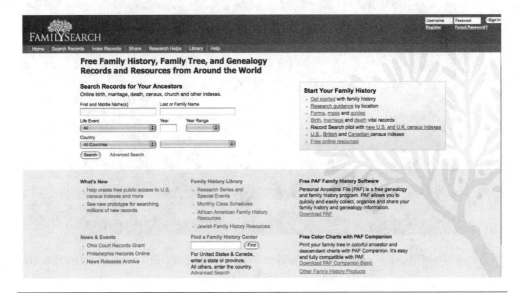

FIGURE 11-5   Main page of the LDS Church's FamilySearch.org site

- **Pedigree Resource File**   This resource indexes the materials that have been submitted by individuals to the LDS Church. Many of these materials have been placed on CD-ROM and can be ordered through the LDS FHC rental program. There are errors in these materials but they can provide pointers for your research.
- **US Social Security Death Index**   This resource can be found here and at several other websites and can be an excellent finding aid.
- **Vital Records Index**   This database currently contains records for only Mexico and Scandinavia.
- **Search Family History Web Sites**   This is a collection of websites indexed by the LDS Church's search engine and references URLs submitted by individuals.
- Footnote.com (subscription databases)   **www.footnote.com**
Footnote.com is the fastest-growing collection of digitized, indexed records of genealogical interest on the Internet. At this writing, Footnote.com is adding approximately 2 million new images to its website each month. Many of these images come from microfilmed records at the National Archives and Records Administration (NARA), including Revolutionary War, War of 1812, and Civil War documents for service, pensions, and more. Naturalization index cards, city directories, and many other document types are available. Figure 11-6 shows a search result for the author's ancestor, John Swords. The Revolutionary War Pension database includes the complete file of 45 pages of digitized original documents for John Swords.

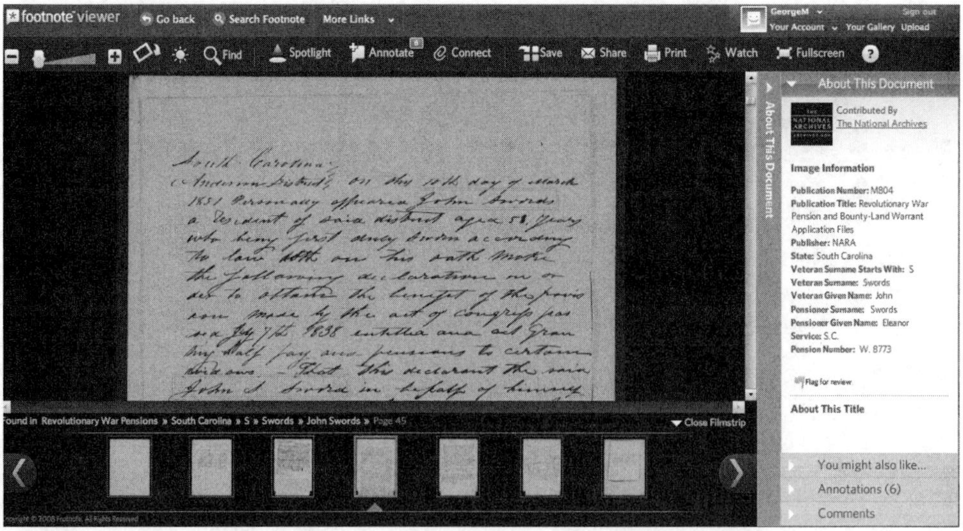

FIGURE 11-6   Revolutionary War Pension file for John Swords. (Used with permission of Footnote.com.)

- Genealogy.com (free and pay databases)   **www.genealogy.com**
  You will find some databases on this site, some of which have been created as a result of individuals submitting their own GEDCOM files. Other databases include the International and Passenger Records, a newspaper database, and several others.
- Library and Archives Canada (free databases)   **www.collectionscanada.gc.ca**
  This resource was discussed in some detail in Chapter 5, concerning census records. Library and Archives Canada has, in its online Canadian Genealogy Centre, a variety of articles, links, and some images.
- The National Archives (U.K.) (pay U.K. census databases)   **www .nationalarchives.gov.uk**
  The former Public Record Office (PRO) and the Historical Manuscripts Commission (HMC) were merged in April 2003 to form The National Archives (TNA). The Family Records Centre (FRC) was relocated to TNA in 2008. The website is a great compendium of information, online exhibits, educational tutorials, and much more. TNA's main web page is shown in Figure 11-7. Of special interest to family history researchers are the digitized census images from TNA's DocumentsOnline collection. Browse the full list of collections in the Family History category under the "Research and learning" tab and "Starting your research" sub-tab.

FIGURE 11-7   Main page of The National Archives (U.K.)

Did You Know?

GEDCOM is an acronym for Genealogy Electronic Data COMmunication, and refers to a specific computer file format. GEDCOMs are extracted data files produced from genealogy database software programs in a common structured format. A GEDCOM from one genealogy database program can be imported into another genealogy database program, and uploaded to certain genealogy websites, complete with individuals' information. Multimedia file data is not supported in the GEDCOM format at this time.

Genealogical Societies

Genealogical societies can offer a wealth of information to you, including reference and referrals, education, companionship, and publications, and may well possess important genealogical records found nowhere else. You will want to investigate the societies at the national, regional, state or provincial, county, parish, and local levels where your ancestors and family members lived. The following are some of the major ones of interest to researchers:

- Canadian Genealogical Societies   **www.generations.on.ca/genealogical-canadian.htm**
  This web page is a subsidiary of the Generations website and provides a list of links to the provincial genealogical societies' websites. There are, however, hundreds of genealogical societies in Canada and you may locate information for and links to a more extensive list of local societies at the provincial societies' sites.
- Federation of Family History Societies (FFHS)   **www.ffhs.org.uk**
  This international organization, based in the United Kingdom, has more than 180,000 members worldwide. It provides education and support to individuals and to genealogical societies, and coordinates a number of national projects in order to integrate the efforts of multiple societies, publish the efforts, and publicize the results.
- Federation of Genealogical Societies (FGS)   **www.fgs.org**
  This organization consists primarily of United States and Canadian genealogical societies. Individual societies join FGS and it, in turn, provides a forum for society education and communications, and hosts an annual conference. The list of member societies is available at **www.fgs.org/membership/members.php**.

You also can search for a particular genealogical society by using your favorite search engine and typing the name of the area and the quotation mark-enclosed phrase **"genealogical society"** or **"genealogy society"** in the search box.

Structure Effective Searches to Locate Information

The Web is an enormous place, currently consisting of billions of individual pages. In reality, we can only guess at its actual size, and it is growing at a fast pace. Because it is relatively easy for anyone to put information on the Web, there is a good possibility that somebody, somewhere, has created a web page that contains information you might find useful for your genealogical research. The trick, then, is to locate that one useful page among the billions of pages out there.

It is important that you learn how to use, in a logical, structured way, the two primary search tools on the Internet: search engines and directories. We're going to explore each one in detail, after which you should practice, practice, and practice in order to become an expert Internet searcher.

Define the Difference Between Search Engines and Directories

Early in the development of the World Wide Web, directories were the way of the world. Before long, search engines appeared. The problem is, however, that over time the directories have added search facilities to their sites and search engines have added directories to their sites. For example, the largest of the directories, Yahoo!, now embeds a search engine that can either search within Yahoo! itself or reach out onto the Web to search millions of web pages. Google, on the other hand, as the largest search engine currently, also has created other facilities. *Both* Yahoo! *and* Google include facilities to search the Web for graphics and audio files, as well as to locate news and financial information. Google also includes an impressive Maps facility. With that in mind, let's define each of the tools and what distinguishes one from another.

A *search engine* is an index of web pages that has been created by a mechanical contrivance known as a spider, a robot, or simply a "bot." The key here is that the index is mechanically created, with very little human intervention. There are three indexed components in a web page that a search index indexes. They are the title, the meta tags, and the body of the web page.

When you enter a single word for a search, it might be located anywhere within these areas of the web pages. As you'll see later, the Advanced Search facility of many search engines may allow you to specify where in the web page the word or phrase is to be sought.

Search engines employ the use of structured searches, using words, keywords, and phrases to match entries in their indexes. Search engines offer both a simple and an Advanced Search facility, the second of which allows you to select criteria to narrow your search results.

Examples of the leading search engines today include Google (shown in Figure 11-8 and located at **www.google.com**, **www.google.co.uk**, and other addresses in other countries), Ask.com (**www.ask.com**), MSN (**www.msn.com**), and a number of others.

A *directory* is another Internet tool that, unlike the search engine, is created entirely by human editors who look at web pages and assign them to logical or appropriate categories. Broad categories can be broken down into narrower subcategories and sub-subcategories. This hierarchical structure can be used to browse deeper and deeper

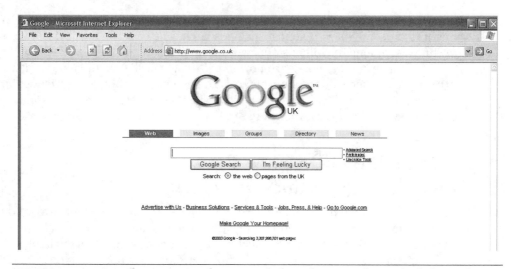

FIGURE 11-8   Search engines such as Google have become the tool of choice for searching the Internet.

to narrow your focus and to locate materials you seek. A directory may also embed a search facility, which enables you to search in just that hierarchical category or to search the entire directory. Some hybrid directories also may allow you to expand your search onto the Web to locate non-categorized materials that are not included in the directory, graphic files, audio files, news wire services, and other resources.

Among the largest directories today are Yahoo! (shown in Figure 11-9 and located at **www.yahoo.com**), Open Directory Project (**http://dmoz.org**), MSN (**www.msn .com**), and several others. Other important reference directories you will want to include in your Favorites list are the Librarians' Internet Index (**www.lii.org**) and the Internet Public Library (**www.ipl.org**). Each of these large directories has links to several million different web pages that have been compiled by their human editors. Because editors add new links to a directory, it may take some time (months, perhaps) before a new web page will appear in a general directory.

There is one more search tool that should be mentioned: the *metasearch engine.* A metasearch engine is another hybrid creature, one that allows you to enter a search in one place and have that engine simultaneously search multiple search engines for you. Does this sound like Nirvana? Hardly! The results may be overwhelming, often coming from lightweights in the searching stratosphere of the Web, often yielding duplicate search results, and/or omitting important leads. Many experienced researchers use metasearch engines only to learn which of the individual search engines has the most or the better search results. However, a metasearch tool can save a great deal of time and can often locate higher-quality results very quickly. Among the major metasearch engines in use today are Dogpile (shown in Figure 11-10 and located at **www.dogpile.com**), MetaCrawler (**www.metacrawler.com**), Mamma (**www.mamma.com**), and Vivisimo (**http://vivisimo.com**).

FIGURE 11-9   Main page at Yahoo!

FIGURE 11-10   Main page of metasearch engine Dogpile.com

Select a "Comfortable" Search Engine and Really Get to Know It

Once you've had the opportunity to peruse the impressive lists of available search engines, and to explore some of them for yourself, you will want to select one or two that you want to use for much or most of your Web research. Just because you've always used Google, though, don't become complacent and just decide that's the one you already know and love.

While Google's index is large and the screen is easy to use (uncluttered, in other words), that doesn't mean that it does everything. You can use a "wildcard" in your Google search query to replace a word when you're unsure of the exact term that you'd like to use. However, if you were unsure how to spell the word "gray" or "grey," some search engines allow you to use what is called a wildcard character in place of the "a" or "e" in the word in order to get matches on both spellings. Google doesn't allow the use of a wildcard for a single character. However, you can still enter **grey or gray** and Google will search for all instances of the word spelled either way.

Once you have selected the "most comfortable" search engine for you, you want to become really comfortable with it. What does that mean? It means you want to learn how to *really* use it and use it effectively—first time and every time from now on out. The way to do this is to locate its Help materials, read them, print them, try the examples provided, reread the text again, memorize it, and then place the text in a polypropylene sheet protector close to your computer for easy reference.

If you are looking for the Help material for Google, go to the main screen and then click the Advanced Search link to the right of the search box. Then, on the Advanced Search screen, click the Advanced Search Tips link. Each search engine (and directory) will have online help. The key to your success is really getting to know the tool and getting to know its strengths (and any weaknesses). Your investment of time now will pay huge dividends later when you're heads-down seeking that research path around the ubiquitous brick wall.

Structure Effective Searches to Locate Information

There are some simple rules of thumb to use in your work with searching the Web. These apply to most search engines. However, read the Help materials for your favorite engine to get the best results.

- To enter a word, simply type it in the box—*in all lowercase letters.* (Never use uppercase or mixed case in searching; only use these for entering web addresses.) Most search directories and search engines don't care, but there are a few that still differentiate between uppercase, lowercase, and mixed case. If you use either all uppercase or mixed case, those few that recognize a difference will only return matches on web pages that have your search term(s) typed in the exact same manner. If you type in all lowercase, however, every directory and search engine will return *all* matches, regardless of case in the original web page.

- Avoid the use of a plural if you can avoid it. If you are searching for matches about bluebirds, enter the word as a singular "bluebird" and most search engines will give matches for both "bluebird" and "bluebirds." When entering a surname that ends in an "s," you may want to enter it *without* the "s" in order to see what matches you will get in your search results list.

- To enter an exact phrase in which two or more words must be contiguous to one another in the precise order you type them, make sure you enclose them in the double quotation marks to make them one entity.

These rules will hold true when searching in both a directory and a search engine, but again, check the Help facility in your favorite search tool.

Use a Search Engine to Get Great Results

The Simple Search or Basic Search screen is typically the main screen you reach at any search engine website. It allows you to slap in a word or two or a phrase, and off you go. Too often, though, a researcher may believe that this is all there is to using a search engine. And while it may give you results, those results may be so massive as to be overwhelming, and probably contain a whole lot of garbage. You may get a sense of all this from the first screen of your search results list. No one I know has the time to cull through 2,175,218 results, and I personally would be skeptical of a search result from Billy Ray Bob's Down Home Page of Genieology! (And yes, that would be misspelled, wouldn't it?) You need to narrow the field. That's where the Advanced Search screen options may help. Look at the Advanced Search screen from Google in Figure 11-11.

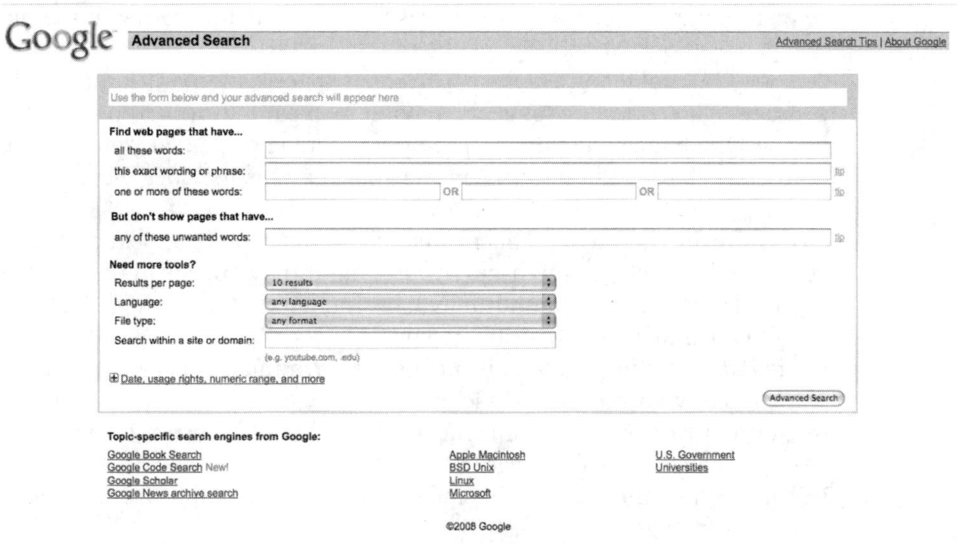

FIGURE 11-11   The Advanced Search page of the Google search engine

Don't forget to check the Advanced Search Tips (the Help text) link in the upper right-hand corner of the screen.

- **all the words**   Entering a single word asks for a search for all web pages that have that word anywhere in the page. Entering multiple words asks for a search for web pages that have *both or all* those words located anywhere in the page and in any order.
- **this exact wording or phrase**   Entering multiple words here will have the same effect as you would have had on the Simple Search screen had you enclosed them in double quotation marks. Here, however, you don't have to enclose them in double quotation marks. You simply enter the words you want treated as a phrase and they will be automatically enclosed in quotation marks when the search begins.
- **one or more of the words**   Entering multiple words asks for a search for web pages that have *any single one* of those words located anywhere in the page.
- **any of these unwanted words**   Entering one or more words here has the effect of excluding from your search results any pages in which one or more of these words might be included anywhere in the page.

The Advanced Search screen also gives you the option of narrowing your search to only web pages written in a specific language. (You may need to download from your browser's development website the character set to install to display certain characters, such as Traditional Chinese, Simplified Chinese, Cyrillic, Korean, Kanji, or others.)

You may opt to have the search engine return only certain document types (or exclude web pages with those types). These include Adobe PDF files, Adobe PostScript files, Microsoft Word files, Microsoft Excel spreadsheets, Microsoft PowerPoint presentations, and Rich Text Format (RTF) files.

You may specify how current a web page must be in order to be returned. However, remember that many web pages contain no date information to make this type of specification 100 percent reliable.

One very helpful feature is the occurrences specification. Click the link labeled "Date, usage rights, numeric range, and more" to expand these additional options. Here you can designate how recently the page was created or updated. You also can indicate where in the web page the term(s)/phrase appears. This includes the following:

- **anywhere in the page**   This means that the term may appear anywhere in the title or the body of the page. In addition, it may appear in the underlying keywords the web page author may have included in his or her HTML document, and the term may not be visible to you.
- **in the title of the page**   This means the term must appear in the blue title bar at the top of your browser window.
- **in the text of the page**   This means the term must appear anywhere in the viewable body of the web page.
- **in the URL of the page**   This means the term must appear somewhere within the web address (URL) of the page.
- **in links to the page**   This means that the term must appear in the text of a link to this specific web page.

The next option, which can narrow your search dramatically, is the selection of Region (or domain). You can specify web pages whose addresses contain the domain(s) you indicate *or* you can cause pages from certain domains not to be included in your search results. Be sure to read the Help material at the search engine you are using to make sure you know how to use this restrictive filter effectively.

The SafeSearch option allows for the filtering of potentially offensive web page content.

Two other options include searches for similar web pages or for web pages that link to a web page. In either case, you may enter a web address (URL) to locate other websites of these types. You can also specify a numeric range. This can be helpful because you can use it to specify year ranges for your searches.

> **Did You Know?** Mailing lists and message boards are among the best tools to use to share and obtain information from other researchers. Both have subjects related to surnames, geographical areas, ethnic groups, and a wide variety of other topics.

Use Mailing Lists and Message Boards to Share Information and Collaborate with Others

Before there was an Internet, genealogists turned to genealogical periodicals (magazines, newsletters, etc.) as a way to publish a question concerning the ancestors they were trying to learn more about. These messages, usually referred to as "queries," were sometimes successful, but even so, they usually were not, since the odds weren't usually very high that the right person (a person who knew the answer to the question) would stumble upon the query. Few genealogists would have the patience to scan every genealogy publication to read every query, especially a backlog of issues going back many years.

Fortunately, the Internet brought a new tool: the electronic mailing list. A query could be sent to a single email address, and it would be automatically re-sent to every mailing list "subscriber." By itself, this was not necessarily a huge improvement over printed queries appearing in subscription magazines or newsletters. However, electronic mailing lists can be archived, and often are. In other words, the older messages can be saved in a database and, as we've already learned, databases can be searched. This means that you can periodically go to the mailing list's archive and search for information of interest.

Online services such as Prodigy, CompuServe, GEnie, and America Online provided another way to exchange queries: a message board (also called a "bulletin board"). Similar message boards could be found on Bulletin Board Systems (BBSs) and as part of another, older tool referred to as Usenet. Eventually, message boards devoted to genealogy were established on the Web, at such places as GenForum at

Genealogy.com (**http://genforum.genealogy.com**) and Ancestry.com (a merger of the old RootsWeb message boards and the newer Ancestry.com boards, located at **http://boards.ancestry.com**).

A message board works like a cork bulletin board found in a typical office or school. Someone posts a message, and hopes that interested parties will see it (and perhaps respond appropriately to it). As with a cork bulletin board, the messages may not remain posted forever. However, as a general rule, genealogy message boards archive messages so that they can be accessed indefinitely. Just to make certain that you clearly understand the differences between a mailing list and a message board, let's explore and discuss both.

What Is a Mailing List?

A mailing list is a facility on the Internet that uses email to distribute a single message to all subscribers. There literally are thousands of genealogical mailing lists to fulfill almost every interest you may have. These include mailing lists dedicated to the following topics: surnames, geographical locations, city directories, record types, ethnic groups, religious groups and records, fraternal organizations, immigration and naturalization, military records, cemeteries, genealogical software, search methodologies, and more.

The organization that hosts the vast majority of genealogical mailing lists is RootsWeb, and you can access their directory of available mailing lists at **http://lists .rootsweb.ancestry.com**.

It is easy to subscribe to a mailing list. For example, let's say that I am researching my ancestors who lived in Rome (Floyd County), Georgia. The Floyd County mailing list would be a good place to learn more from people who also are researching there. I might learn about the history of the area, learn about archives of records of various types, and even meet someone who also is researching the same surnames that I am researching.

From the RootsWeb mailing list directory (see URL above), I entered **georgia floyd** and, on the next page, I clicked on the list for Floyd County, GA. Figure 11-12 shows the web page that is displayed.

If you study Figure 11-12 for a few minutes, you will note several important pieces of information:

- The list is named GAFLOYD-L.
- There is a reference to a web page for this county at the FLOYD COUNTY GAGenWeb Project site that might be of interest to us.
- There are instructions for subscribing to:
  - The GAFLOYD-L mailing list (individual messages)
  - The GAFLOYD-D mailing list (digest mode)
- There are instructions for unsubscribing.
- There is an archive of older messages that may be browsed or searched, using the links shown here.

Georgia Mailing Lists

Floyd County

GAFLOYD-L
lists3

Topic: Floyd County, Georgia. Interested individuals may want to check out the Floyd County GAGenWeb page at http://www.geocities.com/Heartland/Plains /3242/floyd.htm.

There is a Web page for the **GAFLOYD** mailing list at http://www.geocities.com/Heartland/Plains/3242/floyd.htm.

For questions about this list, contact the list administrator at GAFLOYD-admin@rootsweb.com.

- **Subscribing.** Clicking on one of the shortcut links below should work, but if your browser doesn't understand them, try these manual instructions: to join **GAFLOYD-L**, send mail to GAFLOYD-L-request@rootsweb.com with the single word *subscribe* in the message subject and body. To join **GAFLOYD-D**, do the same thing with GAFLOYD-D-request@rootsweb.com.
  - Subscribe to GAFLOYD-L
  - Subscribe to GAFLOYD-D (digest)
- **Unsubscribing.** To leave **GAFLOYD-L**, send mail to GAFLOYD-L-request@rootsweb.com with the single word *unsubscribe* in the message subject and body. To leave **GAFLOYD-D**, do the same thing with GAFLOYD-D-request@rootsweb.com.
  - Unsubscribe from GAFLOYD-L
  - Unsubscribe from GAFLOYD-D (digest)
- **Archives.** You can search the archives for a specific message or browse them, going from one message to another. Some list archives are not available; if there is a link here to an archive but the link doesn't work, it probably just means that no messages have been posted to that list yet.
  - Search the GAFLOYD archives
  - Browse the GAFLOYD archives

RootsWeb is funded and supported by Ancestry.com and our loyal RootsWeb community. Learn more.

About Us | Contact Us | Acceptable Use Policy | PRIVACY STATEMENT | Copyright
Copyright © 1998-2008, MyFamily.com Inc. and its subsidiaries.

FIGURE 11-12   Detail page for Floyd County, Georgia, mailing list

The difference between the GAFLOYD-L mailing list (individual messages) and the GAFLOYD-D mailing list (digest mode) is important to you as a subscriber. Subscribing to the mailing list whose name ends in *L* will result in your receiving a copy of every message as an individual message. This could bury you with email if this turns out to be a busy mailing list. Subscribing to the mailing list whose name ends in *D* will result in your receiving a digest version. This consists of a single email in which all the messages generated in a specific period will be included. There typically is a list of subject headers at the top of the message so that you can tell what types of information are in these messages, followed by the actual messages.

You will remember the Find function discussed earlier in the book (which you can access by pressing the CTRL-F keys on a PC or the COMMAND (⌘)-F keys on a Macintosh). When you subscribe to a digest version of a mailing list and receive potentially a lengthy email with a number of messages inside, the Find function allows you to quickly search for surnames or specific words in which you are interested. This can be a real timesaver.

When you subscribe to a mailing list, you will receive a welcome message. Print and save this message! I personally maintain a file folder labeled "Mailing Lists" in which I keep these messages. The welcome message will provide important information to you to help you maximize your use of the mailing list:

- The purpose of the mailing list
- How to subscribe and unsubscribe
- How to contact the list administrator
- How to browse and/or search the list archives (if available)

By keeping the welcome message, you will be able to quickly locate important information about the mailing list when you need it. In particular, if you decide you want to get off the list, you will have instructions about how to unsubscribe. If there are problems with the list, such as a nasty person who is abusing his or her privilege of participating, the email address of the list owner is invaluable.

When you join a mailing list, it is a good idea to "lurk before you leap." In other words, watch the exchanges of information and messages for a week or two before you jump in. You may find that this isn't really the mailing list you want, and you can unsubscribe.

When you subscribe, also browse or search the archives, if there is one, for answers to any basic questions you have. People on mailing lists cringe when a new person (a "newbie") jumps in and asks a question that has been asked and answered a hundred times.

Last but not least, there are three important rules you should follow:

- Never send an email of a commercial nature unless the description of the list expressly permits it. Sending commercial email on a mailing list is considered to be spamming and is offensive to subscribers.
- Always be polite and patient. There are always "newbies" and your courtesy is expected and appreciated.
- Never type in all capital letters. It is, in the Internet world, considered to be "shouting," not to mention that all caps are more difficult to read. The only exception is that you *should* type surnames in all caps in order to make them stand out.

What Is a Message Board?

A message board, as explained before, is a place on the Internet where people who share an interest in a topic post electronic messages. The difference between a mailing list and a message board is that, for a mailing list, people subscribe via email and messages arrive in their email mailbox. With a message board, the onus is on you to visit the board, to search out information, and to read the postings there yourself.

The Ancestry.com Message Boards at **http://boards.ancestry.com** are among the best available. Figure 11-13 shows the main screen at the Ancestry.com Message Boards. As you can see, it is easy to locate specific surnames, localities, and topics. It also is easy, using the search template toward the top, to either search *all* message boards for a name or text *or* to find a specific message board. Finding a message board is easy: just fill in the name and go from there. For example, I entered the name **weatherly** (no quotes) in the Find a Message Board box and was presented with a new page for the Weatherly surname.

I simply clicked the link and was taken to the page displayed in Figure 11-14. If you study this screen of the Weatherly message board for a few minutes, you'll see that you can search *either* all the message boards *or* just this one for specific words or terms or names. Just click the radio button you want.

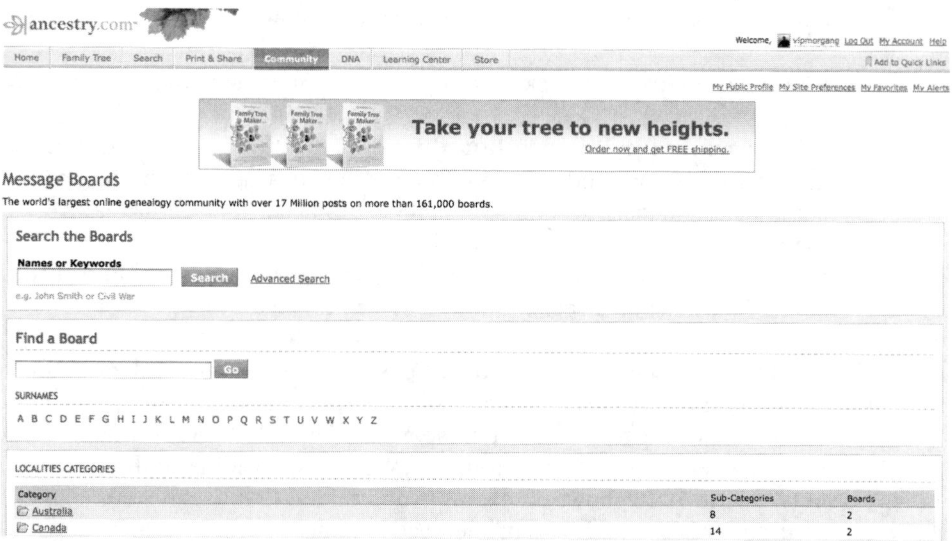

FIGURE 11-13   Main page at the Ancestry.com Message Boards. (Used with permission of The Generations Network, Inc.)

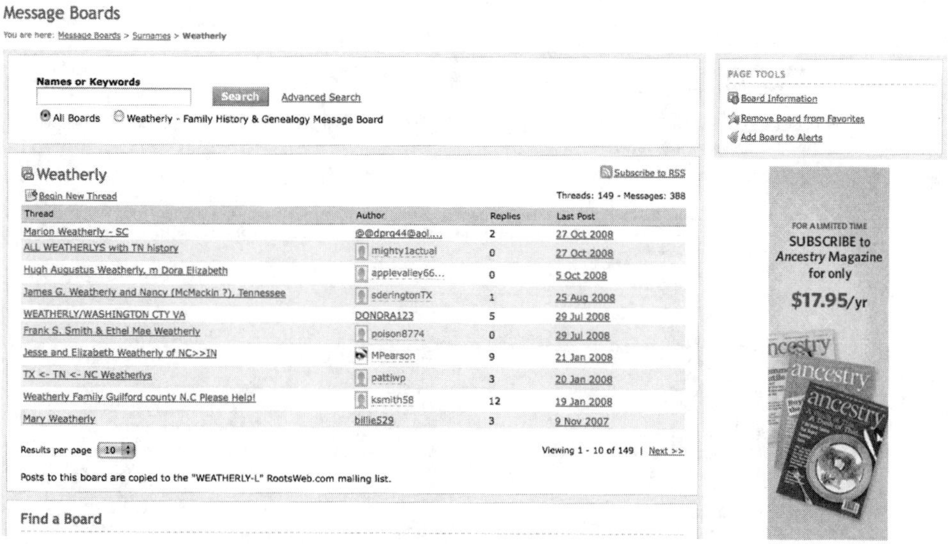

FIGURE 11-14   The Weatherly message board at Ancestry.com. (Used with permission of The Generations Network, Inc.)

You have some other options, including the following:

- **Begin New Thread**   Click this to post a new message on a new topic to this board.
- **Add Board to (or Remove Board from) Favorites**   Whenever you are signed in to Ancestry.com and you visit the message boards, you will have a customized list of places to visit. You must be a registered user to use this feature.
- **Add Board to (or Remove Board from) Alerts**   Allows you to set up a system that sends you an email every time someone posts a message to this message board. You must be a registered user to use this feature.

What you will see in message board postings is something called a "thread." A thread is nothing more than "a thread of conversation" about a single topic. It consists of an original posting and all of the responses to it and the responses to the responses. Each posting is further indented to indicate the response in the thread chain. For example, Figure 11-15 shows an example of a thread that began 9 June 2000 and that has continued through a series of message postings.

There are two display options available when working with the Ancestry.com Message Boards. The first is the "thread view." The page shown in Figure 11-15 is a thread view. The second is the "flat view" in which each message is displayed in its entirety. This is shown in Figure 11-16. Either view can be sorted into oldest first or newest first sequence. You can switch from one display option to the other at will, and

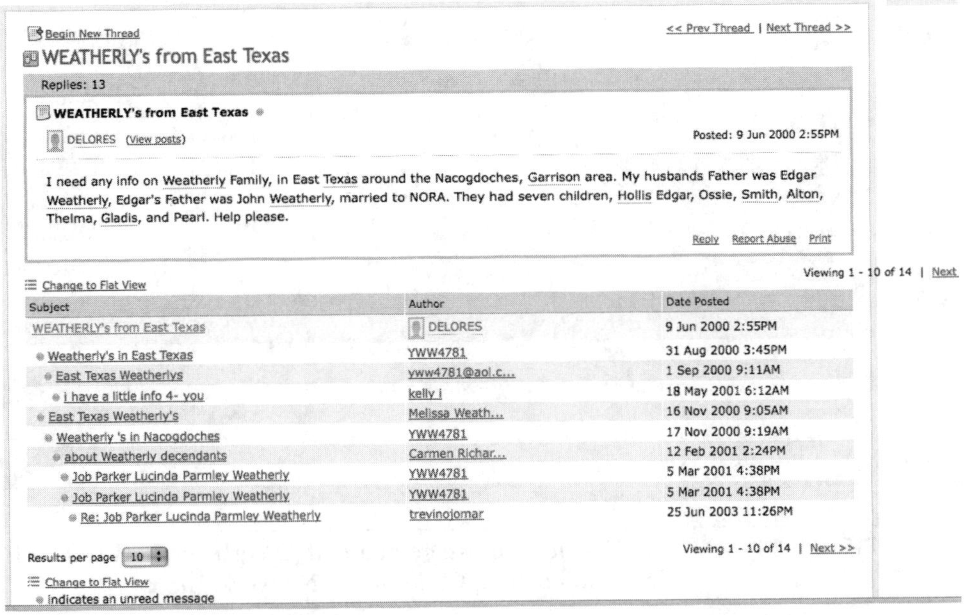

FIGURE 11-15   Messages on the Weatherly message board displayed in "thread view." (Used with permission of The Generations Network, Inc.)

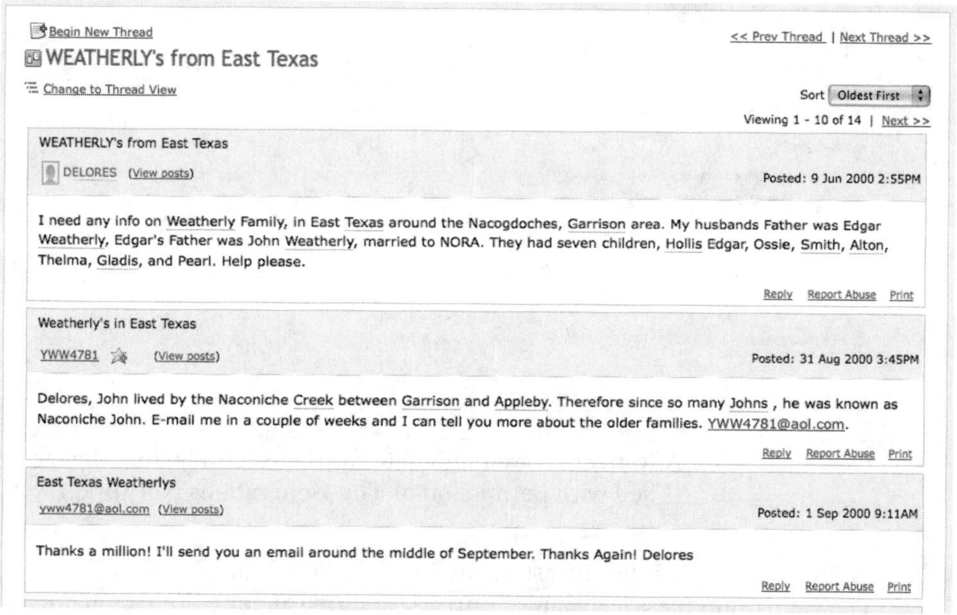

FIGURE 11-16   Messages on the Weatherly message board displayed in "flat view." (Used with permission of The Generations Network, Inc.)

this makes reading the entire correspondence in a whole thread easier than having to click through each one individually. In flat view they are shown on a single screen. What's more, you can use the browser's Find facility to quickly search an entire web page for a specific name or word you want to locate.

You also have the option to display the postings in date sequence in either the collapsed or expanded form. When using the message boards to search for particular text, you may find the Advanced Search feature here as useful as the same function in one of the search engines or directories we have discussed. The Advanced Search template for the Ancestry.com Message Boards is shown in Figure 11-17.

Again, you can search either all the Ancestry.com Message Boards or just the one for this topic, in this case, the Weatherly surname. As you can see, there are some options to help you narrow your search. At the bottom of the screen (not shown) are four additional important links:

- **Request New Board**   You use this if you wish to submit a request to have a new message board established when there is a surname or topic not addressed.
- **Community Guidelines**   This contains guidelines for what is and is not a proper use of the message boards.
- **Board Help**   As always, this is your best friend when you need help and guidance.
- **Board FAQ**   This contains frequently asked questions and answers.

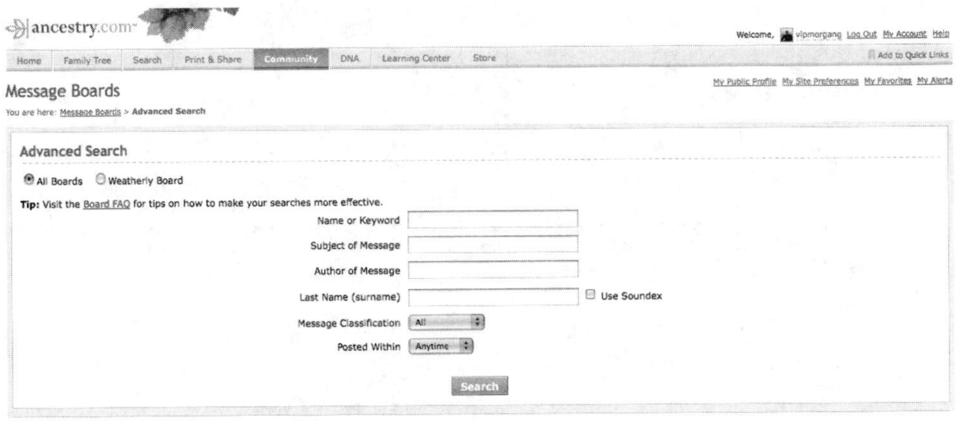

FIGURE 11-17 Advanced Search template for the Ancestry.com Message Boards. (Used with permission of The Generations Network, Inc.)

Remember that the Ancestry.com Message Boards aren't the only ones that exist. The GenForum message boards at **http://genforum.genealogy.com** are a separate group of boards. For maximum exposure for your query, it's a great idea to post messages at *both* sites.

Write Effective Messages and Postings That Get Results

Well-constructed, well-written messages get results. However, you need to know how to create an effective message. A great message really starts with a great subject line that captures the readers' attention. The subject line should be brief but descriptive. It should tell the reader what is inside the message and help him or her determine whether to read the message at all. The subject line content should include details such as the following:

- Name of person sought
- Location
- Time period
- All of the above or other data

Let's look at three examples of potential subject lines. The first is for Rebecca MONFORT who lived in Greene County, Georgia, and her life dates were 1819 to 1886. Please note that the surname is in all uppercase letters to make spotting the surname simpler. This subject line tells the reader who, where, and when. This should be enough to help the reader decide if this is a person about whom he or she would like to learn more or if he or she has something to share. The reader *will* open this message.

Rebecca MONFORT—Greene Co., GA -1819-1886

The second example tells the reader that the author has or wants information concerning a church in a particular location: Madison, North Carolina, in the county of Rockingham.

Zion Baptist Church—Madison (Rockingham) NC

In the third example, the subject tells the reader a lot of information. In this case, the author is seeking information about Brisco HOLDER, who was born in 1879 and who died in the 1920s. Mr. Holder was in Georgia, and then moved to Alabama, and then to Kentucky, and then to some unknown place until his death certificate was located in the city of St. Louis, Missouri. (The greater than character, >, indicates that the person moved.) Reading just this header, you might determine (correctly) that the author is seeking to learn exactly where and when Mr. Holder died and where he was buried.

Brisco HOLDER—1879-ca. 1925—GA > AL > KY > ? > MO

These are all examples of good subject headers. A subject line that reads "Help!" or "Wilson Family" or "Want Grandpa's Dates" is not effective.

The body of the message is just as important as the subject line. It should be concise and should indicate the following:

- The full name (and any nickname or alias) of the individual
- The location in which the person was located
- The time period about which you are interested
- What it is specifically that you are seeking
- Any research you have already conducted or sources you have checked, regardless of whether they helped your search or not
- What else you might be willing to share with another researcher
- How someone can contact or respond to you

Let's look at an example of the body of a good message in Figure 11-18. The author wrote a subject line that clearly provided the surname and the location of the query.

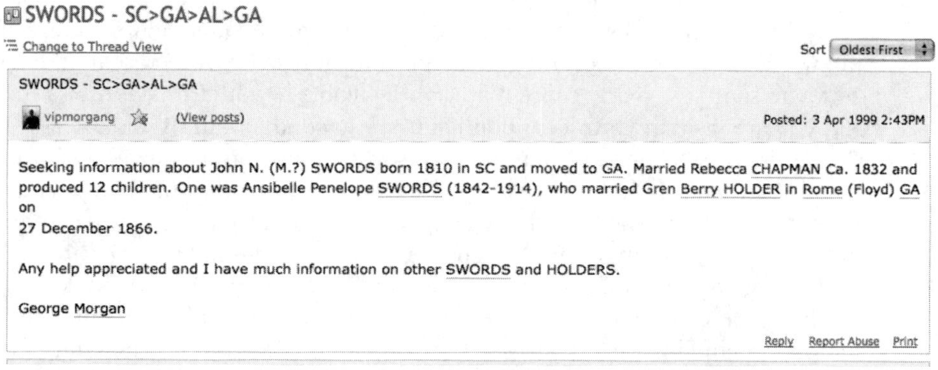
SWORDS - SC>GA>AL>GA

Change to Thread View

Sort Oldest First

SWORDS - SC>GA>AL>GA

vipmorgang (View posts)

Posted: 3 Apr 1999 2:43PM

Seeking information about John N. (M.?) SWORDS born 1810 in SC and moved to GA. Married Rebecca CHAPMAN Ca. 1832 and produced 12 children. One was Ansibelle Penelope SWORDS (1842-1914), who married Gren Berry HOLDER in Rome (Floyd) GA on
27 December 1866.

Any help appreciated and I have much information on other SWORDS and HOLDERS.

George Morgan

Reply Report Abuse Print

FIGURE 11-18 Example of a good message board posting. (Used with permission of The Generations Network, Inc.)

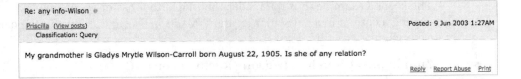

FIGURE 11-19   Example of a less than great message board posting. (Used with permission of The Generations Network, Inc.)

The body of the message indicated that the author was seeking information on one John N. (or M.) SWORDS, his wife, and other members of the family. He provided a detailed description of what he knew, and hoped that this would help the reader determine what he or she might be able to share with the author.

In contrast, let's look at an example of the body of a bad message in Figure 11-19. The author posted this message with the impossible subject line of "any info-Wilson" on the WILSON surname message board. I seriously doubt that anyone read the message, because of the subject line. The author has posted a detailed name and date of birth, but no location. The reader would need to dissect the message, reorganize its content, and further correspond with the author to really determine what the author is seeking.

As you can see, the use of electronic mailing lists and message boards can really expand and extend your research range by providing the ability to advertise the fact that you are seeking information. You will be surprised how many other researchers, even your own cousins, are out there using these electronic queries. Whereas in our discussion of other Internet resources, now *you* have the opportunity to actively participate in requesting and sharing data *and collaborating* with others!

Locate and Use Additional Resources in Your Research

Everything we have discussed so far can contribute to your understanding of how and where to locate important genealogical resources for your research. However, there are so many, many more materials available to you! Consider for a moment that you are visiting your local public library to conduct family history research. You certainly will spend time in the genealogy collection. However, you are sure to encounter material that will cause you to want to use additional library materials that are not physically located within the genealogy and local history department. You will want to consult maps and atlases, and these may be in another part of the library. Encyclopedias, biographies, dictionaries, and language translation books are also in another area. Calendar and timeline books are elsewhere, as are telephone directories and other people-finder materials. The list goes on and on. And hopefully, in the course of your library visits, you are utilizing *all* of the resources there already, and not just the genealogy books.

Let's explore a number of additional Internet-based resources that may be of help to you in your research. In the following sections, I will suggest some examples of Internet searches to help you locate materials for that genre, and will include some of my favorite sites for your review and enjoyment. Your job in all of this is to search for materials that will be of use in your own research, *and* to incorporate these tools into your search strategies.

Online Map Resources

Maps are an essential part of your research work. It is imperative that you use historical maps to locate precisely where your ancestors lived at the time they were there. Contemporaneous historical maps, compared with today's maps, can help you focus in on the places where documents may now reside. Political boundaries have altered tremendously over the centuries. Nations have come and gone, counties and provinces have been formed and divided into smaller, more easily governed areas, towns have been founded and disappeared, places have been renamed, and some places have simply disappeared. It is therefore important to be able to locate historical maps, atlases, and gazetteers (place name dictionaries) of all types.

Following are some examples of Internet searches that might be of help to you. Substitute the place name you are seeking for the one(s) shown in the following examples. Please note that Boolean search characters + and – are being used, as are the double quotation marks (" ") that form an exact phrase. You may use any search engine you like, and may want to use the Advanced Search facility to exclude some materials. For example, for the map searches, perhaps you will want to exclude commercial sources and therefore use the Advanced Search facility to exclude the .com sites from your results. (Remember: You've learned a lot already about how to search the Internet more effectively. Don't slip back into your old ways!)

map "south carolina"
map persia
atlas Georgia 1895
gazetteer ireland 1800s -site:.com

(This search was conducted using Google, and locates pages with the words "gazetteer," "Ireland," and "1800s," and excludes the commercial [.com] sites. Be sure to check the Help of your favorite search engine to verify the correct format for including and excluding specific domains and other data.)

I have a number of favorite websites where I find historical maps. I encourage you to try some of these terrific resources for yourself:

- Perry-Castañeda Library Map Collection   **www.lib.utexas.edu/maps**
- David Rumsey Historical Map Collection   **www.davidrumsey.com**
- Library of Congress Geography & Map Division   **www.loc.gov/rr/geogmap**
  The Library of Congress Geography & Map Reading Room website is an excellent

place to begin searching the facility's extensive collection. Be sure to visit the American Memory Map Collections page at **http://lcweb2.loc.gov/ammem/ gmdhtml/gmdhome.html**.

- The U.S. Geological Survey's Geographic Names Information System (GNIS)   **http://geonames.usgs.gov**
  This is a database that is searchable by name and also by *Feature Class*, such as cemetery, to locate places. The resulting list will provide you all known sites. Select one and you'll be supplied with the latitude and longitude, and if you scroll down you will see an option to click a link titled Show Feature Location, and this will access and display a map for you from the U.S. Census Bureau's Tiger Map Server. This is a great resource for traveling, and the latitude and longitude are excellent if you plan to use a GPS unit to help locate a place.

Dictionaries

There are hundreds of sources for dictionaries online, for English and for other languages that may be helpful for translation purposes. Some excellent sites may be found in the following directories:

- Librarians' Internet Index, under the Reference category   **http://lii.org**
- The Internet Public Library, under Ready Reference   **www.ipl.org**
- Wikipedia, the largest online reference compendium   **www.wikipedia.com**
- Yahoo! Directory in the Reference category   **http://dir.yahoo.com/Reference**

Language Translation

The SYSTRAN site (located at **www.systransoft.com**) remains one of the very best resources for language-to-language translation. The SYSTRAN *BOX* provides you with two methods you can use:

- You may type up to 150 words of text and translate it. This can be helpful when trying to translate foreign languages into English, or for translating into another language when writing letters of inquiry and for record copies.
- You may enter a web address and it will be translated from its original language into English or one of a number of other languages.

The Google Language Tools page at **www.google.com/language_tools** includes a language translation tool.

Please recognize that no online translation is ever going to be perfect. The idiomatic variations and vernacular may not translate well. However, the translation you obtain should be sufficient to help you gather the meaning of the text. For more precise translations, you may want to seek a professional or contact a college or university where students are learning the language. A professor may be willing to have a student assist you as a for-credit project.

Historical and Biographical Resources

Information abounds on the Internet about history and about the lives of notable or historical figures. The databases at Ancestry.com, at Footnote.com, at WorldVitalRecords.com, and in the HeritageQuest Online databases available in libraries and archives include a number of important resources in this area.

Wikipedia provides excellent historical and biographical reference articles. In addition, you can use your favorite search engine to search for information. (Remember to use your critical thinking skills to evaluate the authority of the information you find on websites.) Here are some examples of searches you might employ using your Internet browser and a search engine:

"george washington" biography
"george washington" genealogy
"richard ball" genealogy
pedigree "mark twain"
life "queen Victoria"–albert

Note in the last example that the minus sign (–) should be placed immediately in front of the word or phrase to be excluded. In this case, the search would attempt to exclude details about Prince Albert.

Calendars

You may find good use for calendars in your research. Remember that there was a switch from the Julian calendar to the Gregorian calendar in 1752 in Britain and the British Empire. The changeover in other parts of the world occurred at different times. A good place to find a reference table for the changeover is located at **http://en.wikipedia.org/wiki/Gregorian_calendar#Timeline**. You also can search for calendar converters using the keywords **julian gregorian jewish** and others as needed.

Perhaps you want to know on what day of the week an ancestral event occurred, in which case a perpetual calendar is just what you want. There are many on the Internet, but one of the easiest to use is at **www.wiskit.com/calendar.html**.

People Finders and Telephone Directories

In the course of your research, you are going to want to try to locate "lost relatives" and others. There are many online telephone and people finder resources on the Internet and most are geographically specific. Be aware that there are a couple of drawbacks to using these facilities:

- People with unlisted telephone numbers are not included in the telephone number and people finder databases.
- People's cellular telephone numbers are not included in these databases.

- Email addresses are seldom if ever updated. Therefore, if you find an old email address for someone, a message you send may not be delivered, and some email service providers do not generate "postmaster" messages indicating a failed delivery attempt.

Among the most prolific of the people finder facilities for U.S. residents and businesses are the resources shown in the list below. You will want to search regional versions of Yahoo! and Google for other countries to locate online telephone, email, and people finder services.

- Yahoo! People Search **http://people.yahoo.com**
- The Ultimates **www.theultimates.com**
- Internet Address Finder (IAF) **www.iaf.net**
- PeopleSpot **www.peoplespot.com**
- PeopleSearch.net **http://peoplesearch.net**
- superpages.com **www.superpages.com**

All of your reading and studying will not pay off until you apply what you've learned in a practical way—*and* do it on a regular basis. Throughout this book, you have learned the foundations for research and analysis, applying your critical thinking skills to both the traditional genealogical resources and items and to electronic materials of all sorts. All types of materials can, individually, be used as important tools for your investigative work. By themselves, they are great reference materials. However, when you combine them and work them in tandem with one another, they become a powerful toolkit for your work. That includes the home sources you have found, the documentary evidence you have located and personally reviewed, the databases you have researched, and the Internet resources you have accessed. It is important that you recognize how important working all of these together can be.

You're really on your way now!

12

Research and Verify Your Ancestors Using Genetic Genealogy (DNA)

HOW TO...

- Learn about DNA and its place in genealogical research
- Discover the difference between paternal and maternal testing and the results
- Determine what tests are appropriate for you and other family members
- Learn about genetic testing services
- Join a DNA surname project on the Internet
- Learn more about genetic genealogy

You've probably heard other genealogists talking about using DNA to assist with their research. One of the most recent additions to the genealogist's toolkit is genetic testing. Like learning how to use the Internet and databases, you'll want to learn about DNA and genetic testing in order to understand it and apply it in your own research. Because this chapter cannot possibly address everything about genetic genealogy, I'll discuss some basic concepts and then refer you to other books at the chapter's end that will provide you with an in-depth understanding.

We all have physical traits that distinguish us from one another. You've often heard the comment that someone has his mother's eyes, his father's hair coloring, or some other physical attribute. We know that genetics, the science of biology and heredity, plays a central role in how we are formed. Our genes provide the template for our physical development, from the single-cell fertilized egg to the human form that we become. The basis of this genetic template is DNA.

Learn About DNA and Its Place in Genealogical Research

DNA is an acronym for deoxyribonucleic acid, a chemical that is the blueprint for every cell in all living organisms and in some viruses. DNA molecules store the information and instructions for all the components of cells. DNA carries the genetic information, called genes, that is involved with how the entire organism is formed.

You may have heard the structure of DNA referred to as a "double helix." DNA physically consists of two long strands of organic material called nucleotides. The nucleotides are formed from sugars and phosphate groups that are joined together. These long strands run in opposite directions and form the twisted double helix. One of four types of molecules is attached to each sugar in each strand, and these molecules are called bases. The sequence of the bases is the coding that determines the genetic coding for each cell. The coding is replicated into ribonucleic acid, known as RNA, a single strand of nucleotides.

DNA is organized into structures called chromosomes, and these building blocks are duplicated before cells divide and replicate themselves. All of this information is integral to the creation of life. Scientists have been working for decades to decode the genetic sequences and understand the function of each gene. The Human Genome Project began in 1990 with the goal of identifying all of the human genes and to study their physical structure and their function.

Although this is a simple description of DNA, it will suffice for the rest of the discussion in this chapter.

Both genetics and genealogy focus on heredity:

- *Genetics* is a branch of biology that concentrates on scientific study of the heredity of an individual organism's physical traits. It also is used to demonstrate relationships between individuals.
- *Genealogy* is the study of families and includes tracing the lineage and history of families and demonstrating kinship and history. It seeks to establish proof of relationships from one generation to another.

As you can see, the two research disciplines share a somewhat common goal. DNA has been used in medical and forensic applications for quite some time. Amniocentesis is a method in which a small amount of a pregnant woman's amniotic fluid is removed and tested. It is an important procedure used to diagnose chromosomal irregularities and infections and employs genetic testing. Paternity tests use DNA to confirm or refute the relationship of a man to a child. We've also seen many episodes of television dramas in which DNA evidence has been used to identify a body, to determine the relationship between individuals, or to link a suspect to a crime scene or a victim.

DNA in your genealogy can similarly be used to prove or disprove relationships between individuals and family groups. While not as precise as forensic DNA analysis, modern DNA testing for genealogical purposes has advanced to include more genetic marker tests. These provide a broader range for comparison with other people's test results.

There are three timeframes with which DNA testing can help genealogists:

- **Modern Era**   This period covers the last 500 years, which encompasses the time when the first surnames began being used in England and elsewhere.
- **Historical Era**   This period includes the time before surnames were used; generally speaking between 1 A.D. and 1500 A.D. Written names were, however, recorded.
- **Ancient Era**   This period extends backward before the historical era. This is often referred to as the period of "deep genealogy" when it is possible only to trace migrations of groups.

Each of the three time periods can provide insights into your genealogical research and your deep geographical and ethnic heritage. The modern era is the period in which you are most likely to be able to achieve the most value from DNA testing in your genealogical research. However, the testing also can identify your haplogroup. *Haplogroups* are the main branches of the human genealogical tree, and they consist of haplotypes. *Haplotypes* are closely linked genes and genetic markers that are shared by a closely related group of people. These people typically are from a specific geographical area and/or part of the same ethnic origin. Haplogroups correspond to early human migrations between distinct geographical regions. Your haplogroup is indicative of your deep ancestral origin. Figure 12-1 shows an example of a haplogroup report from Ancestry.com.

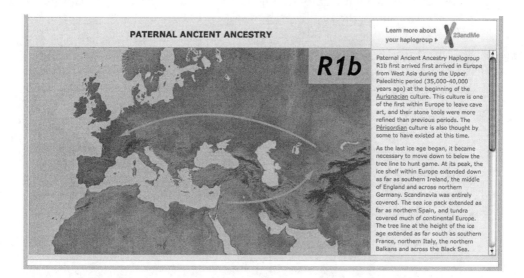

FIGURE 12-1   Sample of haplogroup results. (From the author's collection.)

Discover the Difference Between Paternal and Maternal Testing and the Results

DNA testing, also referred to as genetic profiling or genetic "fingerprinting," is used to identify individuals based on their DNA profile. You order a test kit from a DNA testing company. It typically consists of two or more sterile cotton swabs, an envelope that you seal and label, and a return mailer. The actual test consists of rubbing the cotton swabs inside your mouth. Your oral epithelial cells and saliva contain DNA, and it is that which is captured on the swab. You return the swabs to the testing company and, after some weeks, you receive your test results.

The test determines the values of a set number of markers, and the resulting values can be compared against other people's results. The test uses highly variable repeat sequences that can identify closely related individuals *or* differentiate between unrelated individuals. It also is used to study mutations in the marker values. It is both the similarities *and* the mutations that help determine the number of generations backward that there may be a "most recent common ancestor" (also referred to as the MRCA). The mutations occur at a comparatively regular rate, and these changes can be statistically used to project the number of generations between you and your MRCA.

It is important to know that humans, and most other mammals, have one pair of sex-determining chromosomes in each cell. Males have one Y chromosome and one X chromosome, while females have two X chromosomes. The Y chromosome is present only in males and can therefore reveal information only about the paternal line. The test for the Y chromosome is referred to as a Y-DNA or paternal DNA test. Figure 12-2 shows the results of my paternal DNA test.

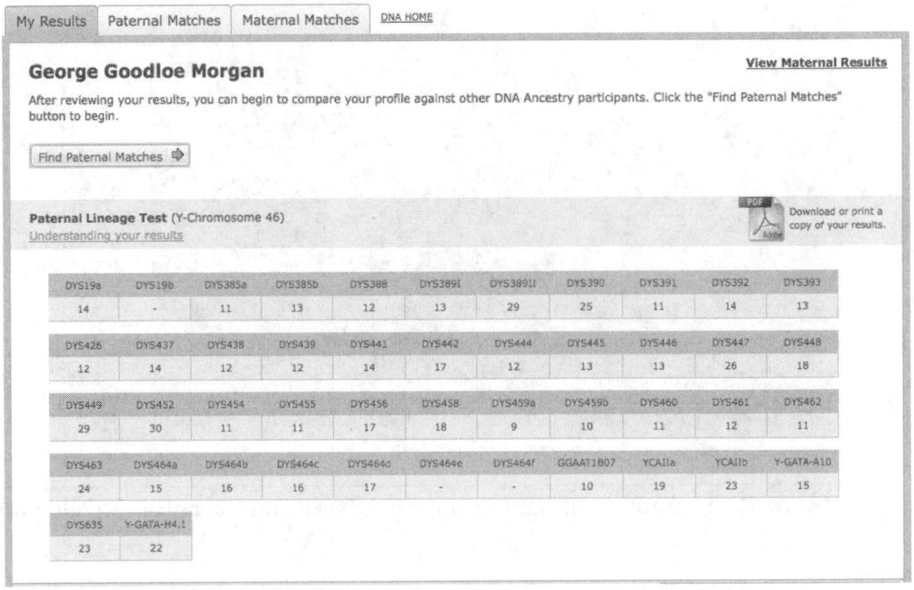

My Results | Paternal Matches | Maternal Matches | DNA HOME

George Goodloe Morgan

View Maternal Results

After reviewing your results, you can begin to compare your profile against other DNA Ancestry participants. Click the "Find Paternal Matches" button to begin.

Find Paternal Matches

Paternal Lineage Test (Y-Chromosome 46)

Understanding your results

Download or print a copy of your results.

DYS19a	DYS19b	DYS385a	DYS385b	DYS388	DYS389I	DYS389II	DYS390	DYS391	DYS392	DYS393
14	-	11	13	12	13	29	25	11	14	13

DYS426	DYS437	DYS438	DYS439	DYS441	DYS442	DYS444	DYS445	DYS446	DYS447	DYS448
12	14	12	12	14	17	12	13	13	26	18

DYS449	DYS452	DYS454	DYS455	DYS456	DYS458	DYS459a	DYS459b	DYS460	DYS461	DYS462
29	30	11	11	17	18	9	10	11	12	11

DYS463	DYS464a	DYS464b	DYS464c	DYS464d	DYS464e	DYS464f	GGAAT1B07	YCAIIa	YCAIIb	Y-GATA-A10
24	15	16	16	17	-	-	10	19	23	15

DYS635	Y-GATA-H4.1
23	22

FIGURE 12-2 Sample of Y-DNA test results. (From the author's collection.)

Mitochondria are structures within cells that convert energy from food into a form that cells can use. The mitochondria contain a small amount of their own DNA. This genetic material is known as mitochondrial DNA, or mtDNA. This mtDNA is passed only from mother to child, and there is usually no change from parent to child. It is therefore a powerful tool for tracing ancestry through the female line.

As a result, there are two types of DNA test available to assist in your genealogical research:

- **Y-DNA Test**   This is a test available only for males to help determine their direct paternal line.
- **mtDNA Test**   This is a test available to males and females to help trace their maternal line.

The Y chromosome can reveal that a man is related to other males—with the same surname or not. It indicates that there is a common male ancestor, but there may be no way to determine how many generations back that the MRCA lived. The value, however, is in comparing the Y-DNA test results with other people. We'll discuss this later in the chapter when we cover DNA surname projects.

The mtDNA test allows you to undertake research into the records of your mother's maternal ancestors. This can be a daunting task. However, the mtDNA test results can be used to definitively confirm your research and the relationships in your maternal lineage (see Figure 12-3).

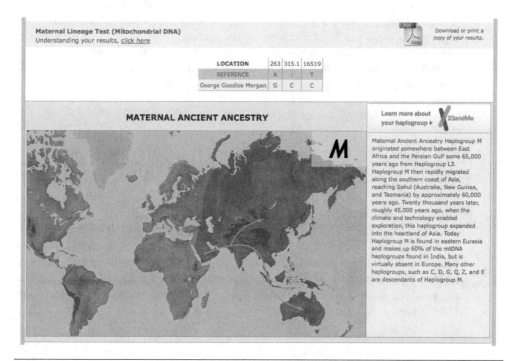

FIGURE 12-3   Sample of mtDNA test results. (From the author's collection.)

Genetic genealogy gives genealogists a means to check or supplement the historical record with information from genetic data. It can be used to solve gaps in your documentary research. However, there are other possibilities. A positive test match with another individual may

- Validate your existing research
- Suggest geographical areas for genealogical research
- Help determine the ancestral homeland and/or ethnic origin
- Discover living relatives
- Confirm or refute possible connections with other individuals and/or families
- Prove or disprove theories concerning ancestry

There also is resistance to DNA testing by some individuals. The reasons may include

- Uncertainty about which testing company to use
- Cost of the test
- Quality of the testing
- Variation in the number of markers tested by the companies
- Privacy issues
- Identity concerns

You may want to seek the participation of other relatives to help expand your genetic genealogy research. The Y-DNA and mtDNA tests each only trace a single lineage, such as your father's father's father's (etc.) lineage or your mother's mother's mother's (etc.) lineage. Many genealogists encourage cousins, aunts, and uncles to submit DNA test kits, even offering to pay for the testing in order to gather more sample data. You may want to consider this incentive approach in order to extend the range of your genetic research.

Learn About Genetic Testing Services

There are many commercial DNA testing services available. You will want to conduct a little research about the number of markers tested, the price of the tests, and any affiliations they may have with other companies and with surname DNA projects on the Internet. You may, in fact, be able to obtain a lower price as part of a surname group, discussed in the next section. Prices differ between the Y-DNA and mtDNA testing, and prices also vary between testing services, dependent on the number of markers tested and other factors. In the meantime, you want to select a testing service whose results are used for genealogical heritage purposes. A DNA paternity test kit and a forensic DNA testing service are not going to be of value to your genealogical research.

The following table lists some of the major DNA testing services. Some of these are ethnicity-specific and provide specialized test results.

23andMe	**https://www.23andme.com**
African Ancestry	**www.africanancestry.com**
DNA Ancestry	**http://dna.ancestry.com**
DNA Heritage	**www.dnaheritage.com**
DNA Tribes	**www.dnatribes.com**
Family Tree DNA	**www.familytreedna.com**
GeneTree	**www.genetree.com**
Jewish DNA Central	**www.jewishgen.org/dna**
Oxford Ancestors	**www.oxfordancestors.com**
Sorenson Molecular Genealogy Foundation	**www.smgf.org**

Join a DNA Surname Project on the Internet

Genealogists who have had their DNA tested are trying to locate matches to other researchers. This is particularly true of those who have had their Y-DNA tested and are seeking matches with others with the same surname. A surname DNA project is the ideal place to make connections with other researchers.

A surname project is a genetic genealogical project in which the results from Y-DNA testing are used to trace male lineage. Surnames are passed down from father to son in many cultures, and Y chromosomes are passed from father to son with a predictable rate of mutation. People who share the same surname can use genealogical DNA testing to determine if they share a common ancestor within recent history. It is certainly possible for persons with a different surname to share the same Y-DNA test results. Don't jump to any conclusions, however. Yes, there may have been an illegitimate child, but other factors may account for the discrepancy. There may have been a change of surname due to adoption; a man may have taken his wife's name; frequent misspelling of an earlier surname may have resulted in a man taking another surname; a surname may have been changed by a male immigrant in order to "fit in;" a nickname or alias may have been used and was then taken as the surname.

The results of a Y-DNA test checks the values of Y-chromosome markers. Depending on the number of markers tested, the results can be compared to someone else's results and can reveal whether the two individuals share a common male ancestor. The number of markers tested and the number of matches at those markers determines the range of generations until their most recent common ancestor (MRCA) would be expected. Let's say that two men are tested using 37 genetic markers. If the two tests match on 37 markers, there is a 50 percent probability that the MRCA was less than 5 generations ago and a 90 percent probability that the MRCA was less than 17 generations ago. A further comparison with other persons' test results might indicate a familial relationship.

A DNA surname project takes the comparison another step. By joining such a project on the Internet, you not only share your test results, but also provide documentation of that surname in your ancestry back to the earliest known male ancestor in that surname line. The administrator of the project adds your test results into a grid that allows for easy comparison of each marker's value with that of other people. The name of each participant's earliest documented ancestor is included, as is his or her haplotype. (See the example in Figure 12-4.) The results are typically grouped together by haplotype and infer clustering. You can make contact with other researchers, usually with the project administrator acting as intermediary to help preserve each person's identity and privacy until they both may indicate their desire to communicate directly. You can then share more detailed genealogical information and collaborate to further one another's research.

#	Kit	Last Name	Haplo	393	390	19	391	385a	385b	426	388	439	389i	392	389ii	458	459a	459b	455	454	447	437	448	449	464a	464b	464c	464d	460	GATA H4	YCAIIa	YCAIIb	456	607	576	570
E1b1a (was E3a)																																			
1	N29270	Currie	E1b1a	13	21	17	10	18	18	11	12	12	13	11	30																					
2	A1574	Wilson	E1b1a	14	21	16	10	16	16	11	12	12	13	11	31	18	8	10	11	11	26	14	21	31	13	16	16	18								
E1b1b1 (was E3b)																																			
3	94078	Wilson	E1b1b1	13	23	13	10	15	16	11	12	11	13	11	31	17	9	9	11	11	25	14	20	34	14	15	15	17	11	11	19	22	15	12	18	18
4	115432	Wilson	E1b1b1	13	23	13	10	15	16	11	12	12	13	11	31	17	9	9	12	11	25	14	20	34	14	15	15	17	11	11	19	22	15	12	18	18
5	54348	Wilson	E1b1b1	13	24	13	10	15	19	11	12	12	13	11	30																					
6	75825	Wilson	E1b1b1	13	24	13	10	16	18	11	12	12	11	11	29	15	9	9	11	11	26	14	20	33	14	16	17	17	9	11	19	21	18	12	16	19
7	74582	Wilson	E1b1b1	13	24	14	10	16	18	11	12	11	13	11	30	15	6	9	11	11	26	14	20	30	15	15	16	18								
8	115118	Wilson	E1b1b1	13	24	14	10	17	19	11	12	11	13	11	30																					
9	54449	Wilson	E1b1b1a3	13	24	14	10	17	19	11	12	11	13	11	30	15	9	9	11	11	26	14	20	31	15	15	16	18	10	12	19	22	15	12	17	20
10	84491	Wilson	E1b1b1	13	24	14	10	18	19	11	12	11	13	11	29																					
11	25780	Wilson	E1b1b1	13	25	13	10	16	18	11	12	12	13	11	31	14	9	9	11	11	26	14	20	31	14	16	16	18	10	11	19	21	17	12	17	20
G2																																			
12	63174	Wilson	G	13	22	15	10	13	14	11	13	11	12	11	28	16	9	9	11	11	23	16	21	30	12	13	13	14	10	11	20	20	15	12	15	18
13	N54969	Wilson	G	14	22	15	10	14	14	11	13	11	12	11	29																					
14	9951	Wilson	G2a	14	22	15	10	14	15	11	13	11	12	11	30	14	9	9	11	11	24	16	21	31	12	13	13	14	11	10	20	20	15	13	15	18
15	105757	Wilson	G2a	14	23	16	11	15	15	11	12	12	12	11	28	16	9	9	11	11	23	16	22	31	12	13	14	14	10	11	20	21	15	13	16	20

FIGURE 12-4 Portion of the Wilson Surname DNA Project page

Learn More About Genetic Genealogy

There is obviously much more that you can learn about genetic genealogy and using DNA test results in your research. There are some excellent books available on the subject. I personally recommend all of the following titles:

- Fitzpatrick, Colleen, and Andrew Yeiser. *DNA & Genealogy*. Fountain Valley, CA: Rice Book Press, 2005.
- Pomery, Chris. *Family History in the Genes*. Kew, Richmond, Surrey, UK: The National Archives, 2007.
- Smolenyak, Megan, and Ann Turner. *Trace Your Roots with DNA: Using Genetic Tests to Explore Your Family Tree*. Emmaus, PA: Rodale, Inc., 2004.

The possibilities offered by DNA testing are increasing and improving each year. You will want to incorporate genetic genealogical research into your research toolkit, and gain another strong research facility for your family history.

13

Follow Alternative Research Paths to Locate Difficult Records

HOW TO...

- Recognize when you have hit a "brick wall"
- Take a fresh look at old documentation
- Reevaluate the quality of your sources
- Widen the scope of your search to include new and different sources
- Use photographs
- Develop an ancestor profile/timeline
- Switch to another family member to bypass your roadblock
- Seek help from libraries, archives, and societies
- Engage the help of a professional researcher

Inevitably you will confront the genealogist's worst nightmare: the dreaded "brick wall." Despite all your best research efforts, your careful assessment of the evidence, documentation, facts, the quality of your source materials, and your best hypotheses, you'll find you just can't progress any farther. It happens to all of us, but the situation isn't always hopeless.

We have explored the most common types of record types, and you have learned about methodologies for using them to discover and document more about your ancestral families. There are literally hundreds of other types of records and artifacts that may provide valuable clues or data to expand your research. The chapter will provide an introduction to some of these resources.

Recognize when You Have Hit a "Brick Wall"

Sometimes the people you think are going to be the simplest to locate become a research nightmare. Every avenue you explore seems to come to an abrupt dead end. One of the most frustrating things is not being able to locate even the most basic vital or civil records that should have been where you expected to find them. Worse, however, is the discovery that the person who you *thought* was your ancestor and in whom you've invested so much research effort actually is not related to you at all. You've been researching someone *else's* ancestor!

Unfortunately, it is easy to become so consumed with the "ordinary" search that you may not even realize you've hit the proverbial "brick wall." You may think that the next record is just around the corner when, in fact, you may never find another record for the person in the place you've identified as the "correct location." Now is the time to step back, put all your knowledge and experience to the test, and employ your most creative thought processes to locate alternative sources. The work you've done to hone your critical thinking skills can provide a big payoff.

There are several keys to solving your problem. The first thing to do is to recognize the fact that you really *do* have a brick wall, and that you haven't just made an oversight. Identify and literally describe the scope and symptoms of the problem. Write a description of your problem, including what you know to be fact and the sources of every fact in evidence. Include what you *want* to find out, what you *already* have searched, and the results you have *or* have not achieved. Often, just putting the facts and the actions you've already taken into words on paper can help focus your attention on the real issues. Here are examples of just a few of the more common categories of research brick walls you can expect to encounter:

- You can locate no records for your ancestor—anywhere!
- You cannot identify your ancestor's parents or cannot link him or her with people who you believe are the parents.
- Records have been lost, stolen, destroyed, or transferred elsewhere.
- Records that you want to access are private, restricted, or entirely closed to the public.
- No resources can be found on Internet web pages, in Internet-based genealogical subscription databases, and/or in those databases accessible through libraries and archives.

Using your written description of the problem *and* the resources you have already researched, now develop a list of alternative research paths, records, and other sources that might help resolve the problem. You may need to conduct some additional research to put your ancestor into geographical, historical, and/or social context and to determine what records might or might not exist to help you locate more information. You may not know about all the various alternative resources that might be available. Your continued reading, research, and collaboration with other genealogists can help you learn about these resources and how to maximize your use of them. Here are some examples of problems and possible solutions.

Problem: A Person's Parents Cannot Be Identified

The person's parents cannot be identified or traced. This is perhaps the most common brick wall genealogists face. Moving backward one more generational step can be exceptionally challenging.

Possible Solutions   Search for ecclesiastical records for your person that may indicate previous membership in another congregation elsewhere. I was able to trace one of my grandfathers from the church in North Carolina in which he was a member at the time of his death back to the church in which his family were members in Georgia, then back to another church in Alabama, and finally to the church in Tennessee in which he was christened. Another possible solution, which we will discuss in further detail later in the chapter, involves researching one or more family members.

Problem: A Person's Previous Place of Residence Can't Be Identified

The person's previous place of residence cannot be identified or traced. This is perhaps the second most common brick wall genealogists face.

Possible Solutions   The ecclesiastical membership record search could work here as well. Common alternative records to help locate previous places of residence include voter registration records, school records, census indexes and population schedules, immigration and naturalization documents, land and tax records, probate packet inventories and heir lists showing property ownership and/or the residences of heirs in other locations, military service records, and obituaries.

Problem: Records Are Missing or Have Been Destroyed

The records you wanted or expected to find are missing, lost, or have been destroyed. Records do disappear, sometimes through misfiling and sometimes by having been removed or stolen. Consider my dismay to find evidence of an ancestor's considerable estate documented in probate court minutes, only to find that the entire probate packet was not in the probate clerk's files. The will and the executor's/administrator's documentation could have provided definitive proof of the names of my ancestor's children and whether they were living or deceased at the time of his death. It could have identified other relatives, land and property holdings, and other pointers to other documentation.

Possible Solutions   Locate all the probate court minutes for hearings concerning the estate. Some of the probate file materials may actually have been read into evidence in the probate court minutes when the report was introduced. Seek newspaper announcements concerning the settlement of the estate. Determine the name(s) of the executor/administrator(s) of an estate through the use of probate court's minutes, and then check the probate files in the event your ancestor's packet was incorrectly filed under the executor/administrator's name rather than under your ancestor's or family member's name. In addition, it is not unheard of to find that a probate packet was removed by a lawyer or other representative and retained in that person's professional files. Investigate the possible existence of transcriptions, extracts, or abstracts of the original will in books, genealogical society publications, and elsewhere. Contact libraries, archives, and genealogical and historical societies to determine if they are aware of the existence and/or disposition of the records you are seeking.

Some of the records you seek may actually have been microfilmed after they were separated, and your research may require that you reunite and reconstruct the different materials from different locations.

Problem: Records Have Been Discarded or Destroyed

The records you are seeking have been discarded or destroyed. Perhaps the courthouse or other government repository ran out of space and determined that records older than a certain date were no longer needed. Originals of records may have been microfilmed and then destroyed, and then the microfilm might have been lost. There may have been a fire, tornado, hurricane, earthquake, flood, or other calamity in which the courthouse or archive was damaged or destroyed, and records were lost.

Possible Solutions   Consider substitute records that might provide identical or similar information. Contact archives, libraries, and genealogical and historical societies that might have acquired or salvaged any records. Investigate the possible existence of transcriptions, extracts, or abstracts of the original materials made or published prior to the records' loss. Don't overlook the possibility that records could have been duplicated and sent/transferred to another agency.

Problem: Records Were Destroyed During Wartime

Records were destroyed during a time of war. Contrary to what you may have heard, General William Tecumseh Sherman did *not* destroy every courthouse in his march through Georgia during the U.S. Civil War. However, some county government buildings and their records were lost. During World War II, there was so much bombing and fire damage in Antwerp, Belgium, that only a few individual ships' passenger lists survived.

Possible Solutions   Look for possible duplicate or substitute records. Investigate the possibility that the records were copied or microfilmed prior to their loss, that transcripts were published elsewhere, or that indexes survived when the actual records did not.

Problem: No Evidence Exists That a Person Lived in a Certain Place

There is no evidence the person ever lived in that place. Your research has led you to a specific place where, no matter what type of records you investigate, there are no records that your ancestor was ever there.

Possible Solutions   Perhaps the lead you had was incorrect. Or maybe the governmental jurisdiction has changed and the records are really in another place. Stop and reexamine all of your information to look for clues you may have missed or information that may have been incorrect.

Problem: Names and Dates Don't Fit

The names and/or dates are all wrong. I was searching for the origin of one of my great-great-grandfathers, Jesse Holder. I knew he lived in Georgia after he was married, but U.S. federal censuses indicated he was born in North Carolina. Searches of records in North Carolina yielded nothing, and so I transferred my attention to the possibility that he may have lived in South Carolina during some period. I found a Jesse Holder in Laurens County, South Carolina. Unfortunately, his year of birth didn't seem to fit. I then determined that this Jesse Holder had married another woman and had died prior to when my great-grandfather was born in Georgia. My own Jesse Holder had been born on 13 August 1810 in North Carolina, and the other Jesse Holder had been born well before his inclusion as a head of household in the 1790 U.S. federal census. That Jesse may, in fact, have been the uncle and person after whom *my* maternal great-great-grandfather was named. As you can see, I still have research to do.

Possible Solutions   Retrace the research steps to determine if you are on the right track or took a wrong turn. Look also in the same area for other branches of the same family that really might be yours. Naming patterns sometimes show that children may have been named for one of the parents' parents, an aunt or uncle, or a sibling.

Problem: You Can't Link Your Ancestor with Possible Family Members

There is no discernable link between *your* ancestor and the people you think could be the parents, siblings, spouse, and/or other relatives.

Possible Solutions   Examine census records in the area in which your person lived and look for other persons in the vicinity with the same surname, and begin to research them. Examine wills, probate records, and ecclesiastical records and look for any family relationship or common denominator linking them together. Consider cemetery records and monumental descriptions to help you relate persons to one another, and then conduct research on those people.

Problem: Person Has Vanished

The person has just simply vanished into thin air. (I call this the "my ancestor was abducted by an alien spaceship" problem.)

Possible Solutions   Reexamine census records for your ancestor *and* for the four to six neighboring families on either side of your ancestor. Locate your ancestor in the last census where you found him or her. Look, then, at the next available census for the neighbors. If they are all still in the same place and your ancestor is gone, you know you have looked in the correct place. If one or more of the neighbors also is gone, start looking for your ancestor *and* the neighbor in available census indexes in that location and surrounding parishes, counties, provinces, or states. Work in concentric circles, using a map and considering the migration routes and social trends of the time, and move outward seeking your ancestor in records that might likely have been created at the time. For example, if you know your ancestor was a Methodist, start looking at Methodist church membership records. Look for voter registration records if the period coincides with a major national election year. Check land and property records to determine if there was a change in property ownership—property sold, different property purchased, relocation to another location, *or* reference to the death of the property owner and the inheritance by an heir.

Problem: Adoption Records Are Sealed

Adoption records are sealed by a court and not accessible to the public.

Possible Solutions   Formally petition the court in whose jurisdiction the adoption took place for access to names and dates of the parties. Be prepared to demonstrate your relationship to any and all parties. (Be sure to check the more recent legislation of the locations involved, as some of these adoption records are being made available, especially in the United States.)

Problem: Records Are Private

The records you want are the property of a private corporation and you are refused access to them.

Possible Solutions   Prepare evidence of your relationship to the person whose records you require and a solid reason for your request. Instead of access to the entire body of records, request an exact extract of the content you want to obtain. If you are refused, be prepared to escalate your request to the headquarters and/or executive officer(s) of the corporation. I have used this tactic in order to access personnel records and funeral home/mortuary records of individual family members.

These examples are not, of course, comprehensive in the scope of possible alternative sources and strategies, but they will give you some ideas to contemplate. Again, it is important to understand your ancestor in context, *all* of the record types that might have been created, possible repositories, and individuals and organizations that may be of help to you.

Take a Fresh Look at Old Documentation

One strategy that I constantly use is the reexamination of documentation and other evidence that I collected previously. It amazes me how much information can be gleaned from taking a fresh look at something that I thought I knew so well.

Remember that over time you will gather new evidence; learn more about history, geography, and other influences; and become acquainted with new people in your family history. Let me give you a good example of how just reexamining census population schedules clarified my research.

My great-grandmother, Caroline Alice Whitefield, was born on 23 August 1853 to William A. Whitefield (also spelled Whitfield) and his second wife, Sophia D. Briggs. Caroline was their fourth and last child. William had fathered nine other children by his first wife, Rozella H. Moore, who died on 25 September 1841. William died on 18 September 1857 and Sophia died on 29 April 1859, both in Person County, North Carolina. Guardianship was granted in Person County in September of 1857, following her father's death, to Caroline's 35-year-old half-brother, LeGrande Whitefield of Montgomery County, Tennessee. I could not find Caroline with LeGrande in the 1860 census, nor could I locate her in North Carolina. However, in working my way through the U.S. federal census of 1870, a portion of which is shown in Figure 13-1, I found Caroline living in the home of Dolphin D. Villines (age 52) and his wife, Emily (age 49), and 80-year-old Sallie Villines, in Person County. When I first acquired the census page in 1989, I did not know why Caroline might be living with this family. It was not until 1999 when I reexamined the record that I realized that Emily Villines was, in fact, Sophia's older sister. Her maiden name had been Emily L. Briggs.

In the intervening years between examining the census population schedule, I had learned more about the family and had actually researched both of William Whitefield's wives' lineages. The connection between the Whitefield and Villines families would not have been clear unless I had reexamined the 1870 census. I now knew that, even though guardianship had been granted to LeGrande Whitefield, he did *not* relocate his half-sister to Tennessee to live with him and his wife. Instead, she remained in the area where she was born and lived with her maternal aunt and uncle.

Even though you think you are familiar with the details of all the evidence you have located for a particular ancestor or family member, look at it again. I like to organize the materials in chronological sequence and read through it all, page by page, as if it is a biography. This gives me a sense of order to the life of the individual. By approaching the person's life story sequentially as documents and other materials were produced, I begin to get to really know and understand the person better. Sometimes this is extremely helpful because, knowing their history, I may be able to anticipate a decision about migration, settlement, occupation, or some other life factor. Try it for yourself and see what you learn.

FIGURE 13-1   Portion of the 1870 U.S. federal census showing Caroline Whitefield in the home of her aunt and uncle. (Used with permission of The Generations Network, Inc.)

Reevaluate the Quality of Your Sources

Scholarly work is one of the foremost goals of genealogical research and we are therefore always searching for the best evidence we can find. It is certainly gratifying to locate an original marriage certificate, created at the time of the marriage and bearing the actual signatures of the bride and groom. Few things are as exciting as holding and touching a document that was handled and signed by our ancestors and that was as important to them as a marriage certificate. The next best thing, of course, is seeing a facsimile of such a document on a photocopy, on microfilm, or as a digitized image. You already know that there are more and more digitized images being made available on the Internet every month.

Not all of our source materials, however, can be such excellent forms of evidence. As you've learned, genealogists work with primary *and* secondary sources; with data transcribed, extracted, and abstracted from original documents; and with a vast array of published materials in all types of formats. In our quest to locate facts about our family, we often must use sources that may be one or more times removed from original source material, and often this information is less than 100 percent accurate. There is something lost in the transfer, diluted as it were, and it is for that reason that we must maintain a keen awareness of primary *vs.* secondary materials and be prepared to carefully analyze the quality of our sources.

I often tell fellow genealogists, "Two secondary sources do not a primary source make." Perhaps it sounds a little corny, but it is emphatically true. I recommend maintaining a healthy skepticism of almost any information until its authority can be proved, and evaluate the weight that it may provide to the big picture.

One major factor contributing to many of our research brick walls can be a problem with the quality of the information we may have obtained from source materials. It is important to take a giant step back from a problem and reexamine all of our evidence. I don't mean "just" the secondary sources, but everything. As I said earlier, a great way to do this is to arrange every piece of evidence you have in the chronological sequence as it may have occurred in the ancestor's life. Reread everything in order. You are sure to find gaps in what you know. In the meantime, reexamine where your information was derived. What you may think is a solid fact may be well documented by a less than excellent source. Let me give you an example.

A friend in Georgia hit a brick wall in her search to prove the identities of the parents of her grandmother and locate other documentation about them. She had a death certificate for her grandmother that documented the date of death as 4 October 1935 and indicated the place of burial was to be in Munford, Alabama. It indicated that her grandmother had been born on 22 June 1859 in Atlanta, Georgia, and that she was 78 at the time of her death. The only information my friend had about the names of her great-grandparents came from the death certificate, and she inferred from the place of birth listed on her grandmother's death certificate that her great-grandparents had lived in Atlanta.

You will remember that a death certificate can be one of those "combination" sources: a primary source for the death information and a secondary source for everything else. My friend knew that well, but still had entered the information she found on the death certificate into her genealogical database and documented the source. However, in her concentration on locating documentation on her great-grandparents, she failed to recognize that the *only* information she had about their names and the place they lived was the information on this death certificate. It turned out that the informant who provided the information for the death certificate was a nephew, and that he did not know the facts about the date and place of birth, the names of the parents, and their place of residence. One glaring error was in the age shown on the certificate. Wait a minute! When I subtract 1859 from 1935, I come up with 76, not 78! Something was amiss here. And why was she to be buried in Alabama?

My friend backed up and began her research again, this time with a fresh perspective. She knew that she had made an error in judgment and assumed that the names, dates, and locations on the death certificate were "probably correct." She now knew that she needed to search for additional source materials. Her next step was to begin again with what she really knew to be factual based on primary sources. She developed a list of document sources that might be available and that might help her solve her research problem. She did some research to determine where those documents might be located, and then began making contact with those locations to see what she could obtain by mail or email. She ultimately arranged to make two short trips to conduct research on-site.

After about a year, she told me that she had solved some problems and had finally gotten around her brick wall. There were four important pieces of information she had obtained from other materials that helped her:

- She located a copy of her grandmother's obituary, which indicated that she grew up in Greensboro, Georgia. It listed her age as 78, and not 76, and confirmed that burial was to occur in Munford, Alabama.
- She traveled to Alabama and located the cemetery where her grandmother was buried. Her grandmother's grave was next to that of her grandfather in *his* family's cemetery lot. That made sense. She also noted on her grandmother's gravestone the birth date of 22 June 1857, yet another confirmation of the age of 78 and not 76 years.
- She reexamined her grandparents' marriage certificate and noted the marriage date of 24 November 1881 and the place of issue as Greene County, Georgia. As it was customary for a bride to be married at home or in her church, my friend believed it made sense to pursue research in Greene County, Georgia, and not in Atlanta.
- She traveled to Greensboro, Georgia, to search for records of her grandmother's family. She located microfilmed copies of the local newspaper in the public library and began searching for marriage announcements. She found the announcement in a newspaper dated Thursday, 8 September 1881, and the notice included her grandmother's name, the name of her fiancé, and the names of *both* sets of parents and their places of residence.

Armed with the new information, my friend continued her research in Greene County, Georgia, and located a vast amount of information about her grandmother's family. She found church records, land and property records, tax rolls, and a probate packet for her great-grandfather in which all of his children's names were listed. Knowing the correct county, she continued by working with the 1880 federal census records to verify the family's residence there, the names of the children, and their ages. Furthermore, my friend learned that her great-grandfather had been the county sheriff for many years, including at the time that her grandmother had been born in 1857. She is now trying to determine whether her grandmother really had been born in Atlanta or in Greensboro, Georgia. However, that is another research story.

My friend's story is not uncommon. Even though her brick wall is a comparatively simple problem, it illustrates how a small error in judgment can result in a major blockage in a person's research. It required stepping back and reexamining the source material, followed with the development of an additional research plan, and some concentrated research to get around her brick wall. Since that time, she has extended her research to include other of her grandmother's siblings and has been able to identify and document her great-grandmother's parents and grandparents. She is still on the right research track, and she has extended her factual evidence by two more generations at last report.

Widen the Scope of Your Search to Include New and Different Sources

One of the joys of genealogy is learning about different resources that can be used to document your family history. Discovery of these materials is exciting and invariably leads to a desire to learn more about them. I remember my excitement at learning about transit permits, those documents that are used to facilitate the transport of bodies across state or national borders to a hometown or some other place of interment. A transit permit can contain a great deal of information about the individual and, prior to the use of official death certificates, can provide details about the cause of death. In the course of my research, I have encountered transit permits in cemeteries' files for soldiers in the U.S. Civil War who died in battle or from disease. I even found a death certificate for my great-uncle, Luther Moffett Holder, who died of tuberculosis en route by train from New Mexico to Georgia. A digital image found on Footnote.com gave me the documentary proof I needed to confirm his death in 1908 (see Figure 13-2).

I've also seen transit permits for a woman killed by a train, people killed by gunshot wounds, several suicides, and for people who died from any number of different diseases. Transit permits that allowed the transport of Civil War soldiers' bodies from one state to another may still be inside cemeteries' administrators' files or inscribed in interment books. These may be the only records of the causes of death of these soldiers. This certainly is not unusual in the offices of administrators and sextons in Canada, the United Kingdom, Australia, and in other places worldwide.

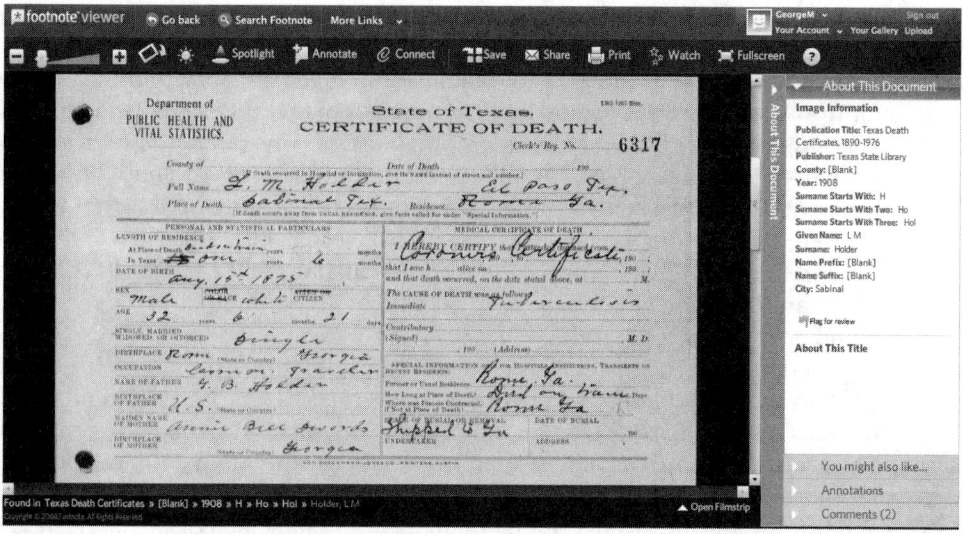

FIGURE 13-2 Death certificate of the author's great-uncle, Luther Moffett
Holder. (Used with permission of Footnote.com.)

There are literally hundreds of documents you might never have imagined existed
that could help you document your ancestors and family members. Beyond the record
types I've covered in this book, you will want to consider other sources. How do you
find out about them? Well, there are all sorts of books available that can introduce you
to descriptions and samples of these records. Let me share a few of my favorites.

Hidden Sources: Family History in Unlikely Places, by Laura Szucs Pfeiffer, is a
compilation of more than a hundred different record types that may be of help to your
personal research. Each record type is described in detail, along with information
about places where it can be located and how it can be used. You will find an
illustration included for each record and a bibliography for additional reading and
reference. Some of the more interesting records are almshouse records, coroner's
inquests, bankruptcies, Freedmen's Bureau records, name change records, orphan
asylum records, passport records, school censuses, street indexes, post office guides
and directories, patent records, and voter registration records.

Another excellent compilation is *Printed Sources: A Guide to Published Genealogical
Records*, edited by Kory L. Meyerink. This impressive book contains authoritative chapters
concerning different record categories, written by a number of eminent genealogical
experts. For example, if you are looking for a more thorough understanding of U.S.
military records, David T. Thackery's chapter, "Military Sources," is a comprehensive
study of what types of records are available and a selective description of published
sources for major military conflicts. Records at the federal, colonial, and state level are
addressed in detail; histories, rosters, and important reference works are described; and
a vast, definitive biography is included.

A study of English parish records requires some understanding of the structure of the parish system *and* of the social responsibilities of the parish officer. *The Compleat Parish Officer* is a reprint by the Wiltshire Family History Society of a 1734 handbook for those persons "who had to apply and interpret the increasingly complex laws enacted to deal with the various social problems as they arose, its starting point being the Great Poor Law Act of 1601 and its various amendments." This compact little book details the authorities and responsibilities of parish constables, churchwardens, overseers of the poor, surveyors of the highways and scavengers, and other officials in the parish operational hierarchy. It is an invaluable primer for genealogists and family historians in understanding the English parish environment and the records that are found documenting your ancestors.

A companion to *The Compleat Parish Officer* is Anne Cole's *An Introduction to Poor Law Documents Before 1834*. This volume describes the parish documents, explaining the reasons for each one's creation, the contents, and what can be gleaned from them. The settlement certificate, for example, was an exceptionally important document for those to whom it was issued. It provided legal proof of residence in the parish and thus, in time of need, entitled the person to financial assistance. However, more importantly, the settlement certificate was used to provide permission to persons to relocate their place of residence from one parish to another. These two books, used together, provide excellent insight for the researcher of English parish records.

And do you have an ancestor who was a midwife in 17th- or 18th-century England? If you do, or if you are simply interested in childbirth in this period, Joan E. Grundy's book *History's Midwives* is a fascinating read. Childbirth was a dangerous process in those times and many women died in labor. Midwifery became an important medical profession and midwives were required by law to be licensed. The requirements for their licensing and their responsibilities are documented in this book. Examples of licensing documentation are included. The author has prepared and included an index of 17th- and 18th-century midwives nomination lists from Yorkshire for those family historians who have an ancestor who was a midwife.

The few examples I've provided here merely begin to scratch the surface of the wide range of record types that can be found and used for your genealogical documentation. I urge you to use the resources of library and archive catalogs, particularly the subject and title search facilities of their online catalogs, to locate books of interest for these topics. In addition, you will find that using the bibliographies included in many genealogical and historical publications will lead you to more reference materials.

Use Photographs in Your Family Research

If you're like most people, you have a collection of photographs stored somewhere in your home. Many of these may be identified and labeled, but you probably have a group of unlabeled photographs that I refer to as "the unknowns." You will find that photographs can, indeed, be helpful in identifying persons and placing them in a specific place at a particular point in time.

Photographs have been around since the production of the first photographic image in the summer of 1826, which is universally credited to Frenchman Joseph Nicéphore Niépce. Over time, other processes and methods of mounting or displaying photographs were developed and introduced. You will find that the type of photograph and its physical attributes, the mountings used, the clothing worn by the subjects, and the background or surroundings can be used to date your photographs with surprising accuracy. It is important to understand a little history of photography first.

Learn About the Types of Photographs

Louis Daguerre's technique of capturing an image on a silver-clad copper plate was officially announced in 1839. These first commercially successful photographs were known as *daguerreotypes* and were, at the time, quite expensive. A daguerreotype was usually attached to a sheet of glass using a decorative frame made with a sheet of gold-colored heavy foil. The decoration was usually embossed into the foil material before enclosing the daguerreotype and its glass. This unit was then press-fitted into a wooden case specifically designed to hold a daguerreotype and sometimes padded with satin, silk, or velvet. The case also may have been a two-piece, hinged affair with a clasp that closed and protected the daguerreotype.

The *calotype* was the first paper photograph, and it was made using a two-step process. The first step involved treating smooth, high-quality writing paper with a chemical wash of silver nitrate. This wash process was performed in a dim, candlelit room and the paper was then exposed to a little heat until it was almost dry. While still somewhat moist, the paper was soaked in a solution of potassium iodide for several minutes, then rinsed and gently dried. The chemical processes in effect iodized the surface of the paper to prepare it for its ultimate exposure to light. The slow drying process preserved the smooth texture of the paper, preventing wrinkling and puckering of its surface. The iodized paper could be stored for some time in a dark, dry place at a moderate temperature. The second step occurred almost immediately before the iodized paper was to be used for a photograph. The photographer mixed a solution of equal parts of silver nitrate and gallic acid that, because of its inherent instability, had to be used right away. Once again, in dim candlelight, the iodized paper that had been prepared in the first step was dipped in this solution, rinsed with water, and blotted dry. It was then loaded in complete darkness into the camera and the calotype photographic image was captured. While the paper treated to the second solution could be dried and stored for use a short time later, the most reliable images were captured using paper still moist with the solution. Calotypes were made for perhaps a decade, from approximately 1845 until 1855. The main problem with them was that because the silver nitrate–gallic acid solution was not chemically stable, many of the images faded over a relatively short time. The surviving examples of many of these early calotypes appear as shadows or "ghosts" on the paper.

The *ambrotype* was introduced in 1854 and became very popular throughout the United States during the Civil War period. An ambrotype is a thin negative image bonded to a sheet of clear glass. When the negative image is mounted and displayed against a black background, the image appears as a positive. Ambrotypes were mounted in display cases much like those used for daguerreotypes.

Photography gained huge popularity in Great Britain when it was showcased at the Great Exhibition of 1851 in London. Both Queen Victoria and her husband, Prince Albert, were fascinated with photography and there are numerous photographs of the couple and other members of the Royal Family dating back to the 1840s. The public was introduced to several displays of photographs in various locations at the Exhibition and a subsequent increase in photographers' business in England has been attributed to that event.

The *tintype* was introduced in the early- to mid-1850s and was in use until the early 1930s. It became hugely popular in both the United States and Great Britain because it was cheap to produce and therefore accessible by almost everyone. Advertisements of the time touted them as the "penny photograph," and street photographers became commonplace sights in towns, cities, and at resort areas such as Brighton, England, and Atlantic City, New Jersey, and also at carnivals and fairs. Tintypes were extremely popular during the U.S. Civil War when soldiers wished to have a picture made of themselves in uniform with their rifle or sword to send home to loved ones. Since a tintype is an image made on metal instead of on a glass plate, it could be mailed without concern for breakage. There is no "tin" in a tintype; it actually is a thin sheet of black iron. The original name for the tintype was *melainotype*, but the more common name is *ferrotype*, which refers to the ferrous base on which the image is recorded. It has been suggested that the term "tintype" was derived from the use of tin sheers used to cut and trim the images on the metal plates. Many tintypes will be irregular in shape, such as the one shown in Figure 13-3, because of the imprecise trimming work. It is possible to narrow the dating of tintype

FIGURE 13-3   The irregular shape of this "tintype" is due to how the photographer cut the piece from the iron sheet. (From the author's collection.)

photographs produced during this extensive period based on a number of criteria, especially in the United States:

- **1856–1860**   The iron plate stock used in this period is thicker than at any other time, and plates are typically stamped on the edge with "Neff's Melainotype Pat 19 Feb 56." They may be found in gilded frames reminiscent of those used with ambrotypes or in leather sleeves.
- **1861–1865**   During the Civil War years, their paper display sleeves may help to date tintypes. These "frames" may bear patriotic symbols such as stars and flags, and early ones bear the imprint of Potter's Patent. After 1863, the paper holders became fancier, with designs embossed into the paper holder rather than printed. In an effort to raise revenue to help fund the Union Army, the U.S. Congress imposed a tax to be collected on all photographs sold between 1 September 1864 and 1 August 1866. A revenue stamp was required to be adhered to the reverse side of the photograph, either on the photographic plate itself or in the case. The tax was based on the amount of the sale, and these revenue stamps are highly prized by stamp collectors. Some photographers initialed the stamps to cancel them and included the day's date and this provides a precise date for the completion of the sale of the photograph.
- **1870–1885**   This period is referred to as the "Brown Period" because one company, the Phenix Plate Company, introduced a ferrous plate with a chocolate-tinted surface. Soon photographers across the United States were clamoring to use this new style of plate. The tintype shown in Figure 13-4 dates from this period.

FIGURE 13-4   Tintype photograph of the author's grandfather, Samuel Goodloe Morgan, taken circa 1880. (From the author's collection.)

You should also know that photographers began using painted backgrounds reflecting a "country" look, with fences, trees, stones, and other rural images in this time period. The painted rural background in these photographs is a telltale indicator that the photograph was made after 1870.

- **1863–1890** Photographer Simon Wing patented a multiplying camera that captured multiple images on a single plate. These photographs measured approximately .75" × 1" and became known and marketed as "Gem" or "Gem Galleries" photographs. These tiny portraits were typically mounted in ovals and attached to a larger mounting card. Some were even cut to fit into pieces of jewelry, such as lockets, cameo frames, cufflinks, and stickpins.

- **Circa 1866–1906** A new method of mounting photographs was introduced and is referred to as the "cabinet card." The photograph was adhered to a piece of cardboard stock. Early cabinet card stock is rather plain, with designs printed on the card. The type and color of the card stock and its decoration changed over the years, with embossed designs, colored inks, beveling, gilded or silvered card edges, and scalloped corners and edges being used at different periods. Photograph mountings were a point of high fashion, and you can use these distinctive traits, card sizes, and card thicknesses to date the period in which the photograph was made. The example shown in Figure 13-5 can be dated by the

FIGURE 13-5 This photograph of the author's great-grandmother, Ansibelle Penelope Swords Holder, was taken circa 1885. (From the author's collection.)

card stock to the period between 1880 and 1890 because the card stock is quite heavy, the front and back sides are of different colors, and the front surface is textured, rather than smooth. The woman's hairstyle indicates a bun worn high in the back. The not-so-high collar, the ornamental pleating on the shoulders of her dress, and the detailed, raised embroidery along the neckline and down the front of the bodice are indicative of fashion three to five years prior to the explosive couture of the 1890s.

- At the same time that cabinet cards were being used, other sizes and styles of photographic mountings came into use. One very popular format was a smaller mounting referred to as the *carte-de-visite*, or visiting card. These cards, like the example shown in Figure 13-6, typically measured 4 1/4" × 2 1/2" and were made of heavy, often glossy card stock. They became the rage and were used as souvenirs and, true to their name, were left as calling or visiting cards.
- Other popular styles and sizes included the Victoria (5" × 3 1/4"), the Promenade (7" × 4"), the Boudoir (8 1/2" × 5 1/4"), the Imperial, shown in Figure 13-7 (9 7/8" × 6 7/8"), the Panel (8 1/4" × 4"), and the stereograph (3" × 7").

FIGURE 13-6   A typical *carte-de-visite*. (From the author's collection.)

FIGURE 13-7   The Imperial size cabinet card was one of the larger, more formal photograph mountings and dates from circa 1900. (From the author's collection.)

- The stereoscope became a tremendously popular form of entertainment and education, beginning in approximately 1849 and continuing until the mid- to late-1920s. The apparatus consisted of a viewing hood with two lenses and an attached arm on which a sliding holder was mounted. The stereoscope was used to view *stereographs* such as the one shown in Figure 13-8, which depicts destruction following the San Francisco earthquake of 18 April 1906. A stereograph is a card on which two almost identical photographs are mounted side by side. When viewed with the stereoscope, the effect is that of a three-dimensional view of the subject. Tens of thousands of stereographs were made for the huge consumer demand for more and more subjects. In fact, you might draw an analogy between the stereograph and a modern television/DVD setup. People could not seem to get enough of them. Subjects included Civil War battlefields and scenes, world travel photographs, public figures, expositions such as the St. Louis and Pan-American Expositions, Americana, African-American subjects, children's games and antics, costumes, cemetery tours, and even series of stereographs telling a story.

- **Circa 1889 to Present**   Photography historians argue about who invented photographic film. However, an Englishman named John Carbutt, who also was an accomplished stereographer living and working in the United States, is credited with coating sheets of celluloid with a photographic emulsion while working in Philadelphia in 1888. In that same year, George Eastman introduced a new camera called the Kodak that used a roll of photographic film. The camera with the film still inside was sent to his company for processing, and the camera

10. Looking east from corner Ellis and Jones.

FIGURE 13-8   A stereograph looking east from the corner of Ellis and Jones in San Francisco, California, following the devastating earthquake on 18 April 1906. (From the author's collection.)

FIGURE 13-9 Photographs were printed to make personalized postcards, such as this one of the author's maternal grandmother on her honeymoon in Washington, D.C., in September 1908. (From the author's collection.)

and a new roll of film were returned to the customer. Within a year, the Kodak name was a household world in the United States, Great Britain, Canada, France, and elsewhere, and the public was hooked on photography. People even had a choice of the way photos were printed, including as a face side for a postcard. The photograph on the postcard in Figure 13-9 was taken by my maternal grandfather and shows my grandmother. The card is dated 18 September 1908, two days after they were married in Rome, Georgia, and was taken in Washington, D.C., on their honeymoon.

- Over the years, several film base materials and a number of emulsion processes were used, each having specific attributes. You can learn more about 20th-century photography and fashions in books on the subjects and on the Internet.

Date Photographs Using Clothing and Hair Fashions

You probably never knew there was so much to learn about photographs, did you? One of the best books on the subject of dating photographs is Maureen A. Taylor's *Uncovering Your Ancestry through Family Photographs.*

Don't overlook the fact that clothing and hairstyles shown in photographs can be very important research clues. Studio photographs were often made with the subject wearing his or her very best clothing, sometimes purchased specifically for the occasion. A photograph of a woman wearing a dress with a wasp waist and balloon sleeves, mounted on a cabinet card with a buff-colored, matte front and a dark-gray back, with gold beveled edge can be dated to within a year or so of its creation date. Add a printed or embossed studio name (and location), and you are helping to narrow the focus of your genealogical search to a time and place.

Be sure to examine photographs for tiny details that might yield clues. Pay attention to buildings, signage, the presence or absence of electric and telephone wires, the styles of wagons and carriages, the sizes of trees and shrubs, and every detail that might communicate location and time period. Researching an old photograph is much like reading between the lines in a book. Enlarge and enhance photographic images to bring out details.

There are a number of excellent books about dating photographs, costume and hairstyles, and other visual history materials that can provide excellent references for you. Search the Internet for such phrases as: "history of photography"; "costume history"; or specific searches such as "Victorian clothing," "women's dresses" + 1830s, history + "men's clothing" 1860s; or other combinations of keywords and/or phrases. There is a wealth of information available to help you narrow the date and place of your photographs.

Switch to Another Family Member to Bypass Your Roadblock

Sometimes, despite all your research, analysis, and troubleshooting efforts, an ancestral brick wall will just be entirely too contrary. Every effort at direct research may be thwarted. What can you do now?

One of my favorite techniques is what I call the "Genealogy Sidestep." This move is simple to perform and involves locating another close family member and switching your research focus. There have been times when I have encountered a brick wall in my research for one person and could not progress to the next generation. What I do then is review all I know about the person through compiling an ancestor profile. If I can identify a sibling or some other blood relative, I move to that person and begin conducting detailed research. I often have found that, while my ancestor may not have a very good paper trail, his or her brother or sister may have. As a result, by researching a sibling, I have sometimes been able to trace the sibling's parents and then, from one or both parents' records, have been able to make the connection downward to my own ancestor.

If you cannot locate or identify a sibling to use in your research sidestep, look for another relative such as an aunt, uncle, cousin, and so forth. If you can identify one person as a focal point, you may just be able to blaze a new research path, albeit sometimes convoluted, up, down, and across the family tree, to locate the link that can then be connected downward to your own ancestor.

Seek Help from Libraries, Archives, Museums, and Societies

It may seem intuitive but I am often surprised that genealogists overlook the services that can be obtained from librarians, archivists, museums, and all types of societies. Librarians and archivists are among my favorite people. They are intelligent and have a nearly unquenchable thirst for knowledge. They love to research interesting and difficult questions and to provide help and instruction to their patrons. These unsung heroes of our communities are trained and skillful professional researchers. They may not know where my Great-grandmother Penelope Swords Holder was born, but they know how to employ their research skills, techniques, and tools to help me locate print and electronic reference materials.

If I have a particularly impossible question about the location of a place that no longer appears on any map, I certainly try to search the materials at my disposal. That includes my own collection of maps, atlases, and gazetteers; online databases and map collections; and any possible Internet resource that I am creative enough with search terms to locate. After my own exhaustive searches, however, I have been known to contact an academic library with a good map collection, a state library or archive, and even the cartographic division of places like the Library of Congress, the National Archives and Records Administration, and the National Geographic Society. The staffs at these places are experts in locating this type of information and are always willing to help.

I encourage you to join genealogical societies in the places in which your ancestors lived and where you are conducting research. The cost is comparatively small but the benefits can be great. The publications of these societies, such as journals, magazines, and newsletters, often contain articles that provide contextual insight about your ancestors' lives and the events in the area. A genealogical or historical society may have conducted a project to identify, document, or otherwise produce. They may even have published some or all of the information in a book or journal, but other materials may not yet have been made publically available. These materials may significantly extend your research. In addition, there is the opportunity to connect with other researchers who might be researching your family or connected collateral lineages.

Genealogical *and* historical societies are excellent resources to assist in your research. Even if you are not a member, you may still make an inquiry of such a group to request information. The society can check its own collection of information and reference material and respond with information for you. Often, too, a society member will make an extra effort to help by heading to a local library, courthouse, government office, cemetery, or other facility to do a quick look-up for you. These "genealogical angels" perform extraordinarily kind services, and while it often is not expected or requested, I always offer to reimburse the person for the cost of their mileage, photocopies, postage, and other expenses. Don't overlook the Federation of Genealogical Societies (FGS) and the New England Historic Genealogical Society

(NEHGS) in the United States and the Federation of Family History Societies (FFHS) in the United Kingdom as resources to help connect you to important organizations and resources in their areas.

Heritage and lineage societies are another excellent source of information. Their staffs and members often maintain extensive collections of printed materials, as well as genealogical records and data submitted by members. These people are experts in genealogical problem solving and know how to address difficult questions and help find answers to obscure facts. There are scores of different such societies, many with regional chapters, lodges, or branches. One of the best websites for learning about such societies around the world and their contact information is Lineages.com at **www.lineages.com**.

You may also determine that your ancestor or another family member was a member of a particular professional, fraternal, trade, alumni, or similar membership organization. If so, consider locating their headquarters and inquiring about any records that may exist about your ancestor, website where they might be located, and how to proceed to request them. Almost all of them will have a website that you may locate using an Internet search engine.

All of these entities exist to serve their members, and their membership operational staffs may be able to help you locate information on your ancestor. They provide yet another resource to help you locate information to get past your brick wall.

Engage the Help of a Professional Researcher

There may come a time when you simply cannot get past your most stubborn brick wall. After trying everything you can think of and following every link you can discover, you may realize that you need the help of a professional genealogical researcher.

A professional genealogical researcher can help you in one of two ways. First, he or she can perform research for you on a fee basis or, second, he or she can act as a paid consultant to you and provide guidance and advice. Before engaging a professional, it is important to identify one who is qualified to provide the service(s) you wish performed, reach agreement on the scope of the work, and define the guidelines that will govern the arrangement.

Locate a Qualified Professional Genealogical Researcher

Anyone who has experience in genealogical research can assist and advise you. However, your best guidance will come from an individual who has been professionally trained and/or has successfully passed tests administered by a professional genealogy credentialing body. There are a number of organizations whose genealogical credentialing standards are held in high esteem. Let me share some of those with you, along with their websites at which you can learn more.

Association of Professional Genealogists (U.S.)

The Association of Professional Genealogists (APG) is not an accreditation or credentialing body, *per se*. It is, instead, a membership organization consisting of nearly 2,000 members in the United States, Canada, and 20 countries whose primary purpose is to support professional genealogists in all phases of their work, from the amateur genealogist wishing to turn knowledge and skill into a vocation, to the experienced professional seeking to exchange ideas with colleagues and to upgrade the profession as a whole. Located in Westminster, Colorado, the association also seeks to protect the interests of those engaging in the services of the professional. Their website at **www.apgen.org** presents a good primer at their link labeled, "Hiring a Professional." In addition, the site contains a searchable database of all current APG members, their titles and/or certification, organizations with which they are associated, and their area(s) of expertise or specialization.

Association of Professional Genealogists in Ireland

The Association of Professional Genealogists in Ireland (APGI) acts as a regulating body to maintain high standards among its members and to protect the interests of clients. Its members are drawn from every part of Ireland and represent a wide variety of interests and expertise. Applicants are required to submit samples of their work in the form of a report on research conducted over a period of not less than five hours, exclusive of report preparation time. The association's website is located at **www.apgi.ie**.

The Board for Certification of Genealogists

The Board for Certification of Genealogists (BCG) is an independent, internationally recognized organization located in Dublin, Ireland, that certifies qualified individuals in the field of genealogy. They define their mission as follows: "To foster public confidence in genealogy as a respected branch of history by promoting an attainable, uniform standard of competence and ethics among genealogical practitioners, and by publicly recognizing persons who meet that standard." Certification involves preparing a portfolio of materials, which is independently reviewed by a panel of three or four judges. BCG requires different materials for each of the following certification categories (the credential designations are shown in parentheses):

- Certified Genealogist (CG)
- Certified Genealogical Lecturer (CGL)

BCG has published the *BCG Genealogical Standards Manual*, which details the requirements for certification in each category. Certification is for a period of five years, after which time the researcher may apply for renewal of his or her certification.

The BCG website at **www.bcgcertification.org** maintains a current roster of certified individuals, searchable by where they are located and by special interests (Irish, English, Jewish, African-American, church records, and more).

Genealogical Institute of the Maritimes

The Genealogical Institute of the Maritimes (Institut Généalogique des Provinces Maritimes) is a nonprofit organization that examines and certifies persons wishing to establish their competence in the field of genealogical research. The first level of certification is that of Genealogical Record Searcher [Canada] [GRS (C)]; the second is that of certified Genealogist [Canada] [CG (C)]. By completing a preliminary application form that assigns points for education, genealogical research experience, and publication, a candidate is evaluated through a points system to determine if he or she possesses the qualifications required to apply for certification at either of these two levels. More information is available at their website at **http://nsgna.ednet .ns.ca/gim**.

International Commission for the Accreditation of Professional Genealogists

The International Commission for the Accreditation of Professional Genealogists (ICAPGen) is a professional credentialing organization that is involved in testing an individual's competence in genealogical research. Originally established in 1964 by the Family History Department of The Church of Jesus Christ of Latter-day Saints (LDS Church), the program was transferred to ICAPGen in 2000. At the time of the transfer, ICAPGen was affiliated with the Utah Genealogical Society (UGA).

Each applicant for the ICAPGen Accredited Genealogist (AG) credential must demonstrate through extensive written and oral testing, and through production of high-quality, well-researched documentation, that he or she is an expert in a particular geographical or subject area. The current areas of geographical testing are the United States, the British Isles, Scandinavia, Canada, Continental Europe, Latin America, and the Pacific Area. There currently are two subject areas for which testing is administered, and these include American Indians and the records of the LDS Church.

The ICAPGen website at **www.icapgen.org** provides a database of accredited researchers, searchable by name, their place of residence, or area of specialization. PDF files of North American and International researchers are also available for printing.

Other Credentials

Individual genealogical researchers may have been awarded other credentials than those listed above. Some colleges and universities offer courses in genealogical studies, and there are any number of specialized genealogical lecture programs and institutes offering individual classes or immersion conferences. These all may entitle the student or attendee to receive the award of a certificate, diploma, or another document attesting to his or her successful completion of the curriculum. These may be weighed in your decision-making process to determine if an individual has the education, experience, and expertise to perform the service(s) you require.

Define the Scope of the Work to Be Performed

Once you decide which professional researcher you want to hire, he or she will likely ask you to define exactly what you are seeking. You should prepare a written report on the individual or family group for which you want research performed, and provide all the information you have gathered. Include names, dates, and source materials you have located, and a description of each item's contents. Here is where an ancestor profile can really come in handy. What you are doing, in effect, is preparing for your potential researcher a complete picture of what you know.

Once that is prepared, you must decide what it is you want to know, and what you want the professional researcher to find for you. These two items may not be one and the same. For example, you may believe that identifying the parents of one ancestor may be all you need in order to continue your research beyond that point.

On the other hand, you may decide that you want the researcher to accept the commission and pursue your research farther. For example, you may have traced your ancestors back to a point at which they arrived from another country or continent, and you want the researcher to first locate the passenger arrival records in order to first determine their port of departure and then to trace your ancestors back to their native town or village.

Establish Guidelines, Goals, and Milestones

It is important to be precise in determining the goal or goals of your research. Your goal(s) will determine the scope of the work to be performed, and you should also define the scope in writing. This document complements the documentation of your research to date, that is, the ancestor profile.

The professional researcher will now be able to review your research materials and evaluate the scope of your project goals. Request a written research plan, an itemized estimate of research time and expenses, a reasonable timetable for the project, and a list of project deliverables. For example, the researcher may determine that locating your immigrant ancestors' passenger arrival may take 15 hours' work, tracing the ancestors to their native village is another 30 hours' work, and preparation of the final report will take another 5 hours' work, a total of 50 hours' work. In addition, costs of document copies, photocopies, telephone calls, postage, mileage, travel, lodging, and meals may be itemized to present an itemized grand total. A good researcher will generally offer you a list of references, and may provide a sample of a final report to give you an idea of the quality of the final product you would receive.

Take your time to review the researcher's proposal and weigh the expenses against what it might cost you in time and money to perform a similar job. Contact the references the researcher provided and discuss their experience with the researcher. Describe at a high level to each reference what it is you want the researcher to do for you, and ask if the person believes the researcher could and would be able to satisfy your need. Take notes and prepare additional questions for your potential research candidate.

Schedule a time to meet with or talk by telephone with your researcher about any questions you have. Make sure that they are all answered to your satisfaction. At that time, consider all the information you have at hand and make your decision. Investing in a professional researcher's services is much like buying an automobile. It pays to do your advance research and to shop around as necessary for the right researcher. Requesting proposals from two or more researchers is not a bad idea. This advance work may save you money and frustration as the project progresses.

Document the Relationship

Let's say that you have decided to accept the proposal of one professional researcher. The association between the two of you should be a formal employer-employee relationship. As such, it should be documented in the form of a contract. A good contract will detail the scope of the work. It also will specify the exact amount of time the researcher will spend and the precise amount of money that you authorize for the project. Be sure to establish benchmarking milestones in the project schedule. These facilitate communication of status reports from the researcher so that you know what is happening. It will help alleviate surprises later on and will allow you both to determine early on whether the scope and goals of the project need to be adjusted.

The contract should include payment terms, and it is not unusual to use a graduated payment schedule. For example, you might choose to pay 25 percent of the total fee as an advance before the project commences; incremental payments payable at certain milestone points, such as written status reports or some mutually agreeable criteria; and the remainder as a final payment when the final report and documentation are delivered. Include a contract cancellation clause that protects your and the researcher's interests.

A good contract is mutually acceptable to both you and your researcher. It should be designed to provide legal protection for both of you. With the project goals and deliverables clearly defined, and the authorized expenses clearly itemized, your expectations and those of the researcher are set.

Conclude the Relationship

When the research project is completed, and you have received your final report and accompanying documentation, make time to read and study its contents. Prepare a list of any questions you have about the contents or outstanding issues. At that point, you should schedule and conduct a final recap meeting with your researcher. Discuss the report and any questions you have about it, the documentation, the source materials found, where they were located, the source citations, and any other pertinent issues. You may learn a great deal from the researcher's recounting of the research process, including information that he or she may have encountered about other individuals that is not included in the report. These may be leads that you can pursue on your own at a later date.

If your experience with your professional researcher has been a positive one, you can offer to be a reference for his or her future clients' inquiries. In the event that the experience has been problematic or the researcher has not performed in a professional or ethical manner, you should consider contacting the certifying or regulatory body that awarded his or her genealogical credentials and file a formal report. This action will help the organization keep track of problems and consider them when reviewing the renewal of the individual's certification or continuation of accreditation. It also helps protect other genealogists from an unsatisfactory researcher.

You will find that professional genealogical researchers are eager to help you and subscribe to a code of high professional ethics and behavior. Seeking out a credentialed individual with the qualifications and experience in the field of specialization you require is a solid first step to getting what you want from a professional research experience. Carefully setting the goals and establishing the contractual relationship with your researcher is essential. You can encourage the progress of the project by establishing and following up on the milestone status reports along the way.

All of the methods and resources discussed in this chapter should make you feel more confident about the various research routes you have open to you. Difficult-to-trace ancestors will invariably show up in your family tree. However, as long as you know how to conduct scholarly research, learn about and work with all kinds of alternative records, and employ the strategies and methodologies defined here, the chances are excellent that you can knock down those brick walls and keep moving your genealogical research forward.

14

Plan a *Very* Successful
Genealogical Research Trip

HOW TO...

- Determine the scope of your trip
- Develop a research plan
- Plan your time effectively
- Pack the right materials
- Efficiently cover territory while you're traveling
- Perform a daily reassessment of your progress
- Process the materials when you return home

It won't be long before your genealogical interest and curiosity take over and you'll want to start making research trips. Your genealogical research at home and through the Internet will certainly help you prepare to visit libraries and archives, courthouses, government document repositories, churches, cemeteries, and other places where you may locate information and records. You probably will even want to locate and visit the places where your ancestors and family members actually lived. The very thought of these adventures is enough to get your blood pumping, I'm sure. However, a research trip of any type cannot be undertaken with any expectations of great success unless you properly plan and prepare yourself.

Professional genealogical researchers become experts in making the most effective use of their time and resources when they conduct research for a client or for themselves. Since you typically would pay a professional researcher at an hourly rate for his or her time, you would certainly hope that they are "working smart" on your behalf, wouldn't you? Well, you want to accomplish the same result when you conduct the research for yourself. That means working the way professional researchers do, and this chapter is sure to put you into the right frame of mind and help you organize for a *very* successful genealogical research trip.

Determine the Scope of Your Trip

The first and most important part of your planning is to determine who you want to research, what information or evidence you want to locate, and in how much depth you want to go in your research. You already know that it is impractical to think that you can completely research five entire generations in only a few days' time. It is important to set realistic goals for your trip. You have to consider where you are going to conduct your research work, what materials might be available there, and how much time you will need to invest to accomplish your goals.

When planning your research trip, select those individuals whose information provides a foundation for expanding research about them *or* about other persons later. Perhaps you are planning an overseas trip and plan to conduct some research there. In that case, choose those individuals to research whose information may only be obtained at the place you are visiting and in some detail. This is especially important when this may be a once-in-a-lifetime, on-site research opportunity.

A genealogical research trip doesn't have to take you halfway around the world. However, most of our research junkets are to places nearby. If you are like most genealogists, your local public and academic libraries will become something like a second home to you. However, you can maximize the use of your time and conduct highly efficient research there by defining the scope of your research in advance and setting goals for yourself. Let's look at a simple scenario.

I planned to visit the John F. Germany Public Library in Tampa, Florida, recently to conduct research to locate an ancestor in the 1900, 1910, 1920, and 1930 U.S. federal censuses in either North or South Carolina. I was unsure of the state in which he lived during those years, although family tradition indicated that he and his family lived in one or the other state.

In advance of my trip, I accessed the Hillsborough County Public Library Cooperative's website at **www.hcplc.org**, and located the web page for that specific library at **www.hcplc.org/hcplc/liblocales/jfg**. There I quickly found the page for the History and Genealogy Collection (**www.hcplc.org/hcplc/liblocales/jfg/H&G/genealogy.html**). I searched the library's online catalog to find out what books, microform resources, and other materials are available to help in my research. This library's catalog allows me to select titles in the search results list and add them to a facility called My Booklist, and the one I created is shown in Figure 14-1. I can print this page or email it to myself and, as a library cardholder, I also can place a hold on any book in the circulating collection. My Booklist contains the book titles and call numbers, and I will take the printed copy with me to the library to quickly locate these books in the library's collection.

By the way, while at the website I also determined the library's hours of operation and obtained a map and driving directions to the location. And thanks to the Internet, I was able to do all this advance work from the comfort of home at 1:00 A.M. while sitting in my pajamas!

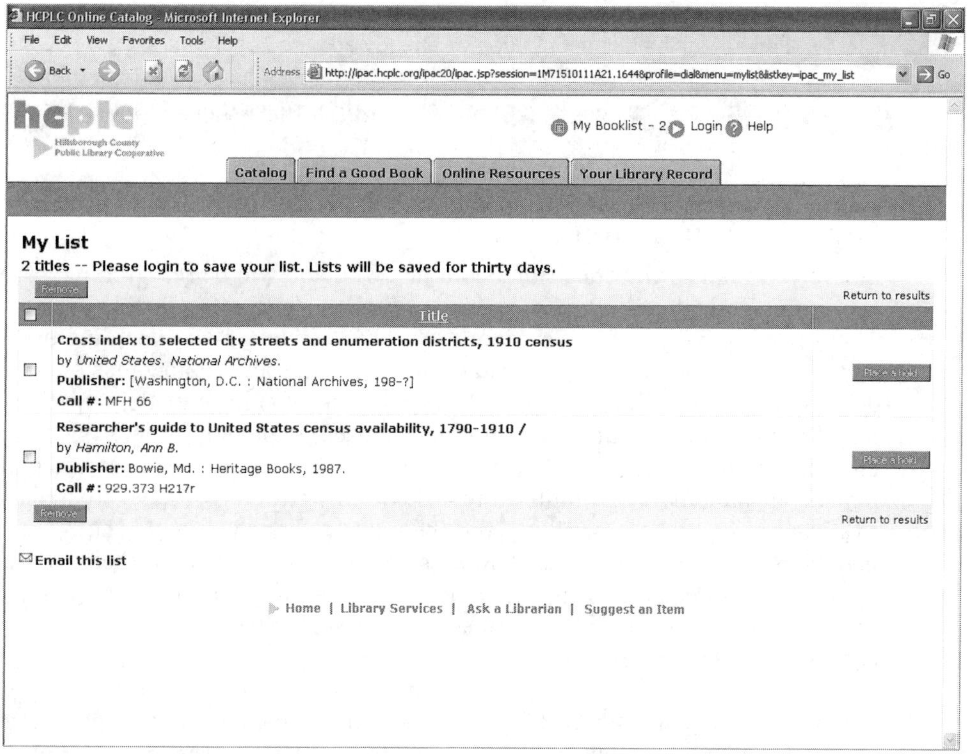

FIGURE 14-1   The My Booklist facility in one library's online catalog allows you to select and print a list of items for use prior to visiting the library.

Develop a Research Plan

A professional genealogical researcher develops a detailed research plan in advance of any trip. Based on the information I obtained from the online catalog, I determined that I would use both of the books I added to the My Booklist facility, and that I would be using the Soundex/Miracode and census population schedule microfilm for North Carolina and South Carolina. Since I was interested in researching records in the four census years of 1900 through 1930, I determined that I would possibly be using 16 rolls of microfilm—4 Soundex rolls and 4 population schedule rolls for each state—to locate my ancestor in the census records.

The selection of the person or persons you plan to research shouldn't be a spur-of-the-moment decision. Chapter 13 discussed the option of hiring a professional researcher to help you, and I told you that the researcher will ask you to be specific about what information and/or evidence you are seeking. The process I described in Chapter 13 is the same one you need to use when you are planning to conduct the research yourself. Let's discuss each of the activities in detail here.

Did You Know? Rereading the documents you've already acquired as if you've never seen them before can help you focus on additional details of your ancestor's life. You may see information that never registered with or seemed important to you before.

Organize Your Materials

Before you finalize your decision about just who you will be researching, gather everything you already have on the individual and/or the family you are considering. That includes every scrap of evidence you have accumulated, including primary and secondary sources, original and derivative materials, photocopies of books and documents you may not have yet processed, notes you have made, hypotheses you may have formulated but have not quite finalized, photographs, letters, and anything else that might be pertinent. If you're like me, you will have come across persons' names and data that don't quite fit into the family structure. I have created a file for every surname I am researching, and the notes and documents I accumulate for these people are filed appropriately. I call these my "Might Be Related" files. If you have materials on some of these people who don't quite fit, gather these together as well. You may finally be able to determine on this research trip whether they really are or are not related after all.

Now is the time to conduct an in-depth review of these materials and get them organized. This will likely be the most time-consuming part of your planning process. Use your critical thinking skills to read, review, and assess the information you have. You will then enter appropriate data into your genealogy database program. (We'll talk about these programs in Chapter 15.) Make certain that you enter your source citations so that you know where your information came from, and add any notations to indicate that a piece of information is not proved or verified, or that it is as yet merely a hypothesis.

File the Documents and Evidence You Have Collected

Next, file the documents in your filing system. We discussed filing options in Chapter 1. As I told you, my own system is arranged in three-ring binders by surname. Your filing system and method of organizing the materials you collect certainly need not mirror mine. On the contrary, whatever system you devise that *works* for you for the long-term is perfectly satisfactory.

Consider Who and What You Want to Research

With your materials all organized and filed, now it is time to consider which person(s) you want to concentrate on in your research trip and what you want to discover. Remember that you have a finite amount of time and that you will want to trace information on key figures whose information forms a foundation on which other work can be done later. Based on this work, you are now prepared to develop a clear research plan.

Prepare Your List of Subjects and Evidence

Make sure you have a copy of a pedigree chart of the direct ancestors and descendants of each person you plan to research. You'll remember that in Chapter 3 we discussed different styles of pedigree charts.

You will also want to produce several family group sheets for these people and their family units. It is important to have a family group sheet that represents your research subject and his or her siblings, because you will want to reference their vital dates of birth, marriage, and death as well as the locations, and the names of their spouses. When you are researching on site, you can never tell when you may want to check a parallel surname line, such as that of a spouse. Make sure that you have a family group sheet for your research subject *and* his or her spouse and children as well. I have encountered situations in which a woman was buried in the cemetery lot of a daughter-in-law's family and, unless I had had reference materials about that surname and relationship, I might never have located the woman's burial site.

This brings us to the next point. Prepare a list of *all* of the surnames of people in the area who might be related to one another. That includes the direct *and* collateral lines—those persons' families into which your relatives married. Make yourself familiar with those names before you begin your research so that they will make an impression whenever you encounter them in an index, a document, a cemetery, or elsewhere. In addition, prepare a list of possible alternate spellings—or misspellings— that might show up.

All of the documents you compile here should include the source citations so that, if necessary, you can quickly determine the origins of your evidence. In Chapter 10, we discussed the use of a research log to keep track of what information you have already researched. A professional researcher will always ask you what you have already found (or not found) and what resources you have already used. He or she doesn't want to duplicate your work unless there is a reason to reexamine or re-verify your findings, hypotheses, or conclusions. Likewise, you don't want to duplicate your research efforts. If you have been using a research log to keep track of the source materials you used when researching a particular individual or family, you have a ready-made reference. If not, either prepare one for your research trip based on the materials you have compiled for your research subject or make sure you continually refer to the source citations embedded in your documentation. Few things are as frustrating as finding that you have wasted precious time and resources re-researching something.

Did You Know? Preparing a list of information you want to locate and then grouping like items together, such as death certificates, deeds, and probate documents, will help you organize your research stops on a genealogy trip.

In order to really organize what you have created, make a folder or envelope for each research individual. Include the documents listed above, and add any notes on "might be related" or "need to research" items. If you think that an image of a specific document, particularly a complex one such as a land record or a will, might be particularly helpful when you are on site, make a photocopy and include it in the appropriate folder. If such a document contains information or applicability to multiple persons you are researching, either add a note in that person's folder cross-referencing another research subject's folder where the copy is filed or make another copy for each applicable research subject's folder. Whatever you do, never take your originals with you! You can always replace a copy but an original may not be replaceable.

All of these folders or envelopes will accompany you on your trip. I find it easier to use folders than to travel with these materials in a binder. A binder is bulkier to carry everywhere than a folder. Instead, I may consolidate the files into a lightweight, portable plastic file box or into a closeable accordion file folder. Everything is still grouped together, but individual file folders can be pulled and carried into research venues only when and where they are actually needed.

Focus on the Evidence You Want

Now that you have all your evidentiary information gathered together and organized for your research trip, you should be feeling like a professional researcher. You're getting very close to having identified what you want to find.

The next step is to go through the folders and the ancestor profiles you've created and identify exactly what you are seeking for each individual. Prepare a list as you do so. For example, on one research trip, I determined that I wanted to locate marriage records, death certificates, and burial locations for my maternal grandmother's six brothers and five sisters, if possible. In preparation, I made three lists—one for each type of record. Here is the information I included on each list

- **Marriage Records**   Full name of family member, name of spouse if known (maiden name used for women), date of marriage, and location
- **Death Certificates**   Full name of family member, date of death if known, and location of death
- **Burial Locations**   Full name of family member, date of death if known, location of death, name of funeral home/mortuary if known

You next need to determine where you can or will find the types of records you want to obtain. That includes the geographical location and the type of facility where the information may be stored, such as libraries and archives, courthouses, health departments, government records offices, civil registries, religious institutions, cemeteries, genealogical and historical societies, relatives, businesses, and so forth.

In the case of the records I was seeking, I did some preliminary research in books and on the Internet for the locations where these people had lived. I determined that the indexed marriage books were to be found in the county courthouse. The death certificates were originally filed with the county health department and copies were furnished to the state bureau of vital statistics. The burial locations could be anywhere, and I knew in advance that my ability to research all of these sites would likely be dependent on information included on the death certificate. However, in advance, I determined that my resources for locating the records would include the following:

- The local public library's online catalog indicated that the genealogy and local history collection contained city directories for tracing residents' addresses, cemetery canvass books prepared and published by the area genealogical society, microfilm of the town's newspapers from the mid-1800s forward (with a few missing years), and a published history of the town. The newspapers could be especially helpful for obtaining obituaries and funeral announcements.
- The online catalogs of the several local colleges' libraries showed that they own some local histories that might include information.
- A municipal cemetery department is responsible for maintenance of the town's three public cemeteries and maintains records of lot ownership and burials.
- The county property clerk's office is responsible for maintaining the records of the sales and transfers of cemetery lots in the three municipal cemeteries.
- The county clerk is responsible for issuing burial permits and transit permits, and their records may include the names and places of interment for specific individuals.
- The area genealogical society has canvassed cemeteries in the area, including the three municipal cemeteries and a number of other public, private, and religious organizations' graveyards. Some of their work has been published but some has not.
- The local historical society has a small collection of materials in a downtown storefront museum. Their collection contains correspondence and photographs.
- The local mortuaries that handled funeral and/or burial arrangements may still be in business. Their files, if they still exist, may provide information about burials.

As you can see, I put a lot of thought into the places where I might be able to locate information and records. You will need to do a similar job as well. Consider what it is you want to locate and where the information or records might be found, including developing a list of likely alternative resources as I did above. In my case, I knew I had a limited amount of time to conduct my on-site research, so I needed to really organize myself for optimizing my time and resources for the trip.

Plan Your Time Effectively

Prepare a research plan far enough in advance to allow time to organize yourself properly and to do some preliminary research work. Defining the records and the places you are likely to find them is only part of the job. The other part is to refine your list of locations so that you can visit only the facilities you really have to in order to obtain what you want. There are a number of ways you can do this, some of which include the use of the Internet, the postal mail and email, and the telephone. Let's examine the primary tools at your disposal and how to use them to your best advantage.

Did You Know?   Organizing the stops on your research trip can help you reduce your on-site travel time. This will give you more time for actual research.

Obtain Information About the Area You Will Be Visiting

You certainly don't want to go into an area without having some idea of its layout, the accommodations, and what resources are available to you. Chambers of commerce and visitors bureaus provide great resources for travel planning. A simple communication with a staff member is usually enough to bring packets of all sorts of information to you. Make sure to specifically request a general area map and a detailed street map, if they are available, and information about libraries, archives, and government offices. Ask for information about historical and genealogical societies in the area, museums, archives, and churches. The bureau is usually happy to compile a custom package for you.

While you're at it, you also might request local residential telephone and business directories, or else contact the telephone company serving that area to request them. Telephone books are relatively inexpensive and the telephone company representative can usually arrange to mail you copies and bill the cost to your own telephone bill. You will find the telephone directory an invaluable research tool, both before your trip and afterward. Prior to your trip, you can learn about the area, the government offices, libraries and archives, churches, funeral homes, and even search for people who may be relatives living in the area. You will use the directory to make calls in advance for appointments and as a resource for addresses when plotting your research stops while on site.

The maps you obtain from a chamber of commerce or visitors bureau may or may not contain the finite amount of detail you want. There certainly are other alternatives. Published atlases and travel books can be helpful for planning your trip. They might even suffice for some of your research forays into neighborhoods, suburbs, and rural regions. However, they may not contain as much detailed information. There are other options available to you. One of these would be a travel or motoring association, such as the American Automobile Association (AAA) in the United States, the Canadian Automobile Association (CAA) in Canada, the Automobile Association (AA) in the United Kingdom, and others. Members enjoy the benefit of obtaining detailed maps of many types and levels of detail either for free or at a considerable savings. Other excellent maps include state highway department maps in the United States and ordnance survey maps in the United Kingdom. These are exceedingly detailed and often include finite details of landmarks such as churches, cemeteries, forts, castles, and parks, and natural features such as rivers and streams, mountains, canyons, and detailed coastline features.

You can also generate maps from websites with mapping resources, such as: Google Maps at **http://maps.google.com**; Yahoo! Maps at **http://maps.yahoo.com** (United States), **http://ca.maps.yahoo.com** (Canada), **http://uk.maps.yahoo.com** (U.K. and Ireland), and **http://au.maps.search.yahoo.com** (Australia); MapQuest at **www.mapquest.com**; Microsoft Multimap at **www.multimap.com**, and many others. I urge you to double-check any driving directions with more than one of the mapping sites. If the maps' directions disagree with one another, you should call ahead to verify directions.

In the United States, you might consider using the Geographic Names Information System (GNIS) of the U.S. Geological Survey at **http://geonames.usgs.gov**. This site allows you to enter a query for a specific location, even using specific feature types such as a cemetery, a church, or a school. The result from your query can be used to produce a detailed map using one of the mapping facilities listed when your search results are displayed.

Invest time *before* your research trip to become familiar with the maps of the area you will be visiting. Study the maps' legends so that you don't have to use valuable on-site research time on that activity. Make note of important landmarks in the area and their directional relationships to one another. This can help keep you on the correct route or alert you to being headed in the wrong direction. You may also want to take along a Global Positioning System (GPS) unit to assist in more precise navigation. GPS units are available for purchase, and some cellular telephones are now available with GPS capabilities built into the phone unit.

Make Hotel Reservations in Advance

I know that some people take trips and travel from one place until they feel the urge to stop at a hotel, motel, or inn. While this may be suitable in some instances, your genealogical research trip requires you to have a comfortable place to stay with space to spread your genealogical materials and do some studying, planning, and paperwork. It is therefore important to do some advance research into housing accommodations. You might find that a bed and breakfast inn is available, and the proprietors may be able to help guide you to people and places in the vicinity that will be helpful. You may, instead, prefer a full-service hotel with a restaurant, a swimming pool, an exercise room, and other amenities. When traveling abroad, consider whether you want an *en suite* accommodation, which includes a private bath, as opposed to sharing facilities with other guests. If you plan to take a portable computer with you, investigate the electrical voltage and outlet plug configuration, the availability of Internet connectivity at your prospective accommodations, and whether it is free or available for a fee.

Use the telephone directories you obtain in advance to locate possible accommodations in the area, and then use your web browser to locate a website to learn more and to comparison shop. Booking hotels on the Internet almost always results in a 10 percent or greater discount even over the motoring clubs' or senior rates in various locations. I advise against the use of the so-called "bargain, last-minute discount" travel sites. My personal experience has been that the rates may not be as good as Internet rates you might book yourself, and that the accommodations you obtain may not be up to the standards you expect. Do your research in advance, and *caveat emptor*!

Search the Internet for Libraries and Archives

You already know how important a library or an archive can be to your research. You will want to take advantage of every opportunity to visit those collections that might hold important information to help with your research. Therefore, it is important to locate these facilities in advance of your trip and do some preliminary research about them.

You can find links for many of these facilities at the LibrarySpot.com website located at **www.libraryspot.com**. From the site's main page, click the Public Libraries link to reach the page shown in Figure 14-2. You can then locate public libraries in the United States, the United Kingdom, and Europe. Similarly, to locate virtually any type of library, including public, academic, national, and special libraries across the United States, Canada, the United Kingdom, and a number of countries around the world, click the lib-web-cats link. This will take you to the web page shown in Figure 14-3, where you can search for libraries by type and country or, at the bottom of the web page, select a location and browse the collection.

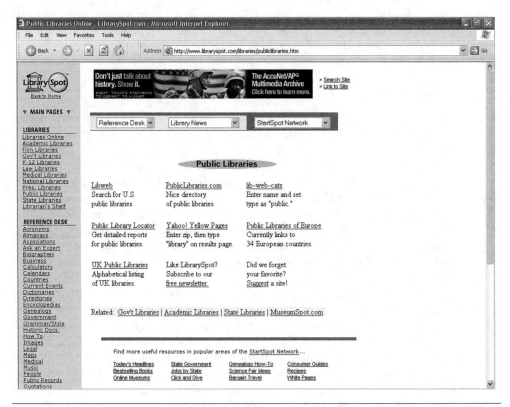

FIGURE 14-2   LibrarySpot.com is an excellent place for locating Internet sites for all types of libraries.

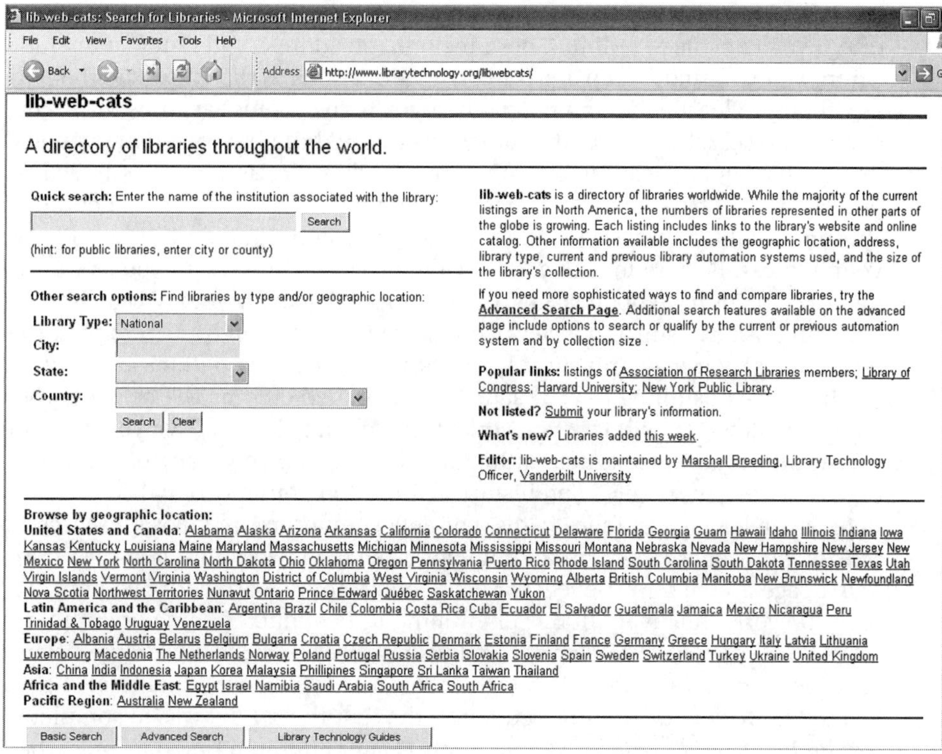

FIGURE 14-3   The lib-web-cats website provides browsable and searchable access to library catalogs around the world.

Alternatively, you can always use your favorite Internet search engine to quickly search for libraries' websites by typing the name of the location where you are going, followed by one or more words, as shown here:

[name of place you're going] library
[name of place you're going] genealogy
[name of place you're going] genealogy library
[name of place you're going] "genealogy library"

In the previous examples, you would omit the use of the square brackets and simply type the place name or, if the place name consists of more than one word or a hyphenated place name, enclose the place name in quotation marks to make it a phrase. You also may wish to specify the type of library by enclosing it in quotation marks as well. Here are some examples:

"fort worth" library
"richmond upon thames" library
"stoke-on-trent" "public library"

When you visit a library's or archive's website, there are a number of important things you can check online. These include the address and hours of operation. Often, you will find a map and/or driving directions at the site. Read the policies for the library to learn what to expect when you arrive. Some facilities may require you to have a researcher's card. If you have not visited the library before, you will need to complete an application form and present identification on your arrival, and this process should be taken into consideration when planning your schedule there. (In some facilities, a passport is not an acceptable form of identification for verifying your address. Be sure to take your current driver's license with you as well.) Some libraries do not have open stacks, or shelves, of books for your access. You may have to complete a call slip and a clerk will locate the item and bring it to you. In some repositories, you may only be able to work with one or two items at a time, and this can be time-consuming to your schedule. By understanding the policies, you can anticipate how you will want to work at that library. Let me give you an example.

At the Library of Virginia, in Richmond, Virginia, you may not bring briefcases or bags into the genealogical and historical area, and you may only use pencils, unbound note paper, legal pads, index cards, portable computers, and loose research notes. You must complete a call slip for an item you wish to view, submit it at the reference desk, and a page is sent to retrieve it for you. You can only work with one item at a time. In order to work effectively in this environment, I conducted some preliminary research in the library's online catalog before I visited and compiled a list of items and their classification/call numbers in advance. Because I knew what materials I probably wanted to work with, and the sequence, the first thing I did was to complete call slips for the first several items I wanted to use. I submitted the first one and, when that item arrived, I submitted the next one. The clerk could then retrieve that item while I worked with the first one. When I returned the first item, the second one was waiting for me and, at the same time, I submitted the slip for the third item. This allowed me to avoid idle time.

If you know that the facility also has microfilm and/or electronic materials you want to use, the library's policy will describe for you whether you need to sign up for time on a microfilm reader or computer, and the time allotted for each user. Costs will usually be listed for photocopies, printed images, scanned documents, and other services. Knowing these facts in advance can help you plan your time effectively. If I know I have to sign up for a microfilm reader/printer, I may plan to arrive early in the morning before there are large crowds and either complete my microfilm work first or sign up for time. Once signed up, I can use the waiting time to locate and work with other materials. The last thing any of us wants to do on site is sit around and wait. If the facility has electronic microform readers, you will want to take a flash drive with you in order to save electronic images on it *and* to avoid copy charges.

Your use of the online catalog to plan your on-site use of the library or archive collection is very important. However, remember that not every single item in the collection is cataloged. Some loose documents may be filed in what librarians refer to as the "vertical files." This is simply another term for a file cabinet. You should be aware that computers in libraries can be very busy, and that you might have to sign up and wait for time to use them. You can avoid some delays by conducting as much of your library catalog work as possible *before* you visit the facility.

I often call the library when I am planning a research trip and ask to speak with the genealogy reference librarian. I introduce myself and tell the librarian that I am planning a visit, and that I have already spent time preparing by researching in the online catalog. I then indicate what it is that I plan to be researching, and ask if there are any items in the vertical files that may be of genealogical and historical significance that might help in my research. Whenever I arrive on site, I generally then ask for the librarian I spoke to, reintroduce myself, and ask for his or her help in locating and accessing those materials. The librarian will appreciate your thorough preparation and will generally give you excellent assistance. The library can be an excellent base of operations for you when you are researching on site. I always check in at the library the first thing when I arrive in a place to do research. I meet and become acquainted with library staff members who work with genealogical and historical materials, and spend time becoming familiar with the library's collection. By doing so, I will know when I'm visiting the area, what materials they might have to help me overcome stumbling blocks. If I know what's there, I can make a quick reference trip to the library, get information I might need, and get back out to continue my research.

Be certain that you get the librarian's name, telephone number, and email address for any follow-up questions. After you return home, it is an excellent idea to perhaps send a thank-you note for such great help. If you *do* have questions after your trip and need follow-up information, you will have a ready-made contact person who will remember you and can help clarify any open item.

Search the Web for Government Offices and Departments

Government offices will frequently be the repositories you visit to obtain many of the official documents you want to review and copy. A research trip may take you to a courthouse, a city or township hall, a public records office, the health department, the vital records bureau, a property and tax assessor's office, or any of dozens of other official agencies' offices. It is not unusual for government offices and departments to be geographically distributed in multiple locations. Sometimes they are logically arranged together or in close proximity based on function or responsibility. However, you can never rely on this.

Did You Know? Telephone directories and Internet websites can be used in tandem with one another to obtain detailed information about government offices you want to visit. The use of a mapping program, such as Google Maps, will help you visualize the offices' proximity to one another and better organize your travel.

Your work with telephone directories can help you tremendously. There is typically a central group of pages in the directory with all government operations and contact information listed. The listings are arranged by government level, such as town/township, parish, county, state, province, and national levels. Review each of these sets of listings for the area you plan to visit, especially in an area you have not visited before and/or if the governmental structure is different from yours at home or unfamiliar. Make note of department names, because the name may be different in one place than in another. For example, an agency responsible for maintaining death records may be called the "State Health Department" in one place, the "Office of Vital Statistics" in another, and the "Civil Registration Office" in yet a third location. And while their functions may be similar and each may maintain copies of death certificates and related records, the nominal difference may be enough to throw you off balance.

Once you have identified the applicable department name, invest some time in locating the government site on the Internet. Here you can verify the structure and departments and their current locations, hours of operation, telephone and fax numbers, and email addresses. Use a web-based mapping program, such as Google Maps, to produce a map showing the locations in relationship to one another. You also can obtain driving directions to and from and between locations, and these can prevent wasted travel time. Read the office's mission statement and policies. Government websites often maintain Frequently Asked Questions (FAQ) collections with answers to the most common questions you might have. If you have other questions or want to obtain details about specific records, feel free to make telephone calls in advance to determine specifics. By communicating in advance, the government representative can probably tell you what materials are and are not available, if any older records are stored off-site and how to gain access to them, and contact names and information for other persons who might be able to provide more information or assistance. You can then make additional contacts as needed. Prepare a list by location and subject to take with you on your trip. You can then make contact when you are en route.

Search the Web for Genealogical and Historical Societies

Genealogical and historical societies are often the keepers of amazing information and materials. They may have gathered and compiled data, documents, correspondence, photographs, and artifacts concerning people in their area. These collections usually are not on display or accessible to the public because these groups may not have the funding needed to provide such access. Most such societies are composed almost exclusively of volunteers and few have a dedicated office or staff. As a result, it is imperative that you make contact in advance to determine what materials or information they might be able to provide. Be sure to let them know you are planning to visit and who and what you are planning to research, and try to make an appointment with an appropriate society officer or member who might be able to help you with your specific research. Be aware that you may have to schedule an evening appointment in order to work around the person's schedule. The contact you make in this manner may be one of the most important you make on your trip, providing you with access to unique materials to help your personal research.

Contact Religious Institutions

One of the biggest challenges in researching some of our ancestors is locating the correct religious institution where their records may be located. Many of these may have websites and email addresses, but some may not. The telephone directories, and the business pages in particular, can be invaluable in locating congregations in the area. It really does behoove you to make telephone calls and write letters far in advance of your trip, because you can expend a huge amount of time researching the wrong church. In addition, many churches do not have full-time personnel in their offices. You will therefore want to make contact in advance and, if you want to visit and examine records, set up an appointment to meet with someone there.

Locate the Cemeteries Where Ancestors May Be Interred

Cemeteries are among the most important and interesting places that we, as genealogists, can obtain information. Many researchers simply show up at a cemetery and wander about in search of grave markers in hopes of locating and transcribing the memorial inscriptions. Cemeteries may actually be a resource for much, much more information than what is on the tombstones. The cemetery's office may have detailed information about the cemetery lots and the persons interred there. I have had great success obtaining important documentary evidence by contacting the cemetery sexton, administrator, or caretaker responsible for a cemetery.

Your challenge is to actually locate the sexton, administrator, or caretaker responsible for the cemetery. A telephone directory listing for a cemetery whose name you already know may provide you with the contact you need. Check the business pages under the listings of "cemeteries" and "memorial gardens" if you don't know the name of the cemeteries you want to check. Don't overlook religious organizations that may own and operate their own graveyards.

Be sure to seek information about local mortuaries, funeral homes, and funeral parlors. These companies are acquainted with many families in the community and are familiar with the public, ecclesiastical, and private family cemeteries in their area. They may be able to direct you to the sexton or administrative contact person for a specific cemetery or to someone else who can. They may even have files for the funeral and burial arrangements that they might share with you.

Did You Know? Schools, colleges, and universities may still have academic files from a century or more ago, and these may be accessible to you. However, the chances are good that older files are in storage. Make contact well in advance of a visit to the institution to request that the files for your ancestor be retrieved for your review.

Contact Schools, Colleges, and Universities

Another resource for genealogical information may be the academic institutions in the area in which your ancestor or family members lived. The registrar's office, office of admissions, records offices, and so on, may still have the original records, microfilmed copies, or transcripts available. Often the older records are stored elsewhere, but if you make contact well in advance of your visit, it is possible that the records you seek might be located and copied for you. Be sure to include time for a visit to the school's library to access and view yearbooks and clipping files that may include details about your ancestor.

Make Appointments in Advance

You should have a good idea by now of the types of organizations at which or through which you might obtain information, copies of records, and referrals. While the telephone directories may be helpful in quickly locating all of these types of facilities, you may find more current, up-to-date information for them on the Internet. I therefore urge you to combine the use of your critical thinking skills and your proficiency at searching the Internet to locate as much quality information as you can well in advance of your research trip. Use print and online information in tandem with one another.

Your trip's success depends on your efforts to determine what organizations located in which places have the information you want to access. Obtain current address and contact information and then make contact *in advance* to set up appointments with organizations and specific, knowledgeable persons. Remember that no one is just sitting there waiting for you to show up. Offices and organizations that are not open and/or do not have personnel available all the time will need advance notice of your visit. While they are usually more than willing to help you, you must work around their schedule for availability.

Set Up a Schedule

If you have identified the individuals you want to research, have defined what evidence it is that you want to discover, and have done all of your advance research and contacts, you should be ready now to put together your research schedule.

Earlier in this chapter, I discussed compiling a list of subjects and evidence. Consider again, now, the types of records and information you want and the places you have identified that possess (or probably possess) those materials. Add notations to the list you prepared earlier, this time indicating the name of the location, its address, its telephone number, and the contact person with whom you communicated. Continue the process until you have dealt with every item on your original list.

At this juncture, your list may look pretty messy, but that won't last long. The next step is to rewrite your list, this time by location and address (and including contact information). For each location, make a checklist of each person and piece of information that is or probably can be found at or through that location. Work your way through all the entries on your original list and make sure each one is listed under a location on your new list.

Your new list is now the research plan we talked about earlier in the chapter. Now you must consider timing and prepare a research schedule for yourself. Determine how long you have on site to perform research. Create a calendar for each day of your research trip and divide each day into one-hour blocks of time.

If some of the locations on your new list involve appointments you made in advance, enter those appointments in the appropriate time block on the calendar pages. These are fixed items. The next step is to consider the physical location of each of the places you want to visit to conduct research, and then how much time you expect to have to spend at each place. You probably already do this in your everyday life, scheduling your errands in a particular sequence based on where you have to stop, hours of operation, and other criteria. You are going to do the same thing with your research trip. Consider everything you have learned about these places already through your telephone calls or Internet research. Are some places only open certain hours? Do some of your tasks, such as visiting a cemetery, have to be done during daylight hours?

Use a map of the area and look at the locations again. Using all the information you have at hand, and recognizing how much time you have to spend researching on site, it is time to fill in the blanks on your schedule. You will work around the scheduled appointments, trying not to schedule an activity in advance that might overflow or conflict with an appointment. Be sure to include transit time between locations in your schedule, as well as time for meals and breaks. Don't expect to last 12 or 14 hours at a time. Your body and mind cannot take that much stress and abuse, and the last hours will not generate quality research.

Fill in the blanks on your calendar and then ask yourself if the schedule makes sense. If you are visiting a town in search of a variety of records, have you included a visit to the library at the beginning for orientation and a review of their collection? Does each location stop on your schedule help create a foundation for the next stop or another progression of research steps? Does your schedule include a lot of backtracking, crisscrossing, or redundancy of effort, time, or visits? Consider all of these factors as you review the schedule. When you are satisfied with the schedule, print it and consider it as "cast in" … well, pencil. You *will* have to maintain flexibility on site.

We'll talk about the on-site work shortly. However, since you have now developed a research plan and your schedule, let's consider the other activities associated with getting ready for your *very* successful research trip.

Take the Right Tools with You

Whenever I make a research trip of any kind, I always prepare a list of the items I need to take along. We've already discussed how to identify the person(s) and information you want to research. That's all part of defining the scope of the research trip. You also have produced a research plan and a schedule of places to go and materials to seek at each place. You've compiled folders containing the pedigree charts, family group sheets, notes, and copies of documents you think may be important to have with you for reference on site. *And* you've prepared or updated your research log containing the places you've already researched and the source materials you've already examined and worked with. This will help alleviate the possibility of duplicating previous research.

All of these things comprise your working research plan and immediate reference materials for the trip. However, in order to make sure you are prepared to capture and record information you acquire along the way, you need to determine the right set of tools to take along. This may be an easier task if you are driving a car and have plenty of space to carry lots of tools and supplies, rather than traveling by airplane, in which case your space is limited. You may have to reduce the amount of tools you take, but that doesn't mean you can't be as effective a researcher. You just have to learn to "pack smart" and consider efficient and economical alternatives when you reach your destination. Let's examine some categories of materials to take with you on your research trip.

Pack the Right Clothing for the Activities

Consider the places you plan to visit, the time of year, the climate, and most of all your comfort. Casual clothes are always your best choice for personal research, and nothing can compare with having a comfortable pair of shoes when you will be on your feet for most of the day. If you have made appointments to meet with individuals, you may want to take some more "dressy casual clothes" for those situations. I would certainly never visit a church in a grubby pair of jeans and muddy shoes if I want to make a good impression and persuade the person I'm meeting that I am a serious professional researcher. You get the idea. Pack the right clothes for the occasions you expect to encounter.

Check the weather forecast for the place you plan to visit if you are not sure what conditions to expect. If you will be working somewhere where the weather is cold, consider taking clothing that allows you to dress in layers.

If you plan to be working in a cemetery or another outdoor area in the summertime, you need to be aware not only of the climate, but of the "critters" you might encounter. Outdoor research forays, especially in wooded or overgrown areas, require attention to your comfort *and* safety with protective clothing. Long pants and a long-sleeve shirt are an excellent choice because they protect you from harmful sunlight and insects. I take rubber bands with me for my shirt cuffs and pants legs to keep insects from getting inside as well. Thick socks and high-top boots may be a better choice for walking in rugged or dense, weedy terrain. Hiking boots provide support for your ankles and protect against sharp objects hidden in deep grass or leaves. The socks and boots also are a preventative defense against snakes and other creatures.

A head covering is wise for all weather conditions. A straw hat or a lightweight cap with a visor will help protect you from the sun's heat and glare in summer and help keep your head warm in winter. Sunglasses are a requirement for outdoor work as well. Choose a pair that is comfortable and scratch-resistant, and invest in a cord so that the sunglasses can hang from your neck when you need to remove them for close examination of things you encounter. Likewise, if you wear glasses, consider another cord for those. You can wear both cords around your neck and alternate between glasses as necessary. You are also less likely to lose your glasses. Clip-on sunglasses are another option, and the ones that attach to your regular glasses and flip up out of the way are simple to use and quite inexpensive.

Last but not least, take a couple of pairs of gloves with you. A pair of heavier garden gloves made of canvas or leather is excellent for pulling weeds, working with a trowel or cutters around gravestones, and for other chores that might injure your hands. A lighter-weight pair that allows you more tactile use of your hands can also be handy to have along. I recommend rubber gloves because they are durable for less rugged chores and are also water-resistant.

Select Other Tools for Outdoor Work

Depending on where you will be working outdoors and the time of year, you may want to take insect repellent along. Always remember to take along and use sunscreen to protect your skin from harmful ultraviolet (UV) rays year round. Your sunscreen should have a Sun Protection Factor (SPF) rating of at least 15 or higher, depending on your skin type and susceptibility to burning. You do not have to, nor should you, apply insect repellent as frequently as sunscreen.

Choose Supplies for Recording Information

So much information, and so little time! Copying and transcribing as fast as you can to cover as many resources in a limited amount of time can be dangerous. We all make errors, but when we rush and don't take time to recheck our work, the potential for errors increases. Taking the right tools for recording the data we find can help reduce the possibility of making on-site errors. You have many choices of materials for "working smart" in this area on your trip. Let's examine them.

Select Writing Tools and Office Supplies

Give some consideration to the types of information you plan to locate and record, and then select a format for paper products for recording your research notes. A spiral-bound stenographer's notebook or composition book is a good, compact choice. Loose sheets of paper can be dropped, become shuffled out of order, or even blow away in a strong wind. A notebook is therefore a better option and has the capacity to help keep your notes organized for easy reference.

If you are researching multiple families or, for whatever reason, want to create separate groups of notes, you might buy a composition book with dividers already included for multiple school subjects. Some of these composition books come with storage pockets inside the front and back covers. These are convenient for tucking in photocopies and document copies as you acquire them on site. You may also choose to use a small package of 3M Post-it® Durable Tabs to create tab dividers as you need them. These give you lots of organizational flexibility.

You will want to take a collection of pencils, pens, and colored highlighters with you. Pencils are your best choice because you can erase and change information as necessary. You should also buy a small pencil sharpener, such as the one you had as a child, to slip into your pocket or purse for quick resharpening. Highlighter pens are good for highlighting information on your copies, but never on any original records nor in any library's or archive's books, of course.

I always take with me a collection of different colored Post-it® Flags, self-adhesive tape flags, and use them in different ways, depending on the need. I sometimes use them to quickly mark pages I plan to photocopy, although some libraries object to or ban their use, especially on older and more fragile materials. However, I use them all the time in the notes I take. For example, I used tape flags on one trip and applied different colored flags to document copies and notes to quickly distinguish which ones contained a specific surname. Red flags were for Morgan, green ones were for Wilson, blue ones were for Patterson, yellow ones were for Alexander, and so on. Some documents that had more than one of these surnames, such as a marriage certificate, had multiple tape flags, each of a different color, attached. Post-it® Notes are also a great tool for note-taking. I use them to remind myself of additional information I need to locate, to make a note of source citation information, and for a hundred other uses. Don't leave home without them!

You will want to take a small collection of basic office supplies with you. These include a small stapler, a supply of staples, and a staple remover. Paper clips of various sizes, rubber bands, some extra blank file folders, and extra large manila envelopes are useful to help organize and store loose papers. You can compile a small kit with some or all of these items, or you can purchase a ready-made travel kit at most office supply stores or a travel cosmetics bag from any pharmacy or variety store.

When traveling by car on what I believe will be an extensive research trip, I also take a cardboard box, a covered plastic file storage box, or an "egg crate" storage container with me to hold all the materials together. I can easily organize everything in one container, quickly locate what files I need, and can carry the entire collection into my hotel room for overnight review work.

Capture Fabulous Images

You are sure to want to take photographs of places you visit and, in some cases, to record information. Modern cameras provide exceedingly high-quality images at a reasonable price, and images can be processed into printed copies or into digitized format, which can be electronically stored, manipulated, enhanced, and then used in multiple ways. I use digitized images as documentation for genealogical facts, include them in my genealogical database, embed them in written and printed materials, add them to family web pages, and exchange them with other family members and researchers.

You have a number of image-capture options available to you. Let's discuss each one briefly.

- **Digital Camera**   A digital camera offers excellent images, like the one shown in Figure 14-4, and control of the quality in a variety of lighting conditions. Digital cameras are commonly available up to 10 megapixels at reasonable costs, and a wide range of settings makes them ideal for indoor, outdoor, and document photographing situations. You also can see the captured image right away to assess its potential quality, albeit in miniature format. The digital image can later be manipulated and enhanced using graphics and photo editing software. Be sure to obtain the permission of the owner, library, archive, or other repository before photographing materials. Some items may be sensitive to light and may require that you photograph without using a flash.

FIGURE 14-4   A digital camera can take high-quality photographs that you can later manipulate and enhance. (From the author's collection.)

- **35mm Film Camera**   Modern 35mm cameras offer high-resolution images and more light-sensitive film choices than ever. They can often be less expensive than a digital camera but do not give you the immediate feedback that the digital model provides. Photo-processing options can include both print and digital images.

- **Disposable Camera Options**   Modern disposable cameras capture remarkably great photographs and come in color, black-and-white, indoor, outdoor, indoor/outdoor, and built-in flash models. In addition, disposable panoramic cameras take magnificent photographs that can be used to place standard-size photographic subjects into a larger context. For example, I often use a panoramic camera to capture a wide-angle picture of a cemetery, such as the one in Figure 14-5. I also take standard-size photographs of individual gravestones and markers, and can cross-reference the images to one another. In the future, when I or another researcher visits the same cemetery and the landmark trees and plantings have changed, these panoramic pictures can help locate the family graves in relation to other markers and landmarks. Again, you can have prints and/or digital images made during the photo processing.

- **Video Recorder**   Video recorders have improved a great deal since their introduction. They are more compact, are all-digital, and come with better image and sound quality than ever before. Rechargeable battery life is longer. Moreover, electronic USB interfaces to computers and software allow you to transfer video and reformat, edit, and enhance the original footage. In addition, some digital cameras and cellular phones can capture short videos.

- **Portable Scanner**   Prices on portable scanners have plummeted the last few years, and economical models can be purchased for less than $100 U.S./£70 U.K., and rebates sometimes reduce the prices still further. Most libraries and archives allow you to bring your notebook computer and a scanner for use with many of their general collection materials, and some provide researcher desks with power sources for every seating position. You may be limited in using scanners with rare and fragile materials, but the ability to scan book and document pages saves photocopy expenses and can pay for the scanner in no time.

FIGURE 14-5   A disposable panoramic camera can be used for wide-angle views of a larger area, and the resultant photos can be paired with smaller, higher-resolution pictures of component subjects to provide a well-documented visual picture. (From the author's collection.)

You also have audio options for your research trip. When working in a cemetery, I may take photographs but will also read tombstone inscriptions word-for-word, spelling and inserting punctuation as inscribed, so that I can accurately record the information in my genealogical database program at home. In the event my photographic images don't come out as clearly and with as much visible detail as I need, I still have the information in audio format.

Digital audio recorders have replaced the once popular compact audiocassette recorders over the past few years. I purchased a small unit made by Olympus a few years ago for less than $100, and I see that the company is now manufacturing a smaller unit that records up to 144 hours and comes with 256MB of internal flash memory for less than $60. The recorder interfaces with my desktop computer via a USB connector and allows for the transfer of sound files.

Oral dictation is much quicker than hand-writing the information. I also use the audio recorder in research facilities when I want to capture larger pieces of information without making photocopies or manually transcribing the material. The recorder also saves time recording source citation information. I can dictate the author name, publication, location, publisher, and date of a reference item on tape and, at the same time, add a simple note with the source name to a photocopy or document copy. I can later match the documentation and a source citation together and enter the full data and the citation into my genealogical database program.

For all of these electronic tools, be sure to take extra batteries, film, and/or tapes. You never want to be caught unprepared to capture that important image.

Consider Taking Some Additional Tools

There are other tools and materials you might consider taking on your trip as well. Some researchers are using portable handheld Global Positioning System (GPS) units, downloading national and local maps to the unit to help find and travel to specific locations. The GPS uses communications with multiple manmade satellites in geosynchronous orbits around the earth to calculate a very precise location at which the electronic GPS unit is located. Do you remember my mention of the Geographic Names Information System (GNIS) of the U.S. Geological Survey earlier in this chapter? I use that site to locate the latitude and longitude of a cemetery, church, or other feature and use my GPS unit to locate it on a map and chart a route there. Also, when I locate a piece of property, a family member's grave in a cemetery, a church, a family residence, or some other site important in my research, I make note of the GPS coordinates and add those to my database for future reference.

A cellular telephone is an absolute necessity for several reasons. First, it provides the ability to make calls while in transit between locations, and perhaps even call home for a check of reference materials you did not bring with you. More important, if you get into difficulty anywhere, you can always call for help. However, modern cellular phones often include other tools that can help you while on a research trip. Some phones come with built-in GPS units. Others include built-in digital cameras, although the quality of the images is often less than that of standalone digital cameras. Software applications (apps) can be downloaded to many phones. These include Google Maps or Google Earth, and genealogy programs to carry your data with you. The choices of new apps are growing every day.

Two-way, portable radios can be an excellent communication tool for pairs of researchers working together. These include "walkie-talkies" and FRS (Family Radio Service) models, which have a relatively short broadcasting range and are quite cheap to purchase. You can divide up in a cemetery to locate a particular grave and converse back and forth as you search, and use the radios to share information, ask questions, and call for assistance if needed. These units can be purchased in many department, hardware, and electronics stores, and on the Internet. Shop around for good deals on these very inexpensive units.

A visit to a cemetery might involve clearing overgrown grass, weeds, and brush from gravestones. You may want to take a pair of handheld garden trimmer shears and a small trowel with you. You may not want to or be able to take these on an airplane flight. If you need these tools when you arrive at a site, never fear. Economy and discount stores sell these at such cheap prices that you can almost afford to use them and discard them later. You may also take a few bottles of tap water with you to pour onto gravestones to darken them for photography purposes. Never use any chemicals or stiff brushes to scrub gravestones. Despite their permanent appearance, many older stone monuments and markers are actually quite fragile and may crumble when brushing or when any pressure is applied. Never use shaving cream or other chemicals to "clean" or to highlight inscriptions. If you want to provide contrast of the inscribed characters and images, consider taking a package of cornstarch or flour with you. Use the foot of an old nylon stocking as a pouch and pour some of the powder into it. Lightly tamp the pouch against the inscribed areas of the stone and then use a very soft brush or cloth to lightly dust off the excess. Take your photographs and then use the water to rinse the residue off the stone.

An extra-large aluminum cookie sheet makes a wonderful reflector, propped up with a pencil, pen, or stick, to catch sunlight and reflect it at an angle against gravestone inscriptions. This provides greater contrast for a better photo.

Don't Forget the Money!

When you were doing your advance research on the Internet, you will have noted the prices of photocopies at libraries and archives, document copies at government offices, and the costs of other items. Be sure you know whether the facility accepts credit cards, debit cards, personal checks, travelers' checks, or cash only, and be prepared with the right tender. I carry a small zipper pouch of coins with me for individual photocopies or, if I think I will make a lot of copies and the library offers the option, I may purchase a photocopying card for convenience and cash in the unused portion before I leave the facility.

Cover the On-site Territory Effectively

I talked earlier about the importance of preparing a research plan and a schedule of places to visit for research. It really is like running your personal errands on a Saturday morning, arranging them in a sequence in order to get everything done without having to backtrack. A professional researcher will do the same thing and, in addition, may try to do multiple things at once. Try to think creatively and do this yourself. Let me give you an example.

Earlier I told you that on one of my research trips I wanted to obtain death certificates for my grandmother's siblings—five sisters and six brothers. Having performed some research in advance and summarizing what I wanted, I prepared a list of the eleven people's names, their dates of birth, and the location and date of death of each person, as I knew them. I had contacted the county health department and verified that they maintained death certificates for the area and that the price of a certified copy would cost me $10 each. When I arrived in the town where I was to conduct my research, one of my scheduled stops was the health department. There I provided the list I had prepared to the same clerk with whom I had spoken by telephone. She reviewed the list and told me to come back later. I paid her in advance for the copies and went on my way. Over the next four hours or so, I visited with the recorder of deeds' office in the courthouse and requested copies of specific land records and property tax records. I then had lunch, and visited the library to work with microfilmed newspapers to locate obituary records. When I returned to the health department, the clerk had located and issued certified copies of 10 of the 11 death certificates I had requested; the eleventh one was not on file in that office. She issued a $10 refund to me and I headed out with my copies. I then went to the recorder of deeds' office again, and paid for and collected the records I had ordered there.

What I accomplished was that I had two other people working on gathering together parts of my research material while I did other things elsewhere. You will want to consider how you can multitask in this way when you are on your own research trip. Now that is what I call "working smart!"

Remember to make careful note of names, addresses, telephone numbers, and email addresses of people you talk to or work with. You may want or need to follow up with them later with questions or requests for additional information. You also *will* want to send each person a thank-you note after you return home. You certainly will have appreciated their help, and they will appreciate your kindness. That one courtesy, too, may open doors for future communications with some of these people and they definitely will remember you!

Perform a Daily Reassessment

One of the greatest things about genealogical research is the feeling of accomplishment you get when you have completed a project or found something to further your work. When you locate new information and evidence of an ancestor or family member, it is a cause for personal celebration—what we call "the genealogy happy dance." However, even if you don't find what you wanted or expected to find, that is no reason to be glum or depressed. Actually, the fact that you conducted the research and found nothing also means that you have accomplished something important. You have investigated a research avenue and have eliminated it from the possibilities. Sometimes the absence of documentation, information, or other evidence is indicative that we must search in another direction. As a result, I can tell you that "the genealogy happy dance" has been done in my house (and hotel rooms) on any number of occasions when I *did* find nothing or when I *did* eliminate or disprove a hypothesis.

A vital part of each day of an on-site genealogical research trip should involve sitting back and reviewing what you have and have not found. Examine your research plan again and ask yourself what you accomplished. Mark those items off your list. Make notes on your research calendar or research log sheets to indicate what you have researched, the sources you used, and the outcome of each inquiry. Evaluate all the material you acquired that day, organize it, and file it by individual in the research subject's folder that you brought along.

Now, compare what you did or didn't find with the information, documents, and data in each folder. Analyze what you think the next research step or alternative path might be. Prepare a list of your thoughts for each research individual. Once you've finished your review, you should have a strong feeling of accomplishment. And yes, you can do "the genealogy happy dance" too!

Based on your newly acquired knowledge, evidence, and experience, you should look at your schedule for the next day. Consider whether any of the places you plan to visit and records you plan to access might further extend your research for anyone whose information you acquired today. If so, add that to your list of things to research at that location. If not, consider what alternative research options you might have open to you, and what you might still be able to fit into your schedule.

Essentially what you are doing is performing a daily reassessment of your *actual* versus *planned* research schedule. Your review and analysis will help you regroup for the next day's research. Revise your schedule and alter your "to do" lists accordingly for the remainder of your on-site research. Always try to allow some extra time for the unexpected and extra things you discover. When I make a multiple-day research trip, I try to allow a final half-day for trying to resolve any loose ends I might have.

My last stop in town is usually the library or archive that I used as a home base. I can check any last-minute references I may have missed and explore ideas from the previous night's daily reassessment. And more important, I can personally thank the library personnel again for all of their help.

A *very* successful genealogical research trip, as you can see, is not a haphazard, "pile-in-the-car-and-let's-go" affair. It involves some forethought, summarization of what you know, advance research, formulation of a research plan and a schedule, and a lot of organizational details. This is part of what you pay a professional genealogical researcher to do on your behalf. You may think now that hiring a researcher might just be a pretty good idea. Well, in some cases that may well be true. However, don't you want the thrill and enjoyment that a genealogical research trip can offer? And don't you want to be able to celebrate the discoveries yourself?

Method, planning, and organization are the keys to conducting a successful research trip, whether it's a trip to the nearby library, to another town, or halfway around the world. There is nothing like the thrill of a research trip and, with all you've learned so far in this book, you really are prepared to do it yourself!

15

Harness Technology for Your Genealogical Research

HOW TO...

- Determine what computer equipment is right for your work
- Choose genealogy database software to support your genealogical work
- Integrate handhelds and smartphones into your research
- Get out there!

Most genealogists and family historians have made the move from recording information on paper forms to maintaining their information on a computer. Genealogists have become accustomed to using computers to locate information in online library catalogs, on Internet websites, and in subscription databases in libraries. They also have become conversant with email, mailing lists, and message boards. As they have become more comfortable with using computers, it is natural that they look for genealogical software application programs that can help them manage and analyze their information.

The use of genealogy programs transforms the information that once was kept on paper forms into electronic data, and electronic documents, images, sound, and video can now be stored together on the computer. Of course, hard copies of electronic documents can be quickly printed from your genealogy database program as needed to help analyze the data.

This chapter focuses on the preceding technical aspects of genealogical research. First it discusses how to evaluate which computer equipment and software is right for you, including hardware to transform paper documents into electronic form. It then introduces a variety of genealogical database software programs available to help you maintain your electronic records. The chapter concludes with a discussion of how you can easily take your computer-based research with you on your research trips, through the use of the modern so-called "smartphones" available today.

Determine What Computer Equipment Is Right for Your Work

Technological advances in computer hardware and software never stop. The ideal computer system for you will depend on what things you plan to do with it. Genealogists typically use their computers for a wide variety of activities:

- Connect to the Internet to exchange email with family and other researchers, post and reply to messages on genealogy message boards, research online genealogical resources, search catalogs of libraries and archives, and access databases to which they subscribe
- Use a genealogical database software program to store and maintain data about their ancestors, and use genealogical utility programs
- Print reports from the genealogical database program for analysis and to share with other researchers
- Use a word processor program to write and print letters and other documents
- Use a scanner to digitize family photographs
- Work with a graphics/photo software program to improve the clarity of scanned photographs and other materials
- Print photographs

These are some of the primary computerized activities, and I'm sure you will use your creativity to devise other uses for your computer. However, the essential components of your computer system will include a computer, a printer, a scanner, and a communications connection to the Internet.

Select a Computer

A computer is nothing more than a machine that manipulates and stores data according to a list of instructions. The core set of instructions for a computer is referred to as its operating system. There are several operating systems used in the desktop and notebook computers available today. The two most common are Microsoft Windows, used by PCs (personal computers), and the Mac OS, used by Apple computers. The version of the operating system used by the PC or a Mac (Macintosh) you own or purchase is important because software programs depend on compatibility with a specific operating system.

The PC has provided the most flexibility and software options for several decades but that is changing. There are many PC brands available, and each comes with a version of Windows installed on it. Mac computers come with the Mac OS installed.

One concern among the public is the incompatibility of programs between the PC and the Mac. Fortunately, the newer Mac desktop computers and notebooks released in 2008 and later can optionally also run a copy of the Windows operating system in order to allow the installation and use of Windows-based programs on the Mac. These newer

Macs are running at least the OS X operating system. If a Mac user wants or needs to use Windows-based programs, he or she needs two programs:

- A program that *allows* the Mac to run two operating systems simultaneously. Two current products fulfill that need: Parallels (**www.parallels.com**) and VMWare's Fusion (**www.vmware.com/products/fusion**).
- A copy of the Windows operating system.

After installation, Windows application programs can then be run simultaneously with Mac applications. (We'll discuss some of the genealogy-specific programs of interest to you later in this chapter.) In other words, the Mac now provides the most flexibility in supporting *both* operating systems *and* software programs designed to run with those systems.

Data storage is always important, and both memory *and* disk space are relatively inexpensive when compared with the cost of purchasing a new computer. I recommend that you purchase and install as much memory as your computer will allow. If you need additional disk space on an existing computer, consider the purchase of an external hard drive and attach it to your computer. If purchasing a new computer, choose as much disk space as you can afford.

Consider Printer Options

A printer is essential for your computer work. There are many brands and choices. Any printer will suffice if you plan to only produce documents printed in black and white. However, if you plan to work with any application in which color is used and the quality is important, a color printer is definitely the way to go. Generally speaking, a laser printer is more appropriate for an office or small business user than for a home user. A laser printer may handle a higher volume and print more rapidly (a higher page-per-minute rate) than an inkjet unit. However, a laser printer itself will be more expensive, as the color toner cartridges typically cost more when considering the per-copy cost, and the quality of printed graphic images produced by laser units manufactured for home users is usually inferior to the quality of those produced with inkjet printers. There also are all-in-one printers that combine a printer, a scanner, and a fax as a single single machine.

The quality of the output you produce may be extremely important in many cases. Printing photographs and graphics will require a printer that supports high-definition printing of many dots per inch (dpi) concentration, the use of archival-quality inks, and the use of special photographic paper stock. The printer you select should be able to handle these demands if you plan to do anything with digitized photographs and other graphic images.

Some people actually have two printers: one to print documents and another to print high-quality photographs on special photographic papers. The photo printer is not necessary unless you do a lot of photography or scan a lot of family photos and wish to share printed copies with other people.

Scanners

A scanner is a device that optically scans images, printed text, handwriting, or an object, and converts it to a digital image. Scanners are available as stand-alone units or as an integrated part of the all-in-one printer units. The all-in-one printers may have the ability to scan *and* may come with card slots into which you can insert memory cards from your digital camera and then print. The prices for scanners and all-in-one printer units have dropped in the last 5 to 10 years, and there are excellent inexpensive units available.

Digital Cameras

Digital cameras have taken over much of the photography market. You can, of course, spend anything you want for a digital camera, depending on the features you want, the quality of the images you wish to capture, and the amount of data storage you want. It's a wise idea to assess your needs *before* you walk into the retail store or shop on the Internet. Some retailers categorize camera equipment: point-and-shoot (standard, sleek and slim); advanced; digital single-lens reflex (also known as SLR or DSLR); and packages. For most genealogists, a point-and-shoot camera with a relatively high megapixel rate will suit almost every need. However, there are a few points you will want to consider.

- Megapixels (abbreviated MP) determine the clarity of the photo resolution, and determine how large you can print the image. Most standard cameras on the market today have 6–8MP, and these produce beautiful 8 × 10 photographs. However, a 10MP camera is great for the genealogist who is photographing grave markers, documents, and other subject materials that benefit from higher-resolution images. More megapixels also equates to the need for more storage. Look for cameras that allow you to change the MP setting downward for those times you do not need higher resolution. More advanced (and expensive) cameras may support 12MP and higher, but they are usually more camera than you need.
- Digital zoom and optical zoom are the two options for zooming in and out on your photographic subject. Digital zoom magnifies the image, and this can result in a small loss of resolution. Optical zoom uses an optical lens to enlarge the image without compromising the quality of the image.
- Some cameras support video, and this may be important to you for capturing specific events, people, and places. The clarity of these videos is seldom as good as that acquired from a digital video recorder. High-quality cameras that support high-resolution video capture can add hundreds of dollars to the purchase price and will quickly use data storage.
- Data storage on your camera need not be pricey. Many standard cameras come with 16MB internal flash memory built into the camera, as well as a memory slot for Secure Digital (SD) or SD High Capacity (SDHC) memory.

- Cameras come with multiple settings. You definitely want a flash and no flash setting. Many libraries and archives will allow the use of digital cameras but only if the flash is turned off.
- Among the many settings for different types of pictures, some cameras include a Text setting. This is ideal for capturing images from books, projected microforms (in a "shadowbox" cabinet), maps, and original documents. The text setting typically captures images in black-and-white for better contrast.
- Cables are typically included to provide an interface with your computer. Software may also be provided that organizes and edits your images, and sometimes storage of images in a choice of formats is supported. You can learn about image file formats in Wikipedia's article on the subject at **http://en.wikipedia.org/wiki/Graphics_file_format**.

Choose Genealogy Database Software to Support Your Genealogical Work

You have learned about and seen examples throughout this book of many different types of resources. Many have been in the form of paper documents, and some have been published in or derived from books, indexes, journals, newspapers, and a wide range of periodicals. You also have learned that a growing body of high-quality information is available on the Internet in the form of digitized document images made available in indexed and searchable databases and catalogs. You are prepared to discover new details through your visits and research trips to sites where ancestors and family members lived, died, and are interred. And still more clues are waiting to be revealed through interviews with family members.

Organization of your information and source materials becomes more and more critical over time. Yes, it is important to organize and file your evidence using some method and medium that works and is most efficient for you. You may use binders and place the individual documents in acid-free, archival-safe, polypropylene sheet protectors to organize and preserve them. You might also use acid-free file folders and store your materials in a filing cabinet, using some organizational scheme that facilitates your quick access and reference. You will devise a system that works best for you. I have organized my materials differently over time as my research evolved. I personally use a combination system that incorporates the binders and polypropylene sheet protectors for what I call "processed documents," those that I have analyzed and found the content to be satisfactory. I maintain file folders with the "unprocessed" materials that still need to be reviewed and analyzed, after which they can be filed in the appropriate binder. I also keep ongoing folders of the "unknowns," those people who just might be related but whose information hasn't connected with my proven family lines. Photographs require different organizational schemes and preservation/conservation techniques. I therefore organize and file photographs separately, sometimes making photocopies of one or two pictures to include in the binder files.

All of these different materials, different preservation requirements, and filing systems can present a considerable challenge on many levels. First, when you want to fully examine an individual's information and source materials, you may have to go into multiple filing systems in different places to access what you need. Then, if you want to expand your view to other family members, including ancestors and/or descendants, you will need to pull those documents as well. Finally, in order to really get a clear picture of the person and his or her place in the family, you may have to create a new set of family group sheets and pedigree charts. This can be a massive amount of work! Finally, there is no way to easily take all your genealogical materials with you on a research trip or to share information with other researchers.

Fortunately for us genealogists, there are a number of genealogical database software programs into which we can enter information, create source citations, make notes, and even incorporate digitized photographs, video clips, and sound files. There are some essential functions offered by genealogy software packages that you just cannot do without. Additional features can expand the amount of data you can include and structure the input in such a way that it can be sorted, analyzed, compared with other persons' information, and presented in reports in many formats. I refer to this as "slice and dice" analysis, simply because you can manipulate the information in your database in different ways *and* do it quickly.

Your organizational system will be influenced by the people you are researching, and perhaps by geographical area, ethnic or religious group, time period, or some other factor. Your choice of genealogical database software also will be influenced by a number of factors, most of all by what you want it to do for you.

The purpose of this section is to help you understand the major genealogical database software programs that are available for the PC and Macintosh computer operating systems discussed earlier in the chapter. These will be noted with "(PC)" or "(Mac)" to indicate on which operating system each program runs. Remember, though, that newer Macs can also run the Parallels or VMWare Fusion program and the Windows operating system, thereby making the use of a PC program on a Mac a viable choice. The prices shown for the genealogical database software programs were in effect at the time of this writing.

The equipment and software choices discussed in this chapter are constantly evolving. As a result, I have not included screen images. I urge you to visit the websites listed to read about software and look at current screenshots of the products. You will certainly be interested in visiting the GenSoftReviews site at **www.gensoftreviews.com** to review the database programs and the software utilities available. The site was created in September 2008 by Louis Kessler, and provides an excellent message board forum for each program for user comments.

As an experienced computer user and family history investigator, you are capable of conducting savvy consumer research to determine what models and features are available, and locate competitive pricing information.

Family Historian

Family Historian (PC) is published by Calico Pie, Ltd., in England, and offers a full-feature genealogical database for users of Microsoft Windows 98 and subsequent Windows operating systems. The software offers an intuitive graphical user interface that is at once, both engaging and simple to use. Four diagram-icon buttons open the Diagram Window to show different views: an Ancestor diagram, a Descendants diagram, an Ancestors *and* Descendants diagram, and an All Relatives diagram. Data entry is easy and intuitive, with strong support for source citations. Among all the genealogy programs, its support for the entry, linking, and labeling of photographs is perhaps the most comprehensive and elegant. Standard reports can be customized and can be saved in simple text format (TXT); Rich Text Format (RFT), which can then be opened by any word processor; and in HTML format for use in building your family history website. The software also offers a merge-and-compare-files function and backup and restore functions to help safeguard your genealogical data. Visit the website at **www.family-historian.co.uk** for a comprehensive tour of the software and details about its features and functions. The price is $56 U.S./£35.50 U.K.

Family Tree Maker

The Family Tree Maker (PC) database software, also known as FTM, has been around a long time and Family Tree Maker 2009 was released in 2008. The software was originally developed and marketed by Broderbund and its ownership has passed through several companies. It is now part of The Generations Network, Inc., owner of Ancestry.com and other genealogy sites. The website for the product is **www .familytreemaker.com**.

FTM has grown in functionality over the years and was completely rewritten in 2007. It includes most of the standard data entry and reporting functions you might expect. It supports opening two database files simultaneously and cutting-and-pasting individuals and data between files. The package supports a scrapbook function that allows you to add photographs and graphics from files, photo CDs, and other sources, and the option to include or exclude the graphic from a scrapbook or slide show. A single graphics file of a photograph, digitized document, or some other image can be linked to multiple individuals' scrapbooks with different descriptive text added to that person's scrapbook record.

The package connects to web locations to search predefined databases, particularly the Ancestry.com sites. Reports can be produced in standard formats and using filters that you define for individuals and data fields to include or exclude. You can create custom reports as well as focus on the people whose history you want to investigate on a research trip.

A user manual, published by Ancestry Publishing, is available for $24.95 U.S. The software sells for $39.95 U.S. (plus shipping and tax) in the store at Ancestry.com and elsewhere.

HEREDIS

HEREDIS (Mac) is a product offered by a French company, BSD Concept. It is available at **www.myheredis.com**. (A free trial version is available for download.) The software boasts an unlimited number of individuals, generations, events, data, and notes. All of the functions can be displayed simultaneously on a single screen, making this a true multitasking genealogical database. It incorporates a significant number of report functions and formats, among other bonuses. The graphical 3-D family tree is a compelling, innovative approach to display relationships and data, and both the database filtered search and source citation facilities are reported to be strong in all the packages. In addition, you can interface with your Palm OS handheld device to take your genealogy data with you. The price is $69 U.S. at the website.

Legacy Family Tree

The Millennia Corporation's Legacy Family Tree (PC) (**www.legacyfamilytree.com**) is a full-feature genealogy database program for Microsoft Windows that is available in two versions. The Standard Edition allows you to input data and source citations, add notes, produce reports, merge files, import and export data, and do all the other standard functions. It has a great deal of power and flexibility *and* it is free. The Deluxe Edition includes 98 additional functions and warrants the price if these look like useful features for your research. These include: language support for Dutch, French, German, Norwegian, and Spanish; additional views, including a report of multiple lines of descent; the Geo Location Database, a searchable compilation of more than three million current locations; mapping functions; web page creation; and many more. You may want to download the Standard Version, try it, and consider upgrading to the Deluxe Edition to obtain the other features. The Deluxe Edition is $29.95 U.S. as a download only and $39.95 U.S. for a boxed copy with a book.

MacFamilyTree

Synium Software's (**www.synium.de**) MacFamilyTree (Mac) is a full-feature genealogy database program for Macintosh. It has a stunning new 3-D display facility that was introduced in 2008. It contains a strong collection of standard reports and supports powerful custom reporting. It has an embedded support for Google Earth to research the geographical locations of your ancestors. The price is $49 U.S. There is also an application called Mobile Family Tree that can be downloaded from the Synium website or from the iTunes Store that allows you to copy genealogical data from MacFamilyTree to your iPhone. (See "Integrate Handhelds and Smartphones into Your Research" later in the chapter.)

The Master Genealogist

The Master Genealogist (PC), also known as TMG, is a feature-rich genealogical software package offered by Wholly Genes Software (**www.whollygenes.com**). It comes in two editions, Gold and Silver. The Silver Edition has all the data entry and some of the reporting functions. It sells for $34 U.S. (download only) or $39.95 (CD shipped via mail). The Gold Edition, however, has enhanced and expanded search, view, and reporting functions. Integrated web support is included for searching at a number of specific sites, including Ancestry.com, FamilySearch.org (LDS Church), RootsWeb.com, and other sites. Reporting options are extensive, including the ability to export data directly into word processing and spreadsheet applications and embedded production of PDF files. This edition sells for $59 U.S. (download only) or $69.95 (CD shipped via mail). A free trial version is available for download.

TMG allows you to customize your working environment and set up user-defined life events for entry, tracking, and reporting, making it a product that can be used by beginners and advanced researchers alike. TMG also facilitates sophisticated book publishing, complete with table of contents, embedded graphics and photographs, footnotes, multiple indexes, and bibliography. Direct import of data from a number of the other major databases is supported without having to use intermediate GEDCOM files.

Reunion

Reunion (Mac), by Leister Productions, Inc. (**www.leisterpro.com**), is one of the few full-feature genealogical database programs available for the Macintosh operating system. It records names, dates, locations, source citations, and notes. It also supports photographs, graphics, sound files, and video clips. It displays family relationships in a graphical form. Objects in charts can be selected, grouped, and easily aligned. Photographs can be placed inside individuals' information boxes, and display and print report formats can be changed and combined to provide an easily customized look. The software is available internationally, and you can locate retailers at Leister's website. It is also available at the Apple Store. The price is $99.95 U.S. A companion application (app) for users of iPhone and iPod Touch devices is available for $14.99 U.S. at the iTunes Store. (iTunes is a free download from **www.apple.com**.)

RootsMagic

RootsMagic (PC) is a full-feature database from RootsMagic, Inc. (**www.rootsmagic .com**). The software was completely rewritten in late 2008, and new Version 4 is about to be released at this writing. RootsMagic is one of the most robust and comprehensive software packages available. There are several navigation view levels and a simple user interface. You can open multiple databases at once and can drag-and-drop to move and copy persons and their information between databases. Each database can contain an unlimited number of individuals with names, dates, locations, source citations, and notes. The software supports more than 60 predefined fact types and you can create your own. The redesign of the source citation function in the new edition allows you to use standard citation formats or create your own. There are strong publishing capabilities, and you can use the preformatted reports or customize your own, and you can create calendars, mailing labels, and other lists. Version 4 also allows you to take your entire database with you on a flash drive. The price is $29.95 U.S.

The genealogical database software options listed here include the major titles for PC and Macintosh. There are certainly more databases, and there are many utility programs that can enhance your research capabilities. Let's look at software for your handheld computer equipment and smartphones that can help you take your genealogy with you.

Integrate Handhelds and Smartphones into Your Research

Your home computer system is the nucleus of your genealogical work. It is the place where you enter, store, analyze, and publish genealogical data. Your choice of a genealogical database software program, such as those just described, will help you organize, document, and analyze your evidence. You certainly can't take your desktop computer and all that data with you when you make a genealogical research trip or visit the relatives, or can you? And sometimes it also is inconvenient or cumbersome to take a notebook computer along. However, most people now have cellular phones that go with them everywhere.

Today's mobile computing options available allow you a great deal of portability. There are electronic equipment choices available that allow you to take all or part of your genealogical data on the road with you, locate specific places, capture information on site, and some allow you to export and print charts, forms, and reports for analysis while you're on the go.

There are essentially two categories of modern mobile devices: handheld computers and smartphones. Handheld units are mobile computing devices that do not include telephone capabilities. Smartphones are mobile telephones that include advanced capabilities, including computer-like functions. Some of the newer smartphones include Global Positioning System (GPS) capabilities. Typically, though, you can install small application programs, referred to as apps, on a smartphone and increase its functionality.

There are a number of operating systems used on handhelds and smartphones as of this writing, and these operating systems are employed by specific device manufacturers and/or used by specific wireless carriers. The following list is taken from Wikipedia (**www.wikipedia.org**). You can consult that site and search the term "smartphone" to view the most recent list.

- **Android** by Google, Inc. (www.google.com)
- **Binary Runtime Environment for Wireless (BREW)** by Qualcomm, Inc. (www.qualcomm.com)
- **iPhone OS** by Apple, Inc. (www.apple.com)
- **Linux OS** by Linux (www.linux.org)
- **Palm OS** by Palm, Inc. (www.palm.com)
- **BlackBerry OS** by RIM (www.blackberry.com)
- **Symbian OS** by Symbian, Ltd. (www.symbian.com)
- **Windows Mobile** by Microsoft (www.microsoft.com)

There are a number of genealogy programs (apps) available for use with various operating systems for mobile devices. More are being added all the time. The following list is intended as a guide, and prices and availability are subject to change:

- **FamViewer** (iPhone) by Aster Software (www.astersoftware.biz), and available at the iTunes Store (http://store.apple.com), $14.99
- **GedWise** (Windows Mobile and Palm OS) by Battery Park Software (www .batteryparksoftware.com), $19.99
- **Genealogy 1.0** (Palm OS) by Genealogy.org and available at TuCows (www .tucows.com), Freeware
- **MobileFamilyTree** (iPhone) by Synium Software (www.synium.de), compatible only with MacFamilyTree for Mac at the iTunes Store (http://store.apple.com), $4.99
- **My Roots** (Windows Mobile and Palm OS) by Tapperware (www.tapperware.com), $24.95
- **Pocket Genealogist** (Windows Mobile) by Northern Hills Software LLD (http:// northernhillssoftware.com); Basic $20, Advanced $35
- **Reunion** (iPhone and iPod Touch) by Leister Productions, Inc. (www.leisterpro .com), compatible only with Reunion, and available from Leister and at the iTunes Store (http://store.apple.com), $14.99

Get Out There!

Now that you know how to research your genealogy, and you know more about desktop and portable computer software, it's time to *really* get started. Use your new knowledge, your critical thinking skills, research methodologies, and all of your tools to accomplish more effective research than ever. Remember to work all of the resources in print, on the Internet, and in specialized databases, and every other type of resource you can find, and work them in tandem with one another.

Get out there! I wish you great successes and happy hunting along this great journey of discovery.

Index

Page references to figures are in italics.

714 - 487-1244